Speaking Torah

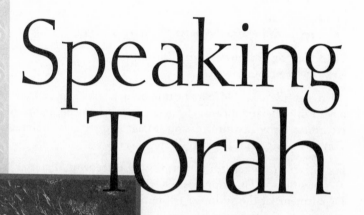

Spiritual Teachings from around the Maggid's Table

Volume 1	Genesis • Exodus • Leviticus

Arthur Green
with **Ebn Leader, Ariel Evan Mayse**
and **Or N. Rose**

For People of All Faiths, All Backgrounds
JEWISH LIGHTS Publishing
Woodstock, Vermont

Speaking Torah:
Spiritual Teachings from around the Maggid's Table—Volume 1

2013 Hardcover Edition, First Printing
© 2013 by Arthur Green

For information regarding permission to reprint material from this book, please write or fax your request to Jewish Lights Publishing, Permissions Department, at the address / fax number listed below, or e-mail your request to permissions@jewishlights.com.

Library of Congress Cataloging-in-Publication Data
Green, Arthur, 1941–
  [Commentaries. Selections]
  Speaking Torah : spiritual teachings from around the Maggid's table / Arthur Green with Ebn Leader, Ariel Evan Mayse, and Or Rose.
    volumes cm
  Includes bibliographical references and index.
  ISBN 978-1-58023-668-3 (alk. paper)
  1. Bible. Pentateuch—Criticism, interpretation, etc. 2. Hasidism. 3. Hasidim—Biography. I. Leader, Ebn D., 1969– II. Mayse, Ariel Evan. III. Rose, Or N. IV. Title.
  BS1225.52.G732 2013
  222'.106—dc23
                                        2013017622

10 9 8 7 6 5 4 3 2 1

Manufactured in the United States of America
Jacket Design: Tim Holtz
Jacket Art: "Seventh Day" was painted by Michael Bogdanow, whose art can be seen at www.MichaelBogdanow.com. The painting was inspired by these words from the Torah portion Emor, Leviticus 23:3: "On the seventh day there shall be a sabbath of complete rest, a sacred occasion."

For People of All Faiths, All Backgrounds
Published by Jewish Lights Publishing
A Division of LongHill Partners, Inc.
Sunset Farm Offices, Route 4, P.O. Box 237
Woodstock, VT 05091
Tel: (802) 457-4000 Fax: (802) 457-4004
www.jewishlights.com

For:
Ma'ayan
Aviv
Sophia
Alma
Ezra
Ezra Elimelech Meir
and ...

ונהיה אנחנו וצאצאינו וצאצאי צאצאינו
כולנו יודעי שמך ולומדי תורתך לשמה

BEIT RABBI (PAGE 130)

It is told that the rabbi from Wolpe [his name is lost to us] was the greatest among the disciples of the great Maggid. In the early days, they would all go to hear him review the words of the Maggid, for he could repeat the teachings precisely and explain them well. But over time the disciples saw that he was being consumed from within and he could not stay there. He fell into drunkenness, may the merciful One save us. And he became a wanderer going from place to place with only his staff and pack....

R. Barukh Mordechai of Bobroysk once ran into him at an inn and recognized him by his behavior. When the Wolper went outside, R. Barukh searched his pack, hoping to find texts of the teachings. But the Wolper came back and caught him and said, "Why are you going through my things? Have I stolen from you?" and R. Barukh said that he was hoping to find written teachings. The Wolper said to him, "With you people the *hasidim* are one thing and the teacher and the teachings are another. That is why you need written texts. We, our teacher, and the teachings were all truly one. We had no need for written texts." He took his staff and pack and left.

SIFTEY TSADDIKIM (FROM VA-YAKHEL)

They said in the name of the holy *tsaddik* R. Leib Sarah's that he used to protest against people "saying Torah."

"What is this 'saying Torah'?" he would ask. A person should rather see to it that all his deeds *be* Torah. The person himself should be Torah. This means behaving according to Torah in all you do, until people can learn from your behavior. It is your behavior itself that is Torah.

Contents

Volume 1

Contents

Volume 2

Contents

To the Reader

What is this book that you have just opened? Think of it as a self-help book in the most profound sense. It offers a way of reading the entire Torah as a guide to helping you find your way out of Egypt. "Egypt" in this sentence means your own enslavement, whatever it may be. The teachings of Torah, from beginning to end, are read here as a path toward liberation, a way of uplifting your soul and allowing it to journey homeward, back to its Source in the oneness of all being. Or, even better, to discover that oneness right here, in a loving but transformative embrace of both world and self.

Written more than two hundred years ago by a circle of Hasidic masters, these teachings have been selected and updated for your use by a small circle of contemporary interpreters. We have selected and translated the sources and have then offered our own attempts to connect the teachings to contemporary readers. But the real work—the true self-help of applying these teachings to your own life—can be done by you alone.

"Speaking Torah"—*zogn toyreh*, in Yiddish—is the unique Hasidic term for the event that underlies the teachings you are about to encounter. The Hasidic master, or *rebbe*, "speaks Torah" with his disciples gathered around his table. This is a linguistic expression of Hasidism's most essential spiritual claim: the *rebbe's* speech is a continuation of the great font of revelation that opened up at Mount Sinai, "a great voice that has not ceased."

The book before you is a selection of spiritual teachings by R. Dov Baer of Mezritch (Miedzyrzec, 1704–1772) and his disciples, founders of the Hasidic movement, following the weekly Torah reading cycle and the Jewish festival calendar. These teachings, originally spoken and then written in Poland more than two hundred years ago, are presented to you, the contemporary reader, in the hope that they will still be found fresh, relevant, and spiritually exciting. While much careful scholarship has gone into the making of this book, it is intended above all to be a work of inspiration to individuals and groups who will study it and use it as a tool of personal spiritual growth and challenge.

Speaking Torah is meant for study and contemplation rather than for casual reading. Each of the four to six teachings offered for a weekly Torah portion or festival is built around an original and often surprising reading of a biblical text. To engage with the Hasidic commentary, always ask yourself two questions: First, "How is the author rereading the passage before him?" Try to see the specific "problem" or opening he finds in the verse, often based on wordplay. Then look carefully at the suggestion offered. Often the "punch" in these teachings lies in the new reading of a familiar verse. Make sure you "get it," consulting the Hebrew if you are able, before moving on. Then ask, "What is he trying to teach?" What is the spiritual or moral message being drawn from this reading of the verse? If your interest is in part historical, you might ask further, "Why is he saying this? Who constituted the audience for such a message?" But if your interest is, as we hope, at least partly personal, you will see yourself/selves as that audience and ask, "What does this reading have to offer us today?" Each translated text is followed by a brief comment of our own, in which we try to build a bridge of understanding between the Hasidic author and the contemporary seeker. At the end of each Torah portion, we print a brief transcription of our own conversation about what we have learned from the Hasidic interpretations of this portion. These "Round Two" conversations of ours are meant to serve as stimulants to your own discussions, which we hope will be personal as well as intellectual. In a certain sense, you may say, we are a teacher and students' circle of today who have the privilege of peering in on a great teacher and his disciples of two hundred years ago. If you should use this book in a similar circle, you will be adding another link to that chain. We hope you do; we urge you too to "speak Torah."

We have presented the original Hebrew texts in this work along with the English translation. If you are able, use our translations as an aid toward studying the texts in the original. While we have worked hard to convey the many plays on words and nuances of meaning in our translations, reading the Hasidic masters in English inevitably has about it something of "kissing the bride through a veil," as has appropriately been said about reading any classic in translation. The language in which these teachings are recorded, an abbreviated Hebrew transcription of longer oral sermons in Yiddish, is poor in vocabulary, syntax, and grammar, but rich in history, symbolism, and allusion. Careful reading and rereading is recommended. These texts are perfect for study in *hevruta*, learning pairs who question and challenge one another and together discover new insights.

The texts selected are taken from a wide range of Hasidic works written by disciples of the great Maggid. Some of these works are well-known classics of Hasidic literature, reprinted many times and widely read in Hasidic circles to this day. These include such books as *Kedushat Levi, Me'or 'Eynayim,* and *No'am Elimelekh.* But many others are quite obscure, known mostly to scholars but forgotten by the general public. The fate of such books often had less to do with their innate quality than with the personal fame (or lack thereof) of the author and the success of his descendants in becoming a major dynastic force within the Hasidic world. We are especially happy to present to you many beautiful gems of teaching and interpretation from authors whose works have been long neglected. Toward the end of volume 2 you will find a brief accounting of each of the more than forty books and authors whose works have been included.

Early Hasidism was primarily an oral movement; it was the spoken rather than the written word that lay at its core. These teachings, spoken around the table, were always offered in a particular context, frequently directed either at an event that had occurred or at the need of a particular hearer. All that was lost once they were written down, translated from oral Yiddish into Hebrew, and published in books.

Concern over this change was not lost on the Hasidic preachers. The point is illustrated, as Hasidic teachings often are, by a story told about the Ba'al Shem Tov, the first Hasidic master and the teacher of Dov Baer. He insisted that his message was only to be delivered orally, never written down. One night the Ba'al Shem Tov had a dream in which he saw a demon prancing about him, carrying a book in his hand. "What is that book?" the master asked. "This is your book; you wrote it," replied the demon. Then the Ba'al Shem Tov knew that someone had violated his orders and had committed the teachings to writing. He called all of his disciples together and demanded to see the notebook. Finally one of them confessed and handed it over. The master read it from cover to cover and proclaimed, "There isn't a single word here that I said."

What did the BeSHT (as he is called) mean by that remarkable statement? His denial may be read in two ways. Perhaps he was saying that the mysterious words spoken were too recondite to be conveyed by pen and ink and simply had no meaning once they were written down. The mysteries are by definition not amenable to the medium of writing; once they are found in books, they have lost their mysterious nature. But he also meant that each teaching was offered at a particular moment, to a certain individual who needed to hear it, and in circumstances that were lost once the teaching was abstracted from its original setting and placed in a book. The Hasidic master is, if anything, a teacher who operates in concrete situations, seeking to deepen and challenge the spiritual life of each of his disciples. Once teachings are generalized and de-contextualized, as is necessarily the case with book learning, they are easily misappropriated, often having a very different effect on latter-day readers than that intended by the master in the moment they were first spoken.

Alas, all we have left of those teachers are their books! And this book is yet another selection and translation, creating another book! But as you read these teachings and drink in their wisdom, you will decide which ones were meant for you and how you are to absorb them. The language in which they are cased is antiquated; their theology may not be one you fully share. But hopefully you will learn to see beyond those barriers and will find a way to take to heart those teachings that you need to make your own.

In presenting eighteenth-century teachings for twenty-first-century readers, we realize that there are a number of cultural hurdles that must be surmounted. While Hasidism belongs chronologically to what is called the early modern period of Jewish history, its rhetoric is entirely medieval. It belongs wholly to the genre of classical Jewish literature that builds on the wisdom of prior generations, reinterpreting but never denying or invalidating any prior source. The most fantastic of biblical and rabbinic tales, while serving as proper subjects for allegorical reinterpretation, are also assumed to be quite literally true. A point may be proved by quoting a verse of Scripture, however totally one may have to reshape that source to provide the meaning desired. So too are the unity of Scripture and the constancy of tradition taken for granted, so that there is nothing strange about Abraham or Moses quoting from writings attributed to King David or Solomon, or observing Jewish rites created only in Talmudic times. Loyalty to the Talmudic tradition, including both the praxis of *halakhah* and the mentality of *aggadah*, Jewish lore and legend, is considered normative, as are the established teachings of both philosophers and mystics of prior generations, even when they seem to contradict one another.

The Hasidic texts are the product of a time and place where religious communities stood over against one another in an aggressive and often dehumanizing or demonizing way. Eighteenth-century Polish and Ukrainian Jews were a despised and persecuted minority. Even in relatively good times, and there were such, their existence was no more than barely tolerated. The Jews in turn looked down on their gentile neighbors, considering them boorish, ignorant, and sometimes even a lesser order of humanity. While we have tended not to select texts that underscore these views, they cannot be escaped entirely. The editors of this collection belong to the neo-Hasidic school of thought pioneered by such as Martin Buber and Hillel Zeitlin, who even a century ago were learning to look at the Hasidic sources of wisdom through a universalizing lens. This means frequently replacing "a Jew" with "a person" as we seek to apply these teachings to contemporary life, though we have taken care not to make this change in presenting the texts themselves.

It is also true that the Hasidic sources were spoken and written entirely by men, assuming also an exclusively male audience of hearers and readers. After much thought, we have attempted to lessen the prevalence of male pronouns by frequent rendering of the Hebrew impersonal third person into the ungendered English second person or first person plural. When that has not been sufficient, however, we have retained the original masculine language, along with frequent metaphors of father and son and male imagery for God. We hope that female readers will not feel excluded by this decision to be faithful to the original texts and their setting. We very much hope that contemporary women as well as men will read these sources, find them inspiring, and respond to them with a creativity emerging from their own experience.

One final word of advice: If you are using this book for personal quest, skip the long introduction for now. Go right to the texts. There is no need to begin at the beginning. Choose this week's Torah portion or an upcoming holiday, or just open the book at random, if you prefer. Eventually you will work your way back, even to the introduction.

Introduction

Hasidism

The First Three Generations (1740–1815)

What Is Hasidism?

Hasidism represents one of the great success stories in the world history of religious movements. When Israel Ba'al Shem Tov, the figure around whose image the movement was to coalesce, died in 1760, there were no more than twenty or thirty people closely linked with him whom we could identify as laying claim to his legacy. All these were within Podolia, a somewhat remote corner of southeastern Poland, up against the Russian and Turkish borders. We have little knowledge of any influence he had beyond this group and his own town of Miedzybozh. Half a century later, ever larger swaths of Eastern European Jewry, majorities in some areas, considered themselves followers of the movement that carried his banner.[1]

The teachings included in this volume were all offered—most of them originally in oral form—by the Ba'al Shem Tov's successor, R. Dov Baer, the Maggid (or preacher) of Mezritch (1704–1772), and his circle of disciples. They belong to what are conventionally called the second and third generations of Hasidic leadership. It was members of this circle who brought Hasidism into the public arena as a distinctive religious phenomenon, arousing both avid support and bitter denunciation. It was largely this group, especially a few key figures within it, who created Hasidism as a historical movement, one that has had a decisive impact upon the history of Jews and Judaism for a quarter millennium, a period often marked by a changing and evolving Hasidic agenda and by conflicts, both between devotees and opponents of Hasidism and within the ranks of the movement itself.

The Mezritch years represent the formation of a close spiritual/ intellectual circle, a group of young men intensely devoted to their master, to a set of ideals, to the task of spreading religious revival, and (for the most part) to one another. Members of the circle continued in this work for decades after their master's death, into the early years of the nineteenth century. The end of this "third generation" of Hasidic leadership, and the waning of its influence, is generally depicted as taking place between 1809 and 1815 with the passing of several key leaders and the emergence of other historical factors to be discussed later.

What was the nature of the shared Hasidic faith that formed the bond among the members of this diverse and highly creative circle? Terms like "popular mysticism" and "revivalism," while appropriate descriptions of Hasidism, do not in themselves tell us very much. Devotion to the personal figures at its center, the BeSHT (a contraction of Ba'al Shem Tov), the Maggid, and their teachings, is another way to define this group. But the intense bonds that constituted this circle were more than either personal loyalty or intellectual commitment. They were based on a degree of shared religious experience, the memory of deep and sometimes transformative spiritual impressions made upon them by their visits to Mezritch and their contact with the Maggid. These experiences, seldom talked about in direct terms, reverberate through their homilies, often spoken decades after those times "around the Maggid's table" had turned into memory. From the texts you will encounter here it is possible to distill the essential teachings that they held in common. A deep contemplation of these texts will sometimes offer the reader a glimpse of the inner experience that lay behind the teachings. We can also see, when we read carefully, what issues divided the members of the circle from one another. What did they argue about around that table in Mezritch or in debates carried on for many years, still with the memory of that formative spiritual hothouse in mind?

Let us begin with some points of general agreement, as a way of defining Hasidism as it existed in those early generations. Although devotional experience rather than doctrine lies at its core, the shared faith of the Maggid's circle can be defined by commitment to the following propositions, articulated partially in language derived directly from the sources.

1. *'Avodah be-Simhah.* The purpose of life is the joyous service of God. God created the world in order to derive pleasure from the devotion of human beings, specifically from the souls of Israel. Our task is to provide that pleasure through constant good works and joyous praise. Be careful of anything that might keep you from that task, especially of excessive religious guilt or calls for self-mortification due to sin. These will only lead you astray from your task of serving God in joy.

2. *Kavvanah.* "God needs to be served in every way." It is not only through Torah study, prayer, and fulfilling specific commandments that we worship God. All of life, including the fulfillment of our physical needs, is to become an avenue of devotion. Transform and uplift every act you do and make it an act of worship.

3. *Penimiyyut.* The essence of religious life lies in inwardness and spiritual intensity. The great battle to be fought is that against "learned" or routinized religious behavior, the opposite of spiritual enthusiasm. Outer deeds are important and the commandments are to be fulfilled, but they are to be seen as means rather than ends, as vessels for the divine light that floods the soul or as concrete embodiments of the heart's inward devotion. *Devekut,* attachment to God, is the goal. All of life, including all the precepts of religion, is to serve as a means toward that end.

4. *Tsimtsum.* Existence originates in the mind of God, where Being is a simple, undifferentiated whole. The words spoken by God to create the world are the essence of existence. Because God is beyond time, that reality has never changed. Our seeming existence as separate beings is the result of *tsimtsum,* the willful contraction or "garbing" of divine presence, a de-intensification of the divine presence so that our minds can stand it and continue to operate as separate selves in order to fulfill our devotional task. In ultimate reality, however, that separate existence is mostly illusion.

5. *Nitsotsot.* God's presence (*shekhinah*) underlies, fills, and includes all of existence. Sparks of divine light are therefore to be found everywhere. The Jew's task is to seek out and discover those sparks, even in the seemingly most unlikely places, in order to raise them up, bring joy to *shekhinah,* and thus reestablish the divine unity that embraces all of being in oneness.

6. *Tefillah.* Prayer is the most essential paradigm of devotional experiences. All of life—including but not limited to Torah study and

mitsvot—should be seen as an extension of the prayer experience, one that involves the entire self and is offered entirely as a gift to God, just as were the sacrifices of Temple times.

7. *Middot.* Our human task is that of uplifting and transforming our physical and emotional selves to become ever more perfect vehicles for God's service. This process begins with the key devotional pair of love and fear. We need to purify these in our lives, coming to realize that the only true love is the love of God and the only worthy fear is our great awe at standing in God's presence. All other loves and fears derive from these, but are in a "fallen" state. True love and fear, and other emotions that follow them, become open channels through which God's blessing can flow into us.

8. *Tsaddik.* The person who lives in accord with these teachings may become a *tsaddik*, a channel for bringing that flow of blessing not only to himself but also to those around him and ultimately to the entire world. Such *tsaddikim* need to enter into the public arena, because they are the only proper leaders of the Jewish people. Combining well-known devotional techniques with his own inner dedication, the *tsaddik* is capable of transforming his consciousness, leaving ordinary perception behind, and rising to states of expanded mind where he sees the divine presence that underlies all existence. These moments are sometime accompanied by apparitions of light or other supernatural manifestations. They are transformative and powerful. In the course of such ascents, the *tsaddik* is able to implant his will for good into the channel of divine blessing that flows through him into the world.

This list, derived from the writings of the Maggid and his disciples, brings together the legacy of the Ba'al Shem Tov, as reported by his followers (especially points 1–3, 6–8), and the Maggid's own enhancement of it (points 4–5). With various slight shifts of emphasis, these views are shared by the entire school, and most are held by other early Hasidic authors as well.

SETTING THE STAGE: ASHKENAZIC PIETY BEFORE HASIDISM

To appreciate the uniqueness of Hasidism and the particular contribution of the Maggid's school, we need to step back in history to a period several generations before it, seeking out the roots of what was to become Hasidism and the reasons for its remarkable success in capturing the hearts and minds of Jews across the reaches of the onetime Polish kingdom and then elsewhere throughout Eastern Europe. Ashkenazic Jewry of the mid-eighteenth century lived in an arc that stretched from Alsace on the Franco-German border in the west to the banks of the Dniepr and the Cossack-dominated steppe to the east. The lingua franca of this highly dispersed community was some form of Yiddish or Judeo-German, spoken in distinctive regional dialects that were largely comprehensible to one another. Although the community's cultural origins lay mostly in the western end of this arc, especially in the ancient communities along the Rhine, its spread and diffusion eastward belonged to the forgotten past, and the communities of Podolia and Volhynia in the Ukraine, where Hasidism first emerged, saw themselves as old and deeply rooted, with memories that extended back to before the great trauma of the peasant uprisings of 1648/49 that resulted in the large-scale murder of Jews and destruction of communities. In fact, by the eighteenth century the pattern of internal migration was beginning to shift toward an east-west direction, including a movement of rabbis and other educated figures from the Polish-Lithuanian heartland to serve communities to their west.

Jews in the easternmost provinces of Poland (until 1772) generally lived in small to midsized market towns (*shtetl*, pl. *shtetlekh*), in which Jews constituted half to threequarters of the population, or in scattered villages and rural hamlets amid the much larger Ukrainian or Belorussian peasant populace. Economically, they often served in various intermediary capacities between the agriculturally based peasantry and their Polish overlords. Small-scale marketplace businesses, trades (especially needle trades), tax-farming, and innkeeping (including production and sale of liquor) served disproportionately as the basis of Jewish economic life. The communities were led by a traditional oligarchy of the few wealthy families (often privileged as such by special connections to the nobility) and a learned rabbinic class that held sway over the internal Jewish court system, governing commerce as well as personal status and ritual matters. The rabbinate also dominated matters relating to education (almost exclusively for boys and men), consisting largely of the passing down of Hebrew literacy and rabbinic lore from one generation to the next.

The intellectual and spiritual life of these communities was shaped by the interplay of two highly developed traditions of post-medieval

Jewry: Talmudism and Kabbalah. Before the modern era, Jews in the Slavic lands lived in a relatively high degree of cultural and linguistic isolation from the surrounding populace. They were thus able to create a separate Jewish civilization, more fully so than in most other Diaspora communities. The model for this was an imaginative re-creation of Babylonian Jewish society as depicted in the Talmud (third to sixth century CE), which they sought to reestablish in Eastern Europe. *Derekh ha-ShaS* ("the Talmudic path") was the way of life in the Ashkenazic communities. Learning, the most highly valued activity for capable Jewish males, was almost exclusively Talmudic in character. Premodern Eastern Europe brought forth rather little creativity in Hebrew poetry, biblical exegesis, or other traditional areas of Jewish literary activity. But it produced a vast and previously unequaled volume of Talmudic commentaries, legal digests, responsa, and other writings around rabbinic law. Ability to study Talmud was the single marker of the educated Jew, and the forms and rubrics of piety were often taken directly from its pages. *Gemore lernen* ("study of Talmud") itself was considered a supreme act of piety, and the text was intoned aloud in a *gemore nign* ("Talmud melody"). The society cultivated a highly unworldly class of pious scholars who dwelt as fully as possible within the world of the Talmudic sages. Revered and idealized for their learned piety, such scholars were depicted as the ideal type of Jewish male and as proper leaders and spiritual exemplars of the Jewish community.

The scholastic traditions of Ashkenazic Jewry had migrated eastward from Germany, Bohemia, and Moravia in the fifteenth and sixteenth centuries. They reached heights of influence over the Polish-Lithuanian communities in the succeeding decades, when works of Talmudic novellae and commentaries on the codes of Jewish law were composed and published by such renowned figures as Rabbi Shmu'el Edels (1555–1631) of Lublin and Ostrog, Rabbi Yo'el Sirkis (1561–1640) of Cracow, and Rabbi Yehoshua Falk (1555–1614) of Lvov, to name but a few. Following this period, Talmudic studies in Poland came to be characterized by an extreme form of casuistry known as *pilpul*, where elaborate argumentation for its own sake or as a display of one's brilliance and erudition became the order of the day. This tendency served to increase the ivory-towered nature of rabbinic learning, keeping these scholars relatively isolated from the daily grind of an existence marked by poverty and insecurity that was the regular lot of most Jews in the region.

The mystical beliefs of Eastern European Jews reflected an amalgam of Kabbalah, a doctrine and symbolic edifice created in Spain and borne eastward by post-expulsion (1492) Spanish exiles, and native Ashkenazic folk beliefs first reflected in the pietistic writings of the medieval Rhineland. These too had moved eastward with the Jewish migration, finding fertile soil as Jews dwelt amid a Christian populace in which folk religion, magic, and demonology flourished, sometimes reflecting old pre-Christian animist traditions that had never been fully eradicated. Popular Kabbalah and magic were fully intertwined and are hard to distinguish from one another. Authors like Moshe of Kiev (fifteenth century) and Shimshon of Ostropolye (d. 1648) were bearers of this popular mystical legacy.

More formal Kabbalistic knowledge includes the symbolic language most fully articulated in the thirteenth-century *Zohar*, its doctrine of emanation and cosmology, and the coordination of its view of the cosmic structure with that of Jewish ritual life and prayer. These secrets came to Poland in the seventeenth century due to the influence of the remarkable mystical revival that was centered in the Galilean town of Safed beginning around 1550. Emissaries from Safed, bearing wondrous tales of this renewed community in the Holy Land, where the mystics walked the same ground once supposedly trodden by Rabbi Shim'on ben Yohai (his grave is just outside Safed) and the other heroes of the *Zohar*, brought their tales northward, disseminating them both orally and in print. Books in which Kabbalistic doctrine was popularized and mixed with moral preaching found widespread acceptance in Eastern Europe. The teachings of classical Kabbalah, as filtered through Safed's Rabbi Moshe Cordovero, arrived in Poland by means of such works as Eliyahu Da Vidas's *Reshit Hokhmah* ("Beginning of Wisdom") and Yeshaya Horowitz's *Sheney Luhot ha-Berit* ("Two Tablets of the Covenant"). Rabbi Yitshak Luria's new Kabbalistic system (often as reshaped by Kabbalists active in northern Italy) also had considerable influence, primarily through widely circulated manuscripts. Mystical prayer manuals by East Europeans in the eighteenth century show particularly strong Lurianic influence.

The intense fascination with Kabbalistic secrets reached a boiling point in the messianic outbreak around Shabbatai Zevi of Izmir, Turkey, beginning in 1666 and reverberating throughout the Jewish world well into the mid-eighteenth century. Scholars remain divided as to the causes of the movement and whether it was the mystical teachings themselves or their interaction with emerging modernity, with Christian-raised Iberian Jewish refugees, or with mercantile society that lent such great power to the Sabbatian dream of imminent redemption. While the movement's greatest strength in its early days lay in the Spanish- and Portuguese-speaking Jewries around the Mediterranean and Atlantic coastlines, by the early 1700s its influence in Central and Eastern Europe was considerable. Jacob Frank, a Polish Jew who crowned himself as a new Shabbatai, led a band of Jewish heretics in the Ukraine in the 1750s, in areas very close to the early centers of Hasidism, leading to fierce persecution by the rabbis and ultimately to the expulsion of Frank and his followers from the community and their conversion to Christianity. Certain devotional tropes were common to the two movements, especially the sense of spiritual adventurism that lay in descending into the depths (intentional sin for the Sabbatians, while only fluttering thoughts of sin or temptation for the *hasidim*) in order to release trapped sparks and souls.

Kabbalistic works, still considered too esoteric for the masses (and thus seldom translated from Hebrew into the vernacular), were taught and studied quite widely by Jews with even a modicum of rabbinic education. As Hebrew printing spread in Eastern Europe after 1750, a great many Kabbalistic and semi-Kabbalistic books appeared in multiple editions. As was the case in Spain, Safed, Italy, and elsewhere, Jewish mysticism tended to be studied and practiced in small closed conventicles of masters and disciples. These groups in the Sephardic lands were known as *havurot* or Kabbalistic *yeshivot* ("fellowships" or "academies"). In Eastern Europe they also took the name *kloiz* (pl. *kloizlekh*), stemming from the small "cloistered" room in which such study took place. By the middle of the eighteenth century we have reports of such *kloizlekh* in a number of towns, in some cases led or taught by an identified charismatic master, but elsewhere seemingly closer to a group of peers drawn to the mystical life—especially to the sharply ascetic practices with which mystical piety had come to be identified.

The nature of these informal groups varied from place to place; each seemed to arise quite spontaneously, perhaps due to the confluence of a charismatic teacher and a generous benefactor willing to sponsor both the place and modest stipends for master and disciples. The *kloiz* presented itself primarily as a study center, featuring a religious activity that was entirely normative for Jewish communities everywhere. Both esoteric and Talmudic studies were pursued by these groups, which belonged in varying degrees to the learned elite class within their communities. In spirit, however, such groups as the *kloiz* in Brody and the *havurah* in Kossov devoted themselves intensely to pursuing a mystical-ascetic regimen of practice, including intense prayer, fasting, and self-mortification, designed to suppress bodily desires (the "evil urge") and all sorts of material concerns in order to bring forth the purest spiritual self.

These proto-Hasidic circles, as we might call them, began to develop certain distinctive practices, setting them off from the community at large. In addition to having separate locations for their prayer and study, they were characterized by early opponents as engaging in lengthy and loud prayer, of drinking to excess (this did not seem to contradict their ascetic aspirations), and of diverting time from Talmud study to carry forth lengthy conversations about moral and spiritual issues. They were known to dress entirely in white on the Sabbath, a custom adopted from Kabbalists in Safed, and to hold communal celebrations of *se'udah shlishit*, the concluding meal of the Sabbath. They also prayed following the Sephardic rite, for its greater affinity to Kabbalistic secrets, rather than following the local Ashkenazic custom.

PERSONALITIES AND HISTORICAL EVENTS: 1740–1762

Sometime in the late 1730s the figure of Yisrael ben Eliezer, later known as the Ba'al Shem Tov, appears at the margins of the Kossov group. He was thought of as somewhat gruff in speech and appearance, having spent a decade or more as a semi-hermit in the untamed wilds of the Carpathian Mountains. His birthplace is disputed, but it seems that he spent at least part of his formative years on the western side of those mountains where the surrounding cultural milieu was Moldavian rather than Ukrainian. The Carpathians were home to numerous Orthodox monasteries of both ethnic groups, among whom ancient traditions of Hesychast prayer (endless devotion through constant repetition of brief prayer formulae focused on the name of Jesus) were maintained. Elements of folk religion and shamanism were also very much alive among the uneducated mountain peasantry of that region.

Yisrael ben Eliezer was known as a *ba'al shem* (lit. "master of the name"), which meant that he was skilled in the art of healing by means of oral formulae or written amulets containing the name of God. The great focus of "practical Kabbalah" on the name or names of God, though often employed in semi-magical ways, bears some interesting resemblance to Christian Hesychasm. Indeed it is not out of the question that these traditions branched forth from a single ancient source. Typically a *ba'al shem* would combine this spiritual legacy of divine names with a knowledge of herbal medicine and other folk traditions of healing, so that the patients who came to them would not know whether it was the herbs, the potions, the holy names, or the sometimes strange behavioral counsels that brought about their healing. There were *ba'aley shem* who were actually shamans who had experiences of transformed consciousness, including visual and auditory experiences of a supernatural sort. The Ba'al Shem Tov belonged to this group. On this level of society there was a great deal of contact and sharing of information across ethno-religious lines. Surely the Ba'al Shem Tov spoke the language(s) of the mountain people and learned from them, perhaps in the spiritual and magical as well as the medicinal skills, in an age and place where the lines between these were anything but clearly drawn.

Understanding Yisrael Ba'al Shem Tov has always rightly been taken as a key to fathoming Hasidism's origins, even though scholars now agree that the phenomenon of proto-Hasidic groups in Eastern Europe preceded him and that the Hasidic movement as such was created by the circle of the Maggid, not appearing on the screen of history until a dozen years after the Ba'al Shem Tov's death. The latter is so important largely because of the role assigned to him by the later movement. Within a generation after his death, the Ba'al Shem Tov had become a mythic figure, taking on a role not unlike that of Rabbi Yitshak Luria in the spreading forth of the legends of Safed some two centuries earlier. All Hasidic groups, both early and late, see themselves as standing in his lineage. In many a Hasidic prayer room around the world one can find a framed print in the form of a tree, showing each school of Hasidism and how it derives through a complex system of limbs and branches from the single root that is the BeSHT. Indeed it is fair to say that in a Hasidic movement large and diverse enough to embrace such varied teachings as those of HaBaD, Bratslav, Komarno, Kotsk, and more, what holds them together is their shared sense of this lineage, each claiming to be a faithful representation of the BeSHT's teachings.

We know about the Ba'al Shem Tov from a rather sparse group of literary sources. He was apparently an entirely oral teacher who did not leave us any books. According to legend, he was even opposed to the writing down of his spiritual counsels, presumably because their freshness in the oral moment and the direct address to a specific hearer would be lost. All we have from his hand are a few letters, including one very important one addressed to his brother-in-law R. Gershon of Kitov, who had settled in the Holy Land in 1747. This highly revealing text, recounting a mystical experience, exists in several recensions and has been analyzed repeatedly by scholars. It is often seen as a cornerstone for understanding the BeSHT and his religious life.

In addition to the letters, we have hundreds of teachings in the Ba'al Shem Tov's name, quoted in the works of his disciples and those who came after them. Particularly reliable are the quotations of authors who knew him personally and in some cases heard the teachings directly from him. Most prominent among these are R. Ya'akov Yosef of Polonnoye, author of the first Hasidic books printed; R. Dov Baer of Mezritch, leader of the circle whose teachings fill this volume; and the BeSHT's own grandson, R. Moshe Hayyim Ephraim of Sudylkow. These quotations are of particular importance because they show us the legacy of the BeSHT as it was transmitted into the nascent Hasidic movement. Both those aspects of the BeSHT's teaching that are emphasized and those that are lacking or downplayed in these quotations offer significant room for investigation.

The teachings quoted are mostly single lines, new and dramatic readings of older sources, often with an ingenious homiletic twist. Occasionally there is a longer parable; the BeSHT was apparently an avid storyteller who favored the parabolic form. The sources he interprets represent a wide swath of Jewish literature, including biblical verses, Talmudic passages, and quotations from the *Zohar* and later Kabbalistic writings. He was an avid reader of the most esoteric strain within Jewish mystical literature, that devoted to inner experience, ascents to higher realms, and mysteries associated with both light and language. His quotations and comments cannot be said to evince scholarship in the conventional rabbinic sense, but they show a highly creative mind exposed to a variety of texts that constantly restimulated his religious imagination, causing him to interpret them in bold and sometimes surprising ways. This surprising of the mind by a new reading of familiar sources served as a kind of awakening device, stimulating the hearer to a deeper sort of consciousness. It was an important part of the BeSHT's legacy to the movement that came after him.

The third source for the Ba'al Shem Tov is the body of Hasidic legends that grew up around him. The first and most important collection of these is known as *Shivhey ha-BeSHT* ("Praises of the BeSHT"), published in 1815 in both Hebrew and Yiddish versions. This hagiographic tour-de-force, probably edited in the 1790s from several different manuscript collections, was meant as a propaganda tool for the popular spread of the movement, particularly supporting the efforts of the emerging HaBaD school in Belorussia. Like parallel volumes honoring Yitshak Luria and Hayyim Vital (and indeed like "saints' lives" in all traditions), it cannot be treated uncritically as a historical source. It includes accounts of miracle working, defeat of werewolves, and other tales that raise the eyebrow of any modern reader. There are tales within it that have been shown to be much older, with only the names of participants and places changed to fit the BeSHT. On the other hand, it is clear that in many ways its original assemblers were very familiar with details of the age in which the BeSHT lived and the people around him as well as the very particular spiritual physiognomy of his circle. Careful scholars have shown that it is possible to sift significant historical information out from among the legendary and literary embellishments. Sometimes this has to be done by sharp critical inquiry, and conclusions drawn remain controversial. If, for example, the legends tell us that the BeSHT carefully appointed R. Dov Baer the Maggid to be his successor, is this tradition to be taken at face value or does it tell us precisely the opposite, that there was controversy about the succession (as indicated by other sources) and that the editors were taking a stand? This and many other questions about the use of *Shivhey ha-BeSHT* continue to vex scholars, but it is no longer regularly dismissed as "mere legend."

It is clear that the Ba'al Shem Tov made his name as a clairvoyant and a wonder-worker or, to use a more controversial term, a magician. He knew enough secrets about the upper worlds and their operation, including those revealed to him in experiences like the "soul ascent" described in his famous letter, to cure the afflicted, to foretell the future, and to look into people's souls. He was a master at the art of prayer, serving as a guide to both ecstatic experiences around liturgical prayer ("come to see the lights within the letters ...") and the raising up of petitions to the heights of divine attention. It is also clear from that document that his interests extended far beyond those of individual clients who might come to him for a magical or medicinal cure. He speaks there of saving entire communities from plagues, both the sort created by the "germs" of evil spirits and those brought about by the hostile environs amid which Jews in his district lived. He had a special spirit-realm master in the biblical prophet Ahijah of Shiloh (cf. 1 Kings 11:29ff.), who is famous mainly because he was also teacher to the prophet Elijah, the original healer/miracle worker of the Jewish tradition.

Despite his ventures into the upper worlds, the Ba'al Shem Tov seems never to have lost the simple touch. He was known throughout his life as loving and caring for ordinary, unlettered people and revering them as repositories of secret wisdom. Many of the tales told about him, as well as some of his teachings, reflect this attraction to simple folk and their faith. While his closest disciples may have been taught a mystical path of gazing into the letters of the prayer book and discerning divine lights within them, the folk tradition of Hasidism has him approving the prayers of a simple Jew who said, "Lord of the World! I have forgotten the prayers I learned as a child. All I remember from school are the letters of the alphabet. But You, Lord, know all the prayers. I will give You the letters, and You put them together." And he prayed, "*Aleph, bet, gimel ...*" A particularly revealing passage in *Shivhey ha-BeSHT* (one hard to imagine as a later invention) says that at an early stage of his mystical development the BeSHT was unable to speak in a normal way, apparently rendered incapable of ordinary conversation by powerful inner experiences. His above-mentioned master came to him and had him recite the verse "Blessed are those of the simple path" (Ps. 119:1) to help him regain his composure. The BeSHT seems to have taken this lesson deeply to heart. Perhaps this tale says something significant about his attraction both to simplicity and to language.

A significant part of the BeSHT's teaching was devoted to techniques of prayer. While mystics of prior ages had always reflected on the liturgy, discovering within its texts repositories of secret lore, and admonitions to pray with intense concentration abound in the tradition, there was relatively little material available on the question of *how* to pray effectively. Prayer instructions abound in early Hasidic writings, many of them attributed to the BeSHT himself. These begin with comments contained in his most famous letter, about counsel on prayer he had received during his heavenly journey:

> In prayer and study, intend every single word coming forth from your lips to be a unification. In each and every letter there are worlds, souls, and divinity. These rise forth and combine with one another. Afterwards the letters themselves unite to form a word. These are truly united with divinity. Bind your soul to them at each and every

one of these levels. Then all the worlds will be united as one, rising in indescribable joy and delight. If you can imagine the joy of bride and groom on the lesser material plane, it is so much greater on this upper level....[2]

The BeSHT called for wholeness in the act of prayer. Widely attributed to him is a play on words based on the identity of the biblical Hebrew *tevah*, meaning "ark" and the rabbinic term for "word." God's instruction to Noah "Come into the ark, you and all your household" (Gen. 7:1) then comes to be read as "Come into the word, bringing along your entire self." Do not be divided in the act of prayer; only as a whole person can you come before the single God. This led to a particularly striking counsel with regard to distractions or even sinful thoughts that arise during prayer. Do not seek to fight them off, the Ba'al Shem Tov taught, because that will only lead to division within the self. Understand rather that these thoughts have come to you in the sacred moment of prayer because they themselves are in need of redemption. Welcome them, strip them of their sinfulness, but then use their energy to activate and strengthen your own prayer. Not surprisingly, this advice was later seen as highly controversial, not least because the example of such sinful thoughts most commonly offered was that of desire for one's neighbor's wife.

The motif of uplifting and transformation was applied by the Ba'al Shem Tov not only to wayward thoughts during prayer but also to a wide range of spiritual phenomena. He was able to see fallen souls, including those already departed, and to work at their redemption. Fallen sparks of divine light might be trapped within nature or even in the alien and hostile realm of the gentiles among whom his Jews dwelled. The Jew's task was ever to seek out and uplift these sparks, even if that meant considerable risk. Thus a marketplace encounter with a peasant or even one of their folk melodies might be raised up to serve as a sacred vessel for God's service. This sense of spiritual adventurism is part of what made Hasidism so attractive to many a young seeker. But we should also note that this is the point at which Hasidism touches most closely on Sabbatianism and its mystical heresy. "Descent for the sake of ascent" is precisely what Shabbatai Zevi's followers had seen in their master's bizarre behavior, and some sought to emulate it in extreme ways. An early tale about the BeSHT says that he once sought to redeem the fallen soul of Shabbatai Zevi. Only at the final stage of uplifting did he realize that in fact the wicked Shabbatai was trying to pull him downward. The

BeSHT broke the connection and cast the false messiah down to hell. Could it be that such a tale recalls an early involvement the BeSHT might have had with Sabbatian believers? Was this notion of "uplifting" a purified version of something valuable and spiritually exciting that he had encountered there?

As an ecstatic and visionary religious personality, the BeSHT was especially attracted to the few surviving elements of the *merkavah* tradition, that earliest stage in Jewish mysticism that described the mystic voyagers' ascent through the heavenly palaces. This ecstatic "journey" finally brought them to stand directly before God's throne and to join into, or even lead, the chorus of heavenly angels. The Ba'al Shem Tov knew such experiences. The letter to R. Gershon describes what he calls "an oath of soul-ascent." The oath formula is derived from the most ancient books of Jewish magic, where the voyager adjures the angels of each heavenly rung not to harm him as he passes through their "territory." As an amulet writer deeply attached to holy names, he was also an adept at the endless permutations and numerical speculations around Y-H-W-H and other names of God, augmented by the Lurianic tradition but rooted in much older mystical/magical texts and praxis. The mysteries of language, both spoken and written, were sources of great fascination to him; those earlier texts that delved into these mysteries spoke to his soul. He discovered new insights into them and made teachings and meditations on speech and the letters of the alphabet a key part of his legacy.

Like most great religious personalities, the BeSHT was a complex individual who cannot be analyzed through a single lens. It should be no surprise to us that some aspects of his vision seem to be in tension with others. The elevation of simplicity and faith in his teachings seems to contradict the ability to foretell the future. Why not just accept life as it comes and place one's trust in God? The great emphasis on humility seems belied by his attempts to affect the will of heaven through his prayers. No simple resolution of these tensions is required; all of them reflect some authentic part of the man and his legacy. He is both humble mystic and bold magician. Somehow those aspects managed to exist side by side within him, as they do in the lives of charismatic religious personalities in all ages and in every tradition.

Possibly the most distinctive feature of the Ba'al Shem Tov's teaching in his own day, and that which set him off from the established pious conventicles that preceded him, was his clear rejection of the ascetic path by which mystical Jewish piety had become so sharply defined in his day. The original Lurianic sources had already tended in this direction, but they were augmented and pulled to greater extremes by a flurry of *Tikkuney Teshuvah*, or Manuals of Penitence, published both during and after the Sabbatian debacle. The earliest of these sought to heighten messianic expectations by creating brotherhoods of extreme penitents, a well-known phenomenon among end-time believers in other religions as well. Afterward, Jews repenting of sins in thought or deed that had led them astray during the messianic outburst also turned to severe prescriptions for their return to the proper path. While all sorts of sins are treated in these manuals, a great deal of emphasis is unsurprisingly laid on sexual misdeeds. The punishments prescribed even for thoughts of temptation or involuntary emission of semen are stupendous, to say nothing of those for the forbidden deeds themselves.

All of this the Ba'al Shem Tov was willing to lay aside. His attraction to simplicity (*temimut*) also bore with it a strong sense of wholeness and self-acceptance. He knew a God who wanted to be served by the entire self, by the evil as well as the good impulse. His counsel regarding prayer was also applied more widely, extending to the entire religious life. So long as you are divided against yourself, he taught, you are not whole enough to come fully before God. He saw great danger in excessive guilt, something that would keep the person from serving God in wholeness. It is a trick of the Evil One, he said, to trip you up in some small sin and then cause you to worry so much about it that you will be unable to open your heart in prayer. Better to leave the sin behind quickly, regret it without dwelling upon it, and return to serving God in joy.

Without psychoanalyzing the BeSHT, it is not possible for us to explain how he was able to make the breakthrough in consciousness that allowed him to liberate himself, and then so many others, from this assumed linking of spiritual intensity and extreme self-mortification and guilt. We may guess, however, based on both tales and teachings, that this was a person who had found healthy fulfillment in his own marital life. How else, for example, would he come up with the suggestion that Israel remain unredeemed "because they do not take long enough in reciting the *ahavah rabbah* prayer [speaking of God's great love, directly preceding the *shema*], which represents the kisses that precede the coupling"? Is there not a certain healthy acceptance of sexuality reflected in his teaching that a Jew should move the body back and forth during prayer, since that is the way one moves in the act of love and "prayer is coupling with the *shekhinah* [the feminine divine presence]"? Of course it was precisely pronouncements like these that so enraged the rabbis who opposed Hasidism.

Later sources, inspired by images already found in *Shivhey ha-BeSHT*, depict the Ba'al Shem Tov as a prominent Hasidic master surrounded by a well-established "court." While this view is almost certainly anachronistic, we do know that he was a figure of some respectability in the important market town of Miedzybozh. From about 1740 he lived tax—and rent—free under the aegis of the Miedzybozh communal leadership, serving as healer, teacher, and Kabbalist-in-residence. He seems to have led his own *kloiz* in Miedzybozh and to have accrued some significant disciples over the two decades of his residence there. Most of these were probably locals, attracted both by the Ba'al Shem Tov's charisma and by the mystical teachings offered in his circle. But as his reputation spread, some came from beyond Miedzybozh as well. These included figures who clearly outshone him greatly in rabbinic learning, the usual measure of status among the intellectual elite, but who nevertheless revered him and repeatedly refer to him in their writings as "my teacher." Two of these disciples require further discussion here.

Ya'akov Yosef of Polonnoye (d. 1783) was rabbi of Szarogrod, one of the largest Podolian Jewish communities, when, in the 1740s, he became attracted to Hasidism of the pre-BeSHTian type, including both self-isolation for meditative prayer and a rigorous pattern of ascetic self-mortification. His community was not pleased with this turn, and he was deposed from his rabbinic post. One of his guides in the ascetic life, a figure known as Aryeh Leib the "reprover" (this term, like *maggid*, meant that he was a preacher but not a rabbi) of Polonnoye, introduced him to the Ba'al Shem Tov, who had begun making a name for himself in these proto-Hasidic circles. Their meeting apparently changed Ya'akov Yosef's life. For the next thirty-some years he humbly referred to Israel ben Eliezer as "my teacher," even though he was by far the greater scholar by any conventional measure of rabbinic knowledge. R. Ya'akov Yosef was author of four volumes of collected sermons, three of which stand among the first printed works of Hasidism, beginning in 1780. In hundreds of places his long and erudite homilies, often quite difficult to follow, are dotted with brief quotations that "I heard from my teacher" or "I heard in my teacher's name."

What was it in the BeSHT's message that was so transformative for Ya'akov Yosef? Fortunately we do not have to resort to guesswork on this question. We have preserved a brief letter the Ba'al Shem Tov wrote to his disciple, published as an addendum to *Shivhey ha-BeSHT* in 1815. The scholarly consensus is that this letter is to be considered authentic. In it the BeSHT, responding to a letter Ya'akov Yosef had written him, says the following:

> I saw from the opening lines of your letter that you consider it mandatory to fast. My stomach was turned when I heard this cry, and I hereby respond. By the word of the angels, the blessed Holy One and His *shekhinah*, you must not endanger yourself in this way! This is an act of melancholy and sorrow. "*Shekhinah* does not come to dwell out of sorrow ... but only out of the joy of performing a commandment" (b. Shabbat 30b). You know this because I have taught it to you several times. You need to keep it upon your heart.... "Do not turn away from your own flesh" (Is. 58:7). God forbid that you fast any more than is obligatory. If you listen to my voice, God will be with you....[3]

This is a remarkable little document, highly revealing of both its author and its recipient. The BeSHT's insistent tone shows that he could be a powerful and highly directive master. The disciple, though having received this message several times in the past, somehow refuses to listen to it. The BeSHT understands that the attraction to asceticism comes from a place of melancholy, probably derived from excessive religious guilt. He is willing to pull out all the stops in combating this, proclaiming his position to be the will of heaven declared by God and the angels. The Talmudic quotation might have been sufficient to make this point, but he insists on presenting it as though freshly revealed to him from above.

The master seals his position by a most powerful reinterpretation of a biblical verse, a good example of the "surprising of the mind" mentioned above. "Do not turn away from your own flesh," a prophetic line well known from the *haftarah* (prophetic reading) for Yom Kippur, means "Do not turn your gaze away from the poor and needy, for they are your own people. You and they are 'one flesh,' as it were." Here the BeSHT reads it to mean "Do not turn away from your *own* flesh," do not reject your own bodily self and its needs. This startling rereading of the familiar line must have had a great impact on Ya'akov Yosef. A man who had both the insight and the daring to transform the meaning of Scripture in this helpful and healing way indeed deserved to be called "my teacher."

The second important disciple is Dov Baer of Mezritch, the central figure of the circle whose writings are represented here. Dov Baer, only a few years younger than the BeSHT, was also much more learned in the sources than the one who was to become his master. But in his case those sources tended more toward Kabbalah than Talmud. Dov Baer was a preacher in an area and generation when homiletics was mostly shaped by the mystical tradition; he was never an ordained rabbi like Ya'akov Yosef. The legendary tradition has it that he too came to the BeSHT quite reluctantly, seeking healing from illness that had been brought on by excessive fasting. The BeSHT healed him in what can only be described as a shamanic ritual, encircling Dov Baer with a magically powered staff while calling out a passage from the *merkavah* tradition. This apparently began a relationship marked by a shared learning of mystical sources in which the more scholarly disciple saw the texts come alive in a new way as read or declaimed by a living ecstatic. According to a famous tale of one of their early encounters, the BeSHT's other followers were duly impressed when Dov Baer came up with a reading of an obscure text that was identical to one they had heard from their teacher. To their "How could he know that?" the BeSHT replied in a formula that was to become typical of Hasidism: "He doesn't just *know* the Torah; he *is* the Torah."

While both the BeSHT and the Maggid bore pieces of the mystical legacy that might have earned them the title "Kabbalist," in fact their bodies of knowledge and the ways in which they knew and taught them were significantly different. The BeSHT, both as an ecstatic religious personality and "professionally" as a *ba'al shem*, was drawn to some of the most directly experiential and formerly most esoteric aspects of Jewish mystical lore. These included fragments of the ancient *merkavah* visions (mostly available only in manuscript, but included in such printed works as *The Book of Raziel the Angel*) and speculations around secrets of letters and numbers that had their earliest root in *Sefer Yetsirah*, The Book of Creation. These had been augmented over the centuries, especially in the thirteenth-century school of Avraham Abulafia, and again in the wake of the Safed revival. While comments on the *Zohar* and other more "mainstream" Kabbalistic works are also attributed to him, these formed the core of his esoteric curriculum.

For the Maggid, study of Kabbalah centered on the *Zohar* and the legacies of Cordovero and Luria, as discussed above. Mystical ideas were also derived from such popular but respectably rabbinic authors as Nahmanides, Bahya ben Asher (both thirteenth-century Spain), and Rabbi Loew, or the MaHaRaL (sixteenth-century Prague). The Maggid was much more a contemplative than an ecstatic, sinking into and ultimately losing himself in the depths of a mystical idea rather than seeing visions, hearing voices, or engaging in shamanic rites. While we have a disciple's testimony that the BeSHT taught the Maggid his supernatural ways, these were notably not passed on to the next generation of followers. The BeSHT surely must have recognized the difference between himself and the Maggid as religious personalities and did not try to make his disciple into a clone of himself. Nevertheless, he taught the Maggid to read classic Jewish sources with a revivalist's eye, cultivating in him his own talent for original and sometimes startling readings that would serve to awaken the soul.

As mentioned above, there is a good bit of attention devoted in *Shivhey ha-BeSHT* and other legendary sources to the Ba'al Shem Tov's designation of the Maggid as his chosen successor. This has rightly led scholars to consider whether this textual certitude might serve to cover over precisely the opposite: a dispute over leadership after the original master's passing. But a more contemporary view of early Hasidic history would have to pose the question differently. Just what was it that the Maggid was to inherit? There was not yet a "Hasidic movement" over which he could preside. Surely he was not being offered leadership of the *kloiz* in Miedzybozh, the only institution over which the BeSHT held sway, or the position of supported "Kabbalist in residence" of that town. It is hard to imagine that this was a transfer of power in the magical dimension, like the prophet Elijah's ordination of Elisha, given our sense that the special powers of the BeSHT in that realm were not what the Maggid in fact most valued. The famous later Hasidic formulation that after the Ba'al Shem Tov died "the *shekhinah* packed her bags and moved to Mezritch" seems retrospective. In fact, not all the Hasidic teachers in that generation became disciples of the Maggid. R. Ya'akov Yosef continued as a lone literary figure, as did several other writers who had clearly been influenced by the BeSHT. Independent circles of master and disciples existed around such distinctive personalities as Pinhas of Korzec (1728–1791) and Yehiel Mikhel of Zloczow (1721–1786).

AROUND THE MAGGID'S TABLE: DRAMATIS PERSONAE

For a period of some ten years Dov Baer, first in Mezritch and then in Rovno, presided as the head of the most significant Hasidic circle. The importance of that circle lies not only in its members' extensive literary output, the basis of our present collection, but also in the fact that it was they who chose to greatly widen the influence of Hasidic teaching and essentially to create Hasidism as a mass movement. In the extensive anti-Hasidic polemical literature of 1772–1800 it is almost always members of the Maggid's circle who stand at the center of controversy. It was they who sought to "conquer" new communities for the movement, to introduce Hasidic practices and customs over wide geographical realms, and when necessary to take on opponents in public disputation and controversy. While there were indeed contemporary Hasidic authors writing and devotional circles flourishing outside the Maggid's domain, we almost never find them embroiled in the great Hasidic versus mitnaggedic ("oppositionist") confrontation.

Because of this, it seems correct to assume that, sometime in the 1760s, a decision was taken by members of this group, probably with the reluctant agreement of its leader, to "go public" with Hasidic teachings and to offer them as an alternative vision of Jewish religious life intended to have mass appeal. Members of the circle spread outward from "around the Maggid's table," especially to the north, taking Hasidic ideas from the two Ukrainian provinces of Podolia and Volhyn across the vast distances of Polesia and Belorussia even to the gates of Lithuania, where they were to meet strong opposition. Within the original Hasidic heartland there seems to have been rather limited controversy regarding the Maggid's disciples and their teachings, possibly because of relatively weak rabbinic leadership. But as their influence spread, rumors of a new "sect" and its dangerous heresies went with it, culminating in a single semi-formal meeting of the disciples in 1772 in response to the publication of the first bans against them, to be discussed below.

The subtitle of this collection of teachings, *Spiritual Teachings from around the Maggid's Table*, might seem to depict a period in which all the authors quoted here, as well as others who did not write, were gathered as one around a great study-hall table in Mezritch. Such a picture is an artifice, however. We do not know how often the disciples visited, how long they stayed during such visits, or how frequently they encountered one another. One author who is here counted among the disciples,

R. Meshullam Feibish Heller, seems to indicate that he visited the Maggid only once (he was primarily a member of the Zloczow circle). Others, including the brothers R. Elimelekh of Lizhensk (Lezajsk) and Zusya of Hanipoli, are said, at least in the legendary materials, to have been much more frequent visitors. Shne'ur Zalman of Lyady seems to have had particularly close friendships with the Maggid's son Avraham ("the angel") and Levi Yitshak of Berdichev (Berdyczow). Some of the younger disciples were brought to Mezritch by older members of the fellowship who were already spreading the teachings. One gets the impression, especially from the Hasidic tales, that the Maggid's disciples formed an intense friendship circle, not just an ideological school. Regardless of whether particular disciples of the Maggid sat facing one another across the table or how often they did so, they surely were exposed to the same sets of ideas, struggled with the same questions, argued with one another about issues raised in the nascent Hasidic body of teachings, and worked cooperatively to some degree in spreading the message outward. The disciples' works from which the teachings included in these volumes are translated were all published at least a decade, some of them several decades, after the Maggid's death. Almost none of the teachings are specifically dated; we therefore cannot know in what year they were spoken or how much later they might have been committed to writing. Nevertheless, the teachers represented here are clearly an intellectual and spiritual school, dealing with a range of issues that recur in variously nuanced ways throughout their writings. It is fair to assume that this school was forged in the years when its master was yet alive, and was driven by memories of the spiritual intensity experienced and shared around the Maggid's table.

The mid-nineteenth-century bibliography *Shem ha-Gedolim he-Hadash* by Aaron Walden lists thirty-one people as disciples of the Maggid. Nearly all are represented in this collection. Judging both from quotations in their works and from later legendary sources, some were close and longtime followers of the Maggid, visiting frequently, while others came to Mezritch only once or occasionally. There was certainly overlap between the Mezritch circle and other early Hasidic groups, especially that around R. Yehiel Mikhel of Zloczow.

While we do not have accounts by the disciples describing their visits to Mezritch, we are in possession of a most remarkable description by a onetime visitor who chose not to become a disciple—indeed who opted for a radically different way of life. I refer to a chapter in the autobiography of Salomon Maimon (c. 1753–1800), Kantian philosopher and member of the Berlin *haskalah*, or "enlightenment," circle. As a precocious adolescent, young Maimon made a visit sometime in the late 1760s to the center of a "new sect" led by a certain R. B. in the town of M., surely referring to Baer of Mezritch. Published only many years later (1793), the description in Maimon's *Lebensgeschichte* is a unique source that tells of a memory seemingly undimmed by the passage of time. Because of its singular importance, it makes sense to quote it at some length:

> I resolved therefore to undertake a journey to M___, where the superior B___ resided. At last I arrived at M___, and after having rested from my journey I went to the house of the superior under the impression that I could be introduced to him at once. I was told, however, that he could not speak with me at the time, but that I was invited to his table on Sabbath along with the other strangers who had come to visit him; that I should then have the happiness of seeing the saintly man face to face, and of hearing the sublime teachings from his own mouth. Although this was a public audience, yet, on account of the individual references which I should find made to myself, I might regard it as a special interview.
>
> Accordingly, on Sabbath I went to this solemn meal, and found there a large number of respectable men who had gathered from various quarters. At length the awe-inspiring great man appeared, clothed in white satin. Even his shoes and snuffbox were white, this being among the Kabbalists the color of grace. He gave every newcomer his greeting. We sat down to table and during the meal a solemn silence reigned. After the meal was over, the superior struck up a solemn inspiring melody, held his hand for some time upon his brow, and then began to call out, "Z___ of H___, M___ of R___," and so on. Every newcomer was thus called by his own name and the name of his residence, which excited no little astonishment. Each recited, as he was called, some verse of the Holy Scriptures. Thereupon the superior commenced to deliver a sermon for which the verses served as a text, so that although they were disconnected verses taken from different parts of the Holy Scriptures they were combined with as much skill as if they had formed a single whole. What was still more extraordinary, every one of the newcomers believed that he had discovered, in that part of the sermon which was founded on his verse, something that had reference to the facts of his own spiritual life. At this we were of course greatly astonished.[4]

We do not know who the others around the table were on the Sabbath of Maimon's visit. Although many of the Maggid's followers were well-known figures by the time his book appeared, its author dwelt in another universe and would not have known whether he had met and chatted with people who subsequently became famous as Hasidic leaders. If we imagine this visit to have taken place in approximately 1768, the Maggid would have been sixty-four years old; most of the disciples would have been slightly older than Maimon, in their twenties and early thirties, but still a relatively young group. Revivalist teachings, as we know from other settings, are often most attractive to footloose young men. We do not know whether Maimon's description of the Maggid's way of constructing his sermon was a regular practice or a high-wire feat that was tried only occasionally (we do possess one other account of a similar technique used by the Maggid's disciple R. Hayyim Hayka of Amdur). Reading his *Maggid Devarav le-Ya'akov* does not immediately reveal it to be a work composed in this extraordinary way, a description that might better fit such a free-associative thinker as R. Nahman of Bratslav. We also have to discount the critical tone of Maimon to some degree. He probably felt, even all those years later, some need to justify why he had not cast in his lot with these partially admirable pietists and had chosen such a different course.

Of the thirty or more people whom Hasidic memory records as disciples of the Maggid, special credit for the spread of Hasidism has to go to seven of the closer disciples. These are the persons mentioned most frequently in the anti-Hasidic writings and known to have been involved in public controversy surrounding their Hasidic views. A brief biographical paragraph on each will follow. The first four listed are those who carried the Maggid's teachings northward, thus encountering particularly strong opposition.

R. Menahem Mendel of Vitebsk (c. 1730–1788)

One of the eldest of Dov Baer's disciples, Menahem Mendel of Vitebsk was the first leader of Hasidism in northern Belorussia. After the Maggid's death, several others in the area saw him as their new master. In 1777, partly in response to the fierce persecution of Hasidism, he led a group of disciples to settle in the Holy Land, creating the first permanent Hasidic community there, centered in Tiberias. In the relative isolation of the Land of Israel, he and his follower Avraham Kalisker (see below) were able to create an intense bond of fellowship among the disciples, unencumbered by the need to popularize their message for a wider audience. His book *Peri ha-Arets* was first published in 1814.

R. Avraham of Kalisk (1741–1810)

Avraham of Kalisk (called the Kalisker) followed R. Menahem Mendel, first to Belorussia and then to Tiberias. After Menahem Mendel's death, he became head of the Tiberias circle. Later he became embroiled in public controversy with R. Shne'ur Zalman of Lyady. This dispute had both ideological (he opposed Shne'ur Zalman's semi-systematic treatise *Tanya* as "garbing the teachings of the BeSHT in those of Rabbi Yitshak Luria") and economic elements, involving the collecting of funds in Belorussia needed to support the Tiberias community. In the midst of this controversy, Shne'ur Zalman accused him of having been responsible for the first opposition to Hasidism, having aroused the 1772 bans by the "childish" ways he had acted in 1770 (called TaLK, based on Hebrew-letter designation of that year, [5]530 AM), overstepping the bounds of respectability by loud outcries during prayer, turning somersaults in front of the ark, and other forms of bizarre behavior. While the conflict between them may have exaggerated these claims, it is hard to think that they were wholly imaginary.

R. Shne'ur Zalman of Lyady (c. 1745–1812)

Shne'ur Zalman was founder of the HaBaD school and the Schneersohn dynasty. He was the youngest and most junior of the threesome who went out to "conquer" his native northern Belorussia for Hasidism, but after the emigration of Menahem Mendel and the Kalisker he became the de facto leader of Hasidism in his area. His following grew vast, both locally and in other parts of Eastern Europe, partly due to the influence of his *Tanya*, first published in 1796. He was the key figure in the final round of the Hasidic-mitnaggedic conflict, and in 1798 he was arrested by the Russian authorities and imprisoned in Saint Petersburg. He was a profound thinker and prolific author, and his homilies read more like extended treatises on mystical ideas than like other Hasidic sermons.

R. Aharon of Karlin (1736–1772)

An early activist among the Maggid's disciples, R. Aharon established a prayer-house in Karlin, a suburb of the important community of Pinsk in Polesia. His prominence in spreading Hasidism is indicated by the fact that many of the early anti-Hasidic tracts simply refer to *hasidim* as "Karliners." His message was significantly simpler and more folk-oriented than that of Shne'ur Zalman. His disciples were also known for loud and lengthy prayer, characterized by wild ecstatic gestures, thus arousing fierce denunciations and parody. He was the one key disciple to predecease the Maggid. His place in Karlin was inherited by his own disciple Shelomoh, creating the Karlin-Stolin Hasidic dynasty that survives to this day, among the earliest still-extant Hasidic dynasties.

R. Levi Yitshak of Berdichev (c. 1740–1809)

Son of a Galician rabbinic family, Levi Yitshak was brought to Mezritch by Shmelke Horowitz, later rabbi of Nikolsburg. Dismissed from rabbinic positions in both Zelichow (south-central Poland; he was the first to attempt to spread Hasidism in that region) and Pinsk because of his Hasidic views, he was named in 1785 rabbi of Berdichev, a major Ukrainian community, where there was little dispute about Hasidism. His concern with issues of leadership and innovation is found throughout his book *Kedushat Levi* (first editions 1798, 1811), showing him to have been actively involved with defining and spreading the movement. His compassion and concern for ordinary Jews and their suffering are documented in his own writings as well as in later legend. In appealing to a mass audience, he made frequent reference to the *tsaddik*'s power to affect the will of heaven. Levi Yitshak served as editor of some versions of the Maggid's teachings.

R. Elimelekh of Lizhensk (c. 1717–1786)

He and his younger brother, R. Zusya of Hanipoli, took on a life of voluntary exile as a sign of piety. In the course of their wanderings they encountered the Maggid, and both became disciples. Elimelekh settled in Lizhensk in central Galicia and was the source of Hasidism's spread throughout both Galicia and Congress Poland. He had a large circle of disciples who carried his message forward in highly varied ways. Still personally committed to a strict ascetic regimen, he addressed his book *No'am Elimelekh* (1788) to his disciples and other would-be *tsaddikim*, setting forth high standards of personal conduct, but also making great claims for the *tsaddik*'s role.

R. Menahem Nahum of Chernobyl (c. 1730–1797)

R. Nahum was one of the few among the Maggid's followers who had also met the BeSHT. He was a popular wandering preacher in the northern Ukraine. His book *Me'or 'Eynayim* is perhaps the most faithful exposition of key themes in the BeSHT's teaching, delivered in homiletic form. His inclusion in this list of key figures (he was not prominently involved in the anti-Hasidic controversies) is partly due to the influence of his son Mordechai of Chernobyl (c. 1770–1837), an active propagandist for Hasidism already during his father's lifetime. He was among the first to claim Hasidic leadership by right of dynastic succession and progenitor of the extensive Twersky family that (along with the Maggid's own offspring, the Friedmans) dominated Ukrainian Hasidic life throughout the nineteenth century.

To this list of key disciples one might add several well-known Hasidic authors, known more for their books than for their personal influence. Chief among these might be R. Ze'ev Wolf of Zhytomir (d. 1780), author of *Or ha-Me'ir*, a major intellectual opus of the Maggid's school, as well as Shelomoh of Lutsk (d. 1813), who served as the first editor of the Maggid's own writings. Others in the group who are known mainly through their writings are to be found in our list of "Sources and Authors," toward the end of volume 2. There were also figures beloved by the Maggid, such as R. Leib Sarah's and R. Zusya of Hanipoli, who were known as saintly non-intellectuals and who did not write at all. Of the latter, legend explains how it was that he had heard very little of the Maggid's teaching. When the master began to speak, he would open by quoting a biblical verse. More often than not, the verse would begin with "God spoke to Moses, saying.... " Apparently, R. Zusya became so excited and agitated each time he heard that God had spoken that he began to scream loudly and would have to be taken out of the room before the Maggid could go on. Even within the highly intellectualized mysticism of Mezritch, there seems to have been room for this very different sort of spiritual figure as well.

What sort of relationship did R. Dov Baer of Mezritch have with the members of his circle? What was the nature or extent of their discipleship? These are difficult questions to answer, except to say that their reverence for him still reverberates in words spoken or written decades after his death. Even a casual reader of the Maggid's teachings will be struck immediately by the prevalence of loving and psychologically sensitive parental metaphors throughout his writings. The love between God and Israel or the *tsaddikim* is always that of father and son, even if he is expounding a passage in the Song of Songs, where another sort of love is the obvious subject. Texts by the Maggid and his disciples repeatedly explain *tsimtsum*, or the contraction of divine light, by analogy to a father who narrows down and simplifies the scope of his knowledge or intellect so that his son might be able to apprehend it. This was a "mysticism" that any parent could appreciate! Dov Baer had only a single son, Avraham "the Angel" (1740–1776), born after a significant period of barrenness in his marriage. He must have been an exceptionally loving father. It seems likely as well that he had fatherly feelings toward his younger disciples. Indeed he may well have served as a significant surrogate father figure to young disciples whose attraction to his path had cost them dearly in their relationships with their own fathers and fathers-in-law. This parental feeling seems to have created a strong sense of filial loyalty within the group that outlived the Maggid himself by several decades.

Both the abstract theology of the Maggid and the lovingly told parables of father and son made deep impressions on the disciples, who carried them forward in homilies preached and volumes published long after their master's death. If there is a certain dissonance between these two methods of teaching, it was bridged by the warmth of personality that became a central value of the movement. The *tsaddik* as a channel of divine blessing was to exude love and generous caring from his own person. Even the more abstract teachings emphasized that the *hasid* had ideally to live as an embodiment of *hesed*, unbounded and nonjudgmental divine love. Now we turn first to the Maggid's essential teachings and then to the figure of the *tsaddik*, where all this will become clearer.

THE PATH TO GOD: KEY TEACHINGS, IDEAS, AND PRACTICES

Dov Baer of Mezritch frames the insights of the Ba'al Shem Tov in a broader metaphysical context, drawing on various works of theoretical Kabbalah. But it is important to remember that he is in essence a revivalist preacher rather than a systematic thinker. Thus he, as well as the school of thought around him, cannot be located specifically in either the Cordoveran or the Lurianic tradition, the two main schools of Kabbalistic thought reaching back to the sixteenth century. It is the way of revivalist preachers to ever be in search of snippets of language and symbolic expressions that will inspire their hearers, lending excitement and profundity to a particular homiletic insight. Consistency does not rank high in their list of virtues. They care little about the source of a phrase or what its original meaning or context might have been, so long as it is somehow within the canon. They also do not care whether a phrase used in this week's sermon originally stood in utter opposition to something they quoted a week, month, or year earlier. Each has power and meaning in the context of the present sacred moment, and that is all that matters.

Nevertheless, it seems fair to say that the Maggid's school stands broadly within the Zoharic and Cordoveran traditions, while adopting certain key phrases and images from the Lurianic sources as well. By the late eighteenth century, the Lurianists had mostly won the battle for definition of Kabbalah. To be considered a Kabbalist, with very rare exception, meant to apply the Lurianic meditative system to one's life of prayer and ritual observance. This was a highly complex hierarchy of contemplative stages, through which one was to effect some piece of the *tikkun*, or restoration, of the broken cosmos. The chief vehicle for this process was a series of *kavvanot* (intentions or directions) and *yihudim* ("acts of unification") that were to accompany each devotional deed and word of prayer. In the Maggid's school these were set aside, sometimes even derided, in a bold move that welcomed non-initiates into the world of intense inner concentration in prayer. The BeSHT had certainly paved the way for this by his wide array of simple, direct prayer instructions. But it was only in the Maggid's generation that these were set into the context of opposition to the conventional Kabbalistic way of praying, much as the BeSHT had opposed those same circles' life of ascetic piety.

The Maggid learned from the BeSHT less of a theology than a way of praying and a path toward mystical awareness. Lights and letters were two key elements in the BeSHT's largely self-created meditational practice, derived from his unique and experience-based readings of various esoteric sources, some quite ancient. These techniques were still alive in the school of the Maggid, and experiences of them, though only rarely discussed in first-person accounts, underlie much of the discourse found in their writings. It was not easy, however, to pass these on to others, especially without some broader framework of understanding. It was this that the Maggid sought to provide. By simplifying and redefining ancient terms, he created a theoretical language within which the spiritual and experiential core of Hasidism could be held and transmitted.

The mystical theology of the Maggid's school is built around a dialectical understanding of being and nothingness, symbolically represented by *hokhmah* and *malkhut*, the first and last of the ten *sefirot*, or divine manifestations, in the system most used by Hasidism. *Hokhmah* represents the mind of God, the fullness of potential existence as it existed (and continues to exist) before and beyond Creation. It is Being (symbolized by the Y of Y-H-W-H) in its purest sense, before any specifying or differentiating lines have been drawn in it. It represents Being at the edge of readiness to become manifest in all beings, but not yet having done so. This fullest font of existence can therefore also paradoxically be described as "Nothing" (the capitalizations are intentional), because it has none of the specific content or "garbing" that alone will render it accessible to human mental perception.

Hokhmah's partner in this existential dyad is *malkhut* (the final H of Y-H-W-H), the "kingdom of God," also called *shekhinah*, or "indwelling presence," since earliest Kabbalistic times. The term *shekhinah* had originally been conceived as a euphemism, a way of referring to God as an immanent presence when the sense of divine majesty might have been demeaned by employing one of the biblical names for God. In this sense it had the same function as *kavod*, or the "glory," of God in Scripture. But the Kabbalists had created a boldly feminine gestalt around *shekhinah*, making her a female embodiment of divinity, the love partner of the blessed Holy One, whose mystical marriage and erotic energy-flow the Kabbalist was ever seeking to strengthen and restore. In this context, and especially in the multitiered universe of later Kabbalah, there had been a shift toward seeing *shekhinah* as a hypostatic entity, a quasi-separate divine being, existing beyond the world and watching over it. The Kabbalist saw himself as the faithful child or knight of *shekhinah*, raising Her from exile and restoring Her to Her Lover's embrace.

The Maggid, picking up the threads of nondominant Kabbalistic teachings, insisted on returning to the term's earliest meaning. "*Shekhinah* is truly in the lower realms," to quote an old rabbinic saying now picked up in the Hasidic context. Everything that exists lies inside *shekhinah*; She is the fullness of being as we know it, with all the definition and specificity that it is ever to have, including past, present, and future.

Shekhinah, sometimes in the form of the divine word, is the true inner core of every existing thing, ensconced in an outer corporeal "shell." All that exists, including each human soul in a particular way, is a "limb" or an aspect of *shekhinah*. She is thus "being," embracing earthly existence, to *hokhmah*'s "Nothingness." But because She is compromised by being wholly cloaked in the garments of physical existence, which themselves are superficial or illusory, She is also "nothing" in contrast to *hokhmah*'s unadulterated "Being."

The dancing interplay of these two (sometimes called by the Zoharic terms *sovev* and *memale*, "surrounding" and "filling," or transcendence and immanence), and the realization that they are ultimately one, is the essential trope of the Maggid's mystical teaching. Everything else is secondary to it and stands to serve it. "The union of blessed Holy One and His *shekhinah*," an inherited Kabbalistic formula still widely in use, now came to mean the absolute union of heaven and earth, the obliteration of any distinction between God, world, and self, or the obliteration of both world and self as they realize their own nonexistence as separate entities before the overwhelming unity of all existence in the oneness of an all-embracing God.

The preceding paragraphs constitute a statement of the Maggid's views in their most radical and unadulterated form. The matter is seldom expressed so boldly in the sources, though there are passages, both in the Maggid and in certain disciples—most notably R. Menahem Nahum of Chernobyl—where it is made quite clear. The hesitancy in most expressions of this view indicates that both master and disciples understood some of the dangers of pantheism and thought it best to cloak this aspect of their theology and experience in more conventional Western religious language. But the strong pantheistic thrust both of their teachings and of the experience that clearly lay behind them was difficult to hide. Such phrases as "The whole earth is filled with His glory!" and "There is no place devoid of Him!" are turned into ecstatic watchwords of early Hasidism.

Hasidism is primarily a devotional mysticism. The question asked over and over again in the sources is not "What is the nature of Being?" but rather "How do I properly serve God?" Unlike the medieval Kabbalist, who depicted esoteric lore as "the way of truth," the Hasidic authors speak of "the way of service" or devotion. Finding God or *shekhinah* everywhere in no way diminished the need to serve. The Maggid's metaphysical insight needs to be seen in this context. It both grows out of and intends to lead the hearer toward an inner state of mind in which this truth of God's nearness is realized. That state, described as *devekut* or intimate attachment to God (but occasionally also as *yihud*, "unity," or even *ahdut 'im ha-kadosh barukh hu*, lit. "oneness with God"), is the goal of the religious life, that toward which both prayer and the life of the commandments are to lead. Arriving at it is mostly a matter of breaking down walls, especially those of ego, defensiveness, and self-delusion that keep us from realizing the divine oneness that flows through all of being. This inward goal of joyous attachment replaces the prior Kabbalistic hierarchy of *tikkun*, or cosmic repair. Its focus is on the inner life of the person praying and the present moment, including the uplifting of *shekhinah*, rather than on the future-oriented redemptive process of restoring the cosmic order.

Hokhmah and *malkhut*, the two ends of the cosmological dyad, need to be seen in this context as representing two states of religious consciousness, not just as metaphysical abstractions. To know God in *hokhmah* is to attain a state of utter obliteration of the self (*bittul*) before the transcendent One. Humility is the moral pathway to this, but its goal is a true mystical self-transcendence, a state associated with *gadlut*, higher mind or expanded consciousness. Such moments of grace are possible, sometimes the result of human spiritual striving but coming also occasionally as divine gift. Inner "ascent" to the state of *gadlut*, when all self-interest and worldly concern must be left behind, is also paradoxically the moment when the mystic may take on supernatural powers, thus affecting the will of heaven and the flow of divine blessing. *Malkhut* as a level of awareness is associated with *katnut*, a "lesser" or ordinary state of consciousness. This is the place for the pantheistic thrust of Hasidic piety, the experience of "the whole earth is filled with His glory." It leads to the attempt to find holiness everywhere, even in the most lowly and unexpected places. That quest, and the effort of uplifting and transformation that follows it, is the *'avodah* ("service") of *katnut*.

The two central myths of Lurianic Kabbalah, *tsimtsum* and *shevirah*, are also reread in uniquely Hasidic ways. *Tsimtsum* (lit. "reduction" or "concentration") originally referred to God's self-withdrawal from primal space in order to leave room for the non-God to exist. God's first creation is thus an empty space, into which His energies are then re-sent in order to create the universe. Following various tendencies in eighteenth-century Kabbalah, Hasidism insists that God's withdrawal from space is not to be taken literally; there is in fact no possibility of anything existing outside God. This too leads to a theology that implies a sort of pantheism. God is fully present in all things; *tsimtsum* is merely the illusion that God and world are separate, a veil placed over our consciousness so that we might do the worldly things required of us. Our task is to gain a glimpse of the truth that lies beyond *tsimtsum*, while still living out our daily existence as though it represented reality. *Shevirah* (lit. "breakage") referred originally to the cosmic cataclysm that occurred as God sought to send His light into the empty space. The contrast between light and emptiness was so great that the vessels containing God's light smashed; this breakage caused sparks of light to spread far and wide, but hidden within the fragments of the broken vessels known as *kelipot* (lit. "shells"). Hasidism devotes little attention to the *shevirah* itself, not wanting to focus on the brokenness of existence. It takes great interest, however, in the sparks, or *nitsotsot*. These are bits of divine light to be found scattered throughout the universe. In the Hasidic reading they seem more to be "sent" by God intentionally, rather than buried by a cataclysm seemingly beyond divine control. The *hasid* is to be constantly seeking out these sparks and uplifting them, restoring them to their source in God. Because all things, moments, and human encounters contain divine sparks, all of them can be uplifted.

Faith in the ubiquity of divine presence also carries a devotional message, one that was to become a central and distinguishing feature of Hasidic piety: "God wants [sometimes 'needs'] to be served in all ways." The well-trodden Jewish paths of studying Torah, fulfilling the commandments, and reciting one's daily prayers are no longer deemed sufficient. They leave vast realms of life untouched! These too must become places to seek and find God. *Everything* is to become an act of service. Some of the Hasidic authors say it in an intentionally provocative way, telling us that we must serve God by means of "our study and our prayer, our eating and our drinking," placing them all on a seemingly equal footing. They especially emphasize that corporeal things and fulfillment of bodily needs are opportunities to appreciate God's creation and to raise awareness. "Even when you are in the lavatory, think, 'Here I am separating bad from good, and the good will remain for His service.'" How strange and daring this must have sounded in a culture where one was supposed to banish sacred thoughts when entering "defiled places"!

This emphasis on the possibility of finding and serving God through all things and in each moment also represents an important change in the understanding of *devekut*, the term closest to "mystical experience" that lies at the heart of Hasidic faith. Unlike generations of Kabbalists who had come before, including the BeSHT himself, the Hasidic adept in the Maggid's circle is not asked to ascend into higher worlds, to contemplate the union of the *sefirot*, or to see himself standing before the Throne of Glory. The trance-like state of vision or integrative contemplation is now mostly set aside in favor of a *gadlut* that means precisely looking at the same world one saw previously, but now seeing nothing in it but the intense and transformative presence of God. *Gadlut* is a perception of *hiyyut*, the divine energy that courses through reality and causes it to exist in each moment. This becomes the object of sacred encounter. The point is to look around at the world and see nothing but God. Scholars have argued as to whether this perception of the vital energy within being is affirmative of this world, embracing material reality as the locus of divine presence, or is meant to lead one to "see through" externals and to disregard all but this divine essence, and is hence ultimately "otherworldly." But this is a matter for reflection on returning from the mystical moment itself. The Maggid's circle is offering a mysticism in which a transformed vision of this world, rather than the substitution of a fantastic alternative, is the core experience.

These formulations represent a radical simplification of the life of mystical piety, a move that renders it accessible to those who had neither the esoteric knowledge nor the spiritual patience to engage in the complex step-by-step devotional exercises demanded by the Lurianic manuals. This deep shift of the spiritual climate is best described by a parable widely found in the early Hasidic sources, most likely created within the Maggid's circle. The king has a treasure that he wants to bequeath to his beloved son. In order to protect it, he seals it up in a treasure-house guarded by multiple locks, each of which has its own unique key. As time goes on the keys to those locks are lost; by the time the king's son reaches maturity and wants to enjoy his fortune, there is no one who knows how to get into the treasury. There is only one thing that can be done: break the locks. The parable is usually followed by the counsel to break your heart in prayer. It is the broken heart that smashes through all the locks, thus taking us directly to our Father and to the reward that He seeks to give us.

This direct appeal to the emotional life brings about changes in both the cosmic and the social orders. Jewish piety had created, over the centuries, a rather crowded picture of the heavens. The monotheistic orthodoxy of a Maimonides was the exception rather than the rule. Folk piety saw the "upper worlds" populated by a host of angels and demons. The latter had a particularly strong hold on the Eastern European Jewish imagination. They needed to be appealed to or placated if the soul was to make progress on its inward journey toward God. Kabbalah alternated between these personified figures and a description of more abstract stages of religious process; for example, crowning the sixth rung in the fourth world with the five graces flowing down from the third world, themselves deriving from the hidden lights that proceed from *malkhut* in the second world, and so on. It was these complexities to which the Lurianic meditations were a guide. Now they are all swept away into irrelevance (though their existence is never formally denied). "There is nothing besides Him!" and "No place is devoid of Him!" take their place. You and God are alone in the universe of your inner life: soul and Source, Father and child, longing to unite with one another. "Smash the locks" means "Break through any illusions that keep you from this truth."

With the emphasis upon *hokhmah* and *malkhut*, the opening and closing elements on the cosmological chart designating the two poles of ultimate reality, the *sefirot* between them lose the importance they once had as stages in the flow of divine energy downward and as stations in the upward journey of the soul. Ultimately, *hokhmah* and *malkhut* (also "being" and "nothingness" or "beyond" and "within") are one; there is no real "journey" needed to get from one to the other, only an opening of the mind. In that case the six *sefirot* beginning with *hesed* or divine compassion (sometimes symbolizing the six weekdays or the six cosmic directions in the old Kabbalah) are available for another, though related, purpose. Hasidism (based on some earlier precedents) turns them into nomenclature for a religious psychology, essential for a mysticism that is mostly about inner human experience. These six are now taken to represent *middot*, understood as qualities of the emotional life that the devotee needs to perfect in order to attain the goal of spiritual wholeness that leads to *da'at*, or awareness. Much attention is devoted to these in the teachings of the Maggid's circle, making Hasidism a system of emotional and moral growth fully linked to its message of self-transcendence: obliteration of self and world in the presence of the One.

The six *middot* are generally understood as *ahavah*, love; *yir'ah*, fear or awe; *tif'eret*, pride; *netsah*, triumph; *hod* (seen artificially as derived from *hodayah*), gratitude; and *yesod*, usually rendered as connectedness or attachment. The last of the six is also called *tsaddik*, which represents the perfected human who has turned all these *middot* toward the good life of faith and devotion. Each of these qualities may also be turned toward ill. Such would include illicit loves; fear of one's enemies or oppressors, but even fear of pain or death; pride in one's accomplishments or possessions; triumph over others; gratitude for worldly things, etc. As mentioned above, love and awe take the lead among these six. The proper balancing of these two most basic religious emotions is understood by Jewish writers long before Hasidism as the key to attaining the life of holiness. The teachings of the early Hasidic masters are filled with admonitions to live always with awareness of these. But each of the six *middot* needs to be saved from misdirection, a distortion of the Creator's intent. Each must be made to serve as a channel for spiritual awareness: love of God, fear of heaven, pride in God's creation, triumph over temptation and evil, gratitude for the opportunity to serve, and so forth. Their fulfillment leads to the seventh rung, *malkhut*, or the fulfillment of God's kingdom on earth within one's daily life.

Hasidism is thus at once a mystical teaching focused on the oneness of being and its realization, and a system of moral growth and self-improvement. From a purely contemplative point of view, the struggle is mainly one of attaining *da'at*, full and intimate awareness of the divinity that radiates through and enlivens all the worlds, from the highest to the very lowest. The perhaps surprising influence of Moses Maimonides (1135–1205), a contemplative of a very different sort, can be seen here in the shaping of a religious goal that is very much about the life of the mind. But this value of awareness is always tied (as indeed in Maimonides) to the goal of moral self-perfection. The moral thrust of Hasidic teaching is to have the devotee reach toward becoming a *tsaddik*, which is Hasidism's term for a fully self-realized person. It is by achieving mastery over these six qualities and acting in accord with them throughout one's life that this goal is realized. The *tsaddik*, in an old phrase widely quoted in the Hasidic sources, is one who "holds fast to both heaven and earth"—indeed becoming a personified link between them.

The attempt to achieve balance between these two goals of mental awareness and moral self-perfection, as well as the interweaving of them, is to be found on virtually every page of early Hasidic teaching. Emphases vary from one person, school, or text to another, giving birth to the great diversity of personal styles and paths of devotion that emerged within Hasidism. But all of the early Hasidic masters were dedicated to teaching and exemplifying both of these values.

THE *TSADDIK* AS HOLY MAN AND HASIDIC LEADER

Faith in the existence of *tsaddikim* in each generation is the bedrock of the Hasidic worldview. It is also fair to say that all of Hasidism accepts that the Ba'al Shem Tov is the ideal embodiment of what the *tsaddik* is supposed to be. As Hasidism spread, it anchored itself around a network of publicly declared *tsaddikim* who were to serve as foci of devotion for ordinary Jews who could not attain their level of either mystical consciousness or moral action. The special attachment to God of these people, and of God to them, including a measure of wonder-working powers, is a part of the BeSHT's legacy to the movement, and that legacy played an essential role in its growth and success.

Hasidism rediscovers and gives new emphasis to an ancient strain of veneration of holy men within Judaism that reaches back as far as the biblical stories of Elijah and Elisha, through the Talmudic *aggadah*, and into the figure of Rabbi Shim'on ben Yohai in the *Zohar*, the ultimate paradigm of *tsaddik* in all later Jewish piety. Jewish folk religion had always known of such saints. Figures like the Talmudic Rabbi Hanina ben Dosa or the later-conceived Rabbi Meir Ba'al ha-Nes come immediately to mind. While the rationalist and legalist elite may have disapproved of such beliefs, even Maimonides himself was turned into such a folk saint by the later Jewish imagination. After the Safed revival of Kabbalah, such folktales became thoroughly intermingled with accounts of the mystics and their extraordinary feats of piety. Stories told about them, including their wonder-working powers, long preceded Hasidism. But, generally speaking, these tales either were told about persons already dead (and continuing to exhibit powers in the world of the living) or were focused on anonymous living *tsaddikim* whom you might encounter without knowing who they were. Such was the widespread Ashkenazic tradition of thirty-six unidentified *tsaddikim* for whose sake the world survived in each generation. The point was that any beggar or unfortunate you might encounter could be one of them; therefore, you should treat each person, especially a stranger, as one of God's elect.

Hasidism took this notion forward in unprecedented ways. A remarkable series of homilies, found scattered throughout early Hasidic writings, makes the point that the true *tsaddik* should not remain in hiding. Becoming a public figure and leading others toward a life of righteousness displays greater courage and integrity than merely serving God in quiet isolation. In a striking act of rereading, the Maggid interprets a Talmudic account of a Temple miracle ("dedicated meat offerings never turned rotten") to mean that "true 'holy flesh' is never corrupted by contact with ordinary people." The hidden *tsaddik* is henceforth to step out of hiding, as it were, and become a source of guidance and blessing to those who gather around him.

As Hasidism began to spread and gain a mass following, veneration of the *tsaddikim* and faith in their supernatural powers became a defining hallmark of the movement. But who was a *tsaddik* and how could one attain this status? Was aspiring toward such righteousness in itself a violation of the virtue of modesty, and hence a paradoxical impediment to one's path? Were *tsaddikim* predestined to be such, chosen by God and "implanted in each generation," or was such righteousness something one could earn by virtue of spiritual struggle? What did discipleship have to do with becoming a *tsaddik*? Were only those who had served apprenticeship under the BeSHT, and then under his immediate followers, to be called *tsaddikim*? Surely, one would think, no one could name *himself* a *tsaddik*; it was up to others to do that. But there are exceptions to that as well. Did being a *tsaddik* perhaps result from achieving a following? Could *anyone*—without pedigree of either discipleship or rabbinic learning—who reputedly worked wonders, prayed with great intensity, and looked the part be set up by followers as a "holy man"? All of these questions swirled about the emergence of Hasidism as a historical force in the last quarter of the eighteenth century. The phenomenon called Hasidism grew in spontaneous and uncontrolled ways, without social controls or rigorous standards of any sort. One might say that it created a situation ripe for abuse, and the many reports of such abuses were not only the product of the anti-Hasidic imagination.

But what of the inner circle that created Hasidism? Surely these were serious religious people, not merely seeking power and control over the masses. They were trying to create nothing less than a spiritual revolution, a transformation of religious values, while still living fully within the framework of normative behavior (*halakhah*, "the path") common to all of premodern Jewry. How did they view the figure of the *tsaddik* and the manner in which such personalities might come to be? It would seem there was a good deal of divergence on this question, even within the circles that took it most seriously. R. Ya'akov Yosef of Polonnoye, a preacher of the old school whose conversion by the Ba'al Shem Tov (as we have seen) did not change him completely, remains an elitist who sees Jewish spiritual life in rather rigidly stratified terms. Using terminology rooted in ancient Platonic tradition, he defines the truly and selflessly pious scholar/sage (he generally prefers the term *talmid hakham* over *tsaddik*) as a "man of form," while the masses of ordinary Jews, sunk in corporeal concerns, are "men of matter." The former are destined to serve as leaders, exemplifying the life of holiness and uplifting the spiritual lives of the communities they serve. He does not give the impression of great flexibility in the social structure as he imagines it, with no "men of matter" growing in such a way that they might enter the category of "men of form." He fulminates frequently and with great vehemence against hypocritical or badly motivated scholars, but he has also come (probably through the BeSHT) to appreciate the pious innocence of simple people. Nevertheless, when he describes the ideal leader he thinks in terms of a refined spiritual/intellectual elite. He devotes much attention in his works to the question of whether Israel, an innocent flock, has been led astray by corrupt leaders or whether a base and materialistic people has pulled its leaders down to its own low level of values. Both, he concludes bitterly, are somewhat the case.

An heir to this elitist view in the next generation, though a disciple of the Maggid and not of R. Ya'akov Yosef, is R. Shne'ur Zalman of Lyady, the founder of the HaBaD school and surely among the most profound thinkers within early Hasidism. He composed a popular semi-systematic introduction to Hasidic teaching (one of very few such works) called the *Tanya*, a book reprinted countless times and considered the spiritual "Bible" of HaBaD Hasidism. There he defines the *tsaddik* in almost inaccessibly elitist terms. The purest *tsaddik* is one who has never even had a thought or temptation that might lead to sin. Such wholeness and innocence has the power to turn evil itself into goodness. Souls like this are very rare and by definition are born rather than made. Indeed, the emergence of such rare souls into the world has much to do, following old Kabbalistic tradition, with the purity of the parents' deeds and thoughts in the moment of their child's conception. The *Tanya* is therefore subtitled *Sefer shel Beynonim*, A Book for Ordinary People, those who seek to lead the good life but entertain no hope of becoming *tsaddikim*. R. Shne'ur Zalman's hope was to create a movement of dedicated strivers seeking to be *beynonim*, itself a high spiritual and moral state. Of course this high standard of what it meant to be a *tsaddik* also served to restrict would-be claimants to the title, thereby creating the basis for what would remain a highly unified HaBaD movement; meanwhile, other Hasidic communities tended to fragment, finding leadership under multiple *tsaddikim*.

The Maggid himself was a great believer in the powers of the *tsaddi-kim*. While we have seen that he maintained a highly abstract theology of God as unknowable *eyn sof*, experienced only through self-negation and entering a state of nothingness, the overflowing parent-like love of God for His creation (especially for Israel and the righteous) causes God to will their good. In exchange for his loyal submission to divine author-ity, the *tsaddik* is given the ability to change the decrees of heaven. This power, an essential part of the supernatural claims made for the BeSHT, was now shared by the various *tsaddikim*. The Maggid provided a theo-logical basis for it. God as *eyn sof*, the endless Source of existence, may seem to be indifferent to the fate of individuals or the outcome of his-torical events. Specific "will" is not easily attributable to such a deity. But God also loves the *tsaddik*, who then can take advantage of this relationship to implant concern for human affairs in God. The ability to "bring about will" in God (the Maggid's daring reading of Ps. 145:19) is no small matter. The transcendent God allows Himself to follow the lead of His earthly elect. In a well-known homily on Numbers 10:12, "Make yourself two silver trumpets," the Maggid reads the word *hat-sotserot* ("trumpets") as *hatsi tsurot* ("half forms"), thus saying that God and the *tsaddik* are two halves, each incomplete without the other.

The Maggid and his disciples were aware of the theological difficul-ties in making such a claim. It was not difficult to foresee the abuses that could emerge from such bold language. They were also aware that extravagant claims for the *tsaddik*'s powers played a key role in the emerging anti-Hasidic critique and the great controversy in which they were embroiled. One strategy for dealing with this problem was a turn to the well-trodden pious path of praying only for the sake of the *shek-hinah*. The *tsaddik* does not seek to wield power in order to benefit himself or his supporters; only the suffering of the exiled divine pres-ence is his concern. But of course the *shekhinah* identifies fully with human (i.e., Israel's) suffering; this is the nature of Her exile. If a Jew acts for the sake of *shekhinah*, he is doing nothing other than fulfilling God's will. But *shekhinah* loves such a devotee; She embraces his intent and causes it to be fulfilled. Bringing blessing upon the *shekhinah*, who is Herself sustainer of the lower worlds, causes Her to overflow with bounty and to shower blessing on this world as well. The *tsaddik* serves as a channel for that blessing, so he and those around him come to be blessed as well. The *tsaddik* is thus not magician, but devoted lover of *shekhinah* and a grateful recipient of Her blessings.

Here it is worth recalling that Hasidism is a movement that was created around the memory of a man who was a *ba'al shem*, a person who had access to supernatural forces (including the all-important power of healing in a society without modern medicine) through knowledge of mysterious holy names as well as through visionary shamanic "ascents of the soul." Of course the BeSHT was much more: a spiritual teacher and charismatic religious personality. But he never abandoned his tradecraft of writing and pronouncing holy names to bring about results that would favor those who came to him seeking help. Surely illness and other sorts of worldly tribulations came about through the will of heaven. A *ba'al shem* is a powerful intercessor who can affect that will. The rabbinate in Eastern Europe was highly intellectualized, ideally the quintessence of the Talmudic tradition described above. Such rabbis had little interest in serving as "holy men" who could respond to the daily needs of ordinary Jews and their sickly children. Classical rabbinic training bore little relationship to this pastoral sense of "spiritual leadership." The *ba'aley shem* stepped into this breach, having the professional role of healers, which also meant intercessors. But they were able to do this not because of claims of special righteousness or moral fitness. Nowhere are we told that *ba'aley shem* in general were great paragons of personal piety. They were masters of powerful esoteric knowledge, using it to ply a holy trade. A *ba'al shem* operates at the juncture point of religion, magic, and medicine; these were quite inseparable in the imaginations of pious Eastern European Jews, especially in the regions where Hasidism first emerged. Nor did a *ba'al shem* need to be a person of especially venerated ancestry. Subject, of course, to the generally expected norms of pious conduct, he was a man living somewhat on the margins of ordinary society, one to whom you could turn when it was necessary to call upon his reserve of supernatural powers.

What happens in Hasidism is that the roles of *tsaddik* and *ba'al shem* come to be amalgamated. Once Hasidism proclaims that there are indeed living *tsaddikim* who can be found, revered, and followed, the functions served by *ba'aley shem* very quickly migrate to these *tsaddikim*. Tellingly, there is no other *ba'al shem* significantly associated with the Hasidic movement after the Ba'al Shem Tov. There is no longer a need for one: the Hasidic *tsaddik* has taken his place. The *tsaddik* is the channel of divine bounty flowing into the world. Surely he can pray for your sick child, your barren wife, or your failing business. He is also the one who can ward off the broader evils that may be affecting the Jewish community as a whole. But he is able to do so with a very important difference. In the emerging Hasidic hierarchy of values, it is personal piety and intensity of prayer that make the *tsaddik* a capable intercessor, not a body of esoteric knowledge about holy names and how to write or pronounce them. The *tsaddik* is a beloved child of God, who rejoices in pouring His bounty upon him. Although many of the early Hasidic masters, including the Maggid himself, were highly learned in the mystical/magical tradition, the focus on the impersonal realm of "practical Kabbalah" or magic became secondary to their own *personal* relationship with divinity. These people were choosing a different path, one in which their healing abilities, though not denied, had mostly to do with personal righteousness and God's love, not technical skill in applied magic. While magic and a belief in its supernatural powers continued to flourish among Eastern European Jews right down to the twentieth century, it was interwoven with faith in the *tsaddik*, the personal beloved of God.

The members of the Maggid's circle vary greatly on the question of how to portray the *tsaddik* and his role. The spiritual hothouse of the Mezritch circle was indeed one intended to cultivate *tsaddikim*, and many of the Maggid's own teachings can be read in that way. The writings of Menahem Nahum of Chernobyl and Elimelekh of Lizhensk, two of the key authors in the circle, seem to be addressed to those struggling to attain a degree of wholeness and perfection in their own spiritual lives, *tsaddikim*-in-training as it were. R. Elimelekh in particular was known for having a close group of disciples around him, continuing the intimate teaching circle of the Maggid into the next generation. He certainly believed in the centrality of the *tsaddik* and the essential role a *tsaddik* needed to play in the spiritual and moral uplifting of ordinary Jews, as well as in the maintenance of the cosmic balance. But his circle of potential *tsaddikim*, like that of the Maggid, seems rather open compared to the views of R. Shne'ur Zalman, at least to those who could live up to the very strict demands he placed upon them.

The homilies of R. Levi Yitshak of Berdichev are preserved in an all-time favorite of Hasidic literature titled *Kedushat Levi* (1798, 1811). While he too had a small coterie of close followers, his teachings are addressed to a more popular audience. Levi Yitshak was the single most activist figure in the popularization of Hasidism in the Ukraine and southeastern Poland. The attacks of Hasidism's enemies in those areas are most often focused on him. He believed that the Maggid's disciples, if they were to spawn a mass movement, would have to respond to people's needs. His most often repeated Talmudic quotation, among the many passages cited in his writings, is the statement that "God issues a decree, but the *tsaddik* may nullify it." This was what ordinary Jews wanted of Hasidism, and he was ready to give it to them. His repeated emphasis on the great powers of the *tsaddik*, especially in overturning harmful divine decrees, sounds like the language of one who was trying hard to build popular support for the nascent movement. Although he shared his teacher's abstract theological concepts, he was a great lover of simple folk and sympathetic to their struggles. He believed firmly in a God who shared that love. He viewed his listeners as people beaten down by oppression, poverty, and the pains of a short and brutish existence, including the sufferings of illness. When God seemed to turn away from such people, it was the *tsaddik*'s most important role to argue their case before God, as Moses had once done at Sinai, even if such intervention seemed contrary to the will of heaven. The *tsaddik* he describes is one who offers hope, caring as does his God for the lives and needs of ordinary people. He is thus there to bring them blessing on the material as well as the spiritual plane.

Popular Hasidism as it began to emerge in the generation after the Maggid accepted, indeed thrived upon, the belief that the *tsaddik* could offer help in the realms of "offspring, life [meaning health and longevity], and sustenance," along with whatever spiritual enlightenment and growth in piety one might attain from basking in his presence. It is fair to assume that the large numbers of Jews who began to visit and seek audiences with *tsaddikim* did so in search of the more material blessings they had to offer. As the movement grew in extent and power toward the turn of the nineteenth century, it became clear that there was a significant livelihood to be made in the provision of such blessings. Competition, controversy, and claims of charlatanism all began to arise as well, though these were much more widespread in the succeeding era. Awareness of such dangers is already present within the Maggid's circle. R. Ze'ev Wolf of Zhytomir, author of *Or ha-Me'ir*, is a cautionary voice; he sees the growth of popular mysticism and shares some of the anti-Hasidic leadership's concerns about it. One would love to know just whom he has in mind in issuing his severe warnings against abuses, but his comments, like nearly all of those in this literature, are kept general and anonymous. Ze'ev Wolf is not the only one of the circle who seems nervous about the popular growth of the movement, especially when figures not part of the BeSHT or the Maggid's circles began setting themselves up as *tsaddikim*. It is not unlikely that there was some tension between Levi Yitshak and other members of the circle, who thought him too generously one-sided in defending Jews and seeking blessing for them, rather than reproaching them for their sins. Levi Yitshak's friend Shne'ur Zalman of Lyady was a purist with regard to the *tsaddik*'s role, refusing requests to pray for his followers' worldly needs. In him and his successors the claim of power to heal or intercede with the divine will would come to be seen as a power not to be used; such claims were overwhelmed entirely by their role as teachers and personal exemplars.

CONTROVERSY AND RELIGIOUS INNOVATION

Latter-day Hasidism, beginning in the early nineteenth century, portrayed itself as an ultra-traditionalist movement, faithful in every way to the classical Jewish way of life, including both religious law and custom. Indeed it certainly appears that way to the outsider; Hasidism is famous for its adherence even to eighteenth-century forms of dress and style. But in its early years Hasidism was fiercely attacked, as we shall see, by the rabbinic authorities of the day as a dangerously innovative, even rebellious, spiritual movement, one that threatened the very pillars of religious authority. Which of these images is true for early Hasidism? How do we sort out the interplay between innovation and conservatism within the Hasidic worldview?

The denunciations of Hasidism, beginning in 1772, point directly to changes in religious practice innovated by the *hasidim*. These include, most prominently, adoption of the Sephardic rather than the Ashkenazic version of the liturgy and a change in the practice of sharpening knives for ritual slaughter, also based on Sephardic practice. Clearly these were ways of distinguishing themselves from the surrounding Jewish community; they required separate quorums for prayer and separate provision of kosher meat, both being methods of establishing borders between themselves and other Jews. Both were technically within the purview of *halakhah*, codified Jewish practice based on respected authorities, although their adoption flaunted the power of *local* authority and tradition.

Alongside these divergences from Eastern European Ashkenazic custom there were accusations of looseness regarding various aspects of practice, particularly around prayer. The Hasidim were notorious for violating the set times for prayer, offering both morning and afternoon prayers when the spirit moved them rather than at the first opportunity; the pious were, after all, expected to comply with the old truth that "those who are careful rush to fulfill the commandments." They would also interrupt their prayers with wordless outcries and melodies, sometimes even with words not in the holy tongue. All of these, from the Hasidic point of view, were ways of underscoring the importance of *kavvanah*, or intense heartfelt direction of prayer, and restoring spontaneity to fixed liturgical prayer. They were seeking to combat their oft-cited bugaboo of "commandments people have learned" (Is. 29:13), or habitual religious behavior. This was the very essence of the Hasidic revival. Nevertheless, in the eyes of the authorities it represented religious deviance and was identified with the even more "strange deeds" of some *hasidim*, which included the cartwheels in front of the holy ark mentioned earlier.

When it came to ritual action (as distinct from prayer), the picture is more complicated. Acts of devotion to the commandments, even to *hiddur mitsvah*, or performing the commandment in a glorified way, are widely attested even in the earliest Hasidic tales. At the same time the Ba'al Shem Tov and others are quoted as warning against extremism, they seem to have encouraged a more relaxed attitude toward certain strictures. As for religious guilt and self-punishment for lack of adequate observance, the voice of Hasidism was clearly on the anti-ascetic side, as we have already seen. The Evil One, the sources say, wants nothing more than to trip you up on some small matter and then to preoccupy your heart with guilt so that you will not be able to serve God with joy and wholeness. Depart from sin, they insist, but depart also from excessive worry about it. Leave the burden behind and rejoice again in God's service.

Perhaps the greatest offense to the rabbinate and its values lay in a certain attitude of derision toward ivory-towered rabbinic learning that is found in Hasidic sources, including the writings of R. Ya'akov Yosef—himself no mean scholar of the tradition. Here we need to be quite careful in our characterization. The early Hasidic authors were not ignorant Jewish peasants or anti-intellectuals, as they were characterized by some early modern romantic descriptions. The Hasidic sources are nearly all written in the form of learned homilies on the weekly Torah portion, replete with quotations from the Talmud, Midrash, *Zohar*, and other classical writings. To offer such a homily, whether orally or in writing, one needed at least a respectable level of traditional education. (In fact, the level of erudition shown in Hasidic works varies significantly.) The point, however, was that the tradition should be used so as to deliver a message of spiritual awakening. It was never "Torah for its own sake" (*Torah li-shemah*), but rather "Torah for God's sake" (*le-shem he, ha-shem*). The penchant of Hasidic preachers for seeking the contemporary relevance of Torah is well known. "Torah is eternal," these passages often begin, "so its words must have meaning in every generation." This would introduce an attempt to find some meaning in a particular verse or portion—often one that no longer applies to contemporary Jewish practice, such as a verse dealing with the Tabernacle, with Temple-based purity laws, or with the sacrificial system—and that therefore has to be reread in some different way, especially a way that would stimulate the hearer toward greater devotion.

Of course Hasidic sources are not the first in the long history of Jewish homiletics and interpretation to seek contemporary relevance in a biblical passage. Preachers of every age need to do that. But in Hasidism there is a new tone of insistence on the legitimacy of this quest, sometimes accompanied by a near petulance that peppers the opening lines of many a Hasidic homily. Torah was given for every generation, so how could it *possibly* say things that are instructions addressed only to Noah for building an ark or to Moses for building a tabernacle?

The quest for relevance and the daring to makes changes (within the broadly conceived normative praxis) are two sides of the same coin. Both reflect the newly asserted and powerful role of the *tsaddik*, who claimed authority in the name of nothing less than the dynamic rabbinic tradition, placing himself in the ongoing chain of interpretation. Listen to the words of the *Degel Mahaneh Efraim* by R. Ephraim of Sudylkow, the BeSHT's grandson:

> "Moses diligently sought out the goat for the sin-offering" (Lev. 10:16). Tradition notes that these words, "diligently sought" [*darosh darash*] are the midpoint in a letter count of the Torah. One needs to understand what is meant by this, what difference it makes. In my humble opinion [it is as follows]: We know that the Written and Oral Torahs are all one, that neither can be separated from the other. Neither is indeed possible without the other, since the Written Torah reveals its secrets through the oral interpretation. The Written Torah without the Oral Torah is incomplete. It was like half a

book until the Sages came and interpreted Torah, lighting up our eyes and revealing its hidden secrets. Sometimes they would uproot something from the Torah, as is the case with regard to [punishment by] lashes. The Torah says: "He shall be stricken forty times" (Deut. 25:3), but the Sages reduced it by one. They did all this by the light of their holy spirit, because the blessed Lord was manifest upon them. [This enabled them] to see the root of everything Written in the Torah in its true state, empowering them to do this. The wholeness of the Written Torah is thus dependent upon the Oral....

This is true of each generation and its interpreters. They make the Torah complete. Torah is interpreted in each generation according to what that generation needs. God enlightens the eyes of each generation's sages [to interpret] His holy Torah in accord with the soul-root of that generation. One who denies this is like one who denies Torah, God forbid.[5]

This is an important claim of interpretive license. *Darosh darash*, "diligently sought" stands at midpoint in the Torah, serving as a link between text and oral interpretation, a process that has never ceased. *Darosh* is the root form of *midrash*, meaning creative reinterpretation of the text. Without this the Torah is but half a book! Parallels to this claim can be found in a number of early Hasidic works. Its seemingly obvious purpose was to defend the often radical interpretive license taken by Hasidic authors, themselves engaged in *derash*, who read Torah texts precisely in ways intended to shock their hearers. This was part of the revivalist practice we have mentioned, a device to awaken the listener out of his conventional mind-set by offering a seemingly simple and yet totally original understanding of the well-known biblical or Talmudic passage. If the quotations in the writings of Ya'akov Yosef of Polonnoye are to be believed, this practice began with the BeSHT himself.

It is significant, however, that the example given by R. Ephraim involves halakhic practice, not just the homilist's claim of interpretive freedom. The reduction of the lashing penalty, already recorded in the Mishnah, is one of several examples one could give (others even involve the death penalty) where the early sages openly demurred from a practice commanded by the Torah text. In commenting briefly on this Mishnah, the Talmud quotes Rava, the third-century Babylonian sage, saying: "How foolish are most people who stand up before a Torah scroll but do not stand in the presence of a great man. The Torah said 'forty lashes' and the sages came and removed one."

R. Ephraim of Sudylkow's choice of this example was probably not accidental. Hasidism was out to proclaim the right of its charismatic leaders, among whom the holy spirit was manifest even in their own day, to change certain practices that had venerable status in the community, if not actual laws. The Hasidic *tsaddik* was heir to the "great man" (*gavra raba*) the Talmud mentions here, and indeed, in the anti-Hasidic bans of the late eighteenth century, the *hasidim* were being accused of "changing the customs of our ancestors" and much worse.

Here we have the Hasidic defense. One *must* believe in the right of each generation's leaders to reinterpret, even to change practice to some degree; to do otherwise is to deny the presence of revelation in Israel's midst, that which makes the Oral Torah still alive and active. Denying that is tantamount to denying Torah itself.

It may also be that R. Ephraim's choice of this example had to do with the well-known tendency of Hasidism to reduce the ascetic burdens that prior generations of Kabbalists and Jewish pietists had taken upon themselves, including voluntary whip-lashings (*malkot*), reaching a crescendo in Eastern Europe of the seventeenth and early eighteenth centuries. Here the author shows that latter-day sages have a right to act precisely in this area where Hasidism was controversial, having compassion upon the sinner to reduce his burden of punishment.

The obligatory character of faith in the ongoing authority of the sages of each generation to reinterpret and actually change the Torah is trumpeted also by Levi Yitshak of Berdichev; he makes frequent use of this claim, which is most likely related to his central place in the controversies around Hasidic innovation. Levi Yitshak compares the authority of Torah and commandments to a royal decree that once issued cannot be revoked. But while the king is still issuing the decree, before he arrives at its conclusion, the generals hearing him might yet interrupt and get him to reconsider. By contrast, because God and revelation exist beyond time, God's speech is never concluded; the conversation between God and Israel, especially the *tsaddikim*, is continuous. Hence they may call upon Him at any time to change His mind, to revoke the decree. In yet another passage Levi Yitshak refers to the well-known popular acronymic reading of the Talmudic term *teku* ("let it stand") for an unresolvable halakhic dispute, taking it to mean that Elijah will come and resolve the dispute. "Why Elijah?" Levi Yitshak asks. He is a figure that has no association with Torah. Why does Moses himself not come to resolve disputes in interpretation of his law? The answer is that

Moses has died, and no one already dead can teach what is appropriate to a yet-living generation. Only Elijah, who never died, can represent that possibility.

What we have here might be called a theology of generational change, a theological reflection on the phenomenon, not unique to the modern world, of a new generation rejecting the cultural truths passed down to it or, in the case of a very conservative culture like this one, seeking a way to recast the meaning of that legacy so that it may at once see itself as both rebellious and loyal. While precedents for it may be found, its centrality and radical adumbration are certainly new and intentionally startling in the Hasidic context. We should note that there is nothing messianic or proto-messianic about these claims. It is not that ours is "the greatest" generation (unlike that of Rabbi Shim'on ben Yohai in the *Zohar*, for example) or the last generation on the cusp of redemption, but merely that *every* generation has the right and need to read Torah in its own way.

I think it fair to say that the interpretive "weapon" wrought by these teachings far outstrips the uses to which they sought to put it. The authority claimed here goes far beyond anything that even the Reformers of mid-nineteenth-century Germany ever dared to claim. With such a "big-stick" authority club in their hands, you might have thought the Hasidim would go farther than to depart from the halakhically prescribed times of prayer or switch to the Sephardic liturgical rite. Undoubtedly the immoderate tone heard in their sermons and published in their early writings only further agitated the *mitnaggedim*, making the latter see them as more dangerous than their actual innovations warranted. But I believe this too was intentional. There was a radical fire being lit here that was set in order to capture the imagination of a generation, especially that of the youth.

The original success of Hasidism has much to do with what might be called the dynamic of "youth culture," found in many different ages and cultural settings. Of course "youth" in the eighteenth-century *shtetl* was quite different from that of later generations. Still, there are enough stories of the young man going off to the *rebbe*, despite his father or father-in-law's opposition, to make us look in this direction. The successful youth-rebellion movement needs to proclaim loudly a total transmutation of values, a rejection *in toto* of the old ways, even if its changes in actual ways of living—especially after an initial phase of experimentation (the *hasidei TaLK* phenomenon?)—might turn out to be rather modest.

49

The enemies of Hasidism were reading its leaders well when they called it a radical or revolutionary movement. Its rhetoric did indeed contain within it the power to shake rabbinic authority to its very foundations. The fact that only rather mild use was made of that great power would eventually allow for the great reconciliation between rabbinism and Hasidism, and the move of Hasidism toward an ultra-traditionalism that would have been quite shocking to the BeSHT and his disciples.

THE EMERGING MOVEMENT AND ITS STRUGGLES: 1772–1795

The year 1772 was a watershed in the history of the young movement. In the spring of that year fierce denunciations and formal bans against Hasidism were publicly proclaimed in Vilna, followed by letters sent to lead communities throughout greater "Lithuania (including Belorussia and Polesia)" asking them to follow suit. The opposition had been simmering in rabbinic circles, especially in these northern regions where the rabbinate had a stronger hand, for at least two years. Tales were being told about "strange deeds" performed by groups of religious enthusiasts, people who had no pedigree of learning or permission from the authorities to diverge from the traditional ways of the community. These people were separating themselves from local synagogues, forming small prayer groups of their own characterized by loud shouting and prayer of extraordinary length, ignoring proper liturgical time boundaries, and even calling out words in the vernacular in the midst of fixed Hebrew prayers, which were not supposed to be interrupted. They called themselves *hasidim*, so it was said, but they were better to be described as *hashudim*, or "suspect ones" (the play on words works especially well in the Lithuanian pronunciation). They made all sorts of exaggerated claims for their leaders, who were probably nothing more than hooligans like themselves or, even worse, charlatans out to deceive their benighted followers.

It was no accident that the bans originated in Vilna, the most important Lithuanian community, long a seat of a distinguished rabbinate characterized by a high degree of Torah learning. They bore the signature, among others, of R. Eliyahu ben Zalman (1720–1797), widely known as the Vilna Gaon, the leading rabbinic scholar of the era. Partly because of his influence (although he held no formal office) the bans were reissued in the name of several other communities, including that of distant Brody in eastern Galicia, another traditional bastion of rabbinic authority. The whole collection of anti-Hasidic polemics was printed in nearby Alexnitsy. The bans aroused great public controversy; attempts were made in various places to break up the emerging Hasidic conventicles and to restore uniform standards of religious behavior. While some such attempts were successful in the short run, most were eventually overcome by Hasidism's broad appeal. Only in Lithuania proper was the effort to quash Hasidism successful.

What was it about the Hasidic revival that caused such great consternation among the rabbis? Several of the practices denounced in the bans (the choice of the Sephardic rite, the wearing of all-white clothes on the Sabbath, etc.) had been practiced by groups of Kabbalists before the BeSHT without great objection. In fact, the Brody version of the ban specifically exempted from it the well-known circle of Kabbalists in that city. After one wades through pages of bombast and mounds of clever wordplay in the anti-Hasidic documents, it is hard to find any examples of true infraction of rabbinic law. But there were several tendencies among the new *hasidim* that certainly must have irked the rabbis significantly. One was a certain disdain for high-powered Torah study within Hasidic circles. Not only did they neglect such study, the proper preoccupation of any literate Jewish male, in favor of telling stories, singing melodies, and smoking their pipes, but in some Hasidic teachings we even find the claim that Talmudic study distracts one from the more important religious pursuit of *devekut*, or intimate attachment to God. The intricate Talmudic arguments (especially given the spread of *pilpul*) are so difficult to comprehend that they engage the entire mind. Where, then, is one to find the energy to contemplate God? Better to rest periodically from such learning, turn the mind wholly to God, and then return to the page. Such a view was shocking to the Talmudist, who saw his own act of study as "life eternal," the very apex of pious devotion. What was being proclaimed here was indeed a revolution in religious values.

The Hasidic teachers were in fact reviving an ancient stream of folk Judaism, one that was especially strong within the Ashkenazic heritage. This was a legacy going back to the Rhineland pietism of the Middle Ages that praised simple faith, love of God, and an inward balance that made one indifferent to mockery or criticism. This sort of faith did not demand great learning and naturally led to the veneration of *tsaddikim*, persons of exceptional piety and the stuff of legend, rather than intellectual giants who had mastered the entire Talmud. The rabbis were right to be shaken by the advent of Hasidism.

The *hasidim* also showed little interest in supporting venerable communal institutions. Not only did they break away from the main synagogue in order to pray in their own style, but they would also study in that same place, where "books of piety" and tales of the *tsaddikim* were welcome parts of the curriculum. Eventually they would come to educate their children separately as well. Charity funds collected in the Hasidic *shtibl* would be sent off to the *rebbe*, supporting his travels and the spread of the movement, rather than given to local sources. The *rebbe* would then give to the poor as he saw fit, of course favoring those loyal to him. The difference in slaughtering knives meant that the *hasidim* would seek out their own sources of kosher meat, often a key element in the economic support of the community. As their numbers grew, the separatist tendencies of the *hasidim* had serious implications, including in the economic realm.

The opposition to Hasidism should not be understood as antimystical or rationalist in bent, as it has sometimes been presented. In fact, the Vilna Gaon was himself a devotee of Kabbalah, as were his immediate disciples. What they objected to was the radical *popularization* of mystical teachings that lay at the very heart of Hasidism. The Jewish mystical tradition had always been associated with esotericism. The texts were written in abstruse symbolic language, thus restricting access to a small subclass within the learned elite. This had been changing since the sixteenth century, with mystical ideas penetrating ethical and homiletical works. But Hasidism took this a significant step farther. In shedding the increasingly complex symbol system of Kabbalah almost in its entirety, it expressed its mystical truth in broad categories that could readily be apprehended by the contemplative-minded seeker, even one with rather little learning. It further claimed that every Jew was capable of *devekut*, that the key to all the secrets was nothing other than a broken heart or an inner awakening to the truth that all but God is illusion. These require no learning, only a cultivation of the spiritual life. The *hasidim* were also not shy about using the often secretive language of the Kabbalists, much of it rooted in the erotic language of the Song of Songs, in plain view of everyone. The learned Kabbalists of Vilna and Brody must have been horrified at what they saw as the utter vulgarization of sacred secrets. Who knows where such teachings could lead if offered to the ignorant masses?

This fear linked up with a claim, found either directly or in hints in several of the bans, that Hasidism was a new Sabbatianism. It was precisely the combination of popular mystical outbursts, leadership by Jews ignorant of or openly hostile to tradition, and sexual irregularities (some real, others just rumored) that had been so traumatic about Sabbatianism in its most recent Frankist garb. The rabbis were fearful that this was yet another round of the mystical heresies that had been plaguing Jewry for the past century in various locations and guises. Superficially there was reason for such concern: the alleged wild practices of early-day Hasidism did indeed look like they might burst across the lines into outright heresy. It is indeed possible to assume that Hasidism's careful avoidance of such extremes was partially a response to this fierce opposition.

The bans engendered sufficient distress for the Maggid's followers that they called a semi-formal meeting of all the close disciples in the town of Rowno, where their leader had moved from Mezritch around 1770. They apparently had decided to take action against their opponents, but the Maggid discouraged them from doing so. The Maggid was deeply shaken by the rabbinic response to his disciples. It seems likely that he had not wanted to go public with disseminating his teachings but would have been content to have a small devotional circle around him like those of the Ba'al Shem Tov's day. He had gone along with his followers' desire to burst forward and spread the word but now saw that the price was a high one. He announced to them that their decision to flout rabbinic authority would be costly in another way as well: "You have lost your head," he told them, meaning that he would no longer be able to remain alive among them. The Maggid died several months later, toward the end of 1772.

It is hard to determine the pace at which Hasidism spread over the last thirty years of the eighteenth century. We do not have the documentary evidence or the detailed studies to tell us the extent of Hasidic penetration into each particular locale. We know of a few places, both small towns (Amdur, Kalisk, Shklov) and cities (Minsk, Vilna), in the northern territories where Hasidic *minyanim* had reared their heads and roused the wrath of communal leaders. In each case these arousals were attributable to specific individuals, some of them the Maggid's own disciples who had returned homeward bringing the new message with them, and others less well-known figures who had been "converted" by these. But for the great majority of locales we have no such complaints. Does that mean that there were as yet no *hasidim* or that there was no opposition?

This question is particularly pertinent with regard to the original Hasidic heartland of Volhyn and Podolia. For those regions we have only the sparsest account of opposition to Hasidism. By the early nineteenth century Hasidism was quite widespread throughout those provinces. The various offspring of the Twersky and Friedman clans (descendants of the *Me'or 'Eynayim* and the Maggid, respectively), who came to dominate that region, had no difficulty in establishing themselves as *rebbes* in town after town, district after district. They only ran into conflict with one another when their territories overlapped, but we hear almost nothing of traditionalist opposition to Hasidism itself. The extensive literature around early Bratslav Hasidism, writing about the first decades in the nineteenth century, uses the term *mitnaggedim* ("opponents") to refer to Hasidic Jews who opposed Bratslav but seems to encounter no trend of opposition to Hasidism as a whole. Still, we do not know exactly when and how Hasidism took hold or how thorough its "conquest" was.

A typical pattern that seems most likely (although the following is a theoretical reconstruction) is one of gradual spread and increasing acceptance over the course of several decades. First there might emerge one or two Hasidic *minyan* groups within the town who set up *shtiblekh* outside the "great" synagogue, often a historic structure and the seat of the town rabbi. These would be founded by young men who had visited either Mezritch or one of the other emerging centers. They might be newcomers to town, including sons-in-law of local families. Such *minyanim* might be augmented by local tradesmen, people who did not have the status—acquired usually by ancestry, money, or learning—to be highly respected within the larger community. In the small *shtibl* they might more easily attain places of honor. They could become enthralled by the warm atmosphere and sense of brotherhood that characterized such small groups, including listening to tales of the righteous and singing Hasidic melodies into the night. There might be conflicts over the kosher meat tax or the distribution of charitable funds, but eventually the *hasidim* would win out by dint of increasing numbers and by their ability to fill the ranks of piety-demanding but low-paying communal functionaries: elementary teachers, preachers, sextons, ritual slaughterers, circumcisers, and the like. Collectively, these had great influence in shaping the tendency of a community. In many places the old synagogue would maintain the Ashkenazic rite for another generation or more, until both rabbi and members of some of the leading families were themselves Hasidic, allowing for the final change. In the course of this process, visits to the town by well-known *tsaddikim*, including healings or other demonstrations of their increasingly believed-in powers, would certainly have moved things along.

Unlike any previous usage of the ancient term *hasid*, one employed by nearly every pietistic movement in Jewish history, in late-eighteenth-century Eastern Europe the word took on the meaning of "disciple." To be a *hasid* in the context of this growing movement usually meant being a follower of a particular teacher figure. *Hasid* and *rebbe* went hand in hand in the emerging lexicon of the movement. Proclaiming oneself a *hasid* would immediately raise the question "To whom do you travel?" meaning "Which Hasidic master is your *rebbe*?" Loyalty to one's own master was often quite fierce, and it was not rare for competitiveness to arise between followers of one *tsaddik* and another, especially in the tales told of their great piety or miracles they had wrought, a characteristic that was to accompany Hasidism throughout its history.

It seems likely that as long as the Maggid was alive, the original effort to spread his teachings forth was shared among the disciples without rancor among them. Menahem Mendel of Vitebsk led the effort in the north, with Avraham Kalisker and Shne'ur Zalman serving loyally under him. R. Aharon Karliner's people and the followers of R. Hayyim Hayka of Amdur were in the same district offering a more popular version of Hasidic life, but we hear nothing of conflict between them. Perhaps they were too busy fighting off enemies from without to become embroiled with one another, or perhaps their shared loyalty to the Maggid kept them at peace. In the south, with Levi Yitshak at the center of conflict, we also do not hear of inner Hasidic strife. R. Nahum was becoming established as preacher and *tsaddik* in the area around Chernobyl, just northwest of Kiev. There may have been some competition between the Maggid's circle of disciples and some outside it, notably the Zloczow and Korzec circles, but it did not reach a serious pitch.

But after the Maggid's death the meager bit of coordination that had existed among those spreading the Hasidic gospel was no more. The closest to continuing the Maggid's pattern of cultivating an intimate circle of disciples was R. Elimelekh, who lived until 1786. Most of the key figures in the fourth generation of Hasidic leadership came out of his school, either taught directly by him or through his own disciples, especially R. Ya'akov Yosef the "Seer" of Lublin (1745–1815). Elimelekh was a figure much like the Maggid in some ways. Himself committed to a rigorously ascetic way of life, he posited high standards for his intimate followers whom he cultivated as *tsaddikim*-in-training. He believed greatly in their potential powers, including what might be called the supernatural, as well as in the bond created between them and their followers as the latter offered them material support. At the same time, his teachings are filled with dire warnings about the sins into which one aspiring to such status might fall, including the great danger of false or excessive pride.

While Levi Yitshak also seems to have had several important close followers, he did not devote the same attention to them as did R. Elimelekh. Levi Yitshak served as rabbi of the major communities of Pinsk (where he was persecuted and driven out because of his role in spreading Hasidism) and Berdichev. He probably did not have the same amount of time to devote to his Hasidic disciples. While the collected teachings of R. Elimelekh may largely be read as admonitions addressed to the circle of disciples, those of Levi Yitshak are more attuned to appealing to the general public, both in the love and concern they show for ordinary Jews and in the relative accessibility of their language.

By the 1780s, other figures from outside the Mezritch circle were exerting major influence on the emerging Hasidic movement. Most notable among these was R. Barukh of Miedzybozh, one of the Ba'al Shem Tov's two grandsons, who established himself as a *rebbe* in his grandfather's town and sought obeisance from the many pilgrims who had begun coming to the Ba'al Shem Tov's grave. Appropriately enough, it was this scion of the BeSHT who seems to have first hit upon the idea that being a *tsaddik* was something to be passed on by heredity. By all accounts Barukh was not particularly talented in either the intellectual or the spiritual realm. He was heir more to the magical and popular aspects of the BeSHT's legacy than to the abstract teachings passed on and refined in Mezritch. He was said to be an angry person, jealous of the dissemination of Hasidic authority outside his family. People were said to be more afraid of his curses than anxious to receive his blessing. Unlike many others of his generation, including his brother R. Ephraim of Sudylkow, he left behind no collection of teachings. The slim volume published in his name a century later offers little opportunity to counter this understanding of him. The notion of inherited leadership seems to have been next picked up by R. Mordechai of Chernobyl; he participated in leadership even during his father R. Menaham Nahum's lifetime, but sought to fully inherit him after his passing in 1797.

We do not know why the pattern of inherited dynastic leadership became dominant in Hasidism. Early scholars saw it as imitation of the noble families among the Poles (*szlachta*); others suggest it is more parallel to the life of the Russian nobility. Indeed there were ways in which Hasidic *rebbes'* families conducted themselves as a sort of royalty or nobility within the Jewish community. But one suspects that this somewhat derisive historical judgment was carried over to the historians from *haskalah* ("enlightenment") barbs against Hasidism. It is just as likely that the ancient Israelite priesthood was the model, the memory of priestly lineage still being passed down in Jewish families from father to son. In the Hasidic literary tradition the *tsaddik* is very often compared to the biblical priest, especially in his ability to bless and to heal. We should remember that there was an active and spiritually powerful non-celibate priesthood functioning across the town square in the Ukrainian Orthodox or Uniate (Eastern-rite Catholic) church, one that in many cases was passed on from father to son. All of the above elements may have combined in creating this characteristic form of Hasidic leadership, which tended in most areas to dominate after a generation or two of master-to-disciple succession.

Other figures from outside the Maggid's circle included R. Yehiel Mikhel of Zloczow (d. 1786) and his five sons, each of whom had his own following as a *tsaddik*. This was another new pattern, Hasidic leadership becoming something of a "family business" to which each male heir had a claim. This too would be picked up, first by the Chernobyl (Twersky) clan and afterwards by the Maggid's own descendants (Friedmans), the sons of R. Yisrael of Ruzhin (d. 1840). As Hasidism grew, new figures without either lineage or discipleship appeared on the scene. Such a personality was Aryeh Leib the *zeide* or "old man" of Shpola (1725–1811), who functioned from the 1790s as a popular Hasidic leader. He was a synagogue sexton who "grew into" the role of *tsaddik*, bringing little to the role beyond an impressive demeanor and the ability to be a convincing wonder-worker. While he had a significant following, his lack of learning or lineage left him wide open to the sharp attacks of his young and unfriendly neighbor Nahman of Bratslav just after the turn of the nineteenth century.

Leadership of Hasidism's spread northward was severely affected by the decision of R. Menahem Mendel of Vitebsk and R. Avraham of Kalisk to settle in the Holy Land in 1777. A great deal has been written about this *'aliyah*, in which the two leaders were accompanied by a band of perhaps eighty faithful followers. Surely the severe persecution they had endured in the five years since the bans, living in a district highly unfriendly to Hasidism, had much to do with their emigration. The positive draw of the Land of Israel for its own spiritual qualities, and possibly because of messianic rumors, was added to this. It may also be that they simply wanted to be left alone to live as an inward-looking spiritual brotherhood, abandoning the attempt to convert large numbers to the Hasidic path. R. Menahem Mendel and R. Avraham settled in Tiberias, forming the basis for the Hasidic community of the Holy Land that was to continue to grow throughout the nineteenth and twentieth centuries. Back home, however, their decision did leave a significant void, one that they first tried to bridge by pastoral letters, but which was filled gradually by Shne'ur Zalman of Lyady as he increasingly felt ready for the role of singular *rebbe* of all Belorussia. Meanwhile there was space for R. Shelomoh of Karlin and his disciple R. Mordechai of Lachowice to offer an alternative model of Hasidic devotion. But Hasidism was significantly weakened for a while in the contested northern districts, growing strong again only after the mid-1790s.

The dissemination of Hasidic ideas began as an oral process. *Maggidim*, or preachers, played a significant part in this, traveling from town to town and delivering sermons on Shabbat afternoons. In an era prior to any sort of mass media, this was an efficient way of disseminating new ideas. It may be that the roles of *maggid* and *tsaddik* were combined in some figures, the pious visiting preacher also making himself available to listen to people's troubles and to offer his blessing. It might be that he would call himself a *maggid*, referring to his own professional role, while believers might begin to consider him a *tsaddik*. The transition from one characterization to the other could be quite subtle.

By the mid-1770s, Hasidic teachings were also beginning to be disseminated in manuscript form. These would most often be disorganized compilations of brief teachings, directions for pious conduct, letters, and parables or stories. Most were attributed to one or another of the great early figures of the movement, above all to the BeSHT himself. But examination of both the surviving manuscripts and the printed versions of these collections, appearing mostly in the 1790s, shows that the same sayings might be attributed here to one master and there to another, including lots of random copying back and forth. There is not much in these essentially anonymous documents, known collectively as *hanhagot*, to distinguish one Hasidic master from another.

The first printed Hasidic book was the *Toledot Ya'akov Yosef* by Ya'akov Yosef of Polonnoye, appearing in Korzec in 1780. Its publication, unaccompanied by any of the usual letters of rabbinic approbation, caused a tremendous stir. Although R. Ya'akov Yosef was a respectable rabbi of several well-known communities, and even a small glance at the volume's contents demonstrates his very considerable learning, his fierce broadsides against the Jewish community's leadership, both rabbinic and lay, left no doubt that its publication was a bombshell. Within a year the bans against Hasidism were pronounced again and a second round of active persecution had begun.

The new bans, announced at the summer fair in the Lithuanian town of Zelva in 1781, followed another appeal directed by R. Eliyahu of Vilna. This time he was joined by R. Avraham Katzenellenboigen, the rabbi of Brest-Litovsk (Brisk), another center of rabbinic learning. The latter writes his own version of the ban, and in it he refers to his defeat of the "chief hooligan" among the *hasidim*, "Yitshak of Zelechow," known to history as R. Levi Yitshak of Berdichev, at a public debate in a suburb of Warsaw. We are not certain when that debate took place, but it was most likely between 1781 and 1784. In fact, by 1781 Levi Yitshak was rabbi of the important Polesian city of Pinsk, one that identified itself as part of anti-Hasidic greater Lithuania, but the name "Zelechower" seems to have stuck with him, even though he had been run out of that town, as he would be from Pinsk.

A short while later, seeing that his alleged triumph in that contest had not stopped the growth of Hasidism, R. Avraham wrote a public letter to Levi Yitshak detailing this debate in writing and listing his objections to Hasidism and its innovations in Jewish life. His complaints were the same as those of 1772, though surrounded by somewhat less innuendo. At least this enemy of Hasidism, while remaining firm in his opposition to the innovations it had made in religious practice, was no longer darkly hinting at other misdeeds or heresies that were too terrible to mention. Levi Yitshak is addressed with a considerable measure of respect as a rabbinic colleague and is urged to repent of his erring ways. This letter was followed by direct attempts to remove Levi Yitshak from the Pinsk rabbinate, an effort that succeeded a year later, making him the central figure and victim of the anti-Hasidic drive.

Among the most interesting documents of the Hasidic struggle against rabbinic opposition is a defense of Levi Yitshak by his friend

R. Elimelekh of Lizhensk, written between 1782 and Elimelekh's death in 1786. Penned by R. Elimelekh's son Eleazar, it answers a *hasid*'s query about how a merciful God could allow a true *tsaddik* like Levi Yitshak to undergo such terrible punishments. Here is an excerpt from the letter:

> I have received your letter, in which you requested that I ask my holy father and teacher about the controversy that has arisen ... around the excellent and famous *hasid*, the rabbi of Zelechow. I asked my father and he answered me in these words:
>
> "Why do you consider this something new? There have always been things like this. Abraham our Father was thrown into the fiery furnace by Nimrod, but he emerged safely. When he arrived in the Land of Israel a famine took place. The local inhabitants said it was because of this heretic who has come into our midst. He went down to Egypt to quiet things down, so [this opposition] would not spread among them. Had this not been the case, he surely would not have gone to Egypt, since God had told him only to go to the Land of Canaan. This was one of his ten trials....
>
> "The truth is that the *tsaddik* serves God in both fear and love. The love drives him nearly crazy, as Scripture says: 'You are ever ravished with Her love' (Prov. 5:19) [taken as referring to *shekhinah*]. We find this to have been the case with King David, who 'jumped about and danced with all his strength' (2 Sam. 6:14–16). The *tsaddik* is constantly going from one rung to the next, every day, and God grants ever new grace to the *tsaddik*, both above and below, each according to his rung. But these gifts of divine grace come about only by means of trials. This is due to the accusing force, since 'there is no *tsaddik* in the world who does [only] good and does not sin' (Eccles. 7:20). The Accuser finds some flaw in the *tsaddik* and goes up to accuse. This is so even though God surely forgives the *tsaddik*, since it is his way to turn immediately to thoughts of penitence and regret. The *tsaddik* is strict with himself down to the finest line and surely will have repented. How then can the Accuser speak against him? Because the Accuser stands above [in heaven, remote from earth] and says that he does these things only to be praised and glorified by others. If people [and their praise] distract him, he would not withstand the test. This would be proof that he was indeed a sinner. Therefore God tries him [by having people denounce him]. This allows God to bring him to a constantly higher level...."[6]

Elimelekh is here defending his friend Levi Yitshak. There is no indication given that he is suffering from the same accusations. The righteous have always suffered, he tells us, offering a typical bit of Hasidic theodicy. His identification of Levi Yitshak with Abraham is particularly striking. Abraham, the true man of *hesed*, was spreading a new faith, "making souls" for it by widely opening his tent and inviting everyone in. He also was willing to argue with God for the sake of Sodom's sinners. This Abraham indeed does sound more than a bit like Levi Yitshak— or perhaps Levi Yitshak is indeed a faithful follower of Abraham our Father. Of course the irony of the fact that Levi Yitshak's chief accuser was named Abraham was probably not lost on R. Elimelekh. Who, indeed, is the real Abraham here?

The growth of Hasidism proceeded, steadily if irregularly, throughout the 1780s. In addition to its original heartland, the movement made significant strides into Galicia and eastern Poland. Members of the Maggid's circle and the local family and followers of Yehiel Mikhel of Zloczow saw eastern Galicia as ripe territory for Hasidic "conquest" almost from the beginning. The presence of R. Elimelekh's circle in Lizhensk in central Galicia seems to have radiated outward sufficiently that the rabbis of Cracow felt a need to issue a ban in 1786, the same year in which R. Elimelekh died. Some members of his circle, including R. Yisrael of Kozhnits (Kozienice) and R. Ya'akov Yitshak Isaac of Lublin (first Lancut), were known to be functioning as *rebbes* in east-central Poland for some time prior to their master's death.

The publication of the *Toledot* was followed by two more books by the same author, as well as by the Maggid's collected teachings in 1781. Shortly after R. Elimelekh's death, his own *No'am Elimelekh* joined the row of Hasidic books, remaining a favorite throughout the movement's history. This list of printed works began to grow longer after 1790; tens, and then hundreds, of Hasidic books were published in each succeeding decade. Still, the movement retained a strong commitment to oral tradition. A teaching by a Hasidic master, and especially a story, was always more powerful if you could begin it with "I heard this from so-and-so, who heard it from his teacher, and he from his," rather than "I read this in a holy book."

The original period of Hasidism's spread coincided with a time of great changes in the political map of Eastern Europe. The old Polish kingdom, weakened over time by diffusion of authority, was seen by the late eighteenth century as ready for dismemberment by its three neighbors, Prussia, Russia, and Austria, all of them more powerful militarily and subject to strong central monarchic leadership. In the first partition of Poland in 1772, eastern Belorussia was taken by the Russians and eastern Galicia by the Austrians. The much-diminished Polish kingdom hobbled on for another twenty years until 1792, when Volhyn and Podolia, the original heartland of Hasidism, went along with western Belorussia to the Russians as well. Finally, in 1795, the Austrians took western Galicia, and Russia annexed Lithuania. With the Prussians accessing its northern and western areas (outside Hasidic influence), historic Poland disappeared from the political map of Europe for the next 120 years.

The acquisition of a large and unassimilated Jewish population was a great shock to Russia's rulers and populace. Until 1772 Jews had been formally excluded from settling in Russian territory. While the first imperial concerns were with the body of Jewry altogether, it was not too many years later that Russian officials began to understand the differences between *hasidim*, their rabbinic opponents, and the earliest *maskilim*, or Westernizing enlighteners, among the Jewish population.

The Austrian empire already had a large Jewish population in prior-held areas (Bohemia, Moravia, Hungary), but the annexation of Galicia greatly increased their numbers and included a population generally less open to the Germanic-Western influence that the empire represented. As early as 1782 the Austrian authorities made efforts both to limit the growth of the Jewish population and to impose on them a requirement of at least minimal German-language education. While both rabbinic and Hasidic leaders were opposed to these early attempts at remaking Galician Jewry, the Hasidic community was particularly firm in rejecting them, seeing them through the lens of "evil decrees" that had been issued throughout Jewish history. This early pattern of opposition to any sort of modernization in Jewish life was the first sign of a new quality within Hasidism that was to characterize it increasingly throughout its entire later history.

While each of the first two rounds of anti-Hasidic opposition caused great consternation to members of the Maggid's circle, leading to a good deal of localized persecution, there is no evidence that they were effective in checking the movement's growth anywhere but in Lithuania. By the mid-1790s Hasidism clearly appeared to be "the wave of the future" for most of Eastern European Jewry. Fixed centers of Hasidism were growing in number and attracting large swarms of pilgrims. Respect for the publicly proclaimed *tsaddikim* and awe before their piety and powers were coming to be taken for granted among ordinary Jews. Hasidic books, aimed at both high- and middle-brow readership, were becoming widely available. It must have seemed like the birth pangs of the new movement were beginning to subside.

THE WELLSPRINGS SPREAD FORTH: 1796–1815

By the closing years of the eighteenth century, distinctive schools and styles were emerging within the widespread Hasidic movement. These variations were determined in part by cultural geography, the differences between Jewries of particular regions, and in part by the distinctive religious personalities and educational philosophies of the various Hasidic leaders.

In the northern districts, R. Shne'ur Zalman of Lyady had begun to assert strong leadership of the growing Hasidic communities already in the 1780s. His distinctive path as a Hasidic leader was shaped by a number of factors. Already an accomplished scholar of the "revealed Torah," or *halakhah*, when he went to the Maggid, Shne'ur Zalman authored his own *Shulhan 'Arukh*, a guide to Jewish praxis within the Hasidic domain. His years of studying the mystical sources with the Maggid and his son Avraham "the Angel" only deepened his commitment to learning and practice on the exoteric level as well. Dealing with the more highly educated Jewish elite that was present in his area, he offered a Hasidism in which both learning and contemplation played a major role. He saw the *tsaddik*'s role chiefly as that of teacher and exemplar, rather than as source or channel of blessing to be brought down to his disciples.

As mentioned earlier, R. Shne'ur Zalman maintained a highly elitist view of the *tsaddik*, urging his disciples to struggle rather to become good *beynonim*, adequate servers of God. Aspiring to more than that was beyond their reach. Listening to the *tsaddik*'s teachings and studying his writings, especially the *Tanya* once it was published (1796), were to play an important part in their ongoing religious growth. But the real work needed to be done by each individual in the cultivation of his own inner life. This effort required much attention to prayer and contemplation. Instructions for these were a regular part of the diet prescribed by Shne'ur Zalman in a series of rulings that he issued for the conduct of his followers' behavior and the inculcation of Hasidic principles. The prayer life of the Hasidic *minyanim* that were springing up all over Belorussia was to be strictly governed. Silent meditation went along with a quiet and contemplative style of prayer, enriched by a particular sort of soulful Hasidic melody that was to become characteristic of HaBaD. Shne'ur Zalman both exemplified and taught a path of restraint, holding the intense passion of Hasidic faith and religious experience within a strong inward container. The force of that passion was to be released slowly and deliberately, so that none of it went to waste. This slow-burning but passionate devotion was to be drawn upon as a protective shield to guard traditional Jewish faith and practice from all the encroachments that were to come.

This Hasidism stood in sharp contrast to the other school of Hasidic devotion that was available in some of the same regions: that being offered by R. Shelomoh of Karlin and offshoots of the Karlin school. Here the spiritual style was entirely different, loud and highly demonstrative, as contrasted with the controlled inwardness of HaBaD. There was nothing in the Karlin school to compare with the high degree of HaBaD intellectuality. Those who gravitated toward it were less educated and not in search of profound learning. They saw worship as an opportunity for great emotional release. What they wanted most was a *tsaddik* who identified with them, concerning himself with their daily struggles in the world of external reality. Such a *rebbe* would be able to offer them assurance that their devotion—to God and to him—would help their prayers be answered.

Karlin, in short, was more like a northern version of popular Hasidism as it was emerging in the Ukraine. For a number of reasons (the higher learning level in the north, the anti-Hasidic pressures, and inferior organizational skills) it was hardly able to hold its own against the growing "empire" of R. Shne'ur Zalman. Forced for a while to relocate in the Ukraine, the Karlin dynasty, when it did return to the Pinsk region, lived very much as the "lesser light" compared to the vast reach of the HaBaD school. This was a far cry from the situation in 1772, when *hasidim* in Lithuania had been generically referred to as "Karliner." (Interestingly, the term survived in the anti-Hasidic documents even when opposing a movement that no longer had any relation to Karlin.)

Within the Ukraine, Hasidism varied from one group to another largely around the personality of the *tsaddik*. Once Levi Yitshak was safely ensconced as rabbi of Berdichev, that large town became a center of Hasidic pilgrimage. So did Chernobyl, northwest of Kiev, and Miedzybozh, where R. Barukh held sway. Less well-known figures, some of them still itinerant preachers, were also very much a part of the Hasidic scene.

Just after the turn of the nineteenth century a new and highly original young Hasidic master appeared on the scene, creating a Hasidic sect that would forever remain different from all others. R. Nahman (1772–1810), great-grandson of the BeSHT and nephew of R. Barukh, began to accept disciples first in Zlotopolye and then in Bratslav (Breslov), the town to which his name is ever linked. As the offspring of such lineage Nahman was expected to become a Hasidic leader, growing up in the years when the new movement was just adopting the hereditary dynastic model. Nahman at first refused, showing considerable disdain for the popular Hasidism of his uncle and others. It was only after his return from a dangerous and highly transformative pilgrimage to the Holy Land in 1798–1799 that Nahman began to gather around himself a small band of followers who constituted the first generation of what were to become Bratslav disciples. In doing so he openly challenged the authority and even the spiritual legitimacy of other *rebbes*, seeing Hasidism already in the early stages of steep spiritual decline.

Bratslav was considered a unique and highly elite religious community; it may be seen as an early attempt at internal reform or regeneration within Hasidism. Nahman claimed that he was training his *hasidim* to become true *tsaddikim*, not merely loyal followers. The relationship of master and disciples was extraordinarily close, a reality that brought forth admiration and envy in some circles but disdain and suspicion in others. In the earliest years Nahman demanded of would-be disciples that they confess all their sins to him. Later this was replaced by such unique religious practices as daily *hitbodedut*, literally meaning "lone meditation," but here referring to verbal "conversations" with God in which the disciple was to pour out his soul in longing and contrition.

The spiritual life of Bratslav is one marked by an awareness of the distance from God felt by the honest seeker, who is deeply attuned to his own shortcomings and failures. In contrast to the simplicity of joyous service idealized by the Ba'al Shem Tov, Nahman experienced and modeled for his followers a life of painful struggle to come into the divine presence. Terms such as *meni'ot* ("obstacles" on the spiritual path) and *ga'agu'im* ("longings"), seldom discussed elsewhere in Hasidism, are key to the Bratslav vocabulary. Joy was indeed the goal, but attaining it was far from simple. Nahman understands the seeming absence of God from much of human life as a divine challenge toward personal growth, demanding a stretching of the soul to reach toward God, but also as resulting from man's sinfulness and especially from the pollution of the human imagination by wicked (often sexual) thoughts.

Largely self-taught, Nahman was clearly a creative religious genius. His collected teachings, *Likkutey MoHaRaN*, published partly in his lifetime (1808) with a second section in the year following his death, display a unique mastery of biblical, rabbinic, and Kabbalistic lore. Although taking the familiar form of Hasidic homilies, Nahman's teachings are marked by several unique characteristics. The associative links between ideas are much looser than in other works, creating a series of wide-ranging discourses in which intellectual argument is replaced by freewheeling imaginative construction. There is often a lyrical quality to Nahman's writing and a passionate form of expression that lends the work a unique place in the Hasidic corpus.

In striving to help redeem the fantasy life of his disciples (and himself) from domination by evil, Nahman in 1806 began to tell fantastic stories derived from East European folkloric motifs but woven with a subtle hinting at Kabbalistic symbols and filled with an air of mythic reality. The intent was to purify the mind by fighting fantasy with greater and richer fantasy than most people could conceive. The most important of these stories were published after his death as *Sippurey Ma'asiyot* (1815) in a Hebrew/Yiddish bilingual edition, a work that has come to be seen as a classic of early modern Jewish literature.

In Nahman's last year he moved to Uman, where he died of tuberculosis and is buried. In his last year he developed a seeming friendship with the town's first *maskilim*, only adding to the fire of controversy that swirled around him both in his lifetime and after his death. The Bratslav sect continued to flourish after Nahman's death under the leadership of his disciple Natan of Nemirov (1780–1845). Neither Natan nor any of the Bratslav leaders who followed him claimed the mantle of *rebbe*, however. Nahman remains the single master of the Bratslav community throughout its history. Because of this the Bratslavers were referred to in Eastern Europe as *di toyte* ("dead") *hasidim*. Their retort, "Better a dead *rebbe* who lives than a living *rebbe* who is dead," tells much about their place within the Ukrainian Hasidic milieu. They remained a much persecuted elite, sustained by a high level of piety and an undying faith in their master. Although the published Bratslav writings are marked by signs of internal censorship, they give a clear impression that at least some of Nahman's followers saw his death rather as a temporary occultation and they hoped for his return. There are various hints, both within Nahman's own writings and in the later Bratslav literature, that link Nahman's soul with that of the messiah. This link has been confirmed by recent publication of long-suppressed Bratslav documents.

The disciples of R. Elimelekh of Lizhensk remained a close circle even after their master's death in 1786. Many of them became followers of R. Ya'akov Yitshak the "Seer" of Lublin. The "Seer" himself is one of the more interesting figures in the world of early Hasidism. His unique epithet indicates that he was reputed to have clairvoyant powers, much like the Ba'al Shem Tov. "All the gates of light were revealed to him, no secret held back." The Seer saw himself as singular heir to the entire tradition of Hasidism, reaching through R. Elimelekh back to the Maggid and the BeSHT. He and his followers were bringing this legacy to Jews in districts where it had not been well known previously, including Galicia and Congress Poland.

The great vehicle for the conversion of these new masses to the path of Hasidism was the person of the *tsaddik* himself. Like Levi Yitshak, the Seer places great emphasis on the supernatural capacities of the *tsaddik*, who is himself an object of mystery and wonder. As Hasidism spreads and becomes a widespread popular movement, it can no longer be expected that all its adherents will live up to the rigorous spiritual standards demanded by the earlier generations, including the Seer's own teacher R. Elimelekh. For them it is sufficient to be attached to a *rebbe* who is the living embodiment of Hasidic truth, an earthly abode (*mishkan*) for the divine presence. The holy radiance that shines outward from such a figure will warm the multitudes by its glow.

It cannot be claimed that R. Ya'akov Yitshak is the founder of this theory; it had been part of Hasidism from the beginning. There was not an original "ideal" period of Hasidism, followed by degeneration into "tsaddikism," as was once claimed. The Hasidic revival was such that profoundly mystical and popular elements had always been thoroughly intertwined. But as memory of the first generations faded in the distance, and as the message was being brought to new generations and masses who cannot have had personal contact with those prior teachers, the centrality of the *tsaddik* as holy man and source of blessing became an increasingly large part of the legacy. The Seer was able to convey this message successfully because he embodied it so fully in his own person, including the varied aspects of powerful leadership indicated by the term "charisma."

Members of the circle branched forth in various directions, creating distinct Hasidic followings. Some were among the founders of Hasidism in Galicia, an increasingly important center of the movement in the nineteenth century. Such figures as R. Mendel of Rymanow (d. 1814) and David of Lelow (1746–1813) were Hasidic masters depicted mostly as kindly patriarchs. They offered neither original teachings nor specifically identifiable paths of devotion, yet they are revered by Hasidic tradition as bearers of warmth and support to Jews in need. The most profound preacher of this circle, R. Kalonymus Epstein of Cracow (d. 1823), is known primarily as an author and did not have a personal following. Another unique offshoot of the group was represented by R. Tsevi Hirsh of Zydachov (d. 1831) and his heirs, who combined Hasidic leadership with profound knowledge of Kabbalah.

Once the Seer moved from Galician Lancut (near Lizhensk) to the historic city of Lublin in eastern Poland, his court became the first major outpost of Hasidism on Polish territory. He and his comrade from R. Elimelekh's circle, R. Yisrael of Kozhnits (d. 1814), are considered the fathers of Polish Hasidism. Like the Seer, R. Yisrael essentially transferred the legacy of prior Hasidism to new territory. Distinguished as an author and scholar, he brought respectability to Hasidism in an area where it had formerly been disdained. But within the circle at Lublin there emerged another highly distinctive sub-school, centered in the town of Przysucha, which created a version of the teaching that is specifically thought of as "the Polish school" within Hasidism.

Its founder was another Ya'akov Yitshak (d. 1813), known as the "Holy Jew" of Przysucha. Like the Seer before him, he set up his own circle during the lifetime of his master, something that was considered a break with tradition. This Ya'akov Yitshak, along with several associates who were treated more like peers than disciples, had developed a complex attitude toward the Hasidic heritage that was imported from Ukraine to Poland. They bore a certain amount of skepticism, especially regarding the supposed wondrous powers of the *tsaddikim*. In any case, they claimed, miracles were beside the point. The real struggle was for a life of faith and the human goodness nourished by it. Too much attention to the lavish tales of wonder-working was just a distraction. Talmudic learning, especially with its emphasis on ethical behavior, was held in high esteem by this group.

The flavor of this group's semi-skeptical Hasidism might best be conveyed by a story. Among the young men drawn to Lublin by tales of the Seer was one named Mendel from the town of Tomaszow, later to be known as R. Mendel of Kotsk (Kock). When he came to meet the Seer for the first time, he was told that it would be some time before the master was free to talk with him. He wandered out to the town market, and while he was there he bought a pocketknife. Later, when he walked into the Seer's chamber, the *rebbe* greeting him by asking, "Did you come to Lublin only to buy a knife?" thus demonstrating his power of clairvoyance. Young Mendel replied, "I sure didn't come to buy the holy spirit!" In other words, "Don't try your wonder act on me. I'm not interested; that's really not what I came here to 'buy.'"

The reader may notice that we have described three distinct schools of Hasidism emerging in the 1796–1815 period: HaBaD (actually beginning earlier), Bratslav, and Przysucha. Although the terms used to describe them may overlap, each has a unique spiritual physiognomy, and they are quite easily distinguished from one another. The first represents a disciplined, restrained, and contemplative intellectuality; the second an emotionally effusive and fantasy-laced creativity; the third a skeptical and earthbound ethical spirituality. Still, one may say that they all have in common a certain inner reformist thrust in the history of Hasidism. Each sees much that it doesn't like as Hasidism has begun to grow into a mass movement, inevitably diluting what is perceived (accurately or not) as the greater spiritual intensity of former times. Each sets out its own path—all of them attempt to restore to Hasidism the devotional gravitas that they felt had gone missing.

The third and final round of anti-Hasidic persecutions seems to have begun with a foolish personal affront. In 1796 a young *hasid* began appearing in various towns of Poland announcing himself as none other than the son of the Vilna Gaon. His aged father, he declared to whoever would listen, greatly regretted his denunciations of Hasidism and wished he could retract them. When word of this imposter, whose message was entirely untrue, reached the Gaon, he became understandably infuriated. Several angry letters ensued, resulting in a renewal of all the former bans again Hasidism by the communities of Vilna and Minsk.

This time the *hasidim* in Vilna were no longer willing to suffer persecution. The movement had grown significantly in the 1790s under the able leadership of R. Shne'ur Zalman. He had just published the *Tanya*, a work that was being widely acclaimed and was to greatly increase his stature within the Hasidic world. Realizing that they were an impotent minority within the formal *kahal* (community) structure, they turned instead to the imperial Russian authorities, their new (since 1795) political overlords. While their true complaint was about the persecution of Hasidism, in order to stimulate the authorities' interest they also included an accusation of malfeasance in the handling of communal funds.

This escalation of hostility crossed a significant line in the mentality of traditional Jewish communities, for whom "informing" to the often harsh and anti-Semitic gentile authorities was considered strictly taboo. Incensed by this new demonstration of audacity by the *hasidim*, the communal authorities were able to turn it around rather deftly: Shne'ur Zalman and several other Hasidic leaders were arrested in October 1798. Although an unbiased reading of the sources makes it clear that involvement of the czarist police began with a Hasidic provocation, the *hasidim* quickly came to see their master as a martyr suffering for the Hasidic cause. His release after less than two months in prison, on the nineteenth of Kislev (December 1798), became the occasion for a festival still widely celebrated in HaBaD Hasidic circles.

The fierce battle between *hasidim* and *mitnaggedim*, particularly in Vilna, continued to flare up for several more years. The passing of the Gaon in the fall of 1797 did nothing to mitigate the harsh feelings, especially because the local *hasidim* refused to tone down their loud Sukkot celebrations on hearing of his death. This last round of controversy brought forth a new leader in the anti-Hasidic struggle: R. Avigdor of Pinsk. He had succeeded to that position after anti-Hasidic forces had driven Levi Yitshak away in 1785. But Pinsk, located on the "border" between areas of strong Hasidic and rabbinic-mitnaggedic influence, gave R. Avigdor little peace. The *hasidim* of Karlin (essentially a suburb of Pinsk) defied his anti-Hasidic proclamations. He too had sought governmental involvement, because he had paid a high price, as was often the custom, to attain this major rabbinic post. Once the third round of hostilities was aflame he took a prominent role in the conflict, resulting in a second imprisonment of R. Shne'ur Zalman and the increase of bitter feelings all around. Other new leaders of the battle also came forward to step into the Gaon's shoes, but the conflict soon began to sputter.

The first fifteen years of the nineteenth century saw the flowering of the varied Hasidic movements we have mentioned. They also saw the firm establishment of Hasidism as a deeply rooted and seemingly permanent feature of Jewish life in Eastern Europe. Increasingly Galicia, Belorussia, and Little Poland (the Lublin district) were seen as areas where Hasidism had important and mostly uncontested influence on Jewish religious life. While it never dominated there as fully as in Podolia and Volhyn, it was no longer considered new or controversial.

We have noted that this period came to a close with the passing of a number of key Hasidic leaders between 1809 and 1815. Memory of what had transpired "around the Maggid's table" could now only be passed on by those who had heard of it from others. So ended the period of Hasidism's original development and spread. From this time forward, Hasidism was viewed more as a part of the religious establishment than as an upstart movement. Throughout the nineteenth century, Hasidism was to see and present itself as the standard-bearer of tradition, master of a legacy handed down from its sacred past, stretching back not only to the Ba'al Shem Tov but also to all the generations that had come before him.

The later history of Hasidism lies beyond the scope of this introduction. The texts before you all represent the generation of the Maggid's disciples, a period that was now at an end. But a few words on the great transformation of Hasidism as it began its next period will help the reader comprehend some of the gap between the spirit and ideas found in these sources and what appears to be the religious tone of latter-day Hasidism.

The first fifteen years of the nineteenth century constituted a critical period in the history of Europe. The armies of Napoleon marched across the continent, seeking to fulfill the French emperor's dream of world conquest. But even though republicans at home viewed Napoleon as the great betrayer of the French Revolution, his advance eastward brought with it many of the radical ideas that had been forged in the heady years of enlightenment; the culmination was the overthrow of the *ancien regime* in ideological as well as political terms. Notions of human rights and liberty were combined with critiques of the older order, particularly the church. Enlightenment religion breathed a spirit of Deism and a disdain for ancient rites that divided people and religious communities from one another. The Napoleonic armies briefly restored Polish political hegemony in the Grand Duchy of Warsaw, established in 1809. In 1812 they were famously defeated at the gates of Moscow, beginning the great retreat that led to the

Congress of Vienna and the reestablishment of old-order authority after 1815. But something important had taken place in those intervening years that could not so easily be brushed aside. Most of the areas where Hasidism had spread were at least briefly under French rule. The possibility of Jewish emancipation and enlightenment, previously confined to very small circles in Western and Central Europe, had now been at least glimpsed by masses of Jews living to the east. The *haskalah*, or Jewish enlightenment, first a literary and philosophical movement of Berlin intellectuals in the 1780s, now began to have adherents scattered across Eastern Europe on both the Austrian and the Russian sides of the reestablished post-1815 borders.

Both the rabbis and the *hasidim*, in many cases sworn enemies a decade earlier, began to see the great dangers confronting their old way of life. The religious authorities, in pondering this new landscape, moved to dramatically change their view of Hasidism. It had proved itself over thirty years of growth not to be a new Sabbatianism. One might find the *style* of Hasidic piety to be offensive, but the fact was that they lived essentially within the bounds of *halakhah*. Moreover, they had managed to generate great enthusiasm for Jewish religious life and were clearly spreading that commitment to a new generation. If a fight had to be led against the inroads of Westernization, educational reforms, and other challenges, why not make common cause with the Hasidic *tsaddikim* in waging that battle?

From the Hasidic side, this unspoken offer by the rabbinate to lay down its weapons was seen as pure victory. Hasidism had become so powerful, everywhere but in Lithuania, that the authorities no longer had either the interest in fighting it or the ability to do so. The *hasidim*, anxious to demonstrate that they were indeed worthy of this acceptance, began to present themselves primarily as defenders of tradition; they were willing to serve as spearheads in the battle against *haskalah*. This willingness was entirely appropriate to a Hasidic leadership that was by this time primarily an inherited one, either by dynastic succession or by second-tier discipleship. Once Hasidism was declared "kosher," one might say, it was rapidly consumed and absorbed by the forces of tradition, who used its remarkable energy to construct a fence that shielded them from modernity for much of the nineteenth and twentieth centuries.

Those who had been around the Maggid's table had thought of themselves as innovators, insisting, as we have seen, on the right of each generation to forge its own path in interpreting the Torah. This generation of post-1815 leaders was in fact fully appropriate to the conservative spirit of those times, committed to preserving and restoring the Hasidic way of life that had been passed on to it by masters and teachers. So it was that Hasidism, denounced as a new, dangerous, and illicitly innovative movement in one generation, became a bastion of ultra-conservative energy for the next. The battle against Hasidism throughout the nineteenth century was waged by modernizers within the Jewish community and agents of assimilation in governmental roles in both the Austrian and the Russo-Polish political establishments. All of these pushed Hasidism ever further into the position of redefining itself as a movement of reaction, hostile to the encroachments of modernity at every turn. History had betrayed the Ba'al Shem Tov. His Judaism of serving God in joy, raising up sparks from every encounter in life, and finding divine presence everywhere took on an increasingly harsh and judging countenance as it struggled against an enemy it could never defeat. While sparks of authentic spiritual life remained—and indeed still do remain—alive within the movement and later generations did produce some masters of depth and originality, much of Hasidism's energy came to be devoted to combating modernity and change on every front. As industrialization, urbanization, and emigration transformed and secularized the lives of Jews throughout Eastern Europe in the late nineteenth and early twentieth centuries, Hasidism came to be seen as a force of the past, struggling to maintain its hold on a dwindling portion of the Jewish population. That remained its situation down to the eve of the Holocaust, the final destruction of most of Jewish life in Eastern Europe. The remarkable postwar revival of Hasidism and the emergence of neo-Hasidic trends within Jewish life outside the Hasidic community are subjects for discussion in another context.

NOTES

1. The following historical summary is based on a wide range of contemporary scholarship, much of it conducted in Hebrew. While I take full responsibility for all views expressed here, I am indebted to many colleagues, both living and dead. Because this work is intended for a general audience, it is published without footnotes, except for a few direct quotations. But I do want to acknowledge here my debt to a number of living scholars, including (but not limited to) David Assaf, Rachel Elior, Immanuel Etkes, Jonathan Garb, Ze'ev Gries, Moshe Idel, Haviva Pedaya, and Ada Rapoport-Albert.
2. My translation. The letter in its entirety is translated and discussed by Immanuel Etkes in *The Besht: Magician, Mystic, and Leader* (Waltham, MA: Brandeis University Press, 2005), 272–288.
3. The entire letter is translated and discussed by Moshe Rosman in *Founder of Hasidism* (Berkeley: University of California Press, 1996), 114–115.
4. Solomon Maimon, *Autobiography* (New York: Schocken Books, 1954). The chapter is reprinted in Gershon Hundert's *Essential Papers on Hasidism* (New York: New York University Press, 1991), 11–24.
5. *Degel Mahaneh Efraim, bereshit* (ed. Jerusalem, 1963), 5b–6a.
6. The letter is published in Mordecai Wilensky's *Hasidim u-Mitnaggedim* (Jerusalem: Mossad Bialik, 1970), 169–176.

בראשית

Sefer Bereshit

The Book of
Genesis

בראשית

Bereshit

ME'OR 'EYNAYIM I

In the beginning, as God created the heavens and the earth, earth was formless and void....
(GEN. 1:1–2)

It was through Torah, called "the beginning of His way" (Prov. 8:22), that God created the world. All things were created by means of Torah, and the power of the Creator remains within the created. Thus Torah's power is present in each thing, in all the worlds, and within the human being. Of this Scripture says: "This is the Torah: a person" (Num. 19:14), as will be explained. Torah and the blessed Holy One are one, [as the holy *Zohar* teaches (1:24a)]. Thus the life of God is present in each thing. "You give life to them all" (Neh. 9:6). God reduced Himself down to the lowliest rung; a portion of divinity above was placed within the darkness of matter. The whole point was that those lowly rungs be uplifted, so that there be "a greater light that emerges from darkness" (Eccles. 2:13).

This is the reason why Joseph went down into Egypt (*mitsrayim*), the lowest rung, the narrow strait of the sea (*meytsar yam*). It was to increase joy, for the "greater light" or greater joy is that which "emerges from darkness." That is why he was called Joseph, which means "increase" (*yosef/yasaf*). This is also the meaning of "Jacob saw that there was produce [*shever*] in Egypt" (Gen. 42:1). He saw "breakage" (*shevirah*) there, the fallen fruits of supernal Wisdom or Torah, since anything that falls from its rung is considered "broken." "In Egypt" means that he saw Torah's fallen fruits even in the narrow straits, needing to be purified and uplifted. He told his sons: "Go down there," to raise them up. He went down in order to restore them to their living root....

Since it is the Torah within all things that gives them life, we should pay attention not to their corporeal form but to their inner selves. "The wise man has eyes in his head" (Eccles. 2:14). The *Zohar* (3:187a) asks on this verse: "Where then should one's eyes be?" The verse rather means that the wise person's eyes are fixed on the head. Look at the "head" of each thing. Where does it come from? Who is its root? This is the meaning of **In the beginning**—it was through Torah that heaven and earth came to be, they and all within them. Thus our sages taught that the particle *et* in this verse is there to include all that was to be born of heaven and earth (*Bereshit Rabbah* 1:14).

Earth was formless and void [*tohu va-bohu*] refers to those who are sunk in earthly concerns. They are indeed "formless and void" because they pay no attention to the life-force. On their own they are indeed empty. RaSHI explained this phrase *tohu va-bohu* to mean "a person would be astonished [*tohe*] at the formlessness [*bohu*] there." He meant to say that a true human being should be astonished at the fool, so busy with the pursuit of material things, when really *bo hu*, it is right there within him. The life of God is there in his very self, but he lacks understanding and keeps at a distance.

A person who pays attention to the life that flows within all things is fulfilling "I place Y-H-W-H ever before me" (Ps. 16:8). In each thing you place before you the Being that causes all things to be....

⟨✺⟩

This opening section of the first teaching in *Me'or 'Eynayim* serves as a unifying introduction to the entire book of Genesis, linking the tale of Creation to Joseph's descent into Egypt. The One allows its divine light to be "broken" or scattered within myriad creatures, even the mostly lowly and earthbound of forms, so that humans will have the opportunity to seek it out, discover it, and uplift it to its Source. Sometimes this requires descent into the lowliest places. This is also a fitting introduction to the key teachings of Hasidism, a path that understands all of Judaism as a way to engage in this transformative inner work.

The final comment here has a very specific address. The true way to "place Y-H-W-H ever before you" is not, as others were teaching, to turn aside from the world and concentrate only on the letters of God's name, but is rather to open your eyes and see the divine presence that truly fills all that is around you.

ME'OR 'EYNAYIM II

In the beginning God created....
(GEN. 1:1)

... Creation took place for the sake of Torah and for the sake of Israel. Its purpose was that Y-H-W-H be revealed to Israel, that we come to know of God's existence. Even though God's true nature lies beyond our grasp, once we recognize that God exists we will surely do all our deeds for the sake of heaven. Thus will "Know Him in all your ways" (Prov. 3:6) become a reality, as we seek to be united with the One. There is none other and there is nothing else! There is no place devoid of God; "the whole earth is filled with God's glory" (Is. 6:3)!

This glory, however, is manifest in the many divine garments; the whole earth is a garbing of God. It is the One who is within all those many garments. This aspect of divinity is called Adonay, related to the word for those "fittings" (*adanim*) by which the Tabernacle was held together. This is God's presence as it has come down into the lower and corporeal rungs. Our task is to unite it with the Source from which it came, Y-H-W-H who calls all the worlds into being. In every act of service, be it study or prayer, eating or drinking, we bring about this unification. All the worlds depend on this: the union of the God within—ADNY—with God beyond, Y-H-W-H.

When these two names are joined together, the letters of each alternating with one another, a combined name is formed: YAHDWNHY, both beginning and ending with the letter *yod*. "You have made them all in wisdom" (Ps. 104:24), and the *yod* represents *hokhmah*, or wisdom, the prime matter out of which all the rest of the twenty-two letters are drawn forth and through which the world was created ... hence it is called by the sages *hyle*, from the words *hayah li*, "it was with Me." All things were within it, and from its potential they emerged into real existence.

Now since *aleph* is the first of the letters, [one might have expected that it should designate the primal substance]. But *aleph* itself is constructed of two *yods*, with a diagonal *vav* between them. The first *yod* represents supernal *hokhmah*, the wisdom in which all the worlds were included. By means of the *vav*, which is a drawing forth of consciousness [extension of the *yod*], all potential was brought to actuality and all the worlds were created. Thus was the final *yod* formed, the lower *hokhmah* or the Wisdom of Solomon [*shekhinah*]. This is the name Adonay, as we have explained, divinity garbed in all things and filling all the worlds.

When you do all your deeds for the sake of heaven, you draw everything in the world, or in the "lower wisdom," close to the "upper wisdom," which is the blessed Creator, the One who calls all into being. Through the consciousness of fulfilling "Know Him in all your ways" (and to "know" in biblical language means "to be joined") you link the lower *yod* to the upper, that sublime point. Then the world and all within it form one single *aleph*. That is why God is called *alufo shel 'olam*, "the Cosmic *Aleph*...."

ᏝᏋᎲᏝᎾ

This text unequivocally lays forth a Hasidic cosmology that is often treated more obliquely. The union of the upper and lower letters *yod*, referring in classical Kabbalistic symbols to the two ends of the divine realm, is here seen as the unification of God and this world. Joining these is the *vav*, which also means "and." It is human consciousness that forms the link, bringing the two *yod*s together. *Shekhinah* is in the fullest sense an indwelling presence, containing within it all that exists. The union of God's two names, or of the blessed Holy One and *shekhinah*, means that world and God are restored to a single wholeness and that all of being is One.

KEDUSHAT LEVI I

> In the beginning God created the heavens and the earth.
> (GEN. 1:1)

The blessed Creator made everything and is everything. In each moment, without ever ceasing, God bestows blessing upon His creatures and upon all the worlds above and below, onto the angels and onto all living beings. It is for this reason that we say in our morning prayers, "Who *forms* light and creates darkness" (based on Is. 45:7) and not "Who *formed* light and created darkness." We use the present tense, because God is constantly forming, revitalizing all of life, moment to moment; all is from the blessed Holy One, who is perfect and all-inclusive....

ᏝᏋᎲᏝᎾ

In his opening sermon on the Torah, the Berdichever articulates a foundational theological claim common to several of his Hasidic colleagues: the act of Creation was not a onetime event but is a continuous process. Moment to moment God breathes new life into all of existence. The *yotser* ("Formation") blessing, recited in preparation for the *shema'*, provides us with the opportunity to focus on this wondrous fact and to give thanks to God for the gift of life here and now.

KEDUSHAT LEVI II

> In the beginning [*bereshit*]....
> (GEN. 1:1)

The word *bereshit* can also be read as *bet reshit* ("two beginnings"). The Holy One bestows bounty upon us, and we, through our prayers, limit and shape this bounty, each of us according to our will. One person forms the letters of the word "life," another the letters of the word "wisdom," and yet another, the letters of the word "wealth." And so it is with all good things, each is shaped according to our will.

Now everything spiritual has a physical counterpart. Sound is undifferentiated, while speech is the concretization of sound through the parsing of the letters of speech. The sound of the *shofar* on Rosh Hashanah is the bounty of the blessed Creator—it is all-inclusive. But the prayers we say on this holiday serve to shape the divine bounty through letters, each according to our will.

The inclusive bounty that emerges from the blessed Creator is the "Written Torah," and that which we shape with this bounty is the "Oral Torah," for Oral Torah is fashioned according to the will of Israel, following our interpretations of the written Word. This is the meaning of *bereshit*: *bet reshit*, "Two beginnings"—Written Torah and Oral Torah.

❧

In this densely symbolic text, Levi Yitshak explores the roles of God and humanity in the creation and renewal of life. Although God provides us with the raw materials of existence, only we can give specific shape and texture to our lives by shaping God's energy through our words and actions. This is an especially important teaching during the early days of the Jewish New Year. While we certainly cannot control all that unfolds in our lives, we can work to fashion lives of holiness through prayer, Torah study, and sacred deeds. Human choice and action are at the center.

KEDUSHAT LEVI III

These are the generations [*toledot*] of heavens and the earth when they were created.
(GEN. 2:4)

This verse comes to teach us the purpose of the creation of the heavens and the earth, because the word *toladah* [singular of *toledot*] can also mean "purpose." This is demonstrated in the continuation of this sentence, which reads: ... on the day Y-H-W-H God made the earth and the heavens. This statement points to the future when "earth" will precede "heaven." This is the purpose of Creation: that the ones above [the celestial forces] will receive from the deeds of the ones below [human beings]. And this is also the meaning of the Psalmist's statement, "God's glory is upon the earth and the heavens" (Ps. 148:13). That is to say, the blessed Holy One's glory emerges when earth precedes heaven, when the upper ones receive from the lower ones. Understand.

☙❧

What does the Divine want of human beings? One answer given repeatedly by Levi Yitshak is that we are to serve as active partners with God in perfecting Creation. While life always begins with divine initiative, we are called upon to take a lead role in completing this great cosmic project. What pleases God most is our acting in a godly manner, using our creative powers to direct the heavens from the earth. In some texts the Berdichever speaks specifically about the need for the *tsaddik* (mystical adept and/or Hasidic leader) to serve in this role. Here, however, the message is addressed to all those who hear or read this teaching.

TORAH OR

> And his brother's name was Yuval; he was the
> ancestor of all who play the lyre and the pipe.
> (GEN 4:21)

Our sages taught: "All [animals] that are led by a chain [*sher*], [may] leave [for a public space] with a chain [on Shabbat]" (m. Shabbat 5:1).

Whenever something rises from one state of being to another, for example when [a soul] ascends from the lower to the higher Garden of Eden, this comes about through song (*shir*), for song allows existence to be nullified. It is known that anything that exists cannot become a different thing unless it first becomes nothing. Then something new can come into existence with greater bounty than before. This may be compared to a seed planted in the ground. It has to decompose in order to bring forth a plant that will carry many seeds. It is the same at higher levels regarding [human] souls or angels. In order to rise to a greater attainment, you have to first go through nullification of what is, and of your current attainment. Only then can you ascend to something greater. The image of the pillar that connects the lower and higher *Gan Eden* symbolizes this nullification.

Thus: "all masters of song [*shir*], leave" their spiritual attainments and are drawn to a higher level "by means of song." This is also the reason that sacrifices [in the Temple] were accompanied by song. The essence of the sacrifice is raising "the flame, the savory smell" from below to a higher level. This ascent calls for song, for nullification as explained previously....

This is the meaning of **Yuval ... the ancestor of all who play the lyre and the pipe.** The word "Yuval" implies flow, directing (*movil*) and drawing upwards by means of **the lyre and the pipe.** These allude to song, since all ascents happen through song, as we explained.

༄࿐ঔ

Behind this play of words on *sher/shir* stands a theology of music, reflecting the great role played by wordless *niggunim* (melodies) in Hasidism. In the course of singing, one goes from the words of a text, repeated many times in refrain, on to a singing of the melody without the words. Ultimately the melody too vanishes into silence. This is an aural expression of the spiritual journey from the concrete world, through successive abstractions, back into the primal Nothing, source of all transformation and renewal.

Bereshit
Round Two

AG: These texts are the Hasidism I love, the unitive vision of being and the human role in bringing that about. They could almost serve as a manifesto for our own neo-Hasidic thought.

EL: Yes, but I especially like the *Torah Or* piece among them, because it talks about how we go about that work. So many of the Jewish texts are weak in proposing method. Here, song is offered as a tool to be used. I also hear a strong environmental echo in this unitive vision, the connectivity that links all of being.

OR: But the tension is always there in the Hasidic sources. Are they about finding God in all that exists, or about overcoming all outer existence to find only God? I want to make sure it's the former, that we do not wind up denying the holiness of the physical world. That's why I am so drawn to the *Kedushat Levi*; it's the worldliness of his vision.

AG: I feel the same about the *Me'or 'Eynayim*. He stays very close to the world-embracing view of the Ba'al Shem Tov.

EL: There is a hidden Maimonidean in me who is always asking: "But how do you know you're not kidding yourself?" Might all this talk of the One within all being just be too facile? The point is that you have to *make* it one through *'avodah*, which means hard work as well as service. You need to "work through" your own stuff until you come through on the other side.

AM: This is all about a conversation between God and ourselves. Language is so fundamental to human experience; here we need to attune our ear to the divine creative voice. We do constitute a half in this dialogue, but we also have to learn to listen.

AG: I don't know a God who speaks in language as we know it. God's language is entirely real, but is also silent. That's why it's so hard for us to listen. We have attributed so many words to God, but to really hear God's voice is to listen to the silence between them.

OR: But we have to notice how universal is the human use of language in search for God, in the quest for meaning. Isn't God present in that very quest? Isn't God's speech woven into the fabric of our own?

EL: Yes, the *Kedushat Levi* has told us that. But there's always the danger of hubris in making such claims for the great human role. Humility is essential to the work. We are shapers of reality through our language, but we are not creators.

OR: But aren't we called *shutafim be-ma'aseh bereshit* ["partners in Creation"]? I agree with your call for humility. But how far need it go? Can we become humble without negating ourselves?

נח

Noah

ME'OR 'EYNAYIM

> ... Noah was a righteous man, wholehearted in his
> generation; Noah walked with God.
> (GEN. 6:9)

RaSHI comments: Of Abraham Scripture says: "The God *before* whom I
walked" (Gen. 24:40). He explains that Noah needed God to support him,
while Abraham was strong enough in his righteousness that he could walk
on his own. But this explanation raises a question.... Are we not told [in
the same verse] that Noah was **righteous** and **wholehearted**? How whole
could he be if he lacked what Abraham had?

It is known [from Kabbalistic teaching] that everything depends upon
the arousal from below, the "feminine" waters, since arousal begins with
woman's longing for the man (cf. Gen. 3:16). We, the Children of Israel,
are "woman" in our relationship with God. We arouse ourselves to become
attached to God from below. As we do so, we awaken in God, as it were, a
desire to extend to us the flowing forth of divine goodness. Then the flow
comes down from above, bearing blessing and compassion, life and peace.

We, the Community of Israel, and our blessed Creator are a single whole
when we are attached to one another. Either without the other is, as it
were, incomplete. Thus He says: "My name is not whole and My throne
is not whole ..." (RaSHI on Ex. 17:16; *Tanhuma Ki Tetse* 11). We are called
the blessed Creator's "throne"; God is not whole without us. Surely we

without God are also incomplete. When we begin the process of arousal by our "female" longing for Him and desire to cleave to Him from below, we awaken His desire for us as well. When these two desires come together there is one whole Self. This is the meaning of "you shall be wholehearted with Y-H-W-H your God" (Deut. 18:13)—you, along with blessed Y-H-W-H, are called one whole Self!

This was the great purpose of Creation: that we first arouse ourselves from below to walk toward God. When this does not happen, God forbid, and there is no arousal from our side, God Himself has to awaken us. But in such a case we accomplish nothing. Noah was one in whom there was no arousal from below. God, wanting the world to survive, had to arouse him first. He had to awaken in Noah the desire to cleave to him. This is "Noah needed God to support him." Abraham our Father was strong in his righteous path, walking on his own, bringing about arousal from below.

Now we can understand why Noah is nevertheless called **righteous** and **wholehearted**. He did in fact cleave to God, though it was not he who had caused this to come about. But it is for those who walk like Abraham that this world was created. Thus Scripture says: "These are the generations of heaven and earth as they were created" (Gen. 2:4). "As they were created" is *be-hibare'am*, the same consonants as *be-Avraham*, "through Abraham," for he was the one who aroused God from below.

⟁

The contrast between Noah and Abraham is a commonplace in the Jewish interpretive tradition. More often they are contrasted as leaders of their generations. Abraham stood up to God when told that Sodom was to be destroyed, demanding justice from the "judge of all the earth." Noah acquiesced too readily to the destruction of those around him. But here the two are contrasted as mystics; Noah needs divine arousal given him as a gift, while Abraham stirs up desire and longing for God from within himself.

It is this, the Hasidic master teaches, that God desires. Yes, religious intimacy is possible as a gift from God; occasionally we humans are blessed in that way. But the reason God created us is that we do the "heavy lifting" in this relationship. We are here to raise human energy back to its source in God. Only in doing so do "we"—creature and Creator—become truly whole.

NO'AM ELIMELEKH I

> ... Noah was a righteous man, wholehearted in his generations; Noah walked with God.
> (GEN. 6:9)

By virtue of holy acts, by doing something holy, a righteous person can draw the exalted and blessed Creator into this world. This benefits the entire generation, for by this they merit to experience the divine presence among them. As the *tsaddik* ascends the rungs of spiritual development, he/she gains a greater ability to connect and draw the Blessed Name into all aspects of the universe. This is the meaning of the verse **Noah was a righteous man, wholehearted in his generations**; the wholehearted nature of his righteousness benefited his generation.

There was yet a further benefit: **Noah walked with God**. This means that he impacted the supernal worlds as well. So the phrase **with God** refers to the supernal worlds. Noah walked there as well. Think about this.

⊙〰〰〰〰⊙

In this teaching the *No'am Elimelekh* may be offering a measure of righteousness. Does the spiritual development of individuals benefit the society they live in? To the extent that it does, the person may have achieved "wholehearted righteousness." And if a life lived this way positively influences the way a generation experiences and understands God, has the Divine not benefited as well?

NO'AM ELIMELEKH II

> ... Noah was a righteous man, wholehearted in his generations; Noah walked with God.
> (GEN. 6:9)

Another understanding of the phrase: **In his generations**. Despite the fact that Noah's life spanned several generations, it seems more appropriate to write "his generation" in the singular form. The main reason for using the phrase **his generations** in the verse is to emphasize his righteousness relative to his generation, as RaSHI explains.

I therefore think it comes to teach us an additional matter. Each and every generation is connected at its root to a specific *mitsvah*, which it needs to establish more than the others. For example, one generation might be connected to the root that leads it to establish the commandment of *tsitsit* (ritual fringes) more than other commandments. So every generation at its root must grasp a specific *mitsvah* more than the others.

Scripture teaches us that Noah was perfect in his generations. This means that in every generation he lived he held and established the root *mitsvah* that was specific to that generation.

⌖

In this teaching Noah is presented as a spiritual leader who is attentive to the changing spiritual needs of his age and who changes the emphasis of his religious teaching in response to those needs. While this is certainly a useful model to emulate, the choice of Noah to represent this sort of leadership is puzzling. Is the *No'am Elimelekh* ignoring the fact that Noah was obviously not successful in impacting his generation prior to the flood, and that while he was saved they all perished?

"What are the unique *mitsvot* of our generations?" we need to ask. Are we being more successful than Noah in helping those around us rise to the challenge?

KEDUSHAT LEVI

> ... Noah was a righteous man, blameless in his age.
> (GEN. 6:9)

... Let us consider RaSHI's comment (on Gen. 7:7) that "Noah was among those of limited faith." How could this be, since the Torah itself testifies that **Noah was a righteous man, blameless in his age**? ... We can explain the matter as follows: There are two types of *tsaddikim* who serve the Creator: there is the *tsaddik* who serves God faithfully and believes that he has the power to direct the cosmos according to his will. As our sages of blessed memory stated, "The Holy One decrees and the *tsaddik* annuls the decree in favor of the good" (b. Mo'ed Katan 16b). There is another type of *tsaddik* who serves the blessed Creator but who is so very lowly in his own eyes that he thinks to himself, "Who am I that I should pray to annul the decree?" and therefore does not pray to do so....

Now even though Noah was a great and blameless *tsaddik*, he was very small in his own eyes and did not have faith that he was a powerful *tsaddik* with the ability to annul the decree of the flood. In fact, he thought of himself as being equal to the rest of his generation. He said, "If I am to be saved in the ark, and I am no more righteous than the rest of this generation, they too will be saved." Therefore, he did not pray to save the people of his generation. This is why RaSHI taught that Noah was among those of limited faith....

❧

One of the hallmarks of early Hasidism is the belief that true *tsaddikim* (mystical adepts and leaders) have the power and responsibility to overturn negative divine decrees. In this paradoxical theological worldview, the Divine actually celebrates the virtuosity of the *tsaddik* and happily cedes control to the holy man working on behalf of the community of Israel. It is based on this ideology that Levi Yitshak portrays Noah as a failed *tsaddik*. While Noah may have been a good man, he misjudged his own abilities and therefore did not act to save his generation from the flood.

What might those of us who struggle with such a magical worldview learn from this text? One lesson might be that there are times when we need to stand tall and take action because we have the talent, power, or opportunity to make a difference. Whether or not we frame such experiences in miraculous terms, each of us has the potential to change reality in big and small ways. The question is whether we choose to stand up and act for the good, even while knowing that we may not succeed and that our actions will be imperfect.

OR HA-ME'IR

> "Now take of all food that is eaten and gather it to you that it be for you and for them as food." Noah did all that God had commanded him.
> (GEN. 6:21–22)

On the latter verse RaSHI comments: "This refers to the building of the ark." And below he says: "This refers to his entering the ark" (Gen. 7:5).

We need to set our hearts to understanding these verses according to our general principle that Torah is eternal [and speaks to each generation], past, present, and future. If that is the case, what does this "building of the ark" come to teach us now? To me it seems to refer to prayer, hinting at the ways we are to arouse ourselves to worship [based on the link between two meanings of *tevah*, "ark" and "word"].

The holy books tell us that in order to attain true inward devotion, to properly bring a word of prayer before God, you have to attach yourself to all creatures [that surround you] during prayer, even to the inanimate things. Scripture says: "You created all in Your wisdom" (Ps. 104:24). Nothing in the world exists without purpose, God forbid. Everything points to a wise and conscious Actor. Everything exists for the sake of God's glory, so that humans will become aware of them all, finding clues to wisdom within them. An enlightened person pays attention to this, seeking out the aspect of wisdom garbed in each thing that exists—animal, vegetable, and mineral, every level of existence. Then you may awaken the heart within yourself and, excited by the wisdom within all creations, speak your words with love and awe. Thus you fulfill the intent of your Creator, the reason that this earth, with all its fullness, came to be....

That is why Scripture has God tell Noah to **take of all food that is eaten and gather it to you**. It was hinting at the varied possibilities of arousal within this service of prayer.... Thus **Noah did all that God had commanded him**.

⟲⟳

Noah's job, according to this version of the Hasidic reading, is that of "building" the word of prayer and then "entering into" it. We build prayer not by detachment or isolation from the world around us, as some might think, but by utter and total *involvement* with the world, indeed with every level of existence. Prayer must begin with an open heart, open wide like the entrance to the ark, taking in every species and all it needs to eat. For us this will mean a prayer life that embraces all the levels of reality with which we are engaged—the physical, the economic, the political, and many more—and bringing them before God, enriching and expanding our understanding of the devotional life. And how many different ways there are to pray—as many and varied as there were animals in the ark and foods needed to sustain them!

Noah
Round Two

AG: The struggle these Hasidic authors have with Noah is really interesting. He is, after all, a *tsaddik*. In fact, he's the only person in the Torah described by that term, one they are using to portray their own ideal leader. So they can hardly shunt him aside. But they keep comparing him negatively to Abraham and then somehow apologizing for him. I think they're just terribly disturbed that he doesn't stand up and fight, that he doesn't do anything to try to save his generation. That's a key part of the *tsaddik*'s job, after all.

EL: There is indeed something strange in the *No'am Elimelekh*'s description of Noah as a leader whose spiritual work benefits his generation and who is attuned to the spiritual needs of his generation. After all, he did not have enough impact to avert the catastrophe of the flood. I wonder if in some ways the Hasidic masters might see themselves in Noah. They know their own imperfections, and while they may be impacting their own circles of disciples, they cannot be sure that they will successfully "save the world." Perhaps in describing what is positive about Noah, they are describing what they think is important about their own leadership, even when there is no guarantee of ultimate success.

OR: One element of this literature that I find most interesting is that it was written by individuals working to create a new religious movement with a new model of religious leadership. In reading these comments on Noah, I hear the Maggid and his disciples struggling to articulate— for themselves, their communities, and their opponents—a compelling vision of leadership for this nascent movement. As you have both commented, in their search for a "usable past" the early Hasidic masters find Noah to be a challenging and unsettling figure, particularly so at this precarious moment in their lives and the life of Hasidism.

AG: Look at our moment. Think about the great "flood" of environmental disaster that is about to come. How are we religious leaders doing at arousing our world to change its ways?

Lekh Lekha

ME'OR 'EYNAYIM I

> Y-H-W-H said to Abram: "Get yourself out of your land, your birthplace, your father's house, unto the land that I will show you."
> (GEN. 12:1)

[On **Get yourself**,] RaSHI comments: "For your benefit, for your own good." But surely Abraham, who is called elsewhere "Abraham My lover" (Is. 41:8), served God for the sake of love alone, not for any "benefit" that might result.

We may answer as follows: Abraham is called doubly by God: "Abraham Abraham!" (Gen. 22:11). Similarly "Jacob Jacob!" (Gen. 42:6) and "Moses Moses!" (Ex. 3:4). This is because "God's people are a part of Him" (Deut. 32:9). While the *tsaddik* lives down here in this lower world, his root continues to exist above. He was created here only so that even one who inhabits a lowly body might still choose the service of God and not deny the seal of the King. He remains as much a *tsaddik* in this world as he is in his root above. This is "Abraham Abraham!"—Abraham the earthly *tsaddik* and Abraham above. So too the other righteous: their names here are the same as their righteous names above.

The souls above bask in the light of *shekhinah*, as is known. Even though they enjoy this light, however, it comes to them as "the bread of shame." A person who eats what is not his own is ashamed to look at it. That is why our blessed God brought the soul down to earth: so that out of our own choice we could serve God and thus receive an earned reward, no longer having to be shamed by the bread we eat. This is the meaning of **Get your-self**—"for your own benefit, for your own good." May pleasure and good come to you as reward for your actions and not as the "bread of shame."

Now even though the soul is clothed in the lowly garb of matter and therefore has bodily and earthly desires, these very desires may lead her back to serve Y-H-W-H. This is **out of your land** [or "earth"]: it is out of your own earthiness that you may turn to God's service....

King David said: "I shall walk before Y-H-W-H in the land of the living" (Ps. 116:9). If you engage in bodily deeds—eating, drinking, and the rest of human needs—just for the sake of fulfilling your desires, these actions have no life. But if you eat to sate your *soul*, uplifting the eating, drinking, and other needs to God by your intentions, then you are fulfilling "Know Him in all your ways" (Prov. 3:6). All your deeds are being done for the sake of heaven. Earth or the land itself then becomes "the land of the living," for in your very earthliness there dwells the Life of Life. This is **to the land that I will show you**—so that it will become the land of the living....

⚭

This is bedrock Hasidism. Like Abraham, we are to serve God out of pure love, with no thought of reward. But God, in loving us, wants us to feel that we have earned love, not merely received it as a gift. The aspect of ourselves that is part of God, ever basking in *shekhinah*'s glow (not only after death, but simultaneous to our lives!), does so knowing that our outermost earthly self has done its part to earn that blessing.

Note that in this tradition there is no debate between "faith" and "works." Of course works, meaning *mitsvot* and good deeds, are essential. In fact, God has done our souls the favor of giving us bodies and placing us in this physical world, just so that we may have the privilege and satisfaction of earning our spiritual keep!

ME'OR 'EYNAYIM II

> Get yourself out of your land ... and I will make you
> a great nation.
> (GEN. 12:1–2)

Nothing is impossible for the Creator! Could He not have made him a great nation right there in his own country?

[handwritten: lower sephirot]

God conducts the world by means of seven qualities. These are represented by the seven-day cycle of the world, known also as the cosmic days or "days of the construct." They begin with *hesed* ("love" or "compassion"), of which Scripture says: "The world is built by *hesed*" (Ps. 89:3). Just as the world is conducted by means of these seven "days," so must the person who serves God be a microcosm, in whom these qualities are implanted. In us they take the form of love, awe, glory, and the rest. Our lives must be conducted in accord with them. Every person is given a choice; we may turn these qualities any way we like. Even though they flow from the highest place, as love is rooted in sublime *hesed*, they may be used for good or ill. We receive them in a fallen state, each containing a mixture of good and evil.

This is what our worship is all about: to purify these qualities within us from their own evil, raising them up to God as we use them in His service. This comes about by means of insight. When a bad form of love or fear comes to you, you must look upon it and tremblingly say in your heart: "This love is fallen from the World of Love, from the love of our blessed Creator. It is my task to raise it up! How, then, can I do an evil act that *[handwritten: A form of psychology]* will cause it to fall still farther? If I find my love energies aroused by this forbidden object, a lowly material creature, how much greater should my love be for God and His Torah, through whom all being was created? He is the joy of all joys!"

Deal similarly with all the other qualities as they arise. You should be too much in awe of God to use the King's own scepter [your sense of fear] to arouse His anger, rebelling against God as though He does not see. When any one of these qualities [or emotions] wells up within you, even if it is manifesting in a negative or superficial way, take it as an opportunity to bind yourself to the same quality as it exists within God. Then you are raising all that has fallen to its root. God has no greater joy!

Abraham our Father held fast to that quality of *hesed* until he became known as "Abraham My lover" (Is. 41:8). It is with *hesed*, love, that we need to begin the repair of our inner qualities. God wanted Abraham to go forth among the nations of the world, where those qualities existed in a deeply fallen state. He was sent especially to Egypt, of which it is written: "Their issue is like that of horses" (Ezek. 23:20) [i.e., an oversexed society]. Abraham, master of love, had to descend to their level in order to uplift the love that had fallen there. In order to raise up any person, as we know, you need to go down to that person's rung. That is why Abraham used to bring in guests, sharing food and drink with them, afterwards saying:

"It is not *my* food you have been eating, [but God's gift]!" It was through their attachment to things of this world, such as eating and drinking, that Abraham was able to bring himself to their level. As he ate and drank with them, he brought them under the wings of the *shekhinah*. That is why we speak of bringing guests *in*, and why hospitality to them is said to be greater than greeting *shekhinah's* face (b. Shabbat 127a). In this way you bind fallen things to their root, providing heaven's greatest joy....

So it was when Abraham set out to repair *hesed*, uplifting the negative forms of love amid those nations among whom there lived holy souls. Then too he had to go down to their level. Of this Scripture says: "There was a famine in the land, and Abraham went down into Egypt" (Gen. 12:10). This was "a famine not for bread and a thirst not for water, but to hear the word of Y-H-W-H" (Amos 8:11). The qualities were very much fallen. Abraham first sought to raise up his own special quality, that of love, from its fallen state. Of this Scripture says: "A man who takes his own sister—that is *hesed*" (Lev. 20:17). The point is that you must come to understand that even this love is a fallen fruit of the divine tree, the attribute of *hesed* above. [Therefore Abraham described Sarah as his "sister."]

As he sought to raise them up, Scripture takes care to say: "Abraham went *down* into Egypt"—an act of descent and self-humbling, lowering himself to their rung so that he be related to them, in order to raise them up. The verse then goes on to say that Abraham went *la-gur sham*, "to dwell there." But this same word can also be translated as "to be fearful there".... Going down to that level demands a certain trepidation. You need to maintain great fear of heaven so that you do not become like them in their failing, making sure that the journey downward is for the sake of ascent on return....

That is what it means that God commanded Abraham to go forth from his land, so that He might make his name great. A person has to humble himself, becoming close to those he seeks to raise up. That way the border of the holy can be expanded and the love of God truly spread forth in the world, as fallen love is restored to its root. One who does this is all the more to be called a lover of God, [making God beloved by many]. This is the meaning of **I will make you a great nation**: by going forth, leaving your land, and proclaiming God's love even in the fallen rungs, you become "Abraham My lover." This will make you a greater lover than you were before....

This teaching is based on the Hasidic understanding of the seven *sefirot* as a guide to human emotional states and moral self-improvement. Our being "in the image of God" means that we contain these seven elements, usually described as love (*hesed*), fear or awe (*gevurah*), pride or glory (*tif'eret*), triumph (*netsah*), gratitude (*hod*, deriving it from *hodayah*), uprightness or connection (*yesod*), and inclusiveness (*malkhut*). Each of these can be used for good or for ill. Our goal should always be to use them as a pathway back to their source in God. The journey begins with love.

This is the energy that drives the true *tsaddik* to enter into the world and engage fully with the lives of ordinary human beings. To love God is to seek out the divine spark of love in all its manifestations, even if they seem grotesque, and bring it back to God. All of love has its root in the single love of God's *hesed*. Our job is to seek out that root, to be clear in our devotion to it, and to lead others toward this deeper and truer path.

NO'AM ELIMELEKH I

> God said to Abram: "Leave your country, the place you were born, your father's house, and go to the land I will show you."
> (GEN. 12:1)

As a *tsaddik,* you know that you can be a source of gifts from heaven, and at times your work may be motivated by the wish to bring such gifts to your companions and students.

Yet God's true will is that you do not think about the benefit you can bring at all. Rather your goal should be to serve God perfectly, and the bounty will come as a result.

This is the meaning of the verse **Leave your country** [Go from your "land"]—you should not be thinking about matters that relate to your earthly gain.

Rather **to the land I will show you**; all your work should be directed toward the "supernal land," and the bounty will come as a result.

This teaching is a caution against expecting a specific benefit to result from the spiritual work done by a person (meaning a need of a specific companion or student). Rather, the *No'am Elimelekh* proposes that true service of God brings about good in ways that we cannot control and of which we may not even be aware. He is not, however, proposing that one should always serve with no thought of benefiting others at all. As he notes elsewhere, the intention to bring benefit to others is both a protection against self-centeredness and a crucial characteristic of leadership.

KEDUSHAT LEVI I

> And you shall be a blessing [ve-heyeh berakhah].
> (GEN. 12:2)

The letters *yod heh* [in *ve-heyeh*] allude to the Holy One, and the letters *vav heh* to Israel [together forming the four letters of the Tetragrammaton, *yod heh vav heh*]. Until Abraham, there was no one to arouse the outpouring of divine blessing from above, and the flow of blessing derived solely from the blessed Holy One. In that sense, *yod heh* preceded *vav heh*. But from the time of Abraham there was an arousal of the blessing from below, and *vav heh* now preceded *yod heh*. This is the meaning of **ve-heyeh berakhah.**

⟆⟪⟫⟎

What does it mean for a person to be a blessing? For the Berdichever, it means that like Abraham we actively engage in spreading God's life-giving force throughout the world. While the Divine can serve as the single source of blessing, what God wants is for us to draw forth God's bounty by means of our sacred thoughts and actions. Through his evocative use of the name "Y-H-W-H," Levi Yitshak teaches that we are called by God to reconfigure reality to such an extent that God's most sacred name, Y-H-W-H, be "misspelled," with human beings (W-H) preceding God (Y-H). God wants us to take the lead!

NO'AM ELIMELEKH II

> There was a famine [*ra'av*] in the land and Abram
> went down to Egypt to dwell there....
> (GEN. 12:10)

A teaching regarding spiritual practice: This is related to the verse "a hunger [*ra'av*] that is not for bread and a thirst that is not for water, but rather to hear the word of God" (Amos 8:11). It follows that the most essential famine is when the people of Israel do not act properly but rather follow their wayward hearts, heaven forbid.

Through this they cause their spiritual leader, even a most perfect *tsaddik*, to lose something of the great and holy spiritual rungs already attained. Thus, "there was a famine in the land," as we explained.

And Abram went down to Egypt implies that because of this famine, the spiritual leader referred to as "Abram" descends from a rung previously reached. But even in this fall the *tsaddik* is not totally lost, heaven forbid. The fall becomes a going **down to Egypt** [*mitsrayim*], which has the same letters as "straits" and "sea" (*meytsar, yam*). This alludes to the spiritual leader's experience of the great holiness, which used to feel as vast as "the supernal sea" (*yam*), now feeling narrow (*tsar*) and constricted.

The blessed Holy One does not bring about this fall just because of the deeds of evil people. **To dwell** in this constricted place actually benefits the *tsaddik*. Without something of a fall, we can become proud and arrogant over our achievements and sanctity. Now, when we see that we have fallen from a prior rung, we feel shame and remorse, like a stranger in the land. We consider ourselves strangers both to the world-that-is and the world-that-is-becoming as we see ourselves fallen from what we thought we had achieved.

❧

In this teaching the *No'am Elimelekh* reminds us how much the community is a part of the spiritual life of its leader. Alongside the image of the leader carrying the community, the *No'am Elimelekh* reminds us that the community also carries the leader. For the leader it is important to remember this as a counterbalance to the tendency toward arrogance. The community needs to remember that far from being insignificant passive recipients, the quality of the community's way of life and behavior is crucial to the leader's ability to offer or attain anything.

KEDUSHAT LEVI II

Melchizedek king of Shalem brought forth bread and
wine; he was priest of the most high God.
(GEN. 14:18)

There are two types of divine servants. One serves God through absolute
devotion [*mesirut nefesh*, implying devotion unto death]; the other serves
by means of *mitsvot* and good deeds. There is a difference between
them: the one who serves solely through devotion, without recourse to
mitsvot or good deeds, is truly in the Nought, while the one who uses the
commandments is serving God by means of an existing thing.... Therefore
the one who serves through devotion cannot draw divine blessing upon
himself, for he is nothing, being so attached to God. The one who serves via
mitsvot and good deeds, being linked to things that exist, can bring divine
blessing to himself [and the world]....

Our sages say that Abraham our Father fulfilled the entire Torah before it
was given, even *'eruvey tavshilin* [a rabbinic device to allow for Sabbath food
preparation on festival days] (b. Yoma 28b). We have tried to understand
how he came to know the entire Torah. Because Abraham separated
himself from the corporeal and thus saw that the life-force sustaining each
of his own 248 limbs was from a particular *mitsvah*, and that without that
mitsvah the limb would have no life (seeing that the life of the head derived
from *tefillin*, for example), he attained all of Torah before it was given....
For this reason Abraham was not able to worship God outside the Land
by means of *mitsvot*. Outside the Land it was impossible to fulfill those
commandments applicable only to those living within it [sabbatical year,
tithing, etc.]. Because the *mitsvot* corresponding to certain limbs could not
be fulfilled, he would have been lacking those limbs.... Thus it was that
so long as Abraham dwelt outside the Land, he served God only through
devotion. But once he entered the Land, he was able to serve through the
mitsvot in such a way as to be a complete form, with all his limbs. Thus he
began to serve in that way....

Outside the Land, serving through *devotion* and thus attached to
the Nought, he was unable to bring the bounty of divine blessing upon
himself.... Thus RaSHI comments on the verse "'Get you forth from your
land' (Gen. 12:1): for your own benefit, for your own good" ... for you will
be able to draw blessing upon yourself.

Now one who serves purely through devotion sees the blessed Creator with his very eyes. But if you worship by means of *mitsvot* and good deeds, you see through a glass, since you are serving through an existing thing. This is the meaning of "After these things, God's word came to Abraham *in a vision*" (Gen. 15:1). Now he saw God only in a vision, through a glass. But God said to him: "Fear not" because you are serving Me in this different way. "Your reward is very great"—this service will be capable of bringing about blessing....

Abraham's fulfillment of Torah was only in the Land, not outside it. But in our case, even though we are outside the Land, we are able to serve by means of *mitsvot*, for the Torah has already been given....

The Midrash (*Bereshit Rabbah* 43:6) discusses this verse: **Melchizedek king of Shalem brought forth bread and wine; he was priest of the most high God.** Rabbi Shmu'el bar Nahmani said that Melchizedek revealed to Abraham the secret of high priesthood, while his colleagues said that it was the secret of Torah. "High priesthood" would mean the service of God by pure devotion, which is the highest form of priesthood, offering oneself as sacrifice to the Creator. "Torah" here would mean the service of God by means of *mitsvot* and good deeds.

Remarkably, Melchizedek here seems to represent the path of the Land of Israel, showing Abraham the very Hasidic truth that it is possible to worship God by means of corporeal things. But the older Abraham, the one who wants to serve by pure devotion, also has his roots in the Maggid's Hasidic circle; this teaching was likely addressed to a fellow disciple "across the table," one who wanted to reach the peak of mystical self-obliteration, often described as the purpose of intense Hasidic prayer. Levi Yitshak, a more popular teacher, sees the goal as bringing Hasidic insight down to earth, and with it offering blessing to those who gathered round. That is what "Abraham," as well as the would-be Hasidic master, needs to learn.

Could Levi Yitshak have had any idea of the role Melchizedek plays in the theology of Christian priesthood? The symbols of bread and wine, the notion of high priesthood, and the final comment about self-sacrifice all bring one close to this tantalizing conclusion, seemingly so unlikely for the context of Jewish-Christian contact in the era in which he lived.

Lekh Lekha
Round Two

OR: Here, like in so many places, they're dealing with the question of the physical. How do we relate to the material world? Here they all see it in *artsekha*, "your land," because *artsiyyut* in their language means "the physical." Levi Yitshak seems to be challenging his teacher the Maggid on this. Melchizedek needs to bring *tsaddik* Abraham down from the heights to teach him a form of worship that will really be effective, that will bring blessing into this world. That's what his Hasidism is all about.

AG: Yes, I think the *Me'or 'Eynayim* sees things similarly. Although the Hebrew doesn't quite preserve it, I think in the oral Yiddish talk behind it he has God saying to Abraham: "Get out of *your way* of seeing the physical world." That would be the way of asceticism and self-denial, the old Kabbalistic path. "Go—for your own good—to the land, to the vision of *artsiyyut*, that I will show you," to the new Hasidic way of worshipping God through every physical act that you perform.

EL: R. Elimelekh is the conservative dissenter in this conversation. He really wants his reader to leave *artsiyyut* behind, to turn wholly toward God in the thought and act of worship. But I think that's because the *No'am Elimelekh* is a different sort of work. It is a training manual for would-be *tsaddikim*, not a set of teachings addressed to the public. The future *tsaddik*, to claim the powers R. Elimelekh wants him to have, will need to be totally selfless and other-worldly. Remember, of these three only he had a real group of disciples and future leaders around him.

Va-Yera

NO'AM ELIMELEKH I

> And God appeared to him by the oak trees of
> Mamre, as he was sitting at the entrance of the tent
> in the heat of the day.
> (GEN. 18:1)

When it arose within the divine will to create the world for the sake of God's creatures, the process began with a retraction of divine energy. Where did that energy go? I heard from my teacher, of blessed memory, that the blessed Holy One became concentrated within the letters of the Torah with which heaven and earth were created....

A *tsaddik* who engages Torah in holiness and with no ulterior motives can draw the blessed Holy One into the letters of Torah, just like at the moment of Creation.

On this basis we can understand the verse **God appeared to him by the oak trees of Mamre**. Mamre alludes to speech (from *amar, amirah*); the tree is Torah and its branches are the *mitsvot*. The verse teaches that the pure utterances Abraham said in the process of engaging in Torah drew the Creator into the letters. **By the oak trees of Mamre** thus means that it was in the "tree" of his utterances that God appeared to Abraham.

What was it that enabled Abraham's Torah study to facilitate a vision of God? The verse explains that this was due to his great humility. This is implied in the phrase **he was sitting at the entrance of the tent**. Despite the fact that he was a great *tsaddik*, he humbly considered himself a beginner—just at the entrance of all that is holy, for the tent alludes to holiness.

In the heat of the day; there are people who appear humble, yet their humility is only a facade. This phrase teaches that Abraham was honestly and wholeheartedly humble. To him, it was as clear as daylight that he was only a beginner in the service of the blessed One. This [clarity] is implied in the words **the heat of the day**.

⟨~~~⟩

This is one of the Hasidic texts that attribute great power to the creative acts of humans. Torah branches out and blossoms through the creative words of the learner, and this in itself constitutes a vision of God. How easily this power and creativity can themselves become the object of idolatrous veneration, if not balanced by true humility.

MAGGID DEVARAV LE-YA'AKOV (#195)

> ... rest beneath the tree.
> (GEN. 18:4)

This verse is linked to "the Tree of Life in the midst of the garden" (Gen. 2:10). The Tree of Life is the holy name Y-H-W-H, as is known. "The midst of the garden" means that this name is garbed within the fifty-three [*GaN*, "garden"] portions of the Torah. Earlier we have taught that this name is clothed within all of speech. It has endless masks and degrees of hiding. It is garbed first within the five openings of the mouth [parts of speech], then successively within letters, combinations of letters, words, and narrations. The Zohar says that one who has eyes [referring to the mind's eye] looks at the inner nature of things; one who lacks such eyes sees only the royal garments. This is especially true of seemingly profane narratives (*Zohar* 3:152a).

Abraham was a teacher to everyone in the world. So this may be what he was showing them, since they appeared to him in human form. He was telling them that when you do a good deed or perform some holy act, think of the inward meaning of that deed, not its simple outer form. That is what he meant by "rest" upon that which is "beneath the tree." He was referring to the life-force that brings all into being, called the Tree of Life. "Tree" can also refer to the human body, as Scripture says: "You shall not destroy its trees ... for a person is a tree of the field" (Deut. 20:19)....

So Abraham was saying to them: **Rest beneath the tree**. Pay no attention to the garments. Look to see what is underneath the tree....

⟐

When the angels come to Abraham in human form, he indeed sees people before him. And he does what the good teacher is always ready to do: he takes the moment and tries to find a profound lesson in it. "Is it a hot day, you weary travelers? Come and rest under this tree. But be sure to look *under* it while you are here, for under each tree, and indeed each physical self, lies the Tree of Life." That is where you should rest your attention.

The message of Hasidism is quite clear. In both ordinary life and engagement with Torah, do not get caught up in the externals. Beneath them, "under the tree," there is always something deeper to be found.

NO'AM ELIMELEKH II

I will bring you bread, to strengthen your hearts;
then you will go on....
(GEN. 18:5)

A *tsaddik* who wants to benefit the world must do so through relationships with other *tsaddikim*. By feeding them in holiness the *tsaddik* draws down a great flow of benefit. That is the meaning of **I will bring you bread, to strengthen your hearts**—by this eating you will fortify your hearts with holiness. The heart is the place where holiness resides, as it says, "that we may obtain a heart of wisdom" (Ps. 90:12). When you do this, you will impact yet others, as the verse continues, "Then you will go on"—you [the receivers] will pass on this benefit to others as well. Think about this.

⟐

At a certain level this teaching is probably the *No'am Elimelekh*'s perception of the table of his teacher the Maggid. Around this table, from its meals and study, the Maggid's students drew sustenance, and from there they went on to spread his teachings and to establish Hasidism in Eastern Europe. In this description turned instruction, the *No'am Elimelekh* emphasizes the mixture of spiritual and physical sustenance, and the importance of thinking of every student as a teacher in potential. These are two lessons we may benefit from thinking about in our times as well. We too set forth a "table" around which our students are nourished.

KEDUSHAT LEVI

> Y-H-W-H said: "Shall I hide from Abraham that which I am doing?... I have known him, that he might command his children and his household after him, that they guard the path of Y-H-W-H, doing justice and fairness."
> (GEN. 18:17–19)

... All the many deeds Abraham performed in God's service, done with both love and great mindfulness, were too little in his own sight. They seemed an inadequate response to the favors and miracles that God had wrought for him.... He therefore decided that his own mindful fulfillment of God's *mitsvot* was insufficient. So another thought entered his mind: Everything I do I will perform in the name of all Israel. All of Israel were bound up in Abraham's thought and mind, just as the potential child is there within the mind of the father. Our ancestor bore within himself the root and seed of the entire Community of Israel, all the way down to the time when messiah's footsteps will be heard. When he performed any *mitsvah* with all his strength, he bore all those future spreading branches in mind.

With this intent, he did a double favor for his offspring. Since Abraham observed all the commandments, as is known, even innovations of the rabbis (like the rules of Sabbath and holiday food preparation; b. Yoma 28b), he did them in all Israel's name as an act of collective worship. Thus each of his descendants had already fulfilled every *mitsvah* in potential. This meant that the way was already paved for them to find great meaning in those deeds, since they had already performed them together with father Abraham. It became easier for each Jew to realize this potential, since the gate was already open since Abraham's day....

This is the meaning of **Shall I hide from Abraham that which I am doing ... I have known him**. "Knowing" is the language of love. God said: "I love him," and began to speak in Abraham's praise. **That he might command his children** does not just mean "commanding" but being linked and bound to them (*mitsvah/tsavta*) in each deed he does. **His children and his household after him** refers to all who will ever come forth from his loins. **That they guard the path of Y-H-W-H** is written as though in the past tense (*ve-shamru*), for it is as though they had already fulfilled all the *mitsvot*. He set forth a way for his offspring so that it would be easier for them ever to act with justice and fairness....

⟨༄⟩

The special warmth and love in Levi Yitshak comes through very strongly in this passage. The Jew has an intimate and loving relationship with the life of the commandments. This is not just because they are familiar to us from our own childhood, as one might think, but because we did them first so very long ago, in the mental embrace of that most loving of all fathers, Abraham, the human embodiment of God's own love.

GINZEY YOSEF

> Maybe there are fifty righteous within the city ... will You not spare the place for the sake of those fifty within it?
> (GEN. 18:24)

The final **within it** is superfluous. Hadn't he already said **within the city?**

Regarding Noah, RaSHI explained the verse saying that "Noah was a righteous man, perfect in his generation" (Gen. 6:9) in a positive way. "Had he lived in a generation of the righteous," he said, "Noah would have been even more righteous."

This is what Abraham meant by adding **within it** to his prayer. They needed only to be righteous enough to be distinguished from the people of Sodom, even if in another city they would not have been considered righteous. Abraham prayed that God nevertheless consider them as though wholly righteous. That's why he said: "Will You kill the righteous with the wicked?" (Gen. 18:25), referring to these righteous who were indeed right there "with the wicked." That is why they are less than perfectly righteous. Were they living among *tsaddikim*, surely they would be even better!

" ... The [fate of] the righteous would be [*ve-hayah*] like the wicked." This is Abraham's prayer: he asks that the righteous of Sodom be seen as perfectly righteous, just as its wicked are perfectly wicked, more so than anywhere in the world! That is why the text uses *ve-hayah* here, a verb form that usually indicates joy (*Bereshit Rabbah* 42:3). It would be a joy indeed if these small-scale *tsaddikim* could be considered wholly righteous, balancing out the wicked among whom they live. That is the reason they are not capable of being more fully righteous, after all! The Hebrew phrasing (*ka-tsaddik ka-rasha'*) points to this [prayer for balanced treatment].

That is why God answered in the same way: "If in Sodom I find fifty righteous within the city" (18:26), again using an extra phrase. If I find fifty righteous only as compared with the rest of the city, not requiring they be as righteous as they would be elsewhere—"I will bear the place."

⟨⟩

Abraham's theory of relativity, we might call it. Here God learns from the human embodiment of His *hesed* that human beings are affected by their surroundings and therefore cannot be held up to absolute standards. Abraham makes a powerful demand that God be as generous with the relatively righteous of Sodom as He was with Noah.

If this was true in Sodom, it must also have been true in Satanow, the Ukrainian town where the author served as preacher. How much more must it be true in our world, given the pressures and temptations that we constantly face. Can we find a *rebbe* who understands and loves us enough to make such a claim for us and our little bits of righteousness?

Va-Yera
Round Two

EL: The opening passage of this *parashah* is such a rich opportunity for Hasidic modeling, it's hard for them to pass it by. Abraham's generous hospitality to unknown strangers conveys much of the feeling of welcome and acceptance that any Hasidic *rebbe* wants to generate.

AM: Yes, that's true of most of these teachings, but not all of them. The first *No'am Elimelekh* text, with which we opened, is purely about personal humility, with no implication about relationship with others.

AG: Yes, that side is there in Hasidism, the focus on your lone relationship with God. But the point is that it prepares you to then go forth in concern for others, as Abraham goes for the people of Sodom in this very interesting *Ginzey Yosef* text.

⟨⟩

חיי שרה

Hayyey Sarah

OR HA-ME'IR I (FROM LEKH LEKHA)

Abraham was old, come into days....
(GEN. 24:1)

I heard from my teacher the Maggid an explanation of "These are the generations of heaven and earth as they were created" (*be-hibare'am*; Gen. 2:4). Our sages read this word [by switching the letters] to mean "through Abraham" (*Bereshit Rabbah* 12:9). The Maggid questioned this teaching, since we have heard about ten generations that passed from Adam to Noah and ten more until Abraham (m. Avot 5:2). How could the world have existed for all those generations before Abraham came into it?

He explained it thus: Indeed, Abraham's own quality was that of *hesed*, or love. In its original state love is so pure that humans could not even grasp its nature. This original love [within the divine realm] is called "Abraham the Elder" [i.e., *hesed*, the prototype of earthly Abraham]. But the human Abraham adorned himself wholly in the service of God through great love; his entire body became a moveable dwelling-place for the quality of love. He made people familiar with this aspect of divinity and enabled them to speak of God's love. The sages paraphrased him as saying [to God]: "Until now You were only called 'God of heaven.' But I have made Your name known among people, so that now You are also known as 'God of earth'" (*Bereshit Rabbah* 59:8). This was because he showed everyone in the world how love flows even into physical reality.

Sefer ha-Bahir (#191) teaches that "the quality of *hesed* said before the blessed Holy One: 'Before Abraham came along, I had to stand my own guard, dealing lovingly with all who come into the world. But now that he exists, I have no need to do so. Thus Scripture says: 'Because Abraham listened to My voice and stood My guard'" (Gen. 26:5). He stood in my place and dealt lovingly with everyone in the world....

This is the meaning of **Abraham was old, come into days**. Read it to mean: "Abraham the Elder came into days"—the original quality of *hesed*, that of Abraham the Elder, "came into days," became embodied and entered into temporal reality in a holy person here in this world, truly.

Now we can understand what the sages meant when they said, "'These are the generations of heaven and earth'—through Abraham." It was by means of that original quality of love, called Abraham the Elder, that the world came to be, existing from Adam through Noah to [the earthly] Abraham. But once he came along and took hold of *hesed*, becoming its embodiment, then "he stood My guard," offering love to all who come into the world....

⟡

It was the quality of *hesed*, which we also call *eros*, that allowed for there to be "generations" from the beginning. The Ba'al Shem Tov and the Freudian agree in not distinguishing *eros* from "*agape*" (erotic love from generous or divine love), but insisting that all of love is one. For the *hasid*, all of love has its root "above," in the pure love of God; all lesser loves and desires represent *hesed* in a fallen or broken state. The Freudian sees the continuum beginning "below," with sexual desire, all the rest being one form or another of sublimation. But the two of them are holding fast to the same continuum.

But suppose we read this text in a contemporary evolutionary context. *Eros*, or the mystery of sexual attraction, making for reproduction and the continuity of life, was indeed there "from the beginning," reaching back (as we understand it today) to our roots in the animal kingdom. The real human love-quality of that generation-bearing process, however, was only manifest when "Abraham" came along. It took an Abraham, meaning a real, fully developed human being, to discover that *eros* is also love, that the biological urge is also the setting for our most sublime human emotions. "Abraham" here, the human representation of *hesed*, but also progenitor of our ancient family, becomes the great embodiment and teacher of divine and human love, sharing it with all around him. We, his spiritual descendants, are charged to do the same.

NO'AM ELIMELEKH

> Abraham was old, come into days....
> (GEN. 24:1)

This verse can be understood based on a Talmudic teaching: "The entire world is sustained for the sake of [*bi-shevil*] my son Hanina, while Hanina my son is satisfied with a bushel of carobs a week" (b. Berakhot 17b).

I have heard people explain that the word *bi-shevil* means that Rabbi Hanina ben Dosa created a pathway (*shevil*) that opened up channels through which the whole world is sustained. This fits our way of interpretation, reading the text as it relates to our service of God.

We see that some *tsaddikim* engage in severe ascetic practices for many years. Through this they achieve great levels of piety. But there are others who do not follow such strict regimens and they too attain great piety and wholeness. The truth is, however, that they too have reached this place because of the [first] *tsaddik*'s efforts. His strict discipline served to remove the separating barrier, sweeping aside the thorns, brambles, and briars that lay in the way, all the external elements that kept people from following this pathway to God. The *tsaddik*'s efforts create the path, a distinct approach to serving the blessed One. The way provided by this path makes it easier for others to approach holiness and to walk in God's ways....

This is the meaning of the verse **Abraham was old, come into days.** "Old" refers to one who has attained wisdom (b. Kiddushin 32b). **Come into days** means that he has brought about unceasing compassion, for the word "day" implies compassion, as is known....

Our father Abraham, through his service, removed the great separating barrier, making it easier for others to approach God in this way. That is what any *tsaddik* wants and longs for—that people be enabled to walk in God's path.

⚭

What is the role of *tsaddik* as spiritual leader? Elsewhere in Hasidic tradition he is seen as a hero who alone can carry the people's prayers to God, going where no one else can enter. This teaching offers a subtler model: the *tsaddik* as path-breaker. Compassion or *hesed* itself is a particular religious path; someone had to open the way to it. The teacher is here to show you that path, but you still have to walk it on your own.

Or ha-Me'ir II

... God blessed Abraham in all.
(GEN. 24:1)

Our sages were aroused to say about this verse (b. Bava Batra 16b) that Abraham had a daughter whose name was *Ba-Kol* (**in all**). We have to interpret their words in connection with the *Tikkuney Zohar's* teaching (*Tikkuney Zohar* t. 69, 116b–117a) about the *shekhinah*: "When She is among birds, She is called 'eagle'; when among plants, 'lily'; when among fowl, 'dove,' and so forth."

We need to understand this matter. If you are a person to whom God has granted a contemplative mind, and you want to enter God's service in an inward and wholehearted way, you will do as follows: In everything you see and hear, you will see and hear only the divine presence that is "garbed" there. You will take it as a clue to a deeper wisdom, awakening you to become attached to God.... Thus you will be raising sparks, limbs of the *shekhinah* that dwell within all (*ba-kol*) and give life to all. This is what they meant by saying "among birds, 'eagle,'" and all the rest. *Shekhinah's* name varies along with all the diversity that exists in the world, all for our sake [that we might recognize and name Her everywhere]....

Abraham our Father, peace be upon him, understood this deeply and tried so hard to find this garbing of *shekhinah* in every (*ba-kol*) place.... He grasped Her presence on all levels, even the most earthly. He was able to see *shekhinah* in everything, to understand under what name She was appearing to him, and to address her properly.

This is the meaning of "Abraham had a daughter whose name was *Ba-Kol*." [He saw that] She is present, garbed in every place and in every creature. "Among birds, She is called 'eagle'; She acquires the name 'eagle' ... among fowl, 'dove,' among plants, 'lily.'" All of these are names for *shekhinah* as She comes to be cloaked in the process of giving life to those diverse rungs. Understand this matter; it is something profound....

☙∞☙

This Hasidic Abraham is a lover of God who celebrates all the great variety of life. Wherever life takes him, he finds yet another occasion to rejoice in God's presence. His link to "in all" is one of love. It may be the love of parent, in this case that of father for a daughter. But he also loved *shekhinah* as she appeared in the forms of birds and flowers. That is the secret of *ba-kol.* The same great love we humans naturally bear for those persons we love was one that Abraham could carry through all of existence.

KEDUSHAT LEVI

> "Behold, I will stand at the well of water. The townsmen's daughters will come to draw water.... In her I will know that You have wrought compassion with my master...." Then Rebecca came forth, who was born to Bethuel.
> (GEN. 24:13–15)

First we must ask why Eliezer needed to mention **the townsmen's daughters** as he did. And why also is Rebecca described as one who **was born to Bethuel,** in the passive form. This seems to hint that her birth came about through someone else, not by himself....

This may be well understood by our approach. Abraham our Father's way was to uplift all the worlds to their root in the infinite, drawing down the forces of compassion from the upper reservoir of blessing. All the compassion flowing through the world came about by his drawing it forth ... opening the channels of compassion.

Now Eliezer his servant knew that all the men of that town were wicked. So he set up the test in this way. When he saw compassion in one of the maidens, he would understand that this had come about because of Abraham, since he was the one causing compassion to flow into the world.... Thus **In her I will know that You have wrought compassion *with my master,*** by means of my master's service ... causing compassion to flow upon all the worlds, including this young woman.

Then Rebecca came forth, who was born to Bethuel. Described in that passive form, since her true birth really came forth from another place.... He saw that her compassionate self surely derived from the root of Abraham our Father....

In her I will know that You have wrought compassion with my master. The *Zohar* tells us that in the days of Rabbi Shim'on ben Yohai, even children were aware of sublime wisdom (1:92b). This was because Rabbi Shim'on served Y-H-W-H through wisdom and mind, causing his quality to flow through all the world, even to children.... Abraham our Father's quality was compassion, causing it to be present throughout the world....

༺◈༻

Rebecca's character is not determined by the destiny of her biological lineage, but by the power of a great soul present in her generation, to whose quality she is inexplicably drawn. Levi Yitshak, who is speaking to young men whose parents often opposed their attraction to the new Hasidic path, might have found the matriarch to be an attractive model. How often we encounter great souls in this world who come from households or circumstances that would not have predicted such a person. Could it be that something in the generation's air—perhaps indeed the hidden presence of a *tsaddik*—draws such special souls to come forth in the world?

Hayyey Sarah
Round Two

AG: We see the creators of Hasidism talking here about a life of *hesed*. Hasidism is to become a Judaism based on love: the love of God, fellow humans, and all creatures, because they all embody the *shekhinah*.

EL: How very different this is from all the earlier uses of "*hasid*" in Jewish history! Usually it meant an extreme religious path, and often included severe ascetic practices. Here they really seem to be talking about simple love and compassion.

OR: I love the way Abraham stands for *hesed*; he embodies it in the real world. Before him it exists only as an ideal; he brings it down to earth. That, too, is very Hasidic.

EL: Yes, but look at how the *No'am Elimelekh* insists that to open the path of compassion, the *tsaddik* needs to work hard at his own ascetic life. Remember that R. Elimelekh was known to be a Hasidic master who never gave up the old path of asceticism. He's justifying that here. What the *rebbe* does is to concretize love, to make it accessible to others.

AG: It seems like the ordinary *hasid* is to be taught the simple life of love and compassion. But behind that teaching there is a really colossal effort that needs to be undertaken in the clearing of channels.

AM: It's surprising that the *Or ha-Me'ir* is the more gentle voice here. If R. Elimelekh is addressing himself to potential *tsaddikim*, R. Ze'ev Wolf seems to be talking to everyone, inviting them to walk this path.

EL: My question for today is about the contemporary rabbi. The *tsaddik* here has to suffer his disciplines in order to give substance and seriousness to the life of *hesed* that he is offering to others. Could we say the same about today's rabbis? They have to study very intensely, knowing the tradition from within, to provide that seriousness for the Judaism practiced in the communities they lead.

AG: Yes, there is a modeling of serious discipline involved in rabbinic learning. But their studies are for the sake of real *content*, so that they have a rich treasury of Torah to share with their communities.

Toledot

These are the generations of Isaac, son of Abraham.
Abraham brought forth Isaac.
(GEN. 25:19)

... A parable: Reuben loves Simeon powerfully. Because Simeon sees that Reuben loves him so much, a love for Reuben is awakened in him as well. Reuben's love for Simeon is called "parental" love; Simeon's love for Reuben is called "generated" love, since it has been brought forth or generated by Reuben's original love.

Now there are two kinds of love that a parent has for a child. The first is just natural love, and this also causes the child to respond and love the parent. But a greater love is aroused when the parent sees the child going in the right path, acting righteously and living wisely. Of this Scripture says: "My son, if you are wise of heart, my heart too will rejoice" (Prov. 23:15). The parent takes great pleasure in the child, and this brings about joy.... The parent's love for the child is greater than ever.

All of the above applies to the realm of people. Before a child is born, or even afterward, we don't know the nature of that child or what sort of deeds the child will eventually do. The second sort of love is hardly present at this stage; the parent's love is primarily that of nature.

But regarding God Scripture says: "Israel, in whom I *will be* glorified" (Is. 49:3). God precedes time; past and future are all the same before God. Before Israel even existed, the deeds and teachings of each and every *tsaddik* were revealed to heaven. As soon as the notion of Israel arose in the divine mind, God was already deriving joy and pleasure from the deeds of each *tsaddik*. This is witnessed in the tale of Moses's ascent to Mount Sinai, during which he found God saying, "My son Eleazar says: 'A two-year-old cow [may be used as the Red Heifer]'" (*Tanhuma Hukkat* 8). This was hundreds of years before Rabbi Eleazar lived! So too did the sages say that "everything a faithful student is ever to say was already given in the law of Moses at Sinai." God said to Moses: "Thus-and-so is scholar x to innovate in that generation" (*Va-Yikra Rabbah* 22:1).

The teachings and deeds of each *tsaddik* give pleasure and delight to our blessed God. This is the sort of love and joy brought about in the Parent by the child's power. This is what the *Zohar* means when it says that "Israel sustain their Father in heaven" (3:7b). This is like the parent being given joy by that beloved child. In the fullness of pleasure the parent may cry out: "I am made strong and healthy by this pleasure!" So it is with the blessed Holy One: the pleasure is so great, it is as though they were sustaining Him!

This is also the meaning of "I was his nursling, his pleasure day by day" (Prov. 8:30). RaSHI explains that the Torah [or "wisdom," the subject of this verse] grew up in God's bosom for two thousand years before Creation. But the simple meaning of this verse claims that wisdom was God's nursemaid or teacher. It is difficult even to say this. Isn't God the First of all firsts? But we can understand it in our way. Torah prides herself on being God's teacher, as it were. This refers to the great pleasure God derives from Torah, from the teachings of each and every *tsaddik* and the good things each one does. These are the commandments that make up the Torah; this becomes a nursing and sustenance for God....

These are the generations of Isaac, son of Abraham. Abraham brought forth Isaac. Scripture speaks in their praise, saying they attained that perfect state where both sorts of love existed between them. This is the meaning of **These are the generations of Isaac, son of Abraham.** "Isaac" means laughter and joy. **Brought forth** means that Isaac, by his great righteousness, brought forth pleasure, joy, and love in Abraham as well.

⊙ﻬﻬﻬ♀

The Maggid's own teachings are especially marked by constant reference to the love of father and child, the ways in which a father can communicate even difficult teachings in a manner appropriate to a child's mind, and the ways in which the child rewards the father. We have no knowledge of R. Dov Baer's own father or the way in which the future Maggid was raised. We do know that he put great and loving effort into instructing his only son, who came to be known as Avraham "the Angel."

The image of God as parent (so much simpler in their age than in ours!) is here given a uniquely Jewish twist. The parent-child relationship is mutual, increasingly so as we go on through life. The parent gives the gift of life to the child, but the "child"—here surely the righteous human of every faith and community—brings plenty of reward to the divine Parent as well.

ME'OR 'EYNAYIM

> Isaac returned and dug the wells of water.... The servants of Isaac, digging in the valley, found a well of living water.
> (GEN. 26:18–19)

... We will begin to understand this passage by turning to the verse "They have forsaken Me, a source of living water, hewing out cisterns, broken cisterns, that cannot hold water" (Jer. 2:13). Y-H-W-H is the Source of life, flowing forth into all living beings in every way. There is none but Him, and all who cleave to Him are attached to the Root of Life whose waters never fail. This is true so long as there is no separation on our part, for if our sins come to separate us from the font, life itself will disappear from our midst. From God's side there is no interruption of the flow; "only your sins separate" (Is. 59:2). But one who draws his life from the "other side," the "broken cisterns" that contain only gathered waters (those into which the sparks of life fell at the time of the breakage, and that is why the cisterns are called "broken"), is cut off from his sublime root and is called a "separator of the One" (Prov. 16:28).

The patriarchs opened up the channels of mind or awareness, teaching all who were to come into the world how to dig within themselves a spring of living waters, to cleave to their font, the root of their lives. Their disciples were called **servants**, as in the servants of Isaac mentioned here, for their service of God came about through the patriarchs.

After the death of Abraham, however, the wellsprings of wisdom were sealed, blocked by the Philistines, representing the evil in humans that overtook the world. The lowest of [the four] elements, earth itself, became the strongest, and the power and spirit of mind were diminished. Then Abraham's son Isaac came along, following in his father's footsteps. He taught the people of his own generation how to dig again into that living font of waters; he taught this by means of various wonderful and mysterious processes of the mind. **Isaac returned and dug the wells of water**. All this came about by means of faith, which is the prerequisite for all. You need full faith that the glory of God fills all the world, that there is no place devoid of Him and none beside Him. By means of that faith you will come to long and desire an attachment to God. This state is referred to as *nahal*, meaning "stream" or "valley," but hinted at by acronym also in the verse *nafshenu hiktah la-Adonay*—"our soul waits for Y-H-W-H" (Ps. 33:20). In this way you come to your root, the spring of living waters. That is **the servants of Isaac, digging in the valley** (*nahal*); they were digging in "our soul waits for Y-H-W-H...."

◠◡◠◡◠

This text offers a beautiful example of the Jewish symbolic imagination and its development. The wells dug by Abraham and Isaac, linked to Jeremiah's description of God as a "Source of living water," create a symbol, often found in Kabbalistic teaching, of God as a well or a fountain. The Hasidic author quite naturally reads this in an internalized way, so that the passage in Genesis becomes an admonition to turn inward, to dig deep wells within the self. This requires faith, leading to the rather exquisite description of the servants, who now include the reader, "digging in 'our soul waits for the Lord.'"

NO'AM ELIMELEKH

> Rebecca said thus to her son Jacob: "I have heard
> your father speaking to Esau your brother, saying...."
> (GEN. 27:6)

The *Zohar* teaches that Rebecca stands for the holy *shekhinah* and Jacob represents the people Israel (*Tikkuney Zohar* t. 18, 34a). We can thus interpret the verses this way. Isaac wanted to offer to Esau the corporeal blessings of this world. But the *shekhinah*, loving Mother of Israel, sharing in all their sufferings, desired greatly that Isaac bless Jacob in this world as well.

How could She bear to look upon Her people's poverty and distress in this world! Therefore she told Jacob to go and receive the blessing from Isaac.

But Jacob was very much afraid of being blessed in the material realm. A panic rose over him. What if he were to become part and parcel of this corporeality, separating him, God forbid, from God's service? Of this Scripture says: "Lest you eat and become sated ... and your heart become haughty and you forget Y-H-W-H your God" (Deut. 8:12–14). He therefore said to Rebecca, the holy *shekhinah*: How can I receive the blessings of this world? "Esau is a hairy man" (Gen. 27:11), meaning that this world is fitting for him. He is a mixed being, walking about in a fog, doing whatever comes his way, whether good or bad. But "I am a smooth man," meaning that I am supposed to be smooth and shiningly pure, without any impurity mixed in. The corporeal world might lead me astray from God's service. Perhaps "my father will touch me," referring to my Father in heaven, my Creator, examining my deeds. "Then I would be in His eyes like a trickster, bringing upon me a curse, not a blessing." This earthly blessing might turn out to be a terrible curse.

"His mother," the *shekhinah*, "said to him: your curse will be upon me" (Gen. 27:13). It will be My responsibility to guard you from such a curse. "But listen to my voice: Go take for me a kid...." Receive the blessings of this world also for My sake. All this should be for God's service. Your intent in all earthly matters, including eating and drinking as well as other corporeal acts, should be only for the sake of heaven. You will bring forth holy sparks from that food that you eat in holiness, giving you strength to worship God through Torah and commandments. In all you do, may your intent be for heaven. "So he went and took it and brought it to his mother...." (Gen. 27:14).

৩᠊᠊᠊᠊৩

This passage was written in an era when poverty and suffering were the lot of most Jews. How could the *tsaddik* not depict *shekhinah* as wanting to preserve them from this fate? But in our day, with circumstances so changed, we might wonder whether Jacob didn't have a point. How much can we count on our turn toward God to keep us free of this world's many temptations? Our task seems to be to make do with less. Can *shekhinah* also lead us away from our over-addiction to too much corporeal bounty?

HAYYIM VA-HESED

Just as Jacob left ... Esau entered from his hunt [*mi-tseydo*].
(GEN. 27:30)

Shavu'ot is the time that Torah is given. It is true that the Torah was given at Sinai, but every year [at the time of Shavu'ot] a new way of thinking is drawn from the Holy Blessed One into the world so that the Torah can be understood through this new perspective.

However, when this new light of understanding leaves its place [to enter our world], it does so with the possibility of choice—for choice is *malkhut* [i.e., inherent in our reality, drawn to both good and evil]. This is the meaning of the verse: **as Jacob left ... Esau came at his side [*mi-tsiydo*].**

Because the evil inclination is joined [with the opportunity for good], you have to outwit it. You have to serve God with the understanding you already have while also constantly focusing on this new light. This will allow you to absorb new perspectives and to serve God with them. Do this throughout your whole life.

❧

A call for constant renewal, done carefully....

Toledot
Round Two

AG: It's a dangerous world we live in. Esau, the evil urge, or the "other side" is everywhere.

AM: Indeed the "other side" is right there at your side, *mi-tsiydo*. We wage a constant battle against self-deception. The evil one can be garbed in some brilliant new insight we have. Esau just loves brilliant new insights!

OR: Do we get any good advice here on how to deal with it?

AM: The Hasidic advice is always two-sided, even contradictory. Battle it and uplift it; uplift it and battle it.

EL: The struggle with evil can lead us to a real fear of this world and its temptations. But Hasidism refused to allow this fear to paralyze it. The

Hasidic masters insisted on embracing this world, even at the risk of temptation.

AM: They were able to do that with some success in a world of poverty, indeed to give hope to people whose worldly existence was pretty miserable most of the time. But what about us, living amid all this wealth and comfort? Jacob's fear seems pretty convincing.

EL: I guess you have to ask whether Mother *shekhinah* really has protected us from being led astray by the things of this world. Or have we turned into Esau, as Jacob feared would happen?

AG: But the message is that She still loves us and believes in us, even when we doubt ourselves.

AM: That is the essential optimism of the Hasidic teachings. There is a profound spiritual dynamism here, a refusal to retreat into fearing the material world. Human actions matter; we can and we must learn to live in the world and do good. Existence itself depends on it.

⟨∭⟩

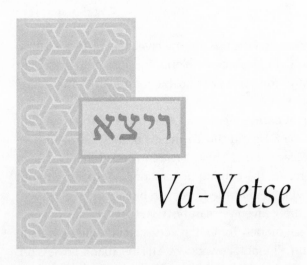

Va-Yetse

ME'OR 'EYNAYIM

> Jacob left Beersheba and set out for Haran....
> (GEN. 28:10)

... Jacob represents *da'at*, meaning "mind" or "awareness." Jacob and Moses are one in this, except that one of them represents it from within and the other from without, internal and external levels of mind. Before Jacob went to Haran, there had been no revelation of this mind or Torah; all was still hidden. The roots of Torah lay scattered about amid the lower rungs of being; no awareness of them yet existed in the world. Such Torah-roots were clothed within the house of Laban. These are the tales written in the Torah of Jacob's deeds in that household, bringing forth and purifying roots of Torah from their hiding place under the powerful "shells" of Laban. We know how powerful those are.

Our father Jacob brought forth those roots in the course of the twenty years he spent there with Laban in Haran. That is why the place is called Haran, referring to *haron* ("anger") of God. Here the Torah-roots were so deeply buried in their shells as to call the place one of divine anger. Everything Jacob had to do with Laban, involving both his daughters and his flocks, was about purifying and revealing those roots, as we know from various esoteric teachings on these passages. His placing of the stripped sticks in the troughs (Gen. 30:38), so that the flock would bear streaked, speckled, and spotted young was all about profound secrets and sublime mysteries. His marriages to Leah and Rachel refer to the Written and Oral

Torahs; he foresaw and prepared the way for the revelation of Torah below. All this had been hidden until Jacob came along. Because he represented *da'at*, Torah could be drawn forth from Beersheba, for upper Torah is called by that name, "Sevenfold Well."

Thus **Jacob left Beersheba**. He went from that place of Torah's hiding to bring it out into the open. He did this by means of the purifications he performed in Haran, the place of the "shells," within which Torah had been hidden. All this was to prepare the coming generations, so that they might attain in a revealed way what had formerly been in hiding. The Ba'al Shem Tov (his soul is among the heavenly treasures!) says that Laban pursued Jacob because some of that hidden Torah, the verses recounting his pursuit and their controversy, plus all that followed, was still in Laban's possession. Jacob hadn't yet transformed it. God thus caused Laban to run after Jacob, bringing to him this portion of Torah that had not yet been made whole. Now, in the course of their conversation, Jacob was able to purify this too, until nothing more remained. Everything he did with Laban, all that is told in the Scriptures, was for the sake of Torah and God's service, to bring Torah forth from the depths beneath which it had been buried in Haran, rejoining it to Torah above.

That is why, when Jacob first came near to Haran, we are told that "he rolled away the stone from the mouth of the well" (Gen. 29:10). He removed the obstacle that blocks the "wellspring of living waters" (Song 4:15), the hidden roots of Torah. He revealed (*va-yeGaL/GiLLaH*) that well, bringing it out into the open from beneath its stone-like shells. Of this Scripture says: "... Remove the heart of stone from your flesh" (Ezek. 36:26), for thus the Torah rooted there comes to be revealed.

꧁꧂

Jacob lived before Moses, at a time when Torah was still completely hidden; he had no clear path of holy living set out for him. Nevertheless, he understood that all that happened to him—his journey to a new and strange place, his difficult relationship with his father-in-law, his long years of service, and his marriages—all were part of the sacred work of uplifting and clarifying a Torah that was not yet known to the world.

We might think all this is just history, retold to glorify the patriarch. But when the author quotes Ezekiel saying "Remove the heart of stone from your flesh," we understand that all of this is instruction to us as well. We too encounter hidden Torah in all that happens in our daily lives. We too can uplift it, transform it, and link it to Torah above, just like Jacob our Father, who represents all of Israel. We only have to move that stone, the one that sits atop our inner well....

OR HA-ME'IR I

> Jacob left Beersheba and set out for Haran. He came upon a certain place....
> (GEN. 28:10–11)

This verse points to the reason why thinking people are forced to turn from thought to speech. Wouldn't it be better to remain always in the mind, contemplating the great and exalted goodness of the blessed Holy One?

The value of turning from thought to speech is that it brings about full expression of God's holy name, as we have explained in various connections. One of these is "Jacob saw that there was produce [*shever*] in Egypt [*mitsrayim*]" (Gen. 42:1). Speech is a "narrow strait [*meytsar yam*]" for thought, a limiting channel for the flow of one's thoughts. Jacob considered all the fragments of pleasure, hinted at in the word *shever*, also meaning "breakage" or "fragment," a breaking up of the wholeness of thought into divisions that fit the five types of sound [lit. "the five openings"] made by the mouth. Each of these has its own delight, and it is this factor that causes thought to proceed into speech.

This is also hinted at here. **Jacob left Beersheba**, the place of his mind and understanding, as in "Moses was willing to explicate (*be'er*, also meaning "wellspring") this entire Torah" (Deut. 1:5) as explained by the *Zohar* (1:147b): he went from thought to speech. This is contained in **and set out for Haran**, since Haran is numerically equal to *garon*, or "throat," the source of speech in Torah or prayer. Then **he came upon**, interpreted to mean "he prayed," **a certain place** [*makom*], which is also a name of God, who is called "Place of the World ..." (*Bereshit Rabbah* 68:9).

❦

Mystics often tend toward the contemplative life; their highest pleasure lies in dwelling within that which they see with their mind's eye. But in Jewish tradition they are forcibly pulled from contemplation into speech, pressing their endlessly expansive thoughts into channels narrow and specific enough for communication. Interestingly, this need is justified here by reference to the divine name. The fact is, however, that this is precisely the word we do not pronounce! It stands nevertheless as the primal font of all language, and all speech proceeds from combinations of its letters. That fact allows human words to become holy and to have transformative power. We cannot do our work of uplifting the broken (*shever*) from "Egypt" until we begin to speak.

KEDUSHAT LEVI

> He saw a well in the field. Three flocks of sheep were resting at it ... there was a large stone at the mouth of the well. When all the flocks were gathered there, they rolled the stone off the mouth of the well.... When Jacob saw Rachel ... he approached and rolled the stone off the mouth of the well....
> (GEN. 29:2–3, 10)

The verses can be interpreted in this way. We know that the Holy One ever longs to have goodness flow upon God's people Israel. It is the evil urge that prevents this flow. But when Israel are aroused in joy, their happiness defeats those "outside" forces, and God's grace and compassion bring forth blessing.

This is **He saw a well**; that is the flow of God's blessing. **In the field** refers to the "holy field of apple trees [*shekhinah*]"; this indicates God's own great joy in giving. **Three flocks of sheep** refers to the three festivals of pilgrimage in the year. The **large stone** is the evil urge, which is called a "stone," as in "if it is a stone, let it crumble" (b. Kiddushin 30b). **At the mouth of the well**, preventing the flow of God's blessing. **All the flocks were gathered there** refers to Israel, assembled together to celebrate the pilgrimage, amid great joy. **They rolled the stone off the mouth of the well**, pushing aside the evil one and all his host, stopping them from holding back the flow. Then blessing and goodness can pour forth upon Israel....

When Jacob saw Rachel refers to the joy of bridegroom and bride, parallel to that of the festival. Scripture says, "I will remove the heart of stone ..." (Ezek. 11:19), referring to the evil urge that dwells in Israel's heart, preventing prophecy from appearing in that heart. Another verse refers to "the prophetic heart of wisdom" (Ps. 90:12), meaning that the heart flows with wise prophecy. **He rolled the stone off the mouth of the well** means that he removed the stumbling-block from the heart that flows (*nove'a*) with prophecy (*nevu'ah*).

⟰⟱⟰

The life that God intended for us is one of constant blessing, a heart ever aware of the divine bounty amid which we live. But our evil urge, that which causes the human ego to assert its own will, blocks us from that vision. Our strongest force in defeating it is that of joy. When we open our hearts and rejoice, especially in the midst of a joyous community, we overcome that need for self-assertion. Then divine blessing can flow upon us, even opening our own hearts to the prophetic witness that is our true natural state of being.

OR HA-ME'IR II

> ... the feeble sheep belonged to Laban, but the robust ones were Jacob's.
> (GEN. 30:42)

There are some people who, even in the course of walking the royal path and doing God's commandments, including study of Torah and prayer, are really doing so for purposes of their own self-glorification and pleasure. They think, "How nicely I speak! How nicely I act!"

Our eyes see this in our own generation, when so many burst forth to wrap themselves up in a *tallit* that is not really theirs. As soon as they see a *tsaddik* or an enlightened person act in a certain way, they try to clothe themselves in the very same actions. Those fools do not understand that even if they lived a thousand years they would not attain such a rung! "How can the fool have the price in his hand [to attain wisdom], when he has no heart" (Prov. 17:16)? He can't even see to his own task of setting right his seven personal qualities, keeping away from their negative sides, but he peers into the actions of others, the pure and enlightened, without any understanding of their secret meaning as a way to pursue the path of truth.

The Torah hints at this by saying that **the feeble sheep** [*ha-'atufim*, also meaning "wrapped up"] **belonged to Laban, but the robust ones** [*ha-keshurim*] **were Jacob's.**

This verse provides a sign. Those who wrap themselves up in a *tallit* not their own, looking to what others do when they don't yet properly see themselves, still belong to Laban. They have false weights in their hands, and do everything by cheating. These are the qualities of Laban the cheat. But the *keshurim* (also "attached"), those who do all their deeds in a bound up or attached way, belong to Jacob. They have conceived how exalted God is, and they take no part of practices that belong to others ... their spirit keeps faith with God; they belong to Jacob our Father, whose quality is truth.

♁

In many ways a conservative within the Maggid's circle, the *Or ha-Me'ir* stands as a warning voice, as Hasidism spreads as a popular movement, against external or imitative acts of piety. His words are appropriate today as well! Immature and imitative piety exists everywhere, not only within the traditional community.

Va-Yetse
Round Two

AG: The world is filled with hidden Torah. The idea that the world was created through Torah means that there is Torah everywhere. All these chapters about life before Sinai are opportunities to deliver that message over and over again.

OR: It's a vision of life that's filled to the brim, both with Torah and blessing, *shefa'*, the bounty that God wants to give us. The question is always how to tap into that blessing. How do we get ourselves enough out of the way so that the channels are clear for that blessing to flow?

EL: It seems that there are both "Sabbath" and "weekday" answers to that question. There is a Shabbat mode, where you just awaken to the reality, then stand aside and let it happen. Levi Yitshak seems especially good at that one. But there is also a weekday model, where you have to struggle and work at it, fighting off the evil urge and the many obstacles it puts in your path. That's more the way of R. Elimelekh.

OR: Why do you think we still find this message so exciting? We live in such different times and have such different concepts, but these teachings still seem to draw us.

EL: It's partly because there's a vision here in which religion is not out to conquer the world, but to find Torah within it. We've had too much of trying to subdue the self, the body, and the natural realm. The battle of spirit against matter is both wearying and ultimately unwinnable. Here we are being told instead to embrace the natural world, finding divinity within it.

OR: This is the adventure. It is a romantic quest for ultimate truth, but one you engage in by going through and into the world, not by evading it.

AG: But then what about the weekday mode? Isn't the struggle against the "evil urge" a battle to conquer nature after all?

AM: Not quite. You aren't supposed to fear the natural, because you know that it too comes from God. Therefore, it can always be transformed and uplifted; it's not your enemy. What you do have to fear is self-deception. Overcome *that* enemy, and you're on your way, in a journey that leads back to your truest self.

EL: Yes, the *Or ha-Me'ir* is especially good at that. In the middle of all this enthusiasm, his self-critical voice provides some healthy leaven. It's good to know that there was room for this in Hasidism, even from its beginning.

Va-Yishlah

NO'AM ELIMELEKH

Jacob sent messengers before him to his brother Esau....
(GEN. 32:4)

We read this with the verse "A person wrestled with him" (Gen. 32:25) and with RaSHI's explanation that the word *va-ye'avek* ("wrestled") is related to raising dust (*avak*).

There is a debate regarding this verse in the Talmud (b. Hullin 91a). One opinion is that Jacob thought the person he wrestled with was a non-Jew, and another opinion is that he thought the person was a rabbinic scholar. This seems like a very strange argument....

To understand this we need to explain the verse "Your word is well refined, and your servant loves it" (Ps. 119:140). It is known that a *tsaddik*'s prayer is answered when praying for a sick person or for others in need. This seems as if the blessed Holy One is subject to change [of will], heaven forbid. But the root of the matter is as follows. The blessed One created letters, which in their original state are pure potential. A *tsaddik* can reconfigure the letters so that they form whatever words are desired. These configurations are what a *tsaddik* does in prayer—making new combinations. The *tsaddik*'s prayer does not cause change in the Creator, as the letters were always there. All the *tsaddik* is doing is creating combinations.

You could still ask: Why is a *tsaddik*'s prayer more effective than the prayer of any other person? Indeed the sages wrote: "If there is a sick person in your home, you should approach a sage to pray" (b. Bava Batra 116a). Why couldn't any person pray and reconfigure the letters? This is because the Torah was created with love, as we say, "the One who chooses the people Israel with love." A *tsaddik* also loves both God and every person in the world. For example, Rabbi Yohanan said: I greet every person in the marketplace, including gentiles, before they have a chance to greet me (b. Berakhot 17a). Most people are not like this, and therefore they do not have the power to reconfigure the letters. Only a *tsaddik* who loves everyone has that power.

This is the meaning of the verse "Your word is well refined [*tserufah*]"; it refers to the supernal letters that have one configuration in potential and are reconfigured (*metsurafim*) into actuality by the all-loving *tsaddik* through the "service of love" (read as *'avadekha ahavah*). That is the meaning of the verse **Jacob sent messengers**. This refers to letters and words, which are called "messengers." **Before him** means that the letters were already there, the potential was there before him. Jacob then made combinations of the letters through the power of his love for all.

This is contained in the words **to his brother Esau** implying that he totally accepted even Esau as a brother, like Rabbi Yohanan, whose love included even non-Jews in the marketplace.

So also we understand the verse "a person wrestled with him." The word *va-ye'avek* refers to traces of something, like in the expression "traces of usury [*avak ribit*]." In reality a person may not love all equally—Jews and gentiles. One's love for a Jew could be complete, while the love for a non-Jew might still be lacking, still retaining the traces of foreignness. This is the Talmudic opinion that Jacob thought the person was not Jewish. That was the struggle—[to rid himself of] the traces [of foreignness] still there.

Similarly, the Talmudic opinion that Jacob thought the person was a scholar implies that Jacob's love for this person was not complete. This was because Jacob realized that this scholar had not yet perfected his personality traits. Jacob did love him, but this love was still incomplete because of these deficiencies. This is the meaning of the verse "A man wrestled with him till the rising dawn [*'alot ha-shahar*]." He struggled to remove the darkness (*shehorut*) within that person, so that he could love him perfectly.

So the Talmudic debate is not so strange after all. Each position highlights a different aspect of Jacob's ability to achieve perfect love for every person.

❧

This is a striking teaching, not only in its description of the power of the *tsaddik*, but also in the limitations it sets to that power. The *tsaddik* cannot create anything new and cannot simply change reality. What he/she can do is to reframe the elements of reality so they are now perceived differently, and thus create a new reality.

It is the *tsaddik*'s capacity for love that enables such miracles. This teaching also stands out in identifying its goal as totally inclusive love and in its recognition of the struggle involved in achieving this goal. Jacob's struggle as depicted here might well be the struggles of the *No'am Elimelekh* himself. It is easy to imagine that the people he would find the most difficult to love would be the local non-Jewish population and the rabbinic scholars among the *mitnaggedim*. And yet he continues to struggle....

KEDUSHAT LEVI I

> Save me from the hand of my brother Esau.
> (GEN. 32:12)

Esau is the [demonic] "Other Side," the angel of death, the evil urge. Jacob's plea is that this Esau not be his brother. **From the hand of my brother Esau** means that it sometimes happens that the evil urge appears like a brother, pushing one to do evil while disguising it as good. In this way a person can be led quickly into evil's trap.

⚬⚬⚬

But what is our "evil urge" if not a shadow-side of our own selves? That seems to be the unspoken meaning of Jacob and Esau as twins. They fight one another, confronting one another in this mysterious struggle by night, and yet we are not sure they are entirely separate from one another. Jacob will become "Israel" in the wrestling match of this portion. Perhaps that means only that he is forever aware of the need to keep wrestling with this "brother" he can never quite fully leave behind.

KEDUSHAT LEVI II

> And when my brother Esau meets you and asks, "Whose are you, and where are you going ...?" and you shall answer, "Your servant Jacob's; they are an offering sent to my lord Esau...."
> (GEN. 32:18–19)

... When you begin to approach God and the evil urge rises against you, think that through your service of God you will also receive the rewards of this world. If you do so, the evil urge will be unable to challenge you about your efforts to cleave to God. Afterwards, once you are already attached to God, your service should be focused exclusively on bringing joy to the Creator and not on the worldly reward.

This is the meaning of the verse **And when my brother Esau meets you and asks, "Whose are you?"**: when the evil inclination, which is called "Esau," meets Jacob's angels—which are your holy thoughts—and Esau challenges these thoughts, saying, **"Where are you going?" you shall answer, "Your servant Jacob's"**—"we are Jacob's messengers; we were created by means of good deeds." Do not challenge Jacob about his good deeds because **they are an offering sent to my lord Esau**—the good [done by Jacob] will also reach you. For by means of Jacob's good deeds the rewards of this world come to him, an offering to the evil urge.

〰〰〰

In this creative rereading of a key exchange between Jacob and his messengers, the Berdichever offers us a strategy for engaging realistically and meaningfully in prayer. While we ultimately seek to transcend our worldly needs and cleave to God, we must also acknowledge and honor our earthly desires. Do not try to avoid "Esau"—the voice of doubt and condemnation—instead, face him, give him his due, and continue the journey.

OR HA-ME'IR

> Jacob named the place Peniel, "for I have seen God face to face, yet my life has been spared."
> (GEN. 32:31)

This seems to accord with the *Zohar*'s teaching (*Tikkuney Zohar* t. 13, 29a) on the verse "Jacob arrived safe" (Gen. 33:18), which it reads to mean "Jacob arrived complete," bearing his entire name, beginning with the *yod*. If you drop the *yod* from Ya'akov, there remains *'ekev*, "heel" [referring to the lowest rung of being]. A wise person is one who knows how to join wisdom, symbolized by the *yod*, to the "heel," those lowly rungs.

Whatever you see or hear, even ordinary conversations between people, as well as whatever happens to you in the course of time, becomes a place where you can find the shining presence, the face of God (*Peney El*). This face of the most supreme God, as it is cloaked in that particular place, reveals itself to the *tsaddik* so that he can raise up from there *shekhinah*'s limbs, which are called *nefesh* or "life."

This is the meaning of our verse. Jacob, the person who is whole or perfect, links the upper wisdom to the lower. Such a person's awareness becomes so clear that any particular place or event only reflects a face of God in one specific configuration or another. This is "I have seen God face to face"—I have come to understand that God is cloaked in multiple faces, throughout the lower rungs. All this is conceived in accord with each *tsaddik*'s own "face" and the strength of his awareness. This is **my life has been spared**, as *shekhinah* is raised up to Her exalted place.

⸙

Hasidism sees Torah as a means toward cultivating awareness. Ultimately that awareness embraces all of life; everything becomes a setting in which to discover another as yet unrevealed face of God. Jacob is a prototype of the seeker, the one who can attach the lowly and ordinary to the highest point of wisdom. He can do this only if he is *shalem*, or whole.

Va-Yishlah
Round Two

EL: The texts are all based on an internalization of the biblical tale. All the characters—Jacob, Esau, Laban—are aspects of the inner self. But at least for the *No'am Elimelekh*, that inner struggle has to lead you to act differently toward the real human beings with whom you share the world.

OR: My question is how well we get to know our own inner Esau. What is our strategy for dealing with "him"? Can we always seek to uplift and transform the Esau impulse within us? Or is there a point at which we just need to say "No" to ourselves, to close the door on a particular form of behavior?

AM: The real struggle is to recognize just what is the "evil urge" in your life. It comes so well disguised as virtue that it's sometimes hard to unmask it.

EL: Sometimes you need to just knock one out, to say: "I'm not going to put the effort into transforming that one. I'm just going to say 'No.'"

AG: I find myself resisting that, still not wanting to insist on closing doors. Wholeness to me means radical self-acceptance. That's a key message that I learn from the Ba'al Shem Tov, and I don't want to compromise it.

OR: But there is a time when you say, "I'm not going to become a new person; I will never be completely victorious in my particular struggles." Sometimes we need to step back a bit and ask, "How will I at least ensure that I do more good than bad in my life?"

AM: We live in a liminal world between the tension of self-transforming aspirations and the need for self-acceptance. The pious denial of both self and surrender to our impulses can lead us into dangerous, even obsessive, places.

OR: Each bears within it its own form of narcissism.

AG: We are saved from this by the Hasidic insistence that we turn outward, away from the self, both toward *shekhinah* and toward others. That's where the true test always lies.

EL: But here the difference between their world and ours really looms large. We are so saturated with stimulation! Temptation comes at us from every side, to a degree that prior generations could hardly have imagined. Could we even begin to keep pace with all the uplifting and transformation that such an environment demands? Or are we kidding ourselves to even try?

AG: A dimension that needs to be considered here is that of varying life stages. To be young and energetic in your spiritual quest is to envision great transformations, moments of rebirth and renewal. Aging makes us more forgiving of ourselves, feeling that we have earned the right to be treated more gently, even by our own self-critical eye. Maybe the time does come to embrace our Esau, to accept our "wicked twin" as none other than our own self.

ᏬᎯᎣ

ויש ב

Va-Yeshev

Maggid Devarav le-Ya'akov (#1)

Jacob settled in the land where his father had dwelt
[*megurey aviv*], the Land of Canaan.
(Gen. 37:1)

The word *megurey* can also be derived from the root of *oger*, "to gather."
Even though Jacob was settled in "land" or earthly existence, he was still
megurey aviv, gathering up his Father. He was gathering the blessed Holy
One into that physical realm.

But there is another way to read this phrase. Every thought is a complete
world, composed of holy sparks. You gather them into their Source. This is
megurey aviv, "gathering his Father," as it were.

This is the meaning of "The eyes of Y-H-W-H are toward the righteous"
(Ps. 34:16). When a child does some childish act, he brings the attention of
his father into those [seemingly trivial] deeds. The righteous are able to do
the same, as it were, bringing the mind of God to rest in the place where
they are thinking. If they think of love, they bring the blessed Holy One
into the world of love. This is the meaning of the *Zohar's* comment on "A
King bound up in tresses" (Song 7:6)—the tresses of the mind (*Tikkuney
Zohar* t. 6, 21a).

This is the meaning of "God concentrated His *shekhinah* to rest between
the two staves of the ark" (*Tanhuma Va-Yakhel* 7). These are the two lungs
of *shekhinah*. God dwells wherever [the righteous one] is thinking. "Eyes"
refers to the mind; the mind [of God] is in the hands of the righteous.

But how do they attain this rung? Only by thinking that they are mere dust, that they can do nothing without the power of God. Whatever they do, it is really being done by God. Without the blessed Holy One, they could accomplish nothing....

🙞🙜

This is a fragment of the long teaching that opens the Maggid's first book, *Maggid Devarav le-Ya'akov*. While somewhat obscure, its strong mystical claim is very clear. The *tsaddik*, in the course of self-negation, directs the eyes or mind of God, bringing into divine focus that quality he wishes to see drawn forth. God is bound up, almost involuntarily, so it seems, with the mind of the righteous one. The *tsaddik* can do this, however, only if he is fully humbled. The original oral sermon surely read *erets kena'an* ("the Land of Canaan") as "humbled down to the earth."

The two readings of "gather" represent in capsule form the twin impulses of Hasidism with regard to the material world. One has the *tsaddik* gathering divinity into the earthly; the other gathers the divine sparks from the physical world to return them to their source. Early Hasidic teaching, even the Maggid himself, taught both of these truths at once.

MEVASSER TSEDEK

> Jacob settled in the land where his father had dwelt,
> the Land of Canaan.
> (GEN. 37:1)

I begin by citing the Mishnah that says: "Pray for the welfare of government [*malkhut*], for without fear of it, people would swallow one another alive" (Avot 3:2).

A person has to serve our blessed Creator in both love and fear. It might seem to people that to serve out of love and fiery devotion is better than service from fear. But if you serve by love alone, you could come to be obliterated, cleaving to God so wholly that you are "swallowed alive" in your Source! That is why you need both of these rungs, love and fear. In that way love will not bring you to self-obliteration; the fear will tamp down the flame of love.

This is the meaning of "the living beings [or 'the life-force'] flow back and forth" (Ezek. 1:14): the fact that a person can go on living in this world, not being wiped out by being joined to God, is because of the "back and forth," the love that takes you forward and the fear that holds you back. That is how life can exist within this world.

This is the meaning of "Pray for the welfare of *malkhut*": pray that the aspect of *malkhut* that includes both love and fear be kept whole. For "without fear of it," if you prayed only with love and not fear, the person would be swallowed alive out of attachment to God. The person's life-force would be reabsorbed in its Source. But this can happen out of fear as well. That's why you need both of these, joined together in prayer.

This is the meaning of **Jacob settled in the land where his father had dwelt**. *Va-yeshev*, the *tsaddik*'s ability to tarry *ba-arets*, in this material world, and not be swallowed back into his Root by his own great love, is *megurey*, which can be rendered both as "dwelling" and as "fear," as in "for I feared" (*yagorti*, Deut. 9:19).... When you serve with both love and fear, you dwell in **the Land of Canaan**. The word "Canaan" can be read as deriving from *hakhna'ah* ("submission"), meaning that you are able, even when in "the land," or worldly things, including eating, drinking, and all the rest, to be humbly serving our exalted Creator, blessed for ever and ever.

⟨⟩∞∞⟨⟩

What a radical rereading of the Mishnah's most this-worldly admonition! It is not earthly government (*malkhut*) you need to pray for, lest we humans consume each other, but rather God's *malkhut*, here meaning the proper balance of sacred forces, lest you be eaten alive in the course of intense prayer!

NO'AM ELIMELEKH

> Jacob settled in the land where his father had dwelt, the Land of Canaan.
> (GEN. 37:1)

... The core of our spiritual work is contemplating the exalted greatness of God. God's name is unified through this and through the fear and awe that result when you contemplate God's wonders and awe-inspiring deeds.

You might ask: if this contemplation is the essence of our spiritual work, why did God give us 613 *mitsvot*? Could we not serve God just through fear and awe, by meditating on God's greatness?

No one could survive the fear and trembling that would result from constant meditation on God's greatness; one's very existence would be negated. God gave us 613 *mitsvot* as an act of divine compassion that enables us to serve God with our bodies. There is tremendous benefit in this [connection of the spiritual experience to the material world], as this makes it possible to cleave to God and continue living.

Thus we explain the verse **Jacob settled in the land where his father had dwelt**. The word used for **had dwelt** (*megurey*) [also means fear] as in "Mo'ab feared (*va-yagor*) [the Israelites]" (Num. 22:3). The sentence implies that he [Jacob] had settled and spent time in this spiritual rung. He was constantly in awe and fear of his Heavenly Father.

Jacob achieved this by serving with his body, by constantly engaging with God's Torah and *mitsvot*. **The Land of Canaan** alludes to the body, which made it possible for him to sustain his mental practice of cleaving to God and meditating on God's greatness....

⟨≈⟩

This teaching presents fear as the main religious experience, rather than love or joy, which we often see emphasized in other Hasidic teachings. It also offers an uncommon explanation for the classic Hasidic teaching on the importance of *'avodah be-gashmiyyut*—serving God through the corporeal world. In this teaching, service through the practicalities of Torah and *mitsvot* is less intense than some meditative experiences, but precisely because of this it is more sustainable. A counterbalance for a group focused on intense spiritual experiences?

KEDUSHAT LEVI

> Jacob settled in the land where his father had dwelt, the Land of Canaan.
>> (GEN. 37:1)

... You must calmly and joyfully accept all that God metes out to you. As our Rabbis taught, loving God "with all your might" (*me'odekha*, Deut. 6:5) means that whatever measure (*middah*) He metes out (*moded*) to you, thank Him (*modeh*) greatly (*me'od*) and say that "all that the Merciful One does is for the good" (b. Berakhot 54a and 60b). You should firmly believe that there is great good even in something that seems to be evil, for evil cannot originate from the Divine. This was the manner of Nahum Ish Gamzu, who, because of his great faith in God, accepted everything that happened as a manifestation of the goodness of the divine will (*gam-zu*, "this too" is for the good; b. Ta'anit 21a). In this way he sweetened the judgments (i.e., transformed the harsh decree into mercy) and changed the evil into the good.

This attitude is reflected in the verse "who brought you water out of flint rock" (Deut. 8:15), which embodies the mystery of raising holy sparks to their divine source. Water symbolizes God's goodness and mercy, while the rock symbolizes His power and might, and hence, judgment. Your pure, firm thoughts can change God's attribute of judgment into the attribute of mercy, when you believe that all God does is for the good, and thus express your great and mighty love for God.

This was the type of faith and trust that characterized Jacob. On the verse **Jacob settled in the land where his father had dwelt**, Rashi explains that Jacob wished to dwell in peace. Jacob always sought to accept, calmly and with equanimity, that all was for the good, even **in the land where his father had dwelt** [*megurey*], even when surrounded by fear (*magor*) and trepidation, the characteristic attribute of his father Isaac. Jacob's righteousness and faith in God provided him with a sense of calm and equanimity, accepting all that befell him.

⟨⟨⟨≈⟩⟩⟩

This text is an interesting contrast to the many legends about Levi Yitshak in which he argues with God on behalf of his community. Here, the Berdichever suggests a different course of action. Rather than confront the Almighty and demand change, understand that our suffering contains goodness within it—like a spark covered over by a dark husk or shell. Once we make this shift in consciousness, says the Rebbe, God's judgment can turn into mercy. But how does this process work? What is the relationship between one's inner state of being and God's actions? Can our faith actually cause God to act toward us with greater kindness? Can we (or the *tsaddik*) negate divine decrees, as the Berdichever claims elsewhere? Or does one achieve a different form of relief simply by shifting consciousness even if the outer reality does not change? How might this teaching relate to contemporary discussions of theology, psychology, and mind-body issues?

GINZEY YOSEF

> They saw him far off and before he drew near to
> them they plotted to kill him.
> (GEN. 37:18)

RaSHI notes that the word *oto* ("him") is in this case unnecessary and is also written as though it might mean "they plotted *with* him." This reading has already been protested by earlier commentators.

The ancients have taught us that if you arouse love in your heart and send forth arrows of love to your fellow person, that one will come to feel love for you as well. This is because of the essential oneness of Israel. Such a sending forth of love can nullify any hatred that person might have felt toward you. Hence "Love your neighbor as yourself" (Lev. 19:18)—as you awaken love, your neighbor will do as you do....

The tribes were jealous of Joseph. Had he made the effort to arouse love in their hearts, that jealousy would have remained, but devoid of hatred. He thus would have been in no danger. But the righteous Joseph could not imagine in advance that they hated him, and thus he did nothing to counter their hatred. Only after the angel told him, "They have journeyed on from here" (Gen. 37:17), to which RaSHI comments "from [your shared] brotherhood," did he begin to consider that they might hate him, and why. While he was contemplating this, **they saw him far off and before he drew near to them**, that is before he became close enough to arouse their love, **they plotted to kill him.**

Had Joseph awakened love as soon as they saw him, their hatred would not have sufficed to kill him. But he was busy absorbing this new idea of their hatred, hinted at by the angel.... This is why the text seems to say that they conspired "*with* him." They and he both caused them to conspire, to bear that great hatred. It was as though he was "with them...."

〇〇〇

What a beautifully insightful and yet sad passage. Joseph somehow shares in the responsibility for his own fate because he could not see the possibility that he had aroused their hatred. Because of that, he did not send forth his love to them soon enough! The limiting phrase "because of the essential oneness of Israel" makes this possibility apply only to relations among Jews. But imagine if the Jewish people could have historically applied this same lesson in our relationships with non-Jews, "because of the essential oneness" of humanity. Might it have made a difference? Might we have "drawn near to them" before "they plotted to kill us"?

MAGGID DEVARAV LE-YA'AKOV (#183)

She grabbed him by his garment, saying: "Lie down with me!" He left his garment in her hand and fled outside.
(GEN. 39:12)

[The Psalmist says:] "He divided the Reed Sea into strips" (Ps. 136:13). The Midrash (*Yalkut Be-Shalah* 241) reads this as "He divided the Sea for the circumcised [*gezarim/gezurin*]...." This is based on the reading of another Psalm verse, "The Sea saw and fled" (114:3). What did it see? It saw the sarcophagus of Joseph [that the Israelites had carried out of Egypt] (*Tanhuma Naso* 30).

The *tsaddik* selects the good out from amid the evil. When coming upon something bad, the *tsaddik* is able to pick out that which is good and use it as a way to unite with God....

This was the situation of Joseph the *tsaddik*. Potiphar's wife tried to persuade him with words and with ever-changed attractive garments (b. Yoma 35b). She was beautiful and showed off her beauty to him. When he looked at her, he selected out the good from her and through it attached himself mentally to *tif'eret* ["Beauty"] above. This is what the sages (b. Sotah 36b) meant when they said that "the image of his father Jacob appeared to him, [because Jacob represents *tif'eret*]." He **fled outside**: the form *ha-hutsah* ("outside") indicates that he fled outside this physical world and attached himself to the world above.

His merit was so great that when the Sea saw his sarcophagus coming, it did the same, leaving this world behind and going to the upper world. But in that place there is no water, as Rabbi Akiva (b. Hagigah 14b) said to his fellow voyagers: "When you reach the place of the pure marble pillars, do not say, 'Water, water!'" So the sea of course had to run dry, all by the merit of that *tsaddik*, guardian of the covenant....

❦

This text is based on an old Midrashic tradition that read "the sea saw and fled" as "the sea saw the 'he fled' of Joseph and split because of his merit." It is not that the *tsaddik* has magical powers; it is rather that his righteousness is so impressive, even to the forces of nature, that they step aside and submit to his will. This subtle distinction was lost in much of popular Hasidism.

The reinterpretation of the rabbis' claim that seeing his father's image kept Joseph from sin is also quite striking. Rather than a classically Freudian father-as-superego reading, we now see Jacob drawn by the woman's beauty to attach himself to the higher beauty of divine *tif'eret*, the source of all beauty in the world.

Va-Yeshev
Round Two

AG: How interesting that here we have four preachers, the Maggid and three disciples, all commenting on the same verse. We should be able to learn something from this.

EL: The *Mevasser Tsedek* and the *No'am Elimelekh* may have heard the same sermon. Both of them are dealing with the question of how to have passionate devotion to God and yet go on living in the world. One sees fear as holding us back from too much love; the other sees the commandments as grounding us in reality so that we cannot fly too high.

AM: They are all talking about "dwelling in the *land*," the physical realm. But is this connection to "land" a positive value or just a protective shield against too much passion?

AG Three of these four texts are about maintaining a sense of balance.

AM: The Maggid himself doesn't seem to care about balance here. He'd just as soon indeed be wholly absorbed in God.

OR: What is R. Levi Yitshak saying about the human mind and the mind of God? Is he making an ontological claim here, or just a psychological statement?

EL: The Maggid is definitely in the realm of ontology here.

OR: I am drawn to this *Kedushat Levi* passage precisely because it is about accepting and living gratefully with the hand God deals you, rather than the audacious claim that we can influence God to change it.

AG: Yes, but remember that we also love Levi Yitshak for that very audacity, which allows him to stand up to God for the sake of Israel! How can those two very different religious emotions live within the same person? Strength is one of the great qualities of the *tsaddik*, but that strength—however paradoxically—derives from the ability to submit.

EL: The Maggid is not interested in bringing material blessing to people, but only in bringing God into the world of love. But both God and the *tsaddik* are transformed by this encounter.

מקץ

Mi-Kets

OR HA-ME'IR (FROM PURIM)

> From the Nile there rose up seven fat and good-looking cows, and they fed in the pasture. But behind them there rose up seven other cows, skinny and bad-looking, thin of flesh.... Seven sheaves ... Joseph said to Pharaoh: "Pharaoh's dream is one; God has declared to Pharaoh what He is doing."
> (GEN. 41:18–25)

We Children of Israel are here to serve in this world, essentially to restore the seven cosmic "days" [the seven *sefirot* from *hesed* to *malkhut*, or the seven personal qualities that embody them]. We are destined to do this day and night, for everything depends on the awakening from below. When we keep our path straight, devoting both study and deeds to serving our Creator, we bring fulfillment and light into these seven "days." But if we do evil, God forbid, we shine light upon their opposite, the seven days of defilement.

Thus the *Zohar* (1:194a) interprets Pharaoh's dreams ... both that of the cows and that of the sheaves. Look there and you will see wonders. **Pharaoh's dream is one**, telling us of the seven "days" and their opposite. "God has fashioned this parallel to that" (Eccles. 7:14). Everything depends on the proper conduct of Israel....

This is the meaning of Pharaoh's dream. **God has declared ... what He is doing**. [In the present tense], from the beginning of Creation until our messiah arrives, speedily and in our day....

This is a person's service, all the hard-working days of our lifetime. That generally lasts about seventy years, through all of which we are to devote heart, soul, and spirit to restoring those seven "days." Of this Scripture says: "The days of our years have seventy within them" (Ps. 90:10). Why did it have to say "within them"? This was to show us that our seventy years are all drawn forth from the seven primal cosmic days. The difference is one of both length and quality; those primal days are great by both measures. Within them are hidden the particulars of each individual soul's seventy years. Our earthly days are low in quality and of short duration. That is what the verse refers to in saying "the days of our years": referring back to those primal days, the seven days of Creation ... those days from which our years are drawn.

⚙︎

Here the sevens of Pharaoh's dream are drawn, almost inevitably, into the sacred structure of sevens around which so much of the Jewish imagination is formed. In this way the dream is one that lays out the cosmic order, both of the universe and of each person's individual life.

ORAH LE-HAYYIM

> Joseph gathered grain, as much as the sand of the sea, so much that they stopped counting, for it was beyond count.
> (GEN. 41:49)

Why does Scripture say **as much as the sand of the sea**? Surely that is an exaggeration! If all of Egypt were to fill up with grain, it would not equal the sand at the sea! Why should the verse exaggerate so?...

The *tsaddik* [and Joseph is his archetype] serves God always, through action, word, and thought. The *tsaddik* is forever linking thoughts to God. But the first thing you have to do in that process is to check against impure motives or extraneous thoughts, being sure that you act for God alone. Only then should you perform the *mitsvot*, and in great awe.

You cannot receive the bounty from above unless you first limit yourself in this way. This was taught by our master Dov Baer around the verse "'Will you not fear Me?' says Y-H-W-H ... 'I who placed sand as the boundary of the sea?'" (Jer. 5:22). What value lies in mentioning this fact? Didn't God create all the worlds? Aren't all of them naught before God? But this verse teaches that we cannot receive God's blessing unless we first limit ourselves. First comes the sand about the sea, setting the limits; only then does the water flow forth into it. When we want to receive God's bounty, we first need to take upon ourselves that sense of complete awe that means self-limitation. Only then can we receive the outpouring of divine love. "Will you not fear Me ..., I who placed the sand as boundary to the sea?" This is the only way to be a receiver....

The one who then serves God by every deed, word, and thought, through all physical things, even within the realm of the permitted, constantly draws forth great blessing and clarity from the world of joy. This is **Joseph gathered,** for he is the *tsaddik*....

So much that they stopped counting. Sometimes you can do so many *mitsvot* and receive such gifts of clarity and joy that you enter a realm of constant joy. But constant joy is no joy at all. I believe that I also heard in the name of our teacher Dov Baer on the verse "His understanding is beyond account" (Ps. 147:5) that *mispar* ("account, counting") can be derived from "sapphire," or shining. This "understanding" is the realm of joy, which cannot shine forth constantly. Then our **so much that they stopped counting** would mean that the *tsaddik* can do so many *mitsvot* that they cease shining or giving off light....

⟨⟩

There seems to be a subtle warning here about certain psychological complexities of the religious life. Humility and awe are its starting points; an act of *tsimtsum*, or self-reduction, is needed to allow divine light into your life. Once you make that space, however, the gifts you receive are beyond limit, overflowing your well-bordered inner "sea." Then you need to take care that you not become an automaton at doing, speaking, and thinking the good, for this too can darken the great gifts that you have to offer. The light needs a background against which to shine.

KEDUSHAT LEVI

> Now Joseph's brothers came and bowed low to him, with their faces to the ground. When Joseph saw his brothers, he recognized them, and he acted like a stranger toward them.
> (GEN. 42:6–7)

What does the Torah wish to teach us when it says, **he acted like a stranger toward them?** This teaches us about Joseph's righteousness. Joseph dreamed that his brothers would bow low to him, as it says, "We were binding sheaves etc.," and "the sun etc." (Gen. 37:7, 9) but his brothers did not accept the notion that Joseph would rule over them.

It is only natural that when a person triumphs over his fellow, and the latter realizes that the other has beaten him, he feels great sadness and pain. But when one triumphs, and the other does not know by whom he has been beaten, the loss is not as painful.

... Now this was Joseph's righteousness: in the moment that his brothers bowed low to him and he actually triumphed over them ... he **acted like a stranger toward them** so that they would not be bitter and it would appear to them that they were bowing to someone else.... Indeed, Joseph [as their brother] was a king, but they were untroubled by this because they thought that they were bowing before another king. When the Torah says that "they bowed low to him ..." and "he recognized them" it means, he recognized that they would suffer if he disclosed his true identity, so "he acted like a stranger toward them," so they would not suffer on account of his victory over them.

MAGGID DEVARAV LE-YAʿAKOV (#68)

> ... and have commerce with the land.
> (GEN. 42:34)

There are two sorts of love. A father may love the actions of his wise child, glorifying in his offspring's clever deeds or the wise words the child speaks. The other sort of parental love is more essential; anything the child says finds favor with the parent, because of this love.

Now God loves us [with both sorts of loves]. The first occurs when the *tsaddik* performs good deeds in a very wise way, raising up the holy sparks that are found in every level of existence. God loves such deeds greatly. Such a person is binding the external worlds to God, since God is present in all the person's actions. This process will only be completed when messiah arrives (speedily, in our day!). Of that time Scripture says: "The whole earth will be filled with knowledge of Y-H-W-H" (Is. 11:9). Even cattle and wild beasts will know God, and then "they will cause no evil or destruction in all My holy mountain."

The second sort of love occurs when the *tsaddik*'s very essence is attached to God. God loves that *tsaddik* greatly, even without the clever deeds of the first one. This *tsaddik* goes about in perfect innocence, always joined to Y-H-W-H. It is this that arouses God's love. This is called raising up the inward worlds, since the *tsaddik* is the innermost part of the world.

That is why Joseph said *ve-et ha-arets* (**with the land**). The particle *et* consists of *aleph* and *tav*, thus including all the letters. Since everything was created through the letters, they are now bound up with the physical world. These letters constitute divine speech, holy sparks. *Tisharu* (**have commerce**) can also mean to surround them and make them "roll" upward.

The Maggid here seems to rejoice in both sorts of divine love. This explains why he could surround himself with activists like Levi Yitshak and Shne'ur Zalman alongside such types as R. Leib Sarah's or Zusya of Hanipoli, who realized the ideal of the *tsaddik* more in simple being than in clever doing.

BEIT AHARON

> Take double the amount of silver in your hands, and the silver that was returned in the mouth of your sacks return on your own.... And may almighty God grant you mercy.
> (GEN. 43:12–14)

Double ... silver (*kesef mishneh*) refers to Torah, to the desire for learning [*kesef*, "longing"; *mishneh*, from *mishnah*, "learning"]. It is called *mishneh* because the desire is doubled. Whenever we long for the Holy One's Torah and commandments and fulfill them, we are blessed twofold from heaven. This means that a person who longs for Torah just a bit is given a double measure of that desire from heaven.

The silver that was returned in the mouth of your sacks refers to this doubled light that was given to you from above. **Return** it above, uplifting everything toward the blessed Holy One. Then you will be doubly blessed again from heaven. This will keep going on, greater each time. This is the real meaning of *kesef mishneh*, an ever-recycling desire. Conduct yourself this way all the days of your life, for "the life-force goes back and forth" (Ezek. 1:14).

When you do this, **almighty God** will **grant you mercy**, giving you the compassion that allows for true prayer.

⟨∭⟩

The heavenly "reward" for devotion, as the true religious soul knows, is more devotion, the opening of the heart to prayer.

Mi-Kets
Round Two

EL: Wherever they turn, these texts seem to find lessons about leadership. "Have commerce with the land." Who would dream that this phrase is a leadership text!

AM: Yes, but does the second type really model leadership? Is there anything that can be imitated in a Zusya or a Leib? Or do they just radiate holiness to those around them?

EL: Yet I think they are models. Just having such persons walking through the world changes it. And that means it will change the behavior of those who are touched by them.

AM: The Maggid is giving us "two types" again here. Yet I feel that even within the first type there are vast differences. Look at Levi Yitshak and Shne'ur Zalman. One leads mostly by example, by loving and defending Jews, while the other creates a disciplined cadre of followers, even composing a text for them to study step-by-step!

EL: Yes, but both are reaching out. A Leib does none of that, but just stands there as the smiling figure at the center, letting others discover what they can of him.

AG: Interesting. Here we are in the Joseph story and they are talking about leadership! That should come as no surprise. The first text too is a modeling text about the leader. Look how Joseph acts to protect the feelings of those who have harmed him!

EL: These are all practices, personal inclinations that need to be nurtured and cultivated. That's how we learn from them.

AM: But are all the models capable of being copied? I'm not so sure. Zusya, in the famous statement, should not try to be Moses. But can we try to be Zusya? Or should we just let ourselves be warmed by the light of his presence?

AG: Here we have the two tendencies within Hasidism. Is the movement meant to cultivate *tsaddikim* or *hasidim*? Leaders or followers? The answer seems clear for the movement's later history. But if we go back to the beginning, trying to pick up the thread ...

Va-Yiggash

OR TORAH

And Judah approached him, saying: "Please, my lord,
let your servant speak a word to my lord; do not
become angry with your servant, for you are the
equal of Pharaoh."
(GEN. 44:18)

The sages taught that "approaching" always means prayer (*Tanhuma Va-Yera* 8).

It seems to me that our verse alludes to this. **And Judah approached
him** refers to any Jewish person, since we are called *yehudim* ["Jews" =
"Judahs"] after him. When you arise to pray before the blessed One, this is
how you should act: the entire intention of your prayer should be to bring
blessing to God's *shekhinah*.

This is the meaning of the sages' statement (b. Berakhot 30b): pray
only with a serious demeanor (*koved rosh*)—be mindful of the Beginning
of all beginnings [*keter*, called *reisha de-kol reishin*, lit. "head of all heads"].
Even though you are asking for something that you need, your intention
should be that whatever it is not be lacking above. Your soul is a part of
God, one of the limbs of the *shekhinah*. The goal of your prayer is that the
lack be fulfilled on high. This will certainly make your prayer acceptable,
and the adversary will be unable to find blame in you. Do not be like those
described in the *Zohar* who act only for themselves, barking out "give,
give" (*Tikkuney Zohar* t. 6, 22a)....

This is the explanation of **And Judah approached** in prayer. **Saying,** fulfill my request for Your sake, for I am a portion of God above. **Please, my lord** [can also mean "the Lord is within me"]. Now **do not become angry.** Do not let the adversaries harass me, since my sole intention is to bring blessing above to the aspect of the Creator inside me; this is **the Lord is within me. For you are the equal of Pharaoh**—Pharaoh's name also means "to reveal" (*para'*, cf. Num. 5:18). Your inner self is being revealed, for He lies within. The World of Speech [*shekhinah*] speaks through you. This is the meaning of **let your servant speak a word.** She is called [the divine] Word, referring to the World of Speech.

♾

Many, but not all, of those gathered around the Maggid's table struggled with the idea of petitionary prayer. If God is within all, and the essence of prayer means removing the ego and forgetting your own individual existence, how can we ask the One to fulfill our very worldly and often mundane needs?

Here the Maggid gives us an answer: *shekhinah* requires our voice. We give Her the words to pray for the world to be healed. Our own unfulfilled needs (both spiritual and physical!) are a part of the fracture. Through the act of prayer we open ourselves up and allow God to speak through us, and in this mystical moment our voice allows the divine element within us to call out to the infinite One above.

PERI HA-ARETS

And Judah approached him, saying: "Please, my lord"....
(GEN. 44:18)

The *Or ha-Hayyim* asks why the term **and Judah approached** is necessary here [since we know Judah was already standing close to Joseph], appropriately explaining that the drawing near to Joseph took place within Judah's heart, as in the verse "As face answers to face in water, so does one man's heart to another" (Prov. 27:19). With these words Judah sought to inspire Joseph's compassion, and therefore he approached him in his heart, drawing near to Joseph and truly loving him, in order to arouse Joseph's love and spark his compassion. The words of the *Or ha-Hayyim* are certainly wise and faithful.

Judah thought that Joseph was an Egyptian, about whom Israel was to be warned "Give them no grace" (Deut. 7:2), meaning that one must not find any beauty in them (b. 'Avodah Zarah 20a). Nevertheless, Judah did not refrain from bringing his heart closer and loving him, [raising up the fallen sparks] as we do through prayer, sacrifices, and eating....

Our Torah is true and trustworthy. It is therefore forbidden to test yourself, to enter into strange thoughts in order to uplift them, heaven forbid. Who knows if you will overcome them like a lion and rise [to the challenge], or descend lower and lower and be unable to withstand the test? But when a test happens that you had not planned, it has certainly come from God. Gird yourself with all your strength, even risking your life in the act of return to God; that is the raising up. Such was the error of King Solomon, who said: "I shall have many [wives] and will not turn aside" (b. Sanhedrin 21b). He set out to uplift the holy sparks, but he did not meet the challenge.

The Sages taught: "One says [the following] blessing upon encountering beautiful creatures, 'Blessed is the One with such in His world'" (b. Berakhot 58b)—even over an attractive gentile. This does not contradict the injunction of "give them no grace." What the verse prohibits is *seeking out* the sight of [the attractive gentile], over whom to say the blessing. This is not the case when the gentile has happened to come before you by chance. Then you must certainly recite the blessing, to uplift the pleasure of seeing. This is what happened with Rabbi Akiva and the Roman matron, when he saw her as he was coming around the corner (b. 'Avodah Zarah 20a/b). To initiate [the test] is certainly forbidden, but in a situation like this one should risk one's life, as in the practice of *nefilat apayim*.

The general rule of uplifting is that you must contemplate everything that happens to you. Discover something of yourself in it, whether for good or ill. Once "like has found like" and [attraction] has been aroused, take heed and immediately connect it with God according to the manner of the event. Realize that certainly this too is God and there is nothing else but Him, as it is said: "His sovereignty rules over all" (Ps. 103:19)....

This is the meaning of **Please, my lord** (*Bi, Adoni*; lit. "my Lord is in me"), since Judah represents the *malkhut* [sovereignty] of David, and "His sovereignty [*malkhuto*] rules over all" and all is included in Him. **And Judah approached him**, binding himself to God. Yet in fact he was Joseph, who is *yesod* and connected to *malkhut*. This is **Please, my lord—my Lord is in me** according to both the simple meaning and the esoteric.

The Vitebsker is urging us to remember that while we should not seek them out intentionally, every test we undergo in life is an opportunity to connect to God, and there are no experiences that we cannot follow back to a divine Source. According to the Kabbalistic tradition, bowing down one's head (*nef-ilat apayim*) during the personal supplications following *shemoneh 'esreh* is an act of descent in order to uplift the fallen sparks. Should we find ourselves in a difficult situation and be forced to go down from our spiritual rung, we must embrace the moment and know that it holds a hidden divine ember waiting to be kindled. This includes the encounter with an attractive gentile!

The Vitebsker's lesson extends to the interpersonal realm as well: each encounter with another human being is an opportunity to discover that both of us share a common Root. The courage to connect yourself to "the other," even when there seems to be no external similarity between the two of you, reveals the immutable bond hidden just beneath the surface and even has the power to bring about the divine unification between the *sefirot* of *yesod* and *malkhut*. This important message is just as relevant in our age as well, when "lines drawn in the sand" still too often obscure our humanity.

OR HA-ME'IR

Judah approached him, saying: "Please, my lord, may your servant speak a word in his master's ear...."
(GEN. 44:18)

We have taught frequently that the essence of God's service and the purpose of both study and prayer is that they be for the sake of *shekhinah*.... Our sages have been aroused to teach us that the ancients had their prayers answered because they prayed with [or "for the sake of"] God's name (*Midrash Tehilim* 91). In last week's Torah portion we saw that Jacob told his sons to "do this [*zot, shekhinah*]" (Gen. 43:11); do all that you do only to make a name, that is for the sake of *shekhinah*, who is God's name.... The verse goes on: "Take of the land's produce [*zimrat ha-arets*] in your vessels." This refers to those songs (*zemirot*) and praises that *shekhinah* is forever singing, following the secret of "God, never be silent" (Ps. 83:2). Take this along in the "vessels" of your speech-letters, recombining those letters by which you sought to ask for your own needs into names by which to address God. These callings will then rise up as they should....

So Jacob told his sons: "Do this." *Shekhinah* is called *zot* ("this"). Be constantly constructing and shaping Her into a perfect form. Do so by your good deeds, especially by the words of study and prayer. "Take of the *zemirot* of the land in your vessels," your entire selves placed into the letters of speech....

Thus **Judah approached him**. The *tsaddik* draws everything near to our blessed Creator, raising up all division to its source in the One. This is the service of Judah, the righteous one in each generation. He says: **"Please, my Lord, may your servant speak a word...."** *Yedabber* ("speak") is a causative form; the whole intent of the true *tsaddik* in prayer is not for himself but for *shekhinah*, to provide words for Her, coming from below. Without them She would be mute, lacking the words to come before God. This is the *tsaddik's* worry, and thus true prayer begins by casting light upon *shekhinah's* needs, She who is called **a word**, giving to Her words, songs, and praises....

꒰ᴥ꒱

Although the author's knowledge of Hebrew grammar may be faulty (*yedabber* is not really a causative), his point is a profound one. True prayer takes place within God, *shekhinah*, or the imminent presence, the God within this world, seeking to unite with the One. But the only language She has to call out for this union is that which we humans provide for Her. That is our role: giving the gift of language to the silent inner longing of being, longing to become One.

Somehow missed in the Hebrew transcription here is the fact that *adoni* ("my lord" of the verse) is graphically identical to Adonay, the divine name most associated with *shekhinah*. "Speaking a word in his master's ear" means giving *shekhinah* the gift of human speech.

MEVASSER TSEDEK

> And we said, "We are unable to go down. If our littlest brother is with us, we shall go down, for we cannot see the man's face if our youngest brother is not with us."
> (GEN. 44:26)

It is known that the *tsaddik* must not descend from his high level, lowering himself in his holy thoughts. This would be like sending holy offerings outside of their proper domain. It is only when someone who is in a constricted spiritual state [*katnut*] needs to be raised up that it is permissible for the *tsaddik* to [go down and] uplift him. This descent is for the sake of the ascent. Through this the *tsaddik* arrives at an even higher spiritual rung, where one may merit seeing the *shekhinah*.

By way of a parable: in the earthly kingdom one cannot easily see the face of the king. Yet suppose the son of the king is lost, taken captive to some faraway place. A certain person travels there, endangering himself so greatly that even he might never return from there, God forbid. Since he did this to give great joy to the king, as soon as he returns he is permitted to gaze upon the face of the king without any barrier.

This is the meaning of the verse: **And we said, "We are unable to go down"**—we are not allowed to descend from our rung, except when **our littlest brother (***ahinu ha-katon***)** is with us. We understand this to mean that we may go down from our level only so that **our brother** who is on a lower rung (*katnut*) **is with us**—become equal to us, since in this way it is possible to lift him up. In this case, **we shall go down**.

The meaning is this: **we cannot see the man's face if our youngest brother is not with us**—the radiant Face is lacking when our littlest brother, whoever is in a constricted spiritual state, remains down below and is not equally with us. Only when we have lifted him up as well are we able **to see the man's face**; He will not abandon the one who is lost. We must see that all the holy sparks are redeemed and purified, and when we raise them up we will be able to gaze upon the pleasantness of God. For this purpose **we shall go down**—in order to lift them up.

⚮

"Descent for the sake of ascent" is a key theme throughout Hasidic piety. Here the poignancy of the Joseph drama is itself "uplifted" to make it a tale of our responsibility for all our brothers and sisters. We may leave no one behind as we seek our path to God. This text serves as a warning to the *tsaddik* not to neglect his communal, earthly mission for the sake of closeness to God. We dare not "go up to our Father" unless the least among us is brought up as well.

KEDUSHAT LEVI

Joseph hitched his chariot and went up to greet his father....
(GEN. 46:29)

Why does the Torah bother to tell us that **Joseph hitched his chariot**? Would it not have sufficed to say that he **went up to greet his father**? We find advice here for every person to keep an open eye on all our deeds. We are not meant to be mere animals, but to weigh our actions, deriving from them wise hints about how to serve God....

Through our deeds we are able to make ourselves into a "chariot" or dwelling-place for God's presence. This is the intent of our verse, to tell us that Joseph was such a person. He had such great joy when he saw his father's face! But this led him to think about what a great joy indeed it would be to behold the face of God. This is what our verse means: he **went up**, he uplifted this moment, **to greet his father**.

In fact this takes place only when you fulfill the *mitsvot* and pray with great intensity. You sometimes get so tired that your own corporeal self begins bit by bit to fade away. Then a spirit flowing forth from God comes upon you. The light that you encounter is like seeing God's own face, as it were. Joseph was so righteous that a bright and pure light shone down upon him, a part of God from above. Thus he was able to transform the joy of seeing his father into a "chariot" for God's presence.

☙☙☙

It does not take much reading between the lines here to see that Levi Yitshak is sharing something of his own religious experience. In a fashion typical of Jewish authors, he ascribes it to a biblical figure of righteousness rather than claiming it as his own.

Va-Yiggash
Round Two

AM: I'm a little disturbed by this final text. Is Joseph still happy to see his father? Or is that moment—like so many others—nothing but an occasion to think about rising up to God?

EL: That's like the classic question about the Kabbalist. Is he so busy concentrating on unifying the *shekhinah* when he makes love that he fails to notice his wife?

AG: Yes, but what about the beautiful gentile in the *Peri ha-Arets* text? Surely he (or she?) is being noticed!

EL: But noticed only in order to take it somewhere else. That text, though, is really flirting with danger!

AM: Yes, but the moment of Joseph's greeting Jacob is so wholly innocent! Why can't we at least enjoy the real human emotion for what it is?

AG: Here's the whole question of Hasidism's love of "descent for the sake of ascent" or "uplifting." I think it's this sense of life as a spiritual adventure—even one that comes close to danger—that makes it so attractive to us.

AM: It tries to strike a balance somewhere between hedonism and asceticism, clearly rejecting both extremes.

AM: What about the other person here? Doesn't the other become an object, an I-It in Buber's terms, if you are just using him or her as a springboard for your return to God?

EL: But Hasidism is supposed to be about the I-Thou, the intimate and open-hearted relationship between masters and disciples.

AM: And among the disciples as well. Yes, this is what Buber loved in Hasidism.

AG: Yes, every *thing* is supposed to be such a springboard. But when it's a person, we get into trouble. Can we somehow preserve that distinction? Can we say it's the *event* of meeting Jacob that takes Joseph back to God, but that his love of Jacob remains real and human, indeed the necessary vehicle for that sacred transformation?

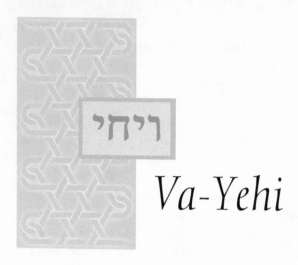

Va-Yehi

OR TORAH

> He blessed Joseph, saying ... "May the angel who
> protected me from all harm bless these lads."
> (GEN. 48:15–16)

The *Zohar* comments that the blessing of children, even though the parent who offers it sees it as complete, does not give the child full pleasure until it is in turn fulfilled [in the next generation] (1:227b). In the sages' words, "May it be God's will that your offspring be like you" (b. Ta'anit 6a). This only applies when there are grandchildren.

The wise son asks for all these blessings in order to give his father pleasure. Seeing this, the father gives him the blessing, for the sake of his children and grandchildren. This is the meaning of "He will turn the hearts of fathers toward their sons and the hearts of the sons toward their fathers" (Mal. 3:24).

This also applies to the blessings that Israel offers to their Father in heaven.

❧

Again the Maggid shows us how profoundly he understands the dynamics of love between parent and child. We ask for our parents' blessing because we know how touched they are to offer it. But they give it thinking not a bit about themselves, but only of their children and grandchildren. This leads to a truly beautiful reading of the verse in Malachi, which of course refers to the final reconciliation that will bring messiah.

But the last line here is no less significant. In giving blessing to God, we cause God to bless us. Each loving side in this relationship is thinking entirely of the other.

OR HA-ME'IR

> Jacob called to his sons and said: "Gather round and I will tell you what will become of you at the end of days."
> (GEN. 49:1)

[The phrase **what will become of you** is written as "how you will be read" at the end of days.] On this verse RaSHI says: "He sought to reveal the end to them, but God's presence departed from him...."

It is also taught that "in the future the righteous will be called by the blessed Holy One's own name" (b. Bava Batra 75b).... The righteous restore the Torah to its original pristine state, Torah as it proceeded from divine Wisdom. The *tsaddik*, by the power of deep understanding, strips Torah of its narrative garb, dressing it instead in spiritual form, sublime lights, and secret Holy names. These names are hinted at in the narratives themselves....

A truly perceptive person can read the entire Torah in God's name Y-H-W-H and can find that blessed name within all the details of the Torah's stories. This is how the *tsaddikim* restore Torah to its original state, before it was dressed up in this world. The Torah had to take on its corporeal form for the sake of Israel, who themselves exist in bodily form. They would never have been able to attain Torah's depths without that narrative garb, which makes it possible for us flesh-and-blood beings to listen to it.

But in the future, when our bodies will be purified of all corporeality and "earth will be filled with the knowledge of Y-H-W-H ... " (Is. 11:9) from great to small, there will be greater understanding in the world and Torah will be stripped of that covering garb. It will exist only as sublime and holy lights, seen by everyone....

Now we can understand what it means that Jacob wanted to reveal the end to his sons. Israel do not have the mind or awareness to fathom how to combine the letters as they were created, to set them forth in a fixed and permanent way....

But if a universally wise sage were to come forth announcing the good, telling each one of Israel: "This is what you need to do, each according to your own will and capacity, in order to reveal those permutations right now" ... who would not listen to such words? Everyone would want to bring about that future state of understanding. Redemption would no longer be delayed.

The trouble is that this powerful teaching would in fact overwhelm the free will that was given to each and every Israelite. Each of us has to come upon those arrangements of Creation's letters that we need to find, each at our own pace and with our own level of awareness, and with intense devotion to God. Without this, our existence as part of Creation has no meaning. What good is it, then, if a great sage comes along and tells us each our own secret, that which we were supposed to discover of our own free will? Our will would be negated by such an act, and it would be of no value!

This is the meaning of **Jacob called to his sons and said: "Gather round and I will tell you...."** The word *agidah* ("tell") also means "to draw forth"; Jacob sought to draw out for them those arrangements of Creation's letters as they would happen to them (or, "as they would be read") at the end of time. He wanted to reveal Torah in its pristine state right then and there, for on this depends redemption. This is why RaSHI says, "He sought to reveal the end to them, but God's presence departed from him." This would have meant the negation of his sons' free choice; each of them would have acted immediately according to those rearranged letters, without any effort or struggle....

⟨⟨⟨⟩⟩⟩

The *Or ha-Me'ir* speaks as a voice of warning within the Maggid's circle. "Beware of giving away too much!" he is saying. Most people aren't ready to hear it; they need to go through their own inner processes of discovery, each at a unique pace. Of course they will seem to respond and follow, if you reveal profound teachings to them. But in the end it will be without value, because they won't have gotten there of their own accord.

KEDUSHAT LEVI I

> Of Asher [Jacob said], "His food is rich; he will
> provide dainties for the king."
>   (GEN. 49:20)

I heard from my saintly teacher Dov Baer on the verse "I will rejoice, rejoice in Y-H-W-H" (Is. 61:10). The word is repeated because I find joy and take pleasure in the fact that I have merited to "behold the beauty of Y-H-W-H" and have delighted in God's service. The fact that I have been so abundantly close to God in itself brings me joy. This is the meaning of "Rejoice, rejoice"....

This is also the meaning of *me-asher. Asher* means "happiness," the World of Joy. We take pleasure in the fact that we have delighted in serving God; that brings us to joy. His food is rich: the word *lehem* ("food") can refer to joy. We are "rich" or joyous in our joy in God's service.

He will provide dainties for the king. I also heard from my teacher Dov Baer that our sages' statement (*Zohar* 3:7b) "Israel provide sustenance for their Father in Heaven" refers to pleasure, which is itself a kind of sustenance. This means that Israel bring joy or pleasure to their heavenly Father. **He will provide dainties for the king** tells us that one who serves in total love provides "love in its delights" (Song 7:7), causing Y-H-W-H to delight in His creatures.

⌒⫘⫘⌒

Simhah shel mitsvah, or "rejoicing in the commandment," is a key element of the religious life as Hasidism teaches it. The joy we take in the pleasure of true worship creates boundless circles of joy, mysteriously embracing God as well as those who serve, binding them ever closer together. In this sense above all others, "the reward of a *mitsvah* is a *mitsvah*"; the life of devotion is its own abundant reward.

KEDUSHAT LEVI II

> Joseph said to his brothers: "Do not fear, for am I instead of God?"
> (GEN. 50:19)

Onkelos rendered **am I instead of God** to mean "I fear God." This Aramaic translation does not make apparent sense.

A general rule: We need to cleave to Y-H-W-H through all of our personal qualities: to be in awe before God's honor with our fear, to love God's greatness with our power of love, and to use our own sense of glory to become "Israel in whom I am glorified" (Is. 49:3). So too all the rest of our qualities. These together compose "the World of Truth."

If you understand this, you will also comprehend such teachings as "Whence do we know that the blessed Holy One called Jacob 'God'" (b. Megillah 18a), or "Just as the blessed Holy One constructs worlds, so too do the righteous" (*Zohar* 1:5a). We are also taught, "In the future the righteous will be called by the name of the blessed Holy One," and "The ministering angels will one day proclaim 'Holy!' before the righteous" (b. Bava Batra 75b).

A person who is attached to our blessed Creator through every personal quality is not **instead of** (or "beneath") God, but is fully joined to Y-H-W-H. Without all those links, we remain "beneath God." This is what Onkelos meant in his translation. He understood Joseph to be asking: "Am I beneath God?" On the contrary, I am wholly attached to God. "I fear God" means that I am linked to the Creator in all those ways.

⟳〜⟲

Joseph, the biblical prototype of *tsaddik*, is attached to God in every dimension of his moral and emotional life, leading with the fear of God. Hasidism also makes this bold claim for the righteous of its own day: they are fully attached to God. This is the source of their healing powers and the special efficacy of their prayers.

In our time we tend to be wary of such claims, having seen them too frequently abused. We tend to settle for the wholeness of devotion, a state of being happily "beneath" God. But do we still seek more? Is there a place in us that longs for all the lines to be erased, to be fully joined to God while still in our bodies? Can we trust those desires?

Va-Yehi
Round Two

AG: This *parashah* of Jacob blessing his sons is a good place to reflect on the wealth of parental metaphors and insights into parenthood we find in the Hasidic sources.

OR: I find myself especially attracted to the first teaching here. The Maggid seems to understand the dynamics of blessing so well, including the complex interplay going on between parent and child. What does a child feel when being blessed? How much is he/she accepting the blessing in order to please the parent?

AM: Blessings can indeed be loaded with all sorts of heavy things.

AG: The second teaching too is part of this conversation. How often parents, out of love, want to give their children too much, instead of letting them learn it on their own!

AM: Both parent and child are in a position of giving. The "wise son" here is actually a kind son; it is an act of kindness on the child's part to seek out the parent's blessing.

OR: You might call it an emotional wisdom.

AM: But it really reflects great emotional maturity, recognizing the parent as a human being with a need to give.

AG: Yes, this is often a great turning point in the parent-child relationship. The child is mature enough to say: I am ready to receive what you have to give.

OR: So, mapped back into cosmic terms, this is our recognizing God's need to give.

AM: Remember that it's not just parent and child. The relationship of teacher and student works in much the same way. Judaism depicts God as both parent and teacher.

OR: It's interesting that the Maggid is surrounded by young men, many of whom struggled with their fathers or fathers-in-law in order to come to him. How much has he taken on the role of loving surrogate parent?

AG: Look then at the last teaching here, a very daring claim for the *tsaddik* by Levi Yitzhak. Might he be claiming that the *tsaddik* really can represent God in the lives of his disciples?

⟨✺⟩

שמות

Sefer Shemot

The Book of
Exodus

שמות

Shemot

ME'OR 'EYNAYIM

We all know the secret meaning of our exile in Egypt: *awareness* itself was in exile. We knew nothing of the Creator or His Torah. In the generation of the flood people had said: "What is God that we should serve Him?" (Job 21:15). Even though Torah hadn't yet been given in the generations before the flood, it existed in this world as the power of the Maker within the made. It had not yet been garbed in specific worldly forms, such as it would have after being given. But there were certain select individuals who fulfilled Torah just as it exists above, having come to grasp it through their own expanded minds. They understood its true inner essence as it was before it was given. Such people were Methuselah, Enoch, and Adam, who were all students of Torah. But at the time of the flood, humans were so wicked that they cut both world and Torah off from their connection to the Creator. Both world and Torah were separated from their Root; that is why the flood came to destroy the world.

Where was Torah cast down at that time? It fell into the "shell" of Egypt. That is awareness in exile, for the Torah represents awareness. And this is why Israel had to go down into Egypt, to raise up fallen Torah....

Once we came out of Egypt, we brought awareness forth from exile. Even though we are indeed still exiled, awareness is not, except for those so totally lost as to deny reality. For most people only the personal attributes [which express that awareness] remain in an exilic state. These include love, fear, glory, and the rest. Everyone knows that God exists and has some degree of awareness. Yet our qualities of acting remain exiled:

we have improper loves, improper fears. These qualities were imprinted within us only for the service of God, but we use them to violate God's will.

That is why the Torah continually admonishes us to "recall the day you came out of Egypt" (Deut. 16:3). This is counsel on how to extricate these qualities from exile as well. If every one of us remembered that awareness itself was once in exile but came forth from it, and we became aware of God's existence, it would be easier for us to bring those personal qualities as well into goodness and away from evil. We would then use them only in ways that accord with awareness of God.

This is what Ben Zoma meant when he interpreted "So that you recall the day you came forth from Egypt all the days of your life" (Deut. 16:3). "The days," he said, "suffices to tell us to remember every day. 'All the days' is there to include the nights as well" (b. Berakhot 12b). Day is a time when the mind is clear, a time when we follow its directives. But we need to remember our liberation from Egypt at "night," as well, when in darkness. If we then recall the existence of a great and awesome God who created everything out of nothing, and in whose hands all remains, "night will shine like the day" (Ps. 139:12) for us and we will come forth from darkness....

⚬⚬⚬⚬

There is a naïve optimism about the *Me'or 'Eynayim*, which today's reader may find both inspiring and difficult. Does mindfulness or awareness indeed solve all our problems? Does the disconnection between our faith, in our best moments, and our actions not continue to distress us? In the Ba'al Shem Tov's tradition, the Chernobyler wants to give us hope, not burden us with guilt. We struggle every day over our *middot*, our moral qualities, and seek to overcome those temptations that keep us from acting on what we know to be our own highest values. But the fact that we are aware of those values, the *Me'or 'Eynayim* tells us, is itself a gift of God, a part of our liberation. That awareness should not be taken for granted. The fact that our eyes are open to them is half the battle, showing us how far we've come from real enslavement of the mind. If we remember that fact every day, and even in times of "night," we'll find the strength to do the rest.

MA'AYAN HA-HOKHMAH

> And these are the names of the Children of
> Israel coming into Egypt; Jacob, the man and his
> household, came.
>   (Ex. 1:1)

We need to know, to pursue God's word, in understanding the distinctions here. Why does the verse first say **Israel** and then **Jacob**? Why first **coming** and then **came**?

This is how it appears to me. **Israel** refers to "Israel arose in thought [before Creation]." This refers to those human beings who serve God through thought, those who look ahead and foresee the negative forces that will arise in the world. They negate these forces by their thought and hold them back from coming into the world.

Then there are the **Jacob** people, standing on a lower rung, who do not know how to combat those forces until they actually come to pass.

These are the names of the Children of Israel refers to those people who contemplate (*beney/bonim = binah*) so that they may be called Israel, coming into Egypt. They understand those narrow straits (*mitsrayim/metsar yam*) and are there to negate them promptly in their contemplative minds.

Then also **Jacob, the man and his household, came.** These are the ones who fight off the negative forces as they arise, only after they **came.**

May God cause good to flow into the world!

☙〰☙

All the categories of the verse and the ensuing story have here been universalized. "Israel arose in thought" refers to people of religious insight and awareness, knowing how to confront "Egypt," the constrictions of vision brought about by *dinim*, ill forces from either within or without, even before they arise. Most of us humans are sadly "Jacobs," perhaps referring to its original meaning as "heels," dealing with problems only after they arise.

NO'AM ELIMELEKH

> An angel of Y-H-W-H appeared to him in flaming fire
> from amid a thornbush. He looked and saw that the
> bush was burning in fire, but was not consumed....
> (Ex. 3:2)

For the righteous, even their evil urge is turned toward good. This is taught on the verse "with all your heart" (Deut. 6:5), meaning "with both urges" (b. Berachot 54a). Nevertheless, you should never trust yourself fully, but remain always on guard.

This is **An angel of Y-H-W-H appeared to him in flaming fire....** The evil urge is also called an angel or messenger of God. It shows itself to the *tsaddik* all wrapped in fiery enthusiasm, as though fully transformed into goodness. **From amid a thornbush**: from formerly having been such a "thorn" in his life. **He looked and saw that the bush was burning in fire**. Even though you see that evil urge all dressed up in passion for the service of God, know that the bush is **not consumed**. Watch out for it until your dying day....

How easy it is to be trapped by our own enthusiasm! How subtle the tricks our ego plays on us! Even this revelation to the great and humble prophet is turned toward delivering this message.

KEDUSHAT LEVI

> And Y-H-W-H said, "I have marked well the plight of
> My people in Egypt and have heeded their outcry
> because of their taskmasters...."
> (Ex. 3:7)

When you ask God for some good thing, do not do so with the intention of satisfying your personal needs; rather, do so to serve the blessed Creator wholeheartedly. When Israel were in Egypt, their awareness was limited, and their outcry emerged from their personal needs. They did not cry out for God to save them from their suffering so that they could better serve the blessed Creator—to be called the "People of Y-H-W-H"—for in Egypt their awareness was constrained.

But the Holy One gifted them in two ways: God saved them from their suffering at the hands of the Egyptians, and He received their outcry *as if* they had been crying out on God's behalf, that is, as if they had cried out that He save them from their suffering so that they could be called the "People of Y-H-W-H."

This is hinted at in the verses, "I have marked well the plight of My people"—that they want to be My people. So, too, in the verse "Now the cry of the Israelites has reached Me" (Ex. 3:9)—as if the primary intention of their outcry was to reach Me ... they cry out with the desire that I save them so that they might serve Me....

✿

In the depths of their oppression, teaches the Berdichever, the Israelites can only cry out for their own physical welfare or freedom; they do not have the capacity to cry out for God—to pray for spiritual redemption. Nonetheless, God invests in them, knowing that once liberated they will grow into a holy community. And so, God acts "as if," investing in the Israelite people of the future. I hear in this commentary the voice of a *rebbe* who understands that when people are in distress, it can be very difficult for them to cultivate their spiritual lives. In such situations, the Hasidic master must follow in God's path and pray for the healing of their bodies and souls, helping them move into a more expansive existence.

Reading this text as an American, one cannot but think of black slaves in the American "Egypt," who did indeed carry on a rich spiritual life while their bodies were yet enslaved.

OR TORAH

> ... He met him [Aaron met Moses] at the mountain of God and he kissed him.
> (Ex. 4:27)

... The reality of God was revealed in Egypt as it is revealed through Creation. Of this Scripture says: "I will pass through Egypt on that night" (Ex. 12:12), and we are taught: "I and no angel...." This had to come about through God's own self, since they were surrounded by such defilement and chicanery that no angel, but only God, had the power to redeem them.

This was testimony to a created universe, one in which God could by will reverse the course of powerful forces.

This revealing of God had to come about through a joining of love and restraint, giving the Israelites the power to [both receive and] withstand God's presence, as was true in Creation. Even though these two forces appeared simultaneously as the world was created, two vessels were needed to contain them. This was how the worlds emerged: All that was a simple unity in the higher world, like the singularity of thought, appeared in a lower world as more fragmented. This was the result of these distinct vessels. But above they remain united to this day, just as thought remains single within the heart. It disperses only in sound and speech, using the distinct vessels of lungs, the organs of articulation, and the windpipe. In the move from speech to physical deed the separation proceeds yet farther.

But in a person of true heart there is no such separation even in the lower realm. Such a person sees that the entirety of life, the full self, comes from above; without its upper root it would not exist at all ... therefore the same unity that exists above should be present here too. No attention is paid to the seemingly different vessels, since they are distinct only as receptacles [of the same essence]. Thus upper and lower worlds are joined, and the person is able to ascend from rung to rung, reaching the very top, where all is a simple unity.

This is why the Torah tells us that Moses refused to rescue Israel from Egypt [on his own]. It was not for naught, but was a reasoned view. Moses represents love alone, "for I drew him from the water [*hesed*]" (Ex. 2:10), meaning love and joy. That is why he was "heavy of speech" (Ex. 4:10), because the mouth restrains and shapes our form of self-expression. Moses had no such restraint, only joy. But God's self was to be revealed here, requiring restraint as well as love. Therefore God said to him: "But your brother Aaron the Levite," the one of restraint, "will serve as your mouth" (Ex. 4:14, 16)....

He met him at the mountain of God. "Mountain" stands for love, like that of Abraham, whom God called "mountain" (b. Pesahim 88a). *Elohim*, the word used for "God," represents judgment and restraint. The two of them met together **and he kissed him**: their spirits were joined, becoming a simple unity.

ᑲᖳᖱᖰᖲᖵ

This passage is interesting mostly as a comment on leadership, on the unique mixture of loving embrace and restrained judicious action that it takes to bring about great things. Wise is the would-be leader who realizes what part of this mix is lacking and goes to seek it in a "brother." If the Maggid is training—or at least inspiring—his disciples to build a great movement, here he is giving them a key piece of advice.

Shemot
Round Two

AG: The Hasidic reading immediately spiritualizes and universalizes the exile in Egypt. The Jewish people's most precious memory is now a description of the human condition; our entire life is lived in a state of denial and unawareness.

AM: And the same is true of redemption. It is all a matter of inner attunement and awakening to awareness. These are the things that bring us forth from the *metsar yam*, our narrow straits.

EL: Redemption has been privatized. They have all heard the Ba'al Shem Tov's reading of the verse in *Lekha Dodi*: "Redemption draws near to my soul"—each soul needs to be redeemed in its own way.

OR: There is such a mix in the Hasidic mind-set of public and private space, the collective and the individual. They're not giving up on the dream of Israel's national redemption, but adding this whole inner dimension to it.

EL: The *Me'or 'Eynayim* and *Kedushat Levi* texts are both talking about the exile of the mind. When your mind is in exile, you don't know you're missing anything. You can't yet long for God, because you don't know what God is. The Israelites are so deeply in slavery that they don't feel this deeper aspect of their own suffering. God has to do it for them.

AG: Yes, I imagine Levi Yitshak is thinking of that phrase *va-yeda' elohim* ["and God knew ..."] left hanging so poignantly at the end of chapter 2.

OR: There's a hierarchy of needs reflected here. You can't expect sophisticated spirituality from people who are in so much direct pain. They want—and deserve—relief from their own pain first.

EL: Yes, but does Levi Yitshak resolve it too easily? God steps in and does it for them, uplifting their outcry as though it were for the sake of heaven. Couldn't we instead get some instruction here, something to tell us *how* to make our outcry into what is truly a call for God?

ואראV

Va-Era

ME'OR 'EYNAYIM

... The secret meaning of the Egyptian exile is that true awareness was in exile; people were unable to attain the awareness required to serve our blessed Creator, that of which Scripture says: "Know your father's God and serve Him" (1 Chron. 28:9). Awareness is the root that brings one to full love and fear of God. Know in faith that "the whole earth is filled with God's glory," "there is no place devoid of God," and that God is the true pleasure of all pleasures and the life of life. Then you will come to realize that within any pleasure, were the flow of divine light and the life-force to disappear from it, that pleasure, like all created things, would return to primal chaos, to the void. This is true of all the worlds, both higher and lower: if one could imagine that God's vitality might depart from them, they would be as naught.

God is thus the essence of all things. One who has faith in this will surely not lust after any this-worldly pleasures. If their essence is the blessed Creator, it would be better to hold fast to that true Pleasure! In this way you do not bring about separation from your Root, taking the pleasure only as it appears in physical form. Doing so would make you a separator, dividing the cosmic One from His own presence. All things are called *shekhinah*; that is the life-force of our blessed God, dwelling within all things. If you conduct yourself as most common folk do, you really become a separator, God forbid.

One who has this awareness should look in all things at the inwardness that gives them life. This is God's blessed presence. Cleave to it and you will come to both awe and love. Of love the Mishnah teaches, on the verse "You shall love Y-H-W-H your God ... with all your might" (Deut. 6:5), that the word *me'od* ("might") indicates that "you should love God with every quality that He measures out to you (*me'od/moded*). You should thank Him profusely for it" (m. Berakhot 9:5).

"With every quality" means the following. God is infinite, having no borders or limitations. But this world is limited. How could it possibly bear the flowing light of divine life that exists within all things? But God rules the world by His divine qualities. God measures and reduces the intensity of His presence in accord with what the world can bear. This is what "measured qualities" means.

All this was brought about by God's unattainable wisdom. Sometimes God calls forth one quality, sometimes another, in accord with what His wisdom dictates is needed at each particular time.... The same is true of each person of Israel: God reduces the intensity of divine presence in accord with each person's mental powers. Sometimes the quality is that of *hesed* [free-flowing love], sometimes of *rahamim* [balanced compassion]. At each particular time, that person is only capable of receiving God through that quality. As a person of awareness, you should accept God's presence as it is measured out to you in that moment, rejoicing to receive it. Serve God in love and awe. Be thankful that you are aware, for awareness (*da'at*) embraces all the qualities....

When Israel were in Egypt, awareness was in exile; the shell, which preceded the fruit, served to cover it. This is the hard shell of the nut spoken of by Scripture in "I went down into the garden of nuts" (Song 6:11), referring to the exile in Egypt. The nut has a hard outer shell and several finer membranes inside it, hiding the meat within. The hard outer shell was broken in Egypt, so that we can see what is inside. The thin membranes are still there, until our messiah comes (speedily, in our day!). Then inwardness will be revealed completely....

◌᷎᷎᷍◌

To be free, to be liberated from Egyptian bondage, is to be aware of God as fully as you are able. This means accepting that God's presence can reveal itself to you in multiple ways. Not all of those are easy to receive; they can include judgment or the "left hand" of God as well as the love that comes from God's right. Part of awareness is the faith that you are being given the particular gift of divine presence that you need and are able to receive.

This gift of awareness serves to break through the hard shell that surrounds us. It is not clear in the text whether this process is fully determined by God or whether all God gives us is a nutcracker, one that we still have to employ to do the work.

OR TORAH

> God [*elohim*] spoke to Moses, saying: "I am Y-H-W-H.
> I appeared to Abraham, to Isaac, and to Jacob as El
> Shaddai; by My name Y-H-W-H I was not known to them."
> (Ex. 6:2–3)

... The blessed Holy One needed to reduce His light in creating the worlds, so that the light could be received and the creatures not be obliterated by it. This reduction (*tsimtsum*) is considered a negative or "judging" force, one that limits the flow of a love that by nature seeks to spread forth. It serves like a vessel that contains water, not allowing it to simply flow. Even though this reduction seems judgmental, in fact it too is an act of love. Everything that exists, anywhere in the worlds, must contain an element of goodness, which is divine love. "The world is built on love" (Ps. 89:3). Even though this is a withholding of love, the worlds would not exist without it.

This aspect of judgment is represented by the name *elohim*. But that very name contains an admixture of love within it, in the name *el*. "God's love [*hesed el*] all the day" (Ps. 52:3). This is also the meaning of "Y-H-W-H *elohim* is sun and shield" (Ps. 84:12). The name Y-H-W-H refers to the sun [*tif'eret*], as is known, [while *elohim* represents its "shield," *malkhut*]. "Sun" and "shield" are like these two names. You cannot stare into the sun without a shield or visor that separates you from it but allows you to take pleasure in its light. So too the name Y-H-W-H: its radiance, meaning the love and compassion contained within it, is so very intense that the world requires a shield or barrier so that we can receive that light. Thus God had to restrain and limit it, using the name *elohim*....

This is the meaning of **I appeared to Abraham, to Isaac, and to Jacob as El Shaddai; by My name Y-H-W-H I was not known to them.** This reduction or *tsimtsum* is called forth by the name *shaddai*, for it means "That [*she*] I said to My world: 'Enough!' [*dai*]." God limited the love, so that it not overflow. Nevertheless, this aspect of judgment is called El Shaddai, reflecting the presence of love within it. This withholding itself was an act of love, so that we could bear the light! Yet **by My name Y-H-W-H I was not known to them**: this name could not yet be revealed in their day; it remained garbed within the name *elohim*. **I am Y-H-W-H**—past, present, and future, concentrated in this withholding....

[*Elohim*] spoke to Moses, saying: "I am Y-H-W-H" also shows that this withholding is itself an act of compassion.... This is the meaning of "I will redeem you from your bondage" (Ex. 6:6). [The *mem* of "from" can be read to mean that] your redemption will come through the bondage itself, the force of judgment. It was by the hard force of your oppression that the predicted four hundred years of bondage in an alien land were fulfilled [in only 210 years]. It was the judgment force that brought forth the brightness, for "Y-H-W-H *elohim* is both sun and shield," as we have explained. This also led to prophecy, an encounter with God face to face, as the sages have taught: "A handmaiden at the Sea saw more than the prophet Ezekiel" (*Mekhilta Be-Shalah*, Shirah ch. 3). That was because they were able to bear the brightness. That which began as harsh ended up being gentle....

✦

The doctrine of *tsimtsum* is a key part of the legacy Hasidism inherited from earlier Kabbalah. The Hasidic sources typically depict it in a psychologized way, a restraint of love or giving that itself turns out to be the greatest gift of all. These portrayals often turn to the parent-child relationship, where the parent needs to at least appear to limit the bestowal of love in order to give the child room to grow and flourish.

It is worth noting that the term for love used throughout this text is *hesed*. To be a *hasid* is to be a devotee of that divine quality in particular and to seek to find it everywhere, even in those moments and events that seem to show a hiding or withholding of God's love. Nevertheless, there is something tough, or seeking toughness, to be found in this text. It was the very pain of exile and oppression that made the Israelites, even the humblest among them, strong enough to receive the vision of God.

MA'AYAN HA-HOKHMAH

> I appeared to Abraham, to Isaac, and to Jacob as El Shaddai, but by My name Y-H-W-H I was not known to them.
> (Ex. 6:3)

... A well-known teaching tells us that every single letter is a name of God. But it would really seem that no letter, sign, or notation could truly apply to God. The teaching is an analogy to the way a person is called by a name bearing that person's unique life-energy. Here's the proof: it's easier to awaken a sleeping person by calling out their name than by touching them. That's because the name is that person's life-energy.

So the blessed Holy One is enwrapped in Torah, in the letters of Torah. A person articulating those letters in study or prayer should do so in awe and fear of the One who created all the many worlds. By those pure and holy letters you are calling upon the exalted Creator. Do so in awe and fear.

How much more should this be true when you speak of other matters! Before opening your mouth you should accept that these holy letters [that constitute all speech] came about because the Creator wrapped Himself in Torah. The Infinite (*eyn sof*) needed to be reduced [in order to enter this world]. Thus every letter really contains the name Y-H-W-H. The name **Shaddai** refers to this reduction (*tsimtsum*).

Numerically, Y-H-W-H [26] and Shaddai [314] together constitute the word *shem* or "name [340]." Thus every letter is a name of God....

꩜

This is a key teaching of Hasidism, built on earlier Kabbalistic insights but here expressed most fully. Language or speech itself is holy, an embodiment of God given to humans as an extension of God's self-manifestation in Torah. Language derives from Torah, not the other way around. Treat it always as a divine gift, never to be defiled.

Va-Era
Round Two

EL: There is so much here of just what we seek in Hasidism. The repeated emphasis on *da'at* reflects a life centered on cultivating awareness.

AG: Yes, although the root is *Y-D-'*, it really doesn't mean just accumulated intellectual "knowledge." It bears what we call "the biblical sense" of knowing. Here we have usually translated *da'at* either as "mind" or "awareness."

EL: *Tsimtsum* is also a major theme here. Isn't it interesting that in talking about our coming forth from the narrow straits of Egyptian bondage, the Hasidic authors wind up discussing how much God has to enter the straits in order to become known to us?

AM: But the *tsimtsum* here has to do with concentration in a particular place or time. God's *tsimtsum* in effect becomes a lens for focusing our awareness.

OR: The question is always how we respond to our imperfect world. Like us, they are much concerned with this question, though in such different terms. The reason for all the darkness is that God's light is reduced or concentrated, so that we might be able to behold it. They are trying to find some good in the bad. *Tsidduk ha-din,* you could call it, or in our language, "making lemonade."

AG: The oppression itself is supposed to bring about the redemption. That really is squeezing the lemon pretty hard.

EL: But Egypt is a state of mind. That means everything depends on you, on how you relate to it. Recognizing that is in itself hard work.

AG: Yes, it all depends on you. But what an odd place in the Torah this is to talk about the need for human initiative or "arousal from below." The Exodus tale, as the Torah tells it at least, is all about God's doing, not ours. We barely even *deserved* to be redeemed.

EL: But remember that they're really talking about our own personal and contemporary *mitsrayim* ["Egypt"]. And that is a redemption that each of us needs to undertake.

OR: That's the difference. For us there are no miracles and wonders, no outstretched arm.

AM: Except for the miracle of awareness, of knowing that we are in Egypt and need to come out. That's pretty big.

בא

Bo

NO'AM ELIMELEKH

> Moses said: "We will all go, young and old; we will go with our sons and daughters, flocks and herds; for we must observe the festival of Y-H-W-H."
> (Ex. 10:9)

The Gemara says: At the celebration of water drawing [the elders] used to say: "Happy is our youth that did not shame our old age" (b. Sukkah 53a). This implies that they followed the right and holy path even when they were young. Thus, in their old age they were not ashamed of the deeds of their youth. But if your youthful behavior is not holy you may be ashamed of your actions when you mature. Then you will have to break your old habits, so it is better to act with sanctity now.

Thus we understand the verse: "Teach a youth according to his way, and he will not leave it even when he ages" (Prov. 22:6). If you educate your children in this way [of holiness] they will not have to change paths in midlife. Rather they will be able to continue on the path of their youth throughout their whole life. It will be much easier for them to serve the blessed Holy One.

Thus the verse says: **We will all go, young and old**, meaning we will act and walk in holiness in both our youth and in our old age. **Our sons and daughters**, we will also guide on holy paths. Our **flocks and herds**, even our material occupations—business, eating, drinking and the like will all be part of our path toward the blessed One. **For we must observe the festival** of Y-H-W-H, meaning a fire of enthusiasm for God's service burns in us. This is easy to understand.

༄

Indeed, this is easy to understand. What parent does not appreciate the good habits acquired in childhood and strive to share them with children? Yet this teaching also reflects a world in which children following the paths of their parents is a primary value. What carries over from this teaching in a world where so many of us have broken radically with the way of our parents? Is shame in "the deeds of youth" the only possible result of midlife change?

Or ha-Me'ir

> Moses raised his hand toward heaven and there was a great darkness in all the Land of Egypt ... people did not see their brothers and no person could rise from where he was seated.
> (Ex. 10:22–23)

Here we derive a moral teaching. People have eyes, yet they do not see the good qualities of the enlightened. They are too busy justifying their own ways, whether good or ill. This keeps them from rising to a higher rung. Thus I have explained the Mishnah (Avot 1:17) "All my days I grew up among the sages" to mean that I was capable of growing, rising from one level to the next, not just standing still, because I was "among the sages." I was able to see how small I was, not yet having learned a single one of my masters' ways.

One who wants to attain a high rung needs to fulfill "I have learned from all my teachers" (Ps. 119:99), as explained by the sages (b. Ta'anit 7a): "I learned much from my teachers, [and more from my companions,] but from my students most of all." This is especially true of all the good qualities each person can learn from a friend or companion (*haver*).

But our generation is filled with lots of ignorant people who do not know their right from their left. Nevertheless they burst forth to take God's name and glory for themselves, while seeking to insult others and to gain glory by deriding them. This leads to baseless hatred, due to our many sins....

This is the **great darkness in all the Land of Egypt**. Where awareness is lacking, there is great darkness. You then fall into the narrow places (*mitsrayim/metsar yam*). But Scripture then tells us what this darkness is: **people did not see their brothers**. "See" means that they didn't consider them ... they didn't take to heart how much they could learn from the goodness of the people around them. On the contrary, they kept finding fault and lack in others, glorifying their own deeds. This led them to walk about in darkness and to see no light. People like that cannot progress from one rung to the next; **no person could rise from where he was seated**. They stood about rather than walking forward, as a Jew is always supposed to do.

❦

Spiritual friendship, seeking to live in a community of like-minded companions and learning from their ways, is among the most precious teachings of Hasidism. While the movement is often seen as built upon the "vertical" relationship of master and disciples, the "horizontal" glance, considering and learning from the practice and goodness of "brothers," is no less important.

ORAH LE-HAYYIM

> Our possessions [lit. "cattle"] too will go along with us; not a portion [lit. "hoof"] of them will remain, for we will take of them to serve Y-H-W-H our God.
> (Ex. 10:26)

... "A mixed multitude went up with them" (Ex. 12:38). Those were the ones in whom holy sparks had become admixed in Egypt. This is why Moses wanted to bring them forth. But the blessed Holy One saw that they were not ready and did not want to bring them out yet.

Before Abraham our Father brought forth either Ishmael or Isaac, he was active in bringing to birth the souls of proselytes. These, his disciples, would convert, and they were considered his children. When Moses addressed the wise elders of Israel saying, "Draw forth and take unto yourselves of the flocks [*tson*] for your families" (Ex. 12:21) ... he was telling them to take those who were coming out (*tson/tsenah*), the mixed multitude of fallen souls, and draw them close, raise them up, and bring them near to the service of Y-H-W-H. Onkelos translates "for your families" to read "as our seed," meaning that you should teach them and draw them near to God's service so that you consider them your own children....

This is what Moses meant when he said: **Our possessions too**—this refers to the mixed multitude, those we have acquired and brought near to ourselves, **will go along with us; not a portion of them will remain behind.** The word *parsah* can mean [either "hoof" or] "portion"; *peres* alone, however, could mean "portion," so that these are "the portion of the letter *heh*," referring to the *shekhinah*, the latter *heh* of Y-H-W-H. It is known from the *Zohar* and other books that proselytes are rooted in that place, and no spark of them was to be left behind in Egypt....

For we will take of them to serve Y-H-W-H our God. It was for the sake of these holy sparks that we came into Egypt, in order to raise them up. We became enslaved in bricks and mortar ... and suffered our own exile in order to do so. It was for the sake of this that we came near to God's service. Therefore **we will take of them to serve Y-H-W-H our God**: it is for this purpose that we ourselves have been drawn near to the service of Y-H-W-H.

⟨⟩

There is no stronger statement anywhere of "the mission of Israel." The Jewish people has been called as a "kingdom of priests" in order to serve God by finding holy souls and sparks throughout the world, beyond their own borders, and drawing them close to the single God who is the source of all. This is why we were sent into Egypt, and this is why God brought us forth. Even if we have to convince God that they are ready to come forth with us, that is part of our role. Is this why we were sent into our present diaspora as well?

KEDUSHAT LEVI

> This month will be the first of the months for you.
> (Ex. 12:2)

RaSHI notes that Moses had difficulty with [calculating] the birth moment of the new moon. Why did Moses have this "difficulty"? Because he wanted full redemption to happen within his lifetime. That would mean an end to the waning of the moon, that "the light of the moon be like that of the sun" (Is. 30:26), as it will be in the days of our righteous redeemer, speedily in our time. Amen.

⟨⟩

This fragment of a teaching shows Levi Yitshak at his most audacious. Moses's "difficulty" is really an objection. Why should the moon have to wane and then have to undergo rebirth every month? The homily was a comment on the Talmudic tale (b. Hullin 60b) about the competition between the "two great lights," in which the moon oversteps her bounds and is punished by the decree of the monthly cycle. God realizes this to be an injustice and seeks atonement for having wronged the moon.

Since the moon is a well-established female symbol in Kabbalah, might it be possible to see Levi Yitshak as protesting the diminished status of women as well as that of the moon? Or is that just wishful thinking?

HAYYIM VA-HESED (FROM VA-ERA)

> This month [hodesh] is the first [rosh] of months for you.
> (Ex. 12:2)

Change and renewal (hithadshut/hodesh) do not apply to the blessed Holy One, who is beyond time. The renewal that God sends us is in fact **for you**, that is, for our sake.... It becomes part of our nature, something we are used to. That is the meaning of "nature" [teva']; the renewal of light is imprinted (nitba') upon us, bringing about a human need.

The time will come in the future when "He will sate your soul with resplendence" (tsahtsehot; Is. 58:11) will be fulfilled in us. The light will be so brilliant that we will ever be thirsting for it; [we will be sated with greater thirst]. The word tsahtsehot comes from tsah, meaning "dry" or "thirsty." But meanwhile the blessed Holy One sends us renewal, so that we are able to raise ourselves up to God.

This is the meaning of **This month [hodesh] is the first [rosh] ... for you**. It is through [paying attention to] the heads of things (rosh) that we are renewed and raise ourselves up to God. That is why the verse is introduced by "Speak to all the community of the Children of Israel...." The whole community can come to behave in such a way because of this renewal.

But "nature" is in fact a lie. The truth is that the blessed Holy One conducts everything: God changes the times, varies the seasons, and orders the stars. The stars and constellations that seem so natural are changed according to God's will. If we were always at the level of clarity to realize that God conducts everything, we would have no need for renewal. But our nature causes us to need it.

When God sends us miracles and the force of renewal, we become able to uplift ourselves above everything in nature so that we come to know that God conducts everything, including nature itself. That is why Scripture refers to *nes le-hitnoses*, "a banner-flying miracle" (Ps. 60:6). God sends us the miracle so that we can fly like a banner, lifting ourselves up to God....

ᘒᘮᘮᘯ

Plays on *hodesh, hiddush*, and *hithadshut*, "month," "innovation," especially in Torah interpretation, and personal "renewal" abound in the early literature of Hasidism, probably reaching back to wordplays and aphorisms of the Ba'al Shem Tov himself. Note that the ideal future is not a time of comfortable satiety, but a time of constant thirst. "The light will be so brilliant that we will be ever thirsting for it."

The illusion of "nature" is a key villain of the Hasidic imagination. The natural quickly descends into become "ordinary" or "habitual." To see life this way is fully as bad as observing Torah as mere habit. World and teaching are both in need of constant renewal, a gift given us by God, if only we open our eyes to it.

Bo
Round Two

AG: Most of these teachings seem to reach out to one or another broader community, whether toward the convert, across generations, or to one's "brother" within the Hasidic community. That's appropriate for the Exodus, such a communal event.

EL: The sense of being there for others is very strong; the passage on the "mixed multitude" is especially impressive. But is there a price to pay here? We are very critical of a Jewish life that is lived "for somebody else"—whether one's kids, one's parents, or one's congregants!

OR: But this is the moment when the people itself is forged. They had to ask (as we do!): "Who are my people? Where are its borders? Who's in and who's out?"

AG: In Egypt they were a forced community, defined as such by their oppressors (think of Jews in the bad old days of the Soviet Union).

Now that they're free, they have to choose the contours of their community.

OR: But they want to take the sparks out of Egypt; that means carrying something of that memory with them.

AM: When you go to a new place (whether physical or psychological) you always have to ask: How much of my past do I want to bring along? And how about the next generation? How much of my past do I want or need to pass on to them?

EL: Remember, not every generation has to rebel. Some generations accept the legacy of the past as a gift. That's what the *No'am Elimelekh* is aiming for here.

OR: We have teachers and students here, parents and children, Israel and the proselytes. Is it always clear who the "giver" is in these relationships, or does each side receive as well as give?

AM: The teachers and friends we really care about are those who see our unique spark. That means they are receiving from us, not just pouring the tradition into us.

EL: Yes, I'm always wary of pious people who love Jews in the abstract but have no room for the real differences between people and their needs.

OR: That somehow is what the Exodus experience is for me. Being out of Egypt, being free, but also being among and surrounded by all those varied people.

⌾⟁⟁⟁☾

בשלח

Be-Shalah

KEDUSHAT LEVI

> Toward morning, the sea returned to its course.
> (Ex. 14:27)

The sea beheld the great pleasure its splitting had brought to God, since it caused Israel to sing. It did not want to return to its normal course. "Let me remain dry land and let Israel go on singing forever!" That is why Scripture had to tell us that it returned to its course (*etano*); it followed the condition (*tena'o*) set for it, that it split only for Moses, but afterwards returned to being an ordinary sea.

This also settles a question raised by the *Or ha-Hayyim*, who asked what was so extraordinary about the sea's splitting. Didn't the Jordan also split [for Joshua], and the River Ginai for Rabbi Pinhas ben Yair (b. Hullin 7a)? But now we understand the difference. Those rivers had already seen the great pleasure God derived from the splitting of the Reed Sea. They therefore lovingly *desired* to split. But the sea hadn't yet seen the joy that was to come to its Creator. That was the difference.

⌘

This is Levi Yitshak's vision of the world. All creatures are as filled as he is with the desire to bring pleasure and joy to God! Even the sea wants only that Israel keep on singing.

ORAH LE-HAYYIM

> Israel saw the Egyptians dead on the shore of the
> sea, and Israel saw the mighty hand that Y-H-W-H
> had raised in Egypt....
> (Ex. 14:30–31)

The Midrash recounts that each Israelite saw his or her own Egyptian oppressor, those who had beaten them and made their burden of work so heavy, dead on the seashore (*Mekhilta Be-Shalah* 6). This demonstrated God's great love for them, wanting to protect them from living for days in the fear that the Egyptians might yet emerge from the sea in some other place and resume pursuing them.

Once they saw how real God's love for them was ... they came to understand that even in Egypt, as their burdens were made heavier when Moses and Aaron came before Pharaoh, God's great love was also present.

This is like the case of a father who has a sick small child. The child needs to take a very bitter medicine that the doctors have prescribed. The child does not want to swallow the medicine. Finally the father has to force the child's mouth open and pour the medicine into it. The child comes to think that his father must hate him. When he grows up, of course, and sees how much his father loves him, he has the mind to understand that the bitter medicine his father forced upon him was a token of great love. It was bitter also for the father that he had to hold his child's mouth open that way and pour in that medicine. But because he knew this cure was needed, he took the pain upon himself and did as was needed....

The first **Israel saw** in these verses refers to sight itself; they really **saw the Egyptians dead on the shore of the sea.** But the second, **Israel saw the mighty hand that Y-H-W-H had raised** *in* **Egypt,** refers to understanding.... They understood that even back in Egypt, when the burdens had been so oppressive, those too were evidence of great divine compassion, like the bitter medicinal herbs one has to take.

It seems to me that I heard something similar from that holy lamp the famous *hasid* R. Zusya of Hanipoli.

⚬⚬⚬

This classic explanation of human suffering has a long history, reaching much farther back than Hasidism. In typically Hasidic fashion, here it is tied to a tale of parental love.

TSEMAH HA-SHEM LI-TSEVI

> Then Moses and the Children of Israel sang this song
> [*shirah*].
> (Ex. 15:1)

[*Yashir* can be read as "will sing" as well as "sang."]

"Hurry down [*tashuri*] from the head of Amana" (Song 4:8). [The verse can also mean "You will sing (*tashiri*) out of the source of faith (*emunah*)"!] Israel are to sing out in the future, as Scripture says: "Sing unto Y-H-W-H a new song, for He has done wonders" (Ps. 98:1)! By what merit will they deserve to sing? By that of Abraham, who had faith in God" (Gen. 15:6). Israel have inherited that faith, as the prophet proclaimed: "The righteous shall live by his faith" (Hab. 2:43). This is "singing out of the source of faith" [i.e., Abraham] (*Shemot Rabbah* 23:5).

The author of *Two Tablets of the Covenant* [Rabbi Yeshaya Horowitz] taught that the righteous, as soon as they are promised some good by God, immediately begin to sing about it, even before it happens, a testament to their great faith. Why is it, then, that Moses delayed singing until after the sea was split, and did not sing when he was first told "to multiply My wonders" (Ex. 11:9), which RaSHI tells us refers to the slaying of the firstborn and the splitting of the sea? The fact is that Israel's faith was not yet strong enough. That is why it says here: "They had faith in God and in His servant Moses" (Ex. 14:31). Then **Moses and the Children of Israel sang....**

There is a difference between singing before or after the event. If the singing follows the miracle, it is a result of the miracle itself. It is out of the love and joy resulting from the miracle that one sings and praises God. Without the miracle there would be no song. This is like a servant who receives a gift from his master. It is for love of the gift that he thanks his master. The miracle is here the "male" or active agent, bringing about the singing; the **song (*shirah*)** is "female," deriving from the miracle....

In the future, preceding the miracle of redemption, we will sing a new song (*shir hadash*), [in the masculine]. The main point will be the singing, as though all the miracles had already taken place. Song will be most important, with the miracle secondary to it. That will put the singing in the masculine [or "giving"] role. The miracle will come about because of faith....

This is a case in which the special Galician pronunciation of Hebrew makes the Midrashic wordplay that reads *tashuri me-rosh amanah* as *tashiri* ("Sing out of the source of faith!") sound like the obvious plain meaning of the Song of Songs verse. A faith in which song is primary and miracle comes second is that which Hasidism strives to create. There is no need to deny miracles; they just have to be kept in their proper place.

PANIM YAFOT

> They were not able to drink the waters, because they were bitter.
> (Ex. 15:23)

I heard it taught in the name of the Maggid that **they were bitter** refers to Israel, for they were embittered at that time. The sick person calls sweet things bitter because of the bitterness in his own mouth. But by the power of Moses, who was already attached to Torah, the "Tree of Life to those who hold fast to it" (Prov. 3:18), the divine presence shone through him to give them the spiritual power to sweeten their mouths with the sweetness of Torah. This is "God showed him a tree, which he cast into the waters, and they were sweetened" (Ex. 15:25).

⟋⟋⟍⟋

May our love of Torah be strong enough to sweeten all the bitter waters we encounter, reminding us that most of the bitterness comes from within ourselves.

OR HA-ME'IR

> Y-H-W-H said to Moses: "Behold I will rain down upon you bread from heaven. The people may go forth to gather it, each day's portion on that day, so that I may test them to see whether they will follow My teaching or not. On the sixth day they shall prepare what they have gathered, collecting double what they did each day...."
> (Ex. 16:4–5)

To understand how these holy verses apply to every person and at all times, we must recall the two ways of serving God. There are some people who have no heart for either knowing or serving the Creator except when they study Torah, pray, or engage in some commandment. But as soon as they go to fulfill their own bodily needs, like eating, drinking, and all the rest, they turn into fools, completely unaware of how to link their thoughts to divinity. [We need rather] to take unto ourselves hints of wisdom, so that we [may] never be separate from our Creator, even in physical matters. We must be aware that there is nothing in the world that does not contain sublime lights, letters of Torah.

Scripture points to this in saying: "Go eat of My bread" (Prov. 9:5). This tells the enlightened how indeed to serve God, to raise up letters of Torah even from the physical act of eating bread. I have explained this also on the verse "At the time of eating, come nigh" (Ruth 2:14). "Nigh" refers to *malkhut*, [the kingdom of God on earth] (b. Zevahim 102a). Even when eating bread and the rest of what is on our table, we should "come nigh" to these limbs of *shekhinah*, dwelling in those lower realms. This is "*My* bread," letters of Torah-bread garbed in the physical bread that we eat....

One who serves the blessed Holy One in this way, uplifting letters of Torah from the earthly world, is called one who eats "bread from the earth" (Ps. 104:14).... The other, who awakens the heart to God's service through Torah and prayer, engages in **bread from heaven**.

The holy books teach us, however, that the holiness of Sabbath depends on that of the weekday. As you act during the week, so will you act on the "Sabbath," that is, when you approach the inner realm of prayer. Everything depends on how you act in the outer physical world. It is proper for those who fear God and contemplate God's name to have some of that "Sabbath" holiness present on each day of the week. They need to stand aside from all evil, ever serving in holiness and purity. They should remain attached to their Creator, linking the most exalted divinity to every act they do, even ordinary conversation with a friend....

⟲∭⟳

Both ways of service are indeed holy, but the author clearly has a message in mind about which is the most important, indeed the key to both. Again one wonders who is "across the table" in this conversation. Is it the *mitnagged* that R. Ze'ev Wolf is addressing here, or might it be another voice from within the Hasidic circle—or indeed from within his own self?

NO'AM ELIMELEKH (FROM TETSAVEH)

> Then, whenever Moses raised his hand, Israel
> prevailed; whenever he let it down Amalek prevailed
> ... and Aaron and Hur supported his hands.
> (Ex. 17:11–12)

You might ask why Moses would put his hand down. The truth is that our teacher Moses, peace upon him, had achieved such great levels of spirituality and holiness that he knew how to awaken [divine] compassion. But if he had actually done this and awakened [only] compassion, the world would have ceased to exist. When God created the world, compassion was included within it. Compassion came alongside judgment so that reward and punishment might exist. If Moses in his practice had awakened compassion exclusively, all would have returned to the primal unity and there would be no punishment even for the wicked. So all Moses could do was sweeten or mitigate judgment. As for us, we wish we could do as much when we try to arouse pure compassion as Moses did when he just sweetened judgment....

This is the meaning of **whenever Moses raised his hand.** "Hand" alludes to authority, for a *tsaddik* has authority over all worlds and can act in them at will ... for the worlds were created to obey the *tsaddik* who is called "this," as in "this man Moses" (Ex. 32:1). So **whenever Moses raised his hand** to assert his authority over all the worlds, **Israel prevailed.** But he had to come down somewhat from his lofty rung, as we mentioned above, [to keep the world existing, and] **Amalek prevailed.**

And Aaron and Hur supported his hands; at their spiritual level, they were trying to awaken compassion.

☙❦❧

A balance of conflicting tendencies. There is a perfect attitude toward the world out there somewhere, one of pure compassion. The *tsaddik* would like to arouse that world to come to be. But doing so would leave no room for the reality of an evil that exists and needs to be confronted, even punished. This teaching recognizes the importance of balancing compassion and boundary setting in the work of the *tsaddik*. On the other hand it acknowledges that most of us are often so overwhelmed by limitation and harsh judgment (against ourselves as well as others) that just attempting to awaken a bit of compassion is a worthy endeavor.

Be-Shalah
Round Two

OR: Things have more to them than first seems to be the case. You always have to look deeper. *Hesed* and *gevurah*, the right and left hands of God, operate and interpenetrate in more complicated ways than we imagine.

AM: Yes, but that message is what's both great and difficult about Hasidism. The call for humility about how much we know provides comfort and meaning. But it does so by denying the reality of evil, including the sometimes great bitterness of life. Human suffering is real and cannot be dismissed. *Tashuri* as "turn it all into singing" is easier said than done.

AG: I'm reminded of Elie Wiesel's confrontation with the *rebbe* at the conclusion of *The Gates of the Forest*. When the survivor challenges the *rebbe* with something like "How can you be singing after what happened to us?" the *rebbe* answers (again, in paraphrase), "What should I do? Scream? Will that lead to greater healing?"

OR: Yes, but we encounter all this in a different era, both post-Freudian and postmodern. We need to recognize that there is a real shadow side to existence. Quietism is not an adequate response. Our question (also a Hasidic one) is "Can we transform it?" We find it unhealthy to deny reality.

AG: That's right. Such denial only leads to blaming yourself. "Ah, it's all good! I am just not whole enough or open enough to see it!" That's a refined guilt trip, but a guilt trip nonetheless. Being a Jew after the Holocaust has to mean confronting the reality of evil and standing up to fight it, not denying its existence.

OR: Your goal remains *yihud*, seeing through to the oneness of all things. But is there room for divine *will* in your thinking? Why does God want there to be evil?

AM: The spiritual optimism of Hasidism is hard for us.

AG: And yet the wholeness they offer is so attractive, so much what we seek!

AM: Yes. Hasidism offers an opportunity for growth, for going up the ladder to higher (or deeper!) understanding, but still insists on self-acceptance as the only path. You have to go up as a whole person, not a divided self. That's how it can still speak to us postmoderns.

 יתרו

Yitro

LIKKUTIM YEKARIM (#135)

> Moses went up to God....
> (Ex. 19:3)

... Our duty to serve our Creator exists in two modes, those of love and awe, as is well known. Even the angels live with these two forms of service. The prophet tells us that "the holy beings ran back and forth" (Ezek. 1:14), which RaSHI explains as their running closer, to gaze upon the *shekhinah* that hovers directly over them, and then moving back and hiding, out of awe. Thus running back and forth can be interpreted as referring to love and fear....

As we start to serve, we begin by drawing forth a sense of awe. This means true awe before our exalted Creator, not a fear of punishment, which is merely superficial. Such real awe does not come to a person easily, but requires a regular determined effort, concentrating on the Creator without a moment's ceasing. This will get you through the first gate, that of awe. "This is the gateway to Y-H-W-H" (Ps. 118:20). It is "with this that Aaron shall enter the holy place" (Lev. 16:3).... But once you have already attained such a sense of awe, it is easy to add the quality of love. Love is called the inner gate. The same is true in an earthly kingdom. A person who wants to come in to the king, having crossed through the outer courtyard, will have an easier time getting through the inner gates. The guards at those gates will see that their compatriots at the outer gates have already let him through....

Thus it says first that **Moses went up to God** (*elohim*), and afterwards: "To Moses He said, 'Ascend to Y-H-W-H'" (Ex. 24:1). The name *elohim* is mentioned first, followed by the Tetragrammaton. This is because *elohim* refers to judgment, the realm of *din* or the awesome. Y-H-W-H refers to pure compassion, leaning toward *hesed*, which is the side of love. The verses mean that first Moses went up to God, the quality of awe. He reached it on his own, by dint of great effort and concentration. Once he was there, he was told to "ascend to Y-H-W-H," to the place of love, which then came easily to him....

৩୷୷৩

Love is indeed a gift, but one that comes only as a reward for our struggle to stand before God in awe.

OR HA-ME'IR

> You have seen what I have done to Egypt [*mitsrayim*], how I raised you upon the wings of eagles and have brought you to Me.
> (Ex. 19:4)

We Children of Israel are called "seekers of Your oneness." We are ever questing after the unity and oneness of God. Even when we are at the lowest of rungs, we search our souls for ways to serve our blessed Creator.... This is logical, since every Jew is obligated not to rest even for a moment, but to go on pursuing that quest. This is the whole of human life, the very purpose of Creation.

We, however, do not possess the breadth of mind needed to know how to rouse our spirits in each and every moment. We see from our own experience that sometimes a person can serve God in a particular way for a certain period of time. But as time passes, this quality of service grows old; its time passes and it is not as vital and beloved as it once was. The Ba'al Shem Tov read the verse: "Cast us not off at the time of our old age ..." (Ps. 71:9) to mean "Do not let time cast you into 'oldness.'" Sometimes a person's way of serving grows old, because of the passage of time....

In the same way I read the verse "May your youth be renewed like that of the eagle" (Ps. 103:5). Our sages were aroused to explain that the eagle [or, "phoenix"] sheds its feathers every thousand years and renews its youth

(RaSHI and Rabbi Moshe Alshekh). "Feathers" indicate a sort of garment. It is well known that all of our devotion, including the actual commandments, are nothing other than a garment…. A person of true insight understands that even the different appearances in which God is "garbed" for the sake of human worship all lead to the same place, indicating His blessed oneness. It is for our sake that the Creator appears in such varied garments, so that each living person [may] be able to arouse the inner heart to constantly discover God anew. When the category through which you now serve grows old for you, you will be able to switch it for another garment, finding a place for it in your soul.

All this is brought about by God for our good and the perfection of our souls, so that we ever remain awake and do not fall into "old age." This is the "shedding of feathers" to which I have referred. When things grow old, you "shed" the former way of service and renew your youth, finding some wise clue that will awaken a renewal within you, leading you to a different garment….

Now we can explain: **"You have seen what I have done to Egypt [*mitsrayim*]; I Myself have brought it about that a person falls into a strait [*meytsar*]."** We have learned that one always has to be in a state of "back and forth" (cf. Ezek. 1:14); it is impossible to stand still on a single rung. But an intelligent person who contemplates this with the inner mind will understand that this too comes from God. God is to be found "garbed" in that very situation for our own sake. It is this that brings us to constant arousal and renewal, giving rebirth to our religious life. "You will come to see and understand that I made this *mitsrayim*."

The value of your seeing this is that I **raised you upon**—higher than—**the wings of eagles and have brought you to Me**. It is all due to God's help. When you reach *hokhmah*, true inner wisdom, you will serve God even without that feathered garment. I **have brought you to Me** (*elay*)—I have brought you to the letter *yod*, *hokhmah*, beyond all the seven categories of garb, to the place where there are no "feathers."

⌘

The moment leading to Sinai has here been entirely personalized. The journey out of Egypt is a coming out of the narrow straits of one's own habitualized religious life. Eventually you come to realize that it is God who is your Liberator from those old and tired ways of service. God is there in such multiple "garments" ever to renew your spiritual youth, but ultimately to bring you "to Me," to the final mystical place where all the varied garments are cast aside.

Read in our day, this is one of those mystical texts that transcends the border of conventional religion. What happens when this ongoing quest for renewal and the shedding of old feathers leads one beyond Judaism? Is that too to be seen as a liberation from Egypt's narrow straits?

TIF'ERET 'UZIEL

I heard this from Levi Yitshak, rabbi of Zhelichow:

Our rabbis said that Israel's soul passed out of them as God spoke each of the ten commandments. They raised the question: But if their soul passed out after the first commandment, how were they able to receive the second? They answered that God brought down some of the dew that He will use to revive the dead [at the end of time] and restored them to life (b. Shabbat 88b–99a).

The commentator MaHaRSHA objects to this: Why do they talk about receiving the second commandment? How could we even exist at all today if their souls had flown away? Why not ask that?

Levi Yitshak answered that the angels denounced the giving of the Torah from above, saying: "Grant Your glory to heaven" (Ps. 8:2)! Moses responded by saying: "Is there any theft among you? Or any hatred [to make you need the Torah]?" It is on this that the Talmud raises its objection. Once Israel's souls had "passed out of them," those souls were on the rung of angels, without bodies. Then how did the second commandment come forth, since Moses's answer to the angels' objection was no longer applicable? Was there any jealousy among Israel's souls? They too were like angels!

So why did Israel, and not the angels, receive the Torah? He answered that God "brought down the dew He would use to resurrect the dead." The emphasis is on "down." He lowered and humbled the spiritual life-force within them, so that it would be on a lower rung. Then Moses's answer became appropriate again. There would indeed be thievery among them, and all the rest, since the holy spirit of Israel had come back to earth.

෴

This early teaching of Levi Yitshak (he was rabbi in Zhelichow before settling in Berdichev) shows that this main theme of his teachings was there from the start. The Torah is for real human beings, given to help us create a human community here on earth, not just to help us reach toward heaven. God does us the favor of humbling us, even allowing some sin to appear in our midst, so that we will have the privilege of receiving God's Torah and with it, the task of turning darkness into light.

KEDUSHAT LEVI I (KEDUSHAT PURIM #1)

... they stood beneath the mountain.
(Ex. 19:17)

Rabbi Avdimi bar Jacob said: This teaches that the blessed Holy One held the mountain over them like a barrel, saying: "If you accept My Torah, it will be well. But if not, this will be your grave" (b. Shabbat 88a). Tosafot notes on this passage: Even though they had already said "We shall do" before "We shall listen" (Ex. 24:7), because they might have turned back due to the great fire, which caused them to faint. [The Talmud adds]: This raises a great objection to Torah [i.e., the question of whether it was willfully accepted].

... We need to understand what they meant by saying "We shall do" before "We shall listen." How do you accept something before hearing what it is? To understand this, we need to turn to the Passover Haggadah's verse "Had He brought us before Mount Sinai and not given us the Torah, it would have been enough." We have to ask what value there would have been in coming near to Mount Sinai without receiving the Torah.

Our sages say that "Abraham our Father fulfilled the entire Torah before it was given, even the laws of Sabbath food preparation on a festival [clearly a rabbinic innovation]" (b. Yoma 28b). How did Father Abraham know the Torah before it had been given? The 248 positive commandments of the Torah parallel our 248 spiritual limbs; Torah's 365 prohibitions are parallel to our 365 spiritual sinews. One who gazes upon his own spiritual limbs and sinews can know them all. Just as our bodily limbs require certain sustenance, so too is each of our spiritual limbs fulfilled by a particular *mitsvah*. And just as our physical limbs do not need to be taught what food they need, so too do our spiritual limbs grasp the *mitsvot* of their own accord. The very life-force of our spiritual limbs and sinews are the commandments themselves. Spirituality is a sublimation of our ordinary mind and thought processes; in its ultimately rarified form it is nothing other than the *mitsvot*....

So it was that before the Torah was given, Israel were able to apprehend all the positive and negative commandments. The reason we cannot do so on our own, through the mind, is because of our own corporeality, which serves as a curtain keeping us from seeing that spiritual light. But a person who transcends the physical self, in whom spirit overcomes matter, can see the Torah in his mind's eye.... So Abraham, whose physical self was so purified, perceived the entire Torah, all 248 plus 365 commandments, from his own limbs, before it was given.

That is what the author of the Haggadah meant in saying: "Had He brought us before Mount Sinai...." In preparing to receive the Torah ... their corporeal selves became so purified that they were able to perceive Torah before it was given, just like Abraham. Therefore "Had He ... not given us the Torah, it would have been enough...."

That is why our sages said that He held the mountain over their heads like a barrel ... even though they had already said "We shall do" before "We shall listen" (Ex. 24:7). In that moment Israel were pure and their minds clear. The divine presence shone upon them and they transcended their bodily selves. But when their minds would be less pure, they would still have to accept the yoke of heavenly rule....

◯⟋⟍◯

A personal note (AG): This was the very first Hasidic text on which I commented, nearly half a century ago. It still has great power, making it clear that the essence of revelation is nothing other than the inward journey, Torah waiting to be discovered within the self. The outer revelation, with all the barrel-over-the-head authority of *halakhah*, is only a backup system, meant to keep us in line when our mind wanders away from that inner truth our mind's eye has already seen.

BEIT AHARON

> The sound of the ram's horn kept growing very much [me'od] louder; Moses spoke [yedabber] and God responded aloud.
> (Ex. 19:19)

The word *me'od* contains the same letters as *adam*, "person." All the thunderclaps and lightning described by the Torah here were nothing extraordinary for God; it was all to teach the people forever. Receiving Torah is eternal; it happens in every generation and for all time....

Moses spoke. The form *yedabber* is actually the future rather than the past tense. In each generation Moses will continue to speak to each and every person. Moses will speak to anyone who seeks to become pure and accept the yoke of Torah. **And God responded aloud**, bringing sound into the word, linking word and thought [thus enabling us to hear Moses's words]. How greatly we should rejoice in receiving Torah, for we each receive according to our capacity and strength.

We must have faith that right now we can turn from our evil way and make ourselves pure.

⚭

This is the simple, direct message of Hasidism. The divine voice has never ceased speaking; Moses has never stopped teaching. Torah is given anew in each moment, if only our hearts are ready to receive it.

KEDUSHAT LEVI II

> "I am the Lord your God...."
> (Ex. 20:2)

Let us explain this verse in light of the following rabbinic teaching: "At the Sea of Reeds He appeared to them as a youth, and at Mount Sinai He appeared to them as an elder" (*Pesikta Rabbati* 21:5).

The blessed Holy One veils (*metsamtsem*, lit. "constricts") Himself in the worlds. However, at the Sea of Reeds, where there was a change in nature, He was not garbed in the worlds, and the Children of Israel saw the Divine unclothed. At Mount Sinai, however, the Holy Blessed One dressed Himself such that the worlds could maintain their existence.

In the writings of Rabbi Yitshak Luria, of blessed memory, clothing is associated with the symbol of hair. That is why at the Sea of Reeds God appeared to them as a youth without facial hair, without any worldly garb. When giving the Torah, God was revealed to them as an elder [*zaken/zakan*, "beard"] with hair, dressed in this-worldly form. This is alluded to in the words of our sages of blessed memory: "At the Sea even the maidservant saw that which the prophet Ezekiel did not see" (*Mekhilta Be-Shalah* 15:2). For Ezekiel and the other prophets saw God clothed in the world, as it were, according to the measure of the worlds. But at the Sea, everyone saw God unclothed.

At Sinai, however, God had to be covered in "garments" so that the Children of Israel would understand the Torah. That is why it is written [in the Rosh Hashanah liturgy]: "You appeared in the cloud of Your glory ..."; that is, by limiting and clothing His great light, for a cloud is a symbol of darkness.... The liturgist then explains why this [darkness] was necessary by saying, "... upon Your holy people to speak to them"; meaning that God spoke to them from within a cloud [i.e., garment], so that they could understand His holy words.

༺❀༻

If the theophany at the Sea of Reeds is a model of unabashed divine power, then the revelation at Mount Sinai is an example of God's power of restraint. Levi Yitshak teaches that the Divine must be limited in the moment of revelation in order to communicate with the people of Israel. It is through self-limitation, *tsimtsum*, that God transmits Torah to the Israelites. To live after Sinai—in the Land of Canaan, Poland, or elsewhere—means that we must become active partners in the covenant, knowing that God is present but that the divine presence is much subtler than in the grand moment of the Exodus. The "garbing of God" in religious forms helps us discover the God who is in fact "garbed" in every form of existence.

HAYYIM VA-HESED

> Moses said to the people: "Do not fear. For it is to test [*nasot*] you that God [*ha-elohim*] has come."
> (Ex. 20:15)

Our sages taught (*Mekhilta Yitro*) that [at Sinai] Moses was set off by himself, Aaron by himself, and the people below. They said to Moses: "You speak to us and we will listen, but let not Y-H-W-H speak to us, lest we die" (20:19), fearing God's great power. Then Moses answered: "**Do not fear**. God does not want you to have only the attribute of fear. [Fear represented by the name *elohim*, **has come** *le-nasot*, to uplift you.] God's intent is that this awe increase your love of God."

That is also the meaning of "God [*elohim*] tested [*nissah*] Abraham" (Gen. 22:1). The quality of *elohim* [fear, awe, judgment] sought to uplift (*nissah*) Abraham, who represents the quality of love.

❦

A very Hasidic reading of both the Sinai and the Abraham texts, the Torah's two most dramatic portrayals of the fear of God. Fear or awe is a vehicle; the goal toward which it leads is greater love.

Yitro
Round Two

OR: The interplay between love and awe is so common in these sources, with awe always coming first. But is it true? Does awe or fear lead to love?

AG: Think about it in human relationships. I'm in awe of the people I love. I'm awed by their ability to give, strength, generosity, or whatever it is. That awe increases my love for the other.

AM: Yes, but in human relationships this had better be mutual. Otherwise one partner is on the pedestal.

OR: But in this case it seems like a senior-junior love relationship. God and the person can hardly be equals.

AG: Maybe that's why the parental metaphor is so widely used in these texts, more than the Song of Songs erotic language. You need some of both.

OR: In romantic relationships too, there are indeed moments of awe; a kind of seeing deeply and appreciating one's lover.

AG: I guess that in the divine-human relationship there is also an attempt to mutualize. God's *tefillin* are supposed to say in them: "Who is like Your people Israel!"

OR: Remember all those Midrashic texts about humans and angels. God prefers real flesh-and-blood humans; God seems to want the adventure that comes along with being engaged with humanity.

AG: I'm noticing the frequency with which God's garments are referred to in these texts. Here we have that moment on eagles' wings, above all those feathers and garments. But do such moments really exist?

OR: Can I dare to say that I want to love God without any *levushim* ["garments"] coming between us?

AM: Or does this lead to paralyzing proximity? Would we just freeze up if we suddenly discovered neither we nor "the Emperor" was wearing any clothes?

OR: Can the candle love the torch? Or is its reality just wiped out when in the torch's presence?

AM: Maybe it's only the garment that allows us to love. Would the term "love" have any meaning without the garments that allow for our separate selfhood?

AM: So we might be glad for the cloud. We might even choose it, so as not to have to see too much.

Mishpatim

MA'AYAN HA-HOKHMAH

> If you acquire a Hebrew servant, six years shall he
> labor, and in the seventh he shall go forth free for
> naught [i.e., without payment].
> (Ex. 21:2)

I can interpret this verse in accord with our sages' teaching that "there is a
person who acquires his whole world in a single hour" (b. 'Avodah Zarah
10b). The Maggid Dov Baer noted that the word *sha'ah* ("hour") may be
related to a word for "turning," as in "to Cain and his sacrifice He did not
turn [*lo sha'ah*]" (Gen. 4:5). Sometimes by a single act of turning one can
repent so fully, with such great passion, as to reach a very high rung indeed.
That person turns toward God all at once, attaining all that he can.

But note that the sages still are careful to say that he acquires *his* world,
not *the* world.... This single act, with all its intensity, will not permit his
ascent step-by-step toward gaining inward fear and love of God. That
higher state is called the [spiritual] "Sabbath," and you have to work hard,
step after step, in order to reach it.

This is the meaning of our verse. Even should you attain a **Hebrew
servant**, [namely a turning toward God] all at once, still **six years shall he
labor**, working as during the six days of the week. **The seventh**, the true
Sabbath of inner fear and love without any intermediary, cannot be reached
by a single act of return. You may indeed have gone **forth free**, but it will
be *be-hinam*, **for naught**.

This reading of the verse is a sharp admonition against the easy path of "pop" religion, which must have existed in the eighteenth century, as it does in the twenty-first. Sometimes indeed you can have a great and sudden awakening, a gift from heaven. But unless you do the hard work of follow-up and growth, it will be for naught, a wasted opportunity. Without preparation there is no Sabbath.

NO'AM ELIMELEKH (FROM *TOLEDOT*)

> If [*ki*] a person [*ish*] opens a pit, or digs a pit and does not cover it and an ox or ass falls into it, the owner of the pit must make restitution. He shall return money [*kesef*] to the owner [of the animal], but the dead animal is his.
> (Ex 21:33–34)

The word *ki* (**if**) functions also as "when," implying that a righteous person, who can rightly be called *ish* (**a person**), has an obligation to open the pit. This alludes to the wellsprings of awe and holiness that can be opened in people's hearts.

Or digs a pit. This alludes to the beginning of the process of digging into people's hearts, and carving out awe and holiness. In this case **an ox or ass falls into it**, meaning that external forces will certainly come into play. **The owner of the pit must make restitution**, referring to the reward of the righteous person, for the Blessed Name who is the master and owner of all holiness and awe will reward this effort in the world-to-come.

But even beyond this—**He shall return money [*kesef*] to the owner**. There is a further reward: the awe and holiness that the righteous person has facilitated in others will come back to that righteous one. It will increase that person's own experience of awe and love and longing in the service of the Blessed Name. For the word *kesef* can also be interpreted as "longing," as in the verse where Laban describes Jacob's longing for his father's home (*nikhsof nikhsafta*, Gen. 31:30). Our verse implies that the longing and love will come back to the owner (the originator).

In this manner I have also interpreted the rabbinic saying: Words that come from the heart enter the heart. The heart that the words came from— those same words enter back into it and increase the holiness within it.

We are here reminded that the actual process of working with people is not an easy one. Hence we have the images of digging and carving. The Hebrew text regarding the external forces is not totally clear. It can be read either as a warning that this process will certainly awaken some of the darker sides of all involved or as a promise that those harsh aspects will ultimately fall away. Both, we hope, are true.

At the same time, the words that we offer as teachers from our open heart facilitate our own growth. That is the wonderful reward of teaching and one of the wonderful gifts that students offer.

MEVASSER TSEDEK

> If you lend money to My people, to the poor amongst you, do not act toward them as a creditor; exact no interest from them.
> (Ex. 22:24)

To explain this we must first understand another verse: "You [Moses] shall enjoin the Children of Israel to bring you clear olive oil" (Ex. 27:20). This means that even though you are Moses their teacher, who instills in them awareness [of God], you must "enjoin the Children of Israel." The word "enjoin" (*tetsaveh*) also means "to connect," as in "the entire world was created only for the sake of this bond" (*tsavat*; b. Berakhot 6b). If you connect yourself to the Children of Israel, then "they will bring you clear olive oil," meaning that they will draw down the highest wisdom for you, and you will be a pipeline for divine bounty in return. Similarly the Sages say, "This one came to teach and wound up learning instead" (b. Hullin 28a)—through the merit of Israel, illumination will be drawn to you from the highest wisdom, which is called clear olive oil.

This is the meaning of **If you lend money (*kesef talveh*)**—if you long to cleave to the blessed One. The word *kesef* refers to longing, as in the verse "You longed [*nikhsof nikhsafta*] for your father's house" (Gen. 31:30). *Talveh* suggests attachment and cleaving, as in "This time my husband will be joined [*yilaveh*] to me" (Gen. 29:34). Our verse continues: **to My people**— you must attach yourself to My people, Israel, and through this you will merit to cleave to the blessed One.

To the poor amongst you—I heard a teaching in the name of R. Yehiel Mikhel [of Zloczow], of blessed memory, about the verse "A prayer of the poor man, when he is faint" (Ps. 102:1): Your own prayer becomes acceptable when you join it to that of the poor. This is also the meaning of **the poor amongst you**: Attach yourself to the prayer of the poor, and then you will merit to cleave to the blessed One evermore.

⊘〰〰〰◡

The whole world was created for the sake of connection! The familiar play on *tsav* ("command") and *tsavta* ("togetherness") is here taken to new heights. Though based on a questionable reading of a Talmudic source, it joins together our longing for connection to God and the ties that link us to one another, including the special bond of caring for the poor. It is because we are joined together that the pure light from above flows down upon us.

How I wish Martin Buber were still alive, so I could show him this one!

ORAH LE-HAYYIM

> When you see your enemy's donkey [*hamor*] crouching beneath its burden, hold back from abandoning him. Release it together with him.
>   (Ex. 23:5)

Our sages said that **with him** means that you are obligated to help the donkey as long as its owner is with it. But if he walks away, saying, "The *mitsvah* obligates you [and not me]," you have no such obligation (*Mekhilta de-RaSHBI*).

There are people who do battle with the evil urge that seduces them to pursue pleasures of the flesh. They take on such serious self-afflictions, intended to break the hold of desire, that they break their bodies themselves. In seeking to escape the evil urge, they destroy their own bodies. Then when they turn to serving God, they find themselves unable. One cannot serve without a body. This is not the path that God has chosen!

... We have to struggle with our urges and break the body bit by bit, gradually, and using good sense. We do not seek to utterly destroy the body. Conduct that war with your urges cleverly and sensibly. Use the powers of that evil urge to serve God; turn the evil urge into an urge for goodness....

When you see your enemy's donkey [*hamor*] refers to the physical (*homer*), corporeal self of **your enemy**, the evil urge overpowering your body. You can so burden your body with afflictions that it is **crouching beneath its burden,** unable to do either good or ill. **Hold back from abandoning** it! Do not do this, but **release it together** *with* **him.** Help your body; lighten these afflictions. Do it bit by bit, carefully and proportionately, so that you do not harm yourself.

As time passes, you will see that God has helped you to turn the evil urge toward good. Use the energy and the passion of the evil urge to serve God. This is the intent of **Release it together with him**—help your body, do not destroy it. **With him** means that [you should work together] with the evil urge and make it into good....

〽

This text should be part of the required curriculum of every religious high school. It clearly shows the wisdom of Hasidism, going back to the Ba'al Shem Tov himself, in opposing the ascetic extremes sometimes associated with Jewish mysticism. But the lesson has to be learned anew in each generation. The urge toward extreme self-affliction, it seems, is one of the hardest to overcome.

ME'OR 'EYNAYIM (FROM *YITRO*)

> All that Y-H-W-H has said we will fulfill and hear.
> (Ex. 24:7)

When Israel said "we will fulfill" before "hear," a heavenly voice came forth and said: "Who revealed this secret to My children, one used by the ministering angels?" (b. Shabbat 88a).

How is it possible to fulfill before obeying, to do the deed before hearing what it is? And why did God take such particular pride in this formulation?

The truth is that human beings cannot remain on a particular rung with constancy, since "the life-force ebbs and flows" (Ezek. 1:14); it comes and disappears. When you are attached to God, you feel the pleasure of that surge of life. But then it vanishes and you fall from your rung.

Why does a person have to fall? The meaning of this contains secrets of Torah. One of these is the possibility of attaining a yet higher rung than one had previously reached. Every being is preceded by non-being. When you want to proceed to a higher rung, you need to lack for something first. Therefore you have to fall from your prior rung.

When you are in such a fallen state, you still need to struggle to rise up to God within your current existence. You need to have faith that "the whole earth is filled with God's glory" (Is. 6:3) and "there is no place devoid of God." God is there in your present state of being, though in highly reduced form....

This is the "doing" or fulfillment that comes before the hearing. Even as we fall from our rung, we cleave to God right where we are. Afterwards we begin to **hear** something, a hearing that really means "understanding." We rise to a higher rung. This is the essence of the Torah that Israel received, and the source of such great divine pride: we attained the great truth that you can be attached to Y-H-W-H always, not being cut off from God even when you fall. This is the essential Jewish path, the way we are to walk.

But how can you come to Y-H-W-H when you are in such a fallen state? Your very awareness and your mental powers have been taken away from you! Nevertheless, you come to know that "the whole earth is filled with God's glory"—even a state that is wholly earthbound, nothing but coarse matter, is filled with the glory of God. Y-H-W-H is called "the Life of life," meaning that the vitality of all life in the world, including that of beasts, cattle, birds, and humans, is God's own Self, the Life of life. God is the life-force within all that lives. When you are in that fallen state, think of this: Am I not alive? Who is this life-force within me? Is it not the blessed Creator? God is indeed present right here, but in this reduced form.

This is why the blessed Holy One said: "Who revealed this secret to My children?" It is the *Who* they contemplate when asking, "Who is the life-force within me?" that reveals to them the secret of how to do before they hear....

Of this King Solomon taught: "Do not say that your former days were better than these, for it is not out of wisdom that you inquire" (Eccles. 7:10). Some fools, when they fall from their rung, just lie there in the dust, not rising back up to Y-H-W-H. They say: "Those days were better than these! Then I was serving God, but now I am fallen!" Do not say this, "for it is not out of wisdom." "Wisdom [*hokhmah*] gives life" (Eccles. 7:12), and "life ebbs and flows." So it is meant to be, and the wisdom of that awareness will bring us back to God.

෴

There is no "place," no inner human state, in which we are utterly cut off from God. To receive Torah is to acknowledge this truth, to know that even in our lowest moments we are filled with the life-giving presence of Y-H-W-H. We only need to pay attention to life itself. This is a message to both the depressed and the doubting—but perhaps most especially to those for whom these two are deeply intertwined.

KEDUSHAT LEVI

> The appearance [mar'eh] of God's glory was like a consuming fire....
> (Ex. 24:17)

One who serves God through Torah and *mitsvot* brings about great joy above. But how do we know if God takes pleasure in our service? The test lies in whether the person's heart burns constantly with the ecstatic flame of God's service. If you have true passion and desire in serving the Creator, you must indeed be bringing such joy to God. You are receiving aid from heaven in these holy thoughts that fill your heart.

This is the meaning of **the appearance [mar'eh] of God's glory was like a consuming fire**. [The word *mar'eh* can also mean "mirror" or "reflection."] When you want to know if you are truly gazing upon God's glory and doing what pleases the blessed Holy One, see whether your heart is burning like a consuming fire.

⚙

This simple trust in one's own inner experience was welcomed in the Maggid's circle and reflects a certain beautiful naiveté to be found in Hasidism. But we may be sure that there was a hearer "across the table," perhaps the *Or ha-Me'ir*, who would have treated Levi Yitshak's embrace of the inner self as a faithful mirror with a bit more suspicion.

Mishpatim
Round Two

AG: This is a great moment of transition in the Torah text, a shift from narrative to code. It's as though we all woke up after sleeping off the great "high" of Sinai, and there was someone calling out: "Okay folks; here's what you signed up for last night!"

EL: Yes, but I see none of that in these Hasidic readings. There's really no difference between the way they read these texts and the way they read a *parashah* in the Abraham or Joseph narratives.

OR: Perhaps that's why we so much like these readings. They allow us to avoid *halakhah* as an issue, taking us right back to the core spiritual questions. Maybe Hasidism is convenient for us liberal Jews.

AG: "Convenient" is usually a dirty word in our circles. Is that how you mean it?

EL: I have a bigger problem. I'm wondering if we like these readings because we live so much in a Christian cultural context. After all, Christianity has been seeking to spiritualize the "Old Testament" for two thousand years, condemning us Jews for being too flesh-concerned in our readings.

AG: And we have always stood up to that and said: "Yes, that's just the point! Judaism is a religion of deeds, one that judges you precisely on how you act down here among real people in the concrete physical universe."

OR: Yes, but we also know the danger that lies in that approach. You get a Judaism that devolves into religious behaviorism, to be viewed through an anthropological lens. You can follow a trajectory from *tikkun ha-middot* [personal moral rectitude] to *tikkun ha-'olam* [restoring the world]. But how do you tie it all back to God and theology?

EL: These texts do nothing to bring the legal and the spiritual realms together. I wanted to see them diving into civil code sorts of questions and uplifting them to a spiritual plane. But they're not going there at all.

AG: There are lots of images of toil and digging here, hard labor. But it is an internal, spiritual digging. They all tend toward their key, unchanging question: What can this text, especially its specific wording, teach me about how to serve God? But the last texts also assure us of the great this-worldly reward we attain through giving and teaching.

Terumah

DIBRAT SHELOMOH

> Tell the Israelites to take Me an offering; from every person whose heart is inspired you shall take My offering.
>
> (Ex. 25:2)

We like to think that the songs and praise we offer to the blessed Creator magnify and make Him even greater, as they would an earthly king. But this is not the case. The Midrash says that we embellish the praises of a king of flesh and blood beyond what he deserves, but the blessed Holy One is extolled and yet remains infinitely more (*Tanhuma Shemot* 2). Regarding this the Talmud teaches: the best thing of all is silence. Like an invaluable pearl, anyone who begins to speak its praise diminishes it (y. Berakhot 9:1).

All the prayers we offer God are a diminution indeed. We try to squeeze the indescribably great divine illumination and life-force into letters. In the words of the *Tikkuney Zohar*, no thought can grasp You at all. We have spoken of this struggle many times.

Yet even so our efforts are quite dear to God and much beloved. By way of a parable: It sometimes happens that when a father and child are playing, the child grabs hold of father's beard, hair, or some other part of his head. The child pulls it down to his little face in order to play with him. This gives the father great pleasure, enjoying it even though it might seem annoying and an affront to his dignity. Were anyone else to do this, it would hurt him. But since the parent loves his child, and sees that the child loves him very much and longs for him as well, it is clear that the child does this out of love. The lesson is clear: even though our words and letters diminish the divine brilliance, [God cherishes them as an expression of our love]....

This is the meaning of **take Me an offering** [*terumah*]. "Even though [in prayer] you are bringing Me down to you, I consider this an act of great uplifting (*haramah*). Should you ask why, Scripture answers: **from every person whose heart is inspired**. I see their inspiration, great longing and their absolute dedication, and therefore **you shall take My offering**." ...

⟋⟋⟋⟋⟋

This moving metaphor of father and child sounds so much like ones used by the Maggid himself. In our songs of praise we cannot hope to fully capture the majesty of the Divine, but the love and desire that infuse prayers can express an affection for our adoring Parent that transcends words.

There is something of this in the biblical story as well. The momentous revelation at Sinai was beyond all words and description. One of our first attempts to deal with that experience was the Golden Calf, a misguided search to concretize the ineffable. In response, God gave us the gift of the *mishkan*. The Tabernacle, with all of its sacrifices and services, is a sanctioned expression of our unending and fully requited love for God. Though our offerings are by definition inadequate, they are beloved indeed.

OR HA-ME'IR

> Take an offering for Me ... acacia wood.
> (Ex. 25:2, 5)

RaSHI asked how they would have had acacia wood available to them in the desert. [He quotes a Midrash teaching that] Rabbi Tanhuma said: Our father Jacob foresaw by the holy spirit that the Children of Israel were to erect a Tabernacle in the wilderness. He brought cedar trees into Egypt and planted them, commanding his descendants to take them along when they would depart from there. [RaSHI assumes the identity of the cedar and the acacia trees]....

We can see their words as pointing to the seven holy qualities that are given to us to repair. "The heavens are the heavens of Y-H-W-H, but the earth has He given to humans" (Ps. 115:16). "Earth" here refers to those seven [earthly = emotional and moral] qualities given to humans. We need to repair them, to build them up; they are called cedars of Lebanon because they are drawn from the uppermost whiteness, the realm of [pure mind or] *binah* (*levanon/loven*).

Our father Jacob was teaching his children the way of God, how divinity flows forth through these qualities and the holy sparks that exist within all creatures. There is no place devoid of Y-H-W-H; the spark residing down in those lower places is that which gives life. It dwells in constraint and darkness, without a glimmer of light, until a sage comes along, one with an all-embracing and expansive mind, who finds a way to serve the Creator through it. This person devotes heart and soul to finding the source whence that quality is drawn, thus becoming aware of how to restore it to that place.

Now we can understand why the sages taught that father Jacob foresaw by the holy spirit the building of the *mishkan* in the desert. This refers to us. We Children of Israel are forever building up our entire selves to become dwelling-places for divinity. That is why they erected the *mishkan* from offerings there in the wilderness. This process has never ceased and goes on in every generation. We Israelites are called upon to build up the full form of *shekhinah* (= *mishkan*) by using our own entire selves. Thus our sages taught on the verse "Let them make Me a Tabernacle and I will dwell within them" (Ex. 25:8). The verse does not say "within it" but "within them"! This teaches that God dwells within every single one of Israel. This is what we have taught: that each of us must build up our entire self to be a fit dwelling for divinity. Then God indeed dwells within us.

This is what the holy *Zohar* meant when it taught that the form in which the world was created, the form of the *mishkan,* and the human form are all the same (2:149a–b)....

⟨⟩

This reading of the *mishkan* as a symbol for the Tabernacle within each human heart is widespread in Hasidic teachings. Here the very earthly elements required for it are linked to the earthly struggles the *hasid* must undergo to build that inner chamber. The search for God everywhere is here directed within the self, seeking to find the root of one's own best inner qualities and to bring them to life. The seven qualities, though rendered in various ways, may most simply be named as love, fear, beauty, triumph, gratitude, righteousness, and authority. For certain members of the Maggid's circle (the *Or ha-Me'ir* and the *Me'or 'Eynayim* in particular), it is the conversion and control of these, directed entirely to God's service, that makes one a *hasid*.

NO'AM ELIMELEKH

> Tell the people of Israel to bring Me an offering. Take these gifts from every person who is inspired to give. (Ex. 25:2–3)

The Mishnah teaches: "Do not be like servants who serve the master only for the reward. Be rather as servants who serve with no anticipation of reward" (Avot 1:3). Why were both halves of this sentence necessary?

There are righteous individuals who serve God by fulfilling the commandments. They are very careful not to transgress even the smallest commandment and do their best to observe it properly. Still, they are not at the level where these commandments bring about attachment and longing for God. Such people can anticipate a reward in the world-to-come.

Then there are righteous individuals who serve by means of their pure thoughts. They use the commandments to connect to the Creator with great passion and attachment, constantly witnessing the greatness of God. They draw the pleasures of the world-to-come to them and they enjoy (as it were) the light of the divine presence in this life. Such righteous ones do not anticipate the pleasures of the world-to-come because they are already enjoying them in this life.

... This is the explanation of the Mishnah: "Do not be like servants who serve the master only for the reward" refers to people who anticipate reward in the world-to-come. In saying "Be rather as servants who serve with no anticipation of reward," the Mishnah tells you to rise to the level where you are rewarded immediately at the moment of fulfilling the commandment, as we have explained. Use the commandments to cleave to God and draw pleasure to yourself.

This is the meaning of **bring Me an offering** (*terumah*, lit. "uplifting"). "Strive to enjoy the light of My divine presence in your life—uplift (*terumah*) and take it from the world-to-come." This is why RaSHI explains the words **bring Me** as "for My [name's] sake." The verse tells you to take and draw the blessed Creator to you and take pleasure in the divine presence. And to whom is this addressed? **Every person who is inspired** to serve the Creator by means of pure thought, and cleaving to God. From such people **take these gifts**.

CRUUNS

While this teaching does not reject outright the hope for a reward in the afterlife, it is certainly clear that the true reward is in the practice itself. In quite a few Hasidic tales and teachings, "world-to-come" is something to be transcended, bartered, or given up.

KEDUSHAT LEVI

> Like all that I show you—the structure of the Tabernacle and the structure of all its vessels—and thus shall you do.
> (Ex. 25:9)

RaSHI comments on **and thus shall you do**—for all generations. But the Tosafot object: The altar that Moses made was not equal to that made by Solomon (b. Shevu'ot 15a)! RaMBaN raises a similar objection.

But following our method, we can understand **and thus shall you do** as referring to something else. Really, the structure of the Tabernacle and all its vessels that had to be of a certain height, weight, and form were all ways of garbing or giving form to some holy spiritual entity. This followed the prophetic vision that Moses had on Mount Sinai, along with all of Israel. As they drew this holy inspiration into their deeds, so it was. This was the way that the garb or vessel, along with the Tabernacle itself, had to be made.

But we also know the Talmudic statement that "no two prophets prophesy in the same style" (b. Sanhedrin 89a). Each does so in his own categories. These follow the path of that person in worshipping God; in that very way does the spirit of prophecy appear to him. This means that Moses and the generation of the wilderness, following the qualities of worship and prophecy they attained at Sinai, had to construct this particular form of Tabernacle, structuring its vessels in just this way so that they would properly garb the spiritual lights of holiness. This is what Scripture means when it says: **Like all that I show you**—according to your framework of prophecy, so should the Tabernacle and vessels be.

Then Scripture adds: **and thus shall _you_ do**—for all generations. This means that in every generation, when you want to build the Temple, the structure should be in accord with the prophecy that is attained at that time. That should determine the form of Temple and vessels. Solomon did it according to his own worship and his prophetic spirit. The form he made followed that which he attained.

Thus RaMBaN's objection can really be dismissed. Of course his altar was different! That was the commandment—that they not do it always in one particular form, but in accord with the flow of prophecy that takes place then. That should determine the form of the earthly vessels.

⌀〰〰⌀

In this and similar passages, the early Hasidic masters make a bold claim for their right, even their need, to innovate in the realm of spiritual praxis (see the discussion of this in our introduction). Interestingly, this theoretical assertion was never used to justify large-scale change. In fact, early Hasidism was fairly conservative with regard to praxis, and later generations of leaders shifted the movement toward an ultra-conservative stance. But these passages remain a part of the Hasidic legacy. How might they be reinvoked today, in a very different age?

ORAH LE-HAYYIM

> On the table place the showbread, before Me always.
> (Ex. 25:30)

Scripture also says: "You shall eat, eat and be sated, and praise the name of Y-H-W-H, who has acted wondrously with you" (Joel 2:26).

That great light our master R. Dov Baer taught that the life-energy within the food is referred to as *okhel*, while the food itself is called *ma'akhal*, since it feeds (*ma'akhil*) the body....

We know that God created the world through Torah, and through Torah all the worlds continue to exist. The life-energy within each thing consists of the letters of Torah; within them is the inward light of Endlessness (*eyn sof*), hidden within the letters that sustain all.

On the verse "If you surely listen" (Deut. 28:1), our sages commented (b. Sukkah 46a–b): "If you listen to the old [familiar teachings], you will hear the new. The blessed Holy One's qualities are unlike those of flesh and blood. Among us, an empty vessel can come to hold things, while a full vessel cannot. But for God, a full vessel can indeed hold [new teachings]."

This is the meaning of "You shall eat, eat"—eat of the life-force of Torah, the sustenance within the food, "and be sated." Once you are sated by words of Torah, becoming a full vessel, then you will absorb the life-energy within the food....

If you attain that energy within the food, your soul will be sustained by its spirit, while your body is nourished by the *ma'akhal*, the physical foodstuff itself. Thus are soul and body joined together. Then "you shall praise the name of Y-H-W-H, who has acted wondrously with you," since this union of spirit and flesh is truly a wonder, sustained by this food.

Our sages taught that as long as the Temple stood, the altar was there to atone for us. Now it is a person's table [and the way we eat at it] that atones (b. Hagigah 27a). Surely they were referring to those who eat in this way, seeking out the life-energy and the holy sparks within the food [joining them] to their souls, allowing them to serve the Creator....

Thus **On the table place the showbread** [*lehem ha-panim*]. This means "the bread of inwardness" (*lehem ha-penimi*), the life-energy within the food. Place this upon your table; then it will be **before Me always**, called "This is the table that is before Y-H-W-H" (Ezek. 41:22).

⟨⁊⁊⁊⁊⟩

This is what the Hasidic masters mean when they speak of eating and drinking as ways of serving God. The this-worldly, non-ascetic affirmation is present, but the true goal is an inward spiritual one. This indeed requires a delicate balance.

Terumah
Round Two

AG: I am impressed that the *mishkan* remains such a powerful set of symbols to the Jewish imagination. It's very different from the Temple in that way. The Temple is a historical memory; the *mishkan* immediately seems to invite spiritualization.

AM: Yes, there is no mourning for the *mishkan*'s loss, which seems to so overwhelm all memory of the Temple.

OR: It's the ultimately accessible symbol for Jews in *galut*, the statement that you can create holiness anywhere.

AG: The play on *be-tokham,* meaning both "in their midst" and "within them," is so widely used; it can be turned toward both inner-life private devotion and building a sacred community as a dwelling-place for God.

AM: The sense of immersion is so strong here. God enters into us; we enter into God. The Midrashic parallels between Creation, the *mishkan,* and the self still seem remarkably powerful.

OR: We are still attracted to the notion of giving something, of having something valuable enough to offer, to God. That's why sacrificial language is so appealing. There is an assertion of human value in it that's very strong.

AG: The Kabbalists were much more daring when talking about sacrifice and *mishkan* than about prayer, precisely because it was theoretical in their day.

OR: Yes, but then Levi Yitshak comes along to tell us that it has to be done differently in each generation. How radically did he mean this?

AG: Or was he empowered to make such claims by the fact that he lived within a halakhic "safety net" that he knew was inviolable?

OR: And then how are we to follow him today, when that framework of self-limitation is lost? That's our big challenge.

❧

Tetsaveh

OR TORAH

> You shall command the Children of Israel to bring to
> you pure olive oil....
> (Ex. 27:20)

The sages taught that Bezalel, who constructed the Tabernacle, knew how to combine those letters by which heaven and earth had been created (b. Berakhot 55a).

The Tabernacle was the life of all the worlds. This can be understood by analogy to the soul. It is the life of the body, even though in itself it has no form. We name it in terms of the body, speaking of the life-energy that animates the arm or the leg. So Bezalel, in making the *mishkan* as the site of this universal life-force, had to understand how to bring life into the worlds, as well as the letters through which the worlds were created. Everything in the worlds was represented in the *mishkan*.

We are taught that "the world was created by ten divine speech-acts" (m. Avot 5:1). The Talmud notes, however, that "God said" appears only nine times in the opening chapter of *Bereshit*. It replies that "In the beginning ..." is also a divine utterance (b. Megillah 21b). But why doesn't the text use "God said" in this first case? Because this act of divine speech is beyond our grasp; only its lower manifestations can be known.... This primal utterance is the raw material out of which all further speech was to emerge.

The same has to be true with regard to the *mishkan*. Parallel to the primal utterance is the *menorah*, which even Moses had difficulty in grasping; it could not be shaped by any human, but formed itself. The *menorah* bore witness to the fact that God's presence now dwelt in Israel's midst. This is the **oil**; the brightness shines right on its surface just like light reflects directly on the surface of the oil. The rest of the utterances are the **olive**, with the oil contained within them.

That is why this chapter does not open with "God spoke to Moses" or even "God said": this "olive oil" is beyond our grasp. Even "saying," which would imply thought, is not appropriate here.

༄

Mishkan ("Tabernacle") and *shekhinah* ("divine presence") are forms of the same Hebrew root, meaning "dwelling." The most secret aspect of the mysterious construction is that of the *menorah*, the form of which had to be revealed by God to Moses. The Maggid suggests that the *menorah* is parallel to *keter*, the highest among the ten *sefirot* and unknowable to the human mind. The divine light shines forth from it so powerfully that we, paradoxically, are not able to see it.

ORAH LE-HAYYIM

> And you, command [*tetsaveh*] the Children of Israel
> that they bring to you pure olive oil....
> (Ex. 27:20)

The leaders of Israel, those who guide and teach the people God's ways and Torah, receive even more from those they teach. ["I learned much from my teachers, more from my compatriots,] but from my students most of all" (b. Ta'anit 7a). In the outflow of mind and awareness that comes from God, they receive more so that they can pass the flow on to others. Proof of this is found in the fact that all the years that Israel were in the wilderness because of the sin of the spies, divine speech stayed away from Moses [because he was not prophesying to Israel].

This is **And you, command [*tetsaveh*] the Children of Israel**. The word may be derived from *tsavta*, "togetherness." Join yourself to the Children of Israel, to teach them and lead them. **They** will **bring to you pure olive oil**: it is they who will cause that pure flow of wisdom and Torah to come upon you.

༄

A good reminder for all of us rabbis and teachers! It is not because of our merits or our brilliance that we receive the insights that we do; it is all brought about by those we teach.

'AVODAT YISRA'EL

> You command the Children of Israel to take unto you pure olive oil....
> (Ex. 27:20)

The Midrash (*Shemot Rabbah* 36:4) quotes the verse: "You call out and I respond to You; You long for the work of Your hands" (Job 14:15). This "longing," it says, is really desire. "In Your light we see light" (Ps. 36:10), yet You command us to kindle lights.

Job spoke this verse out of astonishment. "You call out and I respond," means this: "All the Torah we learn, all the prayers we recite, all the good deeds we do—they all come from You, Master of the World! You gave us the five parts of speech, the five senses, and 248 limbs. You give life to them all, sending energy into them at every moment. Without You we are nothing at all. So whatever holiness we call forth, it is really as though You were calling and doing it all. Our mind and strength are entirely Your own. So it really is as though 'You call out and [Your own] "I" (*anokhi*) responds to You.' All our deeds are nothing more that a response to Your call. When we turn ourselves toward the good, fulfilling Your pure will, it is just like [You] responding [to Yourself]."

Nevertheless, "You long for the work of Your hands"; You desire us, though it is all Yours.

We cannot penetrate Your secret, why it is that You should desire to hear Torah or prayer out of our mouths. The same is true of the candles. "In Your light we see light," yet You command us to kindle lights. "Thought cannot grasp You at all" (*Tikkuney Zohar* 17a); no one can understand the secret of this matter. All we have is "the revealed things for us and our children" (Deut. 29:28) to do. Amen.

The confession of undiminished astonishment is rare in a literature that is so used to providing answers and explanations. In the end, we are being told here, they are all worth nothing. All we can do is stand before the mystery—and go on living and following God's word in this strange world.

KEDUSHAT LEVI

> You shall fill the hand of Aaron and the hand of his sons.
> (Ex. 29:9)

There is no completeness in matters of this world. We always lack for something in the realm of physical pleasures. If you have everything else, you may still want for the pleasure derived from respect. Or you may want because of sexual desire. We always lack for something.

In the religious life, however, the one who serves is whole in every way. "Those who seek Y-H-W-H lack for no good" (Ps. 34:11). Thus the pleasure of serving God is greater than any other. Hold fast to the life-force of serving the Infinite, that which is whole in every way. Then you too will naturally be whole and lack for naught.

This is the meaning of **You shall fill the hand of Aaron and the hand of his sons**. God told Moses to see that he bring Aaron and his sons to that level where they would cleave to holiness. When they came to feel the pleasure of that sublime joy, their hands would be filled with all good and they would lack for nothing.

That is why this period [of dedicating the Tabernacle] is called "the eight days of *milu'im*," meaning "fulfillment." This was when the *shekhinah* came to dwell among them, and they were filled with joy, because of that holiness.

Who ever said that religion was opposed to "the pleasure principle"? It is indeed all about pleasure, the deepest form of human satisfaction, which is also the "sweet savor" that brings pleasure to Y-H-W-H.

Tetsaveh
Round Two

AG: There are two sources of pure oil, a symbol for spiritual blessing and fulfillment, listed here. Our first text sees it as flowing forth from the most mysterious source, the unutterable beginning point of all existence. The second sees it flowing from the relationship between teachers and students, the teacher being blessed by the flow he/she receives back in the course of that communication. Then our fourth text is about fulfillment itself, what it means to be filled with God's presence.

AM: It makes some special sense that these explanations are placed next to one another. Yes, the dynamic flow between people, here seen as exchange of mind, is indeed a source of creativity, what we might call "getting one's juices going." But that in no way detracts from the mystery of it all and our sense that it is indeed a gift of God.

EL: The relationship between people, whether student-teacher, friendship, or coupling, becomes the locus for that mystery. In effect the relationship becomes a *mishkan*, a "place" in which God's glory dwells.

OR: In a post-Temple Judaism it has to be that way. We don't have the *menorah* or other sacred object that holds the presence; we have to reignite the divine light through relationships.

AG: Maybe that is why we are told that once there is no altar, it is either Torah or "a person's table" that takes its place in atonement. Both Torah, transmitted between teacher and student, and the table are scenes of relationship.

AM: These teachings were all spoken around a table. Yes, they were the master's words, but it was the presence of the students that helped bring them forth. Good students do that to you; in their presence you may say things you hadn't known were in you. It is they who brought them forth.

OR: Let me be personal and talk about our experience right here, in these conversations. There is a lot of giving taking place here. We are conducting a series of intimate conversations about that which is ultimately beyond language. But something of that "beyond" slips into the conversation itself.

EL: Like a lot of our best learning and teaching, there is a space created here for opening our hearts, both to one another and to God. This is the sort of moment R. Nahman meant when he talked about turning teachings into prayer. The learning itself becomes an act of devotion.

AG: In our Sephardic/Hasidic liturgy we say *ve-notnim be-ahavah zeh la-zeh*; it is only "through love" that we "give permission" or make space for one another "to sanctify our Creator." The work we are doing here is such an act of love.

Ki Tissa

NO'AM ELIMELEKH

> When you count the heads of the people of Israel by their numbers....
> (Ex. 30:12)

The Talmud teaches: "The western candle (of the *menorah*) would remain lit and he [the priest] would light the other candles from it, and beginning from it would set their wicks and oil [*metiv*]" (b. Shabbat 22b).

The words of our sages allude to the role of the *tsaddik*, who is referred to as the western (*ma'aravi*) candle. The Talmud describes Babylon (*Bavel*) as a place where there is a mixture (*belulah*) of Mishnah, Gemara, and *aggadah* (b. Sanhedrin 24a). The *tsaddik* also contains a mixture (*me'urav*) of various modes of holy service: love and fear, reverence for God, learning, prayer, justice, repentance, acts of kindness, and others like these. The *tsaddik* is referred to as the "combined" (*ma'aravi*) light, containing this mixture (*'eruv*). *Ma'aravi* can also allude to pleasantness (*'arevut*) and sweetness, for the *tsaddik* is pleasant (*'arev*) and sweet in many ways.

This is the meaning of "he would light the other candles from it." Through connecting to the *tsaddik*, the people also light their own candles, which are their souls, with love and fear of the blessed Creator.

"From it he set [*metiv*] their wicks and oil" implies that by means of the *tsaddik*, the blessed One brings goodness (*metiv/tov*) to the world with many forms of blessing.

This is why God said to Moses: **When you count** [*tissa*] **the heads** [*rosh*] **of the people of Israel**. It means that when you raise (*tissa*) their hearts to the peaks, to those upper worlds that are called *rosh*, so that love, fear, and holiness enter their hearts, do so **by their numbers** [*pekudeyhem*], that they will be visited (*pekidah*) [with blessing]. The *tsaddik* issues a decree (*poked*) and the Holy One fulfills it.

⟳⟳⟳

The *No'am Elimelekh* is setting a goal rather than describing reality. Like the *tsaddik*, a teacher for the community must have multiple modes of spiritual engagement, offering varied paths of engagement in order to reach the people. In our day, this requires investing tremendous effort into "feeling at home" in multiple disciplines, without the satisfaction of total mastery of any. The mastery ultimately achieved is that of service and the satisfaction of seeing the people around you "light their own candles."

At the same time, the *No'am Elimelekh* makes the point that spiritual welfare is not divorced from the practical needs of life. The spiritual leader's responsibility does not end with lighting the candles. Making sure the wicks are trimmed and the oil is there requires constant attention.

TIF'ERET 'UZIEL

> ... tablets inscribed on both their sides....
> (Ex. 32:15)

This means that words of Torah are indeed "like a hammer splits the rock" (Jer. 23:29). There are reasons [in interpreting a legal passage in Scripture] to say "Pure!" and reasons to say "Impure!" and similar cases. This is the writing **on both their sides**. One [person's view] may differ from his friend's as widely as possible, but "both are the words of the living God."

⟳⟳⟳

Note how far Hasidism is from scriptural literalism or "fundamentalism." This is an important lesson Judaism has to teach in our world today. Intense piety, love of God, and even reverence for Scripture do not require exclusive devotion to any single reading of the text.

TSEMAH HA-SHEM LI-TSEVI

> Now, if You will bear their sin—but if not, erase me
> from Your book that You have written.
> (Ex. 32:32)

RaSHI comments on **if You will bear their sin**: "It will be good." He feels the absence of a closing phrase [to this conditional sentence]. But to me it seems that the verse concludes properly with **erase me**, that is, "Whether you bear their sin or not," **erase me** [is the conclusion to both openings].

This is like a king's servant who deeply loves his master. He saw that the king's son had rebelled and brought disgrace to his father. It occurred to him that if the king forgave his son, taking on all that shame, he, the king's servant, would not be able to watch. But if he didn't forgive, the servant would also not be able to bear watching the king's pain as he punished his son. Therefore he said ["in either case"] **erase me**. That is why the preceding verse reads: "Please—this people has committed a great sin."

Another reading, based on an interpretation I heard of "Please—this people has committed a great sin." [Moses is saying:] "I have sinned," but in a lesser way—only in thought. But because of this, they have sinned greatly, since he is their root and they are his branches.

Based on this reading, Moses was seeking to find out whether he was the cause. **If You will bear**—I will know it is **their sin**. The root was without sin, and therefore You will forgive. **But if not**, the root too must have sinned in thought, and in that case **erase me**.

These readings reflect the deep attachment the leader feels both to God and to his people. His willingness to die is not the challenge to God that it seems to be, but is either an admission of responsibility (but what is Moses's "sin in thought?") or a touching unwillingness to witness the tragedy about to unfold. God fortunately denies Moses's request.

OR TORAH

> I will give grace to whom I will give grace....
> (Ex. 33:19)

This may be understood in accord with the *Zohar*'s teaching that words brought forth without love and awe cannot fly upward (*Tikkuney Zohar* t. 10, 25b). Speech and voice are a gendered pair, speech being female [representing *malkhut* or *shekhinah*] and voice male [*tif'eret*]. These together comprise *vav* and *heh*, the last two letters of God's name Y-H-W-H. If they emerge without love and awe, representing *yod heh*, the first two letters, which is their birthplace within the name, they bring about division. But the whole purpose of saying the words, both in prayer and in study, is to raise them upward to their [united] Source!

Just as the world's creation began with the twenty-two letters of the alphabet, as the *Zohar* understands God's creation through Torah (1:5a), so does life-sustaining energy flow into all creatures by means of those letters. Our task is to reverse this process, causing words and letters to flow back upward into their Source. This is the process: you link word to word [your word of prayer or study to God's word in creation], voice to voice, breath to breath, thought to thought. These represent the four letters Y-H-W-H. If you do this, all your words fly upward to their Source. You bring your words into God's presence, causing God to look at them.

This is what it means that prayer is "answered." This looking is itself a sort of flow downward, reaffirming the existence of all the worlds. There is no passage of time above.

The divine wellspring gushes forth in each instant. The flow is constant, and its nature is to do good and give blessing to God's creatures. But if you pray or study in this way [with love and awe], you may become a channel for that spring, bringing its blessing and goodness to the entire world....

This is the meaning of the verse **I will give grace to whom I will give grace**. The word *asher* [here meaning "to whom"] has two other meanings. One has to do with praise, as in *ashrey* ("blessed"), the other with seeing, as in *shur*. [The particle *et* is at the center of this verse, composed of *aleph* and *tav*, representing the twenty-two letters.] Read the verse to mean: The one who offers praise (*asher*) by means of those letters, I will turn and see (*asher*). In this way I will then give grace, for the looking itself is the answer to prayer and petition....

⟨ornament⟩

This teaching is a key witness to the abstract theology of the Maggid, in which both prayer and study are transformed into a meditative process, raising the elements of speech and thought back to their source in God. The technique is to bind each stage of one's own inner uplifting to that stage of the Divine as it flows into life. It is significant that the emotional qualities of love and awe are not to be left behind in this journey, but are seen as essential to the very process.

The Maggid's understanding of God's answering of prayer represents Hasidism as a highly refined system of mystical thought. His disciples, seeking to create a popular movement, chose to allow this notion of "answering" to be read on a much more worldly level.

KEDUSHAT LEVI

> ...You may see My back, but My face will not be seen.
> (Ex. 33:23)

Scripture says: "The wise child brings the parent joy" (Prov. 15:20). We are also taught, "Wisdom comes from *ayin* [Nothing]" (Job 28:14). The essence of wisdom is brought forth when a person looks into the Nothing. When you do so, you realize that you lack reality on your own but that the life-force within you comes from that Nothing. You then come to cleave to your root in the Source of life. This attachment of the self to the Creator offers a "garment" to the Creator; this is called by the prophet "covering the Ancient One" (Is. 23:18). The rabbis refer to this when they say that "Israel sustain their Father in heaven" (*Zohar* 3:7b), since clothing is a form of sustenance. That too is why wisdom is called "the returning light," for it is by wisdom's light that you return and attach yourself to your Root. This is hinted at in "I will teach you / '*aleph* you' wisdom" (Job 33:33). Switch around the letters of *aleph* and you get *pele*, "wonder." Your whole life, when you are attached to the root, is one of wonder, beyond comprehension....

So this is the meaning of **You may see My back, but My face will not be seen.** When you look into the Nothing, you become negated. How, then, could your eye be seeing, when you yourself do not exist? Therefore **you may see My back**—when you are on this level of looking into Nothingness, this is what you will see.

But the *ayin* that causes anyone who looks into it to be negated is called Y-H-W-H. The power to look into that *ayin* is called *Ehyeh*, "I shall be." When Israel were in Egypt [as slaves, they had no access to the future; *Ehyeh* represents the future tense] they had not yet gained the ability to gaze at *ayin*. [Therefore the name *Ehyeh* is revealed only at the Exodus.]

Here Levi Yitshak offers a striking personalization of the primal Creation process as described by Kabbalah. You bring wisdom forth from your own inner "Nothing," thus giving to God an embodied ("garbed") presence in the material world. This is effected by the power of human wonder, the ability to marvel at the modest degree of vision we are granted in this life. As we delve deeply into that wonder (*pele*), we are transported back to the realm of cosmic oneness (*aleph*).

Ki Tissa
Round Two

OR: In this *parashah* where Moses stands up to God and offers his life for his people, the *Or Torah* offers an overly subtle notion of prayer. Does God *really* answer prayer? His position sounds more like that of Maimonides than like what you'd expect of a Hasidic master!

EL: The others offer a much more robust *tsaddik*, one who is present to all sorts of people and cares about their woes. To be a leader, you've got to deal with people's needs.

AG: This has everything to do with building a movement. Some of the Maggid's followers saw that the purely mystical teaching would not work for ordinary people.

EL: The *tsaddik's* own spiritual life might inhabit a different plane, one where he prays only for the *shekhinah* and has no personal stake in specific prayers being answered. He is aiming for *bittul*, self-negation, after all.

AG: Yes, but it is precisely this that makes him so attractive to those who want their own prayers answered! This pure *tsaddik* is a blank slate when it comes to desire. If he takes up my petition, how could God deny him?

OR: But even in the Maggid's abstract teaching, God is *hesed*, wanting to flow and bless. The *tsaddik* has to become the personal face on this, the human channel that allows God's blessing to flow.

AG: The *tsaddik* personifies God. That sounds an awful lot like incarnational theology to me.

OR: Judaism should have no problem with incarnation, as long as we are *all* the incarnation of God. That's just another way of saying *tselem elohim*, the divine image.

AG: Yes, but here it's not all of us, just the *tsaddik*.

EL: I'm more interested in the psychology of this, the role the *tsaddik* is taking on. He's being pushed into the father role, becoming the earthly incarnation of the divine parent. What should he do? Can he dodge this role, or must he accept it?

AG: What does the *tsaddik* communicate? Is it a body of teachings, the "content" of the Hasidic message, or is it his own self that he is giving?

EL: How about the future rabbis we are all involved in training? What do we want them to give to their congregants: the "message" of Judaism or their own personal love and caring?

AG: Both, of course. Wrapping these together is what the rabbinate is all about!

ᕼᕼᕼ

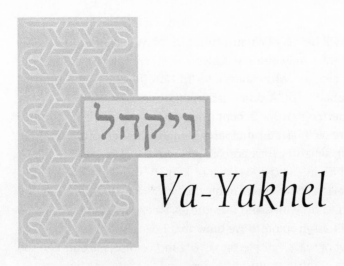

Va-Yakhel

ME'OR 'EYNAYIM (FROM NITSAVIM)

> Moses assembled the whole community of Israel, saying: "These are the things God commanded to do. Six days shall work be done and the seventh day will be holy."
> (Ex. 35:1–2)

Why is **shall work be done** written in this passive form? This seems to indicate that the work is done on its own....

"Know Him in all your ways" (Prov. 3:6) means that everything you do or see should be in accord with the Torah that lies within it. This requires total faith that all things come about in accord with Torah. This is what the prophet Habakkuk meant by summarizing all the commandments in one (b. Makkot 24a): "The righteous shall live by his faith" (Hab. 2:4). Faith lies at the root; with faith you will surely fulfill "Know Him in all your ways," thinking that it is not you, but rather the Torah, that is doing this commercial transaction, or whatever it is. It is the Torah within it [that is active]. By Torah's hand the act gets done on its own, then garbing itself in you the particular person, working through your limbs and speech as you fulfill the *mitsvot* that lie within this deed....

This is what Moses is teaching the people. Even though it is necessary to engage in labor, know that it too is Torah. **These are the things ... Six days shall work be done. These are the things** [or "words"] means that the work that gets done on the six days is also by the hand of Torah. Then

the seventh day will be holy. When you act in this way all through the six days, the seventh will surely be holy, for you will have drawn holiness into the entire week. "The one who makes an effort on the eve of the Sabbath will eat on the Sabbath" (b. 'Avodah Zarah 3a).

The six days are referred to as *hol* ["weekday" or "profane"]. The real meaning is like that of "I have placed sand [*hol*] as a border to the sea" (Jer. 5:22). God willing, when our messiah comes there will be "a day that is entirely Sabbath." Then "all the workers of iniquity will be scattered" (Ps. 92:10); all the "shells" will disappear. Only the holy will exist! But here in our exile, we still need to draw holiness into the six weekdays, the times when holiness faces obstacles in its path. We draw that holiness forth by living out "Know Him in all your ways," not letting the "sand" of *hol* [surrounding the "sea" of wisdom or Torah] become a barrier.

⚬〰〰〰⚬

This is a Hasidism that dignifies worldly labor, recognizing it too as a setting for God's presence. Later Hasidism sometimes misread it to mean that you do not have to labor but should engage in Torah alone. But that is not what is being taught here. It is only by a faith-based transformation of our weekday world that we can hope to merit the holiness of Shabbat. An important lesson, too much forgotten.

TSEMAH HA-SHEM LI-TSEVI

> Each woman [*kol ishah*] who was wise of heart in her hands wove and brought her weaving.... All the women whose hearts lifted them up in wisdom wove the goatskins.
> (Ex. 35:25–26)

[In the first verse,] **in her hands** appears in the singular form, while **wove** is in the plural. Further, why is there need for both this verse and the one that follows, with some differences between them?

I have taught that the Feminine above [*shekhinah*] includes all human women, as is known; She is therefore called *kol ishah*, "the entirety of womanhood" (cf. *Zohar* 1:228a). This is **each woman [*kol ishah*] who was wise of heart**. *Shekhinah* is also called "the lower wisdom," deriving from the thirty-two [*lev*, or "heart"] pathways of wisdom above. **In her**

hands refers to "She holds the distaff in her hands, and her palms grasp the spindle" (Prov. 31:19). **Wove** [in the plural] refers to the [earthly] women who did the weaving. This is similar to what is said about the truly pious, who might pray all day long (b. Berakhot 35b). "How will their work get done?" "If they are so pious, their work will get done by itself," by the hands from above. This would come about through the revealing of upper wisdom.

But the second verse, **All the women ... wove the goatskins**, says that the women had to arouse themselves from below, so that their **hearts lifted them up**, rising upward....

⟨∞⟩

Read this text as a women's version of the preceding one. Yes, the curtains for the *mishkan* were woven by *shekhinah* Herself, acting through the hearts and hands of Israel's women. Yet it was still they, by their own efforts, who got the work done. Our appreciation of the ways God is acting in and through us does not allow us, even for a moment, to hold back from stretching our own souls to reach toward heaven.

KEDUSHAT LEVI

> The work was sufficient for them for all they were to do, and more.
> (Ex. 36:7)

There are two words here that seem to contradict one another. If it was "**sufficient**," what is the "**more**"?

... "Bezalel knew the permutations of letters through which heaven and earth were created" (b. Berakhot 55a). God placed wisdom, understanding, and awareness in their hearts. God grants this power to the righteous of each generation. As the *tsaddikim* engage in Torah and offer new interpretations, they are creating a new heaven and a new earth. In constructing the Tabernacle, its builders directed their holy spirit to be in precise accord with divine wisdom, performing acts of union and permutations [of letters] with each vessel they formed and each deed they undertook. Had they wanted to direct their labors in accord with expansive mind, they could have gone on endlessly, for the spirit of God was upon them. But they had to put limits on their work. Thus they left room for the righteous still to come along in the future to teach about the construction of the Tabernacle, each of them using their minds to uncover secrets of wisdom in every word and in each vessel. Thus they would bring about ever new acts of sublime union.

In creating the world, God left over some of the creative energy, putting a limit on Creation in order to leave room for the righteous yet to come to be creative as well. So too with the building of the Tabernacle. That is why Scripture says both **sufficient for them** [and **more**]. **Sufficient** means that they placed limits on their work. **For all they were to do**, setting it up so that it would bring about unification in the upper mind.

They carried this as far as their own minds would permit. But **more** means that they left room for the righteous and wise in every generation, who would hear and learn of the erection of the Tabernacle, to continue the building and add of their own mind, as far as their own understanding can reach.

⚬⚬⚬

If the building of the Tabernacle is indeed parallel to the creation of heaven and earth, as the sages teach, it must have the same open-ended quality, leaving room for the participation and partnership of new minds as they arise in each generation. It is only a short stretch to say that in this teaching Levi Yitshak understands that both the natural order and human civilization are in a constant state of evolution and the sacred forms of religion must evolve with them.

HAYYIM VA-HESED

He made the ark of acacia wood ... coating it with pure gold both within and without....
(Ex. 37:1–2)

Moses was so attached to the blessed Holy One that his individual existence was negated in the face of God's greatness. He did not see himself at all.

Now "gold" stands for the fear of God (gold = *din*, the left side). Fear (*yir'ah*) has the same letters as "sight" (*re'iyah*). You can only fear One you see. When the human mind steadily contemplates the greatness of God, we fall into a state of awe.

So Moses made something just like himself: he covered the wood, which is the bodily self of the ark, with gold, which stands for fear, **both within**

and without. Note that when Scripture says "Moses! Moses!" (Ex. 3:4), the notes indicate no pause between the names; he paid no attention to his bodily self at all. But in "Jacob! Jacob!" (Gen. 46:2) there is a break between them. Sometimes Jacob did pay attention to his physical self, even though his intent was to raise it up to God. That is the meaning of our sages' saying of Jacob that "his bed [*mittato*] was whole" (*Va-Yikra Rabbah* 46:5), meaning that even his turning (*hattayah*) toward the physical self [conceiving all those children!] was in order to make it more perfect.

⊙ⱲⱲⱲ☉

Both the human self and the Tabernacle are seen as microcosms, miniature re-creations of the sacred order. Here a detail of the *mishkan*'s construction is strikingly described as an outer reflection of Moses's own inner state. Jacob provides a more accessible model; his bodily needs remain present to him, but he works only toward their perfection. It is not his "bed" that is perfect (meaning that all of his offspring were righteous), but rather all his turnings toward worldly things were for the sake of greater wholeness. So should ours be as well.

Va-Yakhel
Round Two

EL: This week the texts all seem to be speaking of the same thing. Who is doing God's work? Are we the active ones, or is God? What does it mean to do God's work?

OR: We have to do the work, but God is doing it, too. This takes different forms: in the *Me'or 'Eynayim*, it is "Torah" working; in the *Tsemah*, it is *shekhinah*. They see a need to strike a balance between God acting through you and the real need for "arousal from below," your own efforts.

EL: Do you make yourself a better tool for God's service by doing or by refraining? Look at the *Hayyim va-Hesed*'s distinction between Jacob and Moses. Who is the proper model?

OR: Moses is so impressive as depicted here, cleaving to God with no self-consciousness.

AG: Yes, but it's by covering himself with *yir'ah*, the *fear* of God. That means maintaining some sense of distance. Even if *yir'ah* is "awe," it still involves a holding back.

EL: Precisely! It's his *yir'ah* that leads him to self-negation. It's being obliterated by one's fear of God, not simple intimacy.

OR: We see this time and again in Hasidism: *yir'ah* is essential to the mystical journey toward self-transcendence. It's not just an end in itself.

AG: That's the great challenge to us moderns in this material. Are we capable of that emotion? We have such a strong sense of self-empowerment and have been taught how positive that is. When do we get beyond it to say, after all, "I am the servant of the blessed Holy One"? Or can we?

EL: Some of it has to do with choices we make. Is it my task to go out into the world, seek injustice, and then try to right it? Or should I just be working on myself, making myself into a more perfect vessel, and then wait for God to choose how to use me?

OR: In conversations like this, I feel something living and breathing in our relationship to these texts. They raise the key questions of our own religious lives.

AG: Something we rarely talk about is how God is working within *us*, using us as a vessel, in a project like this one. Sometimes I feel that I am being led to, or given understanding into, a particular text because a force greater than myself wants it to be available to a reader I don't even know. But I consider it a great privilege; I am grateful to God for using me in this way.

פקודי

Pekudey

RAV YEEVI

These are the precepts [*pekudey*] of the Tabernacle,
Tabernacle of testimony, commanded by the mouth
of Moses, the service of the Levites....
    (Ex. 38:21)

Scripture tells us that "You who cleave to Y-H-W-H your God are alive this day" (Deut. 4:4). But is it possible [the sages ask,] to cleave to God, who is an all-consuming fire (b. Sotah 14a)? It is through fulfilling the commandments, the 248 yeas and the 365 nays, that we cleave to Y-H-W-H. Every *mitsvah* is that name of God, since that word's first two letters *mem* and *tsade* represent *yod* and *heh* in a reverse alphabet. God and Torah are one; by studying Torah and doing *mitsvot* both in deed and in desire of the heart, you draw the *shekhinah* upon yourself....

This is the meaning of **These are the precepts [*pekudey*]**—the *mitsvot* are the visitations [*pikudim*] of God. If you fulfill them, you bring about a dwelling-place for the *shekhinah*. She is represented by the letter *heh*, dwelling with the person. That is: **the Tabernacle**, *ha-mishkan*.

It is called **Tabernacle of testimony** because when we see that the *shekhinah* dwells with someone, this testifies that the person fulfills the Torah, meriting that presence. But this applies not only to the specific precepts mentioned in the Written Torah. Not only these bring about this indwelling of *shekhinah*, but all those things of which we are taught that they were "pathways given to Moses at Sinai," even the oral tradition....

This is what is meant by *pakad*, meaning "visited" or "made present," **by the mouth of Moses**: the Oral Torah as well.

The service of the Levites refers to service that causes you to cleave and be joined to God, as in the verse "this time my husband will be joined to me" (*yilavveh*—the naming of Levi—Gen. 29:34). It means "joining together" and this is the meaning of "Levites" as well....

ᏊᎲᏅᎲ

The work, *'avodah*, is that of cleaving to Y-H-W-H. The tools for that work are the commandments, in which God is present to us. But the term *pekudey* pushes toward an expanded notion of *mitsvot*; it is every bit of oral tradition that makes God present, helping us build our inner *mishkan*. Could the message be any clearer?

HESED LE-AVRAHAM KALISKER (FROM MISHPATIM)

These are the precepts of the Tabernacle [*mishkan*], the Tabernacle of testimony.
(Ex. 38:21)

Everyone knows the rabbinic teaching on this verse—"the Tabernacle [*mishkan*], the Tabernacle" mentioned twice, for twice it was taken in pledge (*nitmashken*) on account of our sins (*Tanhuma Pekudey* 5). The same idea is in the Talmud (b. 'Eruvin 2a)—why is the Temple referred to as *mishkan*? When our sins multiplied and our debt grew, it was taken in pledge for our sins. For this reason we live in exile in the physical realm.

This applies to our spiritual life as well, as each of us can discover within our own self. The holy books teach that everything written about the *mishkan* applies to every person as well.

To understand this you must realize that spiritual exile is just as real, and even more so, than physical exile. Spiritual exile refers to the imprisonment and concealing of the inner point of vitality by multiple garments and coverings ... as it says: "I will conceal, conceal My face at that time" (Deut. 31:18). The Master of the universe [or the cosmic single One] dwells concealed behind many coverings created by the dominance of the material world and by the ascendency of the seven evil attributes. The "seven nations" regarding which we are commanded, "Leave none of them alive, totally destroy them" (Deut. 20:16–17), are a way of speaking about these evil attributes. This is because they are always in opposition to the inner core of life in a person, and the "exile" of a person's spiritual vitality is caused by these seven attributes and their derivatives.

In our physical exile we are dispersed among seventy nations, all branches of the original seven. This is because in the world of evil, things are forever separating; it is a world of fragmentation. On the other hand, in the realm of holiness everything comes together in simple unity.... This should be the guiding principle of your service [spiritual work] as you attempt to redeem your soul and life-force down to its innermost point, freeing it from external forces. Thus you bring [your inner] *mishkan* back into light and eternal freedom.

A powerful lender who is compassionate toward his debtor might allow the pledge (*mashkon*) to be left in the borrower's home, set aside in a special place not to be touched until the loan is paid back. Then the pledge can be used again, and the borrower is redeemed from his pledge.

Thus the BeSHT says: The verse "my soul's redemption is near" (Ps. 69:19) teaches that just as there is a general redemption for all of Israel, so also there is individual redemption for each soul of Israel. Despite what you know of your own coarseness and how immersed you are in the material world, devote your entire will and all your heart constantly to find healing for your soul, to set her free. This involves breaking through the body and material tendencies until you reach their Root in the supernal worlds, the world of freedom.

◌ﻌﻌﻌﻌﻌ◌

Here we see a clear example of the Hasidic way of refocusing Jewish tradition on the internal spiritual work of the individual. Without ignoring the historical reality of exile, the "real" story of the destruction of the Temple is the individual experience of alienation, of living in a fragmented world and life. Only through overcoming personal weaknesses that stand between you and the experience of the unity of all being can "personal redemption" be achieved. All your qualities can be raised up and returned to their sublime Source, the root of all freedom.

ORAH LE-HAYYIM

All the work of the Tent of Meeting was completed.
The Children of Israel did all as Moses had
commanded them; thus did they do.
(Ex. 39:32)

Isn't the verse backwards? Shouldn't it first say that Israel did all Moses commanded, and then that the work was completed? And why the repetition of **thus did they do**? Further, why is **was completed** in the feminine [and passive] voice? Why not say, as it does below, "Moses completed the work" (Ex. 40:33), in the masculine [and active] form?

... Our sages taught that "Bezalel, [who built the Tabernacle,] knew the permutations of letters by which heaven and earth had been created" (b. Berakhot 55a). The Tabernacle was a microcosm, a paradigm of the world. In making each thing he had to consider the permutations by which the aspect of the world being represented had been created. This is "to consider designs" (Ex. 35:32).

So too **the Children of Israel**, meaning these masters of wisdom. The word *yisra'el* is consonantally the same as *li rosh*, "I have a mind." When erecting the Tabernacle, they were considering the meanings of each command and the Torah's inward intent in the building of the Tabernacle and its vessels. Torah has seventy "faces," as is known (*Be-Midbar Rabbah* 13:15). Those masters of service were contemplating the inner direction proceeding from every one of them as they were doing the work.

The root of the word *va-tekhal*, used here for **completed**, can also refer to longing and desire, as in "my soul longs" (*kaltah nafshi*; Ps. 84:3). This is the meaning of [*va-tekhal*] **all the work of the Tent of Meeting**—it all brought about a desire above to have the *shekhinah* dwell in the work of their hands. Their intent reached above this way because **the Children of Israel did all as Moses had commanded them**, bearing all the inner meanings and intentions that had been passed on to Moses regarding each commandment of the building, in all its seventy "faces."

This is why it says: **thus did they do.** *Ken* ("thus") is numerically seventy. Their intent reached upward, causing desire that *shekhinah* dwell below. They did not have the power to bring this about, even with all their intentions and high thoughts. But the *shekhinah* herself came to feel a passionate desire to dwell below. That is why *va-tekhal* is in the feminine, [referring to *shekhinah*'s desire]....

∽∞∞∽

Although the grammatical point is quite a stretch, this reading reflects the ancient view of the power of holy places, well preserved in the Kabbalistic tradition. The inward intentions of the builders were so strong that they aroused a desire of *shekhinah* "above" to descend to earth. How interesting it is to see that here the masculine force is the human one, trying to attract the feminine divine presence to the home we humans have built for Her.

Pekudey
Round Two

EL: How important the *mishkan* is to them! It's the essential spiritual paradigm for bringing God into this world.

AG: That's already true in the *Zohar*, where so much attention is devoted to these seemingly obscure parts of the Torah.

OR: But this is all about the movement inward, the spiritualization of Judaism. "Redemption draws near to *my soul*."

AG: That's true, but remember it's also the ideal way of talking about sacred space for Jews in *galut*, exile.

EL: But for them it's inner space. The revivalist message is that the search for meaning is constant, and these passages are used to stoke that inner fire.

AG: I'd put it this way: the Torah is being read as an instruction manual for bringing God into both world and self.

OR: I feel the tension here between the Hasidic proclamation that "all the world is filled with God's glory!" and the need to construct a *mishkan*, to bring God's glory into the world.

AG: One of my very favorite *midrashim* is the parable about this. "What is the *mishkan* like? A cave at the shore of the sea. The sea comes up and fills the cave, but the sea is no less full." Have you seen Thunder Hole at Acadia Park? That's what it's like.

EL: But the important point is that the *mishkan* can be set up anywhere. This means the same for your life, both your daily life and your inner life. Every place and situation can become a *mishkan*.

OR: It is precisely because "the whole earth is filled with God's glory" that you can build a *mishkan* anywhere. But you do have to build it! The act of *hamshakhah*, drawing it forth, requires a real human struggle.

וִיקְרָא

Sefer Va-Yikra

The Book of
Leviticus

וto the right: ויקרא

Va-Yikra

ME'OR 'EYNAYIM I

> He called to Moses; Y-H-W-H spoke to him from the
> Tent of Meeting.
>   (LEV. 1:1)

The matter is thus: Blessed Y-H-W-H brought us forth from Egypt. Right then He gave us the commandments of Passover and circumcision. Then He split the sea for us, afterwards walking us through the wilderness, leading with a pillar of cloud by day and of fire by night. Then he gave us the Torah and after that commanded us to erect a Tabernacle so that "I might dwell within them" (Ex. 25:8). Scripture does not say "within it," but "within them."

This is like a person who has always dwelt in a place of darkness, never having seen light. If you brought him right out into daylight, he would not be able to stand the brightness. You have to expose it to him gradually. First you make a narrow opening, so that he can see just a bit of light. Then you broaden it until it becomes a window. Only then can you take him out into the open air and show him the light.

So it was with Israel. In Egypt they were immersed in fifty measures of defilement. Had He shown them the brilliance of His presence immediately, they would not have been able to bear it. They needed all these steps along the way. But the whole purpose was "Let them make Me a Tabernacle that I might dwell within them."

The author is introducing his homilies to *Va-Yikra*, trying to show why this book lies at the center of the Torah. He uses a version of the well-known parable of the man dwelling in a cave (deriving from Plato's *Republic*) as a way of saying that all the Torah's narrative has been leading up to this point: the moment of the call to serve. The whole story of Exodus, including the elaborate instructions for the Tabernacle, is preparation for "He called to Moses."

So too our own narratives. All of our life stories up to this moment are there to prepare us for that call. The Hasidic reading of *be-tokham* as "within them," rather than "in their midst," means that the call comes to each person. The Tabernacle is being prepared within our heart; it is from there that the word calls to us. Everything else leads up to this.

ME'OR 'EYNAYIM II

He called to Moses; Y-H-W-H spoke to him from the Tent of Meeting.
(LEV. 1:1)

Our sages taught: "When a person is walking through a dangerous place [and cannot stop to recite his prayers in full], he should recite a short prayer, saying: 'In every time of passage, may their needs come before You.' On this passage the Talmud comments: 'Even when they turn toward transgression ['*ibbur*/'*averah*], may their needs be revealed to You'" (b. Berakhot 28b). [The "danger" is taken to be the danger of sinning.]

God is present in reduced form within every one of Israel. Even the most wicked person contains God's presence. This is seen in the fact that every sinner has some flashes of conscience. This is God calling out and saying: "Return to Me!" But the person just doesn't understand that this is blessed Y-H-W-H calling out to him.

That is why **He called to Moses** is written with a miniature *aleph*. God the cosmic *aleph* is present in miniature form within each Israelite, calling us to return. These are our pangs of conscience, but we do not perceive them as God's own call to us. Thus **He called** is written anonymously in our verse. But when the person understands that this is the voice of God and turns back toward the Creator, then **Y-H-W-H spoke to him from the Tent of Meeting.** When you go to commit a sin and God prevents you from doing so by some means, this too is God speaking to you, calling out: "Come back to Me! How long will you chase after your trivial pursuits?"

This is the "short prayer" the rabbis meant (b. Berakhot 3a). Pray to "shorten" or cut off those forces that separate you from God. "Save Your people, O Y-H-W-H, even when they turn toward transgression!"

⚭

The call of God is present in each of our lives. None of us, despite both our sinfulness and our claims of disbelief, is so far from God that we have no voice of conscience. But recognizing conscience as the voice of our Creator, speaking at first "anonymously" within us, and identifying that call as belonging to the One who has created us and creates us again in each moment—that can be a long journey indeed. We need a "short prayer" for that moment—one that will shorten our journey to that recognition and the change in our lives for which it calls.

NO'AM ELIMELEKH I

> He called to Moses; Y-H-W-H spoke to him from the Tent of Meeting.
> (LEV. 1:1)

It looks as if it would have been better to write, "God called out to Moses and spoke to him," so we knew who called Moses, rather than the existing form of the verse, which is not specific and leaves the identity of the caller unknown.

This can be understood based on the following teaching of the *Zohar* regarding the miniature *aleph* written at the end of the word *va-yikra*. It is small when the *shekhinah* is out of place (1:239a).

Our verse describes the time the people were in the desert rather than at the central place of God's glory, the Temple of Jerusalem. The verse therefore begins with **He called Moses**, implying that She [the *shekhinah*], the miniature *aleph* called out to Moses. But following the initial call, Moses turned to the service of the Creator with all his power, sanctified himself greatly, and achieved the rung of **Y-H-W-H spoke to him**, [Y-H-W-H being] the divine name of compassion.

This is also the meaning of King David's prayer "You Y-H-W-H are enthroned forever" (Ps. 102:13). In our times, due to our sins, the *shekhinah* is in exile. Therefore, when intending to judge the people of Israel, the Holy Blessed One, out of compassion, has to rise from the throne of judgment and sit upon the throne of mercy. In contrast, the messianic time will be an era of absolute compassion, and there will be no need to rise from the throne of judgment and shift from one throne to the other.

This hope is expressed here and in the prayer "You Y-H-W-H are enthroned forever; Your throne endures for all generations" (Lam. 5:19). *Shekhinah*'s glory is [still] present among the righteous. The prayer offered is that despite the decline of the generations (b. Shabbat 112b), may Your throne be upon us in every generation, and in your great compassion may the light of Your presence hover over us. Amen.

⟋⟋⟍⟍⟍

As opposed to our Temple-centered past or our messianic future, our current reality is that of exile. In this reality it is human effort that determines whether God will manifest in harsh judgment or in expansive compassion. In this teaching the Hasidic master has transformed the lament over the destruction of the Temple into a prayer that the righteous people succeed in their work of being the seat of divine compassion in the world.

MAGGID DEVARAV LE-YA'AKOV (#97)

> ... a fire-offering, a pleasing aroma to Y-H-W-H.
> (LEV. 1:9)

The world was created only for the sake of the blessed Holy One's delight and the pleasure God takes in our doing of the *mitsvot*. God speaks and God's will is done. The essence of that pleasure lies in our ecstatic anticipation of doing that which pleases God, fulfilling the divine will. The deed itself is not the essence. Indeed sometimes a person studies Torah just because of an inclination to do so, the same way others pursue business, each following their own desires. What difference is there between them?

God's essential pleasure lies in our desire to serve. Scripture says: "Y-H-W-H your God is a consuming fire" (Deut. 4:24). Read it to mean "A God who consumes fire!" God's main sustenance and pleasure in the commandments is that of our passion's fire in doing them. It is **a fire-offering, a pleasing aroma to Y-H-W-H....**

But enthusiasm alone has nothing in which to garb itself. For that it needs the deed.

༄

The Hasidic rebalancing of religious values is here presented very clearly. "Ecstatic anticipation" is the real point—our burning desire to do God's will, which rises to heaven.

KEDUSHAT LEVI

> If a person offends and performs any one of the commandments of Y-H-W-H that should not be done, and is guilty....
> (LEV. 4:27)

[What is "a commandment of Y-H-W-H that should not be done"?] It is well established that when serving God properly, you should think little about yourself and more about the grandeur of the blessed Creator. However, if a person performs a *mitsvah* and thinks that he does so perfectly, God disregards the *mitsvah*. This is the meaning of the statement **If a person offends**. What is the offense? The person performs the *mitsvah* in a manner that it **should not be done**. Meaning, God disregards this *mitsvah* because of the person's attitude, but the individual assumes that he serves God properly. It is for this reason that he is **guilty**.

༄

What is more important, the performance of a *mitsvah* or the attitude one has when performing it? This is a subject of ongoing conversation throughout Jewish intellectual history. While the early Hasidic masters place great value on the performance of the *mitsvot*, they are most concerned about *kavvanah*—the inner intention of the person carrying out the commandments. Here Levi Yitshak warns us about the danger of becoming self-satisfied in our service of God. Our spiritual practice should engender in us a deep sense of humility as we grow in our awareness of God's infinity and our finitude. The Berdichever intends this teaching to serve as a warning against haughtiness, but as he warns elsewhere, we must also guard against thinking too little of ourselves, lest we become paralyzed by our imperfection.

NO'AM ELIMELEKH II

> Or if one touches a human impurity, anything that
> causes a person impurity, and it be hidden from him,
> [when later] he knows and is guilty....
> (LEV. 5:3)

This alludes to an evil person who has become impure through sins and
mistakes. This gives power and vitality to the supernal persona of unbounded
evil.

The *tsaddik* wants such a person to turn back from sin, and not transgress
any more. This is achieved by **Or if one touches**, meaning that the *tsaddik*
must "touch"—turn toward this matter and deal with it in his own self....

Further, the verse teaches us that it is to be done in this way: **and it be
hidden from him**—the *tsaddik* must do it in secrecy and hiding.... **[When
later] he knows**: this process will become known to the sinner, who will feel
the sin and be overcome by a great fear and motivation for repentance....

And is guilty [*ve-ashem*]; this means the same—the person will be
devastated (*meshomam*) and confused by the act done and will not do it
again.

☙

The "supernal persona of unbounded evil" alludes to a doctrine common in the *Zohar* and particularly in the *Tikkuney Zohar* (cf. 63a, 98b)
that contrasts supernal figures of good and evil. The alignment of positive forces in the universe creates the supernal figure of good, while the
alignment of negative forces creates the evil figure. Just as good deeds
of people strengthen and give life to the cosmic figure of good, evil
deeds strengthen and give life to the cosmic figure of evil. The *No'am
Elimelekh* proposes that the motivation to bring change into other
people's lives should be based on an awareness of the cosmic impact of
each individual life.

In this piece the *No'am Elimelekh* offers a mode of bringing about
change that is directed first inward rather than outward. Rather than
beginning by attempting to uproot the "impurity" in the sinner, the
No'am Elimelekh asks the would-be spiritual leader to approach and
touch the aspect of impurity that he/she is trying to change in others in
his/her own self.

This is a form of activism that seems not to involve active outreach at all. The specific work addressing the evil the spiritual leader wants to change is done in the privacy of inner soul work. This inner work will ultimately impact the leader's interactions with the world, and through this inner process he/she will facilitate development in others as well. In order to do this, we who seek to lead others first have to find the very evil we are trying to change within our own selves.

Va-Yikra
Round Two

AG: The call to Moses gives the Hasidic authors, and us as well, a chance to reflect on the notion of divine call. Much of their reflection concentrates on this single opening word of the *parashah* and the book. What does it mean to be called by God? Does it happen only in biblical times, in literal descriptions like those of Abraham, Moses, and Samuel? Or is any life of devotion a response to God's call, even if it is not heard in words?

The word "vocation" (lit. "calling") is not used very often among Jews attracted to a life in the rabbinate or other positions of Jewish spiritual leadership. I wonder why not. Are we too afraid to sound "prophetic" in describing our own lives? And is that a healthy modesty or an unhealthy awkwardness about expressing our own faith?

EL: I think we have a healthy fear of people hearing the voice of God insofar as it represents an absolute authority that is beyond human judgment. Yet the Hasidic masters may be offering an alternative. When the *No'am Elimelekh* or the *Kedushat Levi* stress the ways in which people influence God's manifestation in the world, the absolute authority of "God's word" is somewhat muted by the recognition that we can only access it through our individual human prism. Given this awareness, is it still meaningful to refer to such a calling as "God's voice"?

OR: Much as I struggle with my own understanding of who or what God is, the metaphor of God's call remains compelling to me. This is true both in my private life and in my life as a Jewish professional. In this context the term "discernment" has been helpful. Like "calling," this word is used much more widely in Christian circles than in Jewish ones. Discernment, as I understand it, requires that we set aside time to explore our core values and commitments and the needs of the world around us. In my experience, much of this practice involves listening—to the wisdom of our sacred traditions, to the voices of trusted conversation partners, and to our own inner voices. As vague as it may sound, I feel comfortable talking about such experiences as attuning myself to "God's call."

Tsav

Or Torah

> Y-H-W-H spoke to Moses, saying: "Command
> Aaron and his sons, saying: 'This is the Torah of the
> ascending-offering, the offering on its stake upon the
> altar, all night until the morning the altar's fire shall
> be lit upon it.... Fire shall constantly burn upon it; it
> shall not go out.'"
> (Lev. 6:1–2, 6)

RaSHI says that the word "command" here shows a special urging,
applicable now and in all generations. Said Rabbi Shim'on: Such urging is
especially needed when there is a cost to the pocketbook.

If this passage is to be understood in its simple sense, why is "special
urging" needed in order to command two daily sacrifices? What "cost to
the pocketbook" is there for these two single communal offerings by the
whole people of Israel? The additional sacrifices were much more costly!
And how are these "applicable now and in all generations"? The two daily
sacrifices were ended when the Temple was destroyed.

We therefore must interpret this passage to conform with our sages'
teaching that "whoever studies Torah is like one who offers all the sacrifices"
(b. Menahot 110a). **This is the Torah of the ascending-offering** [means
that Torah itself rises as an offering]. You may read this entire passage as
pointing in that direction. **Command Aaron and his sons, saying: "This
is the Torah of the ascending-offering"** ... "special urging ... in all

generations" because Torah will never be negated; "it may not be forgotten from the mouth of his seed" (Deut. 31:21). We are being urged to study Torah, that which rises higher than any burnt-offering. What sort of Torah study is this talking about? **The offering on its stake**, meaning teachings offered in ecstasy and close attachment to our blessed Creator, not things that flow only outward from the lips. "Any word that does not come forth in awe and love does not fly upward" (*Tikkuney Zohar* t. 10, 25b) and is not called an **ascending-offering**.

Upon the altar refers to the person, who is called an altar. "Y-H-W-H *elohim* created man out of dust of the earth" (Gen. 2:7); from the place of his future atonement, the "altar of earth" (*Bereshit Rabbah* 14:8). **All night**, all the days of a person's life on earth, which are like a night, **until the morning. The altar's fire**, the fiery teachings of Torah, **shall be lit upon it** [or "within him"], with ecstatic attachment to the Creator.

The passage ends with **Fire shall constantly burn upon it; it shall not go out**. Not for a single moment. "You shall contemplate it day and night" (Josh. 1:8). This indeed requires "urging, now and for all generations," that it will never be ended. Rabbi Shim'on emphasizes this, for he also taught: "If a person concerns himself with seeds at the time of planting and with harvest at its time, when will his learning get done? Therefore study Torah always, and your work will be accomplished by others" (b. Berakhot 35a). This advice indeed is at great "cost to the pocketbook," if one is to leave all worldly work behind and only study Torah.

⸎

Interestingly, the Maggid does not seem to take a stand on the advice of Rabbi Shim'on, but only reports it as a way of explaining his view. The early Hasidic masters were in tension with the elite community of scholars who devoted themselves only to Torah study, while at the same time advocating a life wholly devoted to God's service. Read this text in conjunction with the following one, where a sharper stand is taken on this same question.

ME'OR 'EYNAYIM

Y-H-W-H spoke to Moses, saying: "Command Aaron and his sons, saying: 'This is the Torah of the ascending-offering, the offering on its stake upon the

altar, all night until the morning the altar's fire shall
be lit upon it.... Fire shall constantly burn upon it; it
shall not go out.'"
(LEV. 6:1–2, 6)

The rabbis say that the word "command" here shows a special urging,
applicable now and in all generations. Said Rabbi Shim'on: Such urging is
especially needed when there is a cost to the pocketbook.

This comment is difficult. Weren't all the commandments given for
all generations? And what is the special cost to the pocketbook of this
"ascending-offering"? There are other commandments that can be more
costly, and they are not introduced by a special use of "command" to urge
their observance.

Now the real purpose of the Torah God gave us is that through it we
would bring our evil urge to submission. That is why the *Zohar* refers
frequently to "struggling" with Torah, the same word that is used in the
Aramaic translation of "a man struggled with him" (Gen. 32:25). This is to
say that by means of Torah one can struggle with the evil urge and defeat
it, since the light within Torah can turn the urge back toward goodness
(*Eikhah Rabbah* Petihta 2). Through Torah one can cleave to our blessed
God, who is hidden within Torah. He *is* the light within it....

This is the meaning of "I have seen people of ascent, but they are few"
(b. Sukkah 45b). Through Torah you can rise upward, even setting aright
the damage you had done. This is **the Torah of the ascending-offering—**
that you can rise upward. **All night until the morning**—you can raise up
even your own darkness and turn it into the light of dawn....

Fire shall constantly burn upon it; it shall not go out. By the light
created in the first six days, Adam was able to see from one end of the
world to the other. After he sinned the light disappeared; "the blessed Holy
One hid it away for the righteous in the future." Before that sin the light
was directly visible; only afterward was it hidden in the garments within
which God hid the light, the garments of Torah. This is hinted at by the
verse "God made them garments of skin" (Gen. 3:21), which, in R. Meir's
Torah was written as "garments of light ['or/or]" (*Bereshit Rabbah* 20:12)....
Thus did R. Meir teach the people of his generation, enlightening their
eyes by showing them how to get to that light hidden within the Torah.
Not everyone can reach that light, hidden as it is within the garments. But
R. Meir (his name means "shining" or "bringing light") showed them the
way.

Now we continue where we started. Through Torah a person can rise upward. **This is the Torah of the ascending-offering.** How? This comes about by approaching the hidden light, by looking into that hidden light that extends from one end of the world to the other ("vertically" as well as "horizontally").

This is the meaning of **command,** meaning "urge, now and in all generations." That which happens now and that which will take place in the future will all be the same to you. Present and future will become equal ... in the hidden light of Torah there is no distinction between now and the future. So Rabbi Shim'on had to refer to the "cost to the pocketbook [*kis*]." If you study Torah and come to that hidden light, there it is no longer hidden behind any *kissui,* "covering" or garment. This Torah is like it was before Adam sinned, before God made the garments of light in which it came to be dressed. The light was directly revealed! This is the meaning of *hesron kis,* the "cost to the pocketbook"—the words really mean "the covering is removed"!

That is why the rabbis said: "If only they would abandon Me [*oti*] and keep My Torah!" (*Eikhah Rabbah* Petihta 2, on Jer. 16:11). When you study Torah, you see letters (*otiyot*) before you. When you then meditate upon them, the gates of wisdom open up and you are able to understand the Torah in a mindful way. How do you get there? All you saw, after all, were letters....

It is not that you are so wise and capable of learning on your own; Y-H-W-H is the helpful Teacher. "Y-H-W-H grants wisdom from His mouth, awareness and understanding" (Prov. 2:6).... Indeed, a person who studies in some other way, not seeking the hidden light, will not find much use in such learning. He may become expertly learned in matters of religious practice, that is to say, in the letters of Torah. But that is not what God intended; that is not what is important. Through Torah you are supposed to rise higher than the letters, to that place where the light is without garments. You rise to the place where Torah is light, where it was before Adam sinned and there were no "garments of skin."

This is if only they abandoned *oti,* "My letter," the learning that is mere letters, and truly "kept My Torah," that which rises above the letters, the hidden light.

⌒⍟⍟⍟⌒

Here is Hasidism as its most polemical self. The *Me'or 'Eynayim* is arguing against those who regard only the outer letters, not seeing what dwells within them. The goal is to rise higher than the letters, to the "light without garments." How can we do this without leaving the outer world, even Torah itself, behind? Here there is none of the ambiguity of other texts. The purpose of the outer is only to bring us to the true light within. Otherwise, it is of little value.

TESHU'OT HEN

> Y-H-W-H spoke to Moses, saying: "Command Aaron and his sons, saying: 'This is the teaching of the rising-offering, the rising-offering upon its hearth on the altar....'"
> (LEV. 6:1–2)

Why does **saying** have to be repeated? And what is **this** coming to exclude? The rabbis also taught that the word "command" usually comes in connection with alien worship (*Zohar* 1:27b). It thus seems truly odd and incomprehensible that the text says: **Command Aaron**.

We can explain this in connection with our teaching that [the first two commandments of Sinai] "I am Y-H-W-H your God who brought you forth from the Land of Egypt, the house of bondage" and "You shall not have yourselves any other gods alongside Me" were spoken in a single utterance (*Tikkuney Zohar* t. 22, 63b). The blessed Holy One came forth with a promise for us: As long as "I am Y-H-W-H your God"—as long as you remember Me, and that there is no place where I am not present— then surely "you will not have any other gods," meaning that you will not fall into any sin that involves idolatry. Every sin that a person commits has about it some whiff of idolatry; this comes about because of forgetfulness. "No person commits a sin unless a spirit of folly enters him" (b. Sotah 3a), making his heart swell and causing him to forget. This is like pushing the *shekhinah* aside; thus pride is considered a form of idolatry, as the Lurianic writings teach.

The opposite is also true. "I shall dwell with those who are down and of lowly spirit" (Is. 57:15). Also "There is no forgetfulness before Your Throne of Glory" (b. Berakhot 32b). This quality [of humility] causes a person to be mindful. A sense of "I am Y-H-W-H your God" leads to "In our humility we have memory" (Ps. 136:23). We become mindful and no longer "have other gods" and do not come to sin. This is the secret of the amulet said in the Lurianic writings to aid memory, based on the verse "I am Y-H-W-H your God...."

When the messiah comes, God willing, we will all become completely aware; divinity will be recalled always. I have heard something like this in the name of the Ba'al Shem Tov, on the verse "I, I, am your consoler" (Is. 51:12). When you know there is no "I" but "I" alone, and no other—then you will be consoled. A wise teaching.

We have taught elsewhere that sometimes a *tsaddik* experiences a fall, not because of any personal lack, but for the sake of others who are "branches" [to the *tsaddik*'s "tree"], so that they be uplifted. This is sometimes experienced as a state of spiritual "sleep" or dormancy. We have explained it around the verse "I have placed My bow in the cloud" (Gen. 9:13). The *tsaddik* is called a "bow," but that bow is placed in cloud or darkness. This is to get the righteous one to repent for some small bit of sin brought about in him by the people. Thus the *tsaddik* can raise them up along with himself, planting some thoughts of return within them. The sin, of course, was no real deed, but just a distracting thought or a moment of forgetting God.

So too I heard in the name of the Ba'al Shem Tov: "Happy is the person to whom Y-H-W-H accounts no sin" (Ps. 32:3), who read the words to mean "Happy is the person for whom not thinking of God is the only sin"!...

So we come to the meaning of **Command Aaron and his sons**. God is telling Moses to remind them that sometime "command," or alien worship, will happen to them, meaning that they will forget Y-H-W-H. They need to realize that this is only **the teaching of the rising-offering**; it is there for the purpose of raising up the people, to arouse thoughts of return in their hearts concerning the deeds of their hands. When this course of events becomes known to them, their hearts will boil with great wonder, leading them to mend their ways. **This is the teaching of the rising-offering** means that the descent was for the sake of ascent. "The priest's lips must guard the awareness" (Mal. 2:7) that this is a way of stretching out one's arm to awaken people to return.

⟨ﻬﻬﻬ⟩

"Priest" in this verse, as throughout the Hasidic reading of Leviticus, stands for the *tsaddik* or, even more broadly, for anyone who seeks to serve Y-H-W-H. For such a person the second "commandment" is an assurance following the first. If you truly know "I am Y-H-W-H your

God," you will surely "have no other gods beside Me." But alas, there is no constancy in this assurance. There is no religious life with utter consistency, lacking in moments of "fall," coming in the form of self-doubt, disillusion, or even despair. The challenge to the would-be *tsaddik* is to turn those moments around, to perceive the "teaching" in them, and thus to see them as opportunities and as gifts of God.

NO'AM ELIMELEKH

> And the priest shall wear his linen garment, and linen pants upon his flesh; and he shall raise the ashes to which the fire has reduced the burnt-offering on the altar and place them beside the altar. Then he shall undress and put on other clothes and take the ashes out of the camp to a pure place.
> (LEV. 6:3–4)

... You should wear a **linen garment** (*mido bad*), meaning that you should work on your personal qualities (*middot*) through contemplative reflection (*hitbodedut*). **And linen pants upon his flesh**, meaning you should reflect further "to cover physical nakedness" (Ex. 28:42), meaning [to overcome your sexual] lust.

And he shall raise the ashes.... It is impossible [at first] to overcome all the qualities you were born with. Instead, you should elevate them to holiness. For example, if you tend toward anger, set aside external angers and direct your anger toward the wicked, and likewise with other qualities. **And place them beside the altar** means precisely that—overcome your tendencies and bring your qualities, anger or any other, to holiness.

Then he shall undress and put on other clothes. This teaches you that after this stage there is a greater achievement. It is to totally strip yourself of all those qualities and **take the ashes out of the camp**. This means that those tendencies you were born with will never again rise within you, and you will live in great holiness.

〰️

Every person is a priest in the temple of his/her own soul, working step by step toward holiness. "Cleaning out the ashes" to ensure impure fires don't start up again is a vital part of that work.

Tsav
Round Two

AG: These texts are all classical examples of the spiritualization process at its height. The externals of the Temple cult are all transferred to the realm of the heart. But it's especially interesting to see how the mystical and the moral are completely wrapped together here. Those two sides of Hasidism, the struggle for moral self-improvement and the mystic quest for the original, ungarbed Torah are the same quest.

EL: It's worth noting that in their day books like these were called *sifrey mussar*, "moral treatises," or *sifrey yere'im*, "books for the God-fearing."

OR: I'm so struck by the attempt to find light within Torah, to go back to the garments of light, or even before them. But what about the dark places? Sometimes we are repelled, even horrified, by some things we find in the Torah. What do we do about them?

AG: But that's why the Hasidic masters are such wonderful guides. Look what they're doing here! These are all passages about *terumat ha-deshen*, essentially taking out the ashes from the sacrificial altar. Look how they transformed them!

EL: They are totally unafraid to ask the question "But what does this mean to *us*?"

OR: Yes, that's why they're so attractive. The kind of transformative reading they do with irrelevant passages opens the door for us to do the same, even with offensive passages.

EL: Our answers will of course differ from theirs. But the fact that they were already asking the question makes them our spiritual ancestors; we stand on their shoulders.

AG: But let's go back to Or's challenge. We find a complexity of light and shadow in the text that they did not see. Only occasionally do they tell us that a *peshat* (direct, obvious) reading of the text is offensive to them, that it seems unjust or unduly harsh. We are bothered by issues that caused no problem for them. But still we accept the *tsav* and *zeruz*, the commandment in its most urgent form, to seek the light within and behind the text.

EL: We are still Jews and this is still Torah. Torah remains the battlefield on which we want to fight out the moral and spiritual issues. Like the early *hasidim,* we too see lots of learners and readers around us who just don't get it. Their *mitnaggedim* (opponents) were in the *yeshiva;* ours are more likely critical Bible scholars in the university. Against both, we insist that the way to study Torah is to seek out the hidden light within it.

AG: That is precisely what we mean by a "post-critical" approach to the sacred text. It's all about recovering the holiness, even the holy voice that calls out from within it, without falling back into literalism.

Shemini

> On the eighth day Moses called to Aaron, his sons,
> and the elders....
> (LEV. 9:1)

We need to understand [the current relevance of this, for] whatever happened, happened.

The verse seems to hint that Israel at that time were considered penitents, since the Tabernacle came to atone for the sin of the Golden Calf. The penitent first has to repair his personal qualities; this refers to the seven emotions. These are parallel to the seven days of preparation (cf. Lev. 8:33), during which they were to remain in the sanctuary, separated from all others, in order to repair those seven qualities. Then they could come to the World of Penitence [*binah*, the eighth *sefirah* from below, called *teshuvah*]. **On the eighth day** they reached the eighth world, starting from below, the realm of *teshuvah*, since all had been repaired.

Moses called to Aaron and **his sons.** A person has to serve God with the entire heart. Our sages took this to mean "with both urges, the good and the evil" (m. Berakhot 9:5). But how do we serve God with our evil urge?

A person who has perfected all those qualities has to take care not to become proud on account of that. You always have to remember your sins; "my sin is forever before me" (Ps. 51:5). You should always remain modest, as is taught: "Be of exceedingly humble spirit" (m. Avot 4:4). But if you are too humble in your religious life, saying: "How could I possibly do a *mitsvah* or pray to God for something, a lowly person like me?" such humility is unacceptable. On the contrary, our sages taught "Do not consider yourself evil" (m. Avot 2:13). They also said "You should always see yourself as though the entire world depended upon you. Both you and the world are half guilty and half innocent. Do one good deed ..." (b. Kiddushin 40b). By this they meant to increase the importance of our good deeds in our own eyes, so that we do them with desire and enthusiasm. We can do enough in our service that we bend the entire world toward merit!

Now the first of these qualities, being humble in your own eyes, comes from the good urge. But the second, when you think your own acts, words, and thoughts are important, comes from the evil urge. This is what it means to serve God with both urges....

⟨⟨⟨⟨⟩⟩⟩⟩

The text then moves on in another direction, never quite interpreting this part of the verse. But the intent seems clear enough. Moses, "the most humble man of any on earth" (Num. 12:3), needed to call upon Aaron when he reached the "eighth day." Aaron had enough pride that he could help balance his humble brother, helping him realize the value of his own good deeds. Each of us needs to embody both of these "brothers" within us.

RAV YEEVI

> On the eighth day Moses called to Aaron, his sons, and the elders of Israel, saying to Aaron: "Take unto yourself a calf, a son of the herd, for a sin-offering and a ram for a rising-offering without blemish, and offer them before Y-H-W-H."
> (LEV. 9:1–2)

On the eighth day of the dedication Moses called them forth in order to teach them the way of serving God. Aaron (*aharon*) here represents the sage, since his name derives from the word *mohar*, which means "a gift." Torah is referred to as "necklaces around your throat" (Prov. 1:9). [Torah and its sages or rabbis are both bridal gifts from God to Israel.]

Here the sage is instructed to **take unto yourself a calf**. The author of *Two Tablets of the Covenant* teaches (*Ki Tissa* 11) that the word *'egel* ("calf") is an abbreviation for 'arayot (adultery), gezel (theft), and leshon ha-ra' (wicked speech). The letters come in ascending order of frequency: few are guilty of adultery, more of theft, but everyone of wicked speech, all sins about which people are overly lenient. Then when people come to repent, they waste their strength in fasting.

Therefore Moses is teaching the sage to first **take** the 'egel **unto** himself **for a sin-offering**, to pay attention to all three of those sins. Once you truly consider them sinful, you will not transgress them. **Son of the herd** emphasizes this. Ben ("son") comes from bon, to understand. Bakar ("herd") also means "to distinguish." If you pay attention to these sins, you will understand how to distinguish right from wrong and will keep yourself far from all three.

Then you will have no need of the fasting that diminishes your strength. You will have **a ram**—the word also means "strength" (cf. Ez. 17:13)—**for a rising-offering without blemish.** You will be able to serve God through Torah and prayer in an unblemished way. **And offer them before Y-H-W-H**: the life of Torah and mitsvot.

⟨⟩⟨⟩⟨⟩

Some early Hasidic sources offer a very balanced and rational attitude toward sin and atonement. Know what sin is, including those "little" sins that people tend to ignore. If you keep your guard high, you will not need to waste your energy on excessive acts of penitence. Better to save your strength for more positive ways of serving God.

NO'AM ELIMELEKH

> Moses said to Aaron: "Approach the altar" ... and Aaron approached the altar.
>   (LEV. 9:7–8)

Rashi explains that Aaron was embarrassed and fearful of approaching. Moses therefore said to him: What are you ashamed of? This is what (le-kakh) you were chosen for!

Shame is an essential part of a person. It is a good sign when a person feels shame, and a person who feels shame does not readily sin (b. Nedarim 20a). Aaron's strong feeling of shame came from his great submissiveness. This is the way of a tsaddik: consider yourself a sinner for even a flicker of sin. Treat your small mistakes as if they were major sins. Be humble, think little of yourself, and acknowledge your mistakes publicly. This will inspire thoughts of repentance in those listening to you. They reason—"If the flame has burnt great cedars, what will the lowly mosses on the wall say?" (b. Mo'ed Katan 25b). They will be inspired to full repentance.

This is what Moses told Aaron—why are you ashamed? The fact that you are ashamed and hesitant makes you the perfect spiritual leader, one who is worthy to approach the altar. This is why (*le-kakh*) you were chosen; this is the way the *tsaddik* should act in God's service.

And Aaron approached the altar (Lev. 9:8). Once he heard from Moses that shame and inner submissiveness constitute the greatest spiritual level, he practiced this.

And Aaron approached the altar means he brought himself to the altar, he found shortcomings in himself and constantly sought out an altar of atonement.

ᏳᎻᎵᎯᎧ

What a wonderful psychological reversal. Your sense of unworthiness is what actually qualifies you for leadership....

TSEMAH HA-SHEM LI-TSEVI

> ... Aaron was silent.
> (LEV. 10:4)

Scripture says: "It is good to hope in silence for the salvation of Y-H-W-H" (Lam. 3:26).

There are four levels of existence: the inanimate (*domem*, lit. "silent"), the vegetative, the animal, and the verbal (human). Sometimes a person has to be on the inanimate level, as in "May my self be as dust" (b. Berakhot 17a). Thus you do not feel the pain that another is causing you, or you do not question God's actions, just as the inanimate [soil] feels no pain as the vegetative draws energy out of it. This is the sense of **Aaron was silent** [following the death of his sons]; he brought himself to this inanimate state.

RaSHI says that he received a reward for his silence; the divine Word chose to speak with him. By lowering himself from the verbal to the inanimate or silent level, he allowed the silent *shekhinah* to rise up to the level of speech, as it were. Of this the sages said: "A word is worth a penny; silence is worth two (b. Megillah 18a). And Scripture adds: "He sits alone in silence, for he has taken it upon himself" (Lam. 3:28). He has taken "the burden of silence" upon himself (cf. Is. 21:11).

This is "It is good to hope in silence for the salvation of Y-H-W-H." It is good to hope for the salvation of God [meaning that God is saved], while being silent about oneself. By bringing yourself into silence, you merit to bring about the salvation of Y-H-W-H, which is the emergence of the divine Word.

This is also the meaning of [the fourth child in the Passover Haggadah]: "The one who does not know how to ask, you open for him."

              ᢒᜡᜡᢒ

This is an extraordinarily profound and subtle teaching about silence and religious movement. By silencing his own inner feelings of protest at his sons' death, Aaron overcomes his own place as an articulate, verbal human, sinking into the realm of inanimate silence. This act of self-erasure allows the divine, itself sunk in silence, to rise up into verbal expression. Human silence "saves" the divine word and allows it to be heard.

The fourth child represents none other than *shekhinah*, waiting to be brought forth into speech.

Shemini
Round Two

AG: Look how important sin and repentance remain to them, despite the Ba'al Shem Tov's warning against brooding on one's sins.

EL: When he gets to *Va-Yikra* the *No'am Elimelekh* becomes a stern preacher, warning you about sin. I wonder if this has some relation to the *sefirat ha-'omer* season, when these sections are read.

OR: They may be innovators, but they work so fully within the system.

AG: The struggle for moral self-improvement seems so constant here, overwhelming everything else.

EL: The key issue in most of these teachings is humility. R. Elimelekh seems to be harping on the humility question.

AG: Of course. He's training *tsaddikim*! That's their biggest danger, being put on such a high pedestal. He's telling them that you won't get anywhere as a spiritual teacher unless you can maintain your humility in the face of all that. The modern rabbis we train know a little bit of that struggle as well, and we had better prepare them for it.

OR: Even more so when you're dealing with mystical, almost magical, powers. There's a complex dance here of knowing and accepting how powerful you are, in the heights as well as with people, and yet remaining humble.

EL: That's the legacy of the Ba'al Shem Tov to Hasidism. He taught them to recognize their own power, the ability of their prayer to reach and affect heaven, and not to back down from that awareness.

AG: Yes, and the Maggid taught them humility. His ability, as a learned Kabbalist, to efface himself before the much less learned Ba'al Shem Tov and to call him "my teacher" must have been a very powerful example to his disciples. And the Maggid was a quiet charismatic, leaving his disciples room to each assert his own spiritual strength. That was his greatness as a teacher.

Tazri'a

> ... if a woman be with seed and give birth to a male child....
>
> (LEV. 12:2)

... The *Zohar* (3:42b) notes that from the time a woman becomes pregnant, all she talks of is whether the child will be a boy [or a girl].

I heard my teacher R. Dov Baer comment on the sages' statement "Israel sustain their heavenly Father" (*Zohar* 3:7b). He quoted the verse "The wise child brings a father joy" (Prov. 10:1), saying that our fulfilling the commandments and doing good deeds brings pleasure to our blessed Creator. This is the meaning of the sages' teaching, as pleasure is a sort of sustenance.

But can a Jewish person's *mitsvot* and good deeds really bring God pleasure? Doesn't the blessed Holy One have thousands of angels singing "Holy, holy holy!" in awesome fear? "What is man that You are mindful of him?" (Ps. 8:5).

This can be explained by a parable. The nobles among the gentiles have birds that they are able to train to speak human language. A person who hears this is astonished, running to tell his friends: "Come see and hear this great wonder!" The reference is obvious.

Therefore, you humans, open your eyes and see the great power of your *mitsvot* and good deeds, dwarfing the service of the angels down to nothingness ... and bringing great joy to the Creator.

Sefer Va-Yikra—The Book of Leviticus

In this way the blessed Holy One becomes a "receiver," accepting all that pleasure from us. This too I heard from my teacher R. Dov Baer. "*This* [*zot*] has come from Y-H-W-H; it is a wonder in our eyes" (Ps. 118:23). Note that the word "this" is in the feminine [indicating receptiveness]. If the true purpose of all worship is that of bringing pleasure to God, then God becomes a receiver. That Y-H-W-H can turn into a feminine, receptive Being is clearly a wonder in our eyes. Indeed a great wonder!

Every person contains these three stages: seeding, gestation, and birthing. "Seeding" refers to our first arousal toward serving our Creator. "Gestation" is the developing desire to perform *mitsvot*; "birthing" is the actual deed....

This is what the *Zohar* means by telling us that a "woman," from the moment she becomes pregnant, talks only of her child's sex. From the time we begin to serve our Creator, until we give birth and actually do the *mitsvah*, we think of nothing other than whether our deeds will take on the active ("male") role of bringing blessing into all the worlds. May God give us the merit to serve in such a way! Amen.

༄

Here a biblical passage that is difficult for us is transformed when applied, in good Hasidic fashion, to the spiritual life. The categories of "male" and "female" are widened beyond all limit. All of us are "pregnant" and "birth-givers" here, and God is wondrously "female" as well as "male." True, the ideal form of service is that of the "male," causing blessing to flow, but the feminine-receptive state is elevated to an attribute of God.

As every successful lover knows, the categories of "giving" and "receiving" pleasure are entirely fluid and mutual. My greatest pleasure lies in giving pleasure to the one I love. Is it so difficult to imagine that this is true of our relationship with Y-H-W-H, the One we love indeed?

TESHU'OT HEN

In the Midrash: Rabbi Simlai taught that just as the formation of humans took place after all the beasts, cattle, and birds, so does this teaching regarding humans come after all those regarding cattle, beasts, and birds (*Va-Yikra Rabbah* 14:1).

What is the connection between the placement of this teaching in the Torah and the question of when humans were formed? And why does the Midrash use the word "formed [*yatsar*]" and not "created [*bara*]," when talking about the creation of humans?

All this seems related to "This is the teaching [Torah] of man" (2 Sam. 7:19; cf. Num. 19:14).

Israel and Torah are one. This means that each person's Torah becomes more spiritual or corporeal in accord with the rung that person attains. Before there was sin, Torah was on the level of Adam, who in that sense preceded all other creatures. "Israel [or humanity] arose in thought before the world was created." The combinations of words in the Torah were then in a different order, the teachings about man coming before those of cattle, beasts, and birds. This accorded with the human soul, which was formed before there was any Satan or evil present....

Torah then began with the letter *aleph*, as it will again in the messianic future (speedily, in our day!), when the Torah will be one of *aleph*s. This is the meaning of "Mind is too wondrous for me, so high that I cannot attain it" (Ps. 139:6). The word *peli'ah* ("wondrous") is comprised of *pele* [*aleph* spelled backwards] and God's name, *yod heh*.

King David's soul longed to attain the Torah in the mystery of *aleph*. But this is "I cannot attain it"; this matter cannot be fully grasped until the messiah comes.

Torah in the mystery of *aleph* means that the joining together of all Torah, written and oral, including all the words of the sages, will be clearly manifest in some special permutation. I have heard the preacher [R. Leib of Polonnoye] say in the name of the Ba'al Shem Tov that when messiah comes he will unpack the entire Torah from beginning to end, based on the letter permutations in each word, and then he will make it all into one word. The permutations will be endless, but he will offer insights on them all. This is a good teaching, correct for those who understand it properly.

After the sin [of Adam], when the "bodies of Torah" were given, they came to be garbed in the same material substance as were humans. Torah was given in bodily form, representing the diminished powers of humanity [who could no longer access it in its purely spiritual essence]. So the teaching about humans came to be placed following those of cattle, beasts, and birds. This is what the sages meant when they said that ["if humans are too proud, they will be told] 'this insect preceded you in Creation'" (b. Sanhedrin 28a). But that is also why they taught: "There is no 'former' and 'latter' in the Torah" (b. Sanhedrin 49b); we have it with sections jumbled. That which belonged before was placed later, and vice versa....

Rabbi Simlai is trying to teach us a moral lesson. He said: "Just as the formation [*yetsirah*] of humans took place after all the beasts, cattle, and birds." He did not say "Creation [*beri'ah*]" since that would best apply to souls; therefore he referred instead to "formation." This [present order] refers to something less than "creation." Each person's formation is, as we have said, in accord with his own deeds and sins. It is this that places us even after the insects. So our teaching is laid out only after beasts, cattle, and birds; "the teaching of man" or "a person's Torah" follows his deeds, whether to the right or the left.

⟨ﬦﬦﬦ⟩

Here the Hasidic author takes a daring Kabbalistic formulation, one of several versions discussing a different Torah that existed in primal time and will exist again in the future, to use it in a moralizing vein. He also refers to the hierarchy of multiple worlds, in which *beri'ah* is higher than *yetsirah*. Each person indeed has a unique Torah, according to his/her own personal reach. The message, of course, is to strive higher, to try to reach even a bit closer to the Torah of *aleph*, representing infinity itself.

NO'AM ELIMELEKH I

> She should neither touch anything holy nor enter the sanctuary [*mikdash*] until the days of her purification are completed.
>
> (LEV. 12:4)

When the Temple was standing, the divine presence was in the Temple. Now, during our bitter exile, it is written: "I have become for them a lesser temple [*mikdash me'at*]" (Ezek. 11:16), meaning that the divine presence dwells in the *tsaddik*.

But as for you, do not think you have achieved that level **until the days of her purification are completed**, until you have completed your time, many years of [living in] holiness and purity.

⟨ﬦﬦﬦ⟩

A double-sided metaphor. On one hand the aspiring *tsaddik* is told to be patient—not to claim greatness prematurely. Yet the woman who awaits purity after giving birth is also a symbol of the divine presence waiting for you to perfect yourself, so that you can become a dwelling-place for her.

NO'AM ELIMELEKH II

> When a person has on the body's skin a swelling,
> a rash, or a brightness and it becomes a *tsara'at*
> affliction on the body's skin, the person should be
> brought to Aaron the priest, or to one of his sons,
> the priests. The priest shall examine the affliction
> on the body's skin; if the hair within it has turned
> white, and it is deeper than the [surrounding] body's
> skin, it is *tsara'at*; when the priest sees this he should
> pronounce the person impure.
> (LEV. 13:2–3)

It says: "Y-H-W-H made skin ['or] clothing for Adam and for his woman and dressed them" (Gen. 3:21), and the Talmud teaches that in R. Meir's Torah it said "clothing of light [or]" (*Bereshit Rabbah* 20:12).

This means that indeed initially God created Adam with a body made totally of a great light with no evil inclination.... It was only after Adam sinned by eating from the tree of knowledge that people were given the choice between doing good or, heaven forbid, evil. And if you choose God's ways and fulfill the *mitsvot* of the holy Torah for its own sake, you will transform your body into the "clothing of light" that it was originally created to be. Thus the phrase "R. Meir's Torah" [the name *Meir* means "shining"] means that in his way of life, following the holy Torah, he indeed had "clothing of light." He had reestablished his body and limbs so that they all shone with a great light.

When a person has on the body's skin; "the body" refers to physicality. The verse is thus describing a person who has brought physical lust into the *or* ("skin/light"). Not only did he not transform it into light, but he corrupted the "skin" with sin. **A swelling** refers to bad qualities, which are the root of sin, and the root of all bad qualities is pride. **Swelling** alludes to pride....

Or a rash [*sapahat*]; here Scripture warns us against various causes that can lead a person to arrogance. The first is associating with empty people who spend their days in the streets—such company can lead a person to arrogance very quickly.... [The word used for rash] *sapahat* is used here in the sense of "join me [*sapheni*] to one of the groups" (1 Samuel 2:36).

Or a brightness—this is the second cause. Sometimes the bright light and enthusiasm a person feels from doing a good deed can lead to arrogance. You have to be very careful with this.

And it becomes a *tsara'at* affliction on the body's skin; the words **affliction** (*nega'*) and pleasure (*'oneg*) are written with the same letters. This teaches that you can transform the affliction into [something positive, that causes] pleasure, but if you are not careful it will become *tsara'at*.

Scripture next teaches how to correct your ways—**the person should be brought to ... the priest**—connect with the *tsaddikim*....

When the priest sees this he should pronounce the person impure; the *tsaddik* will demonstrate and explain the great damage you have caused through all this and will teach you the ways of true regret and repentance, so that you can correct the bad attributes and the evil that is within you.

⟨⟩

This is only part of a long reinterpretation of Leviticus, reappropriating the role of the priest to the *tsaddik*. The Hasidic *tsaddik* is not interested in ritual impurity, but rather in helping his/her followers overcome their spiritual shortcomings. Our question today is whether we can allow anyone in our lives to take on the role of looking carefully at our moral blemishes and giving us such clear guidance as to what we need to do about them. Spiritual counselor is neither priest nor therapist, but learns from the skills of both.

MEVASSER TSEDEK

The priest shall see him again [*shenit*] on the seventh day. If his sore is lighter and has not spread in the skin of his flesh, the priest shall declare him pure.
(LEV. 13:6)

Our sages taught that "whoever guards Shabbat in accord with its practice [*halakhah*], even if he has engaged in idolatry as did Enosh [the first idolater], he will be forgiven" (b. Shabbat 118b).

The aspect of soul that we are given on the Sabbath is itself called Shabbat. This soul needs to be guarded in accord with the ways it has walked about (*halikhah*) in the upper worlds, longing only to cleave to God. That is how we are to conduct ourselves on Shabbat, not drawing upon ourselves anything of the snake's skin [defiling worldly concerns]. This is the "guarding" of Shabbat, referring to that special soul; "its practice" is its way of walking in those higher places.

Then all our sins are forgiven. **The priest shall see him** refers to God, who is here called "priest." **On the seventh day** God sees us **again [*shenit*]**, changed or different. God sees how we conduct ourselves differently on Shabbat than we do on weekdays, following pathways of that soul called Shabbat.

Then our **sore is lighter and has not spread in the skin of** our **flesh**; we have not brought the snake's skin upon ourselves. Our afflictions indeed become lighter on that day. Then **the priest shall declare him pure**, forgiving all our sins....

⟨✦⟩

A Jew who observes Shabbat in a truly spiritual way looks different on Shabbat than on weekdays. The "extra soul" of Shabbat is visible as a glowing presence. Here we are told that God too, in the role of cosmic Priest, sees that difference and judges us according to our Sabbath selves.

Tazri'a
Round Two

OR: What a picture of humanity we have here! The soaring heights of human potential and the great abyss, right next to each other.

AG: Even the human body can be turned into a garment of light or a dwelling for the *shekhinah*, and yet the whole thing can come crashing down, especially due to pride.

EL: It's no accident that all this consideration of human nature takes place in these sections, where the human body is so exposed in all its vulnerability. Skin rashes, body sores, birth and death; they're all here. How could one not think about human purity?

OR: They've transferred the whole purity discussion to the moral realm. The *tsaddik* is the priest who can "see the affliction," who knows how to heal our hearts. But what do we do in a world where we don't have—or even want to have—someone in that role? How can we seek purity without a *tsaddik*'s guidance?

AM: Hasidism does offer other resources. Close spiritual friendships can sometimes serve that role. A friend who is a true spiritual *hevruta*, or companion, can save one from pride or pretense. Community, especially the close circle of disciples, is also a big part of the Hasidic legacy.

OR: Some of us are fortunate enough to have marriage partners who play that role, who help keep us honest, humbling us when we need to be brought down and building us up when we think too little of ourselves.

EL: I feel less ready than that to give up on the role of *rebbe*. Look at therapists. Every therapist needs to have his own therapist, someone he can turn to for honest feedback. If you are involved in shaping people's lives, it's awfully important that there be someone who can keep a check on you.

AG: Among Catholics, every priest has his own confessor or spiritual director. Maybe the person doesn't need to be a perfect *tsaddik*, but just to act as an honest listener in this role.

OR: But I'd like something with more mutuality, at least a teacher-*rebbe* whom one also knows as a whole—and even an imperfect—person. I don't think we want the therapist model where your shrink is anonymous to you, hiding behind the professional role.

AG: And so we come to R. Nahman, the original wounded healer. He understands your woes, your suffering, even your doubts, because he's been through them all, and worse. That may be what makes him so popular again today.

ᏜᏢᏔᎧ

מצרע

Metsora'

MA'AYAN HA-HOKHMAH

> Y-H-W-H spoke to Moses, saying: "This shall be the
> teaching of the leper: On the day when he is to be
> purified, he shall be brought to the priest."
> (LEV. 14:1–2)

Here we are being taught how to serve our Creator. When the evil urge
comes along to tempt you with regard to any sin, God intends you to
go perform the *mitsvah* that is that sin's very opposite. That is why the
[temptation to] sin was sent to you, like the shell that you encounter before
getting to the fruit.

When you want to eat a nut, you have to first take it by its shell, breaking
through the shell in order to get at that which lies inside it. You just can't
get to that nutmeat without going through the shell.

The same is true of a *mitsvah*. You can't get to it unless you break through
the shell that opposes it. That is why, when the evil urge tempts you toward
a certain sin, you have to break down that desire by doing the *mitsvah* that
is its opposite. If you do not, even if you break down the evil urge and do
not transgress, it will come to naught. That evil urge will return to you,
because you did not do the *mitsvah*, [the act of turning toward the good].
But when your intent in breaking through evil is to get to the inner *mitsvah*,
God promises that you will complete that journey and truly fulfill it.

This is the meaning of our verse: **This shall be the teaching of the**
leper [*metsoireh*]. Read it as the *motsi ra'* ["defamer," one who speaks ill

of others]. When an opportunity to do evil is at hand, this is what it should teach you: Your intent in breaking through evil should be the brightness of the *mitsvah*, **the day when he is to be purified** [by good speech]. Then, Scripture assures us, **he shall be brought to the priest**, coming before God in perfect service of the *mitsvah*.

⟳ⅧⅧↄ

This teaching reflects a typically Hasidic attitude. "Turn from evil and do good," says the Psalmist (34:15). You must turn from evil in order to do good. A religious life that is all about avoiding sin will turn one toward too much cringing and not enough acting on the love of God. Religion needs to be a positive force in the one's life, not just a protective shield against sin.

NO'AM ELIMELEKH

> This is the teaching regarding the *metsora'*, on the day of his purification when he is brought to the priest.
> (LEV. 14:2)

A great rule of practice is articulated in the verse "walk humbly [*hatsne'a*] with Y-H-W-H" (Mic. 6:8). All deeds done in God's service should be done secretly (*be-tsin'ah*). If they are done in public, they are easily tainted by other personal interests and by arrogance. When you do your work in private, you are less susceptible to arrogance and other ulterior motives, since no one else knows what you are doing.

This is a general rule for people who are attempting to improve their practice. However, if you are repenting for sins of public nature such as gossip or other transgressions like that, the process of repentance must be public as well.

This follows the rule [regarding kashrut] that a substance is expelled the same way it is taken in (b. Pesahim 30b). The same applies to transgressions; they must be rejected in the same way they were adopted. If the sin was private in nature, the repentance should also be private. However, if the sin was in the open and in public, the repentance should also be in public view. Yet how is one to repent publicly when [the publicity could evoke] ulterior motives [that] could undermine the whole process?

The solution to this is to be in the presence of perfect *tsaddikim*. This will certainly save you from ulterior motives, as the evil inclination cannot control you in the presence of such persons. Further, it is impossible to succumb to such interests while witnessing the great deeds of the *tsaddikim*. Your heart will certainly tremble greatly as you say to yourself: "How can I be proud of my own deeds when I compare them to the deeds of the *tsaddikim*?"

This is the meaning of **This is the teaching regarding the *metsora'***; the verse refers to one who has disseminated evil (*motsi ra'*) through gossip. **On the day of his purification**; the [process of] purification and the work of repentance should be public and revealed. This is what "day" symbolizes, for in daylight all is revealed and public.

But what if it [the public nature of the process] evokes arrogance in the sinner?

Therefore Scripture says: **he is brought to the priest**. The solution for this is that the sinner be in the presence of the priest, the great *tsaddik* who serves God with integrity. Seeing the deeds of the *tsaddik* "who loves justice" will distance the sinner from any ulterior motives, and then "the upright shall behold (God's) face" (Ps. 11:7).

༄

As in many other Hasidic teachings, the *tsaddik* takes the place of the priest, and the concern for spiritual welfare replaces the concern for ritual purity. The impact of the presence of the *tsaddik* is explained in both rational and irrational terms. On one hand, the evil inclination has no power in the *tsaddik*'s presence. On the other, who is a better role model for public *teshuvah* than a *tsaddik* who has managed to keep his/her integrity while living in the public eye?

OR HA-GANUZ LA-TSADDIKIM

> The priest shall give the command and take for the one being purified two live pure birds....
> (LEV. 14:4)

These may be said to represent awe and love, by which one's words fly upward like birds. They are called the "wings" [of prayer] (*Tikkuney Zohar* t. 10, 25b) and are both live and pure.

Since the essence of serving God is "to walk humbly with Y-H-W-H" (Mic. 6:8), your service should be more inward than is visible on your outer limbs. That is why we say in the "May it be Your will" prayer, associated with the princes of the twelve tribes [recited in the weeks preceding Passover]: "May You bring that holy bird into the holy place." This is the place "that no eye has seen, O God, except Yours" (Is. 64:3). Your devotion should be interior, in that "holy place."

There are people who like to show others their devotion or how piously they speak. Even though there are times when one has to do this, it is better that it stay within, in that place no other eye has ever seen. Your love and awe, which are the wings of that holy bird, [should be seen by no one else].

ᏎᏇᏬᎥᎩ

The early Hasidic masters, we should recall, were addressing their message primarily to a youthful audience. There is much about Hasidic teaching, including the call for constant spiritual innovation, that reflects this context. It is not surprising, therefore, that warnings against spiritual immaturity are also part of the message. Adolescents (of any age!) within religious communities are often likely to be overly demonstrative of their piety. This call for inwardness, instead of "flapping one's wings" in public, was surely a timely reminder.

Metsora'
Round Two

AG: These two sections, *Tazri'a* and *Metsora'*, are the bane of every Jewish preacher's existence. How does one find anything relevant to say when the Torah is being so concerned with skin diseases and the color of one's lesions?

OR: The Hasidic readings do what they always do: they spiritualize the text. The diseases are moral failings or inner afflictions of the heart. The priest is either God or the *tsaddik*. Everything else follows from these assumptions.

AG: They have an old tradition that sees the skin afflictions as punishment for the sin of gossip or malicious speech. That allows them to read *metsor'a* as *motsi* [*shem*] *ra'*, defamation or character assassination.

OR: That's a sin that is a public act by definition; you therefore have to atone for it publicly as well. The interplay between the public and private realms is very interesting in these teachings. The two shorter texts both push toward inwardness and privacy, so typical of Hasidic readings. But the *No'am Elimelekh* here understands that public sins demand public restitution.

EL: Hasidism itself is worth looking at through the lens of public and private devotion. Even though the teachings are so much about inwardness and one's very personal relationship to God, Hasidism turned into a very public movement, filled with loud and visible displays of piety.

AM: That may be because of the importance lent to community; things have to be visible to be shared in community.

OR: Let's not forget that the *tsaddik* is central to this text. To atone publicly means doing so in the *tsaddik*'s presence, a place where evil cannot dwell.

EL: Yes, but why can't evil dwell there? Because the *tsaddik*, by his very presence, demands absolute honesty of you. You can't hide anything in his presence. The *tsaddik* by force of example demands that you be your best and fullest self.

AM: Who does that in our world? Sometimes it's a close friend, or a circle of close friendship, in whose presence you can be nothing but completely honest. That element is there in Hasidism as well.

OR: But let's not dismiss the *tsaddik* model too quickly. There can be experiences in the presence of a great soul, even in very public settings, that have a deep and transforming effect on those who are present.

EL: I agree. We are too quick to debunk such figures in our age. Even if we have seen that in private they are less than perfect beings, we still can allow ourselves to be moved and changed by the power of their public presence. Many of us know moments like that. We know also that we can and must help create such moments for others, even though we ourselves are far less than perfect.

⊙〰〰〰⊙

Aharey Mot

ME'OR 'EYNAYIM

> Y-H-W-H said to Moses, following the death of
> Aaron's two sons when they approached Y-H-W-H
> and died. Y-H-W-H said to Moses: "Speak to your
> brother Aaron, and let him not come at all times into
> the holy, inside the curtain, facing the atonement-
> cover that is before the ark, and let him not die. With
> this shall Aaron enter the holy...."
> (LEV. 16:1–3)

... Aaron's sons Nadav and Avihu, in their intense devotion and righteousness,
attained fulfillment, giving themselves over to death. They became so
wondrously attached to God that their souls just remained there, cleaving
to the divine light, a channel of energy rising upward. Their souls departed
into the One! This is the meaning of **when they approached Y-H-W-H and
died**. They drew so near, with so much attachment and longing, that their
souls became hidden, cleaving to that which is above.

But really the person who serves in this way and is joined to God in this
mysterious way is able to draw forth divine blessing, bringing it down from
above while remaining alive. "You who cleave to Y-H-W-H your God are
fully alive this day" (Deut. 4:4)! Your attachment to Y-H-W-H has made you
more alive! That is God's will as the Giver of life.

But in them there was some sin that prevented this. Some of our sages
said they were intoxicated; others said they taught a law in the presence

of Moses their teacher (b. 'Eruvin 63a; *Va-Yikra Rabbah* 12:5). Because of this, the downward flow of blessing in the form of returning light was blocked and their souls remained attached there, flowing upward and not returning.

That is why Aaron is now warned not to **come at all times into the holy**. It means to say that all the devotion of the *tsaddik* should be of this sort, handing over their souls as a flow of energy from below. One cannot do this **at all times**. He should indeed come into the holy **with this**, the devotion shown by his sons. But **let him not die**: he should rather add to the life-flow of blessing and holiness pouring forth upon him.

⟵♦⟶

Intense devotion and attachment to God are meant to enhance the gift of life, not to negate it. The *tsaddik*'s real priestly work is to bring God's presence and blessing into this world. Only purity of intention and deed allows one to become such a channel.

NO'AM ELIMELEKH

> With this shall Aaron enter the sanctuary: with a bull of the herd as a sin-offering and a ram as a rising-offering. He shall wear a holy tunic of linen and linen pants upon his flesh; he shall gird himself with a linen sash and don a linen turban. These are holy garments; he should wash his body with water and put them on.
> (LEV. 16:3–4)

These verses begin to discuss the rung of an accomplished *tsaddik*. **Aaron** refers to a great *tsaddik,* one who [wants to] **enter the sanctuary**—the highest realm of holiness.

A bull refers to *dinim*, limitations or boundaries, while **of the herd** [*ben bakar*] alludes to outpouring love as in [the symbol of] morning (*boker*). This is the power of boundaries within love; you should cultivate fear of God (*din*) that derives from love.

As a sin-offering means that you should always reflect upon your actions, search for sin and never think that you have accomplished all that is required of you. You should humble yourself in great submission.

However, **a ram as a rising-offering** refers to intercessory prayer that rises to the heights. Regarding prayer you should be strong as a ram and not abstain from praying for any need. Never say, "Who am I to pray for such matters?" Pray for all things, great and small.

He shall wear a holy tunic of linen means you sanctify your body with such great holiness that it becomes a garment of light (*or*—light/skin). This [the process of becoming a *tsaddik*] is all about creating garments for yourself.

And linen pants upon his flesh, for the pants atone for sexual sins (b. Zevahim 88b). They should always be upon his flesh "to cover the physical nakedness" (Ex. 28:42): overcome your corporeal desires so that they do not rise up in your heart at all.

He shall gird himself with a linen sash—Gird yourself like a hero! You can always do more!

And don a linen turban, which atones for arrogance (b. Zevahim 88b). You must shatter the power of arrogance and sanctify yourself to the extent that you can incorporate aspects of pride into the holy work and make pride itself a holy covering for your head.

These are holy garments—everything. Make all things part of your holy work and they will all be holy garments.

❧

Training instructions for the aspiring *tsaddik*. At the core of all is the divine presence. All of your spiritual work, including both humility and assertiveness, overcoming your tendencies and embracing them, together create a vessel/garment through which God can be accessed and made manifest in the world.

Torey Zahav (from *Tsav*)

> No person shall be in the Tent of Meeting when he comes in to atone for the holy, until he goes out. He shall make atonement for himself and his household....
> (Lev. 16:17)

... In the book *Duties of the Hearts* (Bahya ibn Paqquda; eleventh century) we are told that a person should regularly practice lone meditation, separated from other people. You should reach the state that even when surrounded by a thousand people, you are able to maintain your attachment to God. Nothing should divide you or separate you from that attachment (*Sha'ar Heshbon ha-Nefesh* 3).

Thus I interpret our verse.... We know that before praying you should be stripped of your corporeal self. Your thought should cleave to the exaltedness of God, as though you were standing in the upper worlds among angels, rather than surrounded by people. When you forget that you are among people, you are able to pray with great intensity, without any false motives. This is **No person shall be in the Tent of Meeting**. That refers to the synagogue or house of study, the place where people gather to pray. **No person shall be** there in your thought; you should be so stripped of physical selfhood that you forget you are standing among people. As you **come in to atone for the holy**: the time of prayer, which takes the place of atoning sacrifices. **Until he goes out**: from the beginning to the end of prayer. **He shall make atonement for himself and his household**: prayer of this sort is surely pure.

Thus I also interpreted the sages' saying "In a place where there is no man, try to be a man" (m. Avot 2:5). When you stand in that place of *teshuvah*, strive to be more than an ordinary man; enter the upper realms, where there is no other person. Before you perform a *mitsvah*, set your mind to be attached above, as though there were no person present....

〰〰〰

Prayer is an intensely private and intimate act, even when undertaken in public. Preserving this island of inward intensity in the public setting is a delicate task. Indeed, training in lone meditation is a valuable tool in acquiring it. The Hasidic style of worship emerges from an attempt to foster this inner "space."

YOSHER DIVREY EMET (#10)

> You shall not reveal the nakedness of your sister, your father's daughter, whether born at home or born outside.
> (LEV. 18:9)

This verse is referring to shaming or disgracing Torah, who is called **your sister**, as in the verse "Say to wisdom: You are my sister" (Prov. 7:4). **Your**

father's daughter: this refers to the blessed Holy One. **Born at home** means the hidden Torah; **born outside** refers to revealed teachings. Of both we are told not to **reveal their nakedness**, not to shame them by studying them not for their own sake. [We must study only] for the sake of God's name, in love.

I heard from the mouth of that holy man Dov Baer [of Mezritch], on the Sabbath I spent there during his lifetime, his reply to a question someone asked about a passage in the Midrash. That text compared a student of Torah to a pearl-encrusted clapper inside a golden bell (*Va-Yikra Rabbah* 27:1). He said that this refers to those who study Torah truly for her own sake, in order to be attached to God. Their thoughts are only of God. When Scripture says, "May this book of teaching never depart from your mouth; contemplate it day and night" (Josh. 1:8), the text really meant to "contemplate *Him* day and night"; your thoughts should be of God. The divine presence is concentrated right there in the spirit-breath of Torah as it comes forth from a person's pure mouth. If you can purify both your mouth and heart, you may become a throne for God. So attachment to God is the innermost part [of this act of study]; the teachings one learns are the external form in which this devotion is garbed. That is a proper understanding. This is not true if your desire and love are for anything other than God—if you are still attached to temporal matters or seek even some bit of self-glorification. Then your innermost thought is of that glory, and your learning surrounds that thought. Woe to the disgracing of Torah, making her into a garment for your own foolish thoughts that she has to cover up!

That is why the Midrash compared the student of Torah to a golden bell. The bell is the external section, while the clapper is within it and makes the sound. "Woven gold is her garment," but "the full glory of the king's daughter lies within" (Ps. 45:14). That glory consists of awe before God and the indwelling presence of *shekhinah*, within the heart of every Jew. The "woven gold" is the letters of Torah, in which she is dressed. But the pearl-studded clapper (*'anvil*) is our attachment to God, which is possible only where there is true humility (*'anavah*)....

There is a bilingual play on words hidden in the end of this teaching. R. Meshulam Feibush is suggesting that the unusual noun *'anvil*, used for "clapper," means that the true sage needs to be an *'anav'l*, a humble little guy.... The complete homiletical transposition of a verse like this one, dealing with incest prohibition, to an entirely different realm is quite frequently found in the Hasidic sources.

Aharey Mot
Round Two

EL: Isn't it interesting to see Aaron's sons Nadav and Avihu presented as essentially positive models! That's what the *Me'or 'Eynayim* is doing.

OR: He doesn't even note what their sin is. Usually they are viewed primarily as sinners.

EL: He's not interested in their sin! His goal is total purification of the self, and they look like people who were attempting that.

OR: That's the ideal of *devekut*. Approach the fire as closely as you can; be willing to give up your life for that intensity of devotion. But, at the same time, try to come back.

EL: Of course. This is Hasidism; the goal is always to come back, bring some holiness down to this world, so it can be lifted up.

AG: Think of this as the Yom Kippur experience, because it is the Torah reading for that day. That is Yom Kippur—going all the way, losing the self in the intensity of cleansing prayer—but then coming back, returning to the world, getting to work building your *sukkah* once the day is over.

OR: The *Torey Zahav* also wants us to be able to achieve that *devekut* right in the midst of a sea of people. I find that very moving as a description of religious community.

EL: That's what *tefillah be-tsibbur*, communal prayer (don't call it "public" prayer!), is supposed to provide: a group and setting that support you in your intense and essentially private inward journey. But how rare it is to find a *tsibbur* like that in which to pray! I long for that kind of community.

OR: But isn't there something missing in that? What about dialogue with others in the community? What about mutual caring for one another?

AG: Yes, of course those are part of it. They are what make the support for one's inner life possible.

EL: Maybe we worry too much about togetherness. We pay too much attention to one another's needs, we're too careful never to offend.

Leave it behind! Remember what religious community is really there to do.

AG: But is the horizontal there just for the sake of the vertical? Aren't *mitsvot beyn adam le-havero*, between person and person, a value unto themselves, not just a stepping-stone to *devekut*?

AM: This conversation is hard for us moderns. In the post-Freudian age we are always too busy watching ourselves. We stand too much on the sidelines, being observers. The challenge to us is to walk through the gate, to enter with our whole selves. That's why Nadav and Avihu look so attractive.

קדושים

Kedoshim

OR TORAH

You shall be holy, for I Y-H-W-H your God am holy.
(LEV. 19:2)

The Midrash comments: There will be no death in your midst (*Tanna de-Vey Eliyahu Zuta* 20).

This may be understood as linked to the verse "I shall not die, but live; I will declare [*asapper*] the deeds of YaH" (Ps. 118:17). The *Zohar* teaches that any prayer or word of Torah that does not come forth from the depth of the heart with love and fear [does not fly upward] (*Tikkuney Zohar* t. 10, 25b). Anyone who brings forth a word of Torah or prayer, God forbid, without love and fear, meaning pure thought and an understanding heart, is considered dead. Such a person has no place in Life, the name YaH, which refers to *hokhmah* and *binah* [the deepest inward divine "places"], as is known. "The dead will not praise YaH" (Ps. 115:17).

This is what King David the Psalmist sought in saying: "I shall not die, but live." For as long as I am alive, may I not be considered "dead"; I will maintain pure thought and will speak forth from the depths of my heart. That is *asapper*, here meaning "I will shine," casting a bright light upon the works of YaH. These are *hokhmah* and *binah*, from which all blessings flow. From there I will shine and light up all the worlds.

This is the meaning of **You shall be holy**. When you draw forth those mental energies called "Holy," [from the deep source of *hokhmah*], then you too will be holy, bearing YaH, and then "there will be no death in your midst."

Note that the Midrash does not say "You will not die," but "There will be no death in your midst." This means that throughout your lifetime you will not be considered as though dead.

⚭

This is a very Hasidic definition of holiness: constant attachment to the force of life. You achieve it by intense and constant devotion, including both love and fear. These allow you to shine with the light of YaH, to light up all the worlds. The fact of mortality seems trivial when compared to this great ability to bring forth so much light.

OR HA-ME'IR

> Y-H-W-H spoke to Moses, saying: "Speak to the entire community of the Children of Israel and say to them: 'You shall be holy, for I Y-H-W-H your God am holy.'"
> (LEV. 19:1–2)

Why did this commandment require such an assembling of the Community of Israel? Our sages taught, as is well known, that the most important bodies of Torah's teachings depend on it (*Va-Yikra Rabbah* 24:5).

The main purpose in God's creating the world was for the sake of Israel, who arose in the divine Mind, in order to bring about the great joy and pleasure that God would receive from the souls of the righteous. They have the great power to liken the creature's form to that of the Creator (*Kohelet Rabbah* 2:26)!...

The nature of this matter lies in their clarity of mind, giving them the ability to perceive the sublime lights that spread forth from the highest rung and penetrate even the lowest, such very human pleasures as eating, drinking, sleeping, and all the other forms of this-worldly delight. In their righteousness, acting always out of wisdom and awareness, they are able to conceive the upper through the lower. Not concerned with their own pleasure at all, they raise up those flowing lights to their Source and Root, the place where all is one. These righteous ones have the power and the perception, wherever they look, to see only the divinity that is garbed there. In doing so they necessarily strip away the corporeal and dress it in the form of spirit. This is what it means to "liken the creature's form to that of the Creator."

A person who does this deserves to be called holy. But even such a person, acting with all that wisdom and awareness, raising all to the Root, can only conceive up to the level where that soul is attached to the stature [body-like form] of *shekhinah*.

Each soul of Israel has a particular place in that form to which it is attached; that is where it can affect its work of restoration. It is from there that it can return the lights to the place where they are all one. "One does more, another less, as long as they turn their hearts to heaven" (b. Menahot 110a). Each in accord with that bit of mind and grasping will still be called holy. It is a matter of how you make your own senses pure and holy, fashioning your own entire form into a dwelling-place for God's presence. This is how you come to be called holy....

From the day God created human beings on earth, there have never been two people who stood on exactly the same rung. There are multiple and varied levels of holiness; each person among us Israelites has our own point of attachment among those many rungs. That is what we can attain through our deeds and efforts, and not a hairsbreadth more....

Y-H-W-H spoke to Moses, saying: "Speak to the entire community of the Children of Israel—from the greatest to the least—**and say to them: 'You shall be holy.'"** They are to acquire the name of holiness as we have said, even though they are unequal in the measure of their service of the Creator. Some have mighty, strong consciousness, faithful in spirit unto the end, while others are the smallest of the small. How can we seem to put them all on the same rung by calling them all holy? Their awareness is not at all alike!

Scripture responded to that objection by saying: **for I Y-H-W-H your God am holy.** The phrase **your God** seems superfluous; the verse would make good sense without it. But it comes to say that I [am Your God; I] pronounce My godliness over each one of you. Indeed we find that every one of Israel, from the least to the greatest, claims God as his own in prayer, saying, "Y-H-W-H my God." How do we not hesitate to do so? Are we not grasped by fear and trembling ... in saying "*my* God?..."

But this is God's way, extending his divinity and holiness across the whole community, making **I Y-H-W-H your God am holy** refer to each and every one. "The entire community is holy and Y-H-W-H is in their midst" (Num. 16:3)! Truly "the Compassionate One desires the heart" (b. Sanhedrin 106b). "One does more, another less," as long as we all bend our necks in the yoke of our Lord's service. Then even we of little mind may be called holy....

This text offers a wonderful example of Hasidism's unique combination of democratizing and elitist spirituality. Yes, God created the world for the sake of the *tsaddikim*. But even they, just like the rest of us, can each only reach the place of their own soul-root. Every person's task (again, we must universalize the text!) is to live out the life of holiness from the rung on which we stand. No one can do more than that.

The apex of democratizing enthusiasm comes when the author—surely unwittingly, in a moment of passion—quotes the words of rebellious *Korah*, proclaiming the entire community holy! Sparks of holiness can indeed be found everywhere, even in the words of the wicked.

HAYYIM VA-HESED

Each person fear your mother and father....
(LEV. 19:3)

There are people who are good from the side of their souls, wanting to be joined to their Root. But their physical selves derive from their mothers and fathers, who looked only after their own pleasure as the child was conceived. This is the legacy of the snake, drawing them to the corporeal realm.

This is why the Torah teaches us to **fear your mother and father**. You must struggle hard so that the part of you that you inherit from them is also drawn into your **fear** of God. "Everything is in the hands of heaven except the fear of heaven," our sages taught (b. Berakhot 33b). This is in your power. In doing this, you bring greater delight to the blessed Holy One, who exults in the human being who can subjugate evil to good.

Proof of this is found in Abraham our Father, whom God calls "Abraham My lover" (Is. 41:8). This is not said of Isaac or even Jacob, who is thought of elsewhere as the ideal among the patriarchs (b. Pesahim 117b). This is because Abraham came forth from the deepest "shells"; he was the son of Terah, and he stands first among proselytes. Despite this background, he drew himself near to God. This brought about the greatest of heavenly delight.

❦

While we may be uncomfortable with the rigid body/soul distinction that underlies this text, it strongly states the Hasidic message that "light is greater when it comes out of darkness." Our journey to God cannot be one that leaves the bodily self behind; it too must be uplifted and come with us into God's presence.

SHEMEN HA-TOV

> Love your neighbor as yourself; I am Y-H-W-H.
> (LEV. 19:18)

The author of *Orah le-Hayyim* [R. Avraham Hayyim of Zloczow] once asked R. Shmelke of Nikolsburg how it is possible to fulfill this commandment when my neighbor treats me badly. He gave him a reasonable answer that he was able to accept. "Aren't all the souls of Israel one?" he asked. We were all there together in Adam; each individual soul contains some sparks of that original whole—some from Adam's hands, [some from his feet, etc.], as the holy books tell us.

Now sometimes it happens that a person accidentally strikes himself, even quite hard [on his head]. The head is ruler of the body. But if that person were to pick up a club and strike the hand that had unintentionally hit him, we would consider him a fool. Why should he hurt himself yet again!

The exact same thing is true here. You and your fellow person are a single soul. That person has done you harm due to lack of awareness. When you strike him back, you will be hurting yourself. Think rather that everything that happens comes from God and that God has many emissaries.

But he asked him further: "If you see a person doing what is evil in God's sight, how is it possible to love him?" He replied: "The soul of every person is, as we are taught, a part of God above. Have compassion for God, since one of His holy sparks has become trapped in such a shell!"

⌘

The final comment, without saying so directly, is a reading of the end of this verse. Why should you love your neighbor as yourself? Because you are both part of the single Self of Y-H-W-H. The real tragedy of human evil is that a spark of divinity, capable of endless beauty and elevation, has been dragged into the dust.

TIF'ERET 'UZIEL

... Respect the elder and fear your God.
  (LEV. 19:32)

No animal is considered fit for sacrificial offering unless it is at least eight days old. Our sages said that the reason for this is that it has to have lived through at least one Sabbath (*Va-Yikra Rabbah* 27:10). This means that by being present during a Shabbat, a certain holiness enters into it, rendering it fit for offering.

Now if holiness enters an animal that does nothing active about observing the Sabbath, just by force of the day itself, how much more must this be true of an Israelite, one of this holy people that observes each Shabbat!

The same is true of each and every *mitsvah*. That is why God has commanded us to respect our elders. Think about how much divine holiness must have entered them over the course of all those days and Sabbaths they have lived!

This is **respect the elder and fear your God**. Be in awe of the amount of godly holiness those people bear within them....

෴

There are not two commandments here, but one. True respect for the elderly is recognizing how filled they are—each in a unique way—with God's presence.

Kedoshim
Round Two

AG: Is *kedoshim tehiyu* ["You shall be holy"] always taken as an imperative? Or is it sometimes an assurance? "You will be holy!"

EL: I think the imperative is always there. This is, after all, so much the basis of the Torah's ethos.

AG: But look again at the *Or ha-Me'ir*. I think he's saying: "Recognize that you are holy! Despite the great differences between you, each of you has God within you."

OR: But there remains something aspirational in that as well. You have to live up to that reality.

AM: The *Shemen ha-Tov* piece, seeing each of us as part of the same Adamic body, also implies that we are all holy.

EL: I'll agree that both are present, demand and assurance. But the *Or ha-Me'ir* opens with demand. To "liken the form to its Creator," as he reads it, requires living on a very high level.

AG: He has quietly taken that statement about the prophets' ability to liken God to humans and made it about the ability of the righteous to find God in everything.

OR: We know from elsewhere he means that you do this all the time, even in eating, drinking, and all the rest of your very physical life.

EL: In the first text here, the Maggid is telling us that to be holy is to be truly alive. You get there by intense devotion to God in both love and awe.

AG: The identification of true "living" and holiness is very powerful; vitality itself shows the flow of divine blessing into you.

EL: Look at the last text here. How much holiness had flowed into that old person, who has lived through so many holy Shabbatot!

OR: That's a real statement of faith, judging generously. We all know how easy it is to live through a Shabbat and have nothing of it rub off on you.

EL: There is a message here to young people: Don't miss those opportunities! Holiness is there in each Shabbat, seeking to enter you and transform you.

OR: And to the old as well. "Cast us not off in old age"—see how much of the divine presence we bear within us.

אמר

Emor

RAV YEEVI

> Y-H-W-H said to Moses: "Speak to the priests, sons of
> Aaron, saying to them: 'Do not defile yourselves for a
> person [*nefesh*] among your people.'"
> (LEV. 21:1)

The Talmud tells of Rabbi Zeira that when he became too weak to continue
with his studies, he went to sit at the doorway of Rabbi Natan bar Tuvi.
"When the sages pass by," he said, "I will stand up in their honor, and for
this I will receive reward" (b. Berakhot 28a).

The meaning of this tale is that a person is constantly obligated to "study
them day and night" (Josh. 1:8). This is how we attach ourselves to God.
But Rabbi Zeira, when his heart was so weak that he could not study Torah,
went to fulfill the *mitsvah* "Rise before the whitened head [of the elders
and the wise]" (Lev. 19:32). Thus he would be attached to God always, not
separated for a single moment. Had he turned to wasting time when he
was unable to learn, surely the "other side" would have taken hold of him.
Then, when he went to serve God, he would have been unable, because
of its presence. This is why the sages taught: "If you are neglectful of Torah
study for one day, you have lost two" (*Zohar* 3:35b–36a). And this is also
the meaning of "Sin breeds sin" (m. Avot 4:2).

Thus our verse: **Speak to the priests, sons of Aaron**. These are all who
serve God; they are called "priests" because of their service, and "sons of

Aaron" whose name may be connected to *mohar*, meaning "brideprice" or "gift." Those who serve are indeed of this importance. **Saying to them: "Do not defile yourselves for a person [*nefesh*] among your people."** *Nefesh* can mean "rest," as we are told, "On the seventh day He rested [*va-yinafash*]" (Gen. 2:3). When you want to rest because your heart is weak and you cannot study Torah, do not defile yourselves. You are yet **among your people**; you can fulfill *mitsvot* toward other people, as did Rabbi Zeira....

⟳

Hasidism is addressed to people who live ordinary lives, who cannot fulfill what seems to be a limitless demand of engaging in Torah day and night. "Fear not!" we are told here. Life among people is filled with opportunities to serve and remain close to God.

ME'OR 'EYNAYIM

> Say to the priests, children of Aaron, telling them not to be defiled for anyone among their people.
> (LEV. 21:1)

RaSHI comments: "This is to warn the greater ones [the priests] concerning those who are lesser [*ketanim*] than themselves...."

Every one of Israel surely contains the entire Torah. This includes the sacrificial rites, even though they were performed only by the priests. They exist within every Jew, as in "Whoever studies the burnt offerings, it is as though he had offered one" (b. Menahot 110a).

... Every worshipper is called a "priest." Indeed, when there is no *kohen* present in the synagogue, an ordinary Israelite can be called in his place. Rav [a third-century sage], we are told, read the portion assigned to the *kohen*, even when there was one present (b. Megillah 22a), since everyone who serves God is called a *kohen*.

We read in the Mishnah tractate Avot (1:12): "Be of the disciples of Aaron, loving peace and pursuing peace, loving people and bringing them near to Torah." What does it mean to "love and pursue peace"? It is as the prophet taught: "If he will hold fast to My strength, he will make peace for Me; peace will he make for Me" (Is. 27:5). When you hold fast to God's

Torah ("strength," '*oz*] and service, you bring about peace in the upper "family," the heavenly forces, and that perforce brings about peace in the [earthly] family below. The master asks how we do this, and the answer is by "loving people and bringing them near to Torah."

All the worlds were created through the twenty-two letters of the alphabet. Through Torah the world was created, and by Torah it is maintained. When you study Torah for its own sake in any particular generation, you uplift and draw the world close to its source, which is Torah. Of Torah we read: "All her pathways are peace" (Prov. 3:17). Thus peace is made among the heavenly forces above, causing peace in the lower family as well, and there will be no war.

This is all of human existence: we were created only so that blessed Y-H-W-H would have pleasure. Why would anyone not do the will of our Creator? This could only stem from a lack of religious awareness. We read: "Know the God of your father and serve Him" (1 Chron. 28:9). Without that awareness, whom could one serve? But should you [despair and] say, "What can I do? I have no such awareness," that is not really the case. We see that your mind does have awareness for things of this world. It is just in a lower state (*katnut*), not turned upward toward our blessed Creator. You need to use that same mind to become aware of God....

This is **Say to the priests, children of Aaron.** Those who serve God should be children of Aaron, disciples of the one who makes peace in both the upper and lower worlds. **Telling them**, with RaSHI's comment, that they are indeed "greater ones." We see that they do have mind or awareness for worldly matters. So we need to "warn them concerning ... the lesser [state of mind]." If your mind remains small or childish, even if you are seventy years old you may be considered a child. You have not yet developed the awareness to serve Y-H-W-H. Raise up that small mind of yours! How long will you leave it that way? Rise up and use your mental powers to draw near to God.

෴

Ah, what a world he describes! Every worshipper—in all the world's traditions—becoming a true disciple of Aaron, a lover and bringer of peace both "above" and "below"!

OR HA-GANUZ LA-TSADDIKIM

From the holy place he shall not go forth, so that he
not desecrate the sanctuary of his God, for a diadem
of God's anointing oil is upon him. I am Y-H-W-H.
(LEV. 21:12)

Rabbi Israel Ba'al Shem said that this is the intent of the *Zohar* passage,
saying: "Blessed are the righteous who know how to turn their desire
upward toward the sublime King, rather than toward this world and its
shameful vanity" (2:134b). Your thought should always be attached to the
upper world, to Y-H-W-H.

From the holy place he shall not go forth. But when you need to speak
of worldly matters, have in mind that you are walking downward from the
world above, like a person leaving his home to go outside, but planning to
return home immediately. As you walk along, you think, "When will I return
homeward?" Your thoughts should always be in the upper world; there is
your essential home, cleaving to your Creator. This is the case even though
you may be speaking of worldly matters. Reconnect yourself to that which
is above as soon as you are able.

Thus you will **not desecrate the sanctuary of ... God**, since you serve as
a throne or chariot for the blessed Holy One. **A diadem of God's anointing
oil is upon** you. Of this Scripture says: "Your name is oil pouring forth;
therefore the maidens [*'alamot*] love you" (Song 1:3). This means that
the flow of the divine vitality comes down from world to world (*'olamot*),
until *shekhinah* rests directly with the *tsaddik*. And then, "like a reflection
in the water" (Prov. 27:19). If even the King of kings, the blessed Holy
One who has countless legions in the upper worlds, desires nevertheless to
dwell with man [i.e., the *tsaddik*], how much more do the corporeal worlds
[*'alamot/'olamot*] find themselves attracted to you in love and attachment.

The **diadem of God's anointing oil is upon him.** And what is that
diadem? **I am Y-H-W-H**: I Myself dwell upon him. Therefore he may not
stray from his holiness.

౭ఞఞౢ

Even a passage speaking specifically of the high priest is transferred
directly to the *tsaddik* or the devotee, one who makes it his life's work
never to depart from the inner Temple. Here is a definition of Hasidic

charisma: the *tsaddik* is attractive to followers because they sense the divine presence dwelling with him.

Emor
Round Two

EL: The whole concern here is with living in the world. How do we serve God while living "down here," in ordinary times? *Rav Yeevi* says that we can't always be up there in the intellectual heights. When you need to come down, remember there are lots of *mitsvot* you can do down here as well, among people. But the *Or ha-Ganuz* wants more. In all the time you spend "down here," keep remembering that your home is elsewhere; the land of the soul is where you really dwell. People follow you because they sense that about you. The *Me'or 'Eynayim* is telling you that you *can* be aware of God always. Don't sell yourself short.

AG: It seems like they are all filled up with the question of how to serve God while in this world. It's as though they hadn't yet heard the Hasidic answer of *'avodah be-gashmiyyut*, serving God through corporeal things. I guess that answer wasn't always sufficient for them. It too can become a platitude.

EL: To serve God constantly always remains a struggle. We see that in the rules of monastic communities, just as we see it here.

OR: The fact that all of this comes in *Emor*, which is all about priestly behavior, does indeed make it feel kind of monastic, like a group of monks struggling to fulfill the rule.

EL: It's very clear here that home is in the other world. How much more monastic can you get?

OR: Yes, but it's clear that you have to leave that home sometimes. If these are monks, they are not to remain cloistered; they have to be out in the world.

EL: That's why the voice of the *Me'or 'Eynayim* is so important. Living in the world causes us to lose awareness. We forget our own potential for spiritual greatness. How do we restore it? By doing what a "priest" should do: loving people and bringing them to Torah! That will restore our faith in ourselves, in our own spiritual strength.

AM: That is the real "service through the corporeal." Serving God in *katnut*, in a "lesser" state of mind, brings you back to your own *gadlut*, your higher mind.

EL: Isn't that another version of what the *Or ha-Ganuz* says? Long to go back to your real "upper" home. "Upper world" or "higher mind"— it's all the same!

OR: Yes, that's for the *tsaddik*. But how about the rest of us? Isn't loving people and doing good for them holy enough? Isn't that God's service? Why must we demand more?

בהר

Be-Har

TOREY ZAHAV

Speak to the Children of Israel, saying to them:
"When you come into the land I am giving you, the
land shall observe its Sabbath for Y-H-W-H. Six years
shall you plant your field ... in the seventh the land
shall have a complete Sabbath."
(LEV. 25:2–3)

[The famous sixteenth-century preacher] R. Moshe Alshekh objects to the
phrase **I am giving you**. Isn't that completely obvious? But follow my
reading of "To you and to your seed after you I shall give the land" (Gen.
35:12). There I asked about the phrase "to your seed." If God gives it to
Jacob, isn't it clear that his offspring will possess it as well? But Alshekh
says elsewhere, on the verse "When you come into the land that I Y-H-
W-H bequeath to you and inherit it" (Ex. 12:25), that there is a difference
between a gift and a bequest. A gift may be conditional, giving them the
land if they fulfill the Torah, and stopping that gift if they do not. If the land
is a bequest, there is no taking it back from them.

That is the meaning of our verse: **When you come into the land I am
giving you**, as a gift. See that your deeds are worthy, so that it might [also]
become an inheritance, remaining yours without interruption. Had God
said, "I shall give the land [as an inheritance]," once Abraham observed
the entire Torah, it would have stayed in the inherited possession of his
offspring, even if they hadn't fulfilled the Torah. God would have been

unable to take it from them. Therefore He said: "To you and to your seed after you I shall give," meaning that as I give it to you as a conditional gift, so do I give it to your offspring, depending on their fulfilling the Torah. The Talmud tells us that one who says, "My property goes to you, but afterwards to someone else," must be listened to (b. Bava Batra 133a)....

In this way we understand the Talmudic juxtaposition (b. Berakhot 35a) of the two verses "The earth and all within it belong to Y-H-W-H" (Ps. 24:1) and "The earth has He given to the children of Adam" (Ps. 115:16). Both verses are correct. The latter verse applies when people do God's will, fulfilling the commandments that apply to the land. Then it passes to them as inheritance. But when they do not, "the earth belongs to Y-H-W-H."

How well our generation knows the wisdom of this teaching! The "*mitsvot* that apply to the land" are concerned with the land's rest and proper treatment. We now see that these apply to both the Holy Land and the earth as a whole. May we truly learn their wisdom, before it is too late!

OR HA-ME'IR I

> In all the land that you possess [*ahuzah*], bring redemption to the land.
> (LEV. 25:24)

... The essence of Israel's service in this world is to devote every detail to the building of *shekhinah*'s form. The holy books tell us that we are all a single person; united we compose its complete form. Each of us represents a particular limb in *shekhinah*'s form. That limb is restored in accord with how fully we devote ourselves and act well in our Creator's service. As we adorn our own form by this proper conduct, so is the parallel limb completed in the form of *shekhinah*. When you fulfill, "Surely open your hand to your poor brother" (Deut. 15:11), you are restoring the aspect of "hand." When you fulfill a *mitsvah* that depends upon the feet, you are doing the same for that spiritual limb; "hand for hand, foot for foot" (Ex. 21:24). The *Zohar* calls such devotees "masters of hands and feet" (*Tikkuney Zohar* t. 18, 32b), since they rule over their limbs, directing them according to their will, as a master rules over servants....

We Israelites are capable of building up the *shekhinah* insofar as our soul is attached to her. This is the meaning of "Do [or 'make'] that which is upright in His eyes" (Ex. 15:26). The *Zohar* says that this refers to the joining together of *tsaddik* [the ninth *sefirah, yesod*, with *shekhinah*; *Zohar* 2:60b]. Our building up of *shekhinah*, which is "making" that which is upright in God's sight, allows for the flow into Her of blessing from above, rather than from external [demonic] sources, God forbid.... The verse "The heavens are the heavens of Y-H-W-H, but the land has he given to the children of Adam" (Ps. 115:16) refers to this building of *shekhinah*, who is called [the upper] "land." It is given to us to prepare Her, to build her up, and to adorn Her with Her seven qualities....

"I have done [or 'made'] that which is good in Your sight" (Is. 38:4). The sages applied this verse to the one who [in the prayer service] draws [the blessing of] redemption near to the prayer [the *'amidah*; in other words, one who prays without interruption] (b. Berakhot 10b). But the words of our sages require study. How is this act "doing what is good in God's sight"? To interpret it properly, we must recall that *shekhinah* is called "prayer" (*Zohar* 1:253a). This refers to Her need to be joined to *tsaddik*, who is called Her "redeemer." This is Her redemption from those outside forces, as in "Here the redeemer passes by" (Ruth 4:1), of whom the *Zohar* says that the *tsaddik* comes bearing blessings, that he is the redeemer (*Zohar Hadash* 88a). Thus redemption is brought to the spark that lies hidden in darkness, lost in those lower rungs where no light shines through. When an enlightened person comes and pays attention to uplifting this spark, a limb of *shekhinah* is redeemed....

In all the land that you possess refers to the complete form of the *shekhinah*, from head to heel. **You possess [*ahuzah*]** means that you have the ability to hold fast (*ahaz*) to that place, whether it be hand, foot, or any of your 248 limbs. As you act properly with regard to it, wherever your "possession" is, you do the same to its spiritual parallel in the form of the *shekhinah*.

Whatever we do in this regard brings pleasure to our Creator, of whom Scripture says: "He looks to the ends of the land" (Job 28:24). The blessed Holy One gazes upon the farthest corners of the upper "land" [*shekhinah*], even down to its lowest rung. He hopes that some *tsaddik* there will uplift something of the "legs." Even this will be "making what is upright in God's sight." This is what the verse means by **In all the land that you possess**. The obligation falls upon every one of Israel, and all are equal in this, to bring redemption to the land. We must struggle all our days to "bring redemption near to prayer," to bring redemption to that well-known "land."

The author employs Kabbalistic symbolism to transform both the verse and a mysterious-sounding prayer instruction of the rabbis. "Land" or "earth" is a well-known symbol-term for *shekhinah*, the female aspect of divinity who, in the Hasidic reading, embraces the physical world within Herself, filling all that exists. Our task is to unite Her with Her upper redeemer, who is called *tsaddik*, the heavenly parallel to the righteous of this world.

OR HA-ME'IR II

> When your brother sinks low [in poverty] and sells some of his possession, a redeemer who is close to him shall come forth and redeem that which his brother has sold.
>   (LEV. 25:25)

Brother refers to the blessed Creator, who is called a "Brother" to Israel. As the Holy One descends from diadem to diadem, from crown to crown, that is **sells some of his** upper **possession**, the brilliant lights passing into the lowly realms, all this is being done for you, so that you will increase God's pleasure, which is the essence of Israel's service....

   A redeemer who is close to him shall come forth. This is the *tsaddik*, who is close to God, as in "I shall be sanctified by those close to Me" (Lev. 10:3). **Redeem that which his brother has sold**: he shall devote his intense awareness, in every deed he does, to this act of redemption. This is bringing "redemption to the land" (Lev. 25:24), raising up holy sparks even from the most earthly and corporeal realms, thus uplifting the *shekhinah*'s limbs. This is **that which his brother has sold**. God, the Brother of Israel, has created this world so that the souls of the righteous will uplift all the lower rungs to their source. This is redeeming the limbs of *shekhinah*, who dwells throughout those realms, awaiting the *tsaddik* who will come forth to redeem Her from exile. This is the **redeemer who is close to him**, who has the power to **redeem that which his brother has sold**.

ᏙᏙᏙᎵᎩ

A striking image! We rarely find God depicted as "brother" in Jewish sources. Here God enters in "poverty," as it were, making Himself and His creation needy and vulnerable, all for our sake, so that we may have the privilege of uplifting and transformation.

Be-Har
Round Two

AG: Both processes, the giving of the Land and its redemption, seem here to go on forever. The idea of eternal ongoing revelation has here been expanded into other realms.

AM: But they are processes in which we take an active role. We do the redeeming, transforming our relationship to the "land," in all its levels of meaning.

EL: Every Jew—we would say every person—can become engaged in this. It's another version of the raising up of sparks. God needs you to do it, especially the lower parts of the job, redeeming the "legs" of *shekhinah*. This is what is sometimes called the "democratizing" side of Hasidism, where everyone has a role.

AG: But it's such a different sort of redemption, really quite spiritualized. Here's a Jewish version of redeeming the Land that is neither messianic nor proto-Zionist.

AM: Like the teachings on Exodus from Egypt, redemption here is from *galut ha-da'at*, the exile of mind or awareness.

EL: For the *Torey Zahav* piece, the land is the real Land of Israel. The *Or ha-Me'ir* spiritualizes it entirely, making "land" refer to *shekhinah*. Is there a third alternative, where "land" can mean "earth, soil, land," but any land, not just that of *erets yisra'el*?

AG: The Hasidic teaching wants us to return to *artsiyyut*, the physical realm, and to find holiness there. But then it runs into the strong distinction Judaism makes between the Holy Land and other land. R. Nahman of Bratslav talks about the need to have been in *erets yisra'el* and fulfill the *mitsvot* of the land corporeally, so that afterward he could, even back home, fulfill them spiritually.

EL: But can we see all this in a more expansive way? The "building of the *shekhinah*" would then mean the redeeming of the earthly realm, the corporeal. I have in mind here the new diaspora Jewish "back-to-the-land" movement. Can Hasidic insight help inspire them, even though they are doing it outside "the Land"?

◈

בחוקותי

Be-Hukkotay

OR TORAH

If you walk in My statutes, keeping and performing
My commandments, I will grant your rains
[*gishmeykhem*] in their times....
(LEV. 26:3–4)

... This verse may also be applied to fulfilling the commandments. A person
who understands the meaning of a commandment and its origin will do
it with incomparably more fervor and desire than one who does not, who
follows it as a statute for which no reason is given in the Torah. Even if the
latter person does it to fulfill God's decree, it just cannot bear the same
enthusiasm.

Thus: **If you walk in My statutes.** Even when you don't know the
reasons, **you walk** with devotion and fervor. This will be even more true of
My commandments, where you know the reasons. Then **I will grant your
rains**, [purifying your bodily selves = *gishmeykhem*].

This can be understood through a parable. If a king has servants, they
are to fulfill his wishes even if they do not understand the reason for them
or how the king arrived at them. The servant is not even permitted to ask
the king the reason for his command; he simply has to do it.

But this is not the case with the king's son. His love for his father persuades
him to fulfill all his commands and decrees, even if he does not understand
them. But it is the son's role to ask his father why he commands things. That
is what the king wants as well; he desires that his son ask and come to know

the reasons for things. Suppose the king asks his son to fortify a certain town, or to engage in some tactic of battle. The son asks his father: "Might this be a good way to build the fortification?" or "Is this how the battle should go?" The father will offer his reasons, not objecting at all to the son's questions. The king wants to reveal his wisdom to his child, for one day he too will rule, as he does. He needs to learn from his father's wisdom. The son is permitted to look through all the king's secret treasures. As he does so, he only comes to love his father more, seeing that he is teaching him in such helpful ways.

Of course he also continues to fulfill those commands that he does not understand. He does so out of love. The servant, to whom no meaning has been revealed, fulfills the king's commands only out of fear. He has no enthusiasm, no love for the king.

If you walk in My statutes, fulfilling even the statutes for which you know no meaning, with fervor, **keeping ... My commandments,** when you know the reasons, being precise in their fulfillment, that will show that you have fear of God [as well as love]. One who does things [only] out of love and enthusiasm can sometimes forget to be exact. The one who fears follows them just as they are said. These two are best when together.

၈ထၰၐ

The parable is significantly more daring than the explanation the Maggid offers. If we are to see ourselves as God's children, surely we are to ask, to inquire, even to challenge. All that is part of the child's love, precisely what a good parent wants to see. In the parable, this is clearly a higher rung than that of the servant, who follows blindly, merely out of fear. But in his final comment, the more traditional balance between love and fear seems to be restored.

ME'OR 'EYNAYIM

> If you walk in My statutes and guard My commandments and do them, I will give your rains in their season....
> (LEV. 26:3)

"Statutes" are rules for which there is no reason; "commandments" are those that do have a reason. Why does the text refer to "walking in" rather than "guarding" the statutes? And what is **and do them**? Surely if you guard the commandments, you will do them. Why, the commentators ask, are only material rewards mentioned in the Torah? Surely there is a whole spiritual structure to the commandments: 248 positive *mitsvot*, paralleling the spiritual limbs, and 365 prohibitions, parallel to the spiritual sinews. The body is composed of these same numbers, since the human being is created in the image of God.

We need to understand this matter [of the divine image] properly. Is it really possible to ascribe any such depiction to God? The image we are made in is that of the Torah, which is called "God." Y-H-W-H concentrated the divine Self into the Torah in order that we finite humans be able to attach ourselves to the infinite God. Otherwise it would be impossible for us to be linked to Y-H-W-H.... A perfect person is one in whom the self is one with the image; the physical body is united with the spiritual form of Torah, the "upper human." When such a person moves a physical limb, the same limb is aroused above. This is truly a whole person, the one of whom Scripture says: "A man moves about only with the image" (Ps. 39:7). A person who moves about with the image, who is one with the image, is called a "man." But when you do not perform a *mitsvah* or commit a transgression, you are lacking a limb or sinew and are thus not complete.

That is why we were given these statutes, having no reasons. The reasonable commandments require no faith in order to fulfill them. You just understand that things need to be that way. But in the case of the statutes, there is no reason to do them other than faith that the Creator said to do them and that we need to fulfill His will.

Faith is referred to as "legs," those on which Torah stands. First you need to have faith that there is a Creator, that "He spoke and there was, He commanded and all stood up" (Ps. 148:5). Thus we are taught (b. Makkot 24a) that the prophet Habakkuk established all on one verse: "The righteous shall live by his faith" (Hab. 2:4). He based all of Torah on faith.

Thus: **If you walk in My statutes**, referring to commandments without reason, those that depend wholly on faith, using those "legs" on which to walk. **And do them** means that you cause those *mitsvot* to be done above, establishing the whole cosmic form. **I will give your rains** [*gishmeykhem*] **in their season**: even the physical domain (*gashmiyyut*) in which you act will be connected to the upper form—your eating, your drinking, and all the rest....

Hasidism is very much a form of faith-centered Judaism. But seldom do we find it stated so clearly and directly as here. But what of us, for whom faith is neither so literal nor so simple as he would seem to have it? In what way do unexplained ritual *mitsvot* still give expression to what we call "faith" today?

LIKKUTIM YEKARIM (#118)

> If you walk in My statutes, keeping and performing
> My commandments, I will grant your rains
> [*gishmeykhem*] in their times.
> (LEV. 26:3–4)

"Walking in God's statutes" refers to Torah study, where one must "walk" continuously, not standing on any single rung. You should ever be reaching higher in devotion and passion, until your mind becomes attached to that which transcends all the worlds. Indeed you are like one rising from each world to the next, like "the four who entered the orchard" (b. Hagigah 14b), filled with devotion and pure, holy thoughts.

Then you will attain the state where I will grant that *gishmeykhem*, your physical (*gashmiyyut*), corporeal selves, will become purified....

When a person thinks about something, whatever it is, that thought is composed of letters. When a distracting thought comes to you during study or prayer, its arrival is not by accident. "There is a time for each desire" (Eccles. 3:1). Scripture also says: "As the turn of each maiden came ..." (Esth. 2:12), referring to the holy sparks that lie deeply encased within the shells. The spark is *na'arah* ("maiden") because it is detached (*meno'eret*) from everything, longing to be attached to its root. When its time of holy ascent comes, the person bearing that thought has to be wide awake, since it has hardly come to him for naught, but needs to be uplifted. If not now, when? It may be that this particular "maiden" will never have another chance!

... [As you are purified,] the spark too rises up. **In their times** means that at the time when each of those sparks needs to ascend, this distracting thought comes to you so that **you**, who **walk in My statutes**, may have the merit of raising up that spark....

This method of treating distracting thoughts (described here in some rearranged fragments of a teaching) belongs to the core of the Ba'al Shem Tov's own message, carried on through the early Hasidic generations. Ultimately it comes to mean that there are no real distractions, because any thought may reveal itself as a way back to the One that underlies them all.

TIF'ERET 'UZIEL

> I will remember My covenant with Jacob, even
> My covenant with Isaac, even My covenant with
> Abraham, and I will remember the land.
> (LEV. 26:42)

When they depart from their iniquities and subdue their uncircumcised hearts, I will recall the merits of their ancestors to forgive them.

But we know that if you sin against a fellow human being you are not forgiven until you appease that person. A transgression against a person really involves two sins: one is against God, who commanded you not to oppress your fellow person, and the other is against the person you harmed.

The sin you committed against God by transgressing the commandment may indeed be forgiven by the humbling of your heart. But the sin against the person cannot be forgiven until you seek appeasement directly from the victim.

This is the meaning of **and I will remember the land**. Their transgression against Me, for not having observed the sabbatical, will be forgiven when their hearts are contrite. I will call forth the merits of their ancestors. But still **I will remember the land**. For their sin against the land for not observing the sabbatical, they will need to seek forgiveness from the land. Therefore it says [in the following verse] "... and the land will have its desired Sabbaths" and only afterwards "their sin will be atoned."

༄

No text in the entire early Hasidic corpus is more relevant (we might even say "prophetic") regarding our own day. We will not be forgiven for our sins (gluttony, abuse, overconsumption, among others) until we ask forgiveness of the land we have so abused. But how do we do that? In what language? By what deeds?

Be-Hukkotay
Round Two

EL: The *Me'or 'Eynayim* piece is about faith, total trust in God. But the Maggid in *Or Torah* demands something else. If you are the king's son, you need to understand, not just follow blindly.

AG: I wonder if there isn't a temptation—in our day as well as theirs—to opt for the servant role.

EL: If you want God to be a Father, you need to own up to being a son. That demands that you strive to understand why God's world is built the way it is. You have to prepare to take responsibility.

AG: Yes, the servant has no responsibility, just obedience. But how far does the "son" analogy go? Are we being prepared to rule in our Father's place? Is He looking out at the reality of a human-dominated world, where our learning from God is really an exercise to train us for moral leadership? That's a pretty modern view of religion.

EL: He's thinking more about love and relationship. The king can love the servant for his faithfulness, but there's no real mutuality there. The servant has nothing to offer to the king, beyond loyalty. But the son's love is *needed* by the king who is, after all, a father. The son has something to offer the king.

AM: With our modern skepticism, it's all too easy for us to stand outside when looking at a text like this. The fine line of needing to be *both* son and servant speaks to me, because for us the only real choice is to be both or *neither*. It's that outsider stance that is our real challenge.

AG: "If you walk in My statutes" implies growth, as many of the commentaries say. But can the servant grow? Is there growth without understanding? And can we grow from "servant" to "son"? Or is the dialectic more complex than that?

෴

אינה מקרית, כי יש "עת לכל חפץ" (קהלת ג:א), וכמו שכתוב "ובהגיע תור נערה ונערה" (אסתר ב:יב) שהיא הניצוץ הנתון בעמקי הקליפות הנקראת נערה שמנוערת מכל, ורוצה להתדבק בשרשה. והגיע עת וזמן להעלותה בקדושה, הנה אז צריך האדם להתעורר מאד מאד, כי לא לחנם באה זאת המחשבה, אלא להתעלותה. ואם לא עכשיו אימתי, כי אפשר לא יהיה עוד עת ותור לנערה ההיא...

וגם הניצוץ יעלה. **בעתם**, רוצה לומר בעת הצורך שיוכל לעלות יזדמן לכם המחשבה זרה בכדי לזכות אתכם בהעלאת הנצוצות... **אתם** ההולכים **בחוקותי**...

תפארת עוזיאל

וזכרתי את בריתי יעקוב ואף את בריתי יצחק ואף את בריתי אברהם אזכור והארץ אזכור (ויקרא כו:מב).

כשיעזבו עוונם ויכנע לבם הערל, אזכור זכות אבות למחול עוונם להם. אך ידוע שהעבירות שבין אדם לחבירו [אין יום הכיפורים מכפר] עד שירצה את חברו (מ' יומא ח:ט). ובעוון שבין אדם לחבירו, יש שתי עוונות: אחד נגדו יתברך, שהוא ציוה שלא לעשוק חבירו וכדומה; ואחד מה שחוטא לחבירו. והעון שעבר על רצון קונו כשהרע לחבירו כבר נתכפר על ידי כניעת הלב והוידוי, אבל מה שחטא נגד חבירו לא נתכפר בזה עד שירצה לחבירו.

וזהו: **והארץ אזכור**, כי מה שחטאו נגדי במה שלא שמרו השמיטה, אמחול להם כשיכניעו לבבם. ואזכור זכות אבות. אבל עדיין **והארץ אזכור**, מה שחטאו לארץ שלא שמרו השמיטה. ובזה צריך פיוס לארץ כמדובר למעלה, לכן כתב **והארץ אזכור**. ותרץ "את שבתותיה" (ויקרא כו:מג) , ואז הם ירצו את עוונם לגמרי.

❧ תם ונשלם ספר ויקרא ❧

- קנ"ד -

הצלם, אז נקרא איש. אבל כשלא עשה איזה מצוה או עבר איזה עבירה הוא חסר אבר אחד או גיד אחד ואינו שלם.

והנה מפני מה נצטווינו לעשות החוקים שאין להם טעם, הוא כי במצוות שיש להם טעם אינו צריך שום אמונה בעשייתן, שמבין שצריך לעשות כך. אבל בעשיית החוקים לא יעשה אותם רק כשמאמין שיש בורא ב"ה שאמר לעשות כך וצריך לעשות רצונו. והנה האמונה נקראת רגלין, שהם הרגלין המעמיד את התורה, שקודם כל צריך להאמין שיש בורא ב"ה "הוא אמר ויהי, הוא צוה ויעמוד" (תהלים קמח:ה) כמאמר (מכות כד.): בא חבקוק והעמידן על אחת, "וצדיק באמונתו יחיה" (חבקוק ב:ד), שהעמיד כל התורה על האמונה.

וזהו **אם בחוקותי תלכו**, שחוקים הם מצוות שאין להם טעם והם תלוים באמונה. לכן אמר תלכו שהאמונה נקרא רגלין כנ"ל. **ועשיתם אותם**, רוצה לומר תעשו את המצוות למעלה שתגמרו את הקומה העליונה. **ונתתי גשמיכם בעתם**, רוצה לומר כל מה שתעשו אפילו הגשמיות שלכם יהיה הכל מקושר בקומה העליונה, אפילו אכילה ושתיה ושאר דברים גשמיים...

לקוטים יקרים (ס' קיח)

אם בחוקותי תלכו ואת מצוותי תשמרו ועשיתם אתם: ונתתי גשמיכם בעתם... (ויקרא כו:ג-ד)

אמרו רז"ל: זה לימוד התורה (תורת כהנים). ואמר לשון **תלכו**, כלומר שתלכו תמיד ולא עומדים במקום אחד במדריגה אחת. אלא שתלכו תמיד הילוך העולה ממעלה למעלה בדביקות ובהתלהבות עד שתגיעו למדריגה עליונה לדבק במחשבותיכם למעלה מכל העולמות, כמו מי שעולה מעולם לעולם, כעניין ארבעה שנכנסו לפרדס מרוב הדביקות והמחשבות הטהורות והזכות (חגיגה יד:). ואז תזכו **ונתתי גשמיכם בעתם**, כלומר שגם הגשמיות והחומריות שלכם יזדככו...

והנה האדם כשמחשב איזה מחשבה יהיה מה שיהיה הוא מחשב אותיות, וכבר ידעת שאם באה לאדם איזה מחשבה זרה בלימודו או בתפילתו היא

- קנ"ג -

וממילא עושה גם הציוויים שלא נודע לו הטעמים, כי הוא עושה מאהבה. אבל העבד שלא נתגלה לו שום טעם, אף על פי שהוא מקיים הכל, הוא מיראת המלך לבד, אבל לא מהתלהבות ואהבת המלך.

וזה שאמר **אם בחוקותי תלכו**, אפילו החוקים שאין בהם טעם, תלכו בהם בהתלהבות. **ואת מצוותי** שאתם יודעים הטעמים **תשמרו**, רוצה לומר תדקדקו לעשותם כמאמרם. וזה מורה שיהיה בכם גם מידת היראה, כי העושה מאהבה מגודל ההתלהבות שלו לפעמים אינו מרגיש לדקדק כל כך, אבל הירא שומר הדבר מאד לעשותה כמאמרה. ושניהם כאחד טובים, מידת יראה ואהבה, **אז ונתתי גשמיכם בעתם** כנזכר.

מאור עינים

אם בחוקותי תלכו ואת מצוותי תשמרו ועשיתם אותם: ונתתי גשמיכם בעתם... (ויקרא כו:ג-ד).

הנה חוקים הם מצוות שאין להם טעם, ומצוות הם שיש להם טעם. ולמה אמר כאן תלכו וכאן תשמרו? גם מהו **ועשיתם** - כיון שישמרו בוודאי יעשו! ועוד קושיות המפרשים למה אינו כתוב רק שכר הגשמי. אבל אמת הוא שבתורה יש קומה רוחניות מן רמ"ח [248] אברים רוחניים, היינו רמ"ח מצוות עשה, ושס"ה [365] גידים רוחניים שהם שס"ה לא תעשה. ובאדם יש גם כן רמ"ח אברים ושס"ה גידים.

והנה האדם נברא בצלם אלהים. ולהבין הענין וכי שייך לומר בו יתברך שום תמונה ח"ו? אך הפירוש הוא בצלם של התורה, שהתורה נקראת אלהים שהוא צמצום, שה' יתברך צמצם את עצמו לתוך התורה כדי שיוכל האדם שהוא בעל גבול ותכלית לדבק את עצמו בה' יתברך שהוא בלי גבול ותכלית, ולא היה באפשרי לדבק בו יתברך... והנה האדם השלם הוא כשהוא אחד עם הצלם, דהיינו הקומה גשמיות שלו הוא אחד עם הקומה רוחניות של התורה, אדם העליון. וכשמנענע אבר גשמי מנענע ומעורר אבר העליון וזה נקרא אדם שלם, כמאמר "אך בצלם יתהלך איש" (תהלים לט:ז) - רוצה לומר מי שמהלך עם הצלם, שהוא אחד עם

❧ פרשת בחוקותי ❧

אור תורה

**אם בחוקותי תלכו ואת מצוותי תשמרו ועשיתם אותם:
ונתתי גשמיכם בעתם...** (ויקרא כו:ג-ד).

... יש לומר אף בעשיית המצוות. לפי שאינו דומה העושה מצוה ויודע
טעמה ושורשה, הוא עושה אותה בהתלהבות וחשק גדול, ובין העושה
מצוה שהיא חוקה שאין טעמה מפורש בתורה. אף שהוא עושה אותה
מחמת ציווי וגזירת הבורא יתברך, עם כל זה אינו עושה אותה כל כך
בהתלהבות.

וזהו: **אם גם בחוקותי תלכו,** שאף שאינכם יודעים הטעם, תלכו תמיד
בעשיותם בדביקות ובהתלהבות, ובודאי אין צריך לומר גם **את מצוותי**
שיש להם טעם פשיטא תשמרו כנזכר. **אז ונתתי גשמיכם.**

ויובן על פי משל למלך שיש לו עבדים. והנה כאשר המלך מצוה איזה
ציווי לעבדיו, העבד עושה אותו הציווי אף על פי שאינו יודע טעמו
ושרשו, ומה גם כי העבד אינו רשאי לשאול מאת המלך טעם הציווי, רק
שהוא מחויב לעשות חוק וגזירת המלך.

אבל לא כן מידת הבן. הגם שמגודל אהבת הבן אל האב הוא עושה ומקיים
חוקי המלך וגזירותיו, אף שאינו יודע טעמם ושורשם, אף על פי כן מידת
הבן לשאול מאת האב טעם הציווי, וגם הוא רצון המלך שישאל בנו וידע
טעם של כל דבר ושורשו. למשל, המלך מצוה את בנו לעשות עיר מבצר
או בדבר טכסיסי מלחמה. והנה הבן שואל את אביו, אפשר כך יהיה טוב
המבצר או כך, וכך יערכו המלחמה, ואביו מגלה לו טעם הציווי. ואין רע
בעיני אביו על שאלתו, ואדרבא רצון אביו שיגלה לבנו חכמתו, כי גם הוא
ימלוך כמותו, וצריך לו להתחכם בחכמתו. והרשות להבן לחפש בכל גנזי
אביו ואוצרותיו, ואז נתוסף אהבת אביו על בנו בראותו כי אביו מלמדו
להועיל.

- קנ"א -

320

"גאולה תתנו לארץ" (ויקרא כה:כד), להעלות ניצוצות קדושים אפילו מארציות מדריגות הגשמיים, להעלות משם איברי השכינה. וזה נקרא **ממכר אחיו** - כינוי אליו יתברך, הנקרא אח לישראל כמדובר. ולכוונה זאת היתה עיקר תכלית הבריאה, בשביל נשמת הצדיקים שיעלו כל המדריגות לשרשם. וזה בחינת הגאולה של איברי השכינה השוכנת בכללות המדריגות, וממתינות עת בואו של צדיק לגאול אותה מהגלות, וזה **ובא גואלו הקרוב אליו**, ודאי כמדובר אשר כוחו יפה, **וגאל את ממכר אחיו**.

בכוונות. כי הוא הגואלה מחיצונים, על דרך הכתוב: "והנה הגואל עובר" (רות ד:א), ואיתא בזהר חדש הצדיק בא אתא וטעין ברכאין ונקרא "גואל" - עיין שם (זהר חדש פח.) - שמביא גאולה לניצוץ המלובש במקום חושך, בבחינת מדריגות הנמוכים הנראים לכאורה בלתי הארה. ובבא המשכיל ונותן דעתו לזה מעלה זה הניצוץ, ובזה תולה גאולה של איברי השכינה...

ובכל ארץ אחוזתכם, כלומר בכל קומת ארץ עליונה, מראש עד עקב. **אחוזתכם** שם, מארי דידין אחוזתם ביד, ומארי דרגלין ברגל, כנזכר בפתיחת דברינו. וכיון שכן בהאיך שמתקן מרמ"ח [248] איבריו גורם דוגמתו תיקון אבר רוחני בקומת השכינה.

ויהיה איך שיהיה אחיזתו, משם עושה נחת רוח ליוצרו. והכתוב אומר: "כי הוא לקצות ארץ יביט" (איוב כח:כד), כלומר הקדוש ברוך הוא צופה ומביט לקצות ארץ עליונה, היינו אפילו במדריגה התחתונה. חופש משם אולי ימצא צדיק שתיקן בבחינת רגלין, וגם זה ישר ונכון בעיניו יתברך. ולזה רומז הכתוב כיון שכן אשר **בכל ארץ אחוזתכם** כמדובר. ולכן החיוב מוטל על כל אחד ואחד מישראל וכולם שום לטובה, "גאולה תתנו לארץ," תתאמצו כל ימיכם לסמוך גאולה לתפילה, והיינו גאולה תסמכו לארץ הידוע...

אור המאיר ב'

כי ימוך אחיך ומכר מאחוזתו ובא גואלו הקרוב אליו וגאל את ממכר אחיו (ויקרא כה:כה).

... הבורא ב"ה, הנקרא "אח" לישראל, נעשה כביכול מך וירד מנזרא לנזרא ומכתרא לכתרא. וזהו: **ומכר מאחוזתו** העליונה אורות הבהירים למדריגות התחתונים והנמוכים, הכל בסיבתכם לקבל מכם תוספות תענוג, אשר בזה תולה עיקר עבודת בני ישראל...

וזהו: **ובא גואלו הקרוב אליו,** הוא הצדיק קרוב לה', על שם הכתוב "בקרבי אקדש" (ויקרא י:ג). **וגאל ממכר אחיו,** כלומר לעוצם הכרתו משים מגמתו בפרטי מעשיו לגאול ממכר אחיו, ירצה על דרך האמור

- קמ"ט -

אדם," מה שאין כן אם אין מקיימים מצוות התלויות בארץ, אז הוא "לה'
הארץ ומלואה."

אור המאיר א'

ובכל ארץ אחזותכם גאולה תתנו לארץ (ויקרא כה:כד).

... כי עיקר עבודת אישים הישראלים בעולם הזה לעשות עם פרטי
עובדותיהם קומה לשכינה. כי נודע מספרים אשר אנחנו כולנו איש אחד
נחנו בכלל בחינת קומה שלימה, וכל אחד ואחד מישראל הוא אבר פרטי
של כללות הקומה של השכינה. ולערך הכשר ותיקון מעשיו והתאמצו
בעבודת הבורא ב"ה וקישוט מלא קומתו, כמו כן נתקן אבר דוגמתו
בקומת השכינה, לערך אחיזת נשמתו בקומתה. והיינו כשמקיים "פתוח
תפתח [את ידך לאחיד]" (דברים טו:יא), נתקן בחינת יד. ובעשות מצוה
התולה ברגלים, נעשה דוגמתו אבר רוחני - "יד תחת יד, רגל תחת רגל"
(שמות כא:כד), כמבואר כל זה בתיקונים וזהר. ולכן קורא אותם
התיקונים "מארי דידין, מארי דרגלין (ת' יח לב:), להורות בא, להיות
שכחם יפה לשלוט בבחינת איבריהם לעשות עמהם כרצונם...

כלל הדברים: אשר אנו בני ישראל יש לאל ידינו לעשות קומה שלימה
לשכינה, לערך אחיזת נשמתינו בקומתה. והכתוב רומז "והישר בעיניו
תעשה" (שמות טו:כו), ודרשו בזהר "דא אתחברותא דצדיק" (ח"ב ס:).
והכוונה שיעשה ויתקן קומת השכינה, שהיא הישר בעיניו, להשפיע בה
משפע ברכה עליונה, ולא שתלך ח"ו ההשפעה לחיצונים... ועל דרך
שבארנו למעלה "השמים שמים לה' והארץ נתן לבני אדם" (תהלים
קטו:טז), כלומר תיקון בנין קומת השכינה הנקראת "ארץ," את זאת נתן
בידינו להכינה ולבנותה בקישוט שבע מידותיה...

ובזה מובן "והטוב בעיניך עשיתי" (ישעיה לח:ד), ונתעוררו חז"ל שסמך
גאולה לתפילה (ברכות י:). ודברי חז"ל צריך לימוד, איך נרמז ב"טוב
בעיניך עשיתי" סמיכות גאולה לתפילה? אמנם על פי הנזכר לעיל יתפרש
על נכון, כי נודע השכינה כינויה בשם "תפילה" (זהר ח"א רנג.). משמעו
לשון "חיבור," שצריך לחברה אל בחינת הגאול, כינוי לצדיק עליון כנזכר

- קמ"ח -

ⰣⰉ פרשת בהר ⰄⰉ

תורי זהב

דבר אל בני ישראל ואמרת אליהם כי תבאו אל הארץ אשר אני נותן לכם ושבתה הארץ שבת לה': שש שנים תזרע שדך ושש שנים תזמר כרמך ואספת את תבואתה (ויקרא כה:ב-ג).

והקשה האלשיך ז"ל **אשר אני נותן לכם** מיותר, מי לא ידע שהוא יתברך הנותן כי לו יתברך הארץ ומלואה. ונראה לי על פי שפרשתי פסוק בפרשת וישלח: "לך אתננה ולזרעך אחריך אתן את הארץ" (בראשית לה:יב). והקשיתי ש"לזרעך" הוא מיותר, דאם יהיה שלו ממילא יהיה אחריו לזרעו. ופרשתי דהאלשיך ז"ל מפרש "כי תבא אל הארץ אשר ה' אלהיך נותן לך נחלה וירשתה" (שמות יב:כה). כי החילוק הוא שמתנה הוא על תנאי אם יקיימו התורה, ובאם לאו ח"ו יש הפסק, מה שאין כן בירושה, אין הפסק שאי אפשר ליקח מהם.

וזה שנאמר **כי תבואו אל הארץ אשר אני נותן**, במתנה **לכם** תראו במעשיכם טובים ש"וירשתם אותה," שתשאר אצליכם בירושה, שאין לה הפסק - עד כאן לשונו. ובזה אתי שפיר שבאם אמר יתברך "אתננה," וכשקיים אברהם כל התורה ממילא היה ביד זרעו בתורת ירושה. ואם כן אף כשלא היו מקיימים את התורה, לא היה אפשר לו יתברך ליקח מהם. לכך אמר "לך ולזרעך אתן," רוצה לומר כשם אני נותן לך במתנה כן אני נותן אחריך לזרעך גם כן במתנה על תנאי אם יקיימו את התורה. ובאם לאו, אקח מהם. והוא כדאיתא בגמרא: האומר נכסי לך ואחריך לפלוני, דבריו קיימין (בבא בתרא קלג.)...

ובזה אפשר לתרץ קושית הגמרא (ברכות לה.): כתיב "לה' הארץ ומלואה" (תהלים כד:א), וכתיב "והארץ נתן לבני אדם" (תהלים קטו:טז), דשני הפסוקים צדקו, דכשעושים רצונו של מקום ומקיימים מצוות התלויות בארץ אז הוא בירושה אצלם, ומקום פסוק "והארץ נתן לבני

- קמ"ז -

ובדביקות. וזה שנאמר **כי נזר שמן משחת אלהיו עליו**. ומהו? **אני ה׳,** בעצמי שוכן עליו, על כן ומקדושתו לא יצא.

וזהו **אמור אל הכהנים בני אהרן**, היינו עובדי ה' בני אהרן, שיהיו מתלמידיו של אהרן, דהיינו שיעשה שלום בפמליא של מעלה ובפמליא של מטה. **ואמרת אליהם**, פירש רש"י להזהיר גדולים על הקטנים. דהיינו, שהן באמת גדולים שאנו רואים שיש להם דעת בענייני עולם הזה להזהירם על הקטנים, דכל מי שיש לו דעת בקטנות אפילו הוא בן שבעים שנה נקרא קטן שאין לו דעת בעבודת ה'. וזהו על הקטנים, דהיינו שיעלה על הקטנות כי עד מתי יהיה הדעת להם בקטנות בענייני העולם הזה, אבל יעלו ויתקשרו ויתקרבו באותו הדעת אל ה' יתברך...

אור הגנוז לצדיקים

ומן המקדש לא יצא ולא יחלל את מקדש אלהיו כי נזר שמן משחת אלהיו עליו אני ה' (ויקרא כא:יב).

מהריב"ש ז"ל [הבעש"ט], זה כוונת זהר הקדוש: זכאין אינון צדיקיא דידעון לשוואה רעותהון לעילא לגבא מלכא עילאה, ולא לגבי עלמא דא וכסופא בטילה דיליה [אשרי הצדיקים שיודעים לכוון את רצונם אל המלך העליון, ולא אל עולם הזה והתאוה הבטלה שלו] (ח"ב קלד:). פירוש, שתמיד תהיה מחשבתו דבוקה בעולם העליון - בו יתברך. וזה פירוש **ומן המקדש לא יצא**, וכשצריך לדבר מענייני עולם הזה תהיה מחשבתו שהוא הולך מעולם העליון למטה, כמו אדם ההולך מביתו לחוץ ודעתו לחזור תיכף, ובעת ההליכה חושב מתי לחזור לביתו. כך יחשוב תמיד בעולם העליון, ששם ביתו העיקרי בדביקות הבורא יתברך, אף שהוא מדבר בענייני העולם הזה, ויחזור תיכף מחשבתו לדביקות הראשון.

ולא יחלל את שהוא **מקדש אלהיו**, היינו שהוא כסא ומרכבה להקדוש ברוך הוא. **כי נזר שמן משחת אלהיו עליו**, פירוש כדאמר: "שמן תורק שמך [על כן עלמות אהבוך]" (שה"ש א:ג) - פירוש ששפע וחיות אלוהות יורד מעולם לעולם, ועד לשכון השכינה אצל אדם הצדיק. על כן "כמים הפנים לפנים [כן לב האדם לאדם]" (משלי כז:יט), ומה מלך מלכי המלכים הקדוש ברוך הוא דאין מספר לגדודיו ועולמות עליונים ואף על פי כן נתאוה להיות לו דירה אצל האדם, כל שכן וקל וחומר "על כן עלמות" - הגשמיות - "אהבוך," פירוש ראוי שיתקרבו לך באהבה - קמ"ה -

מאור עינים

ויאמר ה' אל משה אמור אל הכהנים בני אהרן ואמרת אליהם לנפש לא יטמא בעמיו (ויקרא כא:א).

פירש רש"י אמור ואמרת להזהיר גדולים על הקטנים... הנה בכל אחד מישראל מוכרח להיות בו כל התורה ועבודת הקרבנות. אף שהיתה בכהן, מכל מקום יש גם כן בכל אחד מישראל, כל העוסק בתורת עולה [כאילו הקריב] (מנחות קי.).... כי הנה כהן נקרא העובד ה', וכשאין כהן בבית הכנסת קורין ישראל במקום כהן, ורב קרי בכהנא דהיינו אפילו שהיה שם כהן (מגילה כב.), שכל העובד ה' נקרא כהן.

והנה איתא במשנה דאבות (א:יב): הוי מתלמידיו של אהרן - אוהב שלום ורודף שלום, אוהב את הבריות ומקרבן לתורה. ומהו אוהב שלום ורודף שלום? הוא על פי מאמר הכתוב "או יחזק במעוזי יעשה שלום לי, שלום יעשה לי" (ישעיה כז:ה), דהיינו כשמחזיקין בתורתו יתברך ועבודתו עושה שלום בפמליא של מעלה, דהיינו בין השרים עליונים וממילא נעשה שלום בפמליא של מטה. ומפרש התנא, כיצד יעשה זאת? לזה אמר אוהב את הבריות ומקרבן לתורה.

והנה כל העולמות נבראו בכ"ב אותיות התורה; באורייתא ברא קודשא בריך הוא עלמא, ובאורייתא מתנהג עלמא. וכשלומד תורה לשמה בדחילו ורחימו מעלה ומקרב את העולם לשרשו - אל התורה. ובתורה כתיב "וכל נתיבותיה שלום" (משלי ג:יז), ונעשה שלום בפמליא של מעלה בין השרים העליונים וממילא נעשה שלום בפמליא של מטה, ולא יהיו מלחמות.

והנה זה כל האדם לא נברא רק לעשות רצון קונו, שיהיה לה' יתברך נחת רוח. ולמה אינו עושה רצון קונו? הוא רק מחמת שאין לו דעת בעבודות ה' יתברך. וכתיב "דע את אלהי אביך ועבדהו" (דברי הימים א כח:ט) וכיון שאין לו דעת, למי יעבוד? אך אם יאמר מה יעשה שאין לו דעת, זה אינו, שהרי אנו רואין שיש לו דעת בענייני עולם הזה, רק שהדעת אצלו בקטנות שאינו מגביה אותו אל הבורא ברוך הוא, אבל צריך שיתקרב באותו הדעת עצמו אל הבורא ב"ה...

- קמ"ד -

⤳ פרשת אמור ⤳

רב ייבי

ויאמר ה' אל משה אמור אל הכהנים בני אהרן ואמרת אליהם לנפש לא יטמא בעמיו (ויקרא כא:א).

נראה לי בעזרת ה', דהנה במסכת ברכות: ר' זירא כי הוה חלש מגירסיה, הוה אזיל ויתיב אפתחא דרבי נתן בר טובי. אמר כי חלפי רבנן, איקום מקמייהו ואקבל אגרא [ר' זירא כאשר נחלש מלימודו היה הולך ויושב בפתח של רבי נתן בר טובי. אמר כאשר יעברו החכמים, אקום מפניהם ואקבל שכר] (ברכות כח.).

והטעם הוא שהאדם צריך לקיים "והגית בו יומם ולילה" (יהושע א:ח), ועל ידי זה הוא דבוק בה' יתברך. לכך ר' זירא כשחלש לבו ולא היה יכול לעסוק בתורה, הלך לקיים מצות "מפני שיבה תקום" (ויקרא יט:לב), להיות דבוק בה' יתברך תמיד, לא להפרד אפילו רגע אחד מאת ה' יתברך. אבל אם מפנה לבו לבטלה בעת שאינו יוכל ללמוד, אזי שורה סטרא אחרא עליו ונדבק בו. ואחר כך כשרוצה לעבוד לה' יתברך אינו יכול, מפני הסטרא אחרא שנדבק בו, כמו שאמרו רז"ל: אם בטלת יום יומיים בטלת (זהר ח"ג לה:-לו.), וזהו כוונת רז"ל: עבירה גוררת עבירה (מ' אבות ד:ב).

וזהו פירוש הפסוק: **אמור אל הכהנים בני אהרן**. הם העובדים עבודת ה' יתברך נקראים כהנים מלשון שֵירות, ונקראים בני אהרן מלשון "מוהר" ומתן, שהעובדים לה' יתברך הם חשובים. **ואמרת אליהם לנפש לא יטמא בעמיו**, מלשון "שבת וינפש" (בראשית ב:ג), היינו כשרוצה להנפש מחמת שחלש לבו ואין לו כח לעסוק בתורה, **לא יטמא** להיות מפנה לבו לבטלה, בעודו **בעמיו**, שיכול לקיים מצוות עם חביריו, כמו ר' זירא...

- קמ"ג -

תפארת עוזיאל

... והדרת פני זקן ויראת מאלהיך אני ה׳ (ויקרא יט:לב).

כי כל קרבן לא היה כשר להקרבה פחות משמונה ימים. והטעם אמרו חז״ל שצריך שיעבור עליו שבת אחת על כל פנים (ויקרא רבה כז:י). והכוונה ידועה שעל ידי שעבר עליו שבת נכנס קדושה לתוכו, שיהיה כשר להקרבה. ואם בבהמה שהיא לא עושה שום פעולת מצוה בשבת נכנס קדושה על ידי עצומו של יום שבת קודש, ומכל שכן שיכנס לתוך ישראל עם קודש קדושה בכל שבת על ידי שמירת השבת.

וכן על ידי כל מצוה ומצוה. ומטעם זה ציוה הוא יתברך להדר פני הזקן שנכנס בו הרבה קדושות אלהות על ידי רוב הימים והשבתות שעשה. וזה **והדרת פני זקן ויראת מאלהיך אני ה׳**, מחלק קדושות אלהות אשר בקרבו...

- קמ״ב -

329

ואדרבה בזה עושה נחת רוח יותר להקדוש ברוך הוא, ומתענג ומתפאר באותו אדם יותר משמכניע הרע תחת הטוב.

וראיה מאברהם אבינו ע"ה שהקדוש ברוך הוא קראו "אברהם אוהבי" (ישעיה מא:ח), ולא ליצחק ולא ליעקב, אלא הוא היה מובחר שבאבות, כשאמרו רז"ל (פסחים קיז:). אלא לפי שאברהם היה בעומק הקליפות, שבא מתרח וגם ראשון לגרים, ואף על פי כן המשיך אברהם אבינו ע"ה לה' יתברך, ומחמת זה עשה נחת רוח לבורא יתברך יותר ויותר.

שמן הטוב

... **וְאָהַבְתָּ לְרֵעֲךָ כָּמוֹךָ אֲנִי ה'** (ויקרא יט:יח).

שאל הגאון הקדוש בעל "אורח לחיים" להרב שמואל שמעלקע מנקלשפורג ז"ל, היאך מקיימים מצות "אהבת לרעך כמוך," וחברי עושה לי רעות? והשיב לו בשכל שיוכל לקבל ממנו, הלא כל נשמות ישראל אחת הן נשמת אדם הראשון, וכללות ישראל הם כולם ניצוצות מנשמתו, מנהון בידין וכו', כמו שנאמר בספרים. ולפעמים מכה אדם עצמו מכה גדולה בשוגג, בלי דעת. והראש הוא מלך הגוף, אם יקח אדם זה מקל ויכה לידו שהכה אותו בלי דעת, הלא לחסר דעה יחשב, ולמה יכאיב עוד לעצמו?

כן ממש הדבר הזה, שהוא נפש אחת עם חבירו, וחבירו עושה לו רעה מפני חסרון דעת שבו. וכשישלם לו רעה יכאיב לעצמו! אלא יחשוב שהכל מאת ה' יתברך והרבה שלוחין לו יתברך.

ושאל לו עוד, אם רואין אדם רשע לפני המקום, היאך אפשר לאהוב אותו? והשיב לו, הלא נשמות כל אדם חלק אלוה ממעל, ועל כן תהיה לו רחמנות על ה' יתברך שהניצוץ הקדוש שלו נלכד בקליפות.

- קמ"א -

וכמוהו יכול להשיג ולתפוס אלהותו יתברך באמצעות פעולותיו ומדריגותיו ולא יותר אפילו כמלא נימא...

ונחזור לביאור: **וידבר ה' אל משה לאמר: דבר אל כל עדת בני ישראל,** מגדולים ועד קטנים, **ואמרת אליהם קדושים תהיו.** לקנות בעצמם שם קדושה באופן המדובר, הגם שאינם שוים בשיעור עבודתם את הבורא ב"ה. כי יש מי שהכרתו והשגתו עצומה וחזקה ונאמנה את אל רוחו עד כלות נפשו; ויש הרבה, ויש מעט ומעט מן המעט. ואיך יתכן להעמידם על מעלה המעולה והרמה לכנותם בשם קדושים. ובאמת אין דעתן דומה זה לזה.

לזה בא הכתוב כמתרץ ואומר: **כי קדוש אני ה' אלהיכם.** ולכאורה תיבת **אלהיכם** מיותר, ומאי היה המקרא חסר באומרו "כי קדוש אני ה'." אמנם לרמז את האמור, להיות שאני מכנה קדושתי ואלהותי על כל אחד ואחד מכם, ואנו מצינו באמת כל עדת ישראל הקטנים עם הגדולים כל אחד ואחד מכנה אלהות עליו לומר ה' אלהי. ואיך לא יתחמץ לבב אנוש, וחיל ורעדה יאחזון טרם הוציא דיבור לכנות עליו אלהים לאמר "אלהי שלי,"... כי כן דרכו יתברך, שמכנה גם כן קדושתו ואלהותו על כללות העדה, לומר **כי קדוש אני ה' אלהיכם** של כל אחד ואחד מכם, "כל העדה קדושים ובתוכם ה'" (במדבר טז:ג). ובאמת רחמנא לבא בעי (סנהדרין קו:), ואחד המרבה ואחד הממעיט ובלבד שיכניס צווארו בעבודת אדוניו לערך קט שכלו, וגם אליו קדוש יאמר לו...

חיים וחסד

איש אמו ואביו תיראו... (ויקרא יט:ג).

פירוש שיש אנשים שמצד נשמותיהן הם טובים, ורוצים להתחבר בשרשם. אך צד הגשמיות שיש לו מאביו ואמו שכוונו להנאתם הוא מצד הנחש, הם ממשיכין גם כן לצד הגשמיות. ולזה אמר **איש אמו ואביו תיראו,** כלומר גם אותו חלק שיש לך מאביך ואמך צריך להתגבר בתגבורת אחר תגבורת ולהמשיך גם זה החלק הרע להיראה, כי "הכל בידי שמים חוץ מיראת שמים" (ברכות לג:). ויש ברשותך לעשות זאת,

אור המאיר

וידבר ה' אל משה לאמר: דבר אל כל עדת בני ישראל ואמרת אליהם קדושים תהיו כי קדוש אני ה' אלהיכם (ויקרא יט:א-ב).

ולכאורה יש להבין, למה הוצרכה הקהלת כל עדת ישראל בפרשה זו. ודברי חז"ל ידוע: כי רוב גופי תורה תלוים בה (ויקרא רבה כד:ה). והנראה כי הנה כבר נודע עיקר הרצון שעלה ברצונו הפשוט לבריאת העולם, ישראל עלו ברצון הקדום לברוא העולם בשבילם. והכל בשביל התענוג והשעשועים שצפה לקבל מנשמות הצדיקים, שגדול כחם לדמות צורה ליוצרה (קהלת רבה ב:כו).

... בהיות להם בהירות השכל להשיג אורות עליונים, שנתפשטו מרום המעלות עד מדריגות הנמוכים תענוגות בני אדם, כגון אכילה ושתיה ושינה ושארית פרטי תענוגים שיש בעולם, והמה בצדקת מעשיהם בהם הכל בחכמה ודעת, להשיג עליון מהתחתון ולא להנאת עצמם כלום, כי אם להעלות התפשטות האורות למקורם ושרשם מקום האחדות. כי כחם של צדיקים ועיניים להם לראות אל כל מקום שנתנו עיניהם רק אלהות המלובשת לשם, וממילא מפשיטין מצורה גשמית ומלבישים צורה רוחניות, וזהו שמדמים צורה ליוצרה.

ואיש אשר אלה לו קדוש יאמר לו, וראוי לכנותו בשם קדוש. והנה אפילו מי שמעשהו בחכמה ודעת להעלות הכל אל השורש, עם כל זה אינו יכול להשיג יותר מבחינת אחיזת נשמתו בקומת השכינה, כי אם כל אחד ואחד מישראל לערך בחינתו ואחיזת נשמתו, כמו כן גורם תיקונים למעלה ויכול להעלות התפשטות האורות למקום אחדותם - ואחד המרבה ואחד הממעיט ובלבד שיכוין לבו לשמים (מנחות קי.), לערך קט שכלו והשגתו. ועם כל זה קדוש יאמר, לערך קדושתו שמקדש ומטהר פרטי חושיו ומלא קומתו להשראת אלהות, כמו כן קונה בעצמו שם קדושה...

כי הנה מיום ברוא ה' אדם על האדמה, לא היו עדיין שני אנשים להיותם שוה בדומה אחד בבחינת מעלתם, כי מעלות מעלות יש במדריגות הקדושים. וכל אחד מישראל יש לו אחיזה בריבוי המעלות קדושות,

~פרשת קדושים ~

אור תורה

... קדושים תהיו כי קדוש אני ה׳ אלהיכם (ויקרא יט:ב).

במדרש: קדושים תהיו - שלא יהיה בכם מות (תנא דבי אליהו זוטא כ).
ויובן על פי פירוש הפסוק: "לא אמות כי אחיה ואספר מעשי יה" (תהלים
קיח:יז). וקשה, פשיטא אם לא אמות יחיה בוודאי. ויובן במה שנאמר
בזהר: כל צלותא ומלה דאורייתא דלא נפקא בדחילו ורחימו מעומקא
דליבא [לא פרחת לעילא - כל תפילה ודבר תורה שאינה יוצאת ביראה
ואהבה מעומק הלב אינם פורחים כלפי מעלה] (תקוני זהר ת׳ י כה:). ומי
שח"ו מוציא דברי תורה או תפילה מפיו בלא דחילו ורחימו, שהוא
מחשבה זכה וטהורה ובינת הלב, הוא בחייו קרוא מת, שאין לו חלק
בחיים, שם י"ה שהם החכמה ובינה, כידוע. וכתיב: "לא המתים יהללו יה"
(תהלים קטו:יז).

וזהו שביקש דוד המלך ע"ה: "לא אמות כי אחיה." פירוש, כל זמן שאני
בחיים לא אהיה ח"ו חשוב כמת, אלא אהיה מן אותם המטהרים
מחשבותם ורעיונם ומדברים מעמקי הלב, ואז אפשר "ואספר," הוא לשון
"ספיר" ובהירות, ואנהיר ואספר "מעשי יה," שהם חכמה ובינה. שמשם
באות כל ההשפעות, ומהם אנהיר ואספר לכל העולמות.

וזה שנאמר: **קדושים תהיו.** פירוש, כשאתם תמשיכו המוחין הנקראים
"קודש" כידוע, אז תהיו קדושים בבחינת שם י"ה ולא יהיה בכם מות. ולא
אמר לא תמותו, רק בכם דייקא, רוצה לומר כאשר אתם בחיים ולא תהיו
חשובים כמתים ח"ו.

יושר דברי אמת (ס' י)

ערות אחותך בת אביך או בת אמך מולדת בית או מולדת חוץ לא תגלה ערותן (ויקרא יח:ט).

רוצה לומר, קלון וחרפה של התורה הנקרא "אחותך," כמו שכתוב: "אמור לחכמה אחותי את" (משלי ז:ד). **בת אביך** זה הקדוש ברוך הוא. **מולדת בית**, רוצה לומר תורה הנסתרת; או **מולדת חוץ**, רוצה לומר הנגלית, על שניהם אני אומר **לא תגלה ערותן** וקלונם להגות בם שלא לשמה, ח"ו - רק למען שמו באהבה.

ואני שמעתי מפה ק"ק האלהי רבי דוב בער ז"ל, באותו שבת שהייתי אצלו בחיים חיותו, ששאלוהו איזה מדרש, שאמר שם במדרש משל של תלמיד חכם, למה הדבר דומה? לזוג של זהב וענביל של מרגליות (ויקרא רבה כז:א). ואמר כי מי שעוסק בתורה לשמה, רוצה לומר להיות דבוק בה' יתברך ותמיד כל הגיון לבו בה' יתברך, כמו שאמר הכתוב "לא ימוש ספר התורה הזה מפיך והגית בו יומם ולילה" (יהושע א:ח). "בו" דייקא, רוצה לומר בה' יהיה הגיונך, כי הוא שורה ומצומצם ברוחניות הבל התורה היוצאת מפה הטהור של האדם. אם זכה לטהר פיו ולבו שיהיה מרכבה לה' יתברך, נמצא הדביקות שמתדבק בה' יתברך הוא פנימיות, ודברי תורה שלומד היא חיצוניות ולבוש לזה הדביקות, והוא הנכון. מה שאין כן אם אין חשקו ואהבתו בה' יתברך, רק הוא דבוק עדיין בתאות הזמן וחושק לכבוד, אפילו בכל שהוא, אזי פנימיות מחשבתו היא הכבוד, והתורה חיצונית למחשבתו, ואוי לה לאותה בושה שמשים דברי תורה לבוש לפנימיות שטות מחשבתו.

ולזה אמר המדרש: משל תלמיד חכם, למה הדבר דומה? לזוג של זהב. כי ידוע שהזוג הוא חיצונית, וענביל היא הפנימיות, המקשקש בו כענבל בזוג. וזהב נקרא התורה, על דרך "משבצות זהב לבושה" (תהלים מה:יד), רוצה לומר הכתוב אומר "כבודה בת מלך פנימה" (שם), שהיא יראת ה' יתברך, והשראת שכינתו היא פנימה בלב כל ישראל. "ומשבצות זהב," שהם אותיות התורה - "לבושה." וענביל של מרגליות, רוצה לומר הדביקות בה' המכונה לענביל של מרגליות, כי הדביקות בה' יתברך אי אפשר כי אם על ידי הענוה האמיתית... [דורש "ענביל" מלשון "עניו"].

- קל"ז -

334

תורי זהב
(מפרשת צו)

וכל אדם לא יהיה באהל מועד בבאו לכפר בקודש עד צאתו וכפר בעדו ובעד ביתו ובעד כל קהל ישראל (ויקרא טז:יז).

איתא בחובות הלבבות: דצריך האדם להרגיל עצמו במידת ההתבודדות להיות פרוש מבני האדם, עד שירגיל את עצמו כשיהיה בין אלף אנשים יהיה לו גם כן דביקות ליתברך, ולא יהיה שום דבר חוצץ ומפסיק אותו מדביקותו יתברך (שער חשבון הנפש פ' ג). ועל דרך שפרשתי פסוק **וכל אדם לא יהיה באהל מועד בבאו לכפר בקודש עד צאתו וכפר בעדו ובעד ביתו.** כי נודע שקודם התפילה צריך שיהיה לאדם התפשטות הגשמיות ולדבק מחשבתו בהתרוממות האל יתברך, כאלו אינו עומד בין אנשים רק בין מלאכים בעולמות העליונים. ואז כששוכח שהוא עומד בין האנשים יוכל להתפלל בכוונה גדולה ובלי פניות. וזה שאמר: **וכל אדם לא יהיה באהל מועד,** היינו בבית הכנסת או בית המדרש, מקום אשר מתוועדים שם האנשים להתפלל. אז לא יהיה שום אדם במחשבתך, ורוצה לומר שתפשיט הגשמיות כל כך עד שתשכח שעומד בין אנשים. וזהו: **בבאו לכפר בקודש,** היינו בשעת תפילה שהוא במקום קרבנות. **עד צאתו,** היינו מתחילת התפילה עד סופה. ואז בוודאי **וכפר בעדו ובעד ביתו,** כי תפילתו תהיה בוודאי זכה כשתהיה על אופן זה.

ובזה פרשתי: ובמקום שאין אנשים, השתדל להיות איש (מ' אבות ב:ה). רוצה לומר, שהשתדלות שלך להיות איש שהוא בחינת תשובה יותר מגבר אנוש, שיהיה בעולמות של מעלה במקום שאין אנשים. והיינו שקודם עשייתך איזה מצוה, תדבק נפשך למעלה כאלו אין אתה עומד עם בני אדם.

- קל"ו -

335

נועם אלימלך

בזאת יבא אהרן אל הקודש בפר בן בקר לחטאת ואיל לעולה: כתונת בד קודש ילבש ומכנסי בד יהיו על בשרו ובאבנט בד יחגור ובמצנפת בד יצנוף בגדי קודש הם ורחץ במים את בשרו ולבשם (ויקרא טז:ג-ד).

... כאן מתחיל הפסוק לדבר ממדריגת הצדיק הגמור. **בזאת יבא אהרן**, הוא הצדיק הגדול. **יבא אל הקודש**, בקדושה העליונה. **בפר בן בקר: פר**, הוא דינים כידוע. **בקר** רמז לחסד מלשון בוקר, דהיינו גבורה שבחסד, רוצה לומר שתהיה לו יראה מתוך אהבה. **לחטאת**, רוצה לומר לענין חטאים, לפשפש תמיד במעשיו שאינו יוצא ידי חובתו, ויכניע עצמו מאוד בהכנעה גדולה. **ואיל לעולה** רמז, אבל לעולה, היינו תפילה שהיא עולה לגבוה, יתגבר להיות זריז כאיל לבל ימנע עצמו להתפלל על כל דבר ודבר, ואל יאמר מי אנכי שאמלא לבי להתפלל על דברים כאלו - אל יאמר כן, וכגדול כקטן יתפלל תמיד.

כתונת בד קודש ילבש, רמז שיתקן את גופו כל כך בקדושה גדולה, שיהיה כתנות אור בא', וכל זה יעשה לעצמו לבושים. **ומכנסי בד ילבש על בשרו**, דמכנסיים היו מכפרים על גלוי עריות (זבחים פח:), וצריך שיהיו על בשרו תמיד "לכסות בשר ערוה" (שמות כח:מב), דהיינו לכסות כל התאוות הגשמיות, שלא יעלה על לבו כלל שום תאוה. **ובאבנט בד יחגור**, רמז שיאזור כגבור חלציו יותר. **ובמצנפת בד יצנוף**, דמצנפת היה מכפר על גאוה (זבחים פח:), וצריך לקדש עצמו כל כך לשבר כח הגאוה, עד שיבא לקדושה כזאת שגם מהגאוה יכניס לקדושה ויעשה ממנה מצנפת קדש. **בגדי קודש הם**, רוצה לומר כל הדברים יכניס הכל לקדושה, ויעשה מהם לבושי קודשא...

❧ פרשת אחרי מות ❧

מאור עינים

וידבר ה' אל משה אחרי מות שני בני אהרן בקרבתם לפני ה' וימותו: ויאמר ה' אל משה דבר אל אהרן אחיך ואל יבא בכל עת אל הקודש מבית לפרוכת אל פני הכפורת אשר על הארון ולא ימות כי בענן אראה על הכפורת: בזאת יבא אהרן אל הקודש... (ויקרא טז:א-ג).

... כי נדב ואביהו בעבודתם וצדקתם השלימה השלימו את נפשם, ומסרו את עצמם למיתה בהתדבקם בדביקות נפלאה, עד שנשארה נשמתם דבוקה באור העליון בסוד מיין נוקבין, ויצאתה נשמתם כאחד. וזהו **בקרבתם לפני ה' וימותו** שכל כך קרבו ונתדבקו בדביקה ותשוקה גדולה עד שנגנזה נשמתם ונדבקה למעלה.

אמנם באמת העובד עבודה כזו בדביקות נפלאה חוזר וממשיך שפע חיות מלמעלה אליו בחיים חיותו, כאמור "ואתם הדבקים בה' אלהיכם חיים כלכם היום" (דברים ד:ד), שמחמת הדביקות נתוסף חיים. כי זה רצונו יתברך המחיה החיים. אך מפני שהיה בהם חטא המעכב, על פי דברי רז"ל באמרם: שתויי יין או שהורו הלכה [לפני רבם] וכו' (עירובין סג., ויקרא רבה יב:ה), נמנע מהם השתלשלות השפע ההוא באור החוזר אליהם ונשארו נשמתם דבוקות שם בסוד מיין נוקבין. על כן הזהיר את אהרן ואמר **ואל יבא בכל עת** [**אל הקודש**], רוצה לומר שבאמת כל עבודות הצדיקים צריך להיות על דרך זה למסור נפשם בסוד מיין נוקבין. וזהו **ואל יבוא בכל עת,** שבלתי אפשר לבוא בכל עת אל הקודש, כי אם **בזאת יבא,** בבחינת זאת של בניו שהיו בסוד מיין נוקבין. אך לא כדרך שמתו בניו ונשארו גנוזות שם, רק להוסיף שפע חיות וקדושה אליו על ידי זה. וזהו **ולא ימות** כדרך שמתו בניו...

אור הגנוז לצדיקים

וצוה הכהן ולקח למטהר שתי צפרים חיות טהורות... (ויקרא יד:ד).

שהם בדרך משל יראה ואהבה, שעל ידיהם פורחים הדיבורים כצפרים עפות, ונקראים גדפין (תקוני זהר ת' י כה:), והם חיות טהורות.

והנה מפני שעיקר עבודת הבורא הוא "להיות הצנע לכת עם אלהיך" (מיכה ו:ח), שתהיה עבודתו בפנימיות יותר ממה שנראה על האיברים. על כן אומרים בנוסח יהי רצון של הנשיאים: ותעייל הך צפרא קדישא לאתר קדישא [תביא את הצפור הקדושה הזאת למקום הקדוש], דאתמר עלייהו "עין לא ראתה אלהים זולתך" (ישעיה סד:ג). פירוש, שתהיה היראה בפנימיות שנקרא אתר קדישא.

כי יש לך אדם שמראה לבני אדם גם כן שיש לו יראה ושהוא מדבר ביראה. הגם שלפעמים צריך לעשות כן, מכל מקום טוב יותר שתהיה היראה בפנימיות, ושם "עין לא ראתה אלהים זולתך" את היראה ואהבה שנקראין גדפי דצפרא קדישא.

- קל"ג -

338

נועם אלימלך

זאת תהיה תורת המצורע ביום טהרתו והובא אל הכהן (ויקרא יד:ב).

דהנה זה הוא כלל גדול: "הצנע לכת עם אלהיך" (מיכה ו:ח), שכל דרכיו של אדם צריך להיות בהצנע. כי כשאדם עושה דבר בהתגלות, בקל יכול לבא לידי פניה וגדלות בעבודתו. אבל בהצנע אינו יכול לבא לידי פניה, כי אין אדם רואהו. אך זה הוא באדם שרוצה לקרב עצמו לעבודה, צריך לילך בהצנע.

אבל הבעל תשובה שעשה עבירה בפרהסיא, כמו לשון הרע או שאר עבירות, בהכרח תשובתו גם כן בפרהסיא. כי "כבולעו כך פולטו" (פסחים ל:), כלומר כבליעת האיסור שנבלע בו כן צריך לפלוט. אם עבר בסתר, יעשה תשובה בסתר, ואם בגלוי ופרהסיא, צריכה תשובתו גם כן להיות בנגלה ופרהסיא. אבל איך יעשה תשובה בפרהסיא, פן יבא לו איזה פניה בתשובתו ח"ו ויפסיד הכל חלילה? תקנתו שילך אצל הצדיקים השלימים ואז בודאי ינצל מהפניות, כי היצר הרע אין בו כח לשלוט שם במקום הצדיקים. וגם זאת שאינו באפשר לבא לו איזה פניה בראאותו מעשה הצדיקים שהוא רב מאד יחרד לבו בקרבו לאמר: איך אתגאה במעשי נגד מעשה הצדיקים?!

וזהו **זאת תהיה תורת המצורע:** שפירוש מוציא רע, שדיבר לשון הרע. זאת תורתו **ביום טהרתו** - פירוש, צריך לטהר עצמו לעשות תשובה בפרהסיא ובגלוי כיום שהוא גלוי מפורסם. ואם תאמר שמא יבא לו איזה גדלות מזה כנזכר לעיל, לזה אמר **והובא אל הכהן** - תקנתו שילך אצל כהן הוא הצדיק הגדול העובד ה' באמת, וזה ימנעהו מכל פניה בראאותו מעשה הצדיקים אשר צדקות אהב, ואז "ישר יחזה פנימו" (תהלים יא:ז).

- קל"ב -

❧ פרשת מצורע ❧

מעיין החכמה

**וידבר ה' אל משה לאמר: זאת תהיה תורת המצורע ביום
טהרתו והובא אל הכהן** (ויקרא יד:א-ב).

נראה לי שהתורה רמזה לנו בזה דרך בעבודת הבורא, שצריך האדם
להסתכל כשבא יצר הרע באיזה עבירה לפתותו, צריך לידע שבוודאי
כוונת הבורא יתברך שיעשה המצוה שכנגד העבירה הזאת. ולכך שלח לו
זאת העבירה שצריך להיות קליפה קודמת לפרי. למשל: כשאדם רוצה
לאכול אגוז, נוטלו בקליפתו ומשבר את קליפתו ונוטל את האוכל פנימיות
הפרי, ואי אפשר ליטול את האוכל בלא קליפה.

כך אי אפשר לעשות מצוה אם לא שישבר את הרע שכנגד אותה מצוה.
ולכך כשבא יצר הרע לפתותו באיזו עבירה, צריך שישבר התאווה ויעשה
מצוה שכנגדה. שאם לא יעשה המצוה שכנגדה, אף על פי ששבר את הרע
ולא יעשה אותה עבירה, אינו כלום מפני שבוודאי תבוא עוד פעם אחרת
זאת העבירה לידו, מפני שלא קיים עדיין אותה המצוה. אבל כשכוונתו
בשבירת הרע כדי לבא אל פנימיות המצוה מבטיח לו הקדוש ברוך הוא
שבוודאי יבוא לאותה מצוה ויקיימנה.

וזהו כוונת הפסוק **זאת תהיה תורת המצורע**, רוצה לומר מוציא רע.
היינו כשתבוא לידו איזה רע, כנזכר לעיל, זאת תהיה תורתו - שתהיה
כוונתו בשבירת הרע כדי שיבוא בבהירת המצוה טהרתו, על ידי **טהרתו**
כזכר לעיל. אז מבטיח לו הכתוב **והובא אל הכהן**, שיבא אל עבודת
הבורא בשלימות באותה המצוה...

- קל"א -

וזהו **והנה כהה הנגע ולא פשה בעור**: היינו, רוצה לומר שאינו ממשיך עליו ממשכא דחיוויא, והנגעים שלו נעשים כהים ביום זה. אז וטהרו הכהן, רוצה לומר שמוחל לו עוונותיו.

סיבה אחת הגורמת במהרה גאות לאדם, וספחת הוא מלשון "ספחני נא" (שמואל א ב:לו). **או בהרת**, סיבה השנית, הבהירות של אדם. כפירוש רש"י [על] "בהיר הוא בשחקים" (איוב לז:כא), דהיינו לפעמים אם יבא לאדם איזה בהירות והתלהבות על ידי איזה עובדא שעשה, בקל יוכל לבא לידי פניות וגאות אם אינו זהיר וזריז לשמור עצמו.

והיה בעור בשרו לנגע צרעת. דנגע הם אותיות "ענג," דהיינו שהיה אפשר לו להפך הנגע לענג. אך אם אינו נזהר, אז נעשה **נגע צרעת.** ואמר הכתוב איך יעשה ויתקן את מעשיו. **והובא אל הכהן,** דהצדיק גמור נקרא כהן, דהיינו יחבר עצמו לצדיקים.... **וראהו הכהן וטמא אותו,** רוצה לומר יראהו ויבינהו את הפגם הגדול שגרם בכל זאת, ויורהו דרכי התשובה והחרטה באמת לתקן את המדות המגונות והרעות שבו...

מבשר צדק

וראה הכהן אותו ביום השביעי שנית והנה כהה הנגע ולא פשה הנגע בעור וטהרו הכהן מספחת היא וכבס בגדיו וטהר (ויקרא יג:ו).

ואפרש לך: כל שומר שבת כהלכתו, אפילו עבד עבודה זרה כאנוש מוחלין לו (שבת קיח:). כי בחינת נשמה הניתנת לאדם בשבת נקראת שבת, וצריך האדם לשמור הנשמה בשבת כהלכתה של הנשמה בעולמות העליונים, שהנשמה נכספת רק לדבק בו יתעלה. כך צריך האדם להתנהג ביום השבת, ולא להמשיך על עצמו ח"ו ממשכא דחיוויא [עור הנחש]. וזהו כל שומר שבת כהלכתו, רוצה לומר כמו הליכה של הנשמה בעולמות עליונים.

אז על ידי זה מוחלין לו כל עוונותיו. **וזהו וראה הכהן,** הוא ה' יתברך הנקרא כהן. **אותו ביום השביעי שנית:** רוצה לומר, שרואה להארה ביום השביעי, דהוא שבת והוא משנה את מעשיו ביום השבת מבחול ומתנהג כהלכות הנשמה הנקראת שבת.

שכינתו על הצדיק. ואתה אל תחזיק עצמך במדריגה זו **עד מלאת ימי טהרה**, רוצה לומר עד אחר שיתמלאו ימיך ימים רבים בקדושה ובטהרה.

נועם אלימלך ב'

אדם כי יהיה בעור בשרו שאת או ספחת או בהרת והיה בעור בשרו לנגע צרעת והובא אל אהרן הכהן או אל אחד מבניו הכהנים: וראה הכהן את הנגע בעור הבשר ושער בנגע הפך לבן ומראה הנגע עמק מעור בשרו נגע צרעת הוא וראהו הכהן וטמא אותו (ויקרא יג:ב-ג).

דהנה כתיב: "ויעש ה' אלקים לאדם ולאשתו כתנות עור וילבישם" (בראשית ג:כא). ואיתא בגמרא: מצינו בתורתו של רבי מאיר כתנות אור בא' (בראשית רבה כ:יב).

ויש לפרש, דהנה באמת ה' יתברך ברוך הוא ברא את האדם והיה כל גופו אור גדול, בלי שום יצר הרע... ואחר חטא האדם שאכל מעץ הדעת טוב ורע, אז ניתנה הבחירה לאדם לעשות טוב ורע חלילה. וברצות האדם דרכי ה' ותורתו הקדושה לשמור כמצוותה לשמה, אז נעשה גופו גם כן כתנות אור בא', כאשר תחילת הבריאה. וממילא מבואר הפירוש בתורתו של רבי מאיר, שלפי הנהגתו של רבי מאיר שהיה מתנהג בהתורה הקדושה היתה לו כתנות "אור" בא', כנזכר לעיל, לפי שתיקן את גופו ואבריו והיו מאירים אור גדול.

ואמר הכתוב: **אדם כי יהיה בעור בשרו**, הגשמיות נקרא בשם בשר. והיינו שהכניס חלילה תאות הגשמיות בעורו, פירוש לא די שלא תיקן את עורו שיהיה אור בא' אלא שיוסיף חלילה חטאים ועוונות בעורו. ואמר הכתוב מה הם החטאים ועוונות, ומפרש **שאת**, רמז למידות המגונות שהם שורש כל החטאים, שעל ידי מידות רעות בא אדם לכלל חטאים, ושורש המידות רעות היא הגאוה, ושאת רמז לגאוה....

אמר הכתוב לזה יש שתי סיבות. **או ספחת**, דהיינו התחברות מחמת שאדם מחבר עצמו אל אנשים ריקים המהלכים ברחובות ושווקין. זאת

"פליאה דעת ממני נשגבה לא אוכל לה" (תהלים קלט:ו). שמילת פליאה היא אותיות פלא י״ה [״אלף י״ה״], שדוד המלך ע״ה נפשו חשקה בתורה להשיגה בסוד הא׳. וזהו "לא אוכל לה," כי אין הענין הזה מושג בשלימות קודם ביאת המשיח.

וענין התורה בסוד א׳ הוא התכללות תורה שבכתב ושבעל פה, וכל דברי חז״ל יראו בעליל מרומז באיזה צירוף מן הצרופים. וכמו שקבלתי מהרב המוכיח שאמר בשם הבעש״ט נ״ע שכשיבוא משיח במהרה בימינו אמן ידרוש כל התורה מרישא לסיפא על כל הצרופים שבכל תיבה ותיבה, ואחר כך יעשה מכל התורה תיבה אחת. ויעלו צרופים לאין מספר וידרוש על כל צרופים - עד כאן דברי פי חכם חן ונכונים למבין.

והנה אחר החטא שניתנו גופי התורה שנתלבשה התורה אז מחומריות האדם וניתנה בבחינת הגוף כפי תשישת כחו של אדם, נתאחר תורתו של אדם אחר בהמה חיה ועוף. והוא על דרך מאמרם ז״ל שאפילו יתוש קדמך (סנהדרין לח.). ולזה אמרו ז״ל אין מוקדם ומאוחר בתורה (סנהדרין מט:), ועירוב פרשיות יש כאן, כי נתאחר המוקדם והוקדם המאוחר...

רבי שמלאי מעוררנו על ענין מוסר השכל באמרו כשם שיצירתו של אדם, פירוש כי הבריאה יתואר על בחינת הנשמה, שהוא עולם הנשמות. ולזה לא אמר כשם שבריאתו של אדם, רק יצירתו, המורה לנו בחינה קטנה מבריאה כידוע. ויצירתו של אדם דייקא, שכפי בחינת עצמו על ידי פועל כפיו בחטאו שנתאחר להיות אפילו יתוש קדמה ממנו, כך תורתו נתפרשה אחר כל בהמה חיה ועוף, כי זאת תורת האדם מתדמה לפי מעשיו לימין או לשמאל.

נועם אלימלך א׳

... בכל קודש לא תגע ואל המקדש לא תבוא עד מלאת ימי טהרה (ויקרא יב:ד).

כי בזמן המקדש היתה השראת השכינה בבית המקדש. ועתה בגלותנו המר כתיב: "ואהי להם למקדש מעט" (יחזקאל יא:טז), היינו שמשרה

דהיינו, שהקדוש ברוך הוא כביכול יהיה בבחינת נוקבא, בחינת "זאת,"
"היא נפלאת בעינינו" - פירוש, הוא פלא מאד בעינינו. עד כאן דבריו.

והנה בכל אדם יש שלש בחינות הללו: זריעה, והריון, ולידה. "זריעה"
נקראת בחינת התעוררות המעוררת לב בני אדם לעבודת הבורא.
"והריון" נקראת במי שרוצה לעשות המצוות. ו"לידה" הוא כשאדם עושה
את המצוה ההיא...

וזהו שאמר הזהר: איתתא מיומא... - "איתתא" הוא כנסת ישראל. "מיומא
דאיתעברת," דהיינו מעת שמתחיל לעבוד את הבורא, אז נקרא בבחינת
הריון כמו שכתבנו. "עד יומא דילודת," דהיינו עד שעושה המצוה, שאז
נקרא בבחינת לידה כנזכר לעיל. "לית לה בפומא אלא ילידא דילה אי
להוי דכר," דהיינו שיהיה עבודת המצוה בבחינת "דכר," ואז גורם שפע
בכל העולמות. כן יזכנו ה' יתברך לעבוד אותו בבחינות הנזכרות לעיל,
אמן.

תשואות חן

במדרש: אמר ר' שמלאי, כשם שיצירתו של אדם אחר כל בהמה חיה
ועוף במעשה בראשית, כך תורתו של אדם נתפרשה אחר כל בהמה חיה
ועוף - עד כאן לשון המדרש (ויקרא רבה יד:א). יש להעיר בזה איזה
שייכות התדמות יש בתורתו של אדם ליצירתו באמרו "כשם שיצירתו"...
גם הכינוי בלשון יצירה ולא אמר כשם שבריאתו של אדם.

ונראה דהענין הוא על דרך "זאת תורת האדם" (במדבר יט:יד; שמואל ב
ז:יט). שישראל ואורייתא חד הוא, שכפי ערך מדריגתו של אדם כך
מתדמה תורתו להזדכך או להתגשם. והנה לפי זה קודם החטא שהתורה
היתה לפי ערך בחינתו של אדם שהיה אז מוקדם מכל הברואים, על דרך
ישראל עלה במחשבה, היו צרופי התורה אז בדרך אחר, ותורת האדם
נתפרשה אז קודם תורת בהמה חיה ועוף, על פי יצירת נשמתו של אדם,
ואין שטן ופגע רע...

והתורה היתה מתחלת אז בא', וכמו שכן יהיה לעתיד בביאת המשיח -
במהרה בימינו אמן - שהתורה תהיה בסוד אלפים. וזה פירוש הפסוק

❧ פרשת תזריע ❧

קדושת לוי

...אשה כי תזריע וילדה זכר... (ויקרא יב:ב).

איתא בזהר הקדוש על פסוק הנזכר לעיל: "כי תהר" מבעי ליה, אמר רבי יוסי: איתתא מיומא דאיתעברת עד יומא דיולדת לית לה בפומא אלא ילידא דילה, אי להוי דכר [אשה מיום שמתעברת עד יום שיולדת אינה מדברת אלא על הילד שלה, אם יהיה זכר או נקבה]... (ח"ג מב:). דהנה שמעתי ממורי ורבי מורנו דוב בער נ"ע, על מאמר חז"ל: ישראל מפרנסין לאביהם שבשמים (ח"ג ז:). על דרך דאיתא במשלי: "בן חכם ישמח אב" (י:א), דהיינו במה שאנו עושים מצוות ומעשים טובים, אזי גורמים תענוג לבורא ב"ה. וזהו ישראל מפרנסין לאביהם שבשמים, שהתענוג נקרא פרנסה, כביכול. עד כאן.

והנה לפי זה, איך ראוי לכל איש הישראלי לעשות מצוות ומעשים טובים בכדי שיגיע תענוג מזה לבורא ב"ה? הלא להקדוש ברוך הוא יש כמה אלפים מלאכים, שהם אומרים "קדוש, קדוש, קדוש" באימה וביראה (ישעיה ו:ג)! ו"מה אנוש כי תזכרנו" (תהלים ח:ה). ונבאר על דרך משל: כמו שיש לשרי אומות שמלמדים את עוף אחד על לשון בני אדם, והשומע מתמיה כנגדו ואומר לשאר חביריו, בואו ונשמע ונראה דבר חידוש! והנמשל מובן. ואם כן, אתם בני אדם פקחו עיניכם וראו גודל מעלת מצוות ומעשים טובים, עד שכל עבודת מלאכי מעלה חשובים כאין נגד מעשה בני אדם... ובזה מגיע תענוג גדול להבורא ב"ה.

ואז הקדוש ברוך הוא נקרא, כביכול, בבחינת מקבל, על קבלת התענוג כמו שכתבנו. וכמו ששמעתי ממורי ורבי מורנו הרב ר' דוב בער ממעזריטש על פסוק "מאת ה' היתה זאת; היא נפלאת בעינינו" (תהלים קיח:כג). כי מלת "זאת" נקרא על בחינת נוקבא, כידוע. והנה כפי שאמרנו לעיל, שעיקר העבדות יהיה רק על סיבת התענוג המגיע לבורא ב"ה, ואז נקרא כביכול הבורא ב"ה בחינת מקבל. וזהו "מאת ה' היתה זאת":

- קכ"ה -

נטל ממנו הצומח. ועל דרך זה כתיב **וידום אהרן**, שהביא את עצמו למדריגת דומם.

ופירש רש"י: קבל שכר על שתיקתו, ומה שכר קבל? שנתייחד עמו הדיבור. רוצה לומר, על ידי שהוריד את עצמו ממדריגת מדבר לדומם, נתעלה מדומם למדבר דיבור שכינה כביכול, על דרך שאמרו: מלה בסלע, משתוקיתא בתרין [דיבור שוה מטבע אחד, שתיקה שנים] (מגילה יח.). ועל דרך זה "ישב בדד, וידום כי נטל עליו" (איכה ג:כח), פירוש נטל כמו נטל המשא עליו, "משא דומה" (ישעיה כא:יא).

וזה שנאמר "טוב ויחיל ודומם לתשועת ה'," רוצה לומר טוב ויחיל בשביל תשועת ה' כביכול. ודומם, בעניין עצמו, ורוצה לומר שמביא את עצמו למדריגת דומם, ועל ידי זה יזכה לתשועת ה', והיינו שנתייחד עמו דיבור ה' כביכול. ועל דרך זה שאינו יודע לשאול (הגדה של פסח), שהוא במדריגת דומם, "את פתח לו."

נועם אלימלך

ויאמר משה אל אהרן קרב אל המזבח... ויקרב אהרן אל המזבח (ויקרא ט:ז-ח).

פירש רש"י שהיה אהרן בוש וירא לגשת, ואמר לו משה: למה אתה בוש, לכך נבחרת.

דהנה עיקר הוא לאדם הבושה, סימן טוב לאדם שהוא בייש, וכל המתבייש לא במהרה הוא חוטא (נדרים כ.). ואהרן היה מתבייש מאד מגודל ההכנעה שהיתה בו, שכן דרך הצדיק שתמיד הוא בעיניו [מלא] חטאים על כל נדנוד עבירה. ואפילו דבר קל לעבירה חמורה תחשב לו ומכניע עצמו ומשפיל עצמו תמיד, ובפני רבים מוכיח עצמו, ועל ידי זה מכניס הרהורי תשובה בהשומעים באמרם "אם בארזים נפלה השלהבת, מה יעשו אזובי הקיר" (מועד קטן כה:)? והם חוזרים בתשובה שלימה.

וזהו שאמר לו משה רבינו ע"ה: למה אתה בוש? פירוש, בשביל שאתה בוש וירא, ואם כן אתה הוא הצדיק השלם הראוי ליקרב למזבח. לכך נבחרת, שכך הוא ראוי לצדיק להתנהג בעבודתו יתברך. וזהו **ויקרב אהרן אל המזבח**: רוצה לומר, כיון ששמע ממשה שכך הוא המדריגה המעולה הבושה וגודל ההכנעה בלב, ועשה כן. **ויקרב אהרן אל המזבח**: פירוש, שהיה מקרב עצמו תמיד אל המזבח, שהיה מוצא בעצמו חסרונות והיה מחשב תמיד שצריך למזבח כפרה.

צמח ה' לצבי

...וידום אהרן (ויקרא י:ד).

כתיב "טוב ויחיל ודומם לתשועת ה'" (איכה ג:כו). כי המדריגות הם דומם, צומח, חי, מדבר. ולפעמים צריך שיהיה האדם במדריגת דומם, על דרך "ונפשי כעפר" (ברכות יז.), שלא ירגיש בצערו שמצערו חבירו או שלא יהרהר אחר מידותיו יתברך, כמו הדומם שאינו מרגיש בצער אם

ובחינה ראשונה שיהיה שפל בעיניו הוא מצד יצר הטוב, ובחינה השניה
שיגדיל בעיניו מעשיו ודיבוריו הוא מצד היצר הרע. וזהו "בשני יצריך"
...

רב ייבי

**ויהי ביום השמיני קרא משה לאהרן ולבניו ולזקני ישראל:
ויאמר אל אהרן קח לך עגל בן בקר לחטאת ואיל לעולה
תמימים והקרב לפני ה'** (ויקרא ט:א-ב).

נראה לי, בעזרת ה' יתברך, ביום שמיני למלואים קרא משה לאהרן
ולבניו ולזקני ישראל ללמדם סדר העבודה, היאך לעבוד לה' יתברך.
ואמר אל אהרן שהוא התלמיד חכם, נקרא אהרן מלשון "מוהר" ומתן,
והתורה נקראת "ענקים לגרגרותיך" (משלי א:ט). ולימד משה לתלמיד
חכם ואמר **קח לך עגל בן בקר לחטאת**, היינו "עגל" ראשי תבות, כמו
שכתוב בשל"ה: "**ע**ריות, **ג**זל, **ל**שון הרע" (כי תשא ס' יא). והעולם
מקילין בזה, כמו שאמרו: רובן בגזל מיעוטן בעריות כולם בלשון הרע
(בבא בתרא קסה.). ואחר כך כשבא אדם לעשות תשובה מאבד כוחו
בתעניות.

לכך לימד משה לתלמיד חכם שיקח מתחילה **עגל** - היינו עריות, גזל,
לשון הרע - **לחטאת**, וכשיהיה מוחזק אצלו לחטאת, בודאי שלא יחטא.
ולכך אמר **בן בקר**, "בן" מלשון "הבנה," שיבין לבקר בין טוב ובין רע,
וירחיק עצמו מן עגל - עריות, גזל, לשון הרע. ולא יצטרך להתענות אחר
כך לאבד כוחו. ואז **ואיל**, היינו הכח שלו מלשון "ואת אילי הארץ"
(יחזקאל יז:יג), **לעולה תמימים**, שיעבוד בכוחו לה' יתברך בתורה
ובתפילה בתמימות. ואז **הקרב לפני ה'** התורה והמצוות.

❧ פרשת שמיני ❧

אורח לחיים

ויהי ביום השמיני קרא משה לאהרן ולבניו ולזקני ישראל (ויקרא ט:א).

להבין, מה דהוה הוה! נראה שרמז בזה דהנה ישראל היו אז בבחינת בעלי תשובה, שהמשכן היה מכפר על עון העגל. ובעל תשובה צריך לתקן מידותיו, תחילה השבע מידות שלו, והן שבעת ימי המלואים (ויקרא ח:לג), שהיו יושבין בבית המקדש בהפרשה מבני אדם, לתקן השבע מידות ואחר כך יוכלו לבוא לעולם התשובה [ספירת בינה]. וזהו **ביום השמיני**, שהיו באין לעולם השמיני מתתא לעילא, הוא עולם התשובה שנתקן הכל.

קרא משה לאהרן ולבניו... דהנה האדם צריך לעבוד ה' יתברך בכל לבבו, ודרשו חז"ל: "בכל לבבך" (דברים ו:ה) - בשני יצריך, ביצר טוב וביצר הרע (מ' ברכות ט:ה). ולהבין האיך עובדים ה' יתברך ביצר הרע, דהנה האדם השלם בכל מידותיו צריך לראות שלא לבוא לו ח"ו שום גאות מזה, וצריך לזכור בחטאיו בכל עת ולקיים "חטאתי נגדי תמיד" (תהלים נא:ה), ולהיות תמיד בבחינת ענוה, כמו שהזהירו רז"ל: מאד מאד הוי שפל רוח (מ' אבות ד:ד). אבל אם יהיה בעבודה שפל רוח, ויאמר בלבו מה אני שאעשה מצוה או להתפלל ולבקש מה' יתברך שפל כמוני? זהו ענוה פסולה, ואדרבה אמרו רז"ל: אל תהי רשע בפני עצמך (מ' אבות ב:יג), וגם אמרו: לעולם יראה אדם עצמו כאילו כל עולם תלוי בו שהוא חציו חייב וחציו זכאי, וכל העולם חציו חייב וחציו זכאי, עשה מצוה אחת (קדושין מ:)... וכוונתם בזה להגדיל מעשה מצוות בני אדם בעיניהם, שיעשה אותם בחשק ובהתלהבות גדולה שפעל בעבודתו ובמצוותיו שמכריע כל העולם לכף זכות.

נועם אלימלך

ולבש הכהן מדו בד ומכנסי בד ילבש על בשרו והרים את הדשן אשר תאכל האש את העולה על המזבח ושמו אצל המזבח: ופשט את בגדיו ולבש בגדים אחרים והוציא את הדשן אל מחוץ למחנה אל מקום טהור (ויקרא ו:ג-ד).

ולבש הכהן מדו בד: פירוש... צריך להלביש עצמו **מדו בד,** רוצה לומר שצריך לתקן עצמו במדותיו בהתבודדות מחשבתו. **ומכנסי בד ילבש על בשרו,** דהיינו שצריך גם כן התבודדות אחרת "לכסות את בשר ערוותו" (שמות כח:מב), רצה לומר תאוותו. **והרים את הדשן אשר תאכל האש:** רוצה לומר, שזה בלתי אפשרי, שישבר אדם כל מידותיו הנולדים עמו מבטן אמו. רק שצריך להרים אותם אל הקדושה. למשל, מי שיש בו מידת כעס, יסור מכעס החיצוני ויכעוס על הרשעים, וכן בכל המידות. **ושמו אצל המזבח:** פירוש, כנזכר לעיל, שישים המידה אל הקדושה, דהיינו באם יבא לכעס או שאר מידה, ישבר עצמו להביא אותה המידה אל הקדושה. **ופשט את בגדיו ולבש בגדים אחרים:** רוצה לומר, שאחר כך יבא אל מדרגה יותר, עד שיופשט מכל וכל מכל המידות. **והוציא את הדשן מחוץ למחנה:** רוצה לומר, שלא יבא לו בשום פעם מהמידות הנולדות עמו כי אם הכל בקדושה רבה.

עבירה ח"ו. והוא סוד הקמיע המועיל לזכירה על ידי השם היוצא מפסוק "אנכי..." כדאיתא בארז"ל.

ואם ירצה ה', בביאת משיח תושלם כח הזכירה לכולנו ותתמיד זכירתו יתברך שמו. ועל דרך זה שמעתי בשם הבעש"ט ז"ל על פסוק "אנכי אנכי הוא מנחמכם" (ישעיה נא:יב). פירוש, כשתדעו שאין "אנכי" אלא "אנכי" לבדי ואין זולתי, אז ודאי "הוא מנחמכם." עד כאן לשונו, ודברי פי חכם חן.

והנה כבר מוזכר בדברינו, שהצדיק נופל לפעמים ממדריגתו שלא מסיבתו רק לצורך שאר העם שהם ענפיו בכדי להעלותן, והיא בסוד השינה והדורמיטא. וכאשר פירשנו פסוק "את קשתי נתתי בענן" (בראשית ט:יג), שהצדיק מכונה בשם קשת וניתן בענן שהוא החושך, כדי שיתעורר בתשובה על שמץ דבר עבירה שבו על ידי פעולת העם, ויעלה אותם עמו שיכניס בהם ההרהורי תשובה. והשמץ עבירה שבו אינו ח"ו בפועל רק איזה מחשבה זרה או שכחה ממנו יתברך, וכאשר שמעתי בשם הבעש"ט ז"ל על פסוק "אשרי אדם לא יחשוב ה' לו עון" (תהלים לב:ג). פירש, שהפסוק משבח ואומר שאשרי אדם שהחטא אינו אצלו בפועל ח"ו, רק שמה שלא יחשוב ה' - זה לו עון...

ובזה באנו אל הביאור: **צו את אהרן ואת בניו**. פירוש, שצוה ה' יתברך למשה לומר להם שכשיארע להם לפעמים ח"ו בחינת צו, שהיא בחינת עבודה זרה והיא השכחה כנזכר, אין זה אלא **תורת העולה**, שהיא לצורך העלאת שאר העם, בכדי להכניס בלבם ההרהורי תשובה על פועל כפם. וכאשר יוודע להם בחינה זו תרתח לבבם בהפלאה יתירה לחזק בדק. וזהו שמדייק הכתוב: **זאת תורת העולה**, פירוש שהירידה היא צורך עליה, "ושפתי כהן ישמרו דעת" (מלאכי ב:ז), להבין כי היא פשיטת ידו לפנים לעורר בתשובה.

המכוון של ה' יתברך שאין זה העיקר, כי אם שעל ידי התורה יעלה
למעלה מהאותיות, היינו למקום שאין התלבשות להאור, היינו במקום
שהיתה התורה אור קודם חטא אדם הראשון שעדיין לא נעשה כתנות
עור. וזהו "הלוואי אותי עזבו" היינו הלימוד שהוא אינו כי אם אותיות,
"ותורתי שמרו" שהוא למעלה מהאותיות שהוא אור הגנוז הנ"ל.

תשואות חן

**וידבר ה' אל משה לאמר: צו את אהרן ואת בניו לאמר זאת
תורת העולה היא העולה על מוקדה על המזבח...** (ויקרא ו:א-
ב).

יש להעיר באומר **לאמר** פעם שניה ללא צורך. גם מלת **זאת התורה** על
מיעוט אין לו הבנה. גם על פי דברי רז"ל שאמרו: אין "צו" אלא עבודה
זרה (זהר ח"א כז:) - יפלא בעיני כל רואה, והוא כחזיון נסתם לאמר **צו
את אהרן.**

ונראה לפרש על פי המוקדם אצלנו, "אנכי" ו"לא יהיה לך" בדיבור אחד
נאמרו (תיקוני זהר ת' כב סג:). העניין הוא שהקדוש ברוך הוא הופיע
בטחתו אלינו שכש"אנכי ה' אלהיך," פירוש שבעת שתזכור שאנכי ה'
אלהיך ולית אתר פנוי מניה, אז "לא יהיה לך אלהים אחרים," שלא תפול
בשום דבר עבירה שבעולם, שהיא מעניין עבודה זרה. כי כל עבירה שאדם
עובר ח"ו היא משמץ עבודה זרה הנמשכת מבחינת השכחה, כי אין אדם
עובר עבירה אלא אם כן נכנסת בו רוח שטות (סוטה ג.) המגבהת לבו של
אדם ומפילו וכאילו דוחק רגלי השכינה ח"ו, ובחינת הגאוה נקראת
אלהים אחרים, כידוע על פי האריז"ל.

ובהיפוך, כשהאדם הוא בבחינת השפלות, אז ודאי "אני אשכון את דכא
ושפל רוח" (ישעיה נז:טו). ו"אין שכחה לפני כסא כבודו" (ברכות לב:),
ובחינה זו מביא את האדם לזכירה. וזהו "אנכי ה' אלהיך," כשאנכי ה'
אלהיך, אז "בשפלנו זכר לנו" (תהלים קלו:כג) ובא האדם לידי זכירה,
ובודאי לא יהיה שוב לך אלהים אחרים על פני, שלא תבוא לידי דבר

והאש תוקד על המזבח לא תכבה. והענין הוא שאור של ששת ימי בראשית בהם ראה אדם הראשון מסוף העולם ועד סופו, ואחר שחטא נעלם האור; היינו גנזו לצדיקים לעתיד לבוא (חגיגה יב.). כי בתחילה קודם החטא היה האור באתגלייא, ואחר החטא נעלם האור בלבושים שהלבישו את האור, היינו שהאור נתלבש בתוך התורה. וזהו "ויעש ה'... כתנות עור" (בראשית ג:כא), ובתורתו של ר' מאיר היה כתוב כתנות אור בא' (בראשית רבה כ:יב)... [כי רבי מאיר] היה מלמד את בני דורו ומאיר עיניהם, היינו שלימד אותם איך יבואו אל האור הגנוז שבתוך התורה שעל ידי שנתלבש בלבושים לא כל אחד יכול לבוא אל האור הגנוז, ורבי מאיר היה מלמד את בני דורו ומאיר עיניהם איך לבא אל האור הגנוז.

ונחזור לעניינו, כי על ידי התורה נתעלה האדם. **זאת תורת העולה,** ואיך יתעלה האדם על ידי התורה? אין זה כי אם על ידי שיבא אל האור הגנוז, והיינו שיביט על ידי האור הגנוז מה שיהיה מסוף העולם ועד סופו. וזהו **צו** – אין צו אלא זירוז מיד ולדורות – היינו שיהיה שום לו מה שהוא עתה בהווה, היינו מיד, ומה שיהיה לדורות יהיה גם כן שוה למה שהוא מיד... באו אל אור הגנוז ושם אין חילוק בין מיד ובין לדורות, שהוא מקום ששם שוה הווה ומה שעתיד להיות. אמר רבי שמעון: ביותר צריך הכתוב לזרז במקום שיש חסרון כיס, היינו אם לומד התורה ובא לאור הגנוז ושם אין מתלבש האור בשום כיסוי ושום התלבשות, שהוא כמו שהיתה התורה קודם חטא אדם הראשון, שהוא קודם שעשה כתנות אור שלא היתה נתכסה האור בלבושי התורה כי אם האור היה באתגלייא, וזהו חסרון כיס.

וזה שאמרו חז"ל (על ירמיהו טז:יא): הלואי אותי עזבו ותורתי שמרו (איכה רבה פתיחתא ב). פירוש כי האדם הלומד התורה הוא רואה לפניו אותיות, ואחרי זה מתבונן ונפתחין לו פתחי חכמה להבין את התורה בשכל והבנה, מנין לו השכל וההבנה? הלא לא ראה כי אם אותיות!

... והיינו שאין האדם חכם ולמדן מעצמו כי אם ה' הוא המלמד להועיל, והוא "כי ה' יתן חכמה מפיו דעת ותבונה" (משלי ב:ו)... והנה האדם הלומד שלא בדרך הנ"ל שיבוא אל אור הגנוז הוא אינו מועיל לו בלימודו כי אם מה שנעשה למדן ובקי בהלכות, והיינו האותיות שבתורה. ואין זה

- קי"ז -

גדולה ובדביקות הבורא יתברך. ובסוף הפסוק **אש תמיד תוקד על המזבח לא תכבה**, אפילו רגע אחד, רק יקיים "והגית בו יומם ולילה" (יהושע א:ח). וזהו באמת צריך זירוז גדול מיד ולדורות, כי לא תבטל כנזכר. ועל זה אמר רבי שמעון ביותר צריך לזרז. כי רבי שמעון בן יוחאי לטעמיה, דאמר אם יעסוק האדם בזרע בשעת הזריעה... ותורתו אימתי נעשית? אלא יעסוק בתורה [ומלאכתו נעשית על ידי אחרים] (ברכות לה.)... וזהו וודאי חסרון כיס גדול, שיבטל מכל מלאכת העולם הזה ותהיה תורתו אומנתו.

מאור עינים

וידבר ה' אל משה לאמר: צו את אהרן ואת בניו לאמר זאת תורת העולה היא העולה על מוקדה על המזבח כל הלילה עד הבקר ואש המזבח תוקד בו... אש תמיד תוקד על המזבח לא תכבה (ויקרא ו:א-ב,ו).

אין "צו" אלא לשון זירוז, מיד ולדורות. אמר רבי שמעון: ביותר צריך הכתוב לזרז במקום שיש חסרון כיס (תורת כהנים). וקשה הלא כל המצוות נאמרו לקיים לדורות עולם, ומה היא חסרון כיס שבקרבן עולה — הלא יש כמה מצוות שיותר צריך לחסרון בשבילו ולא נאמר בהם צו, לשון זירוז!

ויש לומר כי התורה שנתן לנו ה' עיקרה שעל ידה נכניע את היצר הרע. לכן על פי רוב רוב נזכר בזהר לאישתדלא באורייתא, שהוא תרגום של "ויאבק איש עמו" (בראשית לב:כה), היינו שעל פי התורה יוכל האדם להתאבק עם היצר הרע ולהכניעו, כי המאור שבה [בתורה] מחזירו למוטב (איכה רבה פתיחתא ב). כי על ידי התורה יוכל האדם לדבק אל ה' יתברך, שהוא נעלם בתוך התורה והוא המאור שבה... וזהו "ראיתי בני עלייה והם מועטים" (סוכה מה:), כי על ידי התורה יוכל האדם לעלות למעלה וגם לתקן את אשר קלקל. וזהו **תורת העולה** שעל ידה יוכל להתעלות למעלה. **כל הלילה עד הבוקר**, היינו גם החשכות שלו יוכל להעלותה ולעשות ממנה בוקר אור.

~ פרשת צו ~

אור תורה

וידבר ה׳ אל משה לאמר: צו את אהרן ואת בניו לאמר זאת תורת העולה היא העולה על מוקדה על המזבח כל הלילה עד הבקר ואש המזבח תוקד בו... אש תמיד תוקד על המזבח לא תכבה (ויקרא ו׃א-ב,ו).

פירש רש״י: אין ״צו״ אלא זירוז, מיד ולדורות. אמר רבי שמעון: ביותר צריך הכתוב לזרז במקום שיש חסרון כיס (תורת כהנים). ויש לומר, אם הוא כפשוטו, מה הוא הזירוז להקריב שני תמידין? ומה חסרון כיס זה לכל ישראל להקריב תמידין בכל יום? והלא מוספין הרבה יותר מתמידין, והיה לומר שם צו וזירוז. ועוד, מהו מיד ולדורות? והלא תמידין עתידין ליבטל בחורבן הבית.

יש לומר על פי מה שאמרו רז״ל (מנחות קי.): כל העוסק בתורה כאלו הקריב כל הקרבנות, שנאמר **זאת תורת העולה**. ואפשר לומר על פי רמז כל פרשה זו. **צו את אהרן ואת בניו לאמר זאת תורת העולה**: פירוש, זירוז מיד ולדורות כי התורה לא תתבטל לעולם, ״כי לא תשכח מפי זרעו״ (דברים לא׃כא). לכך זרם שיעסקו בתורה, שהיא העולה למעלה מכל הקרבנות. וקאמר והדר מפרש על איזו תורה זרום? ואמר **היא העולה על מוקדה** - רוצה לומר, שהיא בהתלהבות ובהתדבקות הבורא יתברך, ולא שיהיה ח״ו מן השפה ולחוץ. כי כל מלה דלא נפקית בדחילו ורחימו לא פרחת לעילא [כל מילה שאינה יוצאת ביראה ובאהבה, אינה פורחת למעלה] (תקוני זהר ת׳ י כה׃), ואינה קרויה **עולה**.

ומה שאמר **על המזבח** - הוא האדם הנקרא מזבח, כמו שאמרו רז״ל על פסוק ״וייצר את האדם עפר מן האדמה״ (בראשית ב׃ז): מהיכן נברא? ממקום כפרתו, מן מזבח האדמה (בראשית רבה יד׃ח). ואמר **כל הלילה:** רוצה לומר, כל ימי חיי האדם בעולם הזה, שהוא דומה ללילה. **עד הבוקר... אש תמיד**, היא התורה הנקראת אש. **תוקד בו**, בהתלהבות

- קט״ז -

356

קדושת לוי

ונפש כי תחטא ועשתה אחת מכל מצוות ה' אשר לא תעשינה ואשם (ויקרא ד:כז).

כי הנה ידוע, יותר מה שהאדם עובד את הקדוש ברוך הוא, יותר הוא בעיני עצמו כלא נחשב נגד גדולת הבורא יתברך. אבל כשהאדם עושה מצוה והוא סובר שהוא עובד את ה', זאת המצוה אינה נחשבת לכלום. וזהו פירוש הפסוק **ונפש כי תחטא**: כלומר, מה החטא? **ועשה אחת מכל מצות ה' אשר "לא" תעשינה**. **ואשם**, כלומר שהמצוה הזאת יעשה לו כ"לא," והוא סובר שעובד ה' כראוי, **ואשם**.

נועם אלימלך ב'

או כי יגע בטומאת אדם לכל טומאתו אשר יטמא בה ונעלם ממנו והוא ידע ואשם (ויקרא ה:ג).

רמז לאדם רשע שנטמא בעוונות וחטאים, ועל ידי זה נותן כח וחיות לאדם רע בליעל. והצדיק רוצה שישוב מעוונו, ולא יעשה עוד. וזהו **או כי יגע**: פירוש, שמטה עצמו לדבר זה, כנזכר לעיל. ומלמד הכתוב גם כן שיעשה בדרך זה, **ונעלם ממנו**, שיראה לעשות הדבר הזה בהעלמה ובהסתר. **והוא ידע**: פירוש, ממילא יתוודע לאותו רשע, וירגיש בעוונו ויפול עליו חרדה גדולה והתעוררות תשובה. **ואשם**: פירוש, כנזכר לעיל שיהא משומם ומבולבל מאותו דבר, ולא יעשה עוד.

מטה עצמו לעבודת הבורא ב"ה בכל יכלתו, והיה מקדש עצמו במאוד מאוד ובא למדריגה זו, **וידבר ה' אליו**, שהוא שם הרחמים.

וזהו שהתפלל דוד המלך ע"ה "אתה ה' לעולם תשב" (תהלים קב:יג). כי עתה בעוונותינו הרבים שהשכינה בגלות, כשהקדוש ברוך הוא רוצה לדון את ישראל, צריך ברוב רחמיו לעמוד מכסא דין ולישב עליהם בכסא רחמים. אבל לעתיד לבא יהיה כולו רחמים גמורים, ולא יצטרך לעמוד מכסא דין כלל ולשנות מכסא לכסא. ועל זה התפלל "אתה ה' לעולם תשב כסאך לדור ודור" (איכה ה:יט), דעיקר שכינת כבודו יתברך הוא על הצדיקים. והתפלל לאמר אף על פי שנתמעטו הדורות (שבת קיב:)... אף על פי כן, יהיה כסאך עלינו בכל דור ודור ברוב רחמיך, תחופף עלינו אור שכינתך, אמן.

מגיד דבריו ליעקב (ס' צז)

...**אשה ריח ניחוח לה'** (ויקרא א:ט).

הנה העולם לא נברא רק בשביל שעשוע שהקדוש ברוך הוא ותענוגו כביכול במעשה מצוות, שאמר ונעשה רצונו. פירוש, שעיקר התענוג הוא מה שאדם חושב ומתלהב לעשות נחת רוח לפניו יתברך, והוא למלאות רצונו. כי העבדות עצמה אינה עיקר, כי לפעמים אדם לומד מפני טבעו שיש לו חשק ללמוד, וגם כן אדם עוסק בסחורה שיש לו חשק לזה, ומה ההפרש ביניהם כי אם ממלא תאוותו?

אלא עיקר התענוג של הקדוש ברוך הוא הוא מהחשק שלו לעבודתו יתברך, כמו שנאמר "כי ה' אלהיך אש אוכלה הוא" (דברים ד:כד). פירוש, עיקר אכילתו ותענוגו ממעשה המצוות הוא האש של ההתלהבות, כמו שנאמר **אשה ריח ניחוח לה'**... אך ההתלהבות לבד לא היו לו כלים במה להתלבש, וצריך להתלבש בעובדא...

(ברכות כח:). וקא מפרש בגמרא אפילו בשעה שהם פורשין לעבירה יהיו צרכיהם גלוים לפניך.

העניין הוא שהבורא ב"ה מצומצם אצל כל אחד מישראל, ואפילו רשע גדול יש אצלו עדיין הבורא יתברך. והראיה שלכל רשע באים לו הרהורי תשובה, דהיינו שהקדוש ברוך הוא קורא אותו בעצמו ואומר "שוב אלי," רק שאינו מבין שה' יתברך קורא אותו.

וזהו **ויקרא אל משה** כתיב אלף זעירא, דהיינו שה' יתברך שהוא אלופו של עולם הוא מצומצם אצל כל אחד מישראל וקורא אותו לשוב, דהיינו הרהורי תשובה שבאים לו. רק מפני שאינו מבין שזה קורא אותו ה' יתברך ב"ה, לכן כתיב **ויקרא** סתם, אבל כשמבין שזה קורא אותו ה' יתברך לשוב מדרכו הרעה, והוא משיב עצמו אל הבורא יתברך, אז אחר כך **וידבר ה' אליו מאהל מועד לאמר**, דהיינו כשבא לעשות איזה עבירה והקדוש ברוך הוא מונע אותו על ידי איזה סיבה שלא יוכל לעשות העבירה, הרי הוא כמו שמדבר "שובה אלי, עד מתי תלך אחר הבליך?"

וזהו שאמרו רז"ל: מתפלל תפילה קצרה (ברכות ג.) - לקצר הקליפות. הושע ה' את עמך את עמך, אפילו בשעה שהם פורשין לעבירה...

נועם אלימלך א'

ויקרא אל משה וידבר ה' אליו מאהל מועד לאמר (ויקרא א:א).

לכאורה היה ראוי לכתוב "ויקרא ה' אל משה וידבר אליו," כדי שנדע מי קראו, ולא כן עתה **ויקרא אל משה** סתם, ואינו יודע מי קראו. אך העניין הוא דאיתא בזהר: ויקרא... אלף זעירא, דהשכינה כשאינה במקומה אזי היא זעירא (ח"א רלט:). ואז היו במדבר, ועיקר מקום כבודו הוא בבית המקדש בירושלים. ולכן מתחילה נאמר **ויקרא אל משה**, והיא אלף זעירא קרא אל משה. אך אחר כך, כשכבר קראו והיה משה רבינו ע"ה

- קי"ב -

359

✦ פרשת ויקרא ✦

מאור עינים א'

ויקרא אל משה וידבר ה' אליו מאהל מועד לאמר (ויקרא
א:א).

...הנה הענין הוא שה' יתברך הוציאנו ממצרים, ונתן לנו תיכף מצוות
פסח ומילה, ואחר כך קרע לנו את הים, ואחר כך הוליכנו במדבר בעמוד
ענן יומם ובעמוד אש לילה, ואחר כך נתן לנו את התורה, ואחר כך צוה
לעשות משכן, כאמור "ועשו לי מקדש ושכנתי בתוכם" (שמות כה:ח) -
בתוכו לא נאמר, [אלא בתוכם].

כמשל מי שהיה מעולם במקום חושך ולא ראה אור מימיו, אם היו
מוציאין אותו פתאום לאויר העולם לא היה יכול לסבול האור. ולכן צריך
להראות לו בהדרגה, שמתחילה עושין לו סדק קטן שיכול לראות משם
מעט אור, ואחר כך מרחיבין לו הסדק עד שנעשה חלון, ואחר כך מוציאין
אותו לאויר העולם ומראין לו האור.

כך ישראל במצרים היו משוקעים בחמישים שערי טומאה, ואילו היה
מראה להם תיכף זיו שכינתו לא היו יכולין לסבול. לכן הוצרכו לכל
הדרגות הנ"ל, ועיקר התכלית היה "ועשו לי מקדש ושכנתי בתוכם."

מאור עינים ב'

ויקרא אל משה וידבר ה' אליו מאהל מועד לאמר (ויקרא
א:א).

והנה אמרו רז"ל: המהלך במקום סכנה מתפלל תפילה קצרה, [הושע ה'
את עמך את שארית ישראל,] בכל פרשת העיבור יהיו צרכיהם לפניך

ע׳ קמט **אור המאיר ב׳** - כי ימוך אחיך ומכר מאחוזתו ובא גואלו
הקרוב אליו וגאל את ממכר אחיו (ויקרא כה:כה).

✎ בחוקותי (ע׳ קנא-קנד) ✎

קנא **אור תורה** - אם בחוקותי תלכו ואת מצוותי תשמרו ועשיתם
אותם: ונתתי גשמיכם בעתם... (ויקרא כו:ג-ד).

קנב **מאור עינים** - אם בחוקותי תלכו ואת מצוותי תשמרו ועשיתם
אותם: ונתתי גשמיכם בעתם... (ויקרא כו:ג-ד).

קנג **לקוטים יקרים** - אם בחוקותי תלכו ואת מצוותי תשמרו ועשיתם
אתם: ונתתי גשמיכם בעתם... (ויקרא כו:ג-ד).

קנד **תפארת עוזיאל** - וזכרתי את בריתי יעקוב ואף את בריתי יצחק
ואף את בריתי אברהם אזכור והארץ אזכור (ויקרא כו:מב).

תורי זהב - וכל אדם לא יהיה באהל מועד בבאו לכפר בקודש **ע' קלו**
עד צאתו וכפר בעדו ובעד ביתו ובעד כל קהל ישראל
(ויקרא טז:יז).

יושר דברי אמת - ערות אחותך בת אביך או בת אמך מולדת בית **קלז**
או מולדת חוץ לא תגלה ערותן (ויקרא יח:ט).

קדושים (ע' קלח-קמב)

אור תורה - ... קדושים תהיו כי קדוש אני ה' אלהיכם **קלח**
(ויקרא יט:ב).

אור המאיר - וידבר ה' אל משה לאמר: דבר אל כל עדת בני **קלט**
ישראל ואמרת אליהם קדושים תהיו כי קדוש אני ה' אלהיכם
(ויקרא יט:א-ב).

חיים וחסד - איש אמו ואביו תיראו... (ויקרא יט:ג). **קמ**

שמן הטוב - ... ואהבת לרעך כמוך אני ה' (ויקרא יט:יח). **קמא**

תפארת עוזיאל - ... והדרת פני זקן ויראת מאלהיך אני ה' **קמב**
(ויקרא יט:לב).

אמור (ע' קמג-קמו)

רב ייבי - ויאמר ה' אל משה אמור אל הכהנים בני אהרן **קמג**
ואמרת אליהם לנפש לא יטמא בעמיו (ויקרא כא:א).

מאור עינים - ויאמר ה' אל משה אמור אל הכהנים בני אהרן **קמד**
ואמרת אליהם לנפש לא יטמא בעמיו (ויקרא כא:א).

אור הגנוז לצדיקים - ומן המקדש לא יצא ולא יחלל את מקדש **קמה**
אלהיו כי נזר שמן משחת אלהיו עליו אני ה' (ויקרא כא:יב).

בהר (ע' קמז-קן)

תורי זהב - דבר אל בני ישראל ואמרת אליהם כי תבאו אל **קמז**
הארץ אשר אני נותן לכם ושבתה הארץ שבת לה': שש שנים
תזרע שדך ושש שנים תזמר כרמך ואספת את תבואתה
(ויקרא כה:ב-ג).

אור המאיר א' - ובכל ארץ אחזותכם גאולה תתנו לארץ **קמח**
(ויקרא כה:כד).

ע' קכג   **נועם אלימלך** - ויאמר משה אל אהרן קרב אל המזבח... ויקרב אהרן אל המזבח (ויקרא ט:ז-ח).

קכג   **צמח ה' לצבי** - ...וידום אהרן (ויקרא י:ד).

‫תזריע (ע' קכה-קל)‬

קכה   **קדושת לוי** - ...אשה כי תזריע וילדה זכר... (ויקרא יב:ב).

קכו   **תשואות חן**

קכז   **נועם אלימלך א'** - ... בכל קודש לא תגע ואל המקדש לא תבוא עד מלאת ימי טהרה (ויקרא יב:ד).

קכח   **נועם אלימלך ב'** - אדם כי יהיה בעור בשרו שאת או ספחת... וראה הכהן את הנגע בעור הבשר ושער בנגע הפך לבן... (ויקרא יג:ב-ג).

קכט   **מבשר צדק** - וראה הכהן אותו ביום השביעי שנית והנה כהה הנגע ולא פשה הנגע בעור וטהרו הכהן מספחת היא וכבס בגדיו וטהר (ויקרא יג:ו).

‫מצורע (ע' קלא-קלג)‬

קלא   **מעיין החכמה** - וידבר ה' אל משה לאמר: זאת תהיה תורת המצורע ביום טהרתו והובא אל הכהן (ויקרא יד:א-ב).

קלב   **נועם אלימלך** - זאת תהיה תורת המצורע ביום טהרתו והובא אל הכהן (ויקרא יד:ב).

קלג   **אור הגנוז לצדיקים** - וצוה הכהן ולקח למטהר שתי צפרים חיות טהורות... (ויקרא יד:ד).

‫אחרי מות (ע' קלד-קלז)‬

קלד   **מאור עינים** - וידבר ה' אל משה אחרי מות שני בני אהרן בקרבתם לפני ה' וימותו: ויאמר ה' אל משה דבר אל אהרן אחיך ואל יבא בכל עת אל הקודש ... בזאת יבא אהרן אל הקודש... (ויקרא טז:א-ג).

קלה   **נועם אלימלך** - בזאת יבא אהרן אל הקודש בפר בן בקר לחטאת ואיל לעולה: כתונת בד קודש ילבש ומכנסי בד יהיו על בשרו... (ויקרא טז:ג-ד).

ויקרא (ע' קיא-קיד) ﻪ

ע' קיא מאור עינים - ויקרא אל משה וידבר ה' אליו מאהל מועד לאמר (ויקרא א:א).

קיא מאור עינים ב' - ויקרא אל משה וידבר ה' אליו מאהל מועד לאמר (ויקרא א:א).

קיב נועם אלימלך א' - ויקרא אל משה וידבר ה' אליו מאהל מועד לאמר (ויקרא א:א).

קיג מגיד דבריו ליעקב - ...אשה ריח ניחוח לה' (ויקרא א:ט).

קיד קדושת לוי - ונפש כי תחטא ועשתה אחת מכל מצוות ה' אשר לא תעשינה ואשם (ויקרא ד:כז).

קיד נועם אלימלך ב' - או כי יגע בטומאת אדם לכל טומאתו אשר יטמא בה ונעלם ממנו והוא ידע ואשם (ויקרא ה:ג).

צו (ע' קטו-קכ) ﻪ

קטו אור תורה - ... צו את אהרן ואת בניו לאמר זאת תורת העולה היא העולה על מוקדה על המזבח... אש תמיד תוקד על המזבח לא תכבה (ויקרא ו:א-ב,ו).

קטז מאור עינים - צו את אהרן ואת בניו לאמר זאת תורת העולה היא העולה על מוקדה על המזבח... אש תמיד תוקד על המזבח לא תכבה (ויקרא ו:א-ב,ו).

קיח תשואות חן - וידבר ה' אל משה לאמר: צו את אהרן ואת בניו לאמר זאת תורת העולה היא העולה על מוקדה על המזבח... (ויקרא ו:א-ב).

קכ נועם אלימלך - ולבש הכהן מדו בד ומכנסי בד ילבש על בשרו והרים את הדשן ... ופשט את בגדיו ולבש בגדים אחרים והוציא את הדשן אל מחוץ למחנה אל מקום טהור (ויקרא ו:ג-ד).

שמיני (ע' קכא-קכד) ﻪ

קכא אורח לחיים - ויהי ביום השמיני קרא משה לאהרן ולבניו ולזקני ישראל (ויקרא ט:א).

קכב רב ייבי - ויהי ביום השמיני קרא משה לאהרן ולבניו ולזקני ישראל: ויאמר אל אהרן קח לך עגל בן בקר לחטאת ואיל לעולה תמימים והקרב לפני ה' (ויקרא ט:א-ב).

ספר

ויקרא

להוציאה לחירות, בשברון גופו ומידותיו החומריים, עד שיגיע לשרשן לעולם העליון הנקרא עלמא דחירות.

אורח לחיים

ותכל כל עבודת משכן אהל מועד ויעשו בני ישראל ככל אשר צוה ה' את משה כן עשו (שמות לט:לב).

להבין, לכאורה איפכא הוה ליה למימר **ויעשו בני ישראל** ואחר כך **תכל**. וגם כיון דאמר **ויעשו בני ישראל** וכו', למה אמר אחר כך **עשו** פעם שנית? וגם דאמר **ותכל** לשון נקבה, ולא אמר "ויכל" לשון זכר, כמו שאמר לסוף "ויכל משה את המלאכה" (שמות מ:לג)...

אמרו רז"ל: יודע היה בצלאל לצרף אותיות שנבראו בהם שמים וארץ (ברכות נה.), והמשכן היה דוגמת העולם, וכל מה שעשה דוגמת העולם היה חושב באותן הצירופים שנברא זה הדבר מהעולם. וזה "לחשוב מחשבות" (שמות לה:לב). וכן **בני ישראל** הם אותן בעלי חכמה כידוע, כי אותיות ישראל הם "לי ראש", כשהיו מתעסקין במלאכת המשכן בשעת העשיה היו חושבין טעמי מצוות ופנימיות כוונות התורה במצוות מלאכת המשכן וכליו. וידוע כי שבעים אנפין לתורה (במדבר רבה יג:טו), ובעלי חכמה היו חושבין בשעת עשיה בכל כוונות ופנימיות היוצא מן השבעין אנפין.

והנה מלת **ותכל** לשון חמדה ותשוקה, כמו "כלתה נפשי" (תהלים פד:ג). וזהו **ותכל כל עבודת משכן אהל מועד** - רוצה לומר, כל עבודתן במשכן אהל מועד בא לידי חמדה ותשוקה למעלה להשרות שכינתו במעשי ידיהם, כי כוונתן גדלה למעלה משום **ויעשו בני ישראל ככל אשר צוה ה' את משה** בכל כוונות ופנימיות טעמי תורה שנמסרו למשה בכל מצוות מלאכת המשכן בכל השבעים אנפין. וזה **כן עשה,** כי "כן" גימטריא שבעים, על כן כוונתם גדלה למעלה לחמוד להשרות שכינתו בתחתונים. אבל במדריגתם ומחשבתם לא היה כח, אלא שנכספה וגם כלתה השכינה לשרות בתחתונים. וזהו "תכל" לשון נקבה...

תם ונשלם ספר שמות

חסד לאברהם מקאליסק
(מפרשת משפטים)

אלה פקודי המשכן משכן העדות... (שמות לח:כא).

כי הנה ידוע מאמר רז"ל: **המשכן, משכן** העדות - שנתמשכן בעוונותינו הרבים (תנחומא פקודי ס' ה). וכן אמרו מקדש איקרי משכן (עירובין ב.), כשגברו העוונות ורבו החובות נתמשכן בעוונותינו הרבים, ועל כן אנחנו בגלות בגשמיות.

וכן על זה הדרך ברוחניות כאשר יבחין האדם בעצמו בכל בחינותיו, כמו שנזכר בספרים, שכל מה שהיה במשכן יש באדם. והעיקר להבין העניין כי הנה באמת כמו שיש גלות הגשמי כן יותר ויותר הגלות הרוחני, נקודת חיות הפנימי שהיא אסורה וכבושה בגולה בכמה לבושים והסתרים... שנאמר "ואנכי הסתר אסתיר פני" (דברים לא:יח), שאלופו של עולם יושב בסתר בכמה לבושים מהתגברות החומר, ומה גם מהתגברות שבע מדות רעות רחמנא ליצלן, ומכונים בשם שבעה עממין, שנצטוינו עליהם "לא תחיה כל נשמה" (דברים כ:טז-יז)... שהם מתנגדים תמיד אל נקודת החיות הפנימית שבאדם. וזה הגלות של חיות הרוחניות משבע מידות ותולדותיהן.

וכן בגשמי גלות שבעים אומות מסתעפים מהמכוחות הנזכרים לעיל, כי כל דבר זר וסטרא אחרא היא מעולם הפירוד, מתחלק תמיד, אבל דבר שבקדושה הכל מתיחד לאחד באחדות הפשוטה... וזהו כלל גדול בעבודת ה' יתברך לפדות נפשו וחיותו הפנימית לנקודתה מהמידות החיצוניות, ולהוציא המשכן לאורה חירות עולם. והנה באמת כשבעל המשכון הוא מטיב עם בעל חובו והוא תקיף ממנו מניח משכונו אצלו שיסגירהו בביתו במקום מיוחד לבל יגע בו, עד שיעלה בידו לשלם חובו ואז יחזור להשתמש במשכונו, ואז גאולה תהיה לו.

כמאמר הבעש"ט זי"ע, "קרבה אל נפשי גְאָלָה" (תהלים סט:יט), שכשם שיש גאולה כללית לכלל ישראל, כך יש גאולה פרטית לכל נפש ישראל. ואף על פי שנודע האדם בעצמו גסותו וחומריותו, ואף על פי כן צריך להיות תמיד כל חפצו ורצונו בכל לבבו למצוא תרופה לנפשו

367

פרשת פקודי

רב ייבי

אלה פקודי המשכן משכן העדות אשר פקד על פי משה עבודת הלוים... (שמות לח:כא).

הנה כתוב "ואתם הדבקים בה' אלהיכם חיים כולכם היום" (דברים ד:ד). וכי אפשר לידבק אדם בה', כיון שה' יתברך אש אוכלה הוא (סוטה יד.)? אלא על ידי שיקיים האדם רמ"ח [248] מצוות עשה ושס"ה [365] מצוות לא תעשה הוא מדובק בה' יתברך. כי כל מצוה הוא שם הוי"ה ברוך הוא, כי אותיות "מצ" הוא שם "יה" בא"ת ב"ש. ואורייתא וקודשא בריך הוא חד, ועל ידי שעוסקים בתורה ומצוות בעובדא וברעותא דלבא ממשיך על עצמו השכינה...

וזהו שאמר **אלה פקודי,** היינו המצוות הם פקודים של ה' יתברך. אם מקיימם האדם גורם שעל ידי המצוות ופקודים נעשה משכן לשכינה, שהשכינה שנקראת "ה" כנודע, שוכן על האדם - וזהו **"ה"משכן.** ולפי זה **משכן העדות** אם אנו רואים שהשכינה שורה על האדם הוא עדות וסימן שקיים אדם התורה, לכך זכה להשראת השכינה. ולא תאמר דווקא פקודי המצוות שכתובים בתורה שבכתב גורמים השראת שכינה על האדם, אלא כל מה שנאמר הלכה למשה מסיני, אפילו תורה שבעל פה... וזהו שכתוב **אשר פקד על פי משה,** הוא תורה שבעל פה גם כן. **עבודת הלוים** עבודה שיכול לחבר ולדבק אל ה' יתברך על ידי עבודה זו, כמו "הפעם ילוה אישי אלי" (בראשית כט:לד), שהוא לשון חיבור, כן פירוש **הלוים...**

- ק"ח -

368

רבה מו:ב): פירוש, שכל ההטיה שלו כשהטה עצמו לגופניות היה כדי
לעשות שלימות לזה הדבר.

ודעת. ונתן ה' יתברך זה הכח לצדיקים שבכל דור ודור, כי במה שהצדיקים עוסקים בתורה ומחדשים הם בוראים שמים וארץ חדשים. והם היו מכוונים במלאכת המשכן ברוח קדשם לחכמה עליונה, ועשו יחודים וצרופים קדושים בכל הכלים ובכל המעשים אשר נעשה המשכן. והנה אם היו רוצים לכוין כפי שכלם הרחבה, היה הדבר עד אין שיעור, כי רוח אלהים הופיע עליהם. אך הוצרכו לתת גבול בהדבר, והותירו לצדיקים לעתיד לבוא אשר יבואו וילמדו בספר תורה מעשה מלאכת המשכן. וכל צדיק וצדיק לפי שכלו יכיר תעלומות חכמה בכל דבר ובכל כלי, ויעשה יחוד לדבר רוחני עליונים.

כמו שה' יתברך הותיר כח במעשה בראשית, שהוא נתן גבול והשאיר להצדיקים כדי שיוכלו לחדש דבר בבריאה זו, כמו כן הם במלאכת המשכן. וזה שכתב הכתוב **והמלאכה היתה דים**, שהיו נותנים גבול להמלאכה. **לעשות אותה**, רוצה לומר לתקנו וליחדו בשכל עליון אשר היו יכולים לכוין בכל דבר לפי שיעור שכלם. אך **והותר**, שהותירו להצדיקים והחכמים שכל דור אשר ישמעו וילמדו סדר מלאכת המשכן, והם יגמרו הבנין ויוסיפו מדעתם מה שישיג שכלם.

חיים וחסד

ויעש בצלאל את הארון עצי שטים... ויצפהו זהב טהור מבית ומחוץ ... (שמות לז:א-ב).

פירוש: כי משה היה מקושר בהקדוש ברוך הוא כל כך, עד שהיה בטל במציאות נגד גדלות הבורא, ולא ראה את עצמו כלל. והנה **זהב** הוא יראה, ו"יראה" אותיות "ראיה", כי אי אפשר לירא אלא ממי שרואה. וזהו כשהשכל של אדם רואה תמיד גדלות הבורא, אז נופל עליו יראה.

על כן עשה משה כמו שהיה בעצמו, שכיסה הארון של עץ שהוא עץ הגוף בזהב, שהוא יראה **מבית ומחוץ**. וזהו שאיתא "משה משה" (שמות ג:ד) לא פסיק טעמא, כי לא השגיח על הגוף כלל. אבל "יעקב, יעקב" (בראשית מו:ב) פסיק טעמיה, שלפעמים השגיח על הגוף. אך כוונתו היתה כדי להעלות אותה להקדוש ברוך הוא. וזהו "מטתו שלימה" (ויקרא

- ק"ו -

להמשיך לששת ימי החול, כי אז יש מונעים להקדושה וצריכים אנו להמשיך הקדושה על ידי מה שנקים "בכל דרכיך דעהו" באופן שלא יעכב אותו החול והגבול, והבן.

צמח ה' לצבי

וכל אשה חכמת לב בידיה טוו ויביאו מטווה... וכל הנשים אשר נשא לבן אותנה בחכמה טוו את העזים (שמות לה:כה-ו).

יש לדקדק **בידיה** לשון יחיד, **טוו** לשון רבים. ועוד מה הפרש בין פסוק זה לפסוק השני, ושינוי הלשון ביניהם.

ואמרתי כידוע שהנוקבא דלעילא כוללת כל הנוקבין תתאין, והיא נקראת **כל אשה** על שם שכוללת כל הנשים (זהר ח"א רכח.). וזו כל **אשה חכמת לב**, דאתקריאת חכמה תתאה ומקבלת מן ל"ב נתיבות דלעילא כידוע. **בידיה**, בהידים שלה על דרך שכתוב "ידיה שלחה בכשור וכפיה תמכו פלך" (משלי לא:יט). **טוו** הנשים את המטווה, ועל דרך שאמרו חז"ל: מתוך שחסידים היו, מלאכתן נעשית מאליה (ברכות לה:), והיינו שנעשית על ידי הידים דלעילא. ועיקר היה על ידי שנתגלתה הארת חכמה זו מעילא לתתא, וזה הנרצה מפסוק זה.

ובפסוק שני אמר שהיו גם **נשים** שמתעוררות אתערותא דלתתא, **ונשא לבן אותנה** בחכמה מתתא לעילא.

קדושת לוי

והמלאכה היתה דים לכל המלאכה לעשות אתה והותר (שמות לו:ז).

והנה לכאורה האי **דים והותר** הוא תרתי דסתרי אהדדי, דאם היתה **דים** לא **הותר**!... אמרו חז"ל יודע היה בצלאל לצרף [האותיות שנבראו בהן שמים וארץ] (ברכות נה.). והנה הוא יתברך נתן בלבם חכמה ותבונה

- ק"ה -

≈ פרשת ויקהל ≈

מאור עינים
(מפרשת נצבים)

ויקהל משה את כל עדת בני ישראל ויאמר אליהם אלה הדברים אשר צוה ה' לעשות אותם: ששת ימים תעשה מלאכה וביום השביעי יהיה לכם קודש... (שמות לה:א-ב).

ולהבין מהו לשון תֵּעשה בצירי תחת הת', משמע תיעשה מעצמה?!

וזהו שאמר הכתוב "בכל דרכך דעהו" (משלי ג:ו), כי צריך האדם בכל דבר אשר יעשה או יסתכל שיהא על פי התורה שבדבר ההוא, ויאמין בזה אמונה שלימה. כי כל הנהגת הדברים היא על פי התורה, ועל זה אמרו (מכות כד.): בא חבקוק והעמידן על אחת - "וצדיק באמונתו יחיה" (חבקוק ב:ד). כי העיקר היא האמונה ואז בודאי יקיים "בכל דרכיך דעהו" ויחשוב כי לא הוא העושה המשא ומתן ושארי דברים כי אם התורה שבדבר ההוא, ועל ידה נעשה מעצמו ומתלבשת באדם ההוא ופועלת על ידי אבריו ודיבורו כאמור לעיל, דהיינו בקיימו מצוותיה שבדבר ההוא...

הוא כאמור שמשה רבינו ע"ה לימד דעת את העם בני ישראל ואמר להם אף כי צורך לעסוק בענייני המלאכה, מכל מקום תדעו שזה גם כן תורה. וזהו אומרו **אלה הדברים... ששת ימים תעשה מלאכה. אלה הדברים** דייקא שהוא התורה גם כן מה ששתת ימים תיעשה מלאכה על ידה ויום השביעי קודש. כי בעשותו כך כל השישה ימים אז ביום השביעי יהיה בודאי קודש כי המשיך קדושה לכל השבעה ימים. ואז יהיה יום השביעי קדוש, כי מי שטרח בערב שבת [יאכל בשבת] (עבודה זרה ג.).

כי מה שנקראים השישה ימים חול, הוא מלשון "אשר שמתי חול גבול לים" (ירמיהו ה:כב), כי אם ירצה ה', בביאת משיחנו במהרה בימינו, אזי יהיה יום שכולו שבת כי "אז יתפרדו כל פועלי און" (תהלים צב:י) וכל הקליפות, ולא יהיה רק קדושה לבד. אך היום בגלותנו צריכים אנו

קדושת לוי

... וראית את אחורי ופני לא יראו (שמות לג:כג).

הנה כתיב: "בן חכם ישמח אב" (משלי י:א), וכתיב "החכמה מאין תמצא" (איוב כח:יב). עיקר החכמה הוא כשאדם מסתכל באַין, ויודע שמעצמותו אין בו ממש, רק עיקר חיותו הוא האין ומדבק עצמו בשורשו במקור החיים. וזה שחיותו מתדבק עצמו בבורא יתברך, הבחינה זאת נקרא אצל הבורא יתברך כביכול בחינת לבוש. וזהו הרמז בפסוק "ולמכסה עתיק" יומין (ישעיה כג:יח). וזהו הרמז בגמרא: ישראל מפרנסין לאביהן שבשמים (זהר ח"ג ז:), כי לבוש הוא פרנסה. לכך נקרא חכמה בכל מקום "אור החוזר," כי על ידי חכמה חוזר ומדבק עצמו בשורשו. וזהו הרמז "ואאלפך חכמה" (איוב לג:לג) - אלף אותיות "פלא," כי באמת כל חיותו כשמדבק עצמו בשורשו, שם הוא פלא בלתי השגה.

וזהו הרמז **וראית את אחורי [ופני לא יראו]**, כי המסתכל באין הוא בטל במציאות. ואיך יסתכל בעין הרואה כשהוא בטל במציאות? ולזה אמר **וראית את אחורי**, הוא אשר על ידו תהיה על המדריגה הזאת להסתכל באין זאת תראה.

והנה האין אשר כל המסתכל בו הוא בטל במציאות נקרא הוי"ה, והבחינה הזאת אשר על ידו ישיג להסתכל באין נקרא אהי"ה. וישראל היו במצרים ולא השיגו עדיין להסתכל באין...

- ק"ג -

373

אור תורה

... וַחֲנוֹתִי אֶת אֲשֶׁר אָחֹן (שמות לג:יט).

יובן על פי מה שנאמר בזהר הקדוש, "ההוא מלה דלא נפיק בדחילו
ורחימו לא פרחת לעילא" [הדיבור שיוצא בלי יראה ואהבה אינו פורח
למעלה] (תקוני זהר ת' י כה:). פירוש, כי דיבור וקול הם כנגד זכר
ונקבה, השם ו"ה של שם הוי"ה ב"ה, ואם יצאו בלא דחילו ורחימו, שהם
אבא ואמא, י"ה של השם, הוא עשה פירוד. ובפרט שכל כוונתו בתפילה
ובלימוד הוא כדי להעלות הדיבורים אל שורשם, מתתא לעילא.

כי כמו שתחילת בריאת העולמות היה בכ"ב אותיות התורה, כמו שנאמר
בזהר: באורייתא ברא קודשא בריך הוא עלמא (ח"א ה.). שהם כ"ב
אותיות התורה ומהם הוה ההשפעה וקיום העולמות ולכל הנבראים מעילא
לתתא, כן צריך האדם להעלות הדיבורים מתתא לעילא אל שורשם,
דהיינו כשאדם מדבק ומחבר דיבור עם דיבור וקול עם קול והבל עם הבל
ומחשבה עם מחשבה שהם ארבע אותיות הוי"ה, כידוע. ואם האדם עושה
כן, כל דיבוריו פרחין לעילא אל שורשם, ובזה הוא גורם שהדיבורים
באים לפניו יתברך ומסתכל בהם.

ובזה הוא נענה בתפילתו, כי ההסתכלות הוא כעין השפעה מעילא לתתא.
כי כאשר ה' יתברך משפיע היא קיום העולמות כולם, כי למעלה אין שם
שהות וזמן, כי ברגע אחד באה ההשפעה מהמעיין העליון הנובע תמיד
ודרכו להיטיב ולהשפיע לבריותיו, רק בכשיהיה מקבל ראוי לקבל. ואם
הוא מתפלל או לומד תורה בענין הזה הוא נעשה כצנור אל המעיין העליון
הממשיך ומשפיע שפע טובה לו ולכל העולם כולו.

והנה מלת **אֲשֶׁר** יש לפרש בלשון שבח והלל, כמו "באשרי כי אשרוני
בנות" (בראשית ל:יג). ויש לפרשו גם כן בלשון הסתכלות, כמו "אראנו
ולא עתה אשורנו" (במ' כד:יז). ובזה יובן פירוש הפסוק **וַחֲנוֹתִי אֶת
"אֲשֶׁר" אָחֹן**, למי שמשבח ומהלל אותו ב"את", שהם כ"ב אותיות מא'
עד ת'. באופן אם יגרום בדיבורו ובתפילתו ובלימודו את "אשר" שיעלה
הדיבורים לעילא אל שורשם ויגרום "אשר" השני, שהוא הסתכלות
ובוודאי אז **אָחֹן** אותו. כי ההסתכלות הוא עניית התפילה...

- ק"ב -

374

תפארת עוזיאל

... לוחות כתובים משני עבריהם מזה ומזה הם כתובים (שמות לב:טו).

פירוש, שדברי תורה "כפטיש יפוצץ סלע" (ירמיה כג:כט). יש פנים לטהר ולטמא, וכדומה. וזה **משני עבריהם:** פירוש [אפילו אם] אחד מובדל מחבירו מן הקצה אל הקצה, אלו ואלו דברי אלהים חיים.

צמח ה' לצבי

ועתה אם תשא חטאתם ואם אין מחני נא מספרך אשר כתבת (שמות לב:לב).

וזה לשון רש"י: **אם תשא חטאתם,** הרי טוב. דהוקשה לרש"י על חיסור הסוגר. ונראה לי שהסוגר הוא **מחני נא,** ורוצה לומר בין **אם תשא חטאתם** בין לא, **מחני נא.**

ועל דרך משל, עבד מלך שהיה אוהב למלך מאוד, וראה שבנו מרד בו וביזה את המלך. ועלה בדעתו שאם יש וימחול המלך ביזיונו אינו יכול לראות, וכן אם לא ימחול המלך אין יכול לראות צער המלך על בנו שמענשהו. ולזה אמר **מחני נא.**

וזה שאמר מקודם "אנא חטא העם הזה חטאה גדולה" (שמות לב:לא).

באופן אחר על דרך ששמעתי פירוש על "אנא חטא," כלומר אני [אנא בארמית "אני"] חטאתי במחשבה חטא מועט, ועל ידי זה חטאו העם חטאה גדולה, כי הוא שורשם והם הענפים ממנו.

ועל פי זה יוכל לומר כך, שמשה אמר בזה יוודע לי אם אני הגורם או לאו. **ואם תשא** להם אדע שהוא חטאתם, והשורש לא חטא ולכן מחלת. **ואם אין,** מוכרח להיות כי השורש גם כן חטא במחשבה, לכן **מחני נא.**

- ק"א -

375

פרשת כי תשא

נועם אלימלך

כי תשא את ראש בני ישראל לפקודיהם... (שמות ל:יב).

נראה לי דאיתא בגמרא: נר מערבי היה דולק, ממנו היה מדליק, וממנו היה מטיב (שבת כב:). יש לומר דחז"ל רמזו בדבריהם הקדושים על הצדיק, שהוא נקרא "נר מערבי," על דרך דאיתא בגמרא: למה נקרא שמה "בבל"? שבלולה במשנה וגמרא ואגדות (סנהדרין כד.). כמו כן הצדיק הוא "מעורב" בו כל מיני קדושות, אהבה, ויראה, ורוממות אל, תורה ותפילה, וצדקה, תשובה, וגמילות חסדים, וכדומה. ולכן נקרא "נר מערבי" לשון מעורב, גם מערבי הוא לשון "עריבות" ומתיקות, שהצדיק הוא ערוב ומתוק בכל מיני מתיקות.

וזה הפירוש "ממנו היה מדליק:" הם בני אדם המתחברים עם הצדיק, גם הם מדליקים נרותיהם, הם נשמתם, באהבה ויראה להבורא ברוך הוא. "וממנו היה מטיב" פירוש: על ידי הצדיק מטיב ה' יתברך ברוך הוא לעולם כל מיני השפעות.

וזהו שאמר הקדוש ברוך הוא למשה רבינו ע"ה **כי תשא את ראש בני ישראל**: פירוש, כשתשא לבבם למעלה לראש, הם העולמות עליונים נקראים ראש, למען יכנסו בלבם אהבה ויראה וקדושה. **לפקודיהם** - פירוש, גם זאת יפעלו שיהיה להם פקידה טובה של שפע טוב, שהצדיק גוזר ופוקד והקדוש ברוך הוא מקיים על ידו.

- ק -

376

ואפילו הכי "למעשה ידיך תכסוף" לשון תאוה, כיון שהכל שלך.
אם כן אין לעמוד בסודך למה אתה מתאוה לזה לשמוע תורה ותפילה
מפינו, וכן ענין הנרות "באורך נראה אור" ואתה מצוה אותנו להדליק
נרות. ולית מחשבה תפיסא בך כלל, ואין לעמוד על סוד הענין רק
"הנגלות לנו ולבנינו" (דברים כט:כח) לעשות - אמן.

קדושת לוי

...ומלאת יד אהרן ויד בניו (שמות כט:ט).

דהנה בעניני עולם הזה לא נמצא שלימות, כי תמיד חסר לאדם שרוצה
בתענוגי גשמיות. דהיינו, אם יש לו תענוג משאר דברים, חסר לו תענוג
מכבוד, או תאות המשגל וכדומה, ותמיד הוא חסר. מה שאין כן בעבודת
הבורא, מי שעובד אותו אז הוא שלם בכל, כי "דורשי ה' לא יחסרו כל
טוב" (תהלים לד:יא). וזה התענוג של עבודת ה' עולה על כולם, כי מי
שהוא דבוק בחיות ועבדות של האין סוף, אשר הוא שלם בכל מיני
שלימות, ממילא האדם הדבוק בו אינו חסר לו גם כן שום דבר.

וזהו שכתוב: **ומלאת יד אהרן ויד בניו.** רוצה לומר, שאמר למשה
שיראה להביא את אהרן ובניו למדריגה כדי שיהיו דבקים לבחינות
הקדושה. ואז יהיו ידיהם מלאים כל טוב, כי לא יחסר להם שום דבר
כשירגישו נועם ותענוג עליון. ולכך נקרא שמונת ימי ה"מלואים," כי אז
היתה השראת השכינה ביניהם, והיו "מלאים" תענוג מחמת הקדושה.

אורח לחיים

ואתה תצוה את בני ישראל ויקחו אליך שמן זית זך...
(שמות כז:כ).

דידוע דראשי עם בני ישראל המדריכים את העם ומלמדים אותם בדרכי ה' ובתורתו הם מקבלים יותר מהם, כמו שאמרו רז"ל: [הרבה תורה למדתי מרבותי, ויותר מחביריי,] ומתלמידי יותר מכולם (תענית ז.). וגם בהשפעת השכל והדעת מאת ה' יתברך הם מקבלין כדי שיוכלו להשפיע. והראיה על זה שכל אותן השנים שהיו ישראל במדבר בשביל המרגלים היה הדיבור נפרש ממשה.

וזה שאמר **ואתה תצוה את בני ישראל**, [תצוה מ]לשון "צוותא חדא", כלומר תחבר אותך עם בני ישראל ללמדם ולהדריכם. **ויקחו אליך שמן זית זך**, רוצה לומר שהם יקחו וימשיכו אליך שמן זית זך, חכמה והתורה.

עבודת ישראל

ואתה תצוה את בני ישראל ויקחו אליך שמן זית זך...
(שמות כז:כ).

איתא במדרש (שמות רבה לו:ד): הדא הוא דכתיב "תקרא ואנכי אענך למעשה ידיך תכסוף" (איוב יד:טו), אין תכסוף אלא לשון תאוה. אנו "באורך נראה אור" (תהלים לו:י), ואתה מצוה להדליק נרות.

איוב אמר הפסוק הזה ורמז בזה בלשון תמיה. "תקרא ואנכי אענך," פירוש כי כל התורה שאנו לומדים וכל התפילות שאנו מתפללין וכל מעשים טובים שאנו עושים הכל משלך רבון העולמים, כי אתה נתת לנו חמשה מוצאות הפה וחמשה חושים ורמ"ח [248] איברים, ואתה מחיה את כולם ומשפיע בהם בכל רגע וזולתך אנו אפס ואין. ואם כן כל הקריאה והקדושה שאנו עושים הוי כאילו אתה קראת ועשית, כיון שכל השכל והכח שלך הם, אם כן הוי כאילו "תקרא ואנכי אענך" שכל מעשינו הם רק כענין עונה לקריאה, ואנו מטין את עצמינו לכף זכות לרצונך הטהור והרי זאת רק כמו עונה.

- צ"ח -

❧ פרשת תצוה ❧

אור תורה

ואתה תצוה את בני ישראל ויקחו אליך שמן זית זך...
(שמות כז:כ).

על דרך: יודע היה בצלאל לצרף אותיות שנבראו בהן שמים וארץ
(ברכות נה.). המשכן היה חיות של כל העולמות. ויובן על דרך הנשמה
היא חיות הגוף, והנשמה בעצמה אין לה תמונה. רק אנו מכנים אותה
בשם הגוף, זו חיות היד או הרגל, ואפילו בצלאל שעשה המשכן שהיא
חיות העולמות הוצרך לידע האיך להכניס החיות בהעולמות והוצרך לידע
האותיות שנבראו בהם העולמות.

ואיתא: בעשרה מאמרות נברא העולם (מ' אבות ה:א). ופריך, הלא בתשע
הוויין?! ומשני "בראשית" נמי מאמר הוא (מגילה כא:). וקשה, למה לא
כתוב "ויאמר"? אך המאמר הזה אינו מושג, רק המדריגה תחתונה שלו
מושג... והדבר ההוא הוא היולי של כל המאמרים, שכל המאמרים ממנו
באים.

ובמשכן היה גם כן צריך להיות זאת. וזאת היתה המנורה, שמשה רבינו
ע"ה נתקשה בה ולא היתה יכולה ליעשות על ידי אדם כי אם מאליה,
שעליה העדות שהשכינה שורה בישראל. וזהו נקרא **שמן זית,**
שהבהירות בעצמה שורה עליה כמו האור על השמן. וכל שאר המאמרים
נקראים זית [ז' התחתונים?] שהשמן אגור בתוכו.

ולכך לא כתוב בפרשה זאת "וידבר ה' אל משה" או "ויאמר," כי זה
פירוש של **שמן זית,** והדיבור שלו אינו מושג. אפילו ויאמר, לשון
מחשבה, לא שייך.

- צ"ז -

379

וזה שנאמר **ונתת על השלחן לחם פנים**, רוצה לומר לחם פנימיות. רוצה
לומר, החיות אשר בתוך הלחם זה תתן על שלחנך, ואז **לפני תמיד** ונקרא
"זה השלחן אשר לפני ה'" (יחזקאל מא:כב).

דומה... וזהו אינו, דאדרבה כך היה הציווי שלא יעשה תמיד על ציור אחד, רק כפי השראת הנבואה כך יהיה נצטייר למטה תבנית הכלים.

אורח לחיים

ונתת על השולחן לחם פנים לפני תמיד (שמות כה:ל).

ונראה דהנה כתבתי פירוש הפסוק: "ואכלתם אכול ושבוע והללתם את שם ה' אלהיכם אשר עשה עמכם להפליא" (יואל ב:כו).

דהנה הרב הגדול בוצינא קדישא מורנו הרב דוב בער זלה"ה אמר שהחיות אשר בתוך המאכל נקראת אוכל, והמאכל נקרא מאכל על שם שמאכיל את האדם החיות שבתוכו הנקרא אוכל, עד כאן דבריו. וידוע שבאורייתא ברא הקדוש ברוך הוא, ובאורייתא מתקיימים עלמין. והחיות שבכל דבר הם אותיות התורה ובתוכם אור פנימית אין סוף ב"ה, המתעלם בתוך האותיות המחיה הכל.

וידוע מה שאמרו חז"ל (סוכה מו.-מו:): "אם שמוע תשמע" (דברים כח:א) - אם שמוע בישן, תשמע בחדש. ואמרו שלא כמידת הקדוש ברוך הוא מידת בשר ודם. מידת בשר ודם כלי ריקן מחזיק, כלי מלא אינו מחזיק, אבל מידת הקדוש ברוך הוא כלי מלא מחזיק. וזהו שנאמר "ואכלתם אכול," רוצה לומר שתאכלו חיות התורה אשר בתוך המאכל המחיה אותו. "ושבוע," רוצה לומר אם תהיה שבע בדברי תורה ותהיה כלי מלא, אז תוכלו להחזיק ולהשיג החיות אשר בתוך המאכל...

אם תשיגו החיות אשר בתוך המאכל ותהנה הנשמה מרוחניות שבמאכל והגוף יהנה מגשמיות המאכל, ועל ידי זה יהיו קשורים הנשמה והגוף. "והללתם את שם ה' אלהיכם אשר עשה עמכם להפליא," כי הוא דבר פלא שמקשר רוחני בדבר גשמי ומתקיים על ידי המאכל גם כן.

והנה אמרו רז"ל: בזמן שבית המקדש היה קיים מזבח מכפר, ועכשיו שולחנו של אדם מכפר (חגיגה כז.). בוודאי כוונתם מי שאוכל בדרך זה להוציא חיות אשר בתוך המאכל והניצוצות קדושות אל נשמתו, שיהיה לו כח לעבודת הבורא...

- צ"ה -

שכינתו. ומפרש הכתוב מי הוא שזוכה אל מדריגה זו ואל מי אני מדבר? דהיינו, **מכל איש אשר ידבנו לבו**, דהיינו שנדב לבו לעבוד את הבורא ב"ה במחשבות טהורות ודביקות הבורא ב"ה, **תקחו את תרומתי**, וקל להבין.

קדושת לוי

ככל אשר אני מראה אותך את תבנית המשכן ואת תבנית כל כליו וכן תעשו (שמות כה:ט).

ופירש רש"י: **וכן תעשו** לדורות. ומקשה התוספות (שבועות טו.): הלא לא היה שוה מזבח שעשה משה למזבח שעשה שלמה; וכן הקשה הרמב"ן.

אך לפי דברינו ניחא, דכוונת הכתוב **וכן תעשו** הוא המכוון לדבר אחר. דהנה באמת תבנית המשכן וכל כליו אשר הוכרח הכל להיות מצויר על נכון בגובה ובקומה ובמשקל ובמידה, וזה היה לבוש וציור לרוחניות הקדושה. וכפי הנבואה שראה משה בהר סיני וכל ישראל, וכפי שהמשיכו רוחניות הקדושה בעבדות שלהם, כך היה בערך זה צריך להיות הלבוש דהוא הכלי והמשכן עשוי כתבניתו.

וידוע דברי חז"ל: דאין שני נביאים מתנבאים בסגנון אחד (סנהדרין פט.), רק כל אחד לפי בחינתו וכפי שעובד ה', באותה הבחינה עצמה נראה אליו רוח הנבואה. משום הכי משה ודור המדבר כפי ערך עבודתם ורוח נבואתם אשר השיגו בהר סיני, כך היו צריכין לעשות צורת המשכן ותבנית הכלים, אשר נעשים לבוש לאורות הרוחניים של הקדושה. ואם כן, כך הוא פירוש הכתוב: **ככל אשר אני מראה אותך** - כפי גדר הנבואה, כך יהיה תבנית המשכן וכל כליו.

וכן תעשו לדורות, רוצה לומר בכל דור ודור כשתרצה לבנות בית המקדש, יהיה עשייה כתבנית הנבואה אשר ישיג אז, כך יעשה הציור של המקדש והכלים. ושלמה כפי עבודתו ורוח נבואתו אשר השיג, כך היה עושה הציור. ולא קשה כלל קושית הרמב"ן, דהלא המזבח לא היה

שוכן בכל אחד ואחד מישראל, והיינו באופן המבואר כשבונין מלא קומתו להשרות בקרבם אלהותו יתברך, אזי שוכן יתברך שמו אצלם.

ובאמת איתא בזוהר: ציורא דעובדא דבראשית וציורא דמשכנא וציורא דבר נש חד אינון (ח"ב קמט:א-ב).

נועם אלימלך

דבר אל בני ישראל ויקחו לי תרומה מאת כל איש אשר ידבנו לבו תקחו את תרומתי (שמות כה:ב).

... במשנה: אל תהיו כעבדים המשמשים את הרב על מנת לקבל פרס, [אלא הוו כעבדים המשמשין את הרב שלא על מנת לקבל פרס] (מ' אבות א:ג). ויש לדקדק על כפל הלשון. ויש לומר, דהנה הצדיק העובד ה' במצוות ומשמר את עצמו שלא לעבור ח"ו על איזה מצוה קלה, ומהדר אחריה לעשותה כתיקונה, אבל אינו במדריגה זו שיבא בהמצוות אל דבקות הבורא ב"ה וחשקות גדול אליו יתברך, לזה הצדיק יש לו לצפות לתשלום גמול לעולם הבא.

אבל יש צדיק שעובד במחשבות טהורות, ומדבק את עצמו על ידי המצוות בבורא ב"ה בדבקות וחשקות גדולה ורואה תמיד רוממותו יתברך, הצדיק הזה הוא מושך תענוגי עולם הבא אליו כאלו נהנה מזיו השכינה בעולם הזה. וזה הצדיק אינו מצפה לתענוגי עולם הבא, כי יש לו תענוגי עולם הבא בעולם הזה....

וזהו פירוש המשנה: אל תהיו כעבדים המשמשין את הרב על מנת לקבל פרס - בעולם הבא, היינו שמצפים לתשלום שכר. אלא הוו כעבדים [המשמשין את הרב שלא על מנת לקבל פרס], רוצה לומר שתהיו כל כך צדיקים שתהיה לכם השכר מיד בשעת עשיית המצוה כנזכר לעיל, דהיינו [מ]התדבקות על ידי המצוות תמשיכו את התענוג לכם.

וזהו: **ויקחו לי תרומה**, רוצה לומר שתזכו להנות מזיו שכינתי בעולם הזה, וזהו כמו תרומה והפרשה מעולם הבא. וזהו (פירוש רש"י): ויקחו לי - לשמי, דהיינו שתקחו ותמשיכו את הבורא ב"ה אצלכם, ותהנו מזיו

- צ"ג -

אמר **מאת כל איש אשר ידבנו לבו**, רוצה לומר מפני שאני רואה נדבת לבו וגודל תשוקתו ומסירת נפשו אלי, לכן **תקחו את תרומתי...**

אור המאיר

... ויקחו לי תרומה... ועצי שטים (שמות כה:ב,ה).

... ופירש רש"י: ומאין היו להם במדבר? פירש רבי תנחומא: יעקב אבינו צפה ברוח הקודש שעתידין ישראל לבנות משכן במדבר, והביא ארזים למצרים ונטעם, וצוה לבניו ליטלם עמהם כשיצאו ממצרים...

ויש לרמוז בדבריהם כי נודע ששבע מידות הקדושים הניתן בידינו לתקנם, על שם הפסוק "השמים שמים לה', והארץ נתן לבני אדם" (תהלים קטו:טז). כלומר, שבע מידותיה, את זה נתן לבני אדם לתקנם ולבנות קומתם. והם נקראים ארזים ארזי לבנון, שנמשכו מלובן עליון עולם הבינה.

ויעקב אבינו ע"ה הורה לבניו דרך ה', התפשטות אלהותו יתברך באמצעות מידותיו הקדושים, וניצוציו שישנם בכל הנבראים. ולית אתר פנוי מניה, והניצוץ היושב שם במדריגת התחתונים להחיות אותה, היא במיצר ובחשכת אין נוגה לו, עד בואו של חכם הכולל ויש לו התפשטות הדעת, ליקח לעצמו רמיזא דחכמתא לעבוד את הבורא ב"ה עם זאת הבחינה. והיינו, בשום רוחו ונפשו להבין מאיזה מקום נמשכו, לדעת איך להעלותה אל השורש ומקומה הראשון.

ומעתה תבין אשר חכמים הגידו: יעקב אבינו ע"ה צפה ברוח הקודש שעתידין ישראל לבנות משכן במדבר, והיינו אנו בני ישראל עתידין תמיד לבנות מלא קומתנו מראש ועד עקב בהשראות אלהות, ואזי במדבר בנו את המשכן מתרומה הנזכרת כאן. וכן בכל דור ודור עדיין לא פסק העניין, שאנו בני ישראל מעותדים לבנות תמיד קומת השכינה בתכונות מלא קומתנו. וכאשר נתעוררו חז"ל על פסוק: ועשו לי מקדש ושכנתי בתוכם" (שמות כה:ח) - בתוכו לא נאמר, אלא בתוכם. מלמד שהקדוש ברוך הוא

- צ"ב -

❧ פרשת תרומה ❧

דברת שלמה

דבר אל בני ישראל ויקחו לי תרומה מאת כל איש אשר ידבנו לבו תקחו את תרומתי (שמות כה:ב).

דהנה לפום ריהטא האדם סובר כשאומר שירות ותשבחות ומשבח לבורא יתברך שמגדל בזה אותו יתברך, כמו המלך בשר ודם - להבדיל. ובאמת אינו כן, כמו שכתוב במכילתא: מלך בשר ודם מגדלין ומקלסין אותו במה שאין בו, אבל הקדוש ברוך הוא מקלסין אותו ויש בו יותר ויותר. וכן איתא בגמרא: משל למרגניתא [- סמא דכולא משתוקא למרגלית דלית לה טימי, כל שמשבח בה פגמה; השתיקה עולה הכל. משל למרגלית שאין בה דופי - כל המשבח בה, פוגם בה] (ירושלמי ברכות ט:א). נמצא כל השבחים הוא אצלו יתברך הקטנה, שמביאין בהירותו וחיותו [של] האין סוף באותיות מצומצמין, מה שאין לו תפיסא כלל, כמו שכתוב בתיקוני זהר (יז.): לית מחשבה תפיסא בך כלל ,כמו שכתוב לעיל כמה פעמים.

אמנם עם כל זה הוא חשוב בעיני המקום ואהוב אצלו מאוד. והמשל בזה כמו האב עם בנו הקטן כשמשתעשע עמו, ובנו מושיט ידו ואוחז בזקנו או בשערו או בראשו ומורידו עד למטה נגד פניו הקטן להשתעשע עמו, והאב נהנה מאוד מזה ושמח בבנו העושה זה. והטעם שנהנה מזה, הגם שלפי הנראה הוא פחיתת הכבוד ומטריחו, ואם היה עושה לו זה אדם אחר, אפשר היה כואב לו. רק מחמת גודל אהבת הבן, וגם רואה האהבת בנו ותשוקתו אליו, ומחמת גודל תשוקתו ואהבתו עושה זאת, לכן הוא נאהב מאד אצל אביו. והנמשל מובן: שגם על ידי הדיבורים והאותיות הוא מקטין ומצמצם בהירותו יתברך...

וזהו **ויקחו לי תרומה**, רוצה לומר הגם שיקחו אותי ויורידו אותי אצלם, הוא אצלי תרומה, שהוא הרמה וגדולה אצלי. ואם תאמר מפני מה, לזה

- צ"א -

אותו, ויש לו חשק ורצון בעבודת הבורא, אז בוודאי מוכח שה׳ יתברך יש לו תענוג מעבודתו. ולכך מסייעין לו מן השמים, ושולחין לו מחשבות קדושות לתוך לבו. לזה אמר **ומראה כבוד ה׳**, שהסימן כשירצה אדם לידע אם רואה כבוד ה׳ והקדוש ברוך הוא נהנה ממנו, ולזה **כאש אוכלת**, אם לבו בוער כאש. וקל להבין.

הוא לשון הבנה, דהיינו שבא למדריגה יותר גדולה, כנזכר לעיל. וזה הוא עיקר קבלת התורה שקבלו ישראל, ולכן התפאר ה' יתברך בזה מאד שקבלו התורה בגודל האמת והשיגו האמת שלעולם יהיו דבוקים בה' יתברך, ולא יפרדו ממנו אף בנפלם ממדריגתם. וזהו עיקר ההילוך וההנהגה הישראלית, ובזה צריך להלך.

ובמה יבא לה' יתברך כשנפל ממדריגתו, שהרי ניטל ממנו המוחין והדעת? אך שה' יתברך הוא "מלא כל הארץ כבודו," דהיינו אפילו במקום שהוא כל הארץ שכולו ארציות שהוא רק חומר עב, אף על פי כן מלא כבודו יתברך. והנה ה' יתברך נקרא "חי החיים," דהיינו שכל החיים שבעולם - בהמות, חיות, ועופות ומין האדם - החיות שלהם הוא ה' יתברך. וזהו חי החיים, שהוא יתברך החיות של כל החיים. ויחשוב כשנפל ממדריגתו, הלא חי חי אני! ומי הוא החיות שלי? הלא הבורא יתברך, ונמצא שיש כאן גם כן הוא יתברך, אך שהוא מצומצם מאוד.

וזהו אמר הקדוש ברוך הוא: "מי גילה רז זה לבני"? רוצה לומר "מי," דהיינו כשהם חושבים מי הוא החיות שלהם, זה גילה להם רז זה להקדים נעשה לנשמע כנזכר...

וזהו שאמר שלמה המלך ע"ה: "אל תאמר מה היה שהימים הראשונים היו טובים מאלה, כי לא מחכמה שאלת על זאת" (קהלת ז:י). רוצה לומר שיש שוטים שבנופלם ממדריגתם שוכבים לעפר ואינם עולים שוב אל ה' יתברך. וזהו "אל תאמר שהימים הראשונים היו טובים מאלה," דהיינו שאז הייתי עובד ה' יתברך, ועכשיו נפלתי ממדריגתי. אל תאמר כן, "כי לא מחכמה שאלת על זאת," כי "החכמה תחיה" (קהלת ז:יב), ו"החיות רצוא ושוב." ואם כן מוכרח להיות כך.

קדושת לוי

ומראה כבוד ה' כאש אוכלת... (שמות כד:יז).

דהנה האדם בעבודתו לה' יתברך בתורה ובמצוות מביא תענוג גדול למעלה. וכשאדם רוצה לידע אם ה' יתברך יש לו תענוג מעבודתו, הבחינה הוא על זה: אם אדם רואה שלבו בוער כאש ומתלהב תמיד לעבוד

- פ"ט -

387

שתתעמוס על הגוף סיגופים גדולים אשר תכביד עליו עד שהוא רובץ לגמרי, ואינו יוכל לעשות רע וטוב. **וחדלת מעזוב לו**, לא תעשה כן, אלא **עזוב תעזוב עמו**, רוצה לומר שתעזור את הגוף ותקל הסגופים גדולים רק מעט מעט בהדרגה ובהשגחה שלא תשחית אותו.

ובהמשך הזמן בעזר ה' יתברך תראה לעשות מן היצר הרע יצר הטוב, ובכחות והתלהבות היצר הרע תעבוד את ה'. וזהו **עזוב תעזוב עמו**, רוצה לומר תעזור את הגוף ולא תכלה אותו. **עמו**, רוצה לומר עם היצר הרע גם כן תעזור ותעשה ממנו יצר הטוב...

מאור עינים

... כל אשר דבר ה' נעשה ונשמע (שמות כד:ז).

בשעה שהקדימו ישראל נעשה לנשמע יצתה בת קול ואמרה להן: "מי גילה לבני רז זה שמלאכי השרת משתמשין בו" (שבת פח.)? וצריך להבין איך אפשר לעשות קודם שישמע, מה לעשות? גם מה היה ענין התפארות ה' יתברך שהתפאר בזה כל כך במה שהקדימו נעשה לנשמע?

אך האמת היא שהאדם אינו יכול לעמוד תמיד על מדריגה אחת, כי "החיות רצוא ושוב" (יחזקאל א:יד), שבא ומסתלק. דהיינו כשהוא דבוק בה' יתברך הוא מרגיש חיות ותענוג, ואחר כך מסתלק ונופל ממדריגתו. ויש בזה רזין דאורייתא בטעם הדבר למה צריך ליפול ממדריגתו. וטעם אחד הוא כדי שיבא אחר כך למדריגה יותר גדולה, שבכל דבר צריך להיות העדר קודם להויה, וכשרוצים להגביה למדריגה יותר גדולה צריך להיות העדר קודם. לכן צריך ליפול ממדריגה שהוא עכשיו.

והנה צריך האדם שגם בנפלו ממדריגתו יתאמץ לעלות אל ה' באותה מדריגה שהוא עכשיו, כי צריך להאמין ש"מלא כל הארץ כבודו" (ישעיה ו:ג) ולית אתר פנוי מיניה, ואפילו במדריגה שהוא עכשיו יש גם כן ה' יתברך, כי לית אתר פנוי מיניה, רק שהוא מצומצם מאד...

וזהו נקרא **נעשה** קודם לנשמע. אף בנפילתנו ממדריגתנו להדבק בה' יתברך באותה מדריגה, כנזכר לעיל. ואחר כך **נשמע** שעיקר השמיעה

על דרך "הרי זה בא ללמד ונמצא למד" (חולין כח.), שעל ידי כן בזכות ישראל הומשכה לו נהורא מחכמה עילאה, הנקרא שמן זית זך.

וזהו פירוש הפסוק **אם כסף תלוה**, דהיינו שאתה חומד לדבוק בו יתברך. **כסף**, לשון חמדה על דרך "נכסוף נכספת" (בראשית לא:ל); **תלוה**, לשון חיבור ודיבוק, על דרך "הפעם ילוה אישי אלי" (בראשית כט:לד). ואמר הכתוב **את עמי**, דהיינו שתתחבר עצמך **את עמי** בני ישראל, ועל ידי זה תזכה להיות דבוק בו יתברך. וגם **את העני עמך**, על דרך שאומרים בשם המגיד מורנו הרב יחיאל מיכל זצ"ל על הפסוק "תפילה לעני כי יעטוף" (תהלים קב:א): כשמחבר תפילתו עם תפילת העני אז היא רצויה. וזה **את העני עמך**, שתחבר עצמך לתפילת העני, ואז תזכה להיות דבוק בו יתברך שמו עד עולם, אמן.

אורח לחיים

כי תראה חמור שונאך רובץ תחת משאו וחדלת מעזוב לו עזוב תעזוב עמו (שמות כג:ה).

ורז"ל דרשו: **עמו**, בזמן שבעליו עמו אז מחוייב לעזור לו; אבל הלך לו ואמר לו הואיל ועליך מצוה, אין זקוק לו (מכילתא דרשב"י). ויש לפרש, דיש בני אדם הנלחמים עם יצרם, המסית לרדוף אחר תאות והנאת הגוף, ושוברים את גופם בסיגופים גדולים כדי לשבר תאות הגוף, ומשחיתים את גופם כדי לפטור מיצר הרע האחוז ודבוק אל הגוף. ואחר כך כשרוצים לעבוד ה' יתברך אי אפשר להם לעבוד בלי גוף, ולא בזה הדרך בחר ה'...

אבל האדם צריך ללחום עם יצרו ולשבר הגוף מעט מעט, בהדרגה ובשכל, ושלא להשחית את הגוף לגמרי, ובשכל ובתחבולה יעשה מלחמה עם היצר. ואדרבא, בכחות היצר יעבוד ה' יתברך ויעשה מיצר הרע יצר הטוב...

וזה **כי תראה חמור שונאך**, רוצה לומר החומריות והגשמיות של שונאך הוא היצר הרע הדבוק ומושל על הגוף. **רובץ תחת משאו**, רוצה לומר

נועם אלימלך
(מפרשת תולדות)

וכי יפתח איש בור או כי יכרה איש בור ולא יכסנו ונפל שמה שור או חמור: בעל הבור ישלם כסף ישיב לבעליו והמת יהיה לו (שמות כא:לג-ד).

כי הוא לשון "אשר," דהיינו שהחיוב מוטל על הצדיק הנקרא **איש** שיפתח את הבור. רמז למעייני היראה והקדושה לפתוח לבות בני אדם ביראה וקדושה רבה. או **כי יכרה איש בור** - **יכרה** הוא לשון "חפירה," שמתחיל לחפור ולחקוק בלבות בני אדם יראה וקדושה. **ונפל שמה שור או חמור**, רוצה לומר אז בוודאי יפלו שמה הקליפות. **בעל הבור ישלם**, רוצה לומר זה שכרו של הצדיק הזה, שה' יתברך ברוך הוא שהוא בעל ואדון לכל הקדושות והיראות ישלם לו שכרו לעולם הבא.

ולא עוד אלא **וכסף ישיב לבעליו**, פירוש דגם זה שכרו שהיראה והקדושה הזאת שגורם לבני אדם תשוב אליו, ויוסיף בו עוד יראה ואהבה ותשוקה לעבודתו יתברך שמו. וזהו **כסף** לשון "נכסף נכספת" (בראשית לא:ל), דהיינו התשוקה והאהבה ישיב לבעליו. ועל דרך הזה פרשתי "דברים היוצאין מן הלב נכנסים ללב," פירוש לאותו לב עצמו שיצאו ממנו, באמת אותן הדברים חוזרים ונכנסים בלבו ומוסיפים לו עוד קדושה...

מבשר צדק

אם כסף תלוה את עמי את העני עמך... (שמות כב:כד).

ולפרש זה אקדים לפרש פסוק "ואתה תצוה את בני ישראל ויקחו אליך שמן זית" (שמות כז:כ). דהיינו, "ואתה" - אף שאתה הוא משה רבם, ומלמד דעת לבני ישראל, "תצוה את בני ישראל," דהיינו תצוה לשון חיבור, על דרך "כל העולם לא נברא אלא לצוות לזה" (ברכות ו:). אם תחבר עצמך עם בני ישראל, "ויקחו אליך," דהיינו שהם ימשכו לך "שמן זית," דמרומז על חכמה עילאה. ואתה תהיה הצינור להשפיע בחזרה להם,

๑ פרשת משפטים ๑

מעיין החכמה

כי תקנה עבד עברי שש שנים יעבוד ובשביעית יצא לחפשי חנם (שמות כא:ב).

נראה לי לפרש על דרך שאמרו חז"ל: יש קונה עולמו בשעה אחת (עבודה זרה י:). ופירש הרב המגיד מורנו הרב דוב בער זלה"ה, "שעה" היא לשון "פנה," כמו הכתוב "ואל קין ואל מנחתו לא שעה" (בראשית ד:ה); שאפשר להיות שלפעמים ברגע אחד שאדם עושה תשובה בהתלהבות גדולה הוא בא למדריגה גדולה מאוד. וזהו "יש קונה עולמו בשעה אחת," בפניה אחת, שהוא פונה את עצמו לה' יתברך בתשובה הוא משיג עולמו, כל מה שאפשר לו להשיג.

אלא שחז"ל דקדקו בצחות לשונם שאמרו "עולמו" ולא אמרו "עולם." רמזו בזה שאי אפשר לו להשיג אלא עולמו, אבל אי אפשר לו לילך ממדריגה למדריגה בתשובה זאת לבדה שעושה בשעה אחת. אף על פי שעשה בהתלהבות גדולה, אי אפשר לו לבוא ליראה ואהבה פנימיות, שהיא בחינת שבת, אם לא שילך בתשובתו ממדריגה למדריגה בעמל יגיעה רבה.

וזה הכתוב **כי תקנה,** שאפילו אם תקנה בחינת **עבד עברי** בשעה אחת, כנזכר לעיל, **שש שנים יעבוד,** אינך יכול לעבוד אלא בבחינת ששת ימי חול, שהם בחינת שש שנים. אבל **ובשביעית** שהיא בחינת שבת, בחינת יראה ואהבה הפנימיות בלי שום התלבשות, אי אפשר לו לבוא על ידי תשובה הנזכר לעיל, וזה **יצא לחפשי חנם,** שלא ישיג.

אמנם, במתן תורה היה צריך להתלבש, כדי שיבינו בני ישראל את
התורה. וזהו "אתה נגלית בענן כבודך" (מוסף של ראש השנה). פירוש,
בלבוש וצמצום אורו הגדול, כי "ענן" הוא בחינות חשכות, מורה על
צמצום אורו... על זה אמר "על עם קדשך לדבר עמם," רוצה לומר
שהוצרך לדבר עמהם שיוכלו להבין דיבוריו הקדושים.

חיים וחסד

**ויאמר משה אל העם אל תיראו כי לבעבור נסות אתכם בא
האלהים...** (שמות כ:טז).

והנה אמרו חז"ל: משה מחיצה לעצמו ואהרן מחיצה לעצמו וישראל
לעצמן למטה מהן בדרגה (מכילתא יתרו). וכתיב "דבר אתה עמנו
ונשמעה... פן נמות" (שמות כ:יט) מיראת גדולתו יתברך. ואמר משה
להם **אל תיראו**, כי אין רצון ה' יתברך שיהא בכם רק מידת היראה. רק
כוונת ה' יתברך שהיראה יגדל את האהבה להקדוש ברוך הוא. וזה
"והאלהים ניסה את אברהם" (בראשית כב:א), מידת האלהים מגביה
מידת האהבה. "ניסה," לשון הגבהה.

בית אהרן

ויהי קול השופר הולך וחזק מאד משה ידבר והאלהים יעננו בקול (שמות יט:יט).

מאד הוא אותיות "אדם," כי כל מה שמספר הכתוב מהקולות וברקים אינו דבר חידוש לפני ה' יתברך. רק הכל הוא לימוד לאדם לעולם, כי קבלת התורה היא נצחית בכל דור ודור, ובכל זמן וזמן...

משה ידבר, "דיבר" אין כתיב רק "ידבר," בלשון עתיד. כי עתיד הוא בכל דור ודור לדבר עם כל אחד ואחד, לכל מי שבא לטהר ולקבל עליו עול התורה, מדבר משה עמו. **והאלהים יעננו בקול,** להכניס הקול בהדיבור ולייחד הקול עם הדבור והמחשבה. וצריכין מאוד לשמוח בקבלת התורה, כי כל אחד ואחד מקבל לפי כוחו וערכו. וצריך להאמין כי בוודאי עתה ישוב מאוולתו ויזדכך ויהיה זך.

קדושת לוי ב'

אנכי ה' אלהיך... (שמות כ:ב).

יבואר מאמר חז"ל: בים סוף נגלה להם כבחור, ובמתן תורה נגלה להם כזקן (פסיקתא רבתי כא:ה). דהנה ה' יתברך מצמצם עצמו בעולמות. אמנם בים סוף שהיה שם שינוי הטבע, לא היה מתלבש אז בהעולמות, וראו ה' יתברך בלי שום לבוש. ובמתן תורה התלבש ה' יתברך עצמו כפי שיעור שהעולמות יהיו יכולין להתקיים.

והנה "לבוש" מרומז בכתבי האר"י ז"ל בבחינת שערות. וזהו בים סוף נגלה להם כבחור בלא שערות [הזקן], בלא שום לבוש שהיה מתלבש בעולמות. ובמתן תורה נגלה כזקן, דהיינו שערות, שנגלה להם בלבוש שהתלבש בעולמות. וזהו הרמז בדברי רבותינו ז"ל: ראתה שפחה על הים מה שלא ראה יחזקאל הנביא (מכילתא בשלח טו:ב). כי יחזקאל וכל הנביאים ראו ה' יתברך, כביכול, בהתלבשות בעולמות כפי שיעור העולמות. ובים ראו כולם ה' יתברך כביכול בלא לבוש.

ונראה, שאמרו חז"ל: קיים אברהם אבינו ע"ה כל התורה, אפילו ערובי תבשילין, עד שלא ניתנה (יומא כח:). והנה צריכין להבין, מאין ידע אברהם אבינו ע"ה תורה עד שלא ניתנה? אפס הנה ידוע, כי הרמ"ח [248] מצוות עשה כנגד הרמ"ח אברים הרוחניים, והשס"ה [365] מצוות לא תעשה כנגד שס"ה גידים הרוחניים. והמסתכל ברוחניות אברים שלו וברוחניות הגידין שלו, הוא משיג הרמ"ח מצוות עשה ושס"ה מצוות לא תעשה. וכמו שאברי הגוף צריכין למזון הגשמיות שלו ולדברים הגשמיים הצריכים לכל אבר ואבר, כן האברים הרוחניים צריכין לכל אבר ואבר למצוות שלו. וכשם שאברים הגשמיים אין צריך ללמד אותם הגשמיות שלהם, כן כל אבר ואבר הרוחניים אין צריך ללמד אותם, כי מעצמם משיגים להמצוות שלהם. וגם כי האברים הרוחניים החיות שלהם הם בעצמם המצוות עשה; והשס"ה גידין החיות שלהם בעצמם שס"ה לא תעשה, כי הרוחניות היא דקות השכל ודקות המחשבה, והזדככות המחשבות היא רק המצוות...

ולכן קודם שניתנה התורה הקדושה, היו יכולים להשיג כל התורה - רמ"ח מצוות עשה ושס"ה לא תעשה. אפס מה שאנחנו אין משיגין התורה מעצמנו ומשכלנו, הוא מחמת החומריות אשר הוא מסך המבדיל להשיג אור הרוחניות. אמנם מי שיש לו התפשטות הגשמיות והתגברות הרוחניות, הוא יכול להשיג בעין שכלו מעצמו התורה... ולכן אברהם אבינו ע"ה אשר נזדכך החומר שלו, השיג מרמ"ח איבריו ושס"ה גידיו שלו הרוחניות של כל התורה כולה, עד שלא ניתנה.

וזה אשר יסד בעל הגדה "אילו קרבנו לפני הר סיני..." כלומר, שבהכנת מתן תורה... נזדכך החומר שלהם והשיגו התורה עד שלא ניתנה... וזה "אלו קרבנו לפני הר סיני, ולא נתן לנו את התורה, דיינו..." וזה אשר אמרו חז"ל שכפה עליהם ההר כגיגית... הגם שהקדימו "נעשה" ל"נשמע." אמנם בעת ההיא היו ישראל זכים וברורים וצלולים, והשרה עליהם השכינה, והיתה להם התפשטות הגשמיות. אבל כשמחשבותם לא יהיו זכים וצלולים, אז לא יקבלו עליהם עול מלכות שמים...

- פ"ב -

כפשוטו על שאנחנו בני ישראל חיים עכשיו, מאחר שפרחה נשמתם כבר?

ותירץ [ר' לוי יצחק] דידוע שמלאכי השרת קטרגו למעלה באומרם "תנה הודך על שמים" (תהלים ח:ב), עד שהשיב להם משה רבינו ע"ה, "כלום גזל יש ביניכם, כלום שנאה יש ביניכם"?! ועל ענין זה מקשה הגמרא, מאחר שבדיבור ראשון פרחה נשמתם, ואז כבר היו במדריגת מלאכים בלא גוף, דיבור שני היכי קבלוהו? רוצה לומר, קושית מלאכי השרת, שכבר לא היתה שייכת תשובת משה רבינו ע"ה, כלום קנאה וכו', מאחר שאף ישראל היו כמלאכים.

אם כן, מאיזה טעם יקבלו ישראל התורה ולא המלאכים? ומשני שהוריד להם טל מתחיית המתים, רוצה לומר שהיה הוא יתברך משפיל ומוריד החיות הרוחני שלהם והיתה החיות הקדושה במדריגה התחתונה. ואז שייך שפיר תשובת משה רבינו למלאכים, "כלום גזל" וכו', מאחר שהיתה הרוחניות קדושה של ישראל למטה כמדובר.

קדושת לוי א'
(קדושת פורים א')

... ויתיצבו בתחתית ההר (שמות יט:יז).

אמר רב אבדימי בר חמא: מלמד שכפה הקדוש ברוך הוא עליהם את ההר כגיגית, ואמר להם, אם אתם מקבלין התורה מוטב, ואם לאו, שם תהא קבורתכם, עד כאן לשון הגמרא (שבת פח.). וזהו לשון התוספות: "כפה עליהם ההר כגיגית" - אף על פי שכבר הקדימו "נעשה" ל"נשמע" (שמות כד:ז), שמא היו חוזרים כשראו האש הגדולה, שיצאו נשמותיהם. אמר רב אחא בר יעקב: מכאן מודעא רבה לאורייתא...

ונראה, כי צריכין להבין מה שקדמו ישראל עשיה לשמיעה. האיך עושין קודם ששומעין? אפס נראה לי, כי צריכין להבין על מאמר הגדה [של פסח]: "אילו קרבנו לפני הר סיני, ולא נתן לנו את התורה, דיינו." וצריכין להבין, מה טובה היה בקרבנו לפני הר סיני בלתי קבלת התורה?

נדמה הבורא ב"ה בריבוי בחינת התלבשות, בכדי שהחי יתן אל לבו
לעורר את לבו בקרבו בכל שעה ורגע בבחינה מחודשת, והבחינה זאת
בעצמה שעובד עמה עתה בעת הזאת עבודת בוראו, כשנופלת לידי זקנה
חלוף עבודתו בבחינת התלבשות אחרת, ואזי נותן עצות לנפשו
מהתלבשות זאת.

והכל מאת ה' היתה זאת לטובתו ולהשלמת נפשו, ליתן התעוררות לנפשו
בכל שעה ורגע, לבלתי נופל אצלו העבודה לידי זקנה. וזהו בחינת מריטת
כנפיים, על דרך האמור, היינו כשנופלת אצלו לזקנה מורט את התלבשות
העבודה וחוזר אז לנערותו, ליקח לעצמו רמיזא דחכמתא, לעורר לבו
בקרבו מחדש עם בחינת התלבשות אחרת...

ועתה נבוא לביאור העניין **אתם ראיתם אשר עשיתי למצרים**. כלומר,
אני בעצמי עשיתי זאת שהאדם נופל לפעמים לבחינת "מיצר." כי נודע
מספרים שהאדם צריך להיות בסוד "רצוא ושוב" (יחזקאל א':יד) ובלתי
אפשרי להיות עומד תמיד במדרגה אחת. אמנם אם המשכיל נותן דעתו
לזה ורואה בעין שכלו שהכל מאתו יתברך, והוא כביכול בעצמו מלובש
שם לטובת האדם כמבואר, אדרבא זאת הגורמת בחינת התעוררות וחוזר
לנערותו לבחינה מחודשת לעבודת הבורא.

וזהו **אתם ראיתם** והבנתם **אשר עשיתי למצריים** והתועלת המגיעה
בראותכם ככה, **ואשא אתכם על כנפי נשרים**, כלומר, זה עזר אלוה
כשבא על החכמה עובד את הבורא אפילו בלי התלבשות הכנפיים,
וכאמור. ולזה גמר אומר **ואביא אתכם אלי**, ירצה אל אות י' המורה על
בחינת החכמה למעלה משבעת המידות, אשר שם אין שום בחינת כנפיים.

תפארת עוזיאל

שמעתי מהרב מורנו ר' לוי יצחק, אב בית דין דקהילת הקדוש זאלחאב,
על מאמר ב[מסכת] שבת: מאחר שבדיבור ראשון פרחה נשמתם, דיבור
שני היאך קבלינהו? ומשני שהֶחָיָים בָּטַל שעתיד הקדוש ברוך הוא להחיות
בו את המתים (שבת פח:-פט.). הקשה המהרש"א, למה לא מקשה

ופירוש הפסוק כך הוא, מתחלה **ומשה עלה אל האלהים**, רוצה לומר
עלה אל מידת היראה הנקראת אלהים; עלה אליה והשיגה מעצמו מגודל
השתדלותו והתאמצות והתקשרות שהיו בו כנזכר לעיל. ואחר שכבר
השיג מידה זו, נאמר לו "ואל משה אמר עלה אל ה'," שהוא הוי"ה שהוא
אהבה כנזכר לעיל, כי באה לו בנקל.

אור המאיר

אתם ראיתם אשר עשיתי למצרים ואשא אתכם על כנפי נשרים ואביא אתכם אלי (שמות יט:ד).

... הנה מקראות אלו אומרים דרשינו, והנכון כי הנה אנו בני ישראל
נקראים "דורשי יהודך," על שם שאנו דורשין תמיד יהודו ואחדותו
יתברך. אפילו מפחותי המדריגות נותן האדם עצות לנפשו לעבוד את
הבורא ב"ה... ומצד הסברא החיוב מוטל על כל אחד ואחד מישראל
לבלתי יתן רפיון לנפשו אפילו כמעט רגע מלדרוש אחדותו ויחודו יתברך,
כי זה כל האדם ולזה היתה תכלית הבריאה.

ואולם בעבור זאת, שאין לנו התפשטות השכל להשכיל ולהבין לדעת איך
לעורר רוחו ונפשו בכל שעה ורגע, כי עינינו הרואות לפעמים מעורר
האדם בעצמו איזה בחינה לעבודת הבורא יתברך, ובמשך הזמן נופלת
אצלו זאת הבחינה לזקנה, וחלף ועבר ואינה חשובה וחביבה עליו
כבראשונה. והבעש"ט זללה"ה היה אומר מה שאנו אומרים "אל תשליכנו
לעת זקנה" (תהלים עא:ט)... הכוונה שאל ישליך העת לידי זקנה, כי
לפעמים נופלת העבודה של אדם לידי זקנה באמצעות המשך הזמן...

ואני בארתי הפסוק "תתחדש כנשר נעוריכי" (תהלים קג:ה), ונתעוררו
חז"ל ודרשו מה הנשר לסוף אלף שנה מורט כנפיו וחוזר לנערותו וכו'
(רש"י ואלשיך שם). והכוונה נודע, כנפים מורה על בחינת התלבשות,
וזה נודע ומפורסם לכל היות כל בחינת עובדתנו, ואפילו מעשה המצוות,
אינם כי אם בבחינת התלבשות... ומי שעיני שכל לו יודע באמת אפילו
בשינוי הראות פניו יתברך בהתלבשות מדריגותיו לעבודת האדם, עם כל
זה הכל עולה בקנה אחד, מורה על יחודו ואחדותו יתברך. אכן לטובותינו

๏ פרשת יתרו ๏

לקוטים יקרים (ס׳ קלה)

ומשה עלה אל האלהים... (שמות יט:ג).

הנה ידוע כי עבודת הבורא יתברך המוטל על האדם המה בשני אופנים: באהבה וביראה. והנה מצינו גם במלאכים שתי מידות אלו, שנאמר "והחיות רצוא ושוב" (יחזקאל א:יד), כמו שפירש רש"י ז"ל, רצוא שהם רצים להתקרב ולראות את השכינה אשר למעלה מראשיהם, ומחמת היראה הם שבים ומתחבאים. ויש לומר כי "רצוא ושוב" רומזים אל שתי מידות אהבה ויראה...

והנה תחילת עבודתו צריך האדם להמשיך על עצמו יראת הבורא יתברך, שהיא יראת הרוממות ולא יראת העונש, שזאת יראה חיצונית. רק שזאת היראה האמיתית אינה באה אל האדם בנקל, כי אם אחר טורח גדול והתאמצות והתקשרות גדולה בתמידות במחשבתו אל הבורא יתברך בלי הפסק רגע. ובזה יזכה לכנוס בשער הראשון, שהוא היראה, כמו שכתוב "זה השער לה'" (תהלים קיח:כ), ונאמר "בזאת יבוא אהרן אל הקודש" (ויקרא טז:ג)... אבל כאשר כבר השיג האדם יראת הרוממות, בנקל יכול להשיג מידת האהבה, כי אהבה נקראת מפתחות הפנימיות. וזה נראה בחוש מעניני העולם הזה, הרוצה לבוא אל המלך פנימה, משעבר בשער החצר החיצונה בנקל יכול לכנוס אל שערים פנימיים, בהיות שרואים השוערים ושומרים הפנימים שכבר הניחו אותו לכנוס שומרי שער החיצונה...

וזה שכתוב **ומשה עלה אל האלהים**, ואחר כך נאמר "ואל משה אמר עלה אל ה'" (שמות כד:א). ויש לדקדק, למה בתחילה נאמר שם אלהים ואחר כך נאמר שם הוי"ה? ועל פי הנזכר לעיל יובן, כי ידוע כי שם אלהים הוא דין, שהוא שם "אדני" - "דינא" דמלכותא דינא, שהיא מידת היראה. ושם הוי"ה הוא רחמים גמורים מטה כלפי חסד, שהוא אהבה.

- ע"ח -

בבחינת עוסקיהו במעשהו בחוץ בעניני גשמיותו. כי על כל אלה יאותה ליראי ה' ולחושבי שמו להשפיע מקדושת שבת דבר יום ביומו בששת ימי החול, להיות זהירין ונשמרין מכל דבר רע, לעבוד עבודתם הכל בקדושה וטהרה ודביקות הבורא, ועיקר הדבר לקשור מחשבתו לרוממות אלהות בכל פרטי עניניו, ואפילו דיבור איש אל רעהו...

נועם אלימלך
(מפרשת תצוה)

והיה כאשר ירים משה ידו וגבר ישראל וכאשר יניח ידו וגבר עמלק: ...ואהרן וחור תמכו בידיו... (שמות יז:יא-יב).

ולכאורה למה היה מניח ידו? אך האמת היא מחמת שמשה רבינו ע"ה היו מדריגתו וקדושתו גדולות מאוד, וידע איך לעורר רחמים. ואם היתה עבודתו כזה, לעורר רחמים כמעט היה העולם בטל ממציאות, מחמת שהבורא ב"ה ברא את עולמו ושיתף בו מידת הרחמים, דהיינו דין ורחמים כדי שיהא שכר ועונש. ואם היה משה רבינו ע"ה עבודתו רק לעורר רחמים לבד, היה פועל שיהא הכל אחד, ולא היה עונש אף לרשעים. לכן הוכרחה להיות עבודתו רק בהמתקת הדינים בלבד. אבל אנחנו בעבודתנו אפילו לעורר רחמים הלוואי שנפעול כך כאשר פעל משה רבינו ע"ה בהמתקת הדינים.

וזהו **כאשר ירים משה את ידו**. ד"**ידו**" פירוש רשותו, כי העולמות הם ברשות הצדיק לפעול בהם כרצונו... היינו בריאת העולם היתה למען ישמעו להצדיק הנקרא "זה," כמו שנאמר "זה משה"... (שמות לב:א). וכאשר הרים משה את ידו, היינו כחו ורשותו שיש לו בעולמות, **וגבר ישראל**. אך שהיה צריך לירד קצת ממדריגתו כנזכר לעיל, **וגבר עמלק**. **ואהרן וחור תמכו את ידיו**, במדריגותם לעורר רחמים.

אור המאיר

ויאמר ה' אל משה הנני ממטיר לכם לחם מן השמים ויצא העם ולקטו דבר יום ביומו למען אנסנו הילך בתורתי אם לא: והיה ביום הששי והכינו את אשר יביאו והיה משנה על אשר ילקטו יום יום (שמות טז:ד-ה).

להבין ענין מקראי קודש אלו, שישנה בכל אדם ובכל זמן, כי כבר קדם לנו. מן הידוע שיש שתי בחינות בעבודת הבורא ב"ה. בחינה אחת, שאין לו לב לדעת לעבוד את הבורא ב"ה כי אם בעת עוסקו בתורה או בתפילה, ובעת עוסקו במעשה המצוות. אכן תיכף שהולך לעסוק בצרכי ההכרחי מצרכי גופו שאי אפשר זולתם, כגון אכילה ושתיה ושאר צרכיותיו של אדם המוכרח בהם, אזי הוא איש בער ולא ידע איך לקשור מחשבתו לרוממות אלהותו, לבלתי יהיה נפרד מדביקות הבורא ב"ה אפילו בעניני הגשמיות, ליקח לעצמו רמיזא דחכמתא, לדעת ולהבין שאין דבר בעולם שלא יהיה מלובש שם אורות עליונים אותיות התורה.

והכתוב רומז לזה "לכו לחמו בלחמי" (משלי ט:ה), ירצה לצוות בטוב באזהרה לאישים המשכילים אופן עבודתם עבודת גבוה, להעלות ולהגביה אותיות התורה אפילו מאכילה הגשמית ולחם הגשמי. וכאשר ביארתי במקום אחר פירוש הפסוק "לעת האוכל גשי הלום" (רות ב:יד), ונתעורר: אין הלום אלא מלכות (זבחים קב.). כלומר, אפילו בעת יאכל את לחמו ויתר פרטי מאכל שלחנו, גשי משם הלום, היא איברי השכינה השוכנת במדריגות התחתונים. וזהו "לכו לחמו בלחמי," אותיות התורה נקראות לחם המלובשות בלחם הגשמי שהאדם אוכל...

והנה מי שעובד את הקדוש ברוך הוא על דרך הנזכר ומעלה אותיות התורה מבחינת ארציות, זה נקרא "לחם מן הארץ" (תהלים קד:יד)... ומי שעוסק בתורה ותפילה ולקח לעצמו התעוררות ומתלהב בקרבו לעבודתו יתברך, זה נקרא לחם מן השמים, היינו אותיות שעושה עמהם צירופים בשכליות, וזהו **לחם מן השמים**.

והנה ידוע מספרים שקדושת שבת תולה בימות החול, וכמעשהו בחול כך מעשהו בשבת, בגשתו אל עבודת הקודש פנימה זו תפלה, הכל תולה

לא היתה אמונה חזקה בישראל. הדא הוא דכתיב "ויאמינו בה' ובמשה
עבדו - **אז ישיר משה**" (שמות יד:לא). כלומר, **אז** באותו פעם שר משה,
ולא מקודם מיד שהובטח.

והנפקא מינה אם אומרים שירה קודם או לאחריו. אם אומרים שירה
לאחר הנס, השירה באה מחמת הנס שעשה לו ה' יתברך, ובאהבת
ובשמחת הנס שנעשה לו אומר שירה ושבחים לה' יתברך, ובלא נס לא
היה אומר. וזה דומה לעבד שקיבל מתנה מרבו, מודה ומשבח לו עבור
אהבת המתנה, נמצא לפי זה הנס הוא בבחינת דכר שהוא המשפיע וגורם
לשירה שתאמר אל ידו, והשירה היא בבחינת נוקבא המקבלת מהנס, ולכן
נקרא שירת משה וישראל **שירה** חדשה, לשון נקבה.

ולעתיד לבא יאמרו שירה קודם הנס, מפני שיהיה העיקר אצלם להודות
ולומר שירה, ובאמונה גדולה כאלו נעשו כל הנסים. והעיקר אצלם
השירה והנס טפל, ועל ידי זה השירה הדכר והנס הנוקבא, שהנס בא על
ידי האמונה, והשירה שיאמרו זה גורם לנס שיהיה, לכן נקרא "שיר חדש"
- לשון זכר.

פנים יפות

ויבאו מרתה ולא יכלו לשתות מים ממרה כי מרים הם...
(שמות טו:כג).

שמעתי לפרש בשם הרב המגיד ז"ל מה שכתוב **כי מרים הם** קאי על
ישראל, שהיו בעת ההיא מרים. וכמו שאמרו שהחולה אומר למתוק מר,
מהמרירות שבפיו. זהו שאמר **כי מרים הם**. אמנם בכח משה שהיה דבוק
בעץ החיים שהוא התורה, כמו שכתוב "עץ חיים היא למחזיקים בה"
(משלי ג:יח), הופיע עליו ה' יתברך להשפיע עליהם כח הרוחני להמתיק
בפיהם מתיקות התורה, וזה שכתוב "ויורהו ה' עץ וישלך אל המים
וימתקו המים..." (שמות טו:כה).

- ע"ה -

כאשר ראה אביו לבנו הקטן חולה וצריך לרפואות מרים מאוד על ידי הרופאים ואין הבן הקטן רוצה לקבל ולאכול אותם, אז אביו פותח פיו בחזקה ונותן לתוך פיו הרפואות אשר הם מרים מאד, והבין הבן שאביו שונא אותו. רק אחר כך כשנתגדל השכל אצל הבן וראה אהבת אביו אליו, שזה שהיה נותן לו הרפואות אשר הם מרים מאד, שנתן לתוך פיו בחזקה היתה אהבה יתירה אליו. והיה מר לאביו ביותר שעשה כח זה לבנו ולפתוח פיו בחזקה, וליתן המר מאד לתוך פיו. ומחמת שהבין אביו שזו רפואתו, היה מצטער ועשה לו זאת... וכן בכאן, **וירא הראשון ראייה** ממש, שראו **מצרים מת על שפת הים**. והשני **וירא ישראל את היד הגדולה אשר עשה ה' במצרים** הוא לשון הבנה... שהיו מבינים שגם במצרים שהוכבדה העבודה עליהם היו גם כן חסדים גדולים שהיו צריכין לעשב מר כזה שתתכבד העבודה עליהם.

וכמדומה לי שקרוב לזה שמעתי מפי הרב בוצינא קדישא החסיד המפורסם מורנו הרב משולם זוסמאן מקהילה קדושה אניפאלי.

צמח ה' לצבי

אז ישיר משה ובני ישראל את השירה הזאת לה'... (שמות טו:א).

במדרש: "תשורי מראש אמנה" (שיר השירים ד:ח) - עתידין ישראל לומר שירה לעתיד לבא, שנאמר "שירו לה' שיר חדש כי נפלאות עשה" (תהלים צח:א). ובאיזה זכות אומרים ישראל שירה? בזכות אברהם שהאמין בהקדוש ברוך הוא, שנאמר "והאמין בה'" (בראשית טו:ו), היא אמונה שישראל נוחלין בה. ועליו הכתוב אומר "וצדיק באמונתו יחיה" (חבקוק ב:ד), הוי תשורי מראש אמונה (שמות רבה כג:ה).

הענין כתב בשל"ה (בשלח): מידת הצדיקים מיד שהובטחו לדבר טוב לומר שיר ושבח לה' יתברך מיד קודם שמתקיים, והוא מצד האמונה שמאמינים בהבטחתו יתברך שמו. ומה שמשה רבינו ע"ה איחר מלומר שירה עד שנבקע הים ולא תיכף כשנאמר לו "למען רבות מופתי" (שמות יא:ט), ופירש [רש"י] מכת הבכורות וקריעת ים סוף, שבשביל שעדיין

۞ פרשת בשלח ۞

קדושת לוי

וישב הים לפנות בוקר לאיתנו... (שמות יד:כז).

פירוש מחמת שהים ראה גודל תענוג ה׳ יתברך מהבקיעה, שעל ידו יאמרו ישראל שירה, לא רצה לחזור, שהיה חפץ שיהיה תמיד יבשה, שיאמרו תמיד שירה. משום הכי אמר **וישב הים לפנות בוקר "לאיתנו,"** לתנאי שיקרע רק למשה רבינו ע״ה, אבל אחר כך יהיה ים כמקודם.

ועל פי זה מתורץ קושיית האור החיים, מאי רבותא דים? הלא גם הירדן נבקע, וכן נהר גינאי לרבי פנחס בן יאיר (חולין ז.)! ולפי מה שכתבנו לעיל מתורץ, דהירדן ונהר גינאי שכבר ראו תענוג הבורא ב״ה שהגיע מבקיעת ים סוף, משום הכי באהבה רבה רצו שיבקעו. מה שאין כן הים, דעדיין לא ראה קודם בקיעתו תענוג הבורא, הוי רבותא.

אורח לחיים

... וירא ישראל את מצרים מת על שפת הים: וירא ישראל את היד הגדולה אשר עשה ה׳ במצרים (שמות יד:ל-לא).

ובמדרש מבואר יותר שראה כל אחד ואחד מישראל הנוגש המצרי אשר היה נוגש עליו לכיבוד [כבדות] העבודה, והיה מכה אותו, ראה כל אחד ואחד מישראל הנוגש שלו מת על שפת הים (מכילתא בשלח פ׳ ו). ובדבר זה ראו ישראל אהבה גדולה מה׳ עליהם, שלא רצה שילכו כמה ימים בפחד זה, שמא יעלו המצריים מצד אחר רחוק ממנו וירדפו אחרינו. וכיון שראו ישראל בדבר זה אהבת ה׳ יתברך ממש... היו מבינים שגם במצרים אשר הוכבדה העבודה עליהם, כאשר באו משה ואהרן אל פרעה, היה גם כן אהבה גדולה מה׳ יתברך עליהם.

‏- ע״ג -

שהקדוש ברוך הוא מנהיג הכל, גם הטבע. וזה שנאמר "נס להתנוסס"
(תהלים ס:ו) - הקדוש ברוך הוא שולח לנו נס כדי להתנוסס, כדי להגביה
עצמנו להקדוש ברוך הוא...

קדושת לוי

החודש הזה לכם ראש חדשים... (שמות יב:ב).

עיין רש"י, נתקשה משה על מולד הלבנה. ונראה להבין, למה נתקשה משה במולד הלבנה? כי משה רצה שתהיה גאולה בימיו, להחזיר פגימת הלבנה, ויהיה "אור הלבנה כאור החמה" (ישעיה ל:כו), כמו שיהיה אם ירצה ה' בביאת הגואל צדק במהרה בימינו אמן... (חסר).

חיים וחסד

החודש הזה לכם ראש חדשים... (שמות יב:ב).

פירוש, כי אצל הקדוש ברוך הוא אין שייך השתנות והתחדשות, כי הוא למעלה מהזמן. אך ההתחדשות ששולח לנו ה' יתברך הוא **לכם**, כלומר בשבילנו... ונעשה אצלנו טבע ורגילות. וזהו טבע לשון "נטבע," שנטבע בנו התחדשות האור; על כן צריכים אנו להתחדשות. והנה יהיה עת שיקויים בנו "והשביע בצחצחות נפשך" (ישעיה נח:יא), שתהא כל כך בהירות שנהיה אנו תמיד צמאים להאור. וזהו "בצחצחות," לשון צחה - "צמא" - מחמת גודל בהירות, אבל לעת עתה הקדוש ברוך הוא שולח לנו התחדשות כדי שנגביה עצמנו להקדוש ברוך הוא.

וזה שנאמר **החודש הזה לכם ראש חדשים**, שעל ידי הראשים אנו מתחדשין ומגביהין עצמנו לה'. וזה שנאמר "דברו אל כל עדת בני ישראל," שעל ידי זה ההתחדשות יוכל להתנהג כל עדת ישראל.

והנה הטבע הוא שקר, כי האמת היא שהקדוש ברוך הוא מנהיג כל, והוא משנה עתים ומחליף הזמנים ומסדר כוכבים. הרי שהקדוש ברוך הוא מנהיג המזלות והכוכבים, שהם הטבעים, ומשנה אותם כרצונו. ואם היינו תמיד בזאת הבהירות שהקדוש ברוך הוא מנהיג הכל, לא היינו צריכים להתחדשות, אך מחמת הטבע צריכין אנו להתחדשות.

והנה כשהקדוש ברוך הוא שולח לנו נסים והתחדשות, אז מכח זה אנו יכולים להגביה עצמנו גם על הדבר שהוא בטבע, שתהא לנו ידיעה

- ע"א -

405

אורח לחיים

וגם מקננו ילך עמנו לא תשאר פרסה כי ממנו נקח לעבוד את ה' אלהינו (שמות י:כו).

"וגם ערב רב עלה אתם..." (שמות יב:לח). כי אלו הם ערב רב שנתערבו
ניצוצות קדושות במצרים, ולכן רצה משה להעלותם. אך הקדוש ברוך
הוא ראה שעדיין לא מתוקנים, ולא היה רוצה להוציאם עדיין. והנה
אברהם אבינו קודם שהוליד את יצחק וישמעאל, היה מוליד נשמות גרים,
והיו מגיירין, ותלמידים קרויים בנים. וזה שנאמר אל זקני ישראל, הם
אותם חכמים, כי זקן זה קנה חכמה (קדושין לב:), "משכו וקחו לכם צאן"
(שמות יב:כא) - מלשון "צאינה." רוצה לומר, שימשיכו את הערב רב,
הנשמות שיצאו ונפלו בקליפות, שימשיכו אליהם ולהעלותם ולקרבם
לעבודת ה' יתברך. "למשפחותיכם," ותרגום אונקלוס "לזרעיתכון." רוצה
לומר, שתלמדו ותקרבו אותם לעבודת ה' יתברך, ויהיו חשובים כבנים
שלהם...

וזה שאמר משה **וגם מקננו ילך**, רוצה לומר הערב רב, שהם הקנינים
שלנו שנתקרבו אלינו **ילך עמנו. לא תשאר פרסה**. ומלת פרסה הוא,
פרס "ה", פרס לשון "חתיכה." וידוע בזוהר ובספרים שהגרים שורשם
ב"ה" אחרונה של שם הוי"ה, ולא היה רוצה שישאר שום ניצוץ
במצרים...

כי ממנו נקח לעבוד את ה' אלהינו. רוצה לומר, שבשביל הניצוצות
הקדושות האלו באנו למצרים להעלותם, ונשתעבדנו בחומר ובלבנים...
ואנחנו סבלנו הגלות כדי להעלות אותם הניצוצות קדושות, ונתקרבנו
לעבודת ה' יתברך בעבור זה. וזה **כי ממנו נקח לעבוד את ה' אלהינו,**
רוצה לומר שבשבילם נתקרבנו לעבוד ה'.

אור המאיר

ויט משה את ידו על השמים ויהי חושך אפלה בכל ארץ מצרים... לא ראו איש את אחיו ולא קמו איש מתחתיו (שמות י:כב-כג).

יש לרמוז תוכחת מוסר: אנשים אשר עינים להם ולא יראו כושר מידותיהם הטובים של משכילים, כי אם כל עצמם ליפות את אורחותם, אם טוב ואם רע, הכל נכון לפניהם. וזה הגורם להם שבלתי אפשרי להם לילך ממדריגה למדריגה, וכאשר בארתי פירוש המשנה "כל ימי גדלתי בין החכמים" (מ' אבות א:יז), ועיקר הדברים כל ימי גדלתי והלכתי ממדריגה למדריגה, ולא עמדתי במדריגה אחת, ומה הגורם ככה? להיותי בין החכמים, ואז הבנתי פחיתת ערכי ועדיין לא למדתי אפילו מידה אחת טובה מרבותי.

והכלל, מי שרוצה לעמוד במעלה המובחרת, צריך לקיים בעצמו מה שכתוב "מכל מלמדי השכלתי" (תהלים קיט:צט), וכמאמרם "הרבה למדתי מרבותי, [ומחברי יותר מרבותי], ומתלמידי יותר מכולם" (תענית ז.). ובפרט איש מרעהו וחבירו יכול ללמוד מידות טובות וכדומה מהמעלות. אמנם, עתה בדור הזה רבים עמי הארץ אשר לא ידעו בין ימינם לשמאלם, ועם כל זה הם מתפרצים ומתפארים ליטול את השם והכבוד, וכל מה שיוכלון ליתן דופי באחרים, אזי מתכבדים בקלון חבריהם. ומזה נמשך בעוונותינו הרבים שנאת חנם...

... מול דברינו הנזכר לעיל, **ויט משה את ידו על השמים ויהי חושך אפלה בכל ארץ מצרים**, כלומר בהעדר הדעת **ויהי חושך אפלה**, ונופלים בבחינת "מיצר ים" החכמה. ומפרש הכתוב מה הוא החושך ואפלה, **לא ראו איש את אחיו**... **"ראו"** משמעו לשון חשיבות. לא חשבו בלבם איש את אחיו ללמוד ממעשיהם הטובים. ואדרבא, ממציאים תמיד חסרונות וקלון ודופי, ומיפים מעשה עצמם, ולכן הולכים בחושך ולא אור להם לילך תמיד ממדריגה למדריגה. וזהו **ולא קמו איש מתחתיו**, כי אם המה תמיד במדריגה אחת, והוא רק בחינת עומד ולא הולך, ובאמת איש הישראלי צריך להיות תמיד בחינת הולך.

- ס"ט -

❧ פרשת בא ❧

נועם אלימלך

ויאמר משה בנערינו ובזקנינו נלך בבנינו ובבנותנו בצאננו ובבקרנו נלך כי חג ה׳ לנו (שמות י:ט).

נראה לפרש דאיתא בגמרא: בשמחת בית השואבה היו אומרים ״אשרי ילדותינו שלא ביישה את זקנותנו״ (סוכה נג.). דהיינו, שהיו מתנהגים מיד בנערותם כשורה, ולא היו מתביישים בזקנותם ממעשה נערות שהיו גם כן בקדושה. אבל מי שאינו מתנהג בקדושה בנערותו, אזי לעת זקנותו הוא מתבייש ממעשיו הקודמים. וצריך לסור מדרכו, על כן טוב שיתקדש עצמו מיד.

וזהו שאמר הכתוב ״חנוך לנער על פי דרכו, גם כי יזקין לא יסור ממנה״ (משלי כב:ו). כלומר, שלא יצטרך לסור מדרכו הקודם, ויוכל לילך בעקבות נעוריו כמו שהיה מתנהג עד עתה, ובקל יכול לעבוד ה׳ יתברך ב״ה. וזהו **בנערינו ובזקנינו נלך**, רוצה לומר שנתנהג ונלך בקדושה, הן בנעורינו והן בזקנינו. **בבנינו ובבנותינו נלך**, היינו שנדריך אותם בקדושה. **בצאנינו ובבקרינו נלך**, רמז גם בעובדות הגשמיות, כמו משא ומתן, ואכילה, ושתיה, וכדומה, נלך בכל זה לה׳ יתברך. כי **חג ה׳ לנו**, רוצה לומר כי התלהבות אש בוער בנו לעבודתו יתברך שמו ויתעלה זכרו, וקל להבין.

מעיין החכמה

וארא אל אברהם אל יצחק ואל יעקב באל שדי ושמי ה' לא נודעתי להם (שמות ו:ג).

... ומודעת לכל מאמרם ז"ל: שכל אות ואות שמו של הקדוש ברוך הוא. ולכאורה, לא שייך לומר בו יתברך לא אות, ולא נקודה, ולא טעמים, אלא כביכול נמשל בו כדמיון: כמו אדם ששם שקוראין אותו הוא חיות שלו. וראיה לזה שאדם, כשהוא ישן, קל להקיץ אותו כשקוראין אותו בשמו יותר מהקיצו בגופו, מחמת ששמו הוא חיותו. כך כביכול, קודשא בריך הוא אתעטף באורייתא, היינו באותיות התורה. ואם כן, האדם שמדבר באותיות התורה והתפילה הוא צריך לירא ולפחד מהבורא יתברך שהוא ברא כל העולמות: האצילות, והבריאה, והיצירה, והעשיה. ובאותיות הקדושים והטהורים הוא קורא להבורא יתברך ויתעלה, הוא צריך לירא ולפחד.

וכל שכן כשמדבר שאר הדברים, הוא צריך לישב קודם שמוציא הדיבור מפיו, שעל ידי שה' יתברך מתעטף באורייתא נתהוו אותיות הקדושים. אלא שאדון יתברך, הוא אין סוף ברוך הוא, היה צריך לצמצם. ואם כן, בכל אות ואות הוא שם הוי"ה ברוך הוא, ושם שדי הוא רומז אל הצמצום, והוי"ה [26] ושם שדי [314] הוא גימטריה "שם" [340], וזהו כל אות ואות הוא שמו של הקדוש ברוך הוא...

יבנה" (תהלים פט:ג). ואף שהוא דין מכל מקום אם לא היה צמצום היו העולמות בטלים.

וידוע כי מידת הדין נקרא "אלהים," בתוכו מעורב חסד שהוא שם "אל"... כמו דאמר "חסד אל כל היום" (תהלים נב:ג). וזה שנאמר "כי שמש ומגן ה' אלהים" (תהלים פד:יב): ידוע כי שם הוי"ה נקרא "שמש," וזה שנאמר "כי שמש ומגן" הוא דמיון כמו "ה' אלהים." רוצה לומר כשם שאי אפשר להסתכל בשמש מגודל אור בהירותו אם לא על ידי מגן ומסך המבדיל, שהוא המגן בעד אור השמש שיוכלו ליהנות מאורו, כך הוא שם הוי"ה ברוך הוא שאורו רב מאוד מגודל אור בהירותו, אור החסד והרחמים שבו, אם לא היה לאורו הגדול מסך המבדיל, לא היו העולם יכולים לקבלו. לכך הוצרך לצמצמו ולהגבילו בשם אלהים...

וזה שנאמר **וארא אל** האבות **באל שדי, ושמי ה' לא נודעתי להם**. כי ידוע שמידת הצמצום נקרא שדי, שאמר לעולמו "די." רוצה לומר, שהגביל מידת החסד מלהתפשט יותר מדי. ועל כל זה אף שהוא בחינת דין נקרא אל שדי שמעורב בו החסד הנקרא אל. וזהו גופא חסד כי יוכלו על ידי הצמצום לקבל אורו. **ושמי ה'** שהוא שם הוי"ה **לא נודעתי להם**, רוצה לומר לא היה יכול להתגלות בימיהם והיה מלובש בתוך שם אלהים, שהוא דין וצמצום. **ואני ה'** - היה, הווה, יהיה, ויכולת בידו להתגלות ולפרוע מהם...

עוד נראה לי אומרו **וידבר אלהים אל משה ויאמר אליו אני ה'**, רוצה לומר שזאת המידה הנקראת אלהים, שהוא דין, הוא בעצמו מידת רחמים... וזהו שנאמר "וגאלתי אתכם מעבודתכם" (על פי שמות ו:ו), כלומר מהעבודה גופא שהוא מידת הדין תבא להם הגאולה. וזהו שאמרו רז"ל: קושי השיעבוד השלים ארבע מאות שנה של גירות בארץ לא להם, רמזו אל הנזכר, שמכח מידת הדין בא להם הבהירות כי שמש ומגן ה' כנזכר. ולא עוד אלא שזכו בזה לנביאות פנים אל פנים, כמו שאמרו רז"ל: ראתה שפחה על הים מה שלא ראו ישעיה ויחזקאל (מכילתא בשלח שירה פ' ג), מפני שהיו יכולים לסבול הבהירות. וזהו תחילתו דין וקשה וסופו רך.

וכל זה כפי שגזרה חכמתו יתברך שאינה מושגת. פעם מודד במידה זו,
ופעם במידה אחרת, כפי שגזורת חכמתו יתברך שצריך בעת ההיא
להנהיג עולמו על ידי שפעת חיותו. וכן לכל אדם מישראל, מודד את
עצמו וממצמצם אלהותו יתברך כפי כח האדם ושכלו בזמן ההוא, פעם
בחסד ופעם ברחמים, כי השגחתו יתברך רואה כי אי אפשר לאדם לקחת
אלהותו יתברך בעת ההיא כי אם בזאת המידה דוקא. ואם האדם יש לו
דעת, בודאי מקבל אלהותו יתברך כפי מה שמדד את עצמו אליו בעת
ההיא וישמח בקבלת אלהותו יתברך עליו ויהא מודה לו במאד מאד,
ועובד אותו ביראה ואהבה גמורה מאחר שיש לו דעת, והדעת היא הכולל
אותן כנודע.

והנה כשהיו ישראל במצרים היתה הדעת בגלות, כי קליפה קדמה לפרי.
כי הדעת היתה מכוסה בקליפות, כמו קליפת האגוז, כמו שאמר הכתוב
"אל גינת אגוז ירדתי" (שיר השירים ו:יא), שהוא על גלות מצרים.
ובאגוז יש קליפה חיצונה היותר קשה ומכסה את האוכל, ותחתיה קליפות
דקות זה על זה. ובגלות מצרים נשברה קליפה הקשה כדי שיוכלו לראות
האוכל, הגם שנשארו עדיין קליפות הדקות עד שיבא משיחנו, במהרה
בימינו, שיתגלה הפנימיות לגמרי...

אור תורה

**וידבר אלהים אל משה ויאמר אליו אני ה׳: וארא אל
אברהם אל יצחק ואל יעקב באל שדי ושמי ה׳ לא נודעתי
להם** (שמות ו:ב-ג).

הוצרך הקדוש ברוך הוא לצמצם בהירתו ואורו בבריאת העולמות בכדי
שיוכלו לקבלו ולא יתבטלו ממציאות... ואף שמידת צמצום נקרא דין
המגביל שפע החסד אשר טבעו להתפשט, והדין מגבילו כמו המים שבתוך
הכלי שהכלי מגביל את המים ואינו מניחו להתפשט, והנה לפי הנראה
שהצמצום הוא דין, אבל על כל זה הוא חסד, כי בכל דבר ודבר שבכל
העולמות מוכרח להיות הטוב שהוא החסד מעורב בהם כי "עולם חסד

❧ פרשת וארא ❧

מאור עינים

העניין הוא דנודע סוד גלות מצרים הוא כי הדעת האמיתית היתה בגלות,
שלא היו משיגין הדעת לעבוד הבורא ברוך הוא, כעניין שנאמר "דע את
אלהי אביך ועבדהו" (דברי הימים א כח:ט). כי באמת הדעת היא העיקר
המביא לידי יראה ואהבה הגמורה, כי אחר שידע ויאמין כי מלא כל הארץ
כבודו ולית אתר פנוי מניה, והוא תענוג כל התענוגים ברוך הוא וברוך
שמו חי החיים, אם כן בכל התענוגים אילו יצוייר ח"ו העדר שפעת אורו
וחיותו יתברך בהדברים הנבראים, היו חוזרים הנבראים לתהו ובהו. וכן
בכל העולמות עליונים ותחתונים, אילו יצוייר ח"ו העדר חיותו מהן היו
כלא היו.

ואם כן הוא העיקר בכל הדברים, ואם כן כשיאמין בזה ודאי לא יתאוה
לשום תענוג בעולם, מאחר שעיקרו הוא הבורא ב"ה, ואם כן טוב יותר
לדבק את עצמו בתענוג האמיתי ולא להפריד ח"ו משרשו, ליקח התענוג
כמו שרואה בעין הגשמי ויקרא ח"ו "נרגן מפריד אלוף" (משלי טז:כח) -
מפריד אלופו של עולם משכינתיה. כי כל הדברים מכונים בשם שכינה,
דהיינו חיות ה' יתברך השוכן בכל הדברים. ואם הוא עושה הדבר כמו
שעושים אנשי המונים אזי מפריד ח"ו.

על כן בודאי מי שיש לו דעת זו יראה בכל דבר הפנימיות המקיימו, שהוא
שכינתו ב"ה, וידבק בו ויבא לידי יראה ואהבה. ואהבה נקראת כמו
שנאמר במשנה: "ואהבת את ה' אלהיך... בכל מאדך" (דברים ו:ה) - בכל
מידה ומידה שהוא מודד לך הוי מודה לו במאד מאד (מ' ברכות ט:ה).

להבין הדבר מהו בכל מידה ומידה, דנודע כי ה' יתברך אין סוף, ואם כן
הוא דבר שאין לו גבול ותכלית. והעולם הוא דבר שיש לו גבול. ואם כן
איך אפשר לעולם לסבול אור שפעת חיותו ששוכן בכל הנבראים כנ"ל,
מאחר שאין לו יתברך גבול? אלא הוא יתברך מנהיג עולמו על ידי
מידותיו, והמידות נקראות מה שמדד ה' יתברך וצמצם את עצמו כביכול
באופן שיוכל העולם לסובלו, וזהו לשון "מידה."

- ס"ד -

התחתון לעליון ויכול להעלות ממדריגה למדריגה עד ראש כולם, ששם הכל אחדות פשוטה.

וזהו שנכתב בתורה סירוב משה רבינו ע"ה לילך להוציא בני ישראל ממצרים. לא על מגן אלא להשמיענו דבר הגון. שהדין הוא עמו לפי שהוא היה בחינת אהבה לחוד, כמו שנאמר כי "מן 'המים' משיתיהו" (שמות ב:י), דהיינו בחינת אהבה ותענוג. וזה שנאמר "כי כבד פה [וכבד לשון אנכי]" (שמות ד:י), לפי שדרך הפה לצמצם הקול במבטא כדי לחתוך הדיבור, והוא לא היה מבחינת צמצום, רק מבחינת תענוג לבד. וכאן היה צריך להתגלות אלוהותו יתברך, בחינת אהבה וצמצום. על כן אמר לו ה' יתברך "הלא אהרן אחיך הלוי," דהיינו בחינת צמצום. "והיה הוא יהיה לך לפה" (שמות ד:יד,טז)... **ויפגשהו בהר האלהים. הר** הוא אהבה, כאברהם שקראו "הר" (פסחים פח.), **האלהים** בחינת דין וצמצום, והיינו כשנפגשו היו כבר שניהם כאן. וזהו **וישק לו,** אתדבקו רוחא ברוחא, דהיינו שנעשו שניהם באחדות פשוטה.

באה אלי" (שמות ג:ט), כלומר כאילו עיקר צעקתם "אלי" בשבילי, אשר רוצים וצועקים שאושיע להם בשביל לעבוד אותי.

אור תורה

... וילך ויפגשהו בהר האלהים וישק לו (שמות ד:כז).

... והנה במצרים נתגלה אלהותו יתברך כמו שהיה בחידוש העולם, כנודע, כמו שנאמר "אני ולא מלאך" (שמות יב:יב). כי הוכרח להיות על ידי עצמו יתברך, לפי שהיו מסובבים בטומאות ובכשפים שלא היה יכול להיות כי אם על ידי עצמו יתברך, כנזכר, ולא היה כח בשום מלאך לעשות זה. על כן היה מופת גדול על חידוש העולמות, כי הוא המשדד המערכות כרצונו יתברך.

וכיון שהיה צריך להתגלות אלוהותו יתברך, היה צריך גם כן להיות על ידי אהבה וצמצום, כדי שיוכלו לסבול אותו כמו בחידוש העולם. והנה אף על פי ששם היו אהבה וצמצום הכל ברגע אחד, אף על פי כן בעולם העשיה צריך לזה שני כלים. כי כן הוא דרך העולמות, שמה שבעולם העליון הוא אחדות פשוטה, כמו המחשבה, ובעולם התחתון ממנו נראה יותר פירוד, הוא מצד הכלים. אבל מצד החיות, שהוא מעולם העליון, הוא גם עתה אחדות פשוטה כמו המחשבה, שהמחשבה הוא בלב בלבד, ואחר כך כשרוצה לגלותה על ידי קול ודיבור יש לה כמה כלים נפרדים חמשה כנפי ריאה והמבטאים והקנה. ואחר כך, מזכירה לעשיה, נראה הפירוד עוד יותר.

ובאמת האיש הנלבב אינו עושה פירוד גם בעולם התחתון, כיון שרואה שכל קומתו וחיותו של עולם התחתון הוא מעולם העליון. ואלולי העולם העליון היה העולם התחתון אפס מוחלט, וכן אם יסתלק השפעת עולם העליון אפילו רגע אחד, היה חוזר התחתון לאפס מוחלט. אם כן הוא כמו עולם העליון, וכמו ששם הכל הוא אחדות פשוטה ישים לכאן לאחדותו גם כן. ואינו משגיח על הכלים הנראים מופרדים, כי הוא בבחינת המקבלים. אבל הדיבור בעצמו הוא אחדות פשוטה. ובזה מייחד עולם

- ס"ב -

נועם אלימלך

וירא מלאך ה' אליו בלבת אש מתוך הסנה וירא והנה הסנה בוער באש והסנה איננו אוכל (שמות ג:ב).

... דהנה הצדיקים גם היצר הרע נהפך אליהם לטוב, כמו שאמר "בכל לבבך" (דברים ו:ה), בשני יצריך" (ברכות נד.). אך אף על כן אין להאמין לעצמו, רק צריך תמיד להזהר ולהשמר ממנו. וזהו **וירא מלאך ה' אליו בלבת אש,** דהיצר הרע נקרא גם כן **מלאך ה'.** פירוש והוא מראה עצמו להצדיק בהתלהבות גדולה כנזכר לעיל, שנהפך גם הוא לטוב. **מתוך הסנה,** שהיה בו תחילה כמו סנה. **וירא והנה הסנה בוער באש,** פירוש ואמר הכתוב אף על פי שרואה שהסנה הוא היצר הרע גם כן בוער באש התלהבות לעבודת הבורא יתברך שמו, אף על פי כן **והסנה איננו אוכל,** רוצה לומר וצריך להזהר ולהשמר ממנו עד יום מותו...

קדושת לוי

ויאמר ה' ראה ראיתי את עני עמי אשר במצרים ואת צעקתם שמעתי מפני נוגשיו... (שמות ג:ז).

הנה לבאר, כי כשהאדם מבקש איזה טובה מהבורא יתברך, אזי לא יהיה עיקר כוונתו מחמת דבר הנוגע לעצמותו, רק עיקר כוונתו יהיה שעל ידי זה יעבוד את הבורא יתברך שמו בטוב לב. והנה ישראל במצרים היו בקטנות השכל, וצעקתם היה מחמת דבר הנוגע לאדם לעצמותו, ולא צעקו שיושיע להם מצרתם בכדי שעל ידי זה יעבדו את הבורא ב"ה ויקראו עם ה', כי במצרים היו בקטנות השכל. והנה הקדוש ברוך הוא עשה להם שתי טובות: האחת מה שהושיע להם בצרתם מיד מצרים, ועוד עשה להם טובה גדולה שקיבל צעקתם כאילו צעקו בשבילו, כלומר כאילו צעקו שיושיע להם מצרתם שעל ידי זה יקראו עם ה'.

וזהו רמז בפסוק **ראה ראיתי את עני עמי.** רמז **ראיתי את עני עמי,** אשר רוצים להיות **עמי.** וזהו הרמז בפסוק "ועתה הנה צעקת בני ישראל

מציאת האל יתברך שמו, בודאי נקל גם כן להוציא את מידותיו מהרע ולהביאן אל הטוב כנודע, שלא להשתמש בהן רק כמו שמחייב הדעת.

וכמו שדרש בן זומא: "למען תזכור את יום צאתך מארץ מצרים כל ימי חייך" (שם). "ימי חייך" - הימים; "כל ימי חייך" - הלילות (ברכות יב:). כי בחינת יום נקרא כשהשכל הוא בהיר, ואז בוודאי יפעל בו על ידי זכירת הדעת. אך אפילו בשעת החשכות הנקראת בחינת לילות, אם יזכור בהדעת שיש מציאות אל גדול ונורא שברא יש מאין ובידו הכל בודאי "לילה כיום יאיר" לו (תהלים לקט:יב) ויצא מבחינת החשכות, כי הדעת יתקן הכל...

מעיין החכמה

ואלה שמות בני ישראל הבאים מצרימה את יעקב איש וביתו באו (שמות א:א).

"ונדעה נרדפה לדעת את ה'" (הושע ו:ג), לתרץ הדקדוקים. מפני מה כתיב בתחילה **ישראל**, ואחר כך כתיב **יעקב**? ועוד יש לדקדק, מפני מה בתחילה כתיב **הבאים**, ואחר כך כתיב **באו**? ונראה לי לתרץ על זה הדרך, **ישראל** רמז על ישראל עלה במחשבה, היינו בני אדם שעובדין לה' יתברך במחשבה. אותן בני אדם רואים קודם שבא דין ח"ו בעולם, ומבטלין במחשבה ועוצרים הדינים שלא יבואו לעולם. ובני אדם שהם בבחינת **יעקב**, שהם במדריגה נמוכה, אינם יודעים לבטלו במחשבה, אלא אם כן בא לעולם, ח"ו. וזה **ואלה שמות בני ישראל**, רוצה לומר בני אדם שבוניין, שיהיו נקראים בבחינת ישראל. **הבאים מצרימה**, היינו שהם מבינים שיבא ח"ו "מיצר ים" ומבטלין תיכף ומיד במחשבה. **את יעקב איש וביתו באו**, היינו שהם כך במדריגה כשבאין הדינים ח"ו אז מבטלין. וזה **באו**, רוצה לומר כשבאין לעולם. והבן, וה' יתברך ישפיע שפע טוב לעולם.

- ס -

416

❧ פרשת שמות ❧

מאור עינים

דנודע סוד גלות מצרים הוא כי הדעת היתה בגלות, שלא ידעו כלל מהבורא ב"ה ומתורתו. כי בדור המבול אמרו "מה שדי כי נעבדנו" (איוב כא:טו), כי התורה אף שלא ניתנה קודם המבול מכל מקום היתה גם בזה העולם, כי כח הפועל בנפעל, רק שלא ניתנה בלבושין כמו אחר מתן תורה, שנתלבשה בלבושין כמו זה העולם. והיו יחידי סגולה שהיו מקיימים התורה כמו שהיא במרום מחמת שהיו משיגים אותה במוחין גדולים שהיו להם, עד שהיו משיגים את פנימיותה האמיתית כמו שהיתה מקודם שניתנה, כמו מתושלח וחנוך ואדם הראשון שהיו לומדי תורה כנודע. ובדור המבול היו רשעים גדולים עד שהפסיקו את העולם עם הפועל שהיא התורה מן הבורא ב"ה. על כן כשנפסק העולם והתורה משרשם, על כן חרב העולם באותו זמן והיה מבול.

ולהיכן הפילו את התורה? בקליפת מצרים. על כן באה הדעת בגלות כנודע, שהתורה היא בחינת דעת. על כן הוצרכו ישראל לירד למצרים להעלות את התורה שנפלה בקליפת מצרים...

והנה אחר יציאת מצרים שהוציאו הדעת מהגלות, אף שיש גלות, מכל מקום אין הדעת בגלות, כי אם לתועים גמורים הכופרים במציאות. אבל לרוב העולם אין בגלות כי אם המידות, דהיינו אהבה ויראה והתפארות ואינך המידות. כי הכל יודעים שיש מציאת האל יתברך שמו ויש להם דעת, כל אחד לפי בחינתו. אך המידות מתלבשים בגלות, כגון אהבות אחרות, ויראות אחרות, וכן בכל המידות משתמשין בהם שלא כרצון הבורא יתברך שמו אשר טבע וחקק בהם המידות רק לעבודתו יתברך שמו.

לכן הזהירה התורה בכל מקום "זכור את יום צאתך מארץ מצרים..." (דברים טז:ג), וכן כמה פעמים כי היא נתינת עצה איך להוציא המידות גם כן מהגלות. כי אם יזכור כל אחד כי הדעת יצא כבר ממצרים ונודע לו

- נ"ט -

417

ע׳ קו **חיים וחסד** - ויעש בצלאל את הארון עצי שטים... ויצפהו זהב טהור
מבית ומחוץ... (שמות לז:א-ב).

⚬ פקודי (ע׳ קח-קי) ⚬

קח **רב ייבי** - אלה פקודי המשכן משכן העדות אשר פקד על פי משה
עבודת הלוים... (שמות לח:כא).

קט **חסד לאברהם מקאליסק** - אלה פקודי המשכן משכן העדות...
(שמות לח:כא).

קי **אורח לחיים** - ותכל כל עבודת משכן אהל מועד ויעשו בני ישראל
ככל אשר צוה ה׳ את משה כן עשו (שמות לט:לב).

﷽ שמות (ע' נט-סג) ﷽

ספר
שמות

קדושת לוי ב'

ויאמר אליהם יוסף אל תיראו כי התחת אלהים אני (בראשית
נ:י"ט).

ואונקלוס תרגם "ארי דחלא דה' אנא," [ירא ה' אני]. והנה לפירוש
הפשוט בפסוק, אין להבין התרגום. ונראה כי הכלל האדם בכל מידותיו
צריך להדבק עצמו להבורא ב"ה: במידת היראה, לירא את ה' הנכבד
והנורא; במידת אהבה, לאהוב את ה' הגדול; במידת התפארת, שיקוים בנו
"ישראל אשר בך אתפאר" (ישעיה מט:ג), וכן בשאר המידות וזה הוא
עולם האמת.

ואם תבין זה תבין מאמר חז"ל: מנין שהקדוש ברוך הוא קרא ליעקב אל
(מגילה י"ח.); וגם מאמר חז"ל: מה הקדוש ברוך הוא בונה עולמות, אף
הצדיקים [בונים עולמות] (זהר ח"א ה.); וגם מאמר חז"ל: "עתידין
צדיקים שיקראו בשמו של הקדוש ברוך הוא" (בבא בתרא עה:); וגם
מאמר חז"ל: עתידין מלאכי השרת לומר לפני הצדיקים "קדוש" (שם).

והנה אם האדם דבוק בכל המידות להבורא יתברך, אז הוא אינו **תחת**
אלהים, אדרבה הוא דבוק בה', ואם ח"ו אינו מדבק עצמו במידות כנזכר
לעיל, אז הוא **תחת** אלהים. וזהו הרמז מה שתרגם אונקלוס כי יוסף אמר
התחת אלהים אני, וכי אני תחת אלהים? אדרבה, אני דבוק בה'. וזהו
שתרגם אונקלוס על זה "ארי דחלא דה' אנא," אני דבוק בכל המידות
להבורא יתברך.

❧ תם ונשלם ספר בראשית ❧

כל אחד ואחד יעשה תיכף אותן הצירופים והעובדות, בלי טרחא ובלי יגיעה...

קדושת לוי א'

מַאֲשֵׁר שְׁמֵנָה לַחְמוֹ וְהוּא יִתֵּן מַעֲדַנֵּי מֶלֶךְ (בראשית מט:כ).

דהנה שמעתי ממורי ורבי הצדיק מורנו דוב בער זצ"ל פירוש הפסוק "שׂוֹשׂ אָשִׂישׂ בה'" (ישעיה סא:י), דאני שש ויש לי שמחה ותענוג ממה שזכיתי לחזות בנועם ה' ולהתענג בעבודתו. ומזה עצמו יש לי שמחה, שזכיתי להתקרב לה' יתברך ולהתענג מעבודתו מרוב כל, וזהו "שׂוֹשׂ אָשִׂישׂ"...

וזהו **מַאֲשֵׁר שְׁמֵנָה לַחְמוֹ**. **מַאֲשֵׁר** הוא עולם התענוג, מזה שיש לנו תענוג מעבודת ה' יתברך, מזה עצמו יש לנו שמחה ותענוג שזכינו להתענג מעבודתו יתברך. וזהו **שְׁמֵנָה לַחְמוֹ**, שלחם נקרא תענוג. מזה עצמו שזכינו להתענג מעבודתו, מזה עצמו יש לנו תענוג שזכינו לזה.

וְהוּא יִתֵּן מַעֲדַנֵּי מֶלֶךְ. על פי ששמעתי ממורי הצדיק מורנו דוב בער, על מה שאמרו חז"ל "ישראל מפרנסין לאביהם שבשמים" (זהר ח"ג ז:), היינו שהתתענוג נקרא פרנסה, וה' יתברך מתענג בעבודת ישראל, וישראל גורמים תענוג לאביהם שבשמים. וזהו **יִתֵּן מַעֲדַנֵּי מֶלֶךְ**, שמי שזוכה לעבוד ה' יתברך באהבה שלימה וגמורה "אהבה בתענוגים" (שיר השירים ז:ז), **הוּא יִתֵּן מַעֲדַנֵּי מֶלֶךְ**, שגורם תענוג לה' יתברך, וישמח ה' במעשיו.

אם עיני שכל לו יוכל לקרות כל התורה כולה בשמו של הקדוש ברוך הוא, ולהמציא בפרטי סיפוריה שם הוי"ה ברוך הוא. וזה תכלית הדברים שהצדיקים מחזירים את התורה ליושנה, כמו שהיתה מקודם התלבשותה בזה העולם, וההצריכה להתגשם בסיבת עם ישראל שאנו בני ישראל בעולם הזה בגוף עכור וגשם, ובלתי אפשרי להשיג עומקה כי אם באמצעות התלבשות כזו בכדי שיוכל אוזן הגשמי לשמוע.

אמנם לעתיד לבוא כאשר יזדככו הגופים מחומריות "וימלא הארץ דעה את ה'" (ישעיה יא:ט) מקטנם ועד גדולם גדולות ורוממות אלהותו יתברך ותתרבה ההשגה בעולם, ממילא תתפשט התורה מהגשם גם כן ותהיה רק אורות עליונים ובהירים לעין כל... לכאורה צריך הבנה האיך הוא מרומז בתורה שביקש [יעקב] לגלות להם את הקץ? ולפי הנאמר יתפרש שפיר, כי מחמת שאין להם לישראל שכל ודעת להכיר אותן הצירופים המוטלים עליהם אשר נבראו בעולם, לעשות ולצרף אותן הצירופים ולקבוע אותם בקבע גמור בלתי יתפרדו...

אם בא יבוא חכם הכולל ומבשר טוב, ללמוד וללמד לכל אחד מישראל לומר ככה תעשה ויגלה לנו אותן הצירופים המוטלים עלינו לעשות... בודאי מי הוא זה שלא יסור למשמעתו לעשות אותן העובדות אשר בסיבתם יגרום הצירופים שלעתיד, וממילא לא תמשיך [תארך] זמן הגאולה.

אמנם בעשות ככה אין הבחירה חפשית, כי זה ניתנה ביד עם ישראל כאחד ואחד לערך הכרתו והשגתו והתאמצו בעבודת בוראו, הוא בעצמו יבוא על אותן הצירופים שיש לו באותיות התורה, ואם לאו לא פעל כלום בבריאתו בעולם הזה, ומה אהני לו שחכם הכולל המצוה בטוב גרם ככה, והגיד לו במה יתכן לו לעשות צירופים, אשר זה הוא בחירה בידו, ואם כן בטלה הבחירה.

וזהו: **ויקרא יעקב לבניו ויאמר האספו ואגידה לכם**... וזה ידוע אשר בכל מקום שנאמר "הגדה" רזא דהמשכה, ובכאן הרמז שרצה להמשיך ולהגיד להם אותן הצירופים שיקרה להם באחרית הימים לעת שתחזיר התורה ליושנה, ורצה לגלות להם אז תיכף ונמצא תולה בזה עת הקץ. ולזה פירש רש"י בקש לגלות להם את הקץ, כי בודאי אם אמר להם יעקב אבינו אותן הצרופים שיקראו באחרית הימים, ממילא בטלה הבחירה, כי

- נ"ו -

425

✿ פרשת ויחי ✿

אור תורה

ויברך את יוסף ויאמר... המלאך הגואל אותי מכל רע יברך את הנערים (בראשית מח:טו-טז).

פירש בזהר: ברכתא דבנין, אף על פי שהיא שלם מצדו, מצד הבנין אין תענוגו שלם עד שיגמור שלימותו (זהר ח״א רכז:), כמו שאמרו רז״ל: ״יהי רצון שיהיו צאצאי מעיך כמותך״ (תענית ו.), מה שאין כן לא היו לו בנין, אין צריך לזה.

והבן החכם מבקש הכל בשביל תענוג אביו. ואביו בראותו כי כן נותן לו בשביל בניו. וזהו ״והשיב לב אבות על בנים״ (מלאכי ג:כד), וזהו ענין ברכות שמברכין ישראל לאביהם שבשמים.

אור המאיר

ויקרא יעקב אל בניו ויאמר האספו ואגידה לכם את אשר יקרא אתכם באחרית הימים (בראשית מט:א).

ופירש רש״י: ביקש לגלות להם את הקץ ונסתלקה שכינה ממנו...

ומעתה תבין דברי חכמים ורמיזותם, שנתעוררו: ״עתידין צדיקים שיקראו בשמו של הקדוש ברוך הוא״ (בבא בתרא עה:)... כי הצדיקים מחזירים את התורה ליושנה, לבחינתה. וכבר נודע אורייתא מחכמה נפקית, והצדיק על ידי עומק השגתו מפשיט אותה מהתלבשותה בסיפורי מעשיות ומלביש אותה בצורה רוחניות, אורות עליונים ורזין עלאין משמות הקדושים המרומזים בסיפורים אלה...

- נ״ה -

קדושת לוי

ויאסור יוסף מרכבתו ויעל לקראת אביו... (בראשית מו:כט).

והנה לכאורה מה סיפרה לנו התורה שיוסף אסר, הלא היה די בזה שאמר **ויעל לקראת אביו**. אבל הנראה לנו בזה שיעיין כל אדם בעינא פקיחא על כל מעשיו, שלא ינהג מעשה בהמה ח"ו, רק במאזנים כל מעשיותיו, כדי שיוכל לבא מזה רמיזא דחכמתא לעבודתו יתברך... ואז גורם במעשיו הטובים להיות מרכבה לשכינה. וזהו פירוש הפסוק **ויאסר יוסף מרכבתו**, דהיינו שיוסף היה בבחינה זו.

והנה יוסף היה מתענג בוודאי בראיית פני אביו, ואז היה חושב בעצמו מה אם זה תענוג גדול כל כך אילו הייתי רואה את הקדוש ברוך הוא כביכול, אז היה התענוג יותר גדול מאד מזה התענוג, והיינו **ויעל לקראת אביו**.

אבל באמת זה רק כשאדם עושה מצוות ומתפלל בכוחות גדולים, עד שהוא עייף מאוד ומעט מעט יכול להיות שיוסר מעליו חומריותו, ואז שורה עליו רוח הנאצל מאתו יתברך. וזהו האור הוא כמו ראיית **אביו**, הקדוש ברוך הוא בעצמו כביכול. ויוסף הצדיק מרוב צדקתו בודאי שרתה עליו אור צח ומצוחצח, וזהו חלק אלהי ממעל, ועל זה גרם שעשה ממעשה שהוא התענוג בראיית אביו מרכבה לשכינה.

אלמית שאין לה הדיבורים לומר לפניו יתברך ולזה דוה לבם, ולכן פתיחת דיבורו של צדיק יאיר לשאול עבור השכינה. וזהו **ידבר נא עבדך** פועל יוצא, מוסב על השכינה הנקראת דבר, **ידבר** אותה לגרום לה דבורים וזמירות ותשבחות...

מבשר צדק

ונאמר לא נוכל לרדת אם יש אחינו הקטן אתנו וירדנו כי לא נוכל לראות פני האיש ואחינו הקטן איננו אתנו (בראשית מד:כו).

דהנה ידוע דהצדיק חלילה לו לירד ממדריגתו הרמה לעשות מחשבתו הקדושה, דהוא גורם הוצאת קדשים לחוץ. רק כשצריכין להעלות איזה אדם מישראל אשר הוא בקטנות גדולה, אז מותר לצדיק לירד ממדריגתו ולהעלות אותו האיש מישראל, כי ירידה היא צורך העליה, כי הצדיק בא למדריגה יותר גדולה וזוכה לראות פני השכינה.

על דרך משל מלכותא דארעא אי אפשר לראות בקל פני המלך. אך אם נאבד בן המלך שנשבה למרחקים ואיש אחד הלך לשם וסיכן את עצמו בסכנה עצומה, שגם הוא לא ישאר שם חלילה, והוא עשה כדי לעשות נחת רוח להמלך, אז תיכף בבואו הוא רואה פני המלך בלי שום עיכוב מחמת שגרם שמחה גדולה להמלך. וזהו פירוש הפסוק **ונאמר לא נוכל לרדת,** היינו שאין אנו רשאים לרדת ממדריגתנו אם לא **יש אחינו הקטן אתנו**, היינו נוכל להבין כשנרדה ממדריגתינו יהיה **אחינו** אשר הוא בקטנות **אתנו,** היינו שוה עמנו, שנהיה ביכולת להעלותם, אז **וירדנו.**

והטעם **כי לא נוכל לראות פני האיש** כשאחינו הקטן איננו אתנו, כי יש העדר פנים מאירים כשאחינו הקטן, היינו מי שהוא בקטנות, נשאר שם ואינו אתנו בשוה. אבל כשיעלוהו גם כן אז נהיה ביכולת **לראות פני האיש,** כי "לא ידח ממנו נדח" (שמואל ב יד:יד). וצריכין לתקן שיהיו כל הניצוצות הקדושים יבאו לידי תיקון ובירור, וכשנעלה אז נהיה ביכולת לראות ולחזות בנועם ה', ועל ידי זה **וירדנו** כדי להעלותן.

- נ"ג -

להיות יהודה היה מלכות בית דוד, ומלכותו בכל משלה והכל כלול בו. **ויגש** להתקשר עמו אליו יתברך ועל פי האמת להיותו יוסף הוא היסוד ומתקשר עם המלכות וזהו **בי אדני**, על פי פשוט גם על פי אמת.

אור המאיר

ויגש אליו יהודה ויאמר בי אדני ידבר נא עבדך דבר באזני אדני... (בראשית מד:יח).

הנה זכרנו כמה פעמים היות עיקר עבודת האדם ומגמתו בתורה ובתפילה מהראוי להיות רק עבור השכינה... ומצינו לרז"ל שנתעוררו: מפני מה היו הראשונים מתפללים ונענים? מפני שהתפללו בשם (מדרש תהילים צא). ויש לרמוז בדבריהם על דרך המוזכר בפרשה הקודמת, שאמר יעקב אבינו "אם כן אפוא זאת עשו" (בראשית מג:יא). עיקר עשיותיכם ועובדותיכם רק לעשות שם היא השכינה הנקראת שם... "קחו מזמרת הארץ בכליכם" (שם), היינו אותן הזמירות ותשבחות שהשכינה מזמרת ומשוררת תמיד בסוד "אלהים אל דמי לך" (תהלים פג:ב). קחו זאת באותיותיכם הנקראות כלים, להפוך כל הצירופים שעסק עמהם לצורכי גופו, לעשות צירופי שמות וכינים לקראתו יתברך לפיהם, ואז קריאות שמות עולה לו כהוגן...

ולזאת צוה יעקב לבניו "זאת עשו." השכינה הנקראת "זאת", "עשו" אותה תמיד ותקנו להיות לה בחינת קומה שלימה על ידי עובדותיכם הטובים, ובפרט על ידי דיבורי תורה ותפילה באופן המבואר. "קחו מזמרת הארץ בכליכם," כל עצמכם באותיות של תורה ותפילה הנקראות כלים...

וזהו **ויגש אליו יהודה**, מי שהוא צדיק מקרב הכל אל הבורא ב"ה ומעלה כל בחינת ההתחלקות לשורש האחדות, וכאמור זאת עבודת יהודה מכונה בשם צדיק אשר בכל דור ודור, **ויאמר בי אדני ידבר נא עבדך דבר...** **ידבר** שהוא פועל יוצא, כי באמת כל עצמו של צדיק האמיתי ותשוקתו בתפילה אינו שואל בעבור עצמו כי אם הכל עבור השכינה, שיהא לה הדיבורים להתפאר בהתעוררות התחתונים. ואם לאו היא כביכול בסוד

פרי הארץ

ויגש אליו יהודה ויאמר בי אדני... (בראשית מד:יח).

הנה בספר אור החיים מובא לפרש מלת ויגש - מאי הגשה? והפירוש הוא
כראוי לו, שהגשה היא בלב להיות ידוע "כמים הפנים לפנים כן לב האדם
לאדם" (משלי כז:יט). ובדברים אלו היה רצון יהודה לעורר רחמי יוסף;
לכן הגיש בלבו להתקרב ליוסף ולאהוב אותו באמיתות הלב, בכדי לעורר
אהבת יוסף אליו לעורר רחמיו. והנה יצא מפה קדוש דברי פי חכם חן
אמת ואמונה, אבל אם אמנם לפי דעת יהודה שהיה סבור על יוסף שהוא
מצרי שהוזהרו ישראל "לא תְחָנֵם' (דברים ז:ב) - שלא ליתן להן חן'
(עבודה זרה כ.), לא נמנע יהודה מלקרב לבו לאהוב על דרך הידוע
בתפילה וקרבנות ואכילה...

והנה תורתנו תורת אמת ואמונה, שבודאי אסור לו לאדם להביא את עצמו
לידי נסיון, להכניס את עצמו במחשבה זרה בכדי להעלותה ח"ו, כי מי
יודע אם יתגבר כארי ויתנשא, או אולי ירד מטה מטה ולא יעמוד בנסיון
ח"ו. אם לא כשנסיון נזדמן לפניו בלא מתכוין, בודאי מן ה' לנסותו וצריך
להתגבר בכל כחו ומסירת נפשו על התשובה והיא העליה. וזה היה ענין
שלמה המלך ע"ה שאמר "ארבה [נשים וסוסים] ולא אסור" (סנהדרין
כא:), ומתחילה יצא במתכוין בכדי להעלות ניצוצות קדושות ולא עמד
בנסיון.

וזהו אמרו רז"ל לברך על בריות נאות "ברוך שככה לו בעולמו" (ברכות
נח:), אפילו על גוי נאה. ואינו סותר למאמר "לא תחנם," כי שם מיירי
להכניס עצמו לראותו אינו רשאי בכדי לומר כמה נאה גוי זה. מה שאין כן
כשכבר נזדמן לפניו, בודאי צריך לברך להעלות הנאות הראיה, כמעשה
רבי עקיבא בההיא מטרוניתא, שאמרו רז"ל: קרן זוית הואי (עבודה זרה
כ:), ובתחילה ודאי אסור, והיא מסירת נפש כענין נפילת אפים, כידוע.

והנה כללא דמלתא מענין ההעלאה הוא שצריך האדם להתבונן על כל
המזדמן לפניו שגם בו נמצא שמץ מנהו, מאותו הדבר, אם טוב ואם רע.
ואחר שמצא מין את מינו וניעור, לכן צריך תיכף להתקשר בו יתברך
מעין המאורע שנזדמן לפניו בשומו אל לבו הלא ה' זו ואין דבר בלתו,
כמאמר "ומלכותו בכל משלה" (תהלים קג:יט)... וזהו שאמר **בי אדני**

- נ"א -

430

פרשת ויגש

אור תורה

**ויגש אליו יהודה ויאמר בי אדני ידבר נא עבדך דבר באזני
אדני ואל יחר אפך בעבדך כי כמוך כפרעה** (בראשית מד:יח).

הנה אמרו רז"ל: אין הגשה אלא לשון תפילה (תנחומא וירא ס' ח). ונראה
לי לזה רמז הפסוק **ויגש אליו יהודה**, נאמר [כלומר] איש ישראל הנקרא
על שמו איש יהודי, בעומדו להתפלל לפני ה' יתברך ככה יתנהג, רוצה
לומר שיהיה כל כוונת תפילתו להשפיע בשכינת עוזו. וזה שאמרו רז"ל:
אין עומדין להתפלל אלא מתוך כובד ראש (ברכות ל:), היינו כובד של
רישא דכל רישין [כתר עליון]. ואף שמבקש בקשת צרכי עצמו, יהיה
כוונתו שלא יחסר הדבר לעילא ח"ו, כי הנשמה היא חלק אלוה ממעל,
והיא אבר מאיברי השכינה. וזהו עיקר הבקשה שימולא ויושפע לעילא.
ובוודאי בזה תפילתו רצויה ואין שטן מקטרג עליו, ולא כאותן דעבדין
לגרמייהו וצווחין "הב הב" כדאיתא בספר הזוהר הקדוש (תיקוני זהר ת' ו
כב.)...

וזהו פירוש **ויגש** לתפילה, **ויאמר** עשה הבקשה למענך, כי הרי אני חלק
אלוה ממעל. וזהו **בי אדני**, ואז **אל יחר אפך**, שלא יקטרגו עלי, כיון
שכל כוונתי הוא להשפיע לעילא לחלק הבורא שהוא בי, וזהו **בי אדני**.
כי כמוך כפרעה, רוצה לומר פרעה הוא לשון התגלות, הוא כמוך שהוא
הפנימיות. ומה גם שעולם הדיבור הוא המדבר בי. וזהו **ידבר נא עבדך
דבר**, שהיא המידה הזאת הנקראת דבר, והיא עולם הדיבור.

- ב -

431

משפיעים להם מן השמים פי שנים. היינו, כשאיש ישראל חומד ומשתוקק מעט אל התורה הקדושה או לדבר ה', משפיעים לו מן השמים חימוד פי שנים.

ואת הכסף המושב בפי אמתחותיכם - היינו האור בפי שנים המושב לכם מן השמים. **תשיבו** ותחזירו למעלה בכדי להעלות הכל להקדוש ברוך הוא. ומה שמשפיעים לכם חימוד ותשוקה מן השמים, תשיבו בחזרה להקדוש ברוך הוא. וכמו כן ישיב לכם עוד מן השמים פי שנים, בזה יושפע לכם עוד כפול. וכן יהיה כסדר לכל פעם יותר, וזהו "כסף משנה." וכמו כן צריך להתנהג תמיד כל ימי חיותו, "והחיות רצוא ושוב" (יחזקאל א:יד), וכאשר תעשו כן אזי **ואל שדי יתן לכם רחמים** - זו תפילה.

מגיד דבריו ליעקב (ס׳ סח)

... ואת הארץ תסחרו (בראשית מב:לד).

הנה שתי בחינות אהבות יש: אחת, שהאב אוהב מעשה בנו החכם
ומתפאר במעשה החכמה שעושה, או בדבר החכמה שמדבר; והשנית,
שאוהב את בנו בעצם, וכל מה שמדבר לפניו הכל הגון בעיניו בשביל
אהבתו אותו. והנה באהבת ה׳ יתברך עלינו אהבה אחת, הנזכרת לעיל,
כשהצדיק עושה מצוות ומעשים טובים הכל בחכמה נפלאה ומעלה
ניצוצות הקדושים, מה שבדוממם צומח חי מדבר, ואז ה׳ יתברך אוהב
מעשיו מאוד. ובזה מקשר גם חיצוניות העולמות לה׳ יתברך, שה׳ יתברך
שורה בכל מעשיו. וזה יתוקן לגמרי אם ירצה ה׳ בביאת משיח בבני
ישראל, כמו שכתוב ״ומלאה הארץ דעה את ה׳״ (ישעיה יא:ט), וגם
בהמות וחיות כולם יהיו יודעים את ה׳ יתברך, ״לא יֵרַעו [ולא ישחיתו
בכל הר קדשי].״

והאהבה השנית... הוא כשהצדיק בעצמו מקושר לה׳ יתברך, וה׳ יתברך
אוהבו מאוד, אותו בעצמו. ואינו עושה מעשיו בחכמה כמו הראשון, רק
הולך בתמימות גדולה מקושר לה׳ יתברך, לכן ה׳ יתברך אוהבו. וזה
נקרא עליות פנימיות העולמות, שהצדיק הוא פנימיות העולם. וזהו מה
שנאמר **״ואת״ הארץ**, דהיינו האותיות מא׳ עד ת׳, מה שהם בארציות
כעת. דהכל נברא באותיות, דהיינו הדיבור של הקדוש ברוך הוא, והם
ניצוצות הקדושים. **תסחרו**, לשון עליה דהוא לשון סביב וגלגל.

בית אהרן

**וכסף משנה קחו בידכם ואת הכסף המושב בפי אמתחותיכם
תשיבו בידכם... ואל שדי יתן לכם רחמים...**
(בראשית מג:יב,יד).

וכסף משנה קחו בידכם - היינו התורה. כסף משנה, החימוד והתשוקה
של לימוד. ולכן נקראת ״כסף משנה,״ החימוד נעשה כפול. היינו, כשבני
אדם נכספים לתורתו ומצוותיו של הקדוש ברוך הוא ומקיימים אותה, אזי

- מ״ח -

433

ועובד ה' יתברך בכל מעשיו ודיבוריו ומחשבותיו בכל הדברים הגשמיים, אף בדברים המותרים, אז הוא ממשיך שפע גדול ובהירות מעולם התענוג בכל עת. וזה שאמר **וייצבר יוסף**, מי שהוא בבחינת צדיק...

עד כי חדל לספור, רוצה לומר שעושה מצוות הרבה ומקבל בהירות גדולה ותענוג גדול בכל עת, נמצא הוא תמיד בעולם התענוג, ותענוג תמידי אינו תענוג, כמו שאמר הרב הקדוש בוצינא קדישא מורנו דוב בער זללה"ה. וכדומה לי ששמעתי בשמו פירוש הפסוק על "לתבונתו אין מספר" (תהלים קמז:ה) הוא לשון ספיר והארה, ותבונה הוא עולם התענוג; ותענוג תמידי אינו תענוג. וזהו "מספר" - עד כאן לשונו, ודברי פי חכם חן. וזהו שאמר שעושה מצוות הרבה **עד כי חדל לספור**, רוצה לומר שחדל מלקבל הארה ותענוג **כי אין מספר**, רוצה לומר אין תענוג בתמידי כנזכר לעיל.

קדושת לוי

ויבאו אחי יוסף וישתחוו לו אפים ארצה וירא יוסף את אחיו ויכירם ויתנכר אליהם (בראשית מב:ו-ז).

ויש להבין מה בא להשמיענו בזה שכתוב, **ויתנכר אליהם**. ונראה דהכתוב בא להשמיענו בזה צדקת יוסף הצדיק, כי הנה יוסף חלם לו שאחיו ישתחוו לו, כדכתיב "והנה אנחנו מאלמים... והנה השמש"... (בראשית לז:ז,ט), ואחיו לא רצו במלוכת יוסף עליהם. והנה דרך הטבע כשאדם מנצח את חבירו וזה יודע שהוא מנצח אותו, דהיינו שיודע שמזה האדם היה לו הנצוח, אזי רע לו ויש לו עגמת נפש גדולה. אבל כשהוא מנצח ואין חבירו יודע ממי הוא מנצח, אז אין לו רע כל כך.

וזה היה צדקת יוסף הצדיק, שבשעה שהשתחוו לו ונמצא הוא נצח אותם... **התנכר אליהם** כדי שלא ירע בעיניהם על הניצוח, שהוא מנצח אותם בקיום החלומות, וידמו שהם משתחוים לאחר. ובאמת יוסף הוא מלך, ולא יהיה להם עצבות על השתחויה כי יבינו שהם משתחוים למלך אחר. וזה שאמר הכתוב: **וישתחוו לו... ויכירם** שיהיה להם עגמת נפש, **ויתנכר אליהם** שלא יהיה להם עגמת נפש וצער על שהוא נצח אותם.

- מ"ז -

שנה" (תהלים צ:י), ולכאורה תיבת "בהם" אך למותר. ויש לרמוז כי הנה השבעים שנה של כל אחד ואחד מישראל הכל נמשך משבעת ימי הבנין הקדמונים, אמנם הפרש שביניהם בכמות ואיכות כי ימים הקדמונים המה גדולים בכמותם ואיכותם, ובכל אחד ואחד מימים הקדמונים צפונים וטמונים כללות שבעים שנות פרטיות נפשות ישראל, וימינו החרוצים עלי אדמה המה קטנים באיכותם קצרים ולא ארוכים, וזה נרמז בפסוק "ימי שנותינו," כלומר ימים הקדמונים מורה שבעת ימי בראשית... אותם הימים שנמשך מהם שנותינו.

אורח לחיים

ויצבר יוסף בר כחול הים הרבה מאוד עד כי חדל לספור כי אין מספר (בראשית מא:מט).

להבין דאמר **כחול הים** הוא בודאי דרך גוזמא, כי מלא כל ארץ מצרים לא יספיק לחול הים. והאיך כתוב בפסוק דרך גוזמא?... ונראה דהנה הצדיק שעובד ה' יתברך תמיד בכל מעשיו ודיבוריו ומחשבותיו, ומקשר תמיד את מחשבותיו אליו יתברך, בתחילה הוא רואה שיהא בלי פניה ח"ו ומחשבת חוץ, רק לה' לבדו. ואחר כך כשיעשה המצוה צריך לעשות ביראה גדולה, כי אי אפשר לקבל שום שפע מלמעלה רק על ידי צמצום תחילה, כמו שאמר הרב הקדוש בוצינא קדישא מורנו הרב דוב בער זללה"ה על פסוק "האותי לא תיראו... אשר שמתי חול גבול לים" (ירמיה ה:כב). ומאי רבותיה? הלא ה' יתברך ברא כל העולמות וכולן כאין נגדו, אלא שאי אפשר לקבל שפע מה' יתברך אלא כשמצמצם עצמו תחילה, כמו שבים - תחילה החול גבול סביב הוא הצמצום, ואחר כך התפשטות הים. כן כשאנו רוצים לקבל ממנו יתברך שפע, צריכין לקבל מידת יראה בשלימות הוא הצמצום, ואחר כך יוכל לקבל התפשטות החסדים. וזהו: "האותי לא תיראו... אשר שמתי חול גבול לים," ואי אפשר לקבל אלא בענין זה...

- מ"ו -

✎ פרשת מקץ ✎

אור המאיר
(פורים)

והנה מן היאר עולות שבע פרות בריאות בשר ויפות תואר ותרעינה באחו: והנה שבע פרות אחרות עולות אחריהן דלות ורעות תואר מאד ורקות בשר... שבע שבלים... ויאמר יוסף אל פרעה חלום פרעה אחד הוא את אשר האלהים עושה הגיד לפרעה (בראשית מא:יח-כה).

... אנו בני ישראל זאת היא עיקר עבודתנו בעולם הזה לתקן אותן שבעת ימי הבנין, ולזאת אנו מעותדים יומם ולילה, כי הכל תולה בהתעוררות התחתונים. ובהיות מישרים אורחותם ודרכיהם הטובים ללכת בתורה ועבודה ולהתמיד יומם ולילה בעבודת הבורא, אזי גורמים עם פרטי מעשיהם מילוי והארה בשבעת הימים הידועים שבעת ימי הבנין. וברעות מעשיהם גורמים ח"ו מילוי והארה בשבע תועבות שבע מידות הפכיים.

אתה תחזה מה דאיתא בזהר ענין חלום פרעה... כן ענין השבלים... עיין שם ותבין נפלאות (ח"א קצד.). **וחלום פרעה אחד הוא** להורות על ענין שבעת ימי הבנין ושבעה הפכיים, כי זה לעומת זה עשה אלהים לירא מלפניו כל הימים והכל תולה בכשרון והכשר מעשים טובים של ישראל...

וזה ענין **חלום פרעה... את אשר האלהים עושה הגיד לפרעה**, אשר אלהים עושה תמיד, מראשית הבריאה עד ביאת משיחנו במהרה בימינו.

והנה זאת היא עבודת האדם כל ימי חיים חיותו ומספר ימיו החרוצים עלי אדמה אשר בדרך כלל הן המה שבעים שנה, ישים את לבו ורוחו ונפשו ומאודו לתקן את שבעת הימים. והכתוב רומז "ימי שנותינו בהם שבעים

- מ"ה -

436

דהיינו שהם והוא גרמו בזה שיתנכלו, נמצא הוא והם גרמו לשנאה גדולה, והוא כמו "עמו"...

מגיד דבריו ליעקב (ס' קפג)

ותתפשהו בבגדו לאמר שכבה עמי ויעזוב בגדו בידה וינס ויצא החוצה (בראשית לט:יב).

איתא במדרש: "לגוזר ים סוף לגזרים" (תהלים קלו:יג), לגזורין (ילקוט שמעוני בשלח ס' רמא)... יובן על פי שאמרו רז"ל: "הים ראה וינוס" (תהלים קיד:ג), מאי ראה? ארונו של יוסף ראה (תנחומא נשא ס' ל), ובזה פירוש **ראה וינס ויצא החוצה**. פירוש, הצדיק בורר הטוב מהרע. למשל, אדם אם רואה דבר שאינו הגון במקרה, בורר מזה ועושה יחוד...

וכן היה כאן ביוסף הצדיק, ששידלתו בדברים ובגדים שלבשה לו שחרית [לא לבשה לו ערבית] (יומא לה:), והיתה יפת תואר ומתפארת לפניו. וכאשר ראה אותה בירר הטוב ממנה והתדבק במחשבתו בתפארת ישראל דלעילא. וזה שאמרו רז"ל: דמות דיוקנו של אביו [נראתה לו בחלון] (סוטה לו:). וזהו: **וינס ויצא החוצה** ולא כתיב חוץ; רוצה לומר, שנס ויצא מחוץ לעולם החומרי והתדבק בעולם העליון.

וזכותו גרמה שהים ראה ארונו וינס, גם כן מחוץ לעולם הזה לעולם העליון. ושם אין מים, כמו שאמר רבי עקיבא "כשתגיעו לאבני שיש טהור אל תאמרו 'מים מים'" (חגיגה יד:), וממילא נעשה יבשה. והכל בזכות הצדיק שומר הברית...

- מ"ד -

וזה הבטחון והאמונה תפס יעקב אבינו ע״ה, ועל דא **וישב יעקב בארץ מגורי אביו**, ופירש רש״י ז״ל ביקש לישב בשלוה. כלומר תמיד היה דרכו בכך שביקש לישב בשלוה ונחת רוח ולקבל הכל לטובה, אפילו **בארץ מגורי אביו**, כלומר אפילו כשבא מגור ופחד שהוא מידת **אביו** כנודע, קבל הכל בשלוה ונחת רוח מרוב צדקתו והבטחתו בו יתברך.

גנזי יוסף

ויראו אותו מרחוק ובטרם יקרב אליהם ויתנכלו אותו להמיתו (בראשית לז:יח).

פירש רש״י **[ויתנכלו] אותו** כמו איתו, כלומר אליו. כבר צווחי קמאי דקמאי [ראשוני הראשונים הקשו על פירוש זה]. ונראה לי דהנה כתבו הקדמונים שאם מעורר אחד אהבה בלבו על חבירו ושולח מלבו חצי אהבה ללב חבירו, הוא גורם שחבירו יאהב גם כן אותו ויתעורר חבירו אהבתו מחמת האחדות שיש בין ישראל. ובזה יכול לבטל שנאת חבירו ממנו. וזהו שכתוב ״ואהבת לרעך״ (ויקרא יט:יח), שאם אתה תתחיל לעורר האהבה גם רעך יעורר אהבה ״כמוך״...

והנה כיון דהשבטים מקנאים את יוסף, אם היה יוסף מתגבר [מגביר] האהבה להתעורר ללבם של אחיו, היה מוציא השנאה מלבם. רק שהיה נשאר בהם מהקנאה, שזה לא היה יכול לבטל מלבם. אם כן לא היה בכלל סכנה, רק שיוסף הצדיק לא היה חושד אותם מתחילה שתהיה שנאה בלבם, לכך לא היה בטל השנאה מלבם רק אחר שאמר המלאך ״נסעו מזה״ (בראשית לז:יז), כפירש רש״י מן האחוה, אז התחיל יוסף להרהר בלבו שהם שונאים אותו ועל מה היא השנאה, ובתוך כך שהיה מהרהר **ויראו אותו מרחוק ובטרם יקרב אליהם**, דהיינו קודם שיקריב עצמו ועורר חצי האהבה אליהם, אז מיד **ויתנכלו אותו להמיתו**. נמצא אילו היה יוסף מעורר מיד האהבה תיכף כשראו אותו, לא היה השנאה בהם להמיתו, רק משום שהיה מהרהר בדברי המלאך שהיה אצלו דבר חדש שהם ישנאו אותו, לכך **התנכלו להמיתו...** לכך פירש רש״י כמו איתו,

לעסוק בהם? נעבוד אותו במורא ופחד על ידי הסתכלות ברוממותו
יתברך שמו, כיון שזה היא עיקר העבודה במחשבה. אך אם היה האדם
מסתכל ברוממותו תמיד בלי הפסק היה בטל מהמציאות מהמורא ופחד
ורעדה הבאים לאדם על ידי זה. לכן ה' ברחמיו נתן לנו התרי"ג מצוות
שנעסוק בהם בגופינו לעבודתו, והם תועלת לאדם שיהיה אפשר לו
להתקיים בדביקותו יתברך.

וזהו **וישב יעקב בארץ מגורי אביו**, מגורי לשון "ויגר מואב [מפני בני
ישראל]" (במדבר כב:ג), דהיינו שהיתה לו ישיבה ועכבה במדריגה זאת
תמיד להיותו ביראה ופחד יראת ה' **אביו** שבשמים. **בארץ כנען**, רוצה
לומר על ידי שהיה עובד בגופו ועסק בתורתו ובמצוותיו יתברך תמיד.
ארץ כנען רמז להגוף על ידי זה היה באפשר לו שיתקיים בדביקותו
והסתכלותו ברוממות אל יתברך במחשבה...

קדושת לוי

וישב יעקב בארץ מגורי אביו בארץ כנען (בראשית לז:א).

... גם צריך אדם להתנהג בכל דבר שמביא עליו יתברך יקבל ממנו בנחת
ובשמחה, על דרך שאמרו רז"ל: "בכל מאדך" (דברים ו:ה), בכל מידה
ומידה שהוא מודד לך הוי מודה לו מאד מאד (ברכות נד.), ויאמר "כל מה
דעביד רחמנא לטב עביד" (ברכות ס:), ויבטח ויאמין שיש בזה טובה
גדולה כי מאתו לא תצא רעה ח"ו, כנחום איש גמזו שברוב הבטחתו
ואמונתו בו יתברך אמר על כל דבר "גם זו לטובה" (תענית כא.), ובזה
הוא ממתיק הדינים מעליו, והופך אותם לרחמים ועושה מרע טוב.

ויש גם בזה הדרך העלאת ניצוצות בסוד "המוציא לך מים מצור
החלמיש" (דברים ח:טו), כי מים מרומז על חסדים ורחמים, וצור הוא
לשון תוקף ועוז. והוא "המוציא לך מים" כלומר חסדים, "מצור
החלמיש," כלומר מתוקף משפט שבא עליך, לסוף הוא נהפך לטובה על
ידי מחשבתך הטהורה והנאמנה שאתה מאמין בו יתברך שהכל הוא עושה
לטובה ובזה אתה מורה אהבה עזה ועצומה בו יתברך.

- מ"ב -

הבורא ברוך הוא בדחילו ורחימו, היינו אהבה ויראה. ואף שנראה בעיני האדם שיותר טוב לעבדו באהבה ובהתלהבות גדולה מביראה, אך מחמת גודל האהבה יוכל האדם לבא לביטול ממציאות מחמת הדביקות בבורא יתברך שמו, תהיה חיותו נבלעת בשרשה. ולכן צריך האדם לאלו השתי מדריגות יראה ואהבה, ואז האהבה לא תביאהו לביטול ממציאות כי היראה תכבה לאהבה. וזהו "והחיות רצוא ושוב" (יחזקאל א:יד), היינו מה שיש להאדם חיות בזה העולם ואינו נבלע בשרשו על ידי הדביקות בבורא ב"ה, הוא "רצוא ושוב," היינו רצוי באהבה ושוב ביראה, וזהו קיומו של החיות בזה העולם.

וזהו "הוי מתפלל בשלומה של המלכות," היינו שתתפלל בשלימות של מידת המלכות שכלולה לאהבה ויראה, "שאלמלא מוראה" היינו שאם תתפלל רק באהבה ולא ביראה "איש את רעהו," רוצה לומר היה האדם עם דביקותו בבורא ב"ה [הנקרא רַעַ רק] באהבה, "חיים בלעו," רוצה לומר היתה החיות של האדם נבלעת בשרשה. וכן על ידי היראה יוכל גם כן לבא לביטול ממציאות ולכן צריכין להתפלל בשתי בחינות יראה ואהבה כלולות.

וזהו **וישב יעקב בארץ מגורי אביו**, רוצה לומר מה שיש עכבה להצדיק בזה העולם בארץ, היינו בהארציות בזה העולם ולא נבלעת חיותו בשרשה על ידי האהבה גדולה, הוא **מגורי אביו**, היינו מגורי הוא יראה לשון "כי יגורתי" (דברים ט:יט)... ואז כשהאדם עובד באלו השתי בחינות אז **בארץ כנען**, רוצה לומר אף שעוסק בהארציות, דהיינו האכילה ושתיה ושאר דברי גשמיות, **כנען**, יוכל לעשות הכל בהכנעה גדולה ובפחד הבורא יתברך שמו ויתעלה זכרו לעד ולנצח נצחים אמן.

נועם אלימלך

וישב יעקב בארץ מגורי אביו בארץ כנען (בראשית לז:א).

והנה עיקר העבודה שעל ידה יתייחד שמו יתברך הוא על ידי הסתכלות ברוממות אל יתברך וגדולתו במורא ופחד הבאים לאדם ממילא בהסתכלו נוראותיו ונפלאותיו. ואם תאמר למה נתן ה' יתברך כל התרי"ג מצוות

פרשת וישב

מגיד דבריו ליעקב (ס' א)

וישב יעקב בארץ מגורי אביו בארץ כנען (בראשית לז:א).

מגורי אביו, פירוש לשון "אוגר בקיץ" (משלי י:ה). מאסף הקדוש ברוך הוא לתוכה. או יאמר **מגורי אביו**, דכל מחשבה הוא עולם שלם והם ניצוצות הקדושה, ואסף אותן אל השורש. וזה **מגורי אביו**, פירוש שאסף את אביו, כביכול.

וזה פירוש "עיני ה' אל הצדיקים" (תהלים לד:טז). פירוש כדמיון הבן שעושה מעשה נערות, מביא את השכל של אביו לתוך המעשים האלה, כך הצדיקים עושים כביכול לקדוש ברוך הוא כדמות שכלם, שהוא יתברך חושב מה שהם חושבין. אם חושבים באהבה, מביאים את הקדוש ברוך הוא לעולם האהבה. כמו שכתוב בזהר '"מלך אסור ברהטים' (שה"ש ז:ו), ברהיטי מוחין" (תיקוני זוהר ת' ו כא:).

וזהו פירוש "צמצם שכינתו בין שני בדי הארון" (תנחומא ויקהל ס' ז). פירוש כנפי ריאה, שכינה, והקדוש ברוך הוא שורה כמו שהוא מחשב, ועין נקרא השכל, והשכל הוא ביד הצדיקים. אבל היאך זוכים למדרגה זו? בחשבם שהם עפר ואינם יכולים לעשות שום מעשה בלי כחו של הקדוש ברוך הוא. ונמצא מה שהוא [הצדיק] עושה, עושה זאת הקדוש ברוך הוא, שאם לא הוא יתברך אינו יכול לעשות כלום...

מבשר צדק

וישב יעקב בארץ מגורי אביו בארץ כנען (בראשית לז:א).

ואקדים לפרש לך המשנה "הוי מתפלל בשלומה של מלכות, שאלמלא מוראה איש את רעהו חיים בלעו" (אבות ג:ב). דהנה צריך האדם לעבוד

ומראה את עצמו להצדיק בפנים כזה, בכדי שיעלה משם אברי השכינה הנקראים נפש.

וזה הרמז בכתוב **ויקרא יעקב.** מי שהוא בחינת יעקב, שלם כמדובר, לחבר חכמה עילאה לחכמה תתאה, הכרתו עצומה וכחו יפה, אל כל מקום ממקרי ופגעי הזמנים וכדומה, אינו רואה כי אם פנים של אל באיזה מן המידות שנדמה אליו. **כי ראיתי אלהים פנים אל פנים** - והכוונה ראיתי לשון "הבנה," הבנתי התלבשות אלהים פנים אל פנים, הוא יתברך מלביש את עצמו בכמה ריבויי פנים של מדריגות התחתונים, כפי הפנים של הצדיק וחוזק הכרתו. ועל ידי זה **ותנצל נפשי,** היא השכינה שמעלה הצדיק משם למקומה הרמתה.

קדושת לוי ב'

... כי יפגשך עשו אחי ושאלך לאמר למי אתה ואנה תלך ולמי אלה לפניך: ואמרת לעבדך ליעקב מנחה היא שלוחה לאדני לעשו... (בראשית לב:יח-יט).

דהכלל בתחילת התקרבות האדם לה׳ שיצר הרע מתגבר עליו, יחשוב לו שבעבודתו לה׳ יגיעו לו טובות עולם הזה גם כן, ובזה מוכנע היצר הרע שלא לקטרג אותו על דבקותו בה׳. ואחר כך כשכבר מדבק עצמו בה׳ אז [תהיה] עבודתו רק לעשות נחת רוח ליוצרו ולא לטובת עולם הזה.

וזה **כי יפגשך עשו אחי ושאלך למי**, דהיינו היצר הרע שמכונה בשם עשו, שיפגוש במלאכי יעקב, שהם מחשבות קדושות של יעקב שממנו נבראו מלאכים, והוא יקטרג למחשבות **אנה תלך. ואמרת לעבדך ליעקב**, אנו מלאכי יעקב, שבאמצעות מעשים הטובים אנו נבראים, ואל תקטרג ליעקב על מעשיו הטובים, כי **מנחה היא שלוחה לאדני לעשו**, שגם לך נוגע הטוב, שבאמצעות מעשיו הטובים יגיע לו עולם הזה, שעולם הזה היא מנחת היצר הרע.

אור המאיר

ויקרא יעקב שם המקום פניאל כי ראיתי אלהים פנים אל פנים ותנצל נפשי (בראשית לב:לא).

נראה כוונת הכתוב על דרך שזכרנו, מה דאיתא בתיקונים על פסוק ״ויבא יעקב שלם״ (בראשית לג:יח) עם ה׳״י״ - וכד פרח י׳ מניה, כדין אשתאר ״עקב״ (ת׳ יג כט.). כי מי שהוא איש משכיל ויודע לחבר החכמה, המורה על אות י׳, אל מדריגות התחתונים המכונים בשם ״עקב.״

וכל מה שרואה ושומע, אפילו דיבור איש אל רעהו, וכל הקורה אותו ממקרי ופגעי הזמנים, מוצא שם בחינת התלבשות פנימי המאירים [המאירה]. וזה נקרא פני אל, כלומר הפנים של אל עליון המלובש שם,

וזהו **וישלח יעקב מלאכים**, רוצה לומר האותיות והדיבורים שלח יעקב, דהאותיות והדיבורים נקראים מלאכים. **לפניו**, רוצה לומר שגם מלפנים היו האותיות האלו בכח אצל הבורא ב"ה, ויעקב היה מצרפם מחמת אהבתו שהיה אוהב לכל. וזהו **אל עשו אחיו**, רוצה לומר גם עשו היה שלם עמו כאחיו על דרך "אפילו נכרי בשוק."

וזהו **ויאבק איש עמו**, רוצה לומר כמו אבק ריבית, דהיינו שבוודאי אין כל אהבות שוים כאחד כישראל כגוי, רק שאהבה לישראל היא אהבה שלימה, ואהבה לנכרי אינה שלימה מחמת שיש בו אבק שהוא נכרי. וזהו כמאן דאמר "כגוי נדמה לו," ולכן ויאבק עמו שהיה כמו אבק. וחד אמר "כחכם נדמה לו" ואף על פי כן לא היתה אהבתו שלימה עמו מחמת שהיה יעקב מבין בו שעדיין אין שלם במידותיו. והיה אוהב אותו, רק מחמת החסרונות לא היתה אהבתו שלימה עמו. וזהו **ויאבק איש עמו עד עלות השחר**, רוצה לומר עד אשר יסיר השחרורית שבו ואז תהיה אהבתו שלימה. נמצא אין כאן פלוגתא רחוקה שכל מאן דאמר השמיענו מעלות יעקב איך היתה אהבתו שלימה עם כל אדם, וקל להבין.

קדושת לוי א'

הצילני נא מיד אחי מיד עשו... (בראשית לב:יב).

דעשו הוא הסטרא אחרא, הוא מלאך המות הוא היצר הרע. ובקשת יעקב היה **הצילני נא** שלא יהיה עשו **אחי**. וזהו **מיד אחי מיד עשו**, שלא יתגלגל שהיצר הרע יהיה אחי, שפעמים ח"ו היצר הרע מסית לעבירה ולעין אדם מראה מצוה, ועל דרך זה מתקרב לאדם ללכדו במהרה לעשות עבירה.

444

❧ פרשת וישלח ❧

נועם אלימלך

וישלח יעקב מלאכים לפניו אל עשו אחיו... (בראשית לב:ד).

בצירוף הפסוק **ויאבק איש עמו** (בראשית לב:כה), ופירש רש"י ז"ל
שהיו מעלים אבק. ואיתא בגמרא חד אמר כגוי נדמה לו, וחד אמר כחכם
נדמה לו (חולין צא:), ולכאורה הוא פלוגתא רחוקה.

ונראה לפרש בהקדים לפירוש הפסוק "צרופה אמרתך מאד ועבדך
אהבה" (תהלים קיט:קמ), דהנה הצדיק נענה בתפילתו כשהוא מתפלל על
החולה וכדומה. ולכאורה הוא כמו השתנות אצל הבורא הפשוט אמיתי
חלילה. אך השורש הוא דהנה ה' יתברך ב"ה ברא את האותיות והם בכח
אצל הבורא ב"ה, והצדיק הוא מצרף את האותיות האלו שיהיו נקראים
כרצונו, דהיינו התפילה שהצדיק מתפלל הוא על ידי צרופי אותיות שהוא
מצרף אותם. ונמצא אין כאן שינוי חלילה שהאותיות היו גם כן מתחילה,
רק שהוא מצרף אותם.

ואם תרצה לומר למה דוקא הצדיק נענה בתפילתו? כמו שאמרו חז"ל: מי
שיש לו חולה בתוך ביתו ילך אצל חכם ויתפלל (בבא בתרא קטז.). כל
אדם יתפלל ויהיו האותיות מצורפים! אך מחמת שהתורה הקדושה נבראת
באהבה, כנאמר "הבוחר בעמו ישראל באהבה" (ברכת קריאת שמע),
והצדיק גם כן אוהב את ה' ואת כל אדם בעולם, על דרך שאמר רבן יוחנן
[בן זכאי]: מעולם לא הקדמני אדם שלום בשוק אפילו נכרי (ברכות יז.).
ולא כן הוא מידת כל אדם. ולכן גם האותיות אינם נצטרפים אלא על ידי
הצדיק האוהב לכל.

וזהו "צרופה אמרתך מאד," רוצה לומר האותיות העליונים הם מצורפים
ממילא בכחו על ידי הצדיק האוהב לכל, מצטרפים לפועל וזהו "ועבדך
אהבה."

- ל"ו -

445

נהנים מאומה מן אחרים... אלו הם אנשים כשרים ונאמנה את אל רוחם,
ושייכים למידת יעקב אבינו, שמידתו אמת...

- ל"ה -

מלהמניע השפע מלהשפיע, ואז שופע על עמו ישראל טובות וברכות
וחסדים...

ויהי כאשר ראה יעקב את רחל רמז לשמחת חתן וכלה, שהוא כמו
שמחת הרגל. הנה כתיב "והסירותי את לב האבן" (יחזקאל יא:יט), היינו
הסטרא אחרא השורה על לבות בני ישראל. ומונע הנבואה מלב בני
ישראל, כנאמר "ונביא לבב חכמה" (תהלים צ:יב), שהלב נובע חכמת
הנבואה. וזהו **ויגל את האבן**, הוא האבן המכשול. **מעל פי הבאר**, באר
רומז על הלב שנובע נבואת חכמה.

אור המאיר ב'

... והיה העטופים ללבן והקשורים ליעקב (בראשית ל:מב).

... יש לך אדם אפילו הולך בדרך המלך לעשות מצוות הבורא ולומד
תורה ותפילה וכדומה, כוונתו בהם להנאות עצמו שיגיע לו מזה
התפארות, לומר שהוא נאה דורש ונאה מקיים, כאשר עינינו רואות עתה
בדור הזה רבים הם המתפרצים ומעטפים את עצמן בטלית שאינה שלהם,
כי אם תיכף שרואה איזה הנהגה בצדיק ואיש משכיל, מתעטף גם כן את
עצמו לעשות כמוהו. והכסיל לא יבין את זאת, אלף שנים אילו יחיה לא
יעמוד על מדריגה זאת, ו"למה זה מחיר ביד כסיל [לקנות חכמה] ולב
אין" (משלי יז:טז), כיון ששלו אינו רואה לתקן פרטי מדותיו, לבלתי
אחוז בהם משבע מידות הפכיים. אבל רואה הוא בשל אחרים, אנשים
תמימים ומשכילים, ובודאי לא עמד על סודם, להבין לעשות כמוהם על
דרך האמת. מול זה בא הרמז בתורה, **ובהעטיף... והיו העטופים ללבן
והקשורים ליעקב,** התורה נותנת סימן, ידוע תדע אותן האנשים
המתעטפים את עצמם בטלית שאינה שלהם, שלהם אינם רואים, אבל
רואים של אחרים לעשות כמעשיהם, אלו אנשים שייכים עדיין ללבן. כי
בודאי בידיהם מאזני מרמה לעשות הכל ברמאות, מידותיו של לבן רמאי.
והקשורים ליעקב, כלומר אנשי אמת שכל עצמם עם פרטי עובדותיהם
לעשות הכל בהתקשרות לערך בחינת השגתם ברוממות אלהות, ואינם

בחינת המחשבה, לפרטיות חמשת מוצאות הפה, ויש תענוג בכל מוצא בפני עצמו, וזאת הגורמת לו לצאת מן המחשבה אל בחינת הדיבור. וזה הנרמז בכאן **ויצא יעקב מבאר שבע**, הוא בחינת חכמתו ובינתו, שנקרא באר שבע, על דרך הכתוב "הואיל משה באר את התורה" (דברים א:ה), כנזכר בזהר (ח"א קמז:). יצא מן המחשבה אל הדיבור, והיינו **חרנה**, כי "חרן" גימטריא "גרון" [259], שמשם מוצא הדיבור של תורה ותפילה. וזהו **ויפגע** לשון תפילה, **במקום**, להקדוש ברוך הוא שהוא מקומו של עולם (בראשית רבה סח:ט)...

קדושת לוי

וירא והנה באר בשדה והנה שם שלשה עדרי צאן רובצים עליה... והאבן גדולה על פי הבאר... ונאספו שמה כל העדרים וגללו את האבן מעל פי הבאר... ויהי כאשר ראה יעקב את רחל... ויגש יעקב ויגל את האבן מעל פי הבאר... (בראשית כט:ב-ג,י).

נראה לפרש על דרך רמז, שהנה ידוע שה' יתברך משתוקק תמיד להשפיע טובות על עמו ישראל, אך כביכול הסטרא אחרא מעכב נביעות השפע. רק בזמן שישראל מתעוררים בשמחה, אז זאת השמחה דוחה את החיצונים מלהמניע השפע מלהשפיע, ואז ה' יתברך ברוב רחמיו וחסדיו משפיע שפע ברכה על עמו ישראל.

וזהו: **וירא והנה באר** הוא נביעות השפע. **בשדה**, וידוע ששדה רומז לחקל תפוחין קדישין, שה' יתברך יש לו תענוג גדול להשפיע. **והנה שם שלשה עדרי צאן** רמז לשלש רגלים שבשנה. **והאבן גדולה על פי הבאר** רומז להסטרא אחרא שמכונה בשם אבן, כמבואר במאמר חז"ל: אם אבן הוא נימוח (קדושין ל:). **על פי הבאר**, שמונע כביכול נביעות השפע מלהשפיע. **ונאספו שמה כל העדרים** רומז לכנסת ישראל שבזמן שלש רגלים מתאספים שמה כל ישראל לחוג את חגיהם והשמחה מתרבה. **וגללו את האבן מעל פי הבאר**, ודוחים את הסטרא אחרא וסייעתא דיליה

שאמר הבעל שם טוב זללה"ה שמה שרדף לבן אחר יעקב הוא כי עדיין נשאר אצלו התלבשות התורה ההיא, שהם אלו הפסוקים שנכתבו בתורה איך שרדף לבן אחר יעקב ואיך שנתווכחו זה עם זה עד סוף הפרשה, כל העניין שזאת התורה שבזאת הפרשה נשארה עדיין בהתלבשות אצל לבן, מה שלא בירר עדיין יעקב. וסיבב ה' יתברך כך שירדוף אחריו להביא אליו את התורה שעדיין לא נשלמה להתברר, ששם בהשיגו את יעקב על ידי דיבורו עמו, אלו הדיבורים שנכתבו שם בירר יעקב גם זה עד שלא נשאר אצלו כלום. וכל מה שעשה אצל לבן בכל העניינים הכתובים במקרא היה הכל תורה ועסק העבודה לשמים לגלות התורה מבחינת חרן שהוא עומק הקליפות ועוד להביאה לידי התגלות הקדושה לכוללה לתורה עליונה.

ועל כן נאמר בהגיעו סמוך לחרן "ויגל את האבן מעל פי הבאר" (בראשית כט:י), שהוא סוד אבן נגף שהיה מכסה על ה"באר מים חיים" (שיר השירים ד:טו) שרשי התורה שהיו מלובשים שם והוא גילהו שהביאו להתגלות על ידי שסילק הקליפות שהוא בחינת אבן, כמו שאמר הכתוב "...הסירו את לב האבן מבשרכם" (יחזקאל לו:כו), שאז התחיל לגלות התורה שהיתה מושרשת שם.

אור המאיר א'

ויצא יעקב מבאר שבע וילך חרנה: ויפגע במקום וילן שם כי בא השמש (בראשית כח:י-יא).

יש לרמז בכאן כי הנה מה היא הסיבה המכריחה לו לאיש משכיל לצאת מבחינת מחשבתו אל הדיבור. הלא טוב לו להיות תמיד יושב בסוד המחשבה ולחשוב מרוממות וגדלות הקדוש ברוך הוא! אכן התועלת המגיעה בצאתו ממחשבה לדיבור... שנעשה ונצטרף צירוף [חדש של] שם הוי"ה, כנתבאר לנו כמה פעמים. ועיין פירוש הפסוק "וירא יעקב כי יש שבר במצרים" (בראשית מב:א). ותוכן הדברים, הדיבור הוא "מיצר ים" החכמה, מיצר וגבול התפשטות המחשבה. והבין יעקב בחינת חלקי התענוגים, המרומז בתיבת "שבר," לשון שבירה, והיינו התחלקות כללות

✦ פרשת ויצא ✦

מאור עינים

ויצא יעקב מבאר שבע וילך חרנה... (בראשית כח:יא).

... דהנה נודע כי סוד יעקב הוא הדעת, כי בחינת יעקב ובחינת משה הן אחד, רק שזה מלגאו וזה מלבר, כי זה פנימיות הדעת וזה חיצוניות הדעת כנודע. וקודם הליכת יעקב לבית לבן לא היתה התגלות הדעת והתורה כי אם בהעלם, וכמה שרשי התורה היו מפוזרין במדריגות תחתונים על ידי שלא היתה התגלות הדעת בעולם. ובבית לבן היו כמה שרשי תורה מלובשין שם, וזהו התורה הנכתבת בספר תורה מסיפורי המעשיות שעשה יעקב בבית לבן, שבהם מלובשים היו שרשים ההם שהוציא יעקב ובירר וצירף אותם מעומק קליפות לבן, כנודע גודל הקליפות שלו.

והנה יעקב אבינו ע"ה הוציא משם השרשים ההם בעשרים שנה שהיה שם בחרן אצל לבן, שעל כן נקרא שם המקום חרן, שהוא לשון "חרון אף" של מקום, על שם שהמקום ההוא אשר היו מלובשין שרשי התורה היה מקום קליפות גדולות שהוא בחינת חרון. וכל עסקי יעקב עמו עבור בנותיו וצאנו היה הכל לברר ולגלות שרשי התורה משם, כנודע מסודות התורה שיש על זה הענין. וענין אשר שם יעקב את המקלות ברהטים שעל ידי זה תלדנה הצאן עקודים נקודים וברודים שהן רזין דרזין וסתרין גניזין, וענין שנשא לאה ורחל שהן סוד תורה שבכתב ותורה שבעל פה, שכל זה ראה והתקין התגלות התורה למטה מה שהיה בסתימו עד בוא יעקב. ועל ידי שהוא הדעת נעשה המשכות התגלות התורה מבאר שבע, שהתורה עליונה נקראת באר שבע.

וזהו **ויצא יעקב מבאר שבע**, מבחינת סתימת התורה להביאה לידי התגלות על ידי הבירורין שהלך לבחינת **"חרן,"** שהוא מקום קליפות שהיתה התורה מכוסה ומלובשת בהן. וכל זה לעשות הכנה לדורות הבאים שיוכלו להשיג השגת התורה בהתגלות מה שהיה בהתכסות. וכמו

- ל"א -

בתורתו ובמצוותיו. וכן בכל דבר יהיה כוונתך לשמים. "וילך ויקח ויבא
לאמו" (שם כז:יד)...

חיים וחסד

... וַיְהִי אַךְ יָצוֹא יָצָא יַעֲקֹב וְעֵשָׂו אָחִיו בָּא מִצֵּידוֹ (בראשית
כז:ל)

הנה בשבועות הוא זמן מתן תורה, הנה באמת שעצם התורה ניתנה בסיני.
אך בכל שנה נמשכת שכליות מהקדוש ברוך הוא אל העולם להבין
התורה בשכליות חדשות, ואף על פי כן כשנעתק אור השכליות ממקומו
הוא נעתק עם הבחירה - בחירה הוא מלכות. וזהו **וַיְהִי אַךְ יָצוֹא יָצָא
יַעֲקֹב... וְעֵשָׂו אָחִיו בָּא מִצֵּידוֹ,** כלומר שנתחבר יצר הרע וצריך
להתחכם כנגדו ולעבודת הקדוש ברוך הוא בשכליות הקודש, שהיה לו
להסתכל תמיד על אור החדש ומחמת ההסתכלות יהא נטבע ונכנס השכל
באדם ויכול לעבודת הקדוש ברוך הוא בשכל החדש, והתנהגות האדם כל
שבעים שנה...

-ל-

451

נועם אלימלך

ורבקה אמרה אל יעקב בנה לאמר הנה שמעתי את אביך מדבר אל עשו אחיך לאמר (בראשית כז:ו).

איתא בזהר הקדוש דהשכינה נקראת רבקה, ועם בני ישראל נקראים בשם יעקב (תקוני זהר ת' יח לד.). ויש לפרש בדרך הזה, דיצחק היה רוצה לברך את עשו בגשמיות בעולם הזה. והשכינה הקדושה היא האם המרחמת על בניה בישראל ובכל צרתם לה צר והיתה תשוקתה מאוד שיברך יצחק את יעקב גם בעולם הזה, כי האיך תוכל לראות בעני עמה בצער להם בעולם הזה, ולכן אמרה אל יעקב שילך ויקבל הברכות מיצחק.

ויעקב היה מתירא מאוד שיתברך בעניני גשמיות כי מורא עלה על ראשו פן ואולי על ידי הגשמיות יתגשם ויופרד ח"ו מעבודתו יתברך, כמו שאמר הכתוב "פן תאכל ושבעת... ורם לבבך [ושכחת את ה' אלהיך]" (דברים ח:יב-יד). לזה אמר אל רבקה אמו, היא השכינה הקדושה, האיך אוכל לקבל ברכות עולם הזה? "הן עשו [אחי] איש שעיר" (בראשית כז:יא), רוצה לומר לו ראוי עולם הזה לפי מידתו שהוא איש מעורב בערבוביא הולך בדרך לבו וכל הבא לידו לא ימנע עצמו מלעשות אם טוב ואם רע. אבל "אנכי איש חלק" (שם), רוצה לומר שאני צריך להיות חלק ומצוחצח צח בעבודתו יתברך ויתעלה בלי שום סיג ופסולת, ופן ואולי ח"ו על ידי הגשמיות יומשך לבי מעבודתו יתברך כנזכר לעיל. "ואולי ימושני אבי" (שם כז:יב) שבשמים, הבורא יתעלה ימשש ויפשפש במעשי "והייתי בעיניו כמתעתע והבאתי עלי קללה ולא ברכה" (שם), שעל ידי זאת הברכה יצמיח קללה חלילה וחלילה.

"ותאמר לו אמו" (שם כז:יג), היא השכינה הקדושה, "עלי קללתך בני," רוצה לומר עלי מוטל לשמור אותך מקללה. "אך שמע בקולי ולך קח לי," רוצה לומר שתקבל הברכות בעולם הזה גם כן שיהיה לי, רוצה לומר גם כן לעבודתי לשמו הגדול שתהיה כוונתך בכל עניני עולם הזה הן באכילה ושתיה ושאר גשמיות רק לשמים, להוציא ניצוצות קדושות מתוך המאכל באוכלך בקדושה ובטהרה ושיהיה לך כח לעבוד לו יתברך ולעסוק

- כ"ט -

452

מאור עינים

וישב יצחק ויחפור את בארות המים... ויחפרו עבדי יצחק בנחל וימצאו שם באר מים חיים (בראשית כו:יח-יט).

להבין העניין נקדים פסוק "אותי עזבו מקור מים חיים" (ירמיה ב:יג), כי הוא ה' יתברך הוא המקור שממנו השפעות החיות לכל חי בכל האופנים - "אין עוד מלבדו" (דברים ד:לה). וכל הדבוק בו הוא דבוק בשורש החיות אשר לא יכזבו מימיו, ובלבד אשר לא יהיה הפסקה מצדו, כי אם ח"ו על ידי עוונותיו יפסיק את עצמו מהמקור יעדר חיותו ממנו. אך מצדו יתברך אין שום הפסק, כמו שאמר הכתוב "כי עוונותיכם היו מבדילים [ביניכם לבין אלהיכם...]" (ישעיה נט:ב), ומי שחיותו הוא מסטרא אחרא הנקרא בורות נשברים, שהם מים מכונסים שנפלו שם ניצוצות החיות בעת השבירה, שהם נקראים לטעם זה בורות נשברים, זה נפסק משורשו העליון ונקרא מפריד אלוף.

ולכך אבות העולם שהם פתחו צינורות השכל בעולם ולימדו דעת לבאי עולם איך לחפור את עצמו לבחינת באר מים חיים, להיות דבוקין בהמקור שמשם שורש חיותו, ונקראים תלמידיהם בשם עבדים כמו שאמר הכתוב **עבדי יצחק**. כי עבדות שלהם לבורא יתברך היתה על ידי האבות.

אך אחרי מות אברהם נסתמו מעיינות החכמה ההיא מחמת ש"סתמום פלישתים" (בראשית כו:טו) שהוא בחינת הרע שנקרא באדם שנתגבר על העולם ונתגבר יסוד העפר, וכפי זה נחלש כח הרוחני והשכלי. ובבוא יצחק בנו ואחז בדרך אביו ולימד דעת הנזכר לעיל גם כן לבני דורו לשוב ולחפור לבחינת באר מים חיים בכמה מיני שכליים ועצות גדולות ונעלמות, עד כי **וישב יצחק ויחפור את בארות המים**. וכל זה הוא על ידי האמונה שהוא מבוא לזה, שיאמין באמונה שלימה שה' יתברך מלא כל הארץ כבודו ולית אתר פנוי מיניה ואין עוד מלבדו. ואז על ידי האמונה ישתוקק לו ויתאוה לאחוז ולדבק את עצמו בה' יתברך שהוא בחינת "נחל", שראשי תיבות שלו "**נ**פשי **ח**כתה **ל**ה'" (תהלים לג:כ) שהוא על ידי אמונה ואז על ידי זה יבוא לשורשו שהוא המעיין של באר מים חיים כנזכר לעיל, וזה **ויחפרו עבדי יצחק בנחל**, בבחינת "נחל" כאמור...

- כ"ח -

453

ביאת רבי אלעזר כמה מאות שנים. וכן מה שאמרו רז"ל (ויקרא רבה כב:א): כל מה שתלמיד ותיק עתיד לחדש גם כן, כך הוא הקדוש ברוך הוא אמר למשה כך וכך עתיד תלמיד פלוני בדורו לחדש.

כי תורת הצדיק ומעשיו הם שעשוע ותענוג לפניו יתברך. נמצא כי זה התענוג והשמחה ואהבה נולדה לו להאב מכח בנו. וזהו מה שנאמר בזוהר הקדוש "ישראל מפרנסים [לאביהן שבשמים]" (זוהר ח"ג ז:). כמשל האב שיש לו תענוג מבנו חביבו אזי מגודל התענוג והשמחה אומר האב, כדרך שבריות אומרים בלשון זה, "אני נעשה מהתענוג הזה בריא ושמן," כך מגודל התענוג והשעשוע שיש להקדוש ברוך הוא כביכול כמו שמפרנסים אותו.

וזהו "ואהיה אצלו אמון [ואהיה שעשועים יום יום]" (משלי ח:ל) והנה רש"י ז"ל פירש כי התורה נתגדלה בחיקו של הקדוש ברוך הוא אלפים שנה [לפני בריאת העולם]. אבל פשט הכתוב משמע שהתורה נעשתה אומן להקדוש ברוך הוא. וקשה הדבר לאומרו, והלוא הקדוש ברוך הוא קדמון לכל הקדומים. אבל לפי דרכנו יתורץ שהתורה משבחת את עצמה שהיתה אומן להקדוש ברוך הוא כביכול, דהיינו גודל התענוג והשעשוע שהיה לו יתברך מן התורה, דהיינו מתורת כל צדיק וצדיק ומעשיו הטובים, שהם המצוות הכתובות בתורה, וזה נעשה לו יתברך כביכול אומן ופרנסה...

ואלה תולדות יצחק בן אברהם, אברהם הוליד את יצחק. פירוש הכתוב מספר בשבחם שהגיעו למעלת שלימות שהם שני מיני אהבה בהם. וזהו **ואלה תולדות יצחק בן אברהם,** רוצה לומר שיצחק הוא לשון צחוק ושמחה, **הוליד,** רוצה לומר שגרם והוסיף לאברהם תענוג ושמחה ואהבה מגודל צדקתו...

- כ"ז -

454

פרשת תולדות

אור תורה

ואלה תולדות יצחק בן אברהם אברהם הוליד את יצחק (בראשית כה:יט).

... והנה נמשיל לזה על דרך משל: ראובן שאוהב לשמעון אהבה עזה, ומחמת ששמעון רואה שראובן אוהב אותו ביותר, נתעורר אצל שמעון גם כן אהבת ראובן. נמצא כי אהבת ראובן שאוהב לשמעון נקרא אב, ואהבת שמעון שאוהב לראובן נקרא תולדה, מפני שנולדה אהבת שמעון מכח אהבת ראובן.

והנה יש אהבת אב לבנו בשני ענינים: האחד האב אוהב לבנו מחמת הטבעות, וזה האב גורם שגם הבן אוהב את האב. ויש אהבה אחרת גדולה מזו, שרואה את בנו הולך בדרך הישר ומצדיק מעשיו וחכם בכל החכמות, כמו שכתוב "בני אם חכם לבך ישמח לבי גם אני" (משלי כג:טו). אז יש להאב תענוג גדול מזה ומזה נתהוה השמחה... ונולדה להאב עוד אהבה יותר גדולה אל הבן.

הנה זה המשל שייך לבני אדם. כי קודם לידת הבן או אף אחר לידתו עדיין אינו יודע מה טיבו ומה יהיה מעשה הבן. על כן אין להאב עדיין אהבה כל כך שהוא השנית הנזכרת, רק אהבה הראשונה שהיא מחמת טבעו. אבל אצל ה' יתברך נאמר "ישראל אשר בך אתפאר" (ישעיה מט:ג). כי אצלו יתברך העבר והעתיד הכל בשוה, לפי שהוא קודם הזמן. קודם שהיו ישראל היה גלוי לפניו יתברך כל צדיק וצדיק עם כל מעשיו ותורתו, ומתחילה תיכף כשעלה ישראל במחשבה לפניו היה כבר שעשוע ותענוג כביכול לפניו יתברך מכל צדיק וצדיק ומעשיו. והגם ראיה לזה מה שמצינו שהקדוש ברוך הוא משתעשע בתורתו של הצדיק כמו שאמרו רז"ל כשעלה משה למרום מצא לקדוש ברוך הוא שאומר אלעזר בני אומר פרה [בת שתים ראויה לפרה אדומה] (תנחומא חקת ס' ח), קודם

- כ"ו -

קדושת לוי

הנה אנכי נצב על עין המים ובנות אנשי העיר יוצאות לשאוב מים: ...ובה אדע כי עשית חסד עם אדוני: ...והנה רבקה יוצאת אשר ילדה לבתואל... (בראשית כד:יג-טו).

לכאורה יש לדקדק, מה צורך היה לאליעזר עבד אברהם אבינו להזכיר "בנות אנשי העיר?" ותו יש לדקדק, מפני מה נקוד יַלְדָה בקובוץ, שמשמעה שמצד אחר הוא בא שרבקה ילדה לבתואל, ולא על ידי גרמא דיליה...

אך לפי דרכנו יובן שפיר, דכבר כתבנו שמדריגתו של אברהם אבינו ע"ה היתה להגביה כל העולמות לשורשם, לאין סוף ב"ה, ולהמשיך עליהם חסדים מברכה עליונה. וכל החסדים שנתפשטו בעולם היו באים על ידי המשכתו... על ידי שהוא היה פותח צנורות החסדים. והנה אליעזר עבד אברהם אבינו ע"ה ידע שכל אנשי המקום הזה היו רשעים, ועשה הבחינה על זה האופן. כשיראה באחד מן הבתולות שיש בה מידת החסד, אז בוודאי הוא משורש של אברהם אבינו, שזה בא על ידי השפעתו, שגרם שישפיע מדת חסדים על העולם, ונמשך מדת החסד עליה גם כן...

והנה רבקה יוצאת אשר ילדה לבתואל. השפעות של אברהם אבינו ע"ה ילדה לבתואל, הוא היה הגורם, אבל לא בתואל, ולכן נקד מלת יַלְדָה בקובוץ, שמשמעה שממקום אחר באה הולדת רבקה...

ובה אדע כי עשית חסד עם אדוני. יבואר על פי דמבואר בזהר הקדוש: כי בימי רבי שמעון בר יוחאי אפילו תינוקות ידעו בחכמה עליונה (ח"א צב:). כי רבי שמעון בר יוחאי ע"ה היה עובד ה' בחכמה ובהשכל, עד שהשפיע מדתו בכל העולם שאפילו תינוקות יודעים בחכמה עליונה... והנה באמת אברהם אבינו ע"ה מידתו היתה מידת החסד, והשפיע מידתו בכל העולם, שכל העולם כולו יעשה חסד...

- כ"ה -

456

אור המאיר ב'
(מפרשת לך לך)

... וה' ברך את אברהם בכל (בראשית כד:א).

מאמרם ז"ל שנתעוררו על פסוק **וה' ברך את אברהם בכל**: "בת היתה לו
לאברהם אבינו, ובכל שמה" (בבא בתרא טז:). ויש לכוון על דבריהם
דאיתא בזוהר ובתיקונים שדרשו על השכינה "כד איהי בין ציפרא
אתקריאת נשרא, ובין עשבא אתקריאת שושנה, בין עופא אתקריאת יונה
וכו'" [כאשר היא בין ציפורים נקראת נשר, ובין עשבים נקראת שושנה,
ובין עופות נקראת יונה וכו'] (תקוני זהר ת' סט קטז:-קיז.).

ולהבין את הענין כי באמת מי שחלק לו אלהים בבינה, ורוצה לגשת אל
עבודת אלהים פנימה בלב שלם ובנפש חפצה, זהו דרך יבור לו אדם: אל
כל מקום שרואה ושומע, אל יראה וישמע כי אם אלהות המלובשת שם,
ויקח לעצמו רמיזא דחכמתא ליתן התעוררות לנפשו לדבק ברוממות
אלהותו יתברך... אז מעלה הניצוצין, דהיינו אברי השכינה השוכנת בכל
ומחיה אותם. וזהו כוונת התיקונים: בין ציפרא אתקריאת נשרא וכו'. כי
כפי התחלקות הפעולות בעולם כמו כן יש השתנות שם השכינה לתועלת
בני אדם, אשר משם יכולין להשיגה כפי ההתלבשות...

ובאברהם אבינו ע"ה, לרוב עוצם הכרתו והשתדלותו לראות בכל מקום
התלבשות השכינה, רמזו דבריהם... והשיג אותה בכל מדריגותיה, עד סוף
כל המדריגות אפילו בארציות, מכולם יכול לראות שם השכינה ולהבין
באיזה מן השמות נדמה אליו, לקרותה בשם התלבשותה.

וזהו "בת היתה לאברהם אבינו ובכל שמה," כלומר בכל מקום ובכל
הברואים מלובש שמה, כדברי התיקונים בין ציפרא אתקריאת נשרא...
ובין עופא יונה, ובין עשבין אתקריאת שושנה, כל אלו השמות כינוים אל
השכינה כפי התלבשותה להחיות המדריגות, והבן הענין כי עמוק...

- כ"ד -

457

וביאר שזהו פירוש **ואברהם זקן בא בימים**. כלומר מידת החסד במקומה, נקרא אברהם סבא, **בא בימים**, היינו נשתלשלה ונתגשמה עד שבאה בימים ממש, בגוף קדוש בעולם הזה ימים ממש.

ומעתה מובנים שפיר דברי חכמים באומרם: "אלה תולדות השמים והארץ בהבראם" - באברהם, היינו בבחינת מידותיו אשר במקומה, הנקרא אברהם זקן, נברא העולם ונתקיים מראשית הבריאה מאדם הראשון ועד נח, ומנח עד אברהם. וכיון שבא אברהם ואחז מידת החסד וזכה להיות מרכבה אל עולם האהבה, אזי עמד הוא על משמרתי - מידת החסד - להתחסד עם כל באי עולם...

נועם אלימלך

ואברהם זקן בא בימים... (בראשית כד:א).

נראה לי על פי דאיתא בגמרא: כל העולם כולו ניזון בשביל חנינא בני, [וחנינא בני די לו בקב חרובין מערב שבת לערב שבת] (ברכות יז:). ושמעתי אומרים הפירוש "בשביל," רוצה לומר על ידי שרבי חנינא בן דוסא עשה שביל ודרך ופתח הצינורות, על ידי זה ניזון כל העולם.

ויש לומר גם כן לפי דרכנו בענין עבדות הבורא ב"ה, שאנו רואים כמה צדיקים מסגפים עצמם בסיגופים גדולים כמה שנים ובאים למדריגת חסידות. ויש בני אדם שאינם מסגפים עצמם כל כך ואף על פי כן זוכים לחסידות ושלימות, זה גם כן על ידי סיבת הצדיק שסיגף עצמו והסיר המסך המבדיל הגדול, החרולים והקוצים והברקנים החיצונים המעכבים את האדם לבוא לדרכי ה' ועושה שביל ודרך בעבודתו יתברך. אזי בקל לקרב אל הקדושה וילילך בדרכי ה'...

וזהו **ואברהם זקן בא בימים. זקן**, זה קנה חכמה (קדושין לב:). **בא בימים**, פעל ועשה רחמים שיהיה תמיד בלי הפסק; **ימים** רמז לרחמים כידוע... ונמצא אחר שתיקן אברהם אבינו ע"ה שהסיר המסך המבדיל היה בקל לאחרים לבא לעבדות הבורא, וזהו חשקו ותשוקתו של הצדיק שכולם ילכו בדרך ה'.

- כ"ג -

458

❧ פרשת חיי שרה ❧

אור המאיר א'
(מפרשת לך לך)

ואברהם זקן בא בימים... (בראשית כד:א).

נראה לפרש על דרך ששמעתי מהרב המגיד זללה"ה שביאר מה דאיתא
"אלה תולדות השמים והארץ בהבראם" (בראשית ב:ד). ונתעוררו
חכמינו ז"ל (בראשית רבה יב:ט) "באברהם." והקשה הלא מצינו שמנו
חכמים עשרה דורות מאדם ועד נח, ומנח עד אברהם (מ' אבות ה:ב). ואם
כן קודם שבא אברהם בעולם במה היה מתקיים העולם באותם הדורות?

וביאר, כי הנה באמת מידתו של אברהם אבינו ע"ה היא מידת החסד,
עולם האהבה במקומה הוא עולם בהיר, לית מחשבה תפיסא ביה כלל [אין
מחשבה תופסת בו] מהות ערכה וטיבה, ונקרא אברהם סבא. אמנם להיות
שקישט מלא קומתו לעבוד את הבורא ב"ה באהבה רבה, עד שנעשה כל
גופו מרכבה למידת האהבה והרגיל אלהותו והתפשטות מדה זאת בפי
הבריות, על דרך מאמרם ז"ל לשעבר נקרא אלהי השמים, ועכשיו
הרגלתי שמך בפי הבריות ונקרא אלהי הארץ (בראשית רבה נט:ח),
להיות שהראה לכל באי עולם שיש התפשטות מידת החסד אפילו
בארציות.

וגם איתא בספר הבהיר (ס' קצא): אמרה מידת החסד לפני הקדוש ברוך
הוא, קודם שבא אברהם אני עמדתי על משמרתי להתחסד עם כל באי
עולם, ועכשיו שבא אברהם אני צריך, שנאמר "עקב אשר שמע אברהם
בקולי וישמור משמרתי" (בראשית כו:ה), שעמד על משמרתי להתחסד
עם כל באי עולם...

- כ"ב -

459

בתוך העיר" (בראשית יח:כו) והוא מיותר שכבר אמר "בסדום", אלא הקדוש ברוך הוא השיבו כדבריו, אף שיהיו רק צדיקים בתוך העיר, דהיינו רק נגד אנשי העיר ולא נגד שאר צדיקים שבכל העולם, אעשה כדבריך "ונשאתי לכל המקום" (שם).

כל אחד מישראל יכול להוציא הדבר מכח אל הפועל, ולקיים המצוה בפועל ממש, כיון שהשער הוא פתוח מימות אברהם.

וזה שאמר הכתוב **המכסה אני מאברהם... כי אני ידעתיו**, מלשון אהבה, רוצה לומר אני אוהב אותו. והתחיל לספר בשבח ומעלת אברהם בקיום מצותיו. וזה שאמר **למען** רוצה לומר עבור. **אשר יצוה** רוצה לומר לשון צוותא וחבור, אשר יכוין לחבר בעשותו איזה מצוה אינו עושה אותה הוא לבדו. רק **את בניו ואת ביתו אחריו**: רוצה לומר, שהוא עושה עם כל יוצאי חלציו וזרעו הבאים אחריו. וזהו שאמר **ושמרו דרך ה׳** לשון עבר, רוצה לומר שנחשב כאילו שמרו כבר דרך ה׳, כיון שכבר קיימו כל המצות, וגם עשה דרך לבניו שיהיה להם קל אחר כך לעשות צדקה ומשפט.

גנזי יוסף

אולי יש חמשים צדיקים בתוך העיר האף תספה ולא תשא למקום למען חמשים הצדיקים אשר בקרבה (בראשית יח:כד).

הנה **אשר בקרבה** הוא מיותר, דכבר אמר **בתוך העיר**. ונראה דגבי נח פירש רש״י (בראשית ו:ט): יש דורשין לשבח, שאילו היה בדור צדיקים כל שכן דהוי צדיק יותר. וכך התפלל אברהם **אשר בקרבה**, דכאן הוי צדיקים נגד אנשי העיר, ואפילו [ואילו] נגד צדיקים שבשאר עיירות לא הוי צדיקים. אפילו הכי, ביקש מהקדוש ברוך הוא שיחשב אותם לצדיקים גמורים, ולכך אמר ״להמית צדיק עם רשע״ (בראשית יח:כה), משום שהם ביחד עם רשעים. לכך לא הוי צדיקים גמורים, ואילו היה ביחד עם צדיקים גמורים הוי צדיק ביותר, לכך אמר עם ״רשע״ דייקא.

״והיה כצדיק כרשע״ (שם). והן הדברים שהתפלל שיהיה הצדיק שבקרבה כצדיק גמור, כמו שרשעים שבסדום הם רשעים גמורים יותר מכל העולם, וזהו ״והיה״ לשון שמחה (בראשית רבה מב:ג), שיהיו צדיקים קטנים כצדיק גמור כרשע, כמו שהם רשעים גמורים, ולכך לא יוכלו הצדיקים שבם להיות שלמים ביותר מפני שהם ביחד, ושפיר דייקא כצדיק כרשע בכף כפול. לכן ״ויאמר ה׳ אם אמצא בסדום חמשים צדיקים

- כ -

הקדושה, על דרך שאמר הכתוב "ונביא לבב חכמה" (תהלים צ:יב). ואז כשתעשו כן תשפיע השפעות לאחרים. וזהו **אחר תעבורו**, רוצה לומר שתעבירו השפעה לאחרים גם כן, והבן.

קדושת לוי

וה׳ אמר המכסה אני מאברהם אשר אני עושה... כי ידעתיו למען אשר יצוה את בניו ואת ביתו אחריו ושמרו דרך ה׳ לעשות צדקה ומשפט למען הביא ה׳ על אברהם (בראשית יח:יז-יט).

ונראה פירוש הענין כך הוא, דשורש הדבר דהכתוב מספר צדקתו של אברהם. והנה כל העבדות של אברהם שעשה ועבד את ה׳ באהבה ובשכל גדול, הכל היה מעט בעיניו ולא היו נחשבים לו נגד טובות ה׳ והנסים שנעשה עמו. ולכך לא היה די בעיניו, ואמר בלבו אף אם אתקן את עצמי בכל מיני עשיות ועובדות טובות, מה אני? גלל כן התייישב את עצמו שאין זה מספיק מה שאני לבדי מקיים את המצוות בשכל גדול, רק הכניס עוד כוונה אחרת במחשבתו כשהיה מקיים איזה מצוה, לעשותו בשם כל ישראל.

דהנה כל ישראל היו כלולים במחשבתו ובמוחו של אברהם, כי הבן הוא גנוז בכח האב. והנה במוחו של אברהם היה שורש וכלל מכל כנסת ישראל, וזרע אברהם הבאים אחריו כל דור ודור עד עקבא דמשיחא, ואם כן כשעשה איזה מצוה, עשה עם כל הכוחות שלו, ועם כל הענפים העתידים להתפשט ממנו.

אם כן הגיעו מזה שתי טובות לבניו. אחד, כיון דהוא קיים כל המצוות וכל מצוות דרבנן ודקדוקי המצוות, ואפילו עירובי תבשילין (יומא כח:), אם כן, כשעשה בשם כל ישראל היתה עבודה עבודה דרבים, אשר כל אחד מישראל קיים כל התרי"ג מצוות בכח. ועוד נצמח טובה מזה העבדות, שעשה דרך סלולה לזרעו אחריו שיוכלו להשיג שכליות המצוות ולקיים אותן, מחמת שכבר קיימו אותן פעם אחת בכח, בצוותא עם אברהם אבינו, אשר בקל

מגיד דבריו ליעקב (ס' קצה)

... והשעינו תחת העץ (בראשית יח:ד).

ויש לומר על פי שנאמר "ועץ החיים בתוך הגן" (בראשית ב:י). והנה עץ חיים נקרא שם הוי"ה כידוע. אומרו "בתוך הגן," פירושו שהוא מתלבש בתוכיות ובפנימיות ה"גן" [ב"ג = 53] פרשיות שבתורה, כנזכר בדרושים הקדמונים ששם הוי"ה הוא המתלבש ומתפשט בתוך כל הדיבורים ואמירות. והנה יש לשם הוי"ה ב"ה כמה וכמה לבושים ומסכים עד אין קץ. כי מתחילה הוא מתלבש בה' [חמש] מוצאות הפה, ואחר כך נתהוו ממנו האותיות, ואחר כך הצירופים שמהם נעשים תיבות, ואחר כך הסיפורים. ואמרו בזהר: מאן דאית ליה עינין [מי שיש לו עינים], רוצה לומר עיני השכל, הוא מסתכל בפנימיות הדבר. אבל מאן דלית ליה עיינין הוא מסתכל בלבושי דמלכא [מי שאין לו עינים הוא מסתכל על לבוש המלך], ובסיפורי הגשמיים בפרטן (זהר ח"ג קנב.).

והנה ידוע שאברהם לימד לכל באי עולם. ואפשר לומר שזה רמז להם, כי בדמות אנשים נדמו לו, ואמר להם בעשותכם איזה מצוה או איזה דבר שבקדושה תהיה כוונתכם אל פנימיות הדבר, ולא אל דברי פרטן ולבושם. ולזה אמר **והשעינו** על מה **שתחת העץ**, שהוא החיות והויה המהוה ומחיה לכל החיות. אשר על כן נקרא עץ החיים, כי מלת "עץ" הוא לשון גוף של האדם, כמו שנאמר "לא תשחית את עצה... כי האדם עץ השדה" (דברים כ:יט)... לזה הזהיר והכריז ואמר **והשעינו תחת העץ** - רוצה לומר, אל תסתכלו בכל הלבושים כי אם על מה שתחת העץ...

נועם אלימלך ב'

ואקחה פת לחם וסעדו לבכם אחר תעבורו... (בראשית יח:ה).

דהצדיק הרוצה להשפיע לעולם הוא צריך להשפיע על ידי צדיקים אחרים, בהתחברו עמהם, ועל ידי אכילה שמאכיל אותם בקדושה נמשך השפעה גדולה על ידו. וזה שאמר **ואקחה פת לחם וסעדו לבכם**, דהיינו שתסעדו לבכם בקדושה על ידי אכילה זאת. דלב הוא מקום לשכון בו

- י"ח -

463

✎ פרשת וירא ✎

נועם אלימלך א׳

וירא אליו ה׳ באלוני ממרא והוא יושב פתח האהל כחום היום (בראשית יח:א).

דהנה כשעלה ברצונו יתברך לברוא את העולם להטיב לברואיו, צמצם הקדוש ברוך הוא את עצמו. ולהיכן צמצם את עצמו? שמעתי מפי מורי ז״ל שצמצם עצמו בתוך אותיות התורה, שבהם ברא העולם... והצדיק העוסק בתורה לשמה בקדושה, הוא ממשיך את הבורא ב״ה בתוך האותיות של התורה, כמו בשעת הבריאה.

וזהו **וירא אליו ה׳ באלוני ממרא** - ממרא הוא לשון ״אמירה״ כנזכר לעיל. ואילן הוא התורה, והמצוות הם ענפים. ואמר הכתוב שעל ידי אמרות הטהורות שעסק בתורה, המשיך את הבורא אל תוך האותיות. וזהו **באלוני ממרא**: רוצה לומר, באילן של אמירותיו נראה ה׳ אליו. ואמר הכתוב, מהיכן זכה זאת שנראה ה׳ אליו? על ידי עסק תורתו. זאת היתה לו מחמת הכנעה גדולה שהיתה בו. דהיינו **והוא יושב פתח האוהל**, דהיינו אף שהיה צדיק גדול, אף על פי כן החזיק עצמו בהכנעה גדולה, שעדיין יושב בפתח והתחלה של הקדושה, ד״אהל״ רמז על הקדושה. **כחום היום**: רוצה לומר, שיש בני אדם שנראים שהם מוכנעים, אבל אין תוכו כברו. ואמר הכתוב שאברהם היה מוכנע גדול באמת, בלב שלם ממש וברור כשמש בעיניו שאינו אלא מתחיל בעבודתו יתברך, וזהו **כחום היום**.

והנה זה האדם שעובד הבורא על ידי מסירות נפש, הוא רואה הבורא ב"ה בעין ממש. וזה שעובד הבורא על ידי מצוות ומעשים טובים, הוא רואה את ה' יתברך באספקלריא, כי עובד על ידי "יש". וזהו "אחר הדברים האלה היה דבר ה' אל אברם במחזה לאמר" (בראשית טו:א), פירוש שבעת הזאת עבד לה' יתברך על ידי מצוות. ולכן היה דבר ה' אליו "במחזה", שראה לה' יתברך על ידי אספקלריא. ואמר לו ה' יתברך "אל תירא אברם" (שם), פירוש: שלא תירא שאתה עובד על ידי מצוות ולא במסירות נפש. "שכרך הרבה מאוד" (שם), פירוש: על ידי עבדות שלך במצוות אתה יכול להמשיך עליך שפע...

ונמצא מה שאמרו חז"ל "קיים אברהם כל התורה כולה" היה בארץ ישראל ולא בחוץ לארץ. אמנם מעתה אף על פי שאנו בחוץ לארץ, יכולין אנו לעבוד על ידי מצוות, שכבר ניתנה לנו התורה...

וזהו פירוש המדרש: **ומלכי צדק מלך שלם הוציא לחם ויין והוא כהן לאל עליון,** פליגי רבי שמואל בר נחמן ורבנן (בראשית רבה מג:ו). רבי שמואל בר נחמן אמר "גילה לו סוד כהונה גדולה", ורבנן אמרו "גלה לו סוד תורה." פירוש "סוד כהונה גדולה" היא עבדות על ידי מסירות נפש, שהוא סוד כהונה גדולה, בחינת הקרבה, שמקריב עצמו עבור הבורא. ו"סוד תורה" היא עבדות הבורא על ידי מצוות ומעשים טובים שהוא תורה.

קדושת לוי ב'

ומלכי צדק מלך שלם הוציא לחם ויין והוא כהן לאל עליון
(בראשית יד:יח).

הכלל יש שני עובדי הבורא: אחד שעובד הבורא במסירות נפש, ואחד שעובד הבורא במצוות ובמעשים טובים. וההפרש שזה העובד את הבורא במסירות נפש, לא על ידי מצוות ומעשים טובים, הוא ב"אין" ממש. וזה העובד את ה' במצוות הוא עובד על ידי דבר ה'"יש", כי המצוות הם "יש". ולכן זה שעובד במסירות נפש דהוא ב"אין" אינו יכול להמשיך על עצמו שפע כי הוא אינו כלום, רק שמדבק את עצמו בה' יתברך. וזה שעובד על ידי מצוות ומעשים טובים, הוא על ידי דבר "יש" לכן יכול להמשיך על עצמו שפע מה' יתברך.

והנה אמרו חז"ל: קיים אברהם אבינו כל התורה, אפילו עירובי תבשילין עד שלא ניתנה (יומא כח:). וקרבנו אל השכל, איך ידע כל התורה? אך מחמת שאברהם אבינו הפריד את עצמו מגשמיות וראה הרמ"ח [248] אברים, שכל אבר חיותו ממצוה, וכל אבר ואבר יש לו מצוה שמחיה אותו, שהמצוה שהיא כנגד האבר היא חיות האבר, ומבלעדי המצוה אין חיות לאבר, והשיג שחיות הראש הוא מתפילין, וכן השאר מצוות, משום הכי השיג כל המצוות עד שלא ניתנו... ולכך לא היה אברהם יכול לעבוד את הבורא בחוץ לארץ על ידי המצוות, כי בחוץ לארץ לא היה באפשר לקיים המצוות התלויות בארץ, ולא היה יכול לקיים כמה מצוות שהם כנגד אבריו, והיה נחסר לו כמה אברים... לכן כל זמן היות אברהם בחוץ לארץ היה עובד ה' יתברך על ידי מסירות נפש. אמנם בביאתו לארץ היה יכול לקיים כל המצוות והיתה קומה שלימה בכל אבריו על ידי המצוות, ולכן היה עובד על ידי מצוות.

לכן בחוץ לארץ שעבד על ידי מסירות נפש, היה דבוק ב"אין" ולא היה יכול להמשיך על עצמו שפע. אמנם בארץ ישראל שעבד על ידי המצוות היה בבחינת "יש", והיה יכול להמשיך שפע מהבורא. וזהו פירוש הפסוק "לך לך מארצך" (בראשית יב:א), פירש רש"י ז"ל: "להנאתך ולטובתך"... ותוכל להמשיך עליך שפע. אמנם בחוץ לארץ, שאתה עובד במסירות נפש, דאתה ב"אין", אי אפשר לך להמשיך עליך שפע...

- ט"ו -

466

"וה". ומשבא אברהם והיתה התעוררות השפע מלמטה, נמצא "וה" קודם
"יה", וזהו **והיה ברכה**.

נועם אלימלך ב'

ויהי רעב בארץ וירד אברם מצרימה לגור שם... (בראשית
יב:י).

נראה לפרש על דרך המוסר, כמאמר הכתוב "לא רעב ללחם ולא צמא
למים כי אם לשמוע [את] דבר ה'" (עמוס ח:יא). ונמצא זה עיקר הרעב
אם ח"ו עם בני ישראל אינם מתנהגים כשורה והולכים שובב בדרך לבם
ח"ו. על ידי זה הם גורמים גם לצדיק השלם במעשיו שיורד ממדריגתו
הגדולה הקדושה. וזה שאמר הכתוב **ויהי רעב בארץ** כנזכר לעיל.

וירד אברם מצרימה. פירוש, על ידי זה יורד הצדיק הנקרא בשם
"אברם" ממדריגתו. ואף על פי כן, כי יפול לא יוטל לגמרי ח"ו, רק
שיורד **מצרימה**, דהיינו נוטריקון "מיצר ים," שנעשה לו "צר" ודוחק
בקדושתו העליונה שהיתה לו מקודם; "ים" רמז לקדושה עליונה, ים
העליון.

וכל זאת אין ה' יתברך ב"ה עושה להצדיק שיפול ממדריגתו מחמת רשעת
הרשעים, רק גם זה לטובתו, דהיינו **לגור שם**, דאלולי זאת שיפול
ממדריגתו קצת אפשר שיגבה לבו קצת להתגדל במדריגתו וקדושתו.
ועתה על ידי שרואה הצדיק שנפל ממדריגתו הוא מתבייש מאוד ומתחרט
ואינו מחזיק עצמו רק כגר בארץ, דהיינו שמחזיק עצמו שהוא גר בעולם
הזה ובעולם הבא מאחר שנפל ממדריגתו.

שייכות עמהם להעלותם. וכתיב "לגור שם" מלשון "גורו לכם מפני חרב" (איוב יט:כט), שצריך לאחוז בירידה למדריגתן במידת היראה ולירא מאד מה' יתברך לבל יכשל כמוהם ח"ו בכדי שתהא הירידה צורך העליה...

וזהו שציוהו המקום שילך מארצו ושם יגדל שמו, כאמור למעלה, שצריך להשפיל את עצמו ולהתקרב ולהתקרב אצל אותן שהיה צריך להעלותם ולהרחיב גבול הקדושה, שיתפשט ויתגדל אהבת הבורא ב"ה בעולם על ידי עליות אהבות הנפולות לשרשן, שבזה נקרא יותר אוהבו של מקום. וזהו: **ואגדלה שמך**, שנקראת "אברהם אוהבי" על ידי ההליכה ההיא שתלך מארצך ותתפרסם אהבתו יתברך גם במדריגות נפולין, ותקרא אוהב גדול יותר במעלה מקודם...

נועם אלימלך א'

ויאמר ה' אל אברם לך לך מארצך וממולדתך ומבית אביך אל הארץ אשר אראך (בראשית יב:א).

דהנה הצדיק שהוא יודע שהוא משפיע ומחמת זה הוא רוצה לפעמים להשפיע לקרוביו ולתלמידיו, אבל באמת רצונו של ה' יתברך שלא יעלה על מחשבתו כלל שהוא משפיע, רק שיעבוד ה' יתברך ב"ה בשלימות והשפע ממילא בא. וזהו **ויאמר [ה' אל אברם] לך לך מארצך...** רוצה לומר שלא יעלה במחשבתך כלל דבר הנוגע לארצך, רק **אל הארץ אשר אראך**, רוצה לומר שכל עבודתך תהיה רק אל הארץ העליונה והשפע ממילא יבא.

קדושת לוי א'

... והיה ברכה (בראשית יב:ב).

הכלל: "יה" רמז על ה' יתברך, "וה" על ישראל. ועד אברהם לא היה מי שיעורר השפע מלמעלה, והיה השפע מן ה' לבדו; נמצא השם "יה" קודם

- י"ג -

468

וכיוצא בשאר המידות, בשעה שנתעורר בקרבו איזה מידה מהמידות, אזי יראה ויגור ויחרד להשתמש בשרביטו של מלך מלכו של עולם, להקניטו ח"ו ולעשות נגד רצונו ולמרות עיני כבודו יתברך. ואדרבה, בהתעוררות המידה בקרבו אל הרע ודבר חיצוני ההוא, אז נקל לו לקשר את עצמו עם זאת המידה למעלה בו יתברך שמו מאחר שנתעורר ונפתח פתח המידה ההיא אז. ואז מעלה דברים נפולים לשורשם, שאין תענוג למעלה גדול מזה, שיש לה' יתברך מזה תענוג גדול כנודע כל זה...

והנה אברהם אבינו ע"ה אחז במידת החסד ונקרא "אברהם אוהבי" (ישעיה מא:ח), כמו שכתוב למעלה. כי התחלת תיקון המידות והנהגתן הוא מחסד, ורצה ה' יתברך שירד למדינות העמים ששם היו המדות נפולין מאוד, ובפרט במצרים שהם שטופי זמה, כמו שאמר הכתוב "וזרמת סוסים זרמתם" (יחזקאל כג:כ). והוצרך אברהם, שהוא בעל מידת חסד, לילך ולהשפיל את עצמו אל מדריגתן ולהעלות מידת האהבה הנפולה שם. כנודע שאם ירצו להעלות שום אדם צריך להשפיל את עצמו למדריגתו בכדי שיוכל להעלותו, שעל כן היה אברהם מכניס אורחים ומאכילן ומשקה אותן, ואחר כך אמר להם לא משלי אתם אוכלים. כי על ידי שהן היו שקועים בתאוות עולם הזה, כגון אכילה ושתיה, עם המידות שלהם היה אברהם מקרב את עצמו להם במדריגתן, שהוא אכילה ושתיה, ועל ידי זה הכניסן תחת כנפי השכינה. שזהו כוונת לשון "הכנסת אורחים," שעל כן היא גדולה מקבלת פני השכינה (שבת קכז.) כי על ידי זה הוא מקשר דברים נפולין לשרשן שאין תענוג גדול מזה שיש לה'...

וכן כשרצה אברהם אבינו ע"ה לתקן מידת החסד, שהיא אהבה רעה שהיה בין העמים, שהיו ביניהן נשמות קדושות, הוצרך להשפיל את עצמו למדריגתן שעל כן נאמר "ויהי רעב בארץ וירד אברם מצרימה" (בראשית יב:י), כי היה "לא רעב ללחם ולא צמא למים כי אם לשמוע את דבר ה'" (עמוס ח:יא), שהיו המידות נפולין מאוד ואברהם רצה לתקן מידתו אהבה נפולה, שהיא נפולה ממידת החסד כמו שאמר הכתוב "ואיש אשר יקח את אחותו... חסד הוא" (ויקרא כ:יז), שהכוונה היא שתתן דעתך כי הלא היא אהבה נובלת מפרי אילן העליון מידת החסד.

וברצותו להעלותן נאמר "וירד אברם מצרימה" (בראשית יב:י) לשון השפלה, כמבואר למעלה, שצריך להשפיל את עצמו למדריגתן שיהא לו

- י"ב -

ומעלה האכילות והשתיות ושארי צרכי בני אדם אל ה' בטוב כוונתו, כדכתיב "בכל דרכיך דעהו" (משלי ג:ו) - כל מעשיך יהיו לשם שמים. אז הם נקראים "ארצות החיים," כי בארציות שלו שוכן בהם חי החיים. וזהו: **אל הארץ אשר אראך**, שיהיו נקראים ארצות החיים...

מאור עינים ב'

ויאמר ה' אל אברם לך לך מארצך... ואעשך לגוי גדול (בראשית יב:א-ב).

וכי לא היה אפשר לעשותו לגוי גדול ולגדל שמו בארץ מולדתו, כי אין שום מונע לבורא ב"ה בכל מקום?! אמנם נודע כי ה' יתברך מנהיג את העולם על ידי שבע מידות, שהם שבעה ימים שהעולם סובב בהם. ונקראים ימי עולם וימי הבנין, והתחלתן ממידת החסד, כמו שאמר הכתוב "עולם חסד יבנה" (תהלים פט:ג). וכמו שהנהגת העולמות על ידי שבעה ימים אלו, כמו כן צריך העובד ה', שהוא עולם קטן והוטבעו בו שבע מידות אלו, שהן אהבה ויראה ותפארת וכו' כנודע, וביד האדם הוא להטות המידות לכל אשר יחפוץ. כי זאת הבחירה הנמסרה לאדם, ויכול לפעול על ידם הן לטוב הן למוטב [כלומר לרע] כנודע. ואף שהן נטולין ונאצלין ממקום גבוה, כגון אהבה שבאדם שרשה מעולם האהבה העליונה, וכן יראה וכן שאר המידות, מכל מקום בהשתלשלותן עד קרב האדם הן מעורבין מטוב ורע ונקראים מידות נפולין.

וזה כל עיקר עבודתנו: לטהר המידות שבקרבנו מן הרע, ולהעלותן על ידי שהוא עובד עמהן עבודתו יתברך. וכל זה על ידי טוב הסתכלותו בעת שתבוא לו איזה אהבה רעה או יראה רעה, ח"ו שיסתכל ויחרד. ויאמר בלבו: הלא זאת היא אהבה נפולה מעולם האהבה, אהבת הבורא ב"ה, ואני צריך להעלותה, ואיך אעשה הרעה הזאת להפילה עוד למטה מטה. ואם מה אני אוהב הדבר הרע הזה, שהוא דבר נברא וארציות ונפול, איך יש לאהוב את הבורא ב"ה ותורתו שבה נבראו כל הנבראים והוא תענוג כל התענוגים.

✨ פרשת לך לך ✨

מאור עינים א'

ויאמר ה' אל אברם לך לך מארצך וממולדתך ומבית אביך אל הארץ אשר אראך (בראשית יב:א).

פירש רש"י: "להנאתך ולטובתך." וקשה הא כתיב "אברהם אוהבי" (ישעיה מא:ח), שעבד את ה' מאהבתו אותו ולא משום פנייה. ויש לומר דכתיב "אברהם אברהם" (בראשית כב:יא), "יעקב יעקב" (בראשית מו:ב), "משה משה" (שמות ג:ד), היינו "כי חלק ה' עמו" (דברים לב:ט). והצדיק כמו שהוא כאן בעולם השפל, כן הוא שורשו למעלה. ולזה נברא פה בכדי שאף שהוא נתלבש בגוף עכור, אף על פי כן בטוב בחירתו עובד את ה' ולא מכחיש פומבי דמלכא, היינו חותם המלך. והוא בזה העולם צדיק כמו שהוא צדיק בשרשו שלמעלה. וזהו: "אברהם אברהם," שהוא אברהם פה צדיק כמו שהוא צדיק בשרשו שלמעלה, וכן ביתר צדיקים ששמם פה כמו שהם למעלה צדיקים.

וידוע כי הנשמות נהנים למעלה מזיו השכינה, רק שהוא נהמא דכיסופא [לחם הבושה], כי מאן דאכיל לאו דיליה בהית לאיסתכלא ביה [מי שאוכל מה שאינו שלו מתבייש להסתכל עליו; (ירושלמי ערלה א:ג)]. ולזה הוריד ה' הנשמה למטה, בכדי שבטוב בחירתה שתעבוד אל ה' ישולם לה שכר פעולתה, ולא יהיה לה נהמא דכיסופא. וזהו: **לך לך** "להנאתך ולטובתך," שבשכר פעולתך יתנו לך הנאה וטובה ולא נהמא דכיסופא. והנה הגם שהנשמה היא מלובשת בחומר עכור ומתאווה לתאוות גשמיות וארציות, מזה גופא תוכל לילך בעבודת ה'. וזהו **מארצך** מתוך ארציות שלך תוכל לילך בעבודת ה'.

דוד המלך ע"ה אמר: "אתהלך לפני ה' בארצות החיים" (תהלים קטז:ט), כי דברים גשמיים כגון אכילה ושתיה ושאר צרכי בני אדם, אם עושין אותן בשביל תאוה אין בהן חיות. מה שאין כן אם אוכל לשובע נפשו

אור המאיר

ואתה קח לך מכל מאכל אשר יאכל ואספת אליך והיה לך ולהם לאכלה: ויעש נח ככל אשר צוה אותו אלהים כן עשה (בראשית ו:כא-כב).

ופירש רש"י זה בנין התיבה, ולקמן בפסוק "ויעש נח ככל אשר צוה ה'" (בראשית ז:ה), פירש רש"י זה ביאתו לתיבה. ראוי לשים לב למקראי קודש אלו להבינם, ובפרט מהכלל אשר בידינו שהתורה היא תמידיות בעבר ועתיד והווה. אם כן מה באתה ללמדנו עתה עם בנין התיבה? והנכון בעיני, אשר בכאן נרמז ענין התפילה ואופני התעוררות, איך יעורר אדם את לבו לעבודת אל, זו תפילה.

כי הנה איתא בספרים מי שרוצה לגשת אל העבודה פנימה, להוציא דיבור לפני אלהים בתפילה, צריך לקשור את עצמו בעת עומדו בתפילה אל כל הנבראים והדוממים וכו'. והכוונה כי הנה כתיב "הכל בחכמה עשית" (תהלים קד:כד), שאין שום דבר בעולם לבטלה ח"ו, רק הכל מורה על פועל החכם שמעשהו בדעת. הכל בשביל קילוסו, לדעת כל אנשים מעשיהם ליקח לעצמם רמיזא דחכמתא, ובהיות איש המשכיל נותן דעתו לזה להשיג את הבחינה המלובשת בכל דבר שבעולם, מהנבראים והצומחים והדוממים, ומכל בחינה שבא לכלל הויה ומעורר את לבו בקרבו, ומתלהב את עצמו עם זה החכמה לדבר דיבורים לפניו יתברך בדחילו ורחימו, אזי משלים רצון קונו, אשר לכוונה זו ברא ארץ ומלואה...

ועל פי הדברים האלו יש לרמוז את הכתוב שאמר לו הקדוש ברוך הוא לנח **ואתה קח לך מכל מאכל אשר יאכל**... בכאן רמז לו אופני התעוררות להעבודה זו תפילה... וזהו: **ויעש נח ככל אשר צוה אותו אלהים כן עשה.**

ז"ל (בראשית ו:ט): יש דורשין [לשבח... ויש דורשין לגנאי]. ואם היה
נאמר בדורו, היה גם כן נשמע דרש זה.

ונראה לי דבא לאשמעינן עוד דבר אחד. דהנה בכל דור ודור יש שורש
לתקן מצוה מיוחדת יותר משאר מצות. למשל, בדור הזה יש שורש לתקן
מצות ציצית יותר משאר מצות, וכדומה בכל דור יש שורש להחזיק
במצוה מיוחדת יותר משאר מצות. ובא הכתוב לאשמעינן שהיה נח **צדיק
תמים בדורותיו**; רוצה לומר, בכל דור שהיה חי היה מחזיק ומתקן אותו
שורש המצוה המיוחד יותר לאותו הדור.

קדושת לוי

... נח איש צדיק תמים היה בדורותיו (בראשית ו:ט).

בפירוש רש"י ז"ל (בראשית ז:ז): "אף נח מקטני אמונה היה." האיך יכול
להיות זה, כי הכתוב מעיד עליו **נח איש צדיק תמים היה בדורותיו?**...
נבוא לבאר, כי יש שני מיני צדיקים שעובדים הבורא: יש צדיק שעובד
הבורא ואין לו חשק רק להיות עובד הבורא, ומאמין שיש לו כח בעליונים
להנהיג העולמות כרצונו, כמו שאמרו חז"ל: "צדיק מושל ביראת אלהים"
(שמואל ב כג:ג) - מי מושל בי? צדיק, הקדוש ברוך הוא גוזר וצדיק
מבטל הגזירה לטובה (מועד קטן טז:). ויש צדיק אחר שעובד הבורא
ברוך הוא, והוא שפל בעיני עצמו מאד מאד, וחושב בלבו מי אני
שאתפלל לבטל הגזירה, לכן אינו מתפלל לבטל.

ונח, הגם שהיה צדיק גדול ותמים, היה קטן בעיניו מאוד, ולא היתה לו
אמונה בעצמו שהוא צדיק מושל ויכול לבטל הגזירה. אדרבה, היה חשוב
בעיניו כשאר הדור, והיה חושב אם אני אהיה ניצול בתיבה ואני אין צדיק
יותר משאר הדור המה גם כן ינצלו, לכן לא היה מתפלל על הדור. וזה
שפירש רש"י: "אף נח מקטני אמונה היה."

והנה בנח לא היה אתערותא דלתתא, רק מחמת שה׳ יתברך היה חפץ בקיום העולם שיתקיים על ידי נח; לכן הוצרך ה׳ יתברך לעורר אותו מלמעלה והוצרך להשפיע בנח תשוקה לדבק בו יתברך. וזהו [פירוש רש״י]: נח היה צריך סעד לתומכו, אבל אברהם אבינו ע״ה היה מתחזק בצדקו והולך מאליו באתערותא דלתתא.

והשתא ניחא שנקרא **צדיק תמים**, כיון שהיה דבק בו יתברך אבל לא באתערותא דלתתא, ולכן כתיב ״אלה תולדות השמים והארץ בהבראם״ (בראשית ב:ד), אותיות ״אברהם,״ דהיינו כנזכר לעיל, שעיקר הבריאה היה על ידי כן שיהיה ההילוך כהילוך של אברהם אבינו ע״ה באתערותא דלתתא.

נועם אלימלך א׳

... נח איש צדיק תמים היה בדורותיו את האלהים התהלך נח (בראשית ו:ט).

דהצדיק, על ידי מעשיו הקדושים שעושה איזה דבר קדושה, הוא ממשיך את הבורא ברוך הוא יתעלה לעולם הזה. נמצא עושה טובה לדורותיו, שמזכה להם ששכינתו יתברך עמהם על ידי הצדיק. וכשהצדיק עולה במדריגה יתירה אזי הוא גורם לקשר ולהמשיך את שמו יתעלה בכל העולמות. וזהו: **איש צדיק תמים היה בדורותיו**. רוצה לומר, שתמימות צדקתו היה מועיל לדורותיו. וגם זאת הועילה צדקתו **את האלהים התהלך נח** - פירוש, גם לעולמות העליונים היה משפיע להם. וזהו: **את האלהים**. פירוש, עם אלהים, דהיינו עולמות עליונים גם שם היה מתהלך נח, והבן.

נועם אלימלך ב׳

או יאמר **בדורותיו** (ו:ט). לכאורה ״בדורו״ היה ראוי לכתוב. אף על פי שנח היה חי כמה דורות, אף על פי כן עיקר בא לאשמעינן כפירוש רש״י

✺ פרשת נח ✺

מאור עינים

**... נח איש צדיק תמים היה בדורותיו את האלהים התהלך
נח** (בראשית ו:ט).

פירש רש"י: ובאברהם הוא אומר "אשר התהלכתי לפניו" (בראשית
כד:מ), נח צריך סעד לתמכו, ואברהם היה מתחזק בצדקו והולך מאליו.
וקשה גם כן כנזכר לעיל, הלא הכתוב אומר **צדיק תמים** וכו', ואם כן
הוא, הרי לא היה שלם, שהיה חסר לו המדריגה של אברהם.

אך דנודע שהכל תלוי באתערותא דלתתא, והוא בחינת מים נוקבין, כי
תיאובתא דנוקבא לגבי דכורא [הנקבה תָּאֲוָה לזכר] (על פי בראשית
ג:טז). ואנחנו עם בני ישראל נקראים בחינת נוקבא לגבי קודשא בריך
הוא, וכשאנו מתעוררים לדבק בבוראנו יתברך מלמטה למעלה, אנו
מעוררים כביכול תשוקה בבוראנו יתברך, להשפיע לנו כל טוב סלה,
ומורידים השפעה מלמעלה למטה בשפע וברכה ורחמים וחיים ושלום.

והנה אנחנו כנסת ישראל עם הבורא יתברך דבר אחד שלם כשאנו דבקים
עמו יתברך, וזה בלא זה כביכול אינו נקרא שלם, כמאמר: אין השם שלם
ואין הכסא שלם (רש"י שמות יז:טז; תנחומא כי תצא ס' י"א). שאנחנו
נקראים כסא להבורא יתברך, כי כביכול הבורא ברוך הוא בלעדינו אינו
נקרא שלם. ופשיטא, אנחנו זולתו יתברך. רק כשאנו מעוררים תחלה מיין
נוקבין, דהיינו תשוקתינו ממטה למעלה לדבק בו יתברך, על ידי זה אנו
מעוררים תשוקתו יתברך מלמעלה למטה, ואז כשהשתי תשוקות באות
ביחד אז הוא דבר אחד שלם. וזהו "תמים תהיה עם ה' אלהיך" (דברים
יח:יג), רוצה לומר אתה עם ה' יתברך נקרא דבר שלם.

והנה עיקר הבריאה היה על מנת כן שנלך אל ה' יתברך על ידי אתערותא
דלתתא מתחילה. ואם לאו, ח"ו, דהיינו כשאין אנו מתעוררים באתערותא
דלתתא וצריך ה' יתברך לעורר אותנו מלמעלה, אז אין אנו עושין כלום.

עדן העליון וכדומה הוא על ידי השיר, שהוא בחינת בטול היש. וכנודע שלא יוכל להתהוות מיש ליש אלא אם כן נעשה היש תחילה בחינת אין, אז יוכל להתהוות ממנו יש אחר בתוספת ברכה. כמשל הגרעין הנזרע בארץ, שצריך להיות נרקב בארץ ואחר כך יכול לצמוח מזה הרבה גרעינים. וכמו כן למעלה בנשמות ומלאכים, כדי שיהיה לו עלייה בתוספת השגה צריך מקודם להיות בחינת בטול היש והשגה ראשונה שהיה לו, ואחר כך יוכל לעלות השגה יותר גדולה. וזהו בחינת עמוד שבין גן עדן התחתון לגן עדן העליון הוא בחינת בטול, כנזכר לעיל.

וזהו "כל בעלי השיר יוצאין" בהשגתם ונמשכים לעלות למעלה על ידי השיר, ולכן בשעת הקרבת הקרבן היה צריך להיות גם כן שיר כי ענין הקרבנות הוא העלאה ממטה למעלה "אשה ריח ניחוח" וצריך לזה גם כן בחינת שיר, בחינת בטול כנזכר לעיל שיוכל להתעלות...

זהו ענין **יובל אבי כל תופש כנור וכו'**. פירוש **יובל** לשון הולכה שמוביל וממשיך למעלה על ידי **כנור ועוגב**, בחינת שיר כנזכר לעיל, שעל ידי השיר הוא העלייה **יוצאין בשיר**.

והנה כל מה שיש ברוחניות יש כמוהו בגשמיות. והנה בגשמיות יש קול ודיבור, הקול הוא כלול, והדיבור הוא הצימצום להקול באותיות הדיבור. והנה כן בראש השנה, הקול שופר הוא השפע מהבורא ברוך הוא הוא הכלול, ומה שאנו אומרים מלכיות זכרונות ושופרות הוא הצמצום שאנו מצמצמים בהאותיות את השפע מהבורא ברוך הוא, כל אחד כפי הרצון שלו.

והנה זה שהשפע נשפע כלול מהבורא יתברך זה הוא בחינת תורה שבכתב, וזה שאנו עושין צמצום בהשפע עם האותיות הוא בחינת תורה שבעל פה, כי תורה שבעל פה היא ברצון ישראל, כאשר הם עושין הפירוש בהתורה שבכתב. וזהו **בראשית** - ב' [שתי] ראשית, תורה שבכתב ושבעל פה.

קדושת לוי ג'

אלה תולדות השמים והארץ בהבראם ביום עשות ה' אלהים ארץ ושמים (בראשית ב:ד).

פירוש, זה תכלית של בריאת שמים וארץ, דתולדה הוא לשון תכלית הדבר. **ביום עשות ה' אלהים ארץ ושמים**, פירוש כשיעשה ה' לעתיד ארץ ושמים, שהארץ תהיה קודם לשמים. וזהו תכלית הבריאה, שהעליונים יקבלו ממעשי התחתונים. וזהו "הודו על ארץ ושמים" (תהלים קמח:יג), פירוש "הודו" של ה' יתברך הוא "על ארץ ושמים" כשארץ קודם לשמים, שהעליונים מקבלים מתחתונים, והבן.

תורה אור

ושם אחיו יובל הוא היה אבי כל תופש כנור ועוגב (בראשית ד:כא).

הנה אמרו רבותינו ז"ל: "כל בעלי השיר יוצאין בשיר וכו'" (מ' שבת ה:א). פירוש שכל בחינת העלאה ממהות למהות כמו מגן עדן התחתון לגן

אף שהא' הוא אות ראשונה אך תמונת א' הוא י' בראש, י' בסוף, ו'
באמצע. י' בראש הוא חכמה עילאה חומר הראשון שבתוכו היו כלולים
כל העולמות. ועל ידי הו' שהוא המשכת הדעת נמשך וירד ונשתלשל
למטה ויצאו מכח אל הפועל ונבראו כל העולמות, ונעשה י' בסוף חכמה
תתאה חכמת שלמה דהיינו בחינת אדנ"י הנזכר לעיל, שהוא אלהותו
יתברך שירד ונשתלשל למטה ומלובש בכל דבר שמלא כל הארץ כבודו.

וכשעושה כל מעשיו לשם שמים הוא מקרב כל עניני העולם שהוא חכמה
תתאה אל החכמה עילאה שהוא הבורא יתברך המהוה כל העולמות והיינו
על ידי הדעת שמקיים "בכל דרכיך דעהו" שהוא לשון חיבור והתקשרות
ה' תתאה אל ה' עילאה נקודה עליונה. ואז כל העולם ומלואו הוא בחינת
א' י' בראש י" בסוף ו' באמצע. לכן נקרא ה' יתברך אלופו של עולם...

קדושת לוי א'

בראשית ברא אלהים את השמים ואת הארץ (בראשית א:א).

הכלל שהבורא ב"ה ברא הכל והוא הכל, והשפעתו אינה נפסקת מעולם,
כי בכל רגע משפיע שפע לברואיו ולכל העולמות ולכל ההיכלות ולכל
המלאכים ולכל חיות הקודש. ולכן אנו אומרים "יוצר אור ובורא חושך"
(ישעיה מה:ז), ולא יצר אור וברא חושך, רק "יוצר" בלשון הוה, כי בכל
רגע הוא יוצר, שבכל רגע הוא משפיע חיות לכל חי והכל מאתו יתברך,
והוא שלם והוא כלול מהכל.

קדושת לוי ב'

בראשית ברא אלהים... (בראשית א:א).

ב' ראשית. ה' יתברך משפיע שפע ואנו בתפלתינו עושים צימצום
בהשפע, כל אחד לפי הרצון שלו. זה עושה צימצום עם אותיות ח' י' י' ם'
לחיים, וזה עם אותיות ח' כ' מ' ה' לחכמה, וזה עם אותיות ע' ו' ש' ר'
לעושר, וכן לכל הטובות כל אחד כרצונו.

- ג -

478

בתורה נבראו השמים והארץ שהם כללות הכל וכל דבר שבהם, כמאמר רז"ל (בראשית רבה א:יד): "את" לרבות תולדות. **והארץ**, רוצה לומר מי שמשוקע בארציות **היתה תהו ובהו** מפני שאינו מביט אל החיות, ובאמת מעצמם הם תהו ובהו. ופירש רש"י שאדם תוהא ומשתומם על בוהו שבה. רוצה לומר מי שהוא אדם תוהא ומשתומם על הכסיל המשוקע בארציות, הרי בו הוא! רוצה לומר הרי בו הוא חיות של הקודשא בריך הוא והוא אינו מבין ומתרחק ממנו. וכשהאדם מסתכל בכל דבר אל החיות מקיים "שויתי ה' לנגדי תמיד" (תהלים טז:ח) שבכל דבר משוה נגדו הויה מהווה כל הויה.

מאור עינים ב'

בראשית ברא אלהים... (בראשית א:א).

... דהנה הבריאה היתה בשביל התורה ובשביל ישראל, דהיינו לגלות אלהותו יתברך לישראל שיכירו וידעו מציאותו. אף שמהותו אי אפשר להשיג כשידעו שיש אלוה מצוי יעשו כל מעשיהם לשם שמים לקיים "בכל דרכיך דעהו" (משלי ג:ו) וליחד את עצמם אליו יתברך, כי אין זולתו ואפס בלתו ולית אתר פנוי מיניה, כמאמר "מלא כל הארץ כבודו" (ישעיה ו:ג).

אך שכבודו נקרא לבושין שמלא כל הארץ לבושיו, שמלובש בכל דבר. ובחינה זו נקראת אדני מלשון "אדנים" למשכן, שהוא אלהותו יתברך שיורד למטה במדריגות תחתונים וגשמים, וצריך לייחד זה זה עם המקור אשר ממנו יצאו, דהיינו עם שם הוי"ה ברוך הוא המהוה כל העולמות. ובכל עבודות שלנו, תורתנו ותפלתנו, אכילתנו ושתייתנו, נעשה יחוד זה. וכל העולמות תלוים בזה דהיינו יחוד הוי"ה ואדנ"י.

וכשהשני שמות משולבים הוא י' בראש י' בסוף, כזה יאהדונה"י, ד"כולם בחכמה עשית" (תהלים קד:כד), והחכמה הוא י' וחכמה הוא חומר הראשון של כל האותיות דבאורייתא ברא קודשא בריך הוא עלמא... והוא נקרא בלשון חכמים חומר היולי, לשון "היה לי", רוצה לומר שכל הדברים היו בתוכו וממנו יצאו מכח אל הפועל.

- ב -

479

❧ פרשת בראשית ❧

מאור עינים א'

בראשית ברא אלהים את השמים ואת הארץ והארץ היתה תהו ובהו... (בראשית א:א-ב).

בראשית - באורייתא שנקרא "ראשית דרכו" (משלי ח:כב) ברא קודשא בריך הוא עלמא. נמצא כל דבר נברא על ידי התורה וכח הפועל בנפעל. אם כן בכל דבר ובכל העולמות כח התורה, וכן האדם דכתיב "זאת התורה אדם" (במדבר יט:יד), כאשר יתבאר. והתורה וקודשא בריך הוא חד (זהר א:כד.). נמצא בכל דבר הוא חיות הקודשא בריך הוא. "ואתה מחיה את כולם" (נחמיה ט:ו), וצמצם כביכול עד מדריגות התחתונות והושם חלק אלוה ממעל תוך חשכת החומר, כי כל עיקר הכוונה הוא שיתעלו מדריגות התחתונות למעלה, ולהיות "יתרון האור מן החושך" (קהלת ב:יג).

והוא ענין ירידת יוסף למצרים למדריגות התחתונות - מיצר ים - שעל ידי זה יתוסף תענוג, כדכתיב ויתרון האור, שיש יתרון תענוג כשהועלה מן החשך. ולכך נקרא יוסף מלשון תוספות וזהו "וירא יעקב כי יש שבר במצרים" (בראשית מב:א) - לשון שבירה - שהם נובלות חכמה של מעלה, תורה, מה שנפל ונשבר. כל מה דנחית מדריגה יקרא שבירה. "במצרים" - במיצר ים, שראה שם נובלות התורה שנפלה שם שצריכה להתברר ולעלות. ואמר "רדו שמה" (בראשית מב:ב) להעלות, ונחית להביא אל חיות השרש ועצמי...

כיון שבכל דבר היא התורה המחיה הדבר ההוא, אין להביט בכל דבר אל גשמיותו כי אם אל פנימיות הדבר בסוד "החכם עיניו בראשו" (קהלת ב:יד). ואמר בזהר "וכי באן עיני דבר נש? אלא חכימא מסתכל מאן דקיימא על רישא" [ואיפה עיניו של אדם? אלא חכם מסתכל במי שעומד בראש] (זהר ג:קפז.)! רוצה לומר בכל דבר מביט אל ראשית הדבר ההוא מאין נשתלשל ומי שרשו של הדבר ההוא. וזהו **בראשית ברא וכו'** -

- א -

480

פמקץ (ע' מה-מט)

ע' מה	**אור המאיר** - והנה מן היאר עולות שבע פרות בריאות בשר... והנה שבע פרות אחרות עולות אחריהן... ויאמר יוסף אל פרעה חלום פרעה אחד הוא... (בראשית מא:יח-כה).
מו	**אורח לחיים** - ויצבר יוסף בר כחול הים הרבה מאוד עד כי חדל לספור כי אין מספר (בראשית מא:מט).
מז	**קדושת לוי** - ויבאו אחי יוסף וישתחוו לו אפים ארצה וירא יוסף את אחיו ויכירם ויתנכר אליהם (בראשית מב:ו-ז).
מח	**מגיד דבריו ליעקב** - ... ואת הארץ תסחרו (בראשית מב:לד).
מח	**בית אהרן** - וכסף משנה קחו בידכם ואת הכסף המושב בפי אמתחתיכם תשיבו בידכם... ואל שדי יתן לכם רחמים... (בראשית מג:יב,יד).

פויגש (ע' נ-נד)

נ	**אור תורה** - ויגש אליו יהודה ויאמר בי אדני ידבר נא עבדך דבר ... ואל יחר אפך בעבדך כי כמוך כפרעה (בראשית מד:יח).
נא	**פרי הארץ** - ויגש אליו יהודה ויאמר בי אדני... (בראשית מד:יח).
נב	**אור המאיר** - ויגש אליו יהודה ויאמר בי אדני... (בראשית מד:יח).
נג	**מבשר צדק** - ונאמר לא נוכל לרדת אם יש אחינו הקטן אתנו וירדנו כי לא נוכל לראות פני האיש ואחינו הקטן איננו אתנו (בראשית מד:כו).
נד	**קדושת לוי** - ויאסר יוסף מרכבתו ויעל לקראת אביו... (בראשית מו:כט).

פויחי (ע' נה-נח)

נה	**אור תורה** - ויברך את יוסף ויאמר... המלאך הגואל אותי מכל רע יברך את הנערים (בראשית מח:טו-טז).
נה	**אור המאיר** - ויקרא יעקב אל בניו ויאמר האספו ואגידה לכם את אשר יקרא אתכם באחרית הימים (בראשית מט:א).
נז	**קדושת לוי א'** - מאשר שמנה לחמו והוא יתן מעדני מלך (בראשית מט:כ).
נח	**קדושת לוי ב'** - ויאמר אליהם יוסף אל תיראו כי התחת אלהים אני (בראשית נ:יט).

ויצא (ע׳ לא-לה) ⸙

ע׳ לא | **מאור עינים** - ויצא יעקב מבאר שבע וילך חרנה (בראשית כח:יא).

לב | **אור המאיר א׳** - ויצא יעקב מבאר שבע וילך חרנה: ויפגע במקום וילן שם כי בא השמש (בראשית כח:י-יא).

לג | **קדושת לוי** - וירא והנה באר בשדה והנה שם שלשה עדרי צאן רובצים עליה... והאבן גדולה על פי הבאר...ויגש יעקב ויגל את האבן מעל פי הבאר... (בראשית כט:ב-ג,י).

לד | **אור המאיר ב׳** - ... והיה העטופים ללבן והקשורים ליעקב (בראשית ל:מב).

וישלח (ע׳ לו-לט) ⸙

לו | **נועם אלימלך** - וישלח יעקב מלאכים לפניו אל עשו אחיו... (בראשית לב:ד).

לז | **קדושת לוי א׳** - הצילני נא מיד אחי מיד עשו...(בראשית לב:יב).

לח | **קדושת לוי ב׳** - ... כי יפגשך עשו אחי ושאלך לאמר למי אתה ואנה תלך ולמי אלה לפניך: ואמרת לעבדך ליעקב מנחה היא שלוחה לאדני לעשו... (בראשית לב:יח-יט).

לח | **אור המאיר** - ויקרא יעקב שם המקום פניאל כי ראיתי אלהים פנים אל פנים ותנצל נפשי (בראשית לב:לא).

וישב (ע׳ מ-מד) ⸙

מ | **מגיד דבריו ליעקב** - וישב יעקב בארץ מגורי אביו בארץ כנען (בראשית לז:א).

מ | **מבשר צדק** - וישב יעקב בארץ מגורי אביו בארץ כנען (בראשית לז:א).

מא | **נועם אלימלך** - וישב יעקב בארץ מגורי אביו בארץ כנען (בראשית לז:א).

מב | **קדושת לוי** - וישב יעקב בארץ מגורי אביו בארץ כנען (בראשית לז:א).

מג | **גנזי יוסף** - ויראו אותו מרחוק ובטרם יקרב אליהם ויתנכלו אותו להמיתו (בראשית לז:יח).

מד | **מגיד דבריו ליעקב** - ותתפשהו בבגדו לאמר שכבה עמי ויעזוב בגדו בידה וינס ויצא החוצה (בראשית לט:יב).

ע' טו	**קדושת לוי ב'** - ומלכי צדק מלך שלם הוציא לחם ויין והוא כהן לאל עליון (בראשית יד:יח).

ﭏ וירא (ע' יז-כא) ﭏ

יז	**נועם אלימלך א'** - וירא אליו ה' באלוני ממרא והוא יושב פתח האהל כחום היום (בראשית יח:א).
יח	**מגיד דבריו ליעקב** - ... והשענו תחת העץ (בראשית יח:ד).
יח	**נועם אלימלך ב'** - ואקחה פת לחם וסעדו לבכם אחר תעבורו... (בראשית יח:ה).
יט	**קדושת לוי** - וה' אמר המכסה אני מאברהם אשר אני עושה... כי ידעתיו למען אשר יצוה את בניו... (בראשית יח:יז-יט).
כ	**גנזי יוסף** - אולי יש חמשים צדיקים בתוך העיר האף תספה ולא תשא למקום למען חמשים הצדיקים אשר בקרבה (בראשית יח:כד).

ﭏ חיי שרה (ע' כב-כה) ﭏ

כב	**אור המאיר א'** - ואברהם זקן בא בימים... (בראשית כד:א).
כג	**נועם אלימלך** - ואברהם זקן בא בימים... (בראשית כד:א).
כד	**אור המאיר ב'** - ... וה' ברך את אברהם בכל (בראשית כד:א).
כה	**קדושת לוי** - הנה אנכי נצב על עין המים ובנות אנשי העיר יוצאות לשאוב מים: ...ובה אדע כי עשית חסד עם אדוני: ...והנה רבקה יוצאת אשר ילדה לבתואל... (בראשית כד:יג-טו).

ﭏ תולדות (ע' כו-ל) ﭏ

כו	**אור תורה** - ואלה תולדות יצחק בן אברהם אברהם הוליד את יצחק (בראשית כה:יט).
כח	**מאור עינים** - וישב יצחק ויחפור את בארות המים... ויחפרו עבדי יצחק בנחל וימצאו שם באר מים חיים (בראשית כו:יח-יט).
כט	**נועם אלימלך** - ורבקה אמרה אל יעקב בנה לאמר הנה שמעתי את אביך מדבר אל עשו אחיך לאמר (בראשית כז:ו).
ל	**חיים וחסד** - ... ויהי אך יצוא יצא יעקב ועשו אחיו בא מצידו (בראשית כז:ל).

❧ בראשית (ע׳ א-ה) ❧

ע׳ א **מאור עינים א׳** - בראשית ברא אלהים את השמים ואת הארץ: והארץ היתה תהו ובהו... (בראשית א:א-ב).

ב **מאור עינים ב׳** - בראשית ברא אלהים... (בראשית א:א).

ג **קדושת לוי א׳** - בראשית ברא אלהים את השמים ואת הארץ (בראשית א:א).

ג **קדושת לוי ב׳** - בראשית ברא אלהים... (בראשית א:א).

ד **קדושת לוי ג׳** - אלה תולדות השמים והארץ בהבראם ביום עשות ה׳ אלהים ארץ ושמים (בראשית ב:ד).

ד **תורה אור** - ... יבל הוא היה אבי יושב אהל ומקנה: ושם אחיו יובל הוא היה אבי כל תופש כנור ועוגב (בראשית ד:כ-כא).

❧ נח (ע׳ ו-ט) ❧

ו **מאור עינים** - ... נח איש צדיק תמים היה בדורותיו את האלהים התהלך נח (בראשית ו:ט).

ז **נועם אלימלך א׳** - ... נח איש צדיק תמים היה בדורותיו את האלהים התהלך נח (בראשית ו:ט).

ז **נועם אלימלך ב׳** - ... נח איש צדיק תמים היה בדורותיו את האלהים התהלך נח (בראשית ו:ט).

ח **קדושת לוי** - ... נח איש צדיק תמים היה בדורותיו (בראשית ו:ט).

ט **אור המאיר** - ואתה קח לך מכל מאכל אשר יאכל ואספת אליך והיה לך ולהם לאכלה: ויעש נח ככל אשר צוה אותו אלהים כן עשה (בראשית ו:כא-כב).

❧ לך לך (ע׳ י-טז) ❧

י **מאור עינים א׳** - ויאמר ה׳ אל אברם לך לך מארצך וממולדתך ומבית אביך אל הארץ אשר אראך (בראשית יב:א).

יא **מאור עינים ב׳** - ויאמר ה׳ אל אברם לך לך מארצך... ואעשך לגוי גדול (בראשית יב:א-ב).

יג **נועם אלימלך א׳** - ויאמר ה׳ אל אברם לך לך מארצך וממולדתך ומבית אביך אל הארץ אשר אראך (בראשית יב:א).

יג **קדושת לוי א׳** - ... והיה ברכה (בראשית יב:ב).

יד **נועם אלימלך ב׳** - ויהי רעב בארץ וירד אברם מצרימה לגור שם... (בראשית יב:י).

ספר

בראשית

⚜ הקדמה ⚜

בית רבי (ע' סה:-סו.)

הרב דוואלפא (שמו אינו ידוע לנו) תלמיד הרב המגיד נ"ע מתחילה היה
הוא היותר גדול בחברייא, וכולם היו הולכים לשמוע ממנו חזרת דא"ח
[דברי אלהים חיים] של הרב המגיד, שהיה חוזר הדברים כהוויתן ובטוב
טעם וכו'. אך אחר כך אמרו התלמידים שתולעת אוכלת בו ונדחה משם
ונפל בשכרות, רחמנא לצלן. גם אז היה פה מפיק מרגליות ואדרבה בעת
שהיה נכנס היין היה יוצא הסוד וכו'. ומאז נדחה היה הולך נע ונד בארץ
במקלו ותרמילו...

ושמענו שפעם אחת נזדמן לרב החסיד רב ברוך מרדכי זלה"ה
מבאברויסק לראותו בדרך במלון ומתנועותיו הבין כי הוא זה. וכשיצא
הוואלפער לחוץ חפש הרב ברוך מרדכי בתרמילו, אולי ימצא שם איזה
כתב דא"ח. בתוך כך נכנס הוואלפער ואמר לו לרב ברוך מרדכי: מה
אתם מחפשים אצלי?! האם גנבתי מכם מאומה? והשיב לו הרב ברוך
מרדכי שמחפש אחר איזה כתב. ואמר לו הוואלפער: אצלכם החסידים הם
דבר בפני עצמו, והרב ודא"ח הם דבר בפני עצמו. על כן צריכים אתם
לכתב. אבל אנחנו עם רבינו ועם דא"ח היינו דבר אחד ממש, ולא היינו
צריכים לכתב וכו'. ולקח מקלו ותרמילו והלך לו וכו'.

שפתי צדיקים
(מפרשת ויקהל)

בשם הרב הקדוש ר' **ליב שרה'ס** זלה"ה שהתרעם על "אמירת תורה"
ואמר: מה זה שאומרים תורה? אלא יראה האדם שכל עשיותיו יהא תורה
והוא בעצמו יהא תורה, היינו שיתנהג בכל דרכיו על פי התורה עד
שילמדו בני אדם מהנהגותיו, והנהגותיו עצמו תהא תורה.

דבר אל הקורא העברי

הספר שלפניך נערך בעיקר לצרכי הקורא באנגלית, וחידושו העיקרי הוא התרגום. הפרוש, או ליתר דיוק תגובות העורכים למקורות המובאים בספר, ניתנים באנגלית בלבד והוא הדין גם לשיחות-הרעים שבסוף כל פרשה. הנוסח העברי של המקורות הובא בספר מתוך התחשבות בקורא הנוסח המתורגם שרוצה להשתמש במהדורה דו-לשונית זו כגשר שיעזרנו גם לפיתוח היכולת לקרוא תורות אלו במקורן העברי.

אף על פי כן, יש לדעתנו גם קוראי עברית שימצאו ענין בספר, בעיקר במבחר המקורות שאנו מגישים מתוך כארבעים ספרים של כתבי המגיד ממזריץ' ותלמידיו. לצורך קוראים אלו הוספנו בנוסח העברי מראי מקומות ותרגום ניבים ומובאות מארמית לעברית. כמו כן הכנסנו כמה שינויים לשוניים העשויים להקל על הקורא מבלי לפגוע בסגנון החסידי המיוחד.

מלאכה זו נעשתה על ידינו בדחילו ורחימו, מתוך יראת-כבוד ואהבה מעומק הלב למקורות אלו, בהם אנו שומעים עדיין, מעבר לפער של מאתיים שנה, הדים של "שכינה מדברת מתוך גרונם" של דרשנים אלו מראשית ימי החסידות. תקוותנו היא שגם אתם הקוראים תמצאו בהם קורת רוח ותענוג רוחני.

א"י גרין

אריאל אבן-מעשה

אבן לידר

אור נסתר רוז

אומרים תורה:
סביב שלחנו של המגיד

לקוטי תורות מפי מרן ר׳ דב בער ממזריטש ותלמידיו

לקט תרגם ופירש אברהם יצחק גרין

בהשתתפות:

אריאל אבן-מעשה   אבן דוד לידר   אור נסתר רוז

כרך א: בראשית שמות ויקרא

Bible Study / Midrash

Passing Life's Tests: Spiritual Reflections on the Trial of Abraham, the Binding of Isaac *By Rabbi Bradley Shavit Artson, DHL*
Invites us to use this powerful tale as a tool for our own soul wrestling, to confront our existential sacrifices and enable us to face—and surmount—life's tests.
6 x 9, 176 pp, Quality PB, 978-1-58023-631-7 **$18.99**

The Messiah and the Jews: Three Thousand Years of Tradition, Belief and Hope *By Rabbi Elaine Rose Glickman; Foreword by Rabbi Neil Gillman, PhD; Preface by Rabbi Judith Z. Abrams, PhD*
Explores and explains an astonishing range of primary and secondary sources, infusing them with new meaning for the modern reader.
6 x 9, 192 pp, Quality PB, 978-1-58023-690-4 **$16.99**

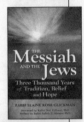

Speaking Torah: Spiritual Teachings from around the Maggid's Table—in Two Volumes *By Arthur Green, with Ebn Leader, Ariel Evan Mayse and Or N. Rose*
The most powerful Hasidic teachings made accessible—from some of the world's preeminent authorities on Jewish thought and spirituality.
Volume 1—6 x 9, 512 pp, Hardcover, 978-1-58023-668-3 **$34.99**
Volume 2—6 x 9, 448 pp, Hardcover, 978-1-58023-694-2 **$34.99**

Masking and Unmasking Ourselves: Interpreting Biblical Texts on Clothing & Identity *By Dr. Norman J. Cohen*
Presents ten Bible stories that involve clothing in an essential way, as a means of learning about the text, its characters and their interactions.
6 x 9, 240 pp, HC, 978-1-58023-461-0 **$24.99**

The Genesis of Leadership: What the Bible Teaches Us about Vision, Values and Leading Change *By Rabbi Nathan Laufer; Foreword by Senator Joseph I. Lieberman*
6 x 9, 288 pp, Quality PB, 978-1-58023-352-1 **$18.99**

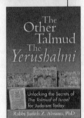

Hineini in Our Lives: Learning How to Respond to Others through 14 Biblical Texts and Personal Stories *By Rabbi Norman J. Cohen, PhD* 6 x 9, 240 pp, Quality PB, 978-1-58023-274-6 **$16.99**

The Modern Men's Torah Commentary: New Insights from Jewish Men on the 54 Weekly Torah Portions *Edited by Rabbi Jeffrey K. Salkin*
6 x 9, 368 pp, HC, 978-1-58023-395-8 **$24.99**

Moses and the Journey to Leadership: Timeless Lessons of Effective Management from the Bible and Today's Leaders *By Rabbi Norman J. Cohen, PhD*
6 x 9, 240 pp, Quality PB, 978-1-58023-351-4 **$18.99**; HC, 978-1-58023-227-2 **$21.99**

The Other Talmud—*The Yerushalmi*: Unlocking the Secrets of The Talmud of Israel for Judaism Today *By Rabbi Judith Z. Abrams, PhD*
6 x 9, 256 pp, HC, 978-1-58023-463-4 **$24.99**

Sage Tales: Wisdom and Wonder from the Rabbis of the Talmud
By Rabbi Burton L. Visotzky 6 x 9, 256 pp, HC, 978-1-58023-456-6 **$24.99**

The Torah Revolution: Fourteen Truths That Changed the World
By Rabbi Reuven Hammer, PhD 6 x 9, 240 pp, HC, 978-1-58023-457-3 **$24.99**

The Wisdom of Judaism: An Introduction to the Values of the Talmud
By Rabbi Dov Peretz Elkins 6 x 9, 192 pp, Quality PB, 978-1-58023-327-9 **$16.99**

From Defender to Critic: The Search for a New Jewish Self
By Dr. David Hartman
A daring self-examination of Hartman's goals, which were not to strip halakha of its authority but to create a space for questioning and critique that allows for the traditionally religious Jew to act out a moral life in tune with modern experience. 6 x 9, 336 pp, HC, 978-1-58023-515-0 **$35.00**

The God Who Hates Lies: Confronting & Rethinking Jewish Tradition
A deeply personal look at the struggle between commitment to Jewish religious tradition and personal morality.
By Dr. David Hartman with Charlie Buckholtz 6 x 9, 208 pp, HC, 978-1-58023-455-9 **$24.99**

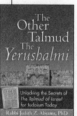

Our Religious Brains: What Cognitive Science Reveals about Belief, Morality, Community and Our Relationship with God
By Rabbi Ralph D. Mecklenburger; Foreword by Dr. Howard Kelfer; Preface by Dr. Neil Gillman
This is a groundbreaking, accessible look at the implications of cognitive science for religion and theology, intended for laypeople. 6 x 9, 224 pp, HC, 978-1-58023-508-2 **$24.99**

The Other Talmud—*The Yerushalmi*: Unlocking the Secrets of The Talmud of Israel for Judaism Today   *By Rabbi Judith Z. Abrams, PhD*
A fascinating—and stimulating—look at "the other Talmud" and the possibilities for Jewish life reflected there. 6 x 9, 256 pp, HC, 978-1-58023-463-4 **$24.99**

The Way of Man: According to Hasidic Teaching
By Martin Buber; New Translation and Introduction by Rabbi Bernard H. Mehlman and Dr. Gabriel E. Padawer; Foreword by Paul Mendes-Flohr
An accessible and engaging new translation of Buber's classic work—*available as an e-book only.* E-book, 978-1-58023-601-0 Digital List Price **$14.99**

The Death of Death: Resurrection and Immortality in Jewish Thought
By Rabbi Neil Gillman, PhD 6 x 9, 336 pp, Quality PB, 978-1-58023-081-0 **$18.95**

Doing Jewish Theology: God, Torah & Israel in Modern Judaism *By Rabbi Neil Gillman, PhD*
6 x 9, 304 pp, Quality PB, 978-1-58023-439-9 **$18.99**; HC, 978-1-58023-322-4 **$24.99**

A Heart of Many Rooms: Celebrating the Many Voices within Judaism
By Dr. David Hartman 6 x 9, 352 pp, Quality PB, 978-1-58023-156-5 **$19.95**

Jewish Theology in Our Time: A New Generation Explores the Foundations and Future of Jewish Belief   *Edited by Rabbi Elliot J. Cosgrove, PhD; Foreword by Rabbi David J. Wolpe; Preface by Rabbi Carole B. Balin, PhD* 6 x 9, 240 pp, Quality PB, 978-1-58023-630-1, **$19.99**; HC, 978-1-58023-413-9 **$24.99**

Maimonides—Essential Teachings on Jewish Faith & Ethics: The Book of Knowledge & the Thirteen Principles of Faith—Annotated & Explained
Translation and Annotation by Rabbi Marc D. Angel, PhD
5½ x 8½, 224 pp, Quality PB Original, 978-1-59473-311-6 **$18.99***

Maimonides, Spinoza and Us: Toward an Intellectually Vibrant Judaism
By Rabbi Marc D. Angel, PhD 6 x 9, 224 pp, HC, 978-1-58023-411-5 **$24.99**

Your Word Is Fire: The Hasidic Masters on Contemplative Prayer
Edited and translated by Rabbi Arthur Green, PhD, and Barry W. Holtz
6 x 9, 160 pp, Quality PB, 978-1-879045-25-5 **$16.99**

I Am Jewish
Personal Reflections Inspired by the Last Words of Daniel Pearl
Almost 150 Jews—both famous and not—from all walks of life, from all around the world, write about many aspects of their Judaism.
Edited by Judea and Ruth Pearl 6 x 9, 304 pp, Deluxe PB w/ flaps, 978-1-58023-259-3 **$19.99**
Download a free copy of the *I Am Jewish Teacher's Guide* at www.jewishlights.com.

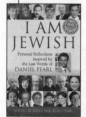

Hannah Senesh: Her Life and Diary, The First Complete Edition
By Hannah Senesh; Foreword by Marge Piercy; Preface by Eitan Senesh; Afterword by Roberta Grossman
6 x 9, 368 pp, b/w photos, Quality PB, 978-1-58023-342-2 **$19.99**

**A book from SkyLight Paths, Jewish Lights' sister imprint*

Spirituality

Amazing Chesed: Living a Grace-Filled Judaism
By Rabbi Rami Shapiro
Drawing from ancient and contemporary, traditional and non-traditional Jewish
wisdom, reclaims the idea of grace in Judaism.
6 x 9, 176 pp, Quality PB, 978-1-58023-624-9 **$16.99**

Jewish with Feeling: A Guide to Meaningful Jewish Practice
By Rabbi Zalman Schachter-Shalomi with Joel Segel
Takes off from basic questions like "Why be Jewish?" and whether the word God
still speaks to us today and lays out a vision for a whole-person Judaism.
5½ x 8½, 288 pp, Quality PB, 978-1-58023-691-1 **$19.99**

The Jewish Lights Spirituality Handbook: A Guide to Understanding,
Exploring & Living a Spiritual Life *Edited by Stuart M. Matlins*
What exactly is "Jewish" about spirituality? How do I make it a part of my life?
Fifty of today's foremost spiritual leaders share their ideas and experience with us.
6 x 9, 456 pp, Quality PB, 978-1-58023-093-3 **$19.99**

Aleph-Bet Yoga: Embodying the Hebrew Letters for Physical and Spiritual Well-Being
By Steven A. Rapp; Foreword by Tamar Frankiel, PhD, and Judy Greenfeld; Preface by Hart Lazer
7 x 10, 128 pp, b/w photos, Quality PB, Lay-flat binding, 978-1-58023-162-6 **$16.95**

A Book of Life: Embracing Judaism as a Spiritual Practice
By Rabbi Michael Strassfeld 6 x 9, 544 pp, Quality PB, 978-1-58023-247-0 **$19.99**

Bringing the Psalms to Life: How to Understand and Use the Book of Psalms
By Rabbi Daniel F. Polish, PhD 6 x 9, 208 pp, Quality PB, 978-1-58023-157-2 **$16.95**

Does the Soul Survive? A Jewish Journey to Belief in Afterlife, Past Lives &
Living with Purpose By Rabbi Elie Kaplan Spitz; Foreword by Brian L. Weiss, MD
6 x 9, 288 pp, Quality PB, 978-1-58023-165-7 **$18.99**

Entering the Temple of Dreams: Jewish Prayers, Movements and Meditations for
the End of the Day By Tamar Frankiel, PhD, and Judy Greenfeld
7 x 10, 192 pp, illus., Quality PB, 978-1-58023-079-7 **$16.95**

First Steps to a New Jewish Spirit: Reb Zalman's Guide to Recapturing the
Intimacy & Ecstasy in Your Relationship with God By Rabbi Zalman M. Schachter-Shalomi
with Donald Gropman 6 x 9, 144 pp, Quality PB, 978-1-58023-182-4 **$16.95**

Foundations of Sephardic Spirituality: The Inner Life of Jews of the Ottoman Empire
By Rabbi Marc D. Angel, PhD 6 x 9, 224 pp, Quality PB, 978-1-58023-341-5 **$18.99**

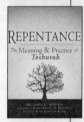

God & the Big Bang: Discovering Harmony between Science & Spirituality
By Dr. Daniel C. Matt 6 x 9, 216 pp, Quality PB, 978-1-879045-89-7 **$18.99**

God in Our Relationships: Spirituality between People from the Teachings of
Martin Buber By Rabbi Dennis S. Ross 5½ x 8½, 160 pp, Quality PB, 978-1-58023-147-3 **$16.95**

Judaism, Physics and God: Searching for Sacred Metaphors in a Post-Einstein World
By Rabbi David W. Nelson 6 x 9, 352 pp, Quality PB, inc. reader's discussion guide,
978-1-58023-306-4 **$18.99**; HC, 352 pp, 978-1-58023-252-4 **$24.99**

Meaning & Mitzvah: Daily Practices for Reclaiming Judaism through Prayer, God,
Torah, Hebrew, Mitzvot and Peoplehood By Rabbi Goldie Milgram
7 x 9, 336 pp, Quality PB, 978-1-58023-256-2 **$19.99**

Repentance: The Meaning and Practice of Teshuvah
By Dr. Louis E. Newman; Foreword by Rabbi Harold M. Schulweis; Preface by Rabbi Karyn D. Kedar
6 x 9, 256 pp, HC, 978-1-58023-426-9 **$24.99** Quality PB, 978-1-58023-718-5 **$18.99**

The Sabbath Soul: Mystical Reflections on the Transformative Power of Holy Time
Selection, Translation and Commentary by Eitan Fishbane, PhD
6 x 9, 208 pp, Quality PB, 978-1-58023-459-7 **$18.99**

Tanya, the Masterpiece of Hasidic Wisdom: Selections Annotated & Explained
Translation & Annotation by Rabbi Rami Shapiro; Foreword by Rabbi Zalman M. Schachter-Shalomi
5½ x 8½, 240 pp, Quality PB, 978-1-59473-275-1 **$16.99**

These Are the Words, 2nd Edition: A Vocabulary of Jewish Spiritual Life
By Rabbi Arthur Green, PhD 6 x 9, 320 pp, Quality PB, 978-1-58023-494-8 **$19.99**

Spirituality / Prayer

Davening: A Guide to Meaningful Jewish Prayer
By Rabbi Zalman Schachter-Shalomi with Joel Segel; Foreword by Rabbi Lawrence Kushner
A fresh approach to prayer for all who wish to appreciate the power of prayer's poetry, song and ritual, and to join the age-old conversation that Jews have had with God. 6 x 9, 240 pp, Quality PB, 978-1-58023-627-0 **$18.99**

Jewish Men Pray: Words of Yearning, Praise, Petition, Gratitude and Wonder from Traditional and Contemporary Sources
Edited by Rabbi Kerry M. Olitzky and Stuart M. Matlins; Foreword by Rabbi Bradley Shavit Artson, DHL
A celebration of Jewish men's voices in prayer—to strengthen, heal, comfort, and inspire—from the ancient world up to our own day.
5 x 7¼, 400 pp, HC, 978-1-58023-628-7 **$19.99**

Making Prayer Real: Leading Jewish Spiritual Voices on Why Prayer Is Difficult and What to Do about It *By Rabbi Mike Comins* 6 x 9, 320 pp, Quality PB, 978-1-58023-417-7 **$18.99**

Witnesses to the One: The Spiritual History of the *Sh'ma*
By Rabbi Joseph B. Meszler; Foreword by Rabbi Elyse Goldstein
6 x 9, 176 pp, Quality PB, 978-1-58023-400-9 **$16.99**; HC, 978-1-58023-309-5 **$19.99**

My People's Prayer Book Series: Traditional Prayers, Modern Commentaries *Edited by Rabbi Lawrence A. Hoffman, PhD*
Provides diverse and exciting commentary to the traditional liturgy. Will help you find new wisdom in Jewish prayer, and bring liturgy into your life. Each book includes Hebrew text, modern translations and commentaries from all perspectives of the Jewish world.

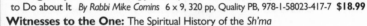

Vol. 1—The *Sh'ma* and Its Blessings
  7 x 10, 168 pp, HC, 978-1-879045-79-8 **$29.99**
Vol. 2—The *Amidah* 7 x 10, 240 pp, HC, 978-1-879045-80-4 **$24.95**
Vol. 3—*P'sukei D'zimrah* (Morning Psalms)
  7 x 10, 240 pp, HC, 978-1-879045-81-1 **$29.99**
Vol. 4—*Seder K'riat Hatorah* (The Torah Service)
  7 x 10, 264 pp, HC, 978-1-879045-82-8 **$29.99**
Vol. 5—*Birkhot Hashachar* (Morning Blessings)
  7 x 10, 240 pp, HC, 978-1-879045-83-5 **$24.95**
Vol. 6—*Tachanun* and Concluding Prayers
  7 x 10, 240 pp, HC, 978-1-879045-84-2 **$24.95**
Vol. 7—*Shabbat* at Home 7 x 10, 240 pp, HC, 978-1-879045-85-9 **$24.95**
Vol. 8—*Kabbalat Shabbat* (Welcoming Shabbat in the Synagogue)
  7 x 10, 240 pp, HC, 978-1-58023-121-3 **$24.99**
Vol. 9—Welcoming the Night: *Minchah* and *Ma'ariv* (Afternoon and
  Evening Prayer) 7 x 10, 272 pp, HC, 978-1-58023-262-3 **$24.99**
Vol. 10—Shabbat Morning: *Shacharit* and *Musaf* (Morning and
  Additional Services) 7 x 10, 240 pp, HC, 978-1-58023-240-1 **$29.99**

Spirituality / Lawrence Kushner

I'm God; You're Not: Observations on Organized Religion & Other Disguises of the Ego
6 x 9, 256 pp, Quality PB, 978-1-58023-513-6 **$18.99**; HC, 978-1-58023-441-2 **$21.99**

The Book of Letters: A Mystical Hebrew Alphabet
Popular HC Edition, 6 x 9, 80 pp, 2-color text, 978-1-879045-00-2 **$24.95**
Collector's Limited Edition, 9 x 12, 80 pp, gold-foil-embossed pages, w/ limited-edition silkscreened print, 978-1-879045-04-0 **$349.00**

The Book of Miracles: A Young Person's Guide to Jewish Spiritual Awareness
6 x 9, 96 pp, 2-color illus., HC, 978-1-879045-78-1 **$16.95** *For ages 9–13*

God Was in This Place & I, i Did Not Know: Finding Self, Spirituality and Ultimate Meaning 6 x 9, 192 pp, Quality PB, 978-1-879045-33-0 **$16.95**

Honey from the Rock: An Introduction to Jewish Mysticism
6 x 9, 176 pp, Quality PB, 978-1-58023-073-5 **$16.95**

Invisible Lines of Connection: Sacred Stories of the Ordinary
5½ x 8½, 160 pp, Quality PB, 978-1-879045-98-9 **$16.99**

The Way Into Jewish Mystical Tradition
6 x 9, 224 pp, Quality PB, 978-1-58023-200-5 **$18.99**; HC, 978-1-58023-029-2 **$21.95**

Inspiration

Saying No and Letting Go: Jewish Wisdom on Making Room for What Matters Most
By Rabbi Edwin Goldberg, DHL; Foreword by Rabbi Naomi Levy
Taps into timeless Jewish wisdom that teaches how to "hold on tightly" to the things that matter most while learning to "let go lightly" of the demands and worries that do not ultimately matter. 6 x 9, 192 pp, Quality PB, 978-1-58023-670-6 **$16.99**

The Magic of Hebrew Chant: Healing the Spirit, Transforming the Mind, Deepening Love   *By Rabbi Shefa Gold; Foreword by Sylvia Boorstein*
Introduces this transformative spiritual practice as a way to unlock the power of sacred texts and make prayer and meditation the delight of your life. Includes musical notations. 6 x 9, 352 pp, Quality PB, 978-1-58023-671-3 **$24.99**

The Bridge to Forgiveness: Stories and Prayers for Finding God and Restoring Wholeness *By Rabbi Karyn D. Kedar* 6 x 9, 176 pp, Quality PB, 978-1-58023-451-1 **$16.99**

The Empty Chair: Finding Hope and Joy—Timeless Wisdom from a Hasidic Master, Rebbe Nachman of Breslov *Adapted by Moshe Mykoff and the Breslov Research Institute*
4 x 6, 128 pp, Deluxe PB w/ flaps, 978-1-879045-67-5 **$9.99**

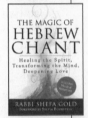

A Formula for Proper Living: Practical Lessons from Life and Torah
By Rabbi Abraham J. Twerski, MD 6 x 9, 144 pp, HC, 978-1-58023-402-3 **$19.99**

The Gentle Weapon: Prayers for Everyday and Not-So-Everyday Moments—Timeless Wisdom from the Teachings of the Hasidic Master, Rebbe Nachman of Breslov
Adapted by Moshe Mykoff and S. C. Mizrahi, together with the Breslov Research Institute
4 x 6, 144 pp, Deluxe PB w/ flaps, 978-1-58023-022-3 **$9.99**

The God Upgrade: Finding Your 21st-Century Spirituality in Judaism's 5,000-Year-Old Tradition *By Rabbi Jamie Korngold; Foreword by Rabbi Harold M. Schulweis*
6 x 9, 176 pp, Quality PB, 978-1-58023-443-6 $15.99

God Whispers: Stories of the Soul, Lessons of the Heart *By Rabbi Karyn D. Kedar*
6 x 9, 176 pp, Quality PB, 978-1-58023-088-9 **$15.95**

God's To-Do List: 103 Ways to Be an Angel and Do God's Work on Earth
By Dr. Ron Wolfson 6 x 9, 144 pp, Quality PB, 978-1-58023-301-9 **$16.99**

Happiness and the Human Spirit: The Spirituality of Becoming the Best You Can Be
By Rabbi Abraham J. Twerski, MD
6 x 9, 176 pp, Quality PB, 978-1-58023-404-7 **$16.99**; HC, 978-1-58023-343-9 **$19.99**

Life's Daily Blessings: Inspiring Reflections on Gratitude and Joy for Every Day, Based on Jewish Wisdom *By Rabbi Kerry M. Olitzky* 4½ x 6½, 368 pp, Quality PB, 978-1-58023-396-5 **$16.99**

Restful Reflections: Nighttime Inspiration to Calm the Soul, Based on Jewish Wisdom
By Rabbi Kerry M. Olitzky and Rabbi Lori Forman-Jacobi 5 x 8, 352 pp, Quality PB, 978-1-58023-091-9 **$16.99**

Sacred Intentions: Morning Inspiration to Strengthen the Spirit, Based on Jewish Wisdom
By Rabbi Kerry M. Olitzky and Rabbi Lori Forman-Jacobi 4½ x 6½, 448 pp, Quality PB, 978-1-58023-061-2 **$16.99**

The Seven Questions You're Asked in Heaven: Reviewing and Renewing Your Life on Earth *By Dr. Ron Wolfson* 6 x 9, 176 pp, Quality PB, 978-1-58023-407-8 **$16.99**

Kabbalah / Mysticism

Jewish Mysticism and the Spiritual Life: Classical Texts, Contemporary Reflections *Edited by Dr. Lawrence Fine, Dr. Eitan Fishbane and Rabbi Or N. Rose*
Inspirational and thought-provoking materials for contemplation, discussion and action. 6 x 9, 256 pp, HC, 978-1-58023-434-4 **$24.99** Quality PB, 978-1-58023-719-2 **$18.99**

Ehyeh: A Kabbalah for Tomorrow
By Rabbi Arthur Green, PhD 6 x 9, 224 pp, Quality PB, 978-1-58023-213-5 **$18.99**

The Gift of Kabbalah: Discovering the Secrets of Heaven, Renewing Your Life on Earth
By Tamar Frankiel, PhD 6 x 9, 256 pp, Quality PB, 978-1-58023-141-1 **$16.95**

Seek My Face: A Jewish Mystical Theology *By Rabbi Arthur Green, PhD*
6 x 9, 304 pp, Quality PB, 978-1-58023-130-5 **$19.95**

Zohar: Annotated & Explained *Translation & Annotation by Dr. Daniel C. Matt; Foreword by Andrew Harvey* 5½ x 8½, 176 pp, Quality PB, 978-1-893361-51-5 **$16.99**
(A book from SkyLight Paths, Jewish Lights' sister imprint)

See also *The Way Into Jewish Mystical Tradition* in The Way Into... Series.

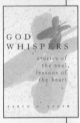